More Praise for *Modern Investment Management*

"This book is likely to become the bible of quantitative investment management."

—Philippe Jorion
Professor of Finance
Graduate School of Management
University of California—Irvine

"A readable book, aimed at the serious investor. It is a comprehensive guide that takes the reader from the theoretical and conceptual all the way through practical application. Our company has been researching and evaluating investment managers for more than 30 years, and yet I am eager to incorporate the insights found in this book into our work. New additions to our staff will be reading it on day one."

—Paul R. Greenwood
Director of US Equity
Frank Russell Company

"Building on the Nobel Prize-winning work of William Sharpe, and on that of their late colleague Fischer Black, Bob Litterman and his colleagues at Goldman Sachs Asset Management have taken the familiar and appealing concept of capital market equilibrium and reshaped it into an approach to asset management. They then extend their reach into many other related topics. Practically all investment managers, plan sponsors, brokers, and other financial professionals will find something of value in this encyclopedic work."

—Larry Siegel
Director, Investment Policy Research
The Ford Foundation

"Equilibrium theory is fundamental to virtually every aspect of modern investment practice. In this book, the team from Goldman Sachs Asset Management provides not only a highly-readable review of the academic theory, but also a very practical guide to applying it to most of the important problems faced by today's institutional investors. Perhaps most impressive is the breadth of this work. From asset allocation, to risk budgeting, to manager selection, to performance attribution, this book touches on the key aspects of professional investment management. This would be a wonderful text to build an applied investment finance course around."

—Gregory C. Allen
Executive Vice President
Manager of Specialty Consulting, Callan Associates

"An elegant, well-written book, which gives the reader a better understanding of the workings of interrelated markets; it explains counterintuitive outcomes in a lucid way. Highly recommendable reading."

—Jean Frijns
Chief Investment Officer
ABP Investments

"*Modern Investment Management* outlines a comprehensive, coherent, and up-to-date road map of the key strategic and implementation issues that institutional investors need to face. This book is destined to become required reading for institutional investors and their advisors."

—Bill Muysken
Global Head of Research
Mercer Investment Consulting

"I found the book to be a valuable A to Z compendium of investment management theory and practice that would be an excellent reference for the experienced investor as well as an educational tool for the less knowledgeable. The book provides a clear and complete guide to both the important technical details and the more practical 'real-world' aspects of portfolio management from 30,000 feet and from ground level. This is certainly another in a long line of high-quality contributions to the investment management industry knowledge base made by Bob Litterman and colleagues at Goldman Sachs Asset Management."

—Tim Barron
Managing Director, Director of Research
CRA RogersCasey

"Early applications of portfolio theory, based on analysts' rate of return forecasts, required arbitrary constraints on portfolio weights to avoid plunging. The path-breaking Black-Litterman equilibrium approach changes focus to the rate of return threshold necessary for a portfolio shift to improve the investor's risk return position. An excellent portfolio theory text based on the Black-Litterman model is long overdue. This book should be required reading for portfolio managers and asset allocators."

—Bob Litzenberger
Emeritus Professor, Wharton
Retired Partner, Goldman, Sachs & Co.

MODERN INVESTMENT MANAGEMENT

Founded in 1807, John Wiley & Sons is the oldest independent publishing company in the United States. With offices in North America, Europe, Australia, and Asia, Wiley is globally committed to developing and marketing print and electronics products and services for our customers' professional and personal knowledge and understanding.

The Wiley Finance series contains books written specifically for finance and investment professionals as well as sophisticated individual investors and their financial advisors. Book topics range from portfolio management to e-commerce, risk management, financial engineering, valuation, and financial instrument analysis, as well as much more.

For a list of available titles, visit our web site at www.WileyFinance.com.

MODERN INVESTMENT MANAGEMENT

AN EQUILIBRIUM APPROACH

Bob Litterman and the Quantitative Resources Group
Goldman Sachs Asset Management

John Wiley & Sons, Inc.

Published by John Wiley & Sons, Inc., Hoboken, New Jersey.
Published simultaneously in Canada.

Library of Congress Cataloging-in-Publication Data:

Litterman, Robert B.

Modern investment management : an equilibrium approach / Bob Litterman and the Quantitative Resources Group, Goldman Sachs Asset Management.

p. cm. — (Wiley finance series)

Published simultaneously in Canada.

Includes bibliographical references.

ISBN 0-471-12410-9 (cloth : alk. paper)

1. Investments. 2. Portfolio management. 3. Risk management. I. Goldman Sachs Asset Management. Quantitative Resources Group. II. Title. III. Series.

HG4529.5 .L58 2003

332.6—dc21 2002154126

Printed in the United States of America.

10 9 8 7 6

About the Authors

Andrew Alford, Vice President, heads the Global Quantitative Equity Research (GQE) team conducting research on fundamental-based quantitative investment strategies. He is also a member of the GQE Investment Policy Committee. Prior to joining GSAM, he was a professor at the Wharton School of Business at the University of Pennsylvania and the Sloan School of Management at the Massachusetts Institute of Technology. Alford has also served as an academic fellow in the Office of Economic Analysis at the Securities and Exchange Commission in Washington, D.C. He has written articles published in the *Journal of Corporate Finance*, the *Journal of Accounting Research*, the *Journal of Accounting & Economics*, and *the Accounting Review.* Alford has a B.S. in Information and Computer Science from the University of California at Irvine (1984) and MBA and Ph.D. degrees from the Graduate School of Business at the University of Chicago (1986 and 1990).

Ripsy Bandourian, Analyst, has been part of the Global Investment Strategies group since its inception in December 2001. She joined Goldman Sachs as an analyst with the Institutional Client Research & Strategy group in July 2001. She assists the team's Research Strategists in advising our clients worldwide as well as participates in research on today's investment issues. She graduated Phi Kappa Phi and cum laude with a B.A. in Economics and Molecular Biology and M.S. in Statistics from Brigham Young University.

Jonathan Beinner, Managing Director, is a portfolio manager and the Chief Investment Officer responsible for overseeing fixed income portfolios, including government, mortgage-backed, asset-backed, corporate, nondollar, and currency assets. Prior to being named CIO, Beinner was co-head of the U.S. Fixed Income team. He joined Goldman Sachs Asset Management in 1990 after working in the trading and arbitrage group of Franklin Savings Association. He received two B.S. degrees from the University of Pennsylvania in 1988.

David Ben-Ur, Vice President, is a Senior Investment Strategist in the Global Manager Strategies group. He is responsible for identifying, evaluating, selecting, and monitoring external managers for all U.S. equity products. Ben-Ur joined Goldman Sachs in January 2000. Previously, he was a Senior Fund Analyst and Assistant Portfolio Strategist at Fidelity Investments in Boston, where he worked for five years. Ben-Ur received his B.A., magna cum laude, in 1992 from Tufts University, where he was inducted into the Phi Beta Kappa National Honor Society. He received his Master's in Public Policy from Harvard University's John F. Kennedy School of Government, with a concentration in International Trade and Finance, in 1995.

Mark M. Carhart, Managing Director, joined GSAM in September 1997 as a member of the Quantitative Strategies team and became co-head of the department in

1998. Prior to joining Goldman Sachs, he was Assistant Professor of Finance at the Marshall School of Business at the University of Southern California and a Senior Fellow of the Wharton Financial Institutions Center, where he studied survivorship and predictability in mutual fund performance. He has published in the *Journal of Finance* and the *Review of Financial Studies* and referees articles for publication in various academic and practitioner finance journals. Carhart received a B.A. from Yale University in 1988, Chartered Financial Analyst designation in 1991, and a Ph.D. from the University of Chicago Graduate School of Business in 1995.

Kent A. Clark, Managing Director, is the Chief Investment Officer of Global Portfolio Management at the Hedge Fund Strategies Group. Prior to that, Clark spent eight years managing the $32 billion U.S. and Global Equities portfolios for the Investment Management Division's quantitative equity management team. In this capacity, he developed and managed equity long/short and market neutral programs. Clark joined Goldman Sachs from the University of Chicago, where he achieved candidacy in the Ph.D. program and received an MBA. He holds a Bachelor of Commerce degree from the University of Calgary. Clark has had research published in the *Journal of Financial and Quantitative Analysis* and in *Enhanced Indexing*. He is a past President of the New York Society of Quantitative Analysts and a member of the Chicago Quantitative Alliance.

Giorgio De Santis, Managing Director, joined the Quantitative Strategies group of Goldman Sachs Asset Management in June 1998. Prior to joining Goldman Sachs, he was an Assistant Professor of Finance at the Marshall School of Business at USC. He has published articles in the *Journal of Finance*, the *Journal of Financial Economics*, the *Journal of International Money and Finance*, and other academic and practitioner journals in finance and economics. He also contributed chapters to several books on investment management. His research covers various topics in international finance, from dynamic models of risk in developed and emerging markets to optimal portfolio strategies in the presence of currency risk. De Santis received a B.A. from Libera Universita' Internazionale degli Studi Sociali in Rome in 1984, an M.A. in Economics from the University of Chicago in 1989, and a Ph.D. in Economics from the University of Chicago in 1993.

Jason Gottlieb, Vice President, is a Senior Investment Strategist in the Global Manager Strategies (GMS) group. He is responsible for oversight of the risk management function within GMS, which includes risk and performance analysis and reporting across GMS products. He is also responsible for identifying, evaluating, and monitoring external managers for all fixed income products. He joined Goldman Sachs in January 1996 and spent four years in the Firmwide Risk Department. Gottlieb received his MBA in Finance from Fordham University and his B.S. in Finance from Siena College.

Barry Griffiths, Vice President, is the Chief of Quantitative Research for the Private Equity Group, and began working with the group in 1996. Prior to joining Goldman Sachs, he was Chief Scientist at Business Matters, Inc., a software firm specializing in business planning software, and previously a Director in the Technology Development Organization at Synetics Corporation, an aerospace research firm.

His recent research includes work on asset allocation in private equity, and on post-IPO performance of venture-funded firms. He is the author of a number of articles on applications of modeling, estimation, and optimization in stochastic systems. He received a B.S. and an M.S. degree in Systems Science from Michigan State University, and a Ph.D. in Systems Engineering from Case Western Reserve University. He is also a Chartered Financial Analyst.

Ronald Howard, Vice President, has worked at Goldman Sachs since 1999 and is currently a Vice President in Foreign Exchange Strategies in the Fixed Income Division. Prior to August 2002, he worked as a Research Strategist in the Global Investment Strategies group in the Goldman Sachs Asset Management Division. He holds a B.A. from the University of Chicago and an M.S. and Ph.D. in mathematics from Princeton University.

Robert Jones, Managing Director, brings over 20 years of investment experience to his work in managing the Global Quantitative Equity (GQE) group. Jones developed the original model and investment process for GQE in the late 1980s, and has been responsible for overseeing their continuing development and evolution ever since. The GQE group currently manages over $28 billion in equity portfolios across a variety of styles (growth, value, core, small-cap, international) and client types (pension funds, mutual funds, foundations, endowments, individuals). Jones heads the GQE Investment Policy Committee and also serves on the GSAM Investment Policy Group. Prior to joining GSAM in 1989, he was the senior quantitative analyst in the Investment Research Department and the author of the monthly *Stock Selection* publication. Before joining Goldman Sachs in 1987, Jones provided quantitative research for both a major investment banking firm and an options consulting firm. His articles on quantitative techniques have been published in leading books and financial journals, including the *Financial Analysts Journal* and the *Journal of Portfolio Management*. A Chartered Financial Analyst, Jones received a B.A. from Brown University in 1978 and an MBA from the University of Michigan in 1980, where he serves on the Investment Advisory Committee for the University Endowment.

J. Douglas Kramer, Vice President, is the head of the Global Manager Strategies group. Kramer is responsible for overseeing the identification, evaluation, selection, and monitoring of Managers in the Program across all asset classes. He joined Goldman Sachs in 1999 as a senior leader of a new business focused on the wealth management market where his responsibilities included product development and management. Prior to joining Goldman Sachs, Kramer was a Director of Columbia Energy Services in Houston, where he managed portfolios of power and weather derivatives. Prior to Columbia, he was a portfolio manager at Fischer Francis Trees and Watts in New York for seven years, managing global fixed income assets, specializing in mortgage-backed securities and corporate bonds. Kramer received his B.S. from the Wharton School of the University of Pennsylvania and his MBA from Columbia University with Beta Gamma Sigma honors.

Yoel Lax, Associate, joined the Global Investment Strategies group in July 2001. Prior to joining Goldman Sachs, he obtained a Ph.D. in Finance from the Wharton

School of the University of Pennsylvania, where he conducted research on life cycle portfolio selection and asset pricing. Lax also holds a B.S. in Economics summa cum laude from the Wharton School.

Terence Lim, Vice President, is a Senior Research Analyst of the Global Quantitative Equity (GQE) group. Lim is responsible for developing and enhancing the group's quantitative models. He also sits on the GQE Investment Policy Committee. Lim joined Goldman Sachs Asset Management in June 1999. Previously, he was a visiting assistant professor of finance at Dartmouth College's Tuck School of Business, and an investment manager at Koeneman Capital Management in Singapore. Lim's research has been published in the *Journal of Finance* and awarded a Q Group grant in 1998. He graduated summa cum laude with dual B.Sc. degrees in engineering and economics from the University of Pennsylvania, and received a Ph.D. degree in financial economics from M.I.T.

Bob Litterman, Managing Director, is the Director of Quantitative Resources within the Investment Management Division of Goldman Sachs. He is the co-developer, along with the late Fischer Black, of the Black-Litterman Global Asset Allocation Model, a key tool in the Division's asset allocation process. During his 15 years at Goldman Sachs, Litterman has also headed the Firmwide Risk department and has been co-director, with Fischer Black, of the research and model development group within the Fixed Income Division's research department. Litterman has authored or co-authored many papers on risk management, asset allocation, and the use of modern portfolio theory. He is a member of the *Risk* magazine "Risk Hall of Fame." Before joining Goldman Sachs in 1986, he was an Assistant Vice President in the Research Department of the Federal Reserve Bank of Minneapolis and an Assistant Professor in the Economics Department at the Massachusetts Institute of Technology. Litterman received a B.S. from Stanford University in 1973 and a Ph.D. in Economics from the University of Minnesota in 1980.

Jean-Pierre Mittaz is the Chief Operating Officer of Global Fixed Income and Currency. He is responsible for ensuring integrated investment infrastructure, continuous improvement of the control environment, and coordinating business financials across New York, London, and Tokyo. Prior to this role, he was the Co-Chief Operating Officer of GSAM's Risk and Performance Analytics Group, where he oversaw risk monitoring, performance analytics, and securities valuation oversight. Mittaz serves on GSAM's Valuation and Risk Committees. Prior to joining the Investment Management Division in 1997, he was a member of Goldman, Sachs & Co.'s Finance Division in Zurich, London, and New York. Mittaz received his Ph.D. from the University of Zurich in Switzerland, where he taught various courses in banking, finance, and accounting. He holds a Master's Degree in Business Administration from the University of Zurich, Switzerland, and is a Chartered Financial Analyst.

Don Mulvihill, Managing Director, is the Senior Portfolio Manager responsible for development and implementation of tax-efficient investment strategies. He works with our investment professionals to integrate income and estate tax considerations into investment decisions. The goal is to enhance the long-term accumulation of wealth, net of taxes, for the benefit of future heirs and charities. Mulvihill joined Goldman Sachs' Chicago office in 1980. There he worked with bank trust departments helping them to manage excess liquidity. In 1985, he moved to New York and spent the next six years managing money market and fixed income portfolios for institutional clients. In 1991, Mulvihill moved to London to help start our international investment management activities and, in 1992, moved to Tokyo as President of Goldman Sachs Asset Management, Japan. He also served as chairman of the American Chamber of Commerce in Japan, Subcommittee on Investment Management and was actively involved in the effort that produced the Financial Services Agreement that was signed by the governments of the United States and Japan in January 1995. Goldman Sachs was the first firm, Japanese or foreign, chosen to manage Japanese equities for the Japanese government pension system. He received a B.A. from the University of Notre Dame in 1978 and an MBA from the University of Chicago in 1982.

Jacob Rosengarten, Managing Director, is the Head of the Risk and Performance Analytics Group within Goldman Sachs Asset Management, a position he held beginning in 1998. Until 1998, he was the Director of Risk Analysis and Quantitative Analysis at Commodities Corporation (acquired by Goldman Sachs in 1997). In this capacity, he directed a group of professionals responsible for measuring risk associated with individual positions, managers, and portfolios of managers who trade a variety of products including futures, derivatives, equities, and emerging markets. In earlier roles at Commodities Corporation, he also functioned as Controller, Assistant Controller, and Director of Accounting. Prior to his tenure at Commodities Corporation, he worked as an auditor for Arthur Young & Company (since 1979); in this capacity he was responsible for managing audits for a variety of diversified clients. Rosengarten holds a B.A. in Economics from Brandeis University and an MBA in Accounting from the University of Chicago. He is also a Certified Public Accountant.

TarunTyagi is an Investment Strategist in the Global Investment Strategies group. His current responsibilities include advising U.S. Institutional clients (corporations, foundations, endowments, and public funds) on strategic investment issues such as asset allocation and risk management policy decisions. Tyagi joined Goldman Sachs Asset Management in July 1999 as an Associate in the Institutional Client Research & Strategy group. Tyagi received an M.S. in Financial Engineering from Columbia University in 1999 and an MBA from the University of Illinois in 1998. During 1997, he was a summer associate at Citibank. Tyagi was employed with India Finance Guaranty Limited as an Assistant Trader and with Tata Consultancy Services as an Assistant Systems Analyst. He received a Bachelor of Technology in Mechanical Engineering from the Indian Institute of Technology, Delhi, in 1995.

Chris Vella, Vice President, is a Senior Investment Strategist for international equities in the Global Manager Strategies group. He is responsible for identifying, evaluating, and monitoring external managers for all international equity products. He joined the firm in February 1999 after six years with SEI Investments where, most recently, Vella was responsible for the evaluation and selection of international and emerging markets equity external managers. He graduated Phi Beta Kappa and magna cum laude with a B.S. from Lehigh University in 1993 in finance and applied mathematics.

Adrien Vesval, Analyst, joined Goldman Sachs Asset Management's Quantitative Strategies Group in January 2002. Vesval received a Master's in Mathematical Finance from New York University in 2001, as well as an M.S. in Applied Mathematics and a B.S. in Economics and Applied Mathematics from Ecole Polytechnique (Paris) in 2002.

Kurt Winkelmann, Managing Director, has been with Goldman Sachs since 1993, and is co-head of the Global Investment Strategy group in Goldman Sachs Asset Management. This effort focuses on strategic issues (including strategic asset allocation) that are of interest to institutional clients. Prior to joining GSAM, Winkelmann spent five years in London as part of the Fixed Income Research Group, where his focus was Global Fixed Income Portfolio Strategy. He has written (or co-authored) several papers with portfolio management themes. Before joining Goldman Sachs, he worked in the investment technology industry (Barra and Vestek) and as an Economist for First Bank Systems. He received a B.A. from Macalester College (St. Paul, Minnesota) in 1978 and a Ph.D. in Economics from the University of Minnesota in 1987.

Peter Zangari, Vice President, is a Vice President in the Quantitative Resources Group at Goldman Sachs Asset Management and Head of the PACE group. The PACE (Portfolio Analysis and Construction Environment) group is responsible for designing, developing, and delivering applications and information to quantitative and active portfolio management teams that support their portfolio construction process, and that are used to measure and identify sources of risk and return in their portfolios. Zangari joined Goldman Sachs Asset Management in August 1998. Prior to joining Goldman Sachs, he was at J.P. Morgan where he was one of the original members of the RiskMetrics group. Later, he became a senior quantitative researcher in the bank's firmwide market risk department. In that capacity, he developed numerous methodologies for measuring market risk. Zangari has done extensive work in the area of financial risk research. He has written several published articles on measuring market risk and currently serves as an associate editor to the *Journal of Risk*. His academic training is in the area of applied econometrics and computational statistics, having earned a Ph.D. in Economics from Rutgers University in 1994.

Preface

A potential reader of this book with a cynical bent might well ask an obvious question: "If those folks at Goldman Sachs who wrote this book really knew anything worthwhile about investing, why would they put it together in a book where all of their competitors could find it?"

It's a good question, because it leads naturally to the kind of thought process this book is really all about. The question might be rephrased in a way that makes our motivation for writing the book a little more clear: "Why, in equilibrium, would a successful investment manager write a book about investment management?" By "in equilibrium" we mean in an investment world that is largely efficient and in which investors are fairly compensated for risks and opportunities understood and well taken. Suppose there is wealth to be created from careful and diligent pursuit of certain rules of investing. Suppose further that one were to write those rules down and publish them for everyone to follow. In equilibrium, wouldn't those sources of success disappear? Somehow it doesn't seem to make sense for good investment managers to write books about their craft. Indeed, many sources of investment success, in particular those with limited capacity, would eventually disappear with increased competition. What we have tried to do in this book is to focus on other types of phenomena, those with a capacity consistent with the equilibrium demand for them. In equilibrium these types of phenomena would remain.

Consider an example of a phenomenon with limited capacity. Suppose it were the case that looking at publicly available information one could easily identify certain stocks (for example, those with small capitalization) that would regularly outperform other stocks to a degree not consistent with their risk characteristics. We would expect that if such a strategy were published and widely recognized, then the prices of such stocks would be bid up to the point where the costs of implementing such a strategy just about offset any remaining excess returns. In other words, we would expect such a phenomenon to disappear.

Now consider a phenomenon in the equilibrium camp. Suppose a rule of portfolio construction, for example a rule suggesting increased global diversification, were published that allows an investor to achieve a higher level of return for the same level of portfolio risk. The actions of investors following this suggestion will increase their expected wealth, but their implementation does not in any way reduce the strategy's effectiveness. Even though other investors might implement the change (in equilibrium all investors will), it will nonetheless remain a rule that makes sense for each investor individually. In this book we write about the latter class of phenomena, not the former. In equilibrium this is what a reader should expect us to do.

Despite this equilibrium approach, our view is that the world is clearly not perfectly efficient, whatever that might mean. There might be a little bit of extra reward for those armed with the most thorough, efficient, and disciplined investment processes, even though competition will certainly quickly eliminate most such opportunities. In equilibrium, markets will be relatively efficient, and to the extent that there are limited opportunities left to create excess returns, why would any profit-seeking investor put such proprietary insights into print? The answer is, of course, that in truth they would not. Let's be honest: To the best of our ability we have tried not to include any proprietary information; there are no secret insights buried in this book about how to beat the market, and no descriptions of the exact factors that enter our quantitative return generating models. Clearly some of the anomalies we rely on to actively manage assets are not equilibrium phenomena, and the process of inviting too many competitors to fish in our pond would diminish our ability to create excess returns in the future.

We do believe, though, that the material we have written here is worthwhile. What we have tried to do is to describe what happens when markets are in equilibrium, and how investors, trying to maximize their investment return, should behave. We also address the question of how investors might, as we do, try to identify and look to take advantage of deviations from equilibrium.

Enough about equilibrium theory. The authors of this book are all market professionals and what we have written is designed to be a practical guide. Although we spend a few chapters in the beginning developing a simple, one-period version of a global equilibrium model, the main body of the text is concerned with what it takes to be a serious investor in the world today. The basics of being a smart investor involve understanding risk management, asset allocation, the principles of portfolio construction, and capital asset pricing. The latter refers to being able to identify the return premiums that are justified by the risk characteristics of different securities, and therefore understanding the basis for being able to identify opportunities.

We have chapters focused on the traditional equity and fixed income asset classes as well as on alternative assets such as hedge funds and private equities. We believe that active management can be productive, and we discuss how to build a portfolio of active managers. We understand, though, that not everyone can outperform the average and that in equilibrium it has to be extremely difficult for a portfolio manager to be consistently successful at the active management game. We have a core focus on the problems faced by institutional funds, but also several chapters on the special issues faced by taxable investors. We hope the book fills a gap by tying together the academic theories developed over the past 50 years with the practicalities of investment management in the twenty-first century.

Finally, we provide here a few words on who we are, and a few words of thanks to those to whom we are indebted. We are the Quantitative Resources Group, a part of Goldman Sachs Asset Management (GSAM). Our group has a number of functions. We manage money using quantitative models, we build financial and risk models, we act as fiduciaries and advisors to institutional funds, and we produce research and market outlooks.

Our debts are many, though clearly our deepest is to Fischer Black, our intellectual leader, a cherished colleague, and the first head of quantitative research in GSAM. Fischer was a great believer in the practical value of the insights provided by equilibrium modeling and he inspired our pursuit of this approach. We also wish to thank our clients whose challenges and questions have sponsored all of the activities we sometimes call "work." Next in line are our colleagues, those in the firm, in our industry, and in academia, who have shared their ideas, suggestions, and feedback freely and are clearly reflected on many of these pages. Many thanks to Goldman Sachs, which supported this project throughout and whose culture of teamwork and putting clients' interests first is embraced by us all. Thanks to Bill Falloon, our editor at Wiley, who suggested we write this book, then waited patiently for several years as the ideas gelled, and finally managed to cajole us into putting thoughts on paper.

And finally, a huge thank-you to our families who most of the time live with the short end of the "balance" that Goldman Sachs affectionately promotes between work and family—and who have contributed even further patience in putting up with our efforts to produce this book. Our domestic accounts are, as usual, hopelessly overdrawn.

ROBERT LITTERMAN

New York, New York
June 2003

Contents

PART ONE
Theory

CHAPTER 1
Introduction: Why an Equilibrium Approach? 3
Bob Litterman

CHAPTER 2
The Insights of Modern Portfolio Theory 7
Bob Litterman

CHAPTER 3
Risk Measurement 24
Bob Litterman

CHAPTER 4
The Capital Asset Pricing Model 36
Bob Litterman

CHAPTER 5
The Equity Risk Premium 44
Mark M. Carhart and Kurt Winkelmann

CHAPTER 6
Global Equilibrium Expected Returns 55
Bob Litterman

CHAPTER 7
Beyond Equilibrium, the Black-Litterman Approach 76
Bob Litterman

PART TWO
Institutional Funds

CHAPTER 8
The Market Portfolio 91
Ripsy Bandourian and Kurt Winkelmann

CHAPTER 9
Issues in Strategic Asset Allocation 104
Kurt Winkelmann

CHAPTER 10
Strategic Asset Allocation in the Presence of Uncertain Liabilities 110
Ronald Howard and Yoel Lax

CHAPTER 11
International Diversification and Currency Hedging 136
Kurt Winkelmann

CHAPTER 12
The Value of Uncorrelated Sources of Return 152
Bob Litterman

PART THREE
Risk Budgeting

CHAPTER 13
Developing an Optimal Active Risk Budget 171
Kurt Winkelmann

CHAPTER 14
Budgeting Risk along the Active Risk Spectrum 192
Andrew Alford, Robert Jones, and Kurt Winkelmann

CHAPTER 15
Risk Management and Risk Budgeting at the Total Fund Level 211
Jason Gottlieb

CHAPTER 16
Covariance Matrix Estimation 224
Giorgio De Santis, Bob Litterman, Adrien Vesval, and Kurt Winkelmann

CHAPTER 17
Risk Monitoring and Performance Measurement 249
Jacob Rosengarten and Peter Zangari

CHAPTER 18
The Need for Independent Valuation 285
Jean-Pierre Mittaz

CHAPTER 19
Return Attribution 297
Peter Zangari

CHAPTER 20
Equity Risk Factor Models 334
Peter Zangari

PART FOUR
Traditional Investments

CHAPTER 21
An Asset-Management Approach to Manager Selection 399
David Ben-Ur and Chris Vella

CHAPTER 22
Investment Program Implementation: Realities and Best Practices 407
J. Douglas Kramer

CHAPTER 23
Equity Portfolio Management 416
Andrew Alford, Robert Jones, and Terence Lim

CHAPTER 24
Fixed Income Risk and Return 435
Jonathan Beinner

PART FIVE
Alternative Asset Classes

CHAPTER 25
Global Tactical Asset Allocation 455
Mark M. Carhart

CHAPTER 26
Strategic Asset Allocation and Hedge Funds 483
Kurt Winkelmann, Kent A. Clark, Jacob Rosengarten, and Tarun Tyagi

CHAPTER 27
Managing a Portfolio of Hedge Funds 501
Kent A. Clark

CHAPTER 28
Investing in Private Equity 516
Barry Griffiths

PART SIX
Private Wealth

CHAPTER 29
Investing for Real After-Tax Results 533
Don Mulvihill

CHAPTER 30
Real, After-Tax Returns of U.S. Stocks, Bonds, and Bills, 1926 through 2001 546
Don Mulvihill

CHAPTER 31
Asset Allocation and Location 565
Don Mulvihill

CHAPTER 32
Equity Portfolio Structure 579
Don Mulvihill

Bibliography 595

Index 605

PART One

Theory

CHAPTER 1

Introduction: Why an Equilibrium Approach?

Bob Litterman

There are many approaches to investing. Ours at Goldman Sachs is an equilibrium approach. In any dynamic system, equilibrium is an idealized point where forces are perfectly balanced. In economics, equilibrium refers to a state of the world where supply equals demand. But it should be obvious even to the most casual observer that equilibrium never really exists in actual financial markets. Investors, speculators, and traders are constantly buying and selling. Prices are constantly adjusting. What then do we find attractive about an equilibrium approach to investing?

There are several attractions. First, in economic systems there are natural forces that come into play to eliminate obvious deviations from equilibrium. When prices are too low, demand will, at least over time, increase. When prices are too high, suppliers will enter the market, attracted by the profitable opportunity. There are lots of interesting, and sometimes uninteresting, reasons why such adjustments take time. Frictions, uncertain information, noise in the system, lack of liquidity, concerns about credit or legal status, or questions about enforceability of contracts all can impede adjustment, and sometimes deviations can be quite large. But financial markets, in particular, tend to have fewer frictions than other markets, and financial markets attract smart investors with resources to exploit profitable opportunities. Thus, deviations from equilibrium tend to adjust relatively rapidly in financial markets.

We need not assume that markets are always in equilibrium to find an equilibrium approach useful. Rather, we view the world as a complex, highly random system in which there is a constant barrage of new data and shocks to existing valuations that as often as not knock the system away from equilibrium. However, although we anticipate that these shocks constantly create deviations from equilibrium in financial markets, and we recognize that frictions prevent those deviations from disappearing immediately, we also assume that these deviations represent opportunities. Wise investors attempting to take advantage of these opportunities take actions that create the forces which continuously push the system back toward equilibrium. Thus, we view the financial markets as having a center of gravity that is defined by the equilibrium between supply and demand.

Understanding the nature of that equilibrium helps us to understand financial markets as they constantly are shocked around and then pushed back toward that equilibrium.

The second reason we take an equilibrium approach is that we believe this provides the appropriate frame of reference from which we can identify and take advantage of deviations. While no financial theory can ever capture even a small fraction of the detail and complexities of real financial markets, equilibrium theory does provide guidance about general principles of investing. Financial theory has the most to say about markets that are behaving in a somewhat rational manner. If we start by assuming that markets are simply irrational, then we have little more to say. Perhaps we could find some patterns in the irrationality, but why should they persist? However, if we are willing, for example, to make an assumption that there are no arbitrage opportunities in markets, which is to assume that there are no ways for investors to make risk-free profits, then we can look for guidance to a huge amount of literature that has been written about what should or should not happen. If we go further and add the assumption that markets will, over time, move toward a rational equilibrium, then we can take advantage of another elaborate and beautiful financial theory that has been developed over the past 50 years. This theory not only makes predictions about how markets will behave, but also tells investors how to structure their portfolios, how to minimize risk while earning a market equilibrium expected return. For more active investors, the theory suggests how to take maximum advantage of deviations from equilibrium.

Needless to say, not all of the predictions of the theory are valid, and in truth there is not one theory, but rather many variations on a theme, each with slightly different predictions. And while one could focus on the limitations of the theory, which are many, or one could focus on the many details of the different variations that arise from slight differences in assumptions, we prefer to focus on one of the simplest global versions of the theory and its insights into the practical business of building investment portfolios.

Finally, let us consider the consequences of being wrong. We know that any financial theory fails to take into account nearly all of the complexity of actual financial markets and therefore fails to explain much of what drives security prices. So in a sense we know that the equilibrium approach is wrong. It is an oversimplification. The only possibly interesting questions are where is it wrong, and what are the implications?

Nonetheless, suppose we go ahead and assume that this overly simple theory drives the returns on investments. One great benefit of the equilibrium approach to investing is that it is inherently conservative. As we will see, in the absence of any constraints or views about markets, it suggests that the investor should simply hold a portfolio proportional to the market capitalization weights. There may be some forgone opportunity, and there may be losses if the market goes down, but returns are guaranteed to be, in some fundamental sense, average.

Holding the market portfolio minimizes transactions costs. As an investor there are many ways to do poorly, through either mistakes or bad luck. And there are many ways to pay unnecessary fees. The equilibrium approach avoids these pitfalls. Moreover, no matter how well one has done, unfortunately there are almost always many examples of others who have done better. The equilibrium approach is likely to minimize regret. If an investor starts with an approach that assumes the markets are close to equilibrium, then he or she has realistic expectations of earning a fair return, and won't be led to make costly mistakes or create unacceptable losses.

Suppose an investor ignores the lessons of equilibrium theory. There are lots of ways the markets can be out of equilibrium. If an investor makes a particular assumption about how that is the case and gets that approach wrong, he or she could easily be out on a limb, and the consequences could be disastrous relative to expectations. The equilibrium approach may not be as exciting, but over long periods of time the overall market portfolio is likely to produce positive results.

Investors today have a lot more opportunity to invest intelligently than did previous generations. Tremendous progress has been made in both the theory and the practice of investment management. Our understanding of the science of market equilibrium and of portfolio theory has developed greatly over the past 50 years. We now have a much better understanding of the forces that drive markets toward equilibrium conditions, and of the unexpected factors that shock markets and create opportunities. In addition, the range of investment products, the number of service providers, and the ease of obtaining information and making investments have all increased dramatically, particularly in the past decade. At the same time, the costs of making investments have decreased dramatically in recent years. Today it is far easier than ever before for the investor to create a portfolio that will deliver consistent, high-quality returns. This book provides a guide to how that can be done.

We have divided the text into six parts. The first presents a simple, practical introduction to the theory of investments that has been developed in academic institutions over the past 50 years. Although academic in origin, this theory is a very practical guide to real-world investors and we take a very applied approach to this material. We try to provide examples to help motivate the theory and to illustrate where it has implications for investor portfolios. Our hope is to make this theory as clear, as intuitive, and as useful as possible. We try to keep the mathematics to a minimum, but it is there to some extent for readers who wish to pursue it. We also provide references to the important original source readings.

The second part is focused on the problems faced by the largest institutional portfolios. These funds are managed primarily on behalf of pensions, central banks, insurance companies, and foundations and endowments. The third part concerns various aspects of risk, such as defining a risk budget, estimating covariance matrices, managing fund risk, insuring proper valuations, and understanding performance attribution. The fourth part looks at traditional asset classes, equities and bonds. We look at the problem of manager selection, as well as managing global portfolios. The fifth part considers nontraditional investments such as currency and other overlay strategies, hedge funds, and private equity. Finally, the last part focuses on the particular problems of private investors such as tax considerations, estate planning, and so on. Paradoxically, the investment problems of private investors are typically much more complicated than those of most institutional portfolios simply because of the unfortunate necessity of private individuals to pay taxes. For example, even in the simplest equilibrium situation, buying and holding a market capitalization portfolio is no longer optimal for a taxable investor. The simple buy-and-hold strategy, while it is generally very tax efficient, can nonetheless still usually be improved upon by selling individual securities when they have encountered short-term losses relative to their purchase prices. Such losses can then generally be used to reduce taxes.

Throughout this book the equilibrium theory is sometimes evident, and sometimes behind the scenes, but it infuses all of our discussions of what are appropriate investment decisions.

CHAPTER 2

The Insights of Modern Portfolio Theory

Bob Litterman

In order to be successful, an investor must understand and be comfortable with taking risks. Creating wealth is the object of making investments, and risk is the energy that in the long run drives investment returns.

Investor tolerance for taking risk is limited, though. Risk quantifies the likelihood and size of potential losses, and losses are painful. When a loss occurs it implies consumption must be postponed or denied, and even though returns are largely determined by random events over which the investor has no control, when a loss occurs it is natural to feel that a mistake was made and to feel regret about taking the risk. If a loss has too great an impact on an investor's net worth, then the loss itself may force a reduction in the investor's risk appetite, which could create a significant limitation on the investor's ability to generate future investment returns. Thus, each investor can only tolerate losses up to a certain size. And even though risk is the energy that drives returns, since risk taking creates the opportunity for bad outcomes, it is something for which each investor has only a limited appetite.

But risk itself is not something to be avoided. As we shall discuss, wealth creation depends on taking risk, on allocating that risk across many assets (in order to minimize the potential pain), on being patient, and on being willing to accept short-term losses while focusing on long-term, real returns (after taking into account the effects of inflation and taxes). Thus, investment success depends on being prepared for and being willing to take risk.

Because investors have a limited capacity for taking risk it should be viewed as a scarce resource that needs to be used wisely. Risk should be budgeted, just like any other resource in limited supply. Successful investing requires positioning the risk one takes in order to create as much return as possible. And while investors have intuitively understood the connection between risk and return for many centuries, only in the past 50 years have academics quantified these concepts mathematically and worked out the sometimes surprising implications of trying to maximize expected return for a given level of risk. This body of work, known today as modern portfolio theory, provides some very useful insights for investors, which we will highlight in this chapter.

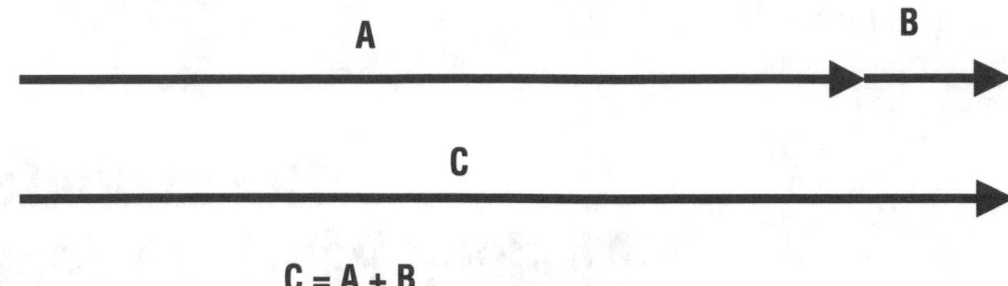

A = Old Portfolio Expected Return

B = New Investment Expected Return

C = New Portfolio Expected Return

FIGURE 2.1 Expected Return Sums Linearly

The interesting insights provided by modern portfolio theory arise from the interplay between the mathematics of return and risk. It is important at this juncture to review the different rules for adding risks or adding returns in a portfolio context. These issues are not particularly complex, but they are at the heart of modern portfolio theory. The mathematics on the return side of the investment equation is straightforward. Monetary returns on different investments at a point in time are additive. If one investment creates a $30,000 return and another creates a $40,000 return, then the total return is $70,000. The additive nature of investment returns at a point in time is illustrated in Figure 2.1.

Percentage returns compound over time. A 20 percent return one year followed by a 20 percent return the next year creates a 44 percent[1] return on the original investment over the two-year horizon.

The risk side of the investment equation, however, is not so straightforward. Even at a point in time, portfolio risk is not additive. If one investment creates a volatility[2] of $30,000 per year and another investment creates a volatility of $40,000 per year, then the total annual portfolio volatility could be anywhere between $10,000 and $70,000. How the risks of different investments combine depends on whether the returns they generate tend to move together, to move independently, or to offset. If the returns of the two investments in the preceding example are roughly independent, then the combined volatility is approximately[3] $50,000; if they move together, the combined risk is higher; if they offset, lower. This degree to which returns move together is measured by a statistical quantity called *correlation*, which ranges in value from +1 for returns that move perfectly together to zero for independent returns, to –1 for returns that always move in oppo-

[1]The two-period return is z, where the first period return is x, the second period return is y, and $(1 + z) = (1 + x)(1 + y)$.

[2]Volatility is only one of many statistics that can be used to measure risk. Here "a volatility" refers to one standard deviation, which is a typical outcome in the distribution of returns.

[3]In this calculation we rely on the fact that the variance (the square of volatility) of independent assets is additive.

site directions. The fact that risks are not additive, but combine in a way that depends on how returns move together, leads to the primary insight of portfolio theory—that diversification, the spreading of investments across less correlated assets, tends to reduce overall portfolio risk.

This risk reduction benefit of diversification can be a free lunch for investors. Given the limited appetite each investor has for risk, the diversification benefit itself creates the opportunity to generate higher expected returns. An additional diversification benefit accrues over time. Due to the relatively high degree of independence of returns during different intervals of time, risk generally compounds at a rate close to the square root of time, a rate that is much less than the additive rate at which returns accrue.[4] This difference between the rate at which return grows over time and the rate at which risk grows over time leads to the second insight of portfolio theory—that patience in investments is rewarded and that total risk should be spread relatively evenly over time.

Consider a simple example. Taking one percentage point of risk per day creates only about 16 percent[5] of risk per year. If this one percentage point of risk per day is expected to create two basis points[6] of return per day, then over the course of 252 business days in a year this amount of risk would generate an approximately 5 percent return. If, in contrast, the same total amount of risk, 16 percent, were concentrated in one day rather than spread over the year, at the same rate of expected return, two basis points per percentage point, it would generate only $2 \cdot 16 = 32$ basis points of expected return, less than one-fifteenth as much. So time diversification—that is, distributing risk evenly over a long time horizon—is another potential free lunch for investors.

All of us are familiar with the trade-offs between quality and cost in making purchases. Higher-quality goods generally are more expensive; part of being a consumer is figuring out how much we can afford to spend on a given purchase. Similarly, optimal investing depends on balancing the quality of an investment (the amount of excess return an investment is expected to generate) against its cost (the contribution of an investment to portfolio risk). In an optimal consumption plan, a consumer should generate the same utility per dollar spent on every purchase. Otherwise, dollars can be reallocated to increase utility. Similarly, in an optimal portfo-

[4]In fact, as noted earlier, due to compounding, returns accrue at a rate greater than additive. To develop an intuition as to why risk does not increase linearly in time, suppose the risk in each of two periods is of equal magnitude, but independent. The additive nature of the variance of independent returns implies that the total volatility, the square root of total variance, sums according to the same Pythagorean formula that determines the hypotenuse of a right triangle. Thus, in the case of equal risk in two periods, the total risk is not two units, but the square root of 2, as per the Pythagorean formula. More generally, if there are the square root of t units of risk (after t periods), and we add one more unit of independent risk in period t + 1, then using the same Pythagorean formula there will be the square root of $t + 1$ units of risk after the t + 1st period. Thus, the total volatility of independent returns that have a constant volatility per unit of time grows with the square root of time. This will be a reasonable first-order approximation in many cases.

[5]Note that 16 is just slightly larger than the square root of 252, the number of business days in a year.

[6]A basis point is one-hundredth of a percent.

lio, the investor should generate the same expected return per unit of portfolio risk created in each investment activity. Otherwise, risk can be reallocated to achieve a portfolio with higher expected returns. The analogy between budgeting dollars in consumption and budgeting risk in portfolio construction is powerful, but one has to constantly keep in mind that in investing, risk is the scarce resource, not dollars.

Unfortunately, many investors are not aware that such insights of modern portfolio theory have direct application to their decisions. Too often modern portfolio theory is seen as a topic for academia, rather than for use in real-world decisions. For example, consider a common situation: When clients of our firm decide to sell or take public a business that they have built and in which they have a substantial equity stake, they receive very substantial sums of money. Almost always they will deposit the newly liquid wealth in a money market account while they try to decide how to start investing. In some cases, such deposits stay invested in cash for a substantial period of time. Often individuals do not understand and are not comfortable taking investment risks with which they are not familiar. Portfolio theory is very relevant in this situation and typically suggests that the investor should create a balanced portfolio with some exposure to public market securities (both domestic and global asset classes), especially the equity markets.

When asked to provide investment advice to such an individual, our first task is to determine the individual's tolerance for risk. This is often a very interesting exercise in the type of situation described above. What is most striking is that in many such cases the individual we are having discussions with has just made or is contemplating an extreme shift in terms of risk and return—all the way from one end of the risk/return spectrum to the other. The individual has just moved from owning an illiquid, concentrated position that, when seen objectively, is extremely risky[7] to a money market fund holding that appears to have virtually no risk at all.[8] Portfolio theory suggests that for almost all investors neither situation is a particularly good position to be in for very long. And what makes such situations especially interesting is that if there ever happens to be a special individual, either a very aggressive risk taker or an extremely cautious investor, who ought to be comfortable with one of these polar situations, then that type of investor should be the least comfortable with the other position. Yet we often see the same individual investor is comfortable in either situation, and even in moving directly from one to the other.

The radically different potential for loss makes these two alternative situations outermost ends of the risk spectrum in the context of modern portfolio theory. And yet it is nonetheless difficult for many individuals to recognize the benefit of a more balanced portfolio. Why is that? One reason is that people often have a very hard time distinguishing between good outcomes and good decisions—and this is particularly true of good outcomes associated with risky investment decisions. The risk is of-

[7]Of course, perceptions of risk can differ markedly from objective reality. This topic has been recently investigated by two academics, Tobias Moskowitz and Annette Vising-Jorgensen, in a paper entitled, "The Returns to Entrepreneurial Investment: The Private Equity Premium Puzzle," forthcoming in the *American Economic Review.*

[8]We will come back to the important point that the short-term stability of the nominal pretax returns from a money market fund can actually create considerable real after-tax risk over longer periods of time.

ten not recognized. Generally speaking, an investor who has just been successful in an investment wants to take credit for the good decisions that created this result and to think of the result as being an almost inevitable consequence of the investor's good decisions rather than to recognize that the outcomes of investment decisions, no matter how good, are, at least in the short run, usually very much a function of luck.

Consider an investor in the situation just described. Such an individual is certainly not typical. He or she has just joined the elite group of people who have experienced the closest equivalent in the business world to winning the lottery. This individual is among the lucky few with a concentrated risk position whose companies have survived, grown profitably, and at an opportune time have been sold to the public. In retrospect, the actions taken by these individuals to create their wealth—the hard work, the business acumen, and in particular the holding of a concentrated position—might seem unassailable. We might even suppose that other investors should emulate their actions and enter into one or more such illiquid concentrated positions.

However, there is a bigger picture. Many small business owners have businesses that fail to create significant wealth. Just as in a lottery, the fact that there are a few big winners does not mean that a good outcome is always the result of a good investment choice. Granting that there may be many psychic benefits of being a small business owner with a highly concentrated investment in one business, it is nonetheless typically a very risky investment situation to be in. When a single business represents a significant fraction of one's investment portfolio, there is an avoidable concentration of risk. The simplest and most practical insight from modern portfolio theory is that investors should avoid concentrated sources of risk.[9] Concentrated risk positions ignore the significant potential risk reduction benefit derived from diversification. While it is true that to the extent that a particular investment looks very attractive it should be given more of the overall risk budget, too much exposure can be detrimental. Portfolio theory provides a context in which one can quantify exactly how much of an overall risk budget any particular investment should consume.

Now consider the investors who put all of their wealth in money market funds. There is nothing wrong with money market funds; for most investors such funds should be an important, very liquid, and low-risk portion of the overall portfolio. The problem is that some investors, uncomfortable with the potential losses from risky investments, put too much of their wealth in such funds and hold such positions too long. Over short periods of time, money market funds almost always produce steady, positive returns. The problem with such funds is that over longer periods of time the real returns (that is, the purchasing power of the wealth created after taking into account the effects of inflation and taxes) can be quite risky and historically have been quite poor.

Modern portfolio theory has one, and really only one, central theme: **In constructing their portfolios investors need to look at the expected return of each investment in relation to the impact that it has on the risk of the overall portfolio.** We will come back to analyze in more detail why this is the case, but because it is, the practical message of portfolio theory is that sizing an investment is best understood

[9]Unfortunately, in the years 2000 and 2001 many employees, entrepreneurs, and investors in technology, telecommunications, and Internet companies rediscovered firsthand the risks associated with portfolios lacking diversification.

as an exercise in balancing its expected return against its contribution to portfolio risk.[10] This is the fundamental insight from portfolio theory. This insight was first suggested by Harry Markowitz (1952) and developed in his subsequent texts (1959 and 1987). Upon first reflection, this insight seems intuitive and not particularly remarkable. As we will see, however, getting it right in building portfolios is generally neither easy nor intuitive.

The first complication is perhaps obvious. It is hard to quantify either expected returns or contributions to portfolio risk.[11] Thus, balancing the two across different investments is especially difficult. Coming up with reasonable assumptions for expected returns is particularly problematic. Many investors focus on historical returns as a guide, but in this book we will emphasize an equilibrium approach to quantifying expected returns. We will return to this topic in Chapters 5 and 6. Here, we focus on measuring the contribution to portfolio risk, which, though still complex, is nonetheless more easily quantified. For an investor the risk that each investment adds to a portfolio depends on all of the investments in the portfolio, although in most cases in a way that is not obvious.

The primary determinant of an investment's contribution to portfolio risk is not the risk of the investment itself, but rather the degree to which the value of that investment moves up and down with the values of the other investments in the portfolio. This degree to which these returns move together is measured by a statistical quantity called "covariance," which is itself a function of their correlation along with their volatilities. Covariance is simply the correlation times the volatilities of each return. Thus, returns that are independent have a zero covariance, while those that are highly correlated have a covariance that lies between the variances of the two returns. Very few investors have a good intuition about correlation, much less any practical way to measure or monitor the covariances in their portfolios. And to make things even more opaque, correlations cannot be observed directly, but rather are themselves inferred from statistics that are difficult to estimate and which are notoriously unstable.[12] In fact, until very recently, even professional investment advisors did not have the tools or understanding to take covariances into account in their investment recommendations. It is only within the past few years that the wider availability of data and risk management technology has allowed the lessons of portfolio theory to be more widely applied.

The key to optimal portfolio construction is to understand the sources of risk in the portfolio and to deploy risk effectively. Let's ignore for a moment the difficulties raised in the previous paragraph and suppose we could observe the correlations and volatilities of investment returns. We can achieve an increased return by recognizing situations in which adjusting the sizes of risk allocations would improve the

[10]In an optimal portfolio this ratio between expected return and the marginal contribution to portfolio risk of the next dollar invested should be the same for all assets in the portfolio.

[11]Each of these topics will be the subject of later chapters. Equilibrium expected returns are discussed in Chapters 5 and 6, and deviations from equilibrium in Chapter 7. Estimating covariance is the topic of Chapter 16.

[12]Whether the unobserved underlying correlations themselves are unstable is a subtle question. The statistics used to measure correlations over short periods of time, which have estimation error, clearly are unstable.

expected return of the overall portfolio. A typical situation would be one in which an asset is relatively independent of other investments in a portfolio and even though it may be risky by itself, it tends to add little to the overall risk of the portfolio. We refer to such investments as diversifiers, and we use them to increase return while living within an overall risk budget. Understanding and being able to measure and monitor the contribution to portfolio risk of every investment becomes a key part of the decision about how much to invest in each asset or investment activity. Assets that contribute less risk to a portfolio are less expensive in terms of using up the risk budget, and, everything else being equal, we should invest more in them.

The intuition behind the mathematics that determines portfolio volatility can be seen in the geometry of a simple diagram. An asset affects the risk of a portfolio in the same way that the addition of a side to a line segment changes the distance of the end point to the origin. This nonlinear nature of adding risks, and the dependence on correlation, is illustrated in Figure 2.2.

The length of the original line segment represents the risk of the original portfolio. We add a side to this segment; the length of the side represents the volatility of the new asset. The distance from the end of this new side to the origin represents the risk of the new portfolio. In the geometry of this illustration, it is clear how the angle between the new side and the original line segment is critical in determining how the distance to the origin is changed. In the case of portfolio risk, the correlation of the new asset with the original portfolio plays the same role as the angle between the new side and the original line segment. Correlations range between –1 and +1 and map into angles ranging from 0 to 180 degrees. The case of no correlation corresponds to a 90-degree angle. Positive correlations correspond to angles between 90 and 180 degrees, and negative correlations correspond to angles between 0 and 90 degrees.

Let us consider a relatively simple example of how to use measures of contribution to portfolio risk to size investments and to increase expected returns. A key question that faces both individual and institutional investors is how much to invest in domestic versus international equities. One school of thought is that as

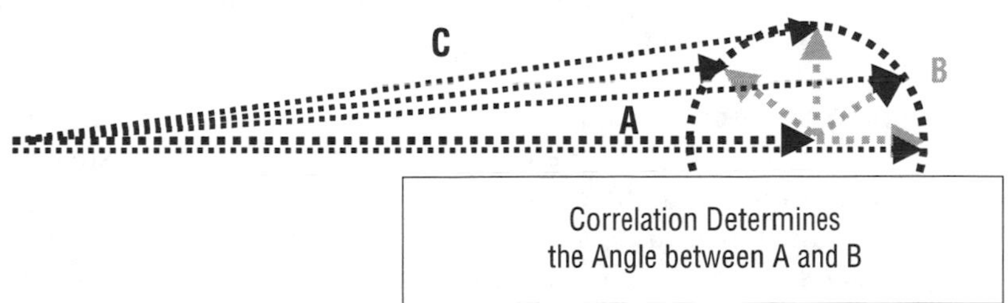

FIGURE 2.2 Summation of Risk Depends on Correlation

global markets have become more correlated recently, the value of diversifying into international equities decreases. Let us see how modern portfolio theory addresses this question. In this example we will initially treat domestic and international equities as if they were the only two asset classes available for investment.

In the absence of other constraints (transactions costs, etc.), optimal allocation of the risk budget requires equities to be allocated from domestic to international markets up to the point where the ratio of expected excess return[13] to the marginal contribution to portfolio risk is the same for both assets. We focus on this marginal condition because it can provide guidance toward improving portfolios. Although a full-blown portfolio optimization is straightforward in this context, we deliberately avoid approaching the problem in this way because it tends to obscure the intuition and it does not conform to most investors' behavior. Portfolio decisions are almost always made at the margin. The investor is considering a purchase or a sale and wants to know how large to scale a particular transaction. The marginal condition for portfolio optimization provides useful guidance to the investor whenever such decisions are being made.

This example is designed to provide intuition as to how this marginal condition provides assistance and why it is the condition that maximizes expected returns for a given level of risk. Notice that we assume that, at a point in time, the total risk of the portfolio must be limited. If this were not the case, then we could always increase expected return simply by increasing risk.

Whatever the initial portfolio allocation, consider what happens if we shift a small amount of assets from domestic equities to international equities and adjust cash in order to hold the risk of the portfolio constant. In order to solve for the appropriate trades, we reallocate the amounts invested in domestic and international equities in proportion to their marginal contribution to portfolio risk. For example, if at the margin the contribution to portfolio risk of domestic equities is twice that of international equities, then in order to hold risk constant for each dollar of domestic equities sold we have to use a combination of proceeds plus cash to purchase two dollars' worth of international equities. In this context, if the ratio of expected excess returns on domestic equities to international equities is less than this 2 to 1 ratio of marginal risk contribution, then the expected return on the portfolio will increase with the additional allocation to international equities. As long as this is the case, we should continue to allocate to international equities in order to increase the expected return on the portfolio without increasing risk.

Let us adopt some notation and look further into this example. Let Δ be the marginal contribution to the risk of the portfolio on the last unit invested in an asset. The value of Δ can be found by calculating the risk of the portfolio for a given asset allocation and then measuring what happens when we change that allocation. That is, suppose we have a risk measurement function, $\text{Risk}(d, f)$, that we use to compute the risk of the portfolio with an amount of domestic equities, d, and an amount of international equities, f.

We use the notation $\text{Risk}(d, f)$ to emphasize that different measures of risk

[13]Throughout this book when we use the phrase "expected excess return," we mean the excess over the risk-free rate of interest.

could be used. Many alternative functional forms have been proposed to measure investors' utility as a function of return distributions. As noted earlier, while investors are generally very sensitive to losses, they often seem much less cognizant of the risk that can lead to losses. We will explore some of these issues in the next chapter. To be concrete, we will here use the statistical measure, volatility, to quantify risk. For example, suppose we have some relevant data that allows us to measure the volatilities and correlation of the returns of domestic and international equities. Let these quantities be σ_d, σ_f, and ρ, respectively. Then one example of a simple risk function would be the volatility of the portfolio, given by:

$$\text{Risk}(d,\ f) = \left(d^2 \cdot \sigma_d^2 + f^2 \cdot \sigma_f^2 + 2 \cdot d \cdot f \cdot \sigma_d \cdot \sigma_f \cdot \rho\right)^{1/2} \tag{2.1}$$

Let us use the notation Δ_d to refer to the marginal contribution to portfolio risk of domestic equities. This quantity is defined to be the derivative of the risk function with respect to the quantity of domestic equity, that is, the difference in the risk of portfolios that have the same amount of international equities, but a small difference, δ, in domestic equities, divided by δ. Thus, we can formalize this as an equation:

$$\Delta_d(\delta) = \frac{\text{Risk}(d+\delta,\ f) - \text{Risk}(d,\ f)}{\delta} \tag{2.2}$$

and let Δ_d be the limit of Δ_d (δ) as δ goes to zero.

Similarly, the marginal contribution to risk of international equities is given by Δ_f, which is defined as the limit of Δ_f (δ) as δ goes to zero, where:

$$\Delta_f(\delta) = \frac{\text{Risk}(d,\ f+\delta) - \text{Risk}(d,\ f)}{\delta} \tag{2.3}$$

These marginal contributions to risk are the key to optimal portfolio allocations. As we shall see, a condition for a portfolio to be optimal is that the ratio of expected excess return to marginal contribution to risk is the same for all assets in the portfolio.

Let us return to the question of whether we can improve the portfolio by selling domestic equity and buying international equity. The ratio of marginal contributions to risk is Δ_d / Δ_f. Let the expected excess returns on domestic and international equities be given by e_d and e_f, respectively. Now suppose e_d / e_f is less than Δ_d / Δ_f. How much international equity must we purchase in order to keep risk constant if we sell a small amount of domestic equities? The rate of change in risk from the sale of domestic equity sales is $-\Delta_d$ per unit sold. In order to bring risk back up to its previous level, we need to purchase (Δ_d / Δ_f) units of international equity. The effect on expected return to the portfolio is $-e_d$ per unit sold of domestic equity and $+(\Delta_d / \Delta_f)e_f$ from the purchase of an amount of international equity that leaves risk unchanged. If, in this context, expected return is increased, then we should continue to increase the allocation to international equity. If expected return is decreased, then we should sell international equity and buy domestic equity. The only case in which the expected return of the portfolio cannot be increased while holding risk constant is if the following condition is true:

$$-e_d + \left(\frac{\Delta_d}{\Delta_f}\right) e_f = 0 \tag{2.4}$$

Rearranging terms, we have:

$$\frac{e_d}{\Delta_d} = \frac{e_f}{\Delta_f} \tag{2.5}$$

Thus, in this simple two-asset example we have derived a simple version of the general condition that the expected return divided by the marginal contribution to portfolio risk should be the same for all assets in order for a portfolio to be optimal. If this condition is not met, then we can increase the expected return of the portfolio without affecting its risk.

More generally, we can consider sales and purchases of any pair of assets in a multiple asset portfolio. The above analysis must hold, where in this context let the risk function, Risk(w), give the risk for a vector w, which gives the weights for all assets. Let $\text{Risk}_m(w, \delta)$ give the risk of the portfolio with weights w and a small increment, δ, to the weight for asset m. Define the marginal contribution to portfolio risk for asset m as Δ_m, the limit as δ goes to zero of:

$$\Delta_m(\delta) = \frac{\text{Risk}_m(w, \delta) - \text{Risk}(w)}{\delta} \tag{2.6}$$

Then, as earlier, in an optimal portfolio it must be the case that for every pair of assets, m and n, in a portfolio the condition

$$\frac{e_m}{\Delta_m} = \frac{e_n}{\Delta_n} \tag{2.7}$$

is true. If not, the prescription for portfolio improvement is to buy the asset for which the ratio is higher and sell the asset for which the ratio is lower and to continue to do so until the ratios are equalized. Note, by the way, that if the expected return of an asset is zero then the optimal portfolio position must be one in which the Δ is also zero. Readers familiar with calculus will recognize that this condition—that the derivative of the risk function is zero—implies that the risk function is at a minimum with respect to changes in the asset weight.

Let us consider how this approach might lead us to the optimal allocation to international equities. To be specific, let us assume the values shown in Table 2.1 for the volatilities and expected excess returns for domestic and international equity, and for cash. Assume the correlation between domestic and international equity is .65.

We will use as the risk function the volatility of the portfolio:

$$\text{Risk}(d, f) = \left(d^2 \cdot \sigma_d^2 + f^2 \cdot \sigma_f^2 + 2 \cdot d \cdot f \cdot \sigma_d \cdot \sigma_f \cdot \rho\right)^{1/2} \tag{2.8}$$

In order to make the analysis simple, let us assume that the investor wants to maximize expected return for a total portfolio volatility of 10 percent. Consider an

TABLE 2.1 Values for Volatilities and Expected Excess Returns

	Volatility	Expected Excess Return	Total Return
Domestic equity	15%	5.5%	10.5%
International equity	16	5.0	10.0
Cash	0	0.0	5.0

investor starting with an equity allocation that is totally domestic. In order to generate a volatility of 10 percent the investor must hold a combination of cash plus domestic equity. In particular, given the assumed 15 percent volatility of domestic equity, the proportion allocated to equity is two-thirds of the total value and the allocation to cash is one-third of the total value.

What happens as the investor starts to sell domestic equity and buy international equity? The marginal contributions to risk are simply the derivatives of this risk function with respect to the two arguments and can easily be shown to be given by the formulas:

$$\Delta_d = \frac{d \cdot \sigma_d^2 + f \cdot \sigma_d \cdot \sigma_f \cdot \rho}{\text{Risk}(d, f)} \tag{2.9}$$

$$\Delta_f = \frac{f \cdot \sigma_f^2 + d \cdot \sigma_d \cdot \sigma_f \cdot \rho}{\text{Risk}(d, f)} \tag{2.10}$$

In the special case when $f = 0$, these formulas simplify to:

$$\Delta_d = \frac{d \cdot \sigma_d^2}{\left(d^2 \cdot \sigma_d^2\right)^{1/2}} = \sigma_d = .150$$

$$\Delta_f = \frac{d \cdot \sigma_d \cdot \sigma_f \cdot \rho}{\left(d^2 \cdot \sigma_d^2\right)^{1/2}} = \sigma_f \cdot \rho = .104$$

Suppose the portfolio has a valuation, v, which is a large number, and an investor sells one unit of domestic equity; that is, let $\delta = -1$. Recalling equation (2.6),

$$\Delta_d(\delta) = \frac{\text{Risk}(d + \delta, f) - \text{Risk}(d, f)}{\delta} \tag{2.11}$$

The risk of the portfolio is decreased by approximately:

$$\text{Risk}(d + \delta, f) - \text{Risk}(d, f) = .15 \cdot \delta = -.15 \tag{2.12}$$

In order to keep risk unchanged, the investor must purchase

$$\frac{\Delta_d}{\Delta_f} = \frac{.15}{.104} = 1.442 \tag{2.13}$$

units of international equity. The sale of one unit of domestic equity reduces portfolio expected excess return by .055.

The purchase of 1.442 units of international equity increases expected excess return by:

$$1.442 \cdot .05 = .07215 \tag{2.14}$$

Thus, at the margin, selling domestic equity and purchasing international equity at a rate that keeps risk constant raises expected excess by

$$.07215 - .055 = .01715 \tag{2.15}$$

per unit of domestic equity sold.

The signal provided by this marginal analysis is clear and intuitive. The investor should continue to sell domestic equity as long as the effect on portfolio expected excess returns is positive and the risk is unchanged. Unfortunately, of course, this increasing of expected return cannot go on indefinitely. As soon as the investor sells domestic equity and purchases international equity, the marginal contribution to risk of domestic equity begins to fall and that of international equity begins to rise. This effect is why the marginal analysis is only an approximation, valid for small changes in portfolio weights.

Before we investigate what happens as the investor moves from domestic to international equities, however, we might consider what is the expected excess return on international equities for which the investor would be indifferent to such a transaction. Clearly, from the preceding analysis this point of indifference is given by the value, e_f, such that:

$$(1.442 \cdot e_f - .055) = 0 \tag{2.16}$$

In other words, the hurdle rate, or point of indifference for expected return, such that expected returns beyond that level justify moving from domestic to foreign equity, is $e_f = 3.8\%$.

To put it differently, if the expected excess return on foreign equity is less than this value, then we would not have any incentive to purchase international equities.

If we were to look only at the risks and not expected excess returns, we might suppose that because of the diversification benefit we would always want to hold some international equity, at least at the margin. In fact, when assets are positively correlated, as they are in this example, even the first marginal allocation creates marginal risk and requires an expected excess return hurdle in order to justify a purchase.

Now suppose the investor has sold 10 percent of the domestic equity. In order to keep risk constant the investor can purchase 13.18 percent of international equity. Using the new values $d = .5667$ and $f = .1318$ in the above formulas we can confirm that the volatility of the portfolio remains 10 percent and that $\Delta_d = .148$ and $\Delta_f = .122$.

The impact on expected excess return of the portfolio per unit sold at this point is given by:

$$\left(\frac{\Delta_d}{\Delta_f}\right)e_f - e_d = (1.212 \cdot .05 - .055) = .01667 \tag{2.17}$$

The investor should continue to sell domestic equity since the value is positive, though at this level the value in terms of incremental expected excess return to the portfolio per unit sold has dropped slightly, from .17 to .1667.

Again we might consider what is the expected excess return on international equities for which the investor would be indifferent to an additional purchase. The point of indifference is the value, e_f, such that:

$$(1.212 \cdot e_f - .055) = 0 \tag{2.18}$$

That is, $e_f = 4.5$.

The hurdle rate to justify continued purchase of international equities has increased from 3.8 to 4.5 because the marginal contribution of international equities to portfolio risk has increased relative to that of domestic equities.

Suppose the investor decides to keep only 10 percent of the portfolio value in domestic equity. In order to keep risk constant, the investor must purchase 56 percent of international equity. Using the new values $d = .10$ and $f = .56$ in the earlier formulas we can confirm that the volatility of the portfolio remains 10 percent and that $\Delta_d = .110$ and $\Delta_f = .159$.

The impact on expected excess return of the portfolio per unit sold at this point is given by

$$\left(\frac{\Delta_d}{\Delta_f}\right) e_f - e_d \tag{2.19}$$

which simplifies as

$$(.691 \cdot .05 - .055) = -.012 \tag{2.20}$$

Now the investor has sold too much domestic equity. The value in terms of incremental expected excess return to the portfolio per unit sold has dropped so far that it has become negative. The negative impact on the portfolio expected return signals that at the margin the investor has too much risk coming from international equity and the expected excess return does not justify it.

The hurdle rate to justify continued purchase of international equities is the value, e_f, such that:

$$(.691 \cdot e_f - .055) = 0 \tag{2.21}$$

That is, $e_f = 8.0\%$.

Clearly this hurdle rate has continued to increase as the marginal contribution of international equities to portfolio risk has continued to increase relative to that of domestic equities.

Throughout this example, we have assumed that the investor has a set of expected excess returns for domestic and international equities. In practice, few investors have such well-formulated views on all asset classes. Notice, however, that given an expected excess return on any one asset class, in this case domestic equities, we can infer the hurdle rate, or point of indifference for purchases or sales of every other asset. We refer to these hurdle rates as the *implied views* of the portfolio. Rather than following the traditional portfolio optimization strategy, which requires prior specification of expected excess returns for all assets, we can take an existing portfolio, make an assumption of excess return on one asset (or more generally on any one combination of assets such as a global equity index), and back out the implied views on all others. Purchases of an asset are warranted when the hurdle rate given by the implied view appears to be lower than one's view of what a reasonable value is. Conversely, sales are warranted when the implied view appears to be above a reasonable value. Implied views provide insight for deciding how large to make investments in an existing portfolio.

There is, however, an additional layer of complexity that we have not yet reflected: the role of correlation in determining optimal positions. In the earlier analysis, the role correlation played, through its impact on portfolio risk and marginal contribution to portfolio risk, was not highlighted.

In order to highlight the role of correlation, we extend the previous example by considering a new asset, commodities, which we suppose has volatility of 25 percent, and correlations of –.25 with both domestic and international equities. Consider again the original portfolio invested two-thirds in domestic equities and the rest in cash. If we consider adding commodities to this portfolio, the marginal contribution to portfolio risk of commodities, Δ_c, is –.066. Because domestic equity risk is the only risk in the portfolio, a marginal investment in commodities, which is negatively correlated with domestic equity, reduces risk.

This negative marginal contribution to portfolio risk for commodities leads to a new phenomenon. Commodities are a diversifier in the portfolio. The previous type of analysis, where we sold domestic equity and bought enough international equity to hold risk constant, doesn't work. If we sell domestic equities and try to adjust the commodity weight to keep risk constant, we have to sell commodities as well. If instead we were to purchase commodities, then we would reduce risk on both sides of the transaction.

Retain the assumption that the expected excess return on domestic equities is 5.5 percent and consider the hurdle rate for purchases of commodities, which is given by the expected excess return, e_c, such that:

$$\left(\frac{\Delta_d}{\Delta_c}\right)e_c - .055 = 0 \tag{2.22}$$

That is,

$$\left(\frac{.150}{-.066}\right)e_c - .055 = 0 \tag{2.23}$$

$$-2.27 \cdot e_c - .055 = 0 \tag{2.24}$$

$$e_c = -2.42\% \tag{2.25}$$

Here we see an interesting result. When there is no existing position in commodities in this portfolio, the implied view for commodities is a negative expected excess return.

Now suppose we assume a 5 percent long position in commodities. Most investors believe that a long position implies a positive expected excess return and that the larger the position, the larger is the implied view. As we shall see here, that is not necessarily the case; the implied view may not even have the same sign as the position. With the commodity position at 5 percent and the domestic equity position unchanged, the portfolio volatility drops to 9.76 percent. The marginal contributions to portfolio risk, Δ_d and Δ_c, become .149 and –.032, respectively. The marginal contribution of domestic equity has declined while the marginal contribution for commodities remains negative, but has increased closer to zero. Consider the new implied view for commodities, the value of e_c such that:

$$\left(\frac{.149}{-.032}\right)e_c - .055 = 0 \tag{2.26}$$

$$-4.65 \cdot e_c - .055 = 0 \tag{2.27}$$

$$e_c = -1.18\% \tag{2.28}$$

Here we see a truly counterintuitive result: Despite our positive holding of a significant 5 percent of the portfolio weight in the volatile commodities asset class, the implied view for commodities is a negative expected excess return.

Perhaps one might at this point jump to the conclusion that this counterintuitive sign reversal will always be the case when the correlations between two assets are negative. However, that is not so. Let us see what happens when we further increase the size of the commodity position from 5 percent to 15 percent of the portfolio. The volatility of the portfolio remains unchanged at 9.76 percent. The portfolio volatility is minimized at 9.68 when there is a 10 percent weight in commodities. At 15 percent commodities the volatility is increasing as more commodities are added. The marginal contributions to portfolio risk, Δ_d and Δ_c, are now .139 and .032, respectively. The contribution of domestic equity continues to decline while the marginal contribution for commodities has increased from a negative value to a positive value.

The new hurdle rate for commodities is given by the expected excess return, e_c, such that:

$$\left(\frac{.139}{.032}\right)e_c - .055 = 0 \tag{2.29}$$

$$4.35 \cdot e_c - .055 = 0 \tag{2.30}$$

$$e_c = 1.26\% \tag{2.31}$$

Clearly at 15 perceent of portfolio weight, the hurdle rate on commodities has become positive. As the weight on commodities increased from 5 percent to 15 percent the impact on the portfolio changed from being a diversifier to being a source of risk. In fact, there is a weight in commodities for which the portfolio volatility is minimized. This risk-minimizing value for commodities, holding all other assets constant, is a special and interesting position. It has the property that this is the point where the marginal contribution to risk, and therefore the implied excess return on commodities, is zero. We can solve for the risk-minimizing position by setting $\Delta_c = 0$, or equivalently, solving for c such that $(c \cdot \sigma_c^2 + \mathrm{d} \cdot \sigma_d \cdot \sigma_c \cdot \rho_{dc}) = 0$ where ρ_{dc} is the correlation between commodities and domestic equity. Holding fixed the two-thirds weight in domestic equity, this risk-minimizing position in commodities is 10 percent.

Thus, an important intuition that helps make sense of implied views is as follows: **Holding fixed the weights in all other assets, there is a risk-minimizing position for each asset. Weights greater than that risk-minimizing position reflect positive implied views; weights less than that risk-minimizing position reflect bearish views.** In terms of implied views, there is nothing special about positions greater than or less than zero; the neutral point is the risk-minimizing position. In a single-asset portfolio the risk-minimizing position is, of course, zero. More generally, however, the risk-minimizing position is a function of the positions, volatilities, and correlations of all assets in the portfolio. Moreover, in multiple-asset portfolios, the risk-minimizing position for each asset can be a positive or a negative value.

We can use the correlations among assets and the risk-minimizing position to identify opportunities to improve allocations in portfolios. In multiple-asset portfolios, the risk-minimizing position will only be at zero for assets that are uncorrelated with the rest of the portfolio. Such uncorrelated assets are likely to be very valuable. Any asset or investment activity that is uncorrelated with the portfolio, but also has a positive expected excess return, should be added to the portfolio. In addition to commodities, such uncorrelated activities might include the active risk relative to benchmark of traditional active asset managers, certain types of hedge funds, active currency overlays, and global tactical asset allocation mandates.

More generally, in the case of assets or activities that do have correlations with the existing portfolio and therefore that have nonzero risk-minimizing positions, any position that lies between zero and the risk-minimizing position is likely to represent an opportunity for the investor. Such positions are counterintuitive in the same sense that the 5 percent commodity position was. The implied view is opposite to the sign of the position. Typically investors hold positive positions because they have positive views, and vice versa. Whenever this is the case and the actual position is less than the risk-minimizing position, it makes sense to increase the size of the position. This situation is an opportunity because increasing the size of the position will both increase expected return and decrease risk.

In terms of asset allocation, the counterintuitive positions described here are not very common. Most positions in asset classes are long positions (very few investors hold short positions in asset classes), most asset returns correlate positively with portfolio returns (commodities are an exception), and most assets are expected to have positive excess returns. More generally, though, we will see that when portfolios of securities are constructed with risk measured relative to a benchmark, such counterintuitive positions arise quite often.

In this chapter we have taken the simple idea of modern portfolio theory—that investors wish to maximize return for a given level of risk—and developed some very interesting, and not particularly obvious, insights into the sizing of positions. We have tried to develop these ideas in a way that is intuitive and which can be used to help make portfolio decisions at the margin. We avoid the usual approach to portfolio construction, which suggests an unrealistic reliance on developing expected return assumptions for all assets and on the use portfolio optimizers.

SUMMARY

Risk is a scarce resource that needs to be allocated in ways that maximize expected return.

The single condition that characterizes optimal portfolios is that at the margin the ratio of the change in expected excess return to the contribution to portfolio risk must be the same for every asset or investment activity.

Marginal contributions to portfolio risk can be measured relatively easily. Together with an expected excess return assumption for one asset class, they determine a set of implied views for all other asset classes.

Implied views provide a set of hurdle rates that can guide portfolio decisions. When the hurdle rates seem to be unreasonably low or high they are useful signals that positions should be either increased or decreased.

The position in an asset that minimizes portfolio risk is an important location, and is not typically zero. Weights greater than the risk-minimizing position represent bullish views; weights that are less than the risk-minimizing position represent bearish views.

Counterintuitive positions, those between zero and the risk-minimizing position, represent opportunities for most investors to add value. Most likely, the investor faced with such a situation will want to increase the size of the position until it is at least larger in absolute value than the risk-minimizing position, perhaps much larger.

CHAPTER 3

Risk Measurement

Bob Litterman

How should investors think about investment risk, and how can they monitor it and manage it in ways to increase expected portfolio returns?

Many investors assume, incorrectly, that the purpose of risk management is to minimize risk. In fact, many investors even go so far as to worry that too much focus on risk management will constrain their portfolio managers and inhibit their ability to generate positive returns. Nothing could be further from the truth.

In an investment portfolio risk is necessary to drive return. The purpose of the risk management function is not to minimize risk, but rather is to monitor the level and sources of risk in order to make sure that they match expectations. In fact, an investor with strong risk management controls ought to feel more comfortable targeting and maintaining a higher overall level of risk, thus leading to higher, rather than lower, returns over time.

Attention to risk management should be a positive contributor to portfolio return. For this to happen investors need to create an investment plan with which they are comfortable, and they need to follow that plan. The plan should have two components: an asset allocation and a risk budget. These two components of the investment plan are critical in defining its risk profile. They will also determine the long-run rate of return on the portfolio.

Nonetheless, risk creates the capacity for losses, and along the path to long-run returns there will be painful bumps, losses of capital that will cause any investor to question the plan. One critical role that risk management can play in generating long-run returns is to provide comfort in such situations that a portfolio remains in adherence to the long-run plan so that the investor does not lose confidence and overreact to short-term market fluctuations.

A useful way to think about risk in a portfolio is to view it as a scarce resource. Just as a family must budget its expenditures against its income, an investor must budget the risk in the portfolio relative to his or her limited ability to accommodate losses. Of course, some investors will be able to accept larger losses than others, so there is no single level of risk that is right for all investors. If we compare portfolios of investors in different countries and at different points in time, we see substantial differences in the average level of risk taken. Even within a particular country at a point in time there will be substantial differences across different investors, even those with the same degree of wealth. Over the course of their lives, many investors show a typical pattern of increasing ability to take risk as they increase their level of savings, followed by decreasing risk as they retire and draw down those savings. But even after accounting for differences in circumstances, age, country, taxes, and other measurable characteristics, there is a strong component of the tolerance for risk taking that simply depends on the preferences of the individual.

Recognizing that risk is a scarce resource and that different investors have different appetites for risk, each investor needs to develop an individually tailored investment plan with a target level of risk for the portfolio based on the investor's preferences and circumstances. For most investment portfolios the dominant risk will be a relatively stable exposure to the traditional asset markets, especially equities and bonds. These long-term stable exposures to asset markets are referred to as the strategic asset allocation.

The construction and management of a portfolio is simplified considerably when the investment plan is divided into two steps: first the development of a strategic asset allocation that leads to the creation of a benchmark, and second the implementation and monitoring of portfolio allocations relative to that benchmark. The strategic asset allocation is designed to be a stable asset mix that maximizes long-run expected return given a targeted level of risk. The strategic asset allocation is a high-level allocation to broad asset classes that determines the overall level of portfolio risk and will be the dominant determinant of long-run performance. For example, a very simple asset allocation might be 60 percent equity (i.e., stocks) and 40 percent bonds. A less risky allocation would be 50 percent equity and 50 percent bonds. Higher equity allocations will create more short-term volatility in the portfolio, but over long horizons can be expected to generate higher returns.

Today most asset allocations also differentiate between domestic and foreign assets and might include other alternative assets such as real estate, private equity, or commodities, as well. In large institutional portfolios, the strategic asset allocation might include as many as 15 or more asset classes, although the complexity of trying to deal with too many asset classes can quickly outweigh any potential benefit. We will have much more to say about the process of developing a strategic asset allocation for institutions and individuals, respectively, in Chapters 9 and 31. Developing the strategic asset allocation is a topic for which the equilibrium approach, which we develop in Chapters 4, 5, and 6, can add considerable insight.

Once the strategic asset allocation is set, the second step is to develop an implementation plan. This plan will vary depending on the nature of the investor, the size of the portfolio, and other constraints that might apply. Two particular issues that all such plans should focus on, though, are first, managing the costs associated with implementation, and second, budgeting and monitoring how much risk and return are generated relative to the strategic benchmark.

A very important consideration that investors need to recognize is that the risk and return characteristics of asset class benchmarks are generally available at very low cost through passive index portfolios, derivative products, or exchange-traded funds (ETFs). Investors should not pay a significant management fee for such a benchmark exposure. These index products provide an efficient, and therefore attractive, way to implement asset allocation decisions. Over time, as these products have become available at low cost, a very significant amount of wealth has, appropriately, moved into passively managed index portfolios.

Nonetheless, most money is still invested with active managers, managers who create portfolios that do not replicate, but rather attempt to outperform, indexes. This is an important distinction. The difference between a passive manager and an active manager can be compared to the difference between a housepainter and an artist. Both work with paint, but they do two completely different jobs, and they get paid very differently. Active managers do not get paid fees for creating passive exposures to broad asset classes. To pay an active fee for benchmark returns would be like paying an expensive artist to paint the walls of a room a solid color—it could be done, but it would be a waste of money.

Active managers earn their fees for taking risk relative to a benchmark, referred to as active risk. Active managers deviate from benchmarks in an attempt to outperform their benchmark. These deviations are the artistry that the active managers use to create the opportunity to outperform the benchmark, but they also create the risk that the manager may underperform. It is the expectation of outperformance generated by active risk, not the exposure to the market risk embedded in the benchmark, that justifies active management fees. Clearly, active risk should be taken only when there is an expected positive net return (after fees and after taxes) associated with it. Just like artists, active managers come in many different styles. Some are very conservative; they take very little active risk and have very low fees. Others take lots of active risk and charge high fees. A common terminology for referring to active management styles, in order of increasing risk, is as follows: enhanced, structured, and concentrated.

We emphasize the distinction between total risk and active risk because it is a key element in the design and overall management of portfolios. Asset allocation balances the risks and returns embedded in benchmarks; risk budgeting revolves around making decisions between passive and active management, choosing different styles of active management, and allocating and balancing the active risk that is created when active managers are grouped together. In the portfolios of most investors, the dominant risk and source of return comes from asset allocation decisions and exposures to broad market indexes. The active risk in a portfolio, representing the aggregation of all deviations from benchmarks, is generally a small contributor to overall portfolio risk and return. When managed carefully it can be an important source of positive returns relative to the benchmark, but otherwise it can be a costly source of risk and underperformance.

Too often portfolio construction is a bottom-up by-product of decisions made about individual managers, funds, or other investment products. Each such decision should not be made independently; rather portfolio construction should start with a top-down asset allocation—the determination of allocations to different broad asset classes. Only after the asset allocation is determined should the implementation decisions be made. The decisions about which products to put into a portfolio and from whom should be part of this process we call risk budgeting.

The choices that need to be made as part of the risk budgeting implementation plan include for each asset class:

- What benchmark or benchmarks to use.
- How much of the portfolio to allocate to index products versus active managers.
- What types of styles of active managers to invest in.
- How many managers to hire or funds to invest in.

- What percentage of the assets to give to each manager.
- Whether, and if so how, to make tactical asset allocation adjustments.
- For nondomestic assets, whether to hedge foreign currency risk.

Chapters 11 through 15 will have much more to say about developing the portfolio implementation plan.

Once the asset allocation and risk budget are in place, the final and ongoing step in portfolio construction is the process of updating the implementation of the plan and monitoring adherence to the plan. This process includes rebalancing different components of the portfolio, reviewing the allocations of external portfolio managers and funds, and adjusting investments for cash flows into or out of the portfolio. The process should also include a regular review of the risk budget to make sure it is on track, an occasional update of the strategic asset allocation benchmark, and finally the monitoring of whether to terminate existing managers and whether to hire new ones.

Risk management is an important aspect of the process of monitoring adherence of a portfolio to the investment plan. As noted above, the primary role of risk management is not to minimize risk, but to make sure the portfolio is on track relative to the asset allocation benchmark and the risk budget. If a manager or some aspect of the investment plan is creating unexpected risk or unusual performance, it is the role of the risk management function to identify, understand, and, if necessary, correct the situation. The risk management function could just as well identify a portfolio that is taking too little risk relative to the budget as find one that is taking too much risk. A portfolio that has a risk allocation that it is not using is not only wasting a scarce resource, the opportunity to use risk to generate returns; it is also likely to be charging fees that are not being earned.

There are many dimensions of risk. We have been focusing on market risk, the term used to describe the gains and losses that can arise from changes in the valuations of securities. For example, changes in the value of a portfolio due to a decline in the general level of valuations in the equity market constitute a form of market risk. Other types of risk that need to be managed include the following:

- *Credit risk*—the risk of loss due to the default of a counterparty.
- *Legal risk*—the risk of loss due to a contract dispute, a lawsuit, or illegal activity.
- *Operational risk*—the risk of loss due to a problem in clearing or settlement of securities or contracts.
- *Liquidity risk*—the risk of loss due to the inability to dispose of securities or contracts in a timely manner

Different approaches are required to monitor these various types of risk. Market risk is somewhat special in that quantitative models play a key role in monitoring market risk. Credit risk also requires quantitative models, but qualitative judgments play a larger role. Qualitative approaches are the key in evaluating the other types of portfolio risk, though quantitative approaches are becoming more and more common in areas such as liquidity risk and operational risk.

The role of risk management in investment management is often misunderstood, in part because the discipline of risk management in financial institutions has grown rapidly in recent years, particularly in banks and securities firms with a significant focus on derivative securities. In banks and securities firms the role of risk management is focused on internal management and control, as well as regulatory reporting. Although there are many common features with portfolio risk management—after all, most large financial institutions are portfolios of risk-taking activities—there are also many important differences.

Perhaps the most important difference between how risk management is practiced in these two worlds is that in financial institutions risk is measured in an absolute sense, whereas in asset management the risk in portfolios is almost always measured relative to benchmarks. Another difference is that in financial institutions risk is aggregated and taken on behalf of the owners of the firm. In the asset management world, risk is often taken on behalf of external clients or investors in a fund. An investment firm will typically have many, perhaps hundreds, of different portfolios to monitor, each with different investors.

In financial institutions traders manage positions that tend to be held for short periods of time. Derivatives are used extensively to manage risk. Complex securities and contracts are created and positioned to facilitate the needs of other businesses. Fees are earned in the process, and traders generally try to hedge the risks of such positions. Positions are most often taken in reaction to client needs. Because they are reacting to external demands, traders in financial institutions are generally in the business of providing liquidity.

In contrast to such traders, portfolio managers tend to rely on simpler, direct investments. Through their investment decisions they most often initiate and intentionally create exposures. They are typically demanding liquidity and creating, rather than hedging, risks. Generally asset managers hold such positions for much longer periods of time.

Finally, in financial institutions decision making tends to be hierarchical, and the primary means of control is through the setting of limits and monitoring various measures of risk relative to those limits. There is shared responsibility. A trader is expected to request permission before exceeding a limit. In investment management firms, decisions are made by portfolio mangers who take primary responsibility for their performance. There are seldom limits. Portfolios tend to have guidelines and/or targets for the amount of risk to be taken, but it would be an unusual circumstance for a portfolio manager to solicit management approval for a change in a portfolio for which he or she is responsible.

All of these differences between the practice of risk management at banks and securities firms and risk management in the investment world have led to a different set of approaches and tools, and even a different language for risk management in the two industries.

For example, Value at Risk (VaR) is a standard measure of risk among financial institutions. The VaR of a set of positions is a measure of the size of loss that is expected to occur with a specified frequency, such as the largest daily loss that is expected to occur with a specified frequency such as once per year. The focus of management tends to be on short-term potential losses—that is, on how much could be lost in an event that could occur over a short period of time. VaR is an attempt to answer the most common question about risk posed by the management of a financial institution: "How much money can I lose?" Of course, VaR does not really answer this question, which is fundamentally unanswerable. VaR is the answer to a slightly different question that *can* be answered. Rather than focus on what is the worst case, it focuses on what will happen in an appropriately defined rare event. A key concern in the calculation of VaR is what happens in these rare, short-term events. This concern is especially relevant with respect to portfolios that incorporate options, since these and other derivatives allow the level of exposure to increase rapidly with changes in the levels of markets.

Investors, in contrast, do not usually focus on rare, short-term events. Investors tend to have much longer horizons, and they have used different risk measures, which reflect that longer focus. The two most common measures of risk in the investment world are annualized volatility and annualized tracking error. Annualized volatility is simply the volatility of portfolio returns over a one-year horizon. Tracking error measures the volatility, measured in percent or basis points—that is, hundredths of a percent—of active risk relative to a benchmark over a one-year horizon.

These different measures of risk, VaR in the case of financial institutions and tracking error or annualized volatility in the case of portfolio managers, are but one reflection of the different needs and concerns of these two different communities. There has been, though, a very beneficial cross-fertilization of ideas. Because the risk management effort grew very rapidly recently in financial institutions, many practitioners with a securities firm background have tried to take the concepts, the language, and even the software of the financial institutions and apply them to the investment world. Despite the occasional confusion and resistance that this transfer has sometimes caused, a positive effect has been the rapid advances in availability of risk management tools in the investment community.

There is a common unifying principle that runs through all financial risk management: In financial planning one needs to recognize and to be prepared for dealing with all possible future outcomes. This principle, as applied to portfolios, implies that the investor needs to have a realistic understanding of potential changes in market levels and valuations of individual securities, and an understanding of how those changes will impact his or her portfolio valuation. Thus, the fundamental focus of risk management is the understanding of this distribution of potential future outcomes. Given this distribution, and comparing it with the distributions of future outcomes associated with other portfolios, the investor can make informed decisions about asset allocation and the risk budget.

In practice there are many complexities to risk management. In general, there is no one characteristic or measure that can summarize the distribution of potential outcomes adequately. Many characteristics of the distribution may affect decisions. For most investors the primary focus is on reducing the probability of bad outcomes. Portfolio decisions are generally driven by the inability to sustain losses above a certain size. While much of the science of modern portfolio theory focuses on the mean and volatility of the distribution of outcomes, these two statistics may not be adequate for the purposes of many investors whose focus is on particular downside events.

Another issue that arises in assessing risk is that picking the appropriate time horizon for decision making is not always obvious, nor inconsequential. On the one hand, decisions can always be revised with new information, suggesting a relatively shorter horizon may be adequate. On the other hand, focusing on a short horizon can have very important, and generally negative, consequences for investment decisions. Avoiding bad outcomes clearly requires either reducing risk or buying securities that have downside protection, both of which negatively impact longer-term expected returns. In the short run, this impact on expected return is not an important consideration in preventing losses. Thus, investors who focus on the short run tend to be relatively more risk averse. If the investor does, in fact, have a short time before the investment must be cashed in, then this is appropriate.

However, in the long run, the increased expected return from careful risk taking clearly has a positive effect and must be taken into account in determining the amount of risk to take and thus in centering the distribution of outcomes. As mentioned in the previous chapter, investors benefit from the fact that returns accumulate more quickly over time than does risk. Other considerations also become more important in the long run. For example, as we will discuss in Chapter 29, over longer periods of time inflation creates considerable uncertainty in the real purchasing power of nominal investments. The benefit of tax deferment of capital gains is another consideration that grows with longer horizons. Thus, time horizon has a major impact on how investors should evaluate the risk and return trade-offs of different portfolio decisions.

Probably the simplest and most important risk management exercise for an investor is the stress test. The stress test is a very simple exercise. A particular dimension of risk is identified and one asks what happens if there is a shock, that is, a major event along this dimension. The change in portfolio value is measured. For example, a stress test might answer the question, "Suppose the stock market were to decline by 10 percent; what would be the impact on my portfolio?" The basis for this measurement is a set of assumptions about how a stock market decline would affect the value of each security in the portfolio. We start by identifying "the stock market" with a particular benchmark. In the United States, we might use the S&P 500 stock index. If one of the investments in the portfolio were an S&P 500 index fund, then the impact on this investment would be simply a 10 percent decline. If there were an investment in a portfolio managed with a small amount of active risk relative to an S&P 500 benchmark, then one would expect the impact to be close to the 10 percent decline. A common statistical measure of equity portfolio risk is the beta, the expected change in value of a stock or portfolio relative to the change in value of the market. If a portfolio has a beta of 1, then its decline is expected to match that of the market, while a portfolio with a beta of .9 would be expected to decline only 9 percent if the market were to decline 10 percent.

There are no set rules for how to measure the beta of a security. One common approach is to look at historical data and use it to statistically estimate a coefficient that measures the degree to which historically the security has, on average, moved when the market has changed. Such an approach is subject to all the usual statistical measurement issues such as how much data to use and whether to look at daily, weekly, monthly, or some other frequency of returns. In this, as in many risk management contexts, however, it is important not to lose sight of the forest for the trees. Accuracy is often not the primary issue. Just getting a reasonably accurate measure of exposure is often close enough to answer the most important questions.

More generally, we want to measure the exposures of a portfolio to a set of common dimensions of risk. In addition to equity market changes, we might like to measure sensitivity to interest rate changes, currency changes, energy prices, credit spreads, foreign market changes, and so on. The particular measures one focuses on will depend on the portfolio characteristics.

Most exposures in investment portfolios are linear. Linearity is simply the property that when the market move is scaled up or down, the gain or loss is scaled the same amount. When exposures are linear, it suffices to measure the response to an event of any given size. All other sized events can be extrapolated from the one. More generally, when exposures are not linear, then we need to measure the response to events of different sizes. Nonlinear exposures most commonly arise from options and other derivatives.

Stress tests are relatively simple to perform and provide a relatively straightforward set of signals of what types of shocks could create portfolio losses. The limitations of stress tests are important to recognize, however. Because the stress test provides no guidance about the likelihood of shocks of different sizes, or the likelihood that different markets will move together or offset each other, it is difficult to measure overall portfolio risk. In order to make sense of stress tests alone, the investor has to have a good intuition about the volatilities and correlations of all the different risk factors.

Another simple risk management tool is the scenario analysis. A scenario is like a stress test, except that generally a number of different risk factors are stressed at the same time. In fact, a stress test can be thought of as one particularly simple version of a scenario analysis. What makes the scenario analysis useful, and conceptually different from a stress test, is that the scenario is generally constructed to represent an event that is likely to constitute a particularly significant risk to the portfolio. For example, a common scenario to analyze is a global recession and the expected impacts on equity, real estate, credit, bond, and currency markets around the world. Such a scenario would most likely include the different impact on cyclically sensitive industries relative to more stable sectors, and it might also include secondary impacts such as increased likelihood of defaults, monetary policy changes, changes in wages and rents, and so on.

The strength of a scenario analysis is that it is an excellent tool for preparing oneself for a particular outcome. Two weaknesses of scenario analysis as a risk management tool, however, are that it is hard to know which scenarios to analyze and how to react. Portfolio managers often try to put probabilities on different scenarios, but it is very difficult to approximate all possible outcomes with a few scenarios, and even more difficult to reasonably put probabilities on such scenarios.

The standard statistical measure of risk is volatility, which measures the size of a typical outcome's deviation relative to its expected value. When quantifying the volatility of portfolios, the volatility is generally measured in terms of percent per year. A balanced portfolio with equities and bonds might, for example, have an annualized volatility of 9 percent. If such a portfolio has an expected return of 10 percent with a 9 percent volatility, that implies that the portfolio returns will typically—that is, about two-thirds of the time—fall between 1 percent and 19 percent.

There are many approaches to measuring volatility. Most such measures rely on extrapolating past behavior into the future. Perhaps the simplest approach, when the portfolio has not changed recently, is to measure the historical volatility of the portfolio returns directly. When the portfolio itself has changed, or when the volatility or correlations of different components of the portfolio have changed, then a more disaggregated approach must be taken. In this case the usual approach is to use stress tests to measure the sensitivity of the portfolio to its different risk factors, and then to estimate the covariance structure—that is, the volatilities and correlations—of those different risk factors.

Depending on whether or not the stress exposures are linear, different methods are available for computing the portfolio volatility. Intuitively, however, the basic idea is that the covariance structure creates a probability distribution for risk factors, and the stress tests provide a basis for valuing the portfolio with respect to each risk factor outcome. Thus, a distribution is implied for portfolio valuations, and we can measure the volatility of that distribution.

The strength of volatility as a measure of risk is that it summarizes many possible outcomes in one number. The weaknesses of volatility as a measure of risk are many, but the most important is that it tries to capture risk, which is generally a multidimensional concept, in a single number. Only in special cases, such as when returns are known to have a normal distribution, does volatility alone provide enough information to measure the likelihood of most events of interest. Another weakness of volatility as a measure of risk is that it does not distinguish upside risk from downside risk—all deviations from the expected value create risk. This weakness is mitigated for portfolios because the distributions tend to be approximately symmetric. Finally, the volatility measure provides no insight into the sources of risk.

Despite these shortcomings, and despite the fact that for all these reasons volatility has been discredited as a measure of risk in the securities and banking industry, volatility is still the most common measure of risk in investment portfolios. This is not, however, necessarily a weakness. It certainly is the case that in the typical investment context, most of the limitations of volatility are less important. For example, over longer periods of time the aggregation of independent returns is likely to create more normally shaped distributions. Investors are less likely to use options or other derivatives that create significant nonlinear responses to market moves. Moreover, in most situations it is very difficult to estimate precise measures of the shape of return distributions. In many contexts a one-dimensional measure is adequate and the primary interest is in whether and to what extent portfolio changes impact the basic shape of the distribution of portfolio returns. For this purpose volatility is the preferred measure. Thus, while it is important to understand the limitations of this statistical measure, it is likely to remain an important tool in the management of risk in investment portfolios.

Economists have struggled for centuries with the problem of measuring investor's utility and how it changes as a function of wealth. There is general agreement on very little other than that this function is concave—that is, that utility increases with wealth, but that the rate of increase gets smaller as wealth increases. When utility has this concave shape it is said to exhibit risk aversion. An investor will prefer a known level of wealth to a distribution of outcomes with the same expected value.

Modern portfolio theory has developed a very elegant set of insights based on a simple utility function, which in turn is based on the idea that utility increases with higher expected returns and decreases with increased volatility. We can write this utility function as:

$$U(r_p) = E(r_p) - .5 \cdot \lambda \cdot \sigma^2(r_p) \tag{3.1}$$

where E( ) is the expected value of the distribution of uncertain returns, r_p, and σ^2( ) is the variance. The parameter, λ, is the degree of risk aversion of the investor. This utility function is usually justified as an approximation. Two conditions under which it will accurately represent an investor's behavior are locally where a more general smooth utility function can be approximated by a quadratic function, or globally for an investor with constant relative risk aversion and for which returns are normally distributed. Our view is that the key trade-offs in portfolio construction are likely to be illuminated with this function, that risk aversion is the key parameter to vary, and that the main insights of modern portfolio theory are likely to be robust with respect to alternative utility functions that might be found to be more accurate.

This equation is the basis for the mean-variance approach to portfolio optimization. Over time this classic utility function became the basis for the equilibrium theory, which we review in Chapter 4, and the large academic literature now referred to as modern portfolio theory. This mean-variance framework is usually represented graphically as in Figure 3.1, which shows the frontier of efficient portfolios. In this figure the horizontal axis shows portfolio volatility, and the vertical axis shows portfolio expected return. The portfolio frontier is a line or a curve that represents the set of all portfolios with the greatest possible expected return for a give level of volatility. Such portfolios are generally termed "Efficient." Curves of constant utility, termed "indifference" curves, show the trade-offs investors are willing to make in this space between expected return and risk. Increasing utility comes from moving from one such curve to another through generating either higher expected return, lower risk, or both.

When portfolios include only risky assets or have other constraints, then the optimal portfolio frontier is likely to be a concave curve as shown in Figure 3.1. If, however, investors are able to borrow and lend freely at a risk-free rate, then the optimal portfolio frontier is a line connecting the risk-free rate with the risky portfolio that has the highest ratio of expected excess return over the risk-free rate per unit of portfolio volatility, a ratio called the Sharpe ratio after Nobel laureate William F. Sharpe. In either case, the portfolio that maximizes utility will be one of the efficient portfolios and thus will lie on the efficient portfolio frontier. For a recent in-depth textbook treatment of modern portfolio theory the interested reader might consult Elton et al. (2002).

Clearly one condition for a portfolio to be optimal is that any change in an asset weight must fail to increase utility. This implies that, unless there are binding constraints, small changes in asset weights of an optimal portfolio must increase or decrease expected return per unit of portfolio volatility at the rate given by the slope of the utility indifference curve at the point of tangency to the efficient frontier. Thus when utility is defined as in equation (3.1) our theme from Chapter 2, that for a portfolio to be optimal the ratio of expected excess return to contribution to portfolio risk be the same for all assets, is justified formally as the marginal condition required for this utility function to be maximized. If for any asset this condition is not true, clearly we could, by adjusting that asset weight, increase the utility of the portfolio, contradicting the assumption that the portfolio is optimal.

Whatever the measure of portfolio risk, it is important to try to understand what the sources of risk in the portfolio are. Simply knowing the volatility of a portfolio, per se, does not provide any insight into what is creating the risk. Risks

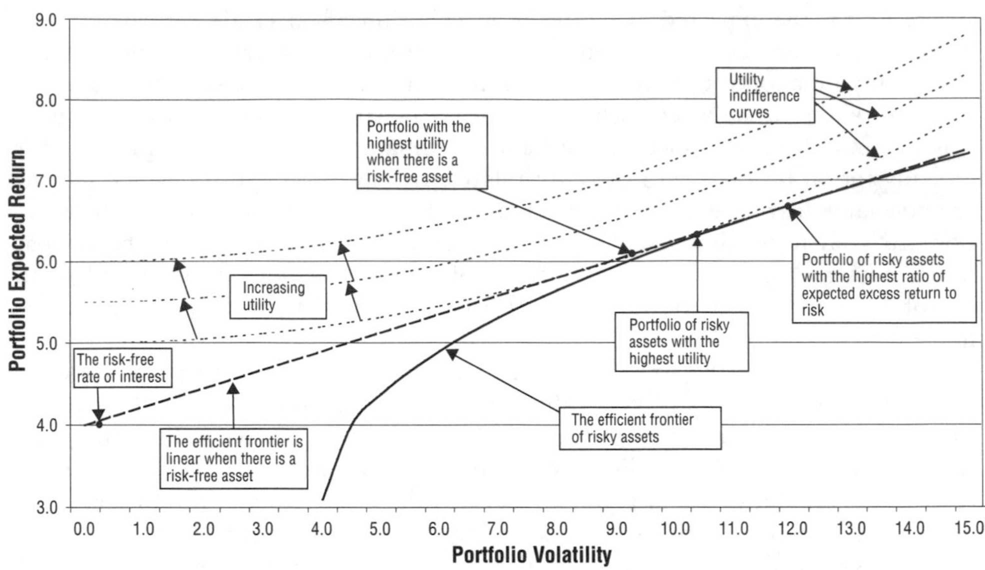

FIGURE 3.1 The Frontier of Efficient Portfolios

can be productive if they are expected to generate return, or unproductive when they are too large or unintended. Thus, knowing the level of risk in a portfolio is not enough. The investor needs to measure where the risk is coming from.

The best way to understand the sources of risk in a portfolio is simply to measure the impact on the overall portfolio risk of separate small changes in each component in the portfolio. This marginal measurement forms the basis for a decomposition of portfolio risk. It identifies the hot spots in the portfolio, the components to which portfolio risk is most sensitive.

The decomposition of risk is similar to but different from the marginal contribution to portfolio risk, which was described in Chapter 2. In forming optimal portfolios we try to equalize across all assets the ratio of the contribution to expected return from each asset with its contribution to portfolio risk. In that case we measure the change in portfolio risk that is caused by a unit addition of the asset to the portfolio. We might, for example, consider adding a unit of a new asset that is not currently in the portfolio. Such an addition will generally impact portfolio risk, either increasing or decreasing it. In measuring the decomposition of risk, though, we focus not on a unit change, but rather on what happens to portfolio risk when there is a percentage change in the portfolio weight. This difference in measuring marginal risk in the context of risk decomposition should be intuitive. In the first context we want to be very cautious about adding an asset to a portfolio. If the asset creates significant risk at the margin, we need to get paid an expected return premium for taking that marginal risk. In contrast, when measuring where risk is in a current portfolio we want to know how important are existing positions; if we don't already own an asset then it cannot be a source of risk in the current portfolio.

For well-behaved measures of risk, the total portfolio risk is equal to the sum of the marginal percentage changes in all the portfolio components. Thus, the percentage contribution to risk of each component of the portfolio is simply the marginal percentage change in risk divided by the total risk. This decomposition is valid for measures of portfolio risk having a property that when all positions are increased by a constant factor, then the portfolio risk increases by that factor. This is true, for example, for all three of the measures of portfolio risk we have mentioned—VaR, volatility, and tracking error.[1]

The portfolio decomposition is a very useful tool for identifying the significant hot spots in a portfolio. When these hot spots represent intended exposures, when the relative sizes make sense, and when the exposures are not too concentrated, then the investor can feel comfortable. Very often, however, the hot spots will reveal unintended risks or concentrations of risk that need to be reduced in size. We will give examples of the use of the portfolio decomposition in Chapter 13.

This chapter on risk management began by emphasizing that risk management is not designed to minimize risk. In the investment world risk management should not be a constraint, but rather a quality control. A sensible approach to risk management is to view it as an important source of investment return.

SUMMARY

Portfolios should have both an asset allocation benchmark, which determines the overall level of risk, and long-run expected return and a risk budget, which is a plan for how the asset allocation is implemented.

The basic role of risk management is to measure the adherence to this plan. The risk management function should identify any areas that are not on track.

Many of the tools of risk management from the securities and banking industries have been usefully imported to the investment world, but there are many contrasts in approach, which reflect important differences in the objectives and horizons of investors as opposed to traders.

The decomposition of risk is a particularly useful risk management tool because it highlights the hot spots, the most important sources of risk, in the portfolio.

---

[1]For a more complete discussion of this decomposition of risk, see the Litterman paper, "Hot Spots and Hedges," published as part of the Risk Management Series at Goldman Sachs, October 1966.

CHAPTER 4

The Capital Asset Pricing Model

Bob Litterman

The Capital Asset Pricing Model (CAPM) developed by Jack Treynor, William F. Sharpe, John Lintner, and Jan Mossin in the early 1960s was an important milestone in the development of modern portfolio theory. It is a simple mathematical model, and it is, like all scientific models, an attempt to capture some aspects of the world around us. But more than being a model, we view the CAPM as a framework for thinking about investments.[1]

The CAPM asks what happens, in the simplest possible world, when markets are efficient, all investors have identical information, and investors maximize the expected return in their portfolios and minimize the volatility. The CAPM is in this sense an equilibrium model. It takes market capitalizations as given and asks what must the levels of expected returns be for all investors to be satisfied holding the outstanding asset weights. The results provide a useful intuition about the long-run expected returns of different assets. The CAPM doesn't tell us what is the right level for the stock market at a point in time, but it does, for example, provide a basis for thinking about issues such as how much return should an investment in equity provide, how should the returns of different stocks differ as a function of their different risk characteristics, and how much equity belongs in a portfolio.

In this chapter we develop the intuition behind the CAPM in a very simple setting. For now we will not investigate deviations from equilibrium. We are not interested in this chapter in modeling the real world or in dealing with realistic portfolios. Rather, we want to develop some intuition, especially about how expected returns must adjust when the world is populated with investors who are attempting to maximize return and to minimize risk. The next two chapters will focus on how to calibrate the premium associated with the equilibrium market portfolio; we will develop a global version of the model and try to calibrate it to more realistic aspects of the world so that we can apply it in practice. In Chapter 7, we will investigate how to use the equilibrium model in a more realistic context in which we have views about how the markets deviate from equilibrium.

---

[1]For a recent review with extensive references to the literature on the CAPM, see William Sharpe's 1990 Nobel Lecture: "Capital Asset Prices with and without Negative Holding," *Nobel Lectures, Economic Sciences 1981–1990*, 312–332.

We start with a world that has a single period of time. Assume there is a fixed supply of two risky assets, which we will call equity and bonds. Let the outstanding supplies (that is, the market capitalization weights) be given by e and b, respectively. There is also a risk-free asset, which we refer to as cash. Cash is risk free in the sense that at the end of the period a unit investment in cash will return a known quantity, $1 + r$. Equity and bonds are risky in the sense that unit investments return random values, $1 + r_e$ and $1 + r_b$, respectively.

We take the risk in this world to be given exogenously. That is, we assume that r_e and r_b are random variables with known, or estimable, volatilities given by σ_e, and σ_b, and a correlation ρ. In contrast, we do not take the mean returns as given, but rather wish to solve for them in equilibrium. While we don't focus on prices, we do assume that investors will bid the prices for individual stocks and bonds up or down until their prices reach levels such that expected returns clear markets—that is, until the demand for each asset equals the outstanding supply. Let these unknown market-clearing expected returns be μ_e and μ_b, respectively.

At the beginning of the period, each investor must choose a set of portfolio weights that represent the proportion of his or her holdings of cash, bonds, and equity. For a representative investor, we express these portfolio weights as a percentage of beginning of period wealth. Let w_e and w_b represent the portfolio weights in equity and bonds, respectively, for the representative investor. The weight in cash is $1 - w_e - w_b$.

The investor chooses asset weights in order to maximize the value of a utility function that rewards higher expected returns and penalizes portfolio risk. In particular, let the expected return on the portfolio be given by μ_p and the volatility of the portfolio be given by σ_p. Assume the utility function has the simple quadratic form described in Chapter 3 and given by the following equation:

$$U = \mu_p - .5 \cdot \lambda \cdot \sigma_p^2 \tag{4.1}$$

The parameter λ gives the investor's risk aversion, the rate at which he or she will trade off a reduction in expected return for a reduction in variance. The quadratic form of the utility function represents the assumption that as risk increases there is an increasing aversion (in the form of willingness to forgo expected return) to additional increases in risk.

Portfolio expected return is given by the asset weights times the expected returns on each asset.

$$\mu_p = r \cdot (1 - w_e - w_b) + w_e \cdot \mu_e + w_b \cdot \mu_b \tag{4.2}$$

Portfolio variance is also determined by asset weights in the risky assets and the assumed volatilities and correlation between these assets. Letting $\sigma_{e,b}$ represent the covariance of equity and bond returns, that is, $\sigma_{e,b} = \sigma_e \cdot \sigma_b \cdot \rho$,

$$\sigma_p^2 = w_e^2 \cdot \sigma_e^2 + w_b^2 \cdot \sigma_b^2 + 2 \cdot w_e \cdot w_b \cdot \sigma_{e,b} \tag{4.3}$$

Thus, for given weights, w_e and w_b, the investor has a utility given by:

$$U(w_e, w_b) = r \cdot (1 - w_e - w_b) + w_e \cdot \mu_e + w_b \cdot \mu_b \\ -.5 \cdot \lambda \cdot (w_e^2 \cdot \sigma_e^2 + w_b^2 \cdot \sigma_b^2 + 2 \cdot w_e \cdot w_b \cdot \sigma_{e,b}) \tag{4.4}$$

For the representative investor, if the parameters of the distributions of returns are known (that is, if r, μ_e, μ_b, σ_e, σ_b, and ρ are given), then it is a relatively easy mathematical optimization exercise to choose asset weights that maximize utility. As was discussed in Chapter 2, the optimal weights must be ones for which the ratio of the marginal contribution to portfolio expected return to contribution to portfolio risk is the same for equity and bonds.

The contributions to portfolio expected returns for equity and for bonds are given by $(\mu_e - r)$ and $(\mu_b - r)$, respectively. Given a set of weights w_e and w_b, the marginal contribution to portfolio risk for an increase in the weight in equity is given by:

$$\frac{w_e \cdot \sigma_e^2 + w_b \cdot \sigma_{e,b}}{\sigma_p} \tag{4.5}$$

Similarly, the contribution to portfolio risk for a marginal increase in the weight in bonds is given by:

$$\frac{w_b \cdot \sigma_b^2 + w_e \cdot \sigma_{e,b}}{\sigma_p} \tag{4.6}$$

Thus, one condition for the portfolio weights to be optimal is that:

$$\frac{\mu_e - r}{w_e \cdot \sigma_e^2 + w_b \cdot \sigma_{e,b}} = \frac{\mu_b - r}{w_b \cdot \sigma_b^2 + w_e \cdot \sigma_{e,b}} \tag{4.7}$$

The risk aversion parameter, λ, determines how much risk is desired given the available expected returns. Given the form of the utility function, it is clear that for the portfolio to be optimal it must be the case that marginal changes in any portfolio weights must create a change in expected return that is equal to $.5 \cdot \lambda$ times the marginal change in portfolio variance. In particular, for a marginal change in the weight in equity, w_e, it must be the case that:

$$\mu_e - r = .5 \cdot \lambda \cdot (2 \cdot w_e \cdot \sigma_e^2 + 2 \cdot w_b \cdot \sigma_{e,b}) \tag{4.8}$$

The quantity in parentheses is the marginal change in portfolio variance given a small change in the weight w_e. The analogous condition must hold for bonds. Thus, we have the additional condition:

$$\lambda = \frac{\mu_e - r}{w_e \cdot \sigma_e^2 + w_b \cdot \sigma_{e,b}} = \frac{\mu_b - r}{w_b \cdot \sigma_b^2 + w_e \cdot \sigma_{e,b}} \tag{4.9}$$

and we can solve these two equations for the optimal weights, w_e and w_b. The result, derived after a bit of algebra, is that:

$$w_e = \frac{\sigma_b^2 \cdot (\mu_e - r) - \sigma_{e,b} \cdot (\mu_b - r)}{\lambda \cdot (\sigma_e^2 \sigma_b^2 - \sigma_{e,b}^2)} \tag{4.10}$$

and

$$w_b = \frac{\sigma_e^2 \cdot (\mu_b - r) - \sigma_{e,b} \cdot (\mu_e - r)}{\lambda \cdot (\sigma_e^2 \sigma_b^2 - \sigma_{e,b}^2)} \tag{4.11}$$

Notice that in these formulas the expected returns show up with the risk-free rate subtracted off. The risk-free rate is the natural reference point for expected returns, and in general, we will find it more convenient to focus on expected excess returns above the risk-free rate. From this point forward we will use the notation $E(r)$ and μ to refer to the expected excess return, and the subtraction of the risk-free rate will be implicit.

The equations shown above for the two risky asset case are quite complicated. The nature of the solution is more obvious when we use matrix notation. More generally, we can write down the optimization problem for n risky assets as follows:

$$\max_{(\text{over } w)} U = E[\mu_p(w)] - .5 \cdot \lambda \cdot \sigma_p^2(w) \tag{4.12}$$

where w is an n-dimensional vector of proportions of portfolio weights in each of the risky assets.

Let μ be the n-dimensional vector of expected excess returns of assets and Σ be the $n \times n$ matrix of variances and covariances of the risky assets. We have:

$$E[\mu_p(w)] = \mu' w \tag{4.13}$$

and

$$\sigma_p^2(w) = w' \Sigma w \tag{4.14}$$

Thus, the optimal portfolio problem is to choose w such that we maximize

$$U = \mu' w - .5 \cdot \lambda \cdot w' \Sigma w \tag{4.15}$$

Taking the derivative with respect to w and setting it equal to zero leads to the optimal portfolio condition:

$$w = \left(\frac{1}{\lambda}\right) \cdot \Sigma^{-1} \mu \tag{4.16}$$

The analysis up to this point follows the original mean-variance optimization developed by Harry Markowitz in his work. What makes the CAPM interesting, however, is that it goes beyond this individual investor optimization problem for given expected excess returns. Rather than take μ_e and μ_b as given, as we did in the two-asset example, CAPM asks for what values of these mean returns will the demand for assets be equal to the outstanding supply. In our simple context of investors holding equity, bonds, and cash, CAPM asks what values for μ_e and μ_b will lead the sum of demands for equity and bonds of the optimizing investors to be equal to the market capitalization weights, e and b.

In this simple world, we can easily develop an intuition of what the answer must be. First, since all investors have identical information, they must each hold the same expected excess returns. In optimizing portfolio allocations the only difference across investors will be the risk aversion parameter.

One might expect investors with higher risk aversion to hold more bonds and less equity, remaining fully invested. In fact, we can see from the above equations that higher risk aversion will cause an investor to hold proportionally more cash and both less bonds and less equity. All investors, however, will hold the same ratio of bonds to equity.

The intuition behind this result follows directly from the requirement that expected excess return be proportional to contribution to portfolio risk. If a more risk-averse investor decided to hold more bonds and less equity than other investors, then the marginal contribution to risk of bonds in that investor's portfolio would be higher than that of other investors. But in equilibrium expected excess returns are assumed to be the same across investors. Thus, following the example in Chapter 2, for the investor holding more bonds and less equity a higher-returning portfolio with the same risk could be obtained by selling bonds and adding a combination of equity and cash.

If all investors hold the same ratio of bonds to equity, then the equilibrium ratio of bonds to equity must be b/e, the ratio of the outstanding market capitalizations. More generally, we see from the matrix version of the equation for optimal portfolio weights that when there are more than two assets the optimal portfolio weights of investors with different degrees of risk aversion will still be proportional. Thus, in the general case each investor must hold some fraction of the market capitalization weighted portfolio and some fraction in cash.

Also notice that the marginal contribution to portfolio risk for each asset is proportional to the covariance of the returns of that asset with the portfolio. For example, the covariance of equity returns with portfolio returns,

$$\begin{aligned}\text{Covariance}(r_e, r_p) = \sigma_{e,p} &= w_e \cdot \sigma_e^2 + w_b \cdot \sigma_{e,b} \\ &= \sigma_p \cdot (\text{Equity marginal contribution to risk})\end{aligned} \tag{4.17}$$

For optimal portfolios the expected excess returns for each asset are also proportional to the marginal contributions to risk. Thus, in optimal portfolios, the expected return of an asset is proportional to the covariance of that asset with the portfolio. That is, for each asset i and a constant proportionality k, the expected excess return, μ_i, is given by the following equation:

$$\mu_i = k \cdot \sigma_{i,p} \tag{4.18}$$

Since in equilibrium the optimal portfolio is proportional to the market capitalization weighted portfolio, we have shown that in equilibrium the expected excess return of each asset must be proportional to the covariance of that asset's return with the returns of the market portfolio. That is, we can substitute the market portfolio for the optimal portfolio in equation (4.18) and obtain:

$$\mu_i = k \cdot \sigma_{i,m} \tag{4.19}$$

In particular, in equilibrium assets whose returns are uncorrelated with the market portfolio have zero expected excess return. This is an important result, and we will return to its implications in Chapter 12.

Switching to vector notation, let ϕ be the vector of returns of all assets and $m'\phi$ be the returns of the market portfolio, then the vector of covariances of asset returns with the market portfolio returns is given by $\text{Cov}(\phi, m'\phi) = \Sigma\, m$. And finally, we can write the formula for the vector of equilibrium expected excess returns for all assets as:

$$\mu = k \cdot \Sigma\, m \tag{4.20}$$

Now, assume there are n investors with the proportion of wealth of the ith investor given by W_i. In the general case, the total portfolio holdings are given by:

$$\begin{aligned} \text{Total portfolio holdings} &= \Sigma_{i=1,n}(W_i) \cdot w_i \\ &= \Sigma_{i=1,n}\left(\frac{W_i}{\lambda_i}\right) \cdot \Sigma^{-1}\mu \\ &= \Sigma_{i=1,n}\left(\frac{W_i}{\lambda_i}\right) \cdot \Sigma^{-1}k \cdot \Sigma m \\ &= \Sigma_{i=1,n}\left(\frac{W_i}{\lambda_i}\right) \cdot k \cdot m \end{aligned} \tag{4.21}$$

However, we know that in equilibrium the total portfolio holdings must equal the market capitalization weights, m. Thus, we can solve for k.

$$k = \frac{1}{\Sigma_{i=1,n}\left(\frac{W_i}{\lambda_i}\right)} \tag{4.22}$$

Substituting back into the formula for the equilibrium expected excess returns, we have for each asset

$$\mu_i = \frac{\sigma_{i,m}}{\Sigma_{i=1,n}\left(\frac{W_i}{\lambda_i}\right)} \tag{4.23}$$

The term in parentheses is the wealth of investor i divided by the investor's risk aversion. The inverse of risk aversion is risk tolerance. Thus, the greater the wealth-weighted average risk tolerance of investors is, the smaller are the equilibrium expected excess returns, also known as risk premiums. Unfortunately it is very difficult to measure or infer risk aversions directly. Thus, it is very difficult to estimate the risk premium of any individual asset or of the market. However, note that without knowing anything about risk aversions we can nonetheless infer that the ratio of any two risk premiums is the ratio of their covariances with the market portfolio.

$$\frac{\mu_i}{\mu_j} = \frac{\sigma_{i,m}}{\sigma_{j,m}} \tag{4.24}$$

In particular, letting μ_m be the risk premium of the market portfolio we have:

$$\frac{\mu_i}{\mu_m} = \frac{\sigma_{i,m}}{\sigma_m^2} \tag{4.25}$$

and thus

$$\mu_i = \left(\frac{\sigma_{i,m}}{\sigma_m^2}\right) \cdot \mu_m \tag{4.26}$$

or using the conventional notation "beta" for this ratio $\beta_i = (\sigma_{i,m}/\sigma_m^2)$ we have that

$$\mu_i = \beta_i \cdot \mu_m \tag{4.27}$$

Thus, for each asset its risk premium is given by the asset's beta with the market portfolio times the market risk premium. The beta, being the ratio of a covariance to a variance, is easily estimated. In a regression projection of an asset's return on the market return, beta is simply the coefficient on the market return. This then is the fundamental insight of the Capital Asset Pricing Model: In equilibrium the risk premium of an asset is the coefficient of the projection of its return on the market return times the market risk premium.

In the next chapter we will review the evidence, weak as it is, on how large the market risk premium ought to be. We will then, in Chapter 6, extend this simple domestic CAPM model to an international setting where currency risk adds a considerable amount of complexity.

SUMMARY

We view the CAPM as a framework for thinking about investments. The CAPM asks what happens, in other words what is the nature of equilibrium, in the simplest possible world, where markets are efficient, all investors have identical information, and investors maximize the expected return in their portfolios and minimize their volatility.

The optimal portfolio problem is to choose w such that we maximize

$$U = \mu' w - .5 \cdot \lambda \cdot w' \Sigma w \tag{4.28}$$

Taking the derivative with respect to w and setting it equal to zero leads to the optimal portfolio condition:

$$w = \left(\frac{1}{\lambda}\right) \cdot \Sigma^{-1} \mu \tag{4.29}$$

In the general case each investor must hold some fraction of the market capitalization weighted portfolio and some fraction in cash.

In optimal portfolios the expected return of an asset is proportional to the covariance of that asset with the portfolio. Thus, in equilibrium the expected excess return of each asset must be proportional to the covariance of that asset's return with the returns of the market portfolio.

The greater the wealth-weighted average risk tolerance of investors is, the smaller are the equilibrium risk premiums.

The ratio of any two risk premiums is the ratio of their covariances with the market portfolio.

Finally, the fundamental insight of the CAPM is that in equilibrium the risk premium of an asset is simply its beta times the market risk premium.

CHAPTER 5

The Equity Risk Premium

Mark M. Carhart and Kurt Winkelmann

As shown in the previous chapter, if markets are efficient, if all investors have identical information, and if investors maximize the expected return in their portfolios and minimize volatility, the expected excess return on the market portfolio is

$$\mu_m = \frac{\sigma_m^2}{E\left(\frac{W}{\lambda}\right)} \tag{5.1}$$

That is, the market portfolio's expected return over the riskless asset is the market portfolio's variance divided by the average across all market participants of the ratio of their wealth to their risk aversion. Unfortunately, to most of us this formula reveals no intuition whatsoever. However, we all agree on the concept of an equilibrium expected return to compensate investors for taking market risk. The difficult question is, how large is the market return premium?

It's clearly not zero or negative, as investors extract a price in order to bear volatility in their wealth. On the other hand, it's probably not 10 percent per year above the riskless asset, because the market's volatility is of the same magnitude, which implies that holding the market causes a relatively small probability of negative return over one year, and even less than this at the end of five years.

In this chapter, we attempt to arrive at a reasonable range for the market risk premium over the riskless asset. More specifically, we evaluate estimates of the *equity* risk premium (ERP), from which the market risk premium is easily derived using the CAPM.

We consider two approaches to measure the ERP. Our first is purely empirical: We study the average returns of equity markets over long periods of time. In addition to looking at long-run averages, we also look at decompositions of these averages, in the hope that they will provide insights into the drivers of equity returns.

Our second approach is more theoretical. In this approach, we look at the theoretical relationship in equilibrium between investor demand and asset supply. In particular, we are interested in exploring the role of investor preferences in shaping the equity premium.

What do we mean by the equity risk premium? We define the ERP as the expected return, in equilibrium, on the capitalization-weighted global equity market in excess of the riskless asset. Since the CAPM is a one-period model, it requires the arithmetic mean return on the market minus the current yield over one period. To apply this in the real world, we must define what is meant by one period. Because we are analyzing an equilibrium concept, we require a fairly long horizon, say five to 30 years. We can think of this as the investment horizon over which investors make strategic decisions on how much market risk to take.

The investment horizon is required to measure the riskless return, as (nominally) riskless securities exist for one day out to 30 years. In this chapter, we take the U.S. 10-year government bond as the proxy for the riskless asset in the United States. Consistent with past research and current practice, we report all mean return estimates using geometric averaging.[1]

HISTORICAL PERSPECTIVE

Roger Ibbotson and Rex Sinquefield (1976) conducted the first major analysis on equity returns using data from the Center for Research in Securities Prices at the University of Chicago. At that time, they estimated that the ERP in the United States since 1926 was 5.1 percent. They derived this from the total nominal annualized equity return of 8.5 percent, inflation of 2.4 percent, and a real risk-free return of 1.0 percent (on long-term government bonds).

When Ibbotson and Peng Chen update the data to 2000, the real risk-free return is somewhat higher at 2.05 percent but the ERP is very similar at 5.24 percent. Of this premium, 1.25 percent per year is explained by expansion of price-earnings multiples since 1976, shown in Figure 5.1. If we postulate that this P/E expansion was a one-time event, not a secular trend or a bubble that will reverse, their adjusted ERP estimate is approximately 4 percent.

Using a slightly longer data set starting in 1872, Eugene Fama and Kenneth French (2002) reach similar conclusions. Over their sample, they estimate the ERP at 5.57 percent. Fama and French conclude that the secular rise in P/E ratios since 1951 is likely to have been a one-time event and conclude the ERP estimate from 1872 to 1951 is more representative of future expectations. Their ERP estimate for this earlier window is 4.40 percent.

These results are effectively averages over many possible regimes. From a more dynamic perspective, Jagannathan, McGrattan, and Scherbina (2000) look at the long-run equity premium in the United States and conclude that it has fallen. They apply a version of the Gordon growth model to different historical time periods and conclude that the long-run experience studied by Ibbotson, Fama and French, and others includes distinct regimes. On the basis of their analysis, they conclude that the U.S. equity premium averaged around 700 basis points during the period 1926 through 1970, and closer to 70 basis points after that.

[1]In the CAPM, the market risk premium is the arithmetic expected return over the investment horizon, but converting arithmetic to geometric returns is straightforward using the following approximation: $R_{geo} = R_{arith} - {}^{1}/_{2}\text{var}(R)$.

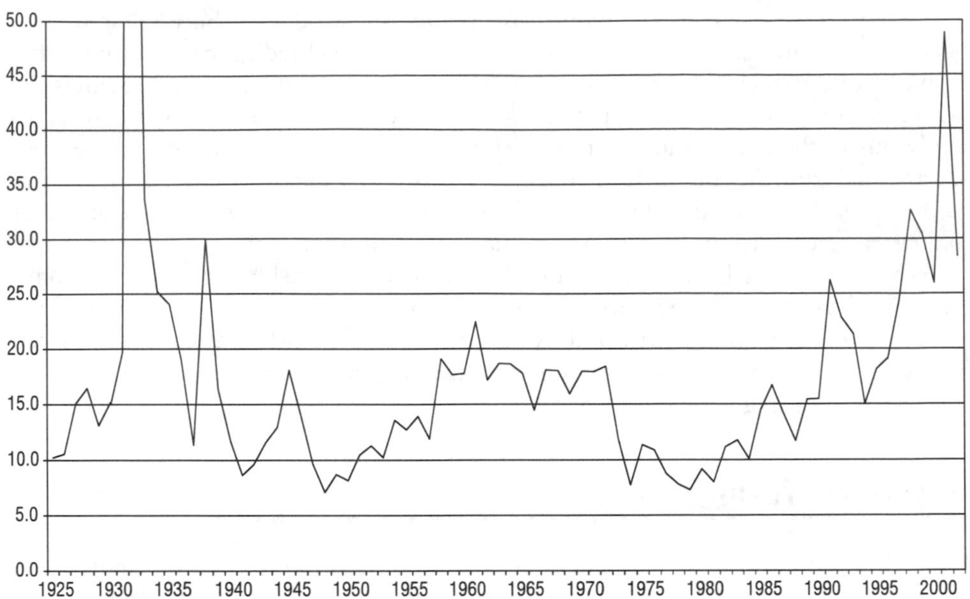

FIGURE 5.1 U.S. Equity Trailing P/E Ratios (January 1926–June 2002)

However, looking only at the U.S. data probably biases our inferences, because our interest and access to this long data series on the United States is conditional on the U.S. market growing from a small, emerging market two centuries ago into by far the largest market in the world today. This survivor bias can only be corrected by painstakingly creating equivalent data sets for every market that existed over the entire time period.

Fortunately, Philippe Jorion and Will Goetzmann (2002) have done this for us. Starting in 1926, they collect equity prices on 39 different equity markets and construct real price return (without dividend) approximations over periods of market disruption, mostly wars and nationalizations. Figure 5.2 displays their real capital gain estimates as a function of length of market survival.

Notably, using this measure the United States was the best-performing market in the world. Whereas the real price return in the United States was 4.32 percent per annum, the median across all markets was only 0.75 percent. This difference does not appear to be explained by higher dividend returns in countries outside the United States, either: The dividend return in the United States was over 4 percent per year during this period and is about the same as a subset of other countries in the sample where Jorion and Goetzmann obtained dividend returns. On a brighter side, a gross domestic product (GDP) weighted estimate across all countries yields a real price return of approximately 4 percent, only 0.3 percent below that of the United States.[2]

[2]Jorion and Goetzmann report that the United States was 46 percent of worldwide GDP in 1921 versus only about 30 percent today.

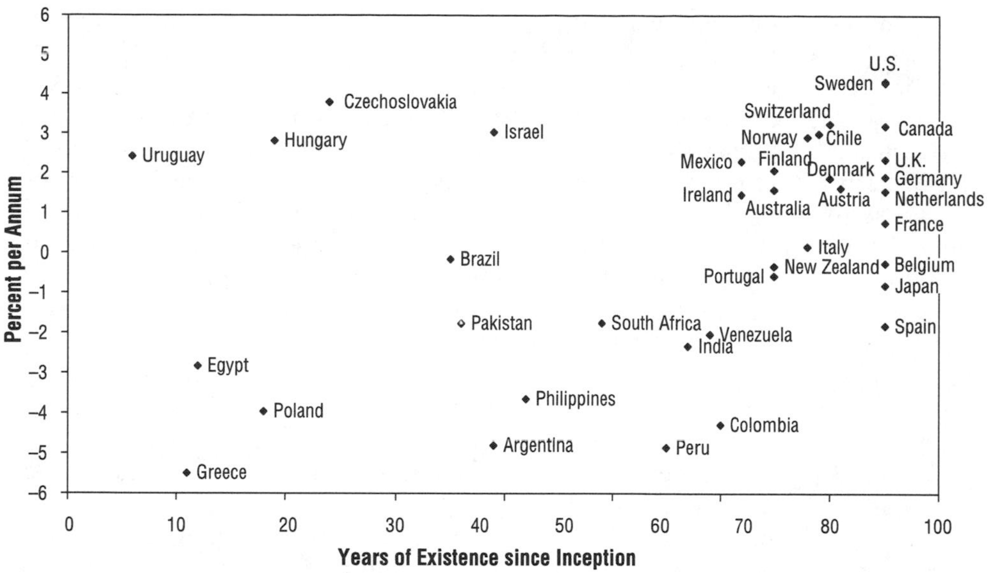

FIGURE 5.2 Compound Annual Real Capital Gains on Global Markets through 1996

Of course, we can do better than merely look at the historical average performance of global equity markets. For investment policy purposes, we should also be interested in the underlying economic drivers of equity markets in general and the equity premium in particular. In principle, the market value of equity should reflect expectations of future earnings growth. Over the long run, these expectations should in turn be linked to economic growth in the long run. Consequently, we have another path to follow in understanding the historical performance.

For example, Ibbotson and Chen show that the realized, long-run real return on equity (not the ERP) is equal to long-run dividend yields plus long-run real earnings growth rates plus expected future P/E growth. Suppose that markets are fairly valued, so that expected P/E expansion (or contraction) is zero. Since aggregate economic growth includes earnings growth, and if the corporate sector is assumed a constant proportion of the overall economy, it follows that long-term real earnings growth is equal to long-term real economic growth.[3]

How are dividends related to real economic growth, then? Some researchers on this topic incorrectly assume that dividends are an independent input into the expected real return on equities. For example, Arnott and Bernstein (2002) take the unusually low current dividend yield as proxy for long-run dividend income and at the same time link long-term real earnings and economic growth.

However, the implication of their assumption is that dividend payout does not affect earnings growth, which is nonsensical because an increased retention in earnings should lead to higher future earnings growth. Take two otherwise identical

[3]One could instead assume that the corporate sector is a growing segment of the economy, but this can't be true in perpetuity and we are talking about equilibrium conditions here.

companies with different dividend payout ratios. Why should the expected return on these two companies differ based to their respective dividend yields? The correct (and intuitive) answer is, they shouldn't.

In fact, there is an equilibrium condition that determines long-term dividend yield. In the long run, dividend yields should equal earnings growth rates. Why? If dividend yields were higher than real earnings growth, the transfers from the corporate sector would exceed its economic growth and corporations could not remain a constant proportion of the economy. The opposite is clearly also the case. Therefore, equilibrium dividend yields equal long-term earnings growth.

All that remains to determine an expected real return on equity, then, is long-term real economic growth. Since 1947, compound real annual GDP growth averaged 3.4 percent per year.[4] Taking a slight haircut from this to reflect survivorship, it seems reasonable to expect future real economic growth in the 2.5 to 3.0 percent range. This implies a real equity return of 5 percent to 6 percent. Taking the midpoint of this range, along with Ibbotson and Chen's real risk-free return estimate of 2 percent, yields an ERP estimate of 3.5 percent.

The decomposition outlined above offers a useful tool for understanding the current debate about the level of the ERP. Since most researchers would agree on the basic structure of the decomposition, the debate can be centered on both the levels of each component (e.g., the real economic growth rate) and the underlying economic fundamentals. For example, Arnott and Bernstein argue forcefully that we are in a bubble, and that P/E ratios will decline substantially from their recent levels. To answer this question, we can reasonably ask what the equilibrium relationships are between equity valuations and the real economy. Thus, in addition to exploring the historical record, we should also include a theoretical understanding of the equity premium.

EQUILIBRIUM ESTIMATES OF THE EQUITY RISK PREMIUM

Gauging the equity risk premium from the demand side requires a model for investor preferences. Two early academics studying the ERP, Mehra and Prescott (1985), report a rather surprising estimate of 0.4 percent for the ERP! This is so low relative to realized equity returns that they called their finding "the equity premium puzzle." Their results spawned a generation of new academic research attempting to rationalize their findings, some of which we describe in this chapter.

Mehra and Prescott's work is an application of a standard dynamic macroeconomic model generalized to allow for asset pricing (see, for instance, Lucas 1978). At its core, this model makes the commonsense assumption that what investors really care about is not investing per se, but rather the consumption stream that such investing will support. That is, an investor's well-being (or utility) depends on the path of current and future consumption. Investors are willing to defer current consumption and invest only if they believe that the return on investing will generate sufficient future consumption to make them feel better off.

---

[4]According to the U.S. Federal Reserve Board, 1947–2001, *Flow of Funds Accounts of the United States*, Washington, DC: Federal Reserve Board.

As a result, the demand for current and future consumption and the demand for investments are interdependent: The effort on the part of investors to select an optimal path for current and future consumption also sets a path for asset demand, and vice versa.

An implication of this type of reasoning is that analysts should first write down (explicitly) a function representing asset demands. This demand function will, of course, reflect all features of the investor's utility function. Equilibrium asset *prices* are found by combining the path of asset demand with a path for asset supply. Asset *returns*, of course, are simply the changes in asset prices over time, and the equity premium is simply the return on a risky asset relative to a risk-free asset. Thus, Mehra and Prescott's model gives us a very elegant way to relate the equity premium to investor preferences about consumption.

To represent investor behavior, Mehra and Prescott use a very standard utility function. They assume that there is a single investor (who is also the single consumer) acting as a stand-in for the entire economy. Again following standard practice, this investor is assumed to want to maximize the following function:

$$E_0\left(\Sigma\beta_t \frac{c_t^{(1-\alpha)}-1}{1-\alpha}\right) \tag{5.2}$$

Several important ideas are expressed in equation (5.2). The first interesting parameter is β. This parameter represents the rate at which the investor is willing to substitute current consumption for future consumption. At one level, we can interpret β as the rate at which the investor discounts future consumption.

The second interesting parameter is α. This parameter governs the investor's level of risk aversion. More risk-averse investors require higher levels of future consumption to keep well-being (as measured by the utility function) constant. The third interesting part of the equation is the variable c_t, or consumption at time t. This part of the equation tells us that the investor's current utility depends on the entire stream of consumption.

Finally, the $E\{\ \}$ represents the mathematical expectation. This part of the equation tells us that the investor is operating in a world of uncertainty. Since α and β are assumed to be fixed, the uncertainty that the investor faces is about the path of consumption. Thus, equation (5.2) tells us that the investor wants to maximize the expected discounted value of the utility of current and future consumption, where the discount rate is the rate of intertemporal substitution and the utility of consumption depends of the level of risk aversion.

To understand the impact of some of the parameters, let's work through a simple example. For simplicity, we'll assume that the path of consumption is known. We'll index consumption to be 100 at date 0, and assume that it grows at a constant rate of 3.0 percent per year: In other words, $c_0 = 100$, $c_1 = 103$, $c_2 = 106.09$, and so on. Now, to calculate total utility, all we need to do is pin down values for α and β. For α, we'll use 1.25 as a starting value.

We'll assume that $\beta_t = \beta^t$ for every date. In other words, the rate of time preference is constant across two adjacent periods. For β, let's assume that the real interest rate is 1.0 percent per annum. Under this assumption, β is equal to .99. For ease of exposition, we'll ignore all dates after 60 in the calculation of total utility.

On the basis of these assumptions, we can calculate the total value of utility at date 0, and then assess the impact of changes in the assumptions on total utility. Our base case total utility value is 135.413. Now we can assess the impact on total utility of changes in the underlying assumptions.

Suppose first that we increase the growth rate in consumption, say from 3 percent to 4 percent. Under this assumption, total utility increases from 135.413 to 138.149. Similarly, if we reduce the growth rate in consumption from 3 percent to 2 percent, total utility declines from 135.413 to 132.394. Clearly our utility function is consistent with the idea that investors prefer higher consumption growth rates to lower.

Now let's explore the impact of changes in the rate of time preference, and let the discount rate increase by 10 basis points to 1.10 percent. Under this assumption, investors value consumption today more highly than consumption in the future: The total utility value declines to 131.697. To keep utility unchanged from the base case, consumption growth must increase from a 3.0 percent annual growth rate to a 4.44 percent annual growth rate. Thus, higher discount rates (lower discount factors) imply that consumption growth must increase to keep utility unchanged.

The final parameter we can change is the risk aversion parameter. Suppose that we increase the risk aversion parameter from 1.25 to 1.30. In this case, consumption growth must increase from 3.0 percent annually to almost 13 percent annually for utility to be unchanged.

How do Mehra and Prescott make use of equation (5.2)? They begin by manipulating this equation to derive demand functions for both assets and consumption. To close the system, Mehra and Prescott need to make assumptions about production and equilibrium. They assume that each period a single perishable good is produced, and that production grows, but at a random rate. Although the growth rate in production is random, its distribution is known, with a long-term average growth rate and a known variance. In this simple economy, the long-term average growth rate is assumed to be given exogenously. Factors such as productivity growth that would naturally be expected to influence the long-term average growth rate are not considered in this model. To close the system, they further assume that in equilibrium consumption equals production of the single good at every date. Thus, uncertainty about future consumption—that is, the quantities in equation (5.2)—is effectively uncertainty about future output. Now, what about asset pricing and asset returns?

Looking at equation (5.2) more closely, we see that in the abstract, the only unknown quantity at any date in time is consumption, or c_t. Mehra and Prescott exploit this point quite explicitly in their analysis. Effectively, they are trying to provide answers to the following questions: What would an investor be willing to pay for an asset whose payoff would look approximately like the path of consumption? What would the return on that asset be over time? And what would give rise to a premium on that asset?

Mehra and Prescott's answers to these questions begin from a very fundamental point: If production (and, in this model, consumption) were known with certainty, then the price of the asset would be the same at each date, and the equity premium would be zero. This works out because if the path of consumption and output are known with certainty at each date, then the investor's utility is also fixed. Consequently, *the existence of a return premium can only be as a payment to the investor for accepting volatility in future consumption.* Equation (5.2) gives us a road map for pinning down the size of the premium.

Since the utility function depends on the mean and variance of the path of consumption, the level of risk aversion, and the rate of intertemporal substitution, it is reasonable that the asset pricing equation should depend on the same parameters. Thus, Mehra and Prescott propose the following: If we know the mean and variance of current and future consumption, the willingness to trade consumption across time, and the level of risk aversion, then we should be able to pin down the size of the equity premium. How would the parameters of the utility function and the economy (e.g., the average growth rate and variance of consumption) affect the equity premium?

Intuitively, more uncertainty about future consumption (expressed, say, through the variance in consumption) should increase the equity premium. The reason for this is because more uncertainty about future consumption translates into more uncertainty about current utility. Similarly, since higher levels of risk aversion have a pronounced impact on utility they should be accompanied by increases in the equity premium, all else being equal. Finally, if an investor were not very willing to substitute future consumption for current consumption, then the equity risk premium should increase.

To test their model, Mehra and Prescott directly estimate the variance of consumption, and find it to be quite low. They rely on the work of other researchers to pin down (or, in the parlance of real business cycle theorists, calibrate) the value of α. More specifically, Mehra and Prescott propose that values of α larger than 10 are not supported by the literature. They focus instead on values of α between one and two. They focus on values of β consistent with discount rates between 1 percent and 2 percent.

The results of their analysis are quite provocative. What they find is that under reasonable assumptions about the mean and variance of consumption, and the willingness of investor/consumers to trade consumption across time, the value of the equity premium should be 40 basis points. This value is quite small relative to the historical average (at the time Mehra and Prescott wrote, the historical average was around 600 basis points). Consequently, Mehra and Prescott coined the term "the equity premium puzzle" to describe the difference between the historical average and the theoretical value of the equity risk premium.

While the model that Mehra and Prescott used to analyze the equity premium is elegant, it is nonetheless an abstraction. In particular, this model assumes a particular utility function and that investors may trade in markets without frictions. As it turns out, in the absence of frictions, it is difficult to construct a function for investor preferences that reconciles observed equity returns with the standard axioms of utility theory used in economics. In response to this dilemma, Epstein and Zin (1991) propose a nonstandard utility function that can explain the equity premium puzzle without frictions. The more accepted resolution to the puzzle is to introduce frictions, an approach that Mehra and Prescott suggest in their original paper.

There are three distinct ways in which frictions can be introduced into the model. The first of these is to introduce transaction costs to trading. Introducing transaction costs means that investor/consumers will not invest at the theoretically optimal level without receiving an additional compensation. An example of this type of research is shown in Aiyagari and Gertler (1991).

A second way to introduce frictions is by changing the nature of the optimization problem that our investor/consumer faces. In particular, a number of researchers have suggested the existence of "habit persistence" in modeling investor/consumer behavior. Equation (5.2) is modified so that an investor's well-being depends not only on the path of current and future consumption, but on the path of past consumption as well. The path of past consumption sets a "habit" level of consumption that investors do not want to fall below. Because investing necessarily means taking on risk, the investor must be compensated by an extraordinary return on equity to compensate for the possibility that consumption will fall below its habit level: At higher habit levels, the impact of potential declines in consumption is more significant than at lower habit levels. Constantinides and Ferson (1991) first develop such a model, and Campbell and Cochrane (1999) provide an example of further research in this direction.

The third way that frictions can be introduced is through the institutional environment. Institutional constraints operate in the same spirit as transaction costs, in the sense that they prevent investors from reaching their theoretically optimal allocations. Examples of institutional barriers include taxes, foreign content legislation, and laws increasing the liability to investment providers. An example of this type of research is given by McGrattan and Prescott (2001), which is discussed in more detail later.

These lines of research suggest a natural resolution between the theoretical value of the equity premium and the observed performance of the U.S. equity market. In particular, these lines of research suggest that the *ex post* behavior of the U.S. equity market can be viewed as the result of a transition between high and low equity premium regimes. Differences between the regimes are produced by declines in transaction costs, taxes, and the regulatory environment (as it relates to equity holdings). Suppose we assume that markets are fairly priced before and after the transition between the two regimes. Since the second regime embeds a lower equity premium than the first, valuations must be higher (but expected returns lower). Consequently, during the transition period between the two regimes, equity prices must increase, thereby producing *ex post* equity returns that are in excess of the *ex ante* returns in the new regime.

For example, McGrattan and Prescott offer an explanation for P/E expansion that does not rely on market disequilibrium: taxes. Most previous research—including Prescott's previously referenced paper on the equity premium puzzle—ignores taxes, but in reality investors consume only after-tax wealth. McGrattan and Prescott point out that the effective dividend tax rate has more than halved over the past 50 years, from around 44 percent in 1950 to about 18 percent today. By their calculations, the change in effective tax rates completely explains the observed shift in price-dividend ratios. Two primary explanations for the lower effective dividend tax rates are the decrease in the highest marginal corporate and personal income taxes and the significantly larger proportion of stocks held by nontaxable entities like pension plans and individual retirement accounts (IRAs).

Unfortunately, precise estimates of the ERP from equilibrium theory lean heavily on estimates of other parameters—like individual investor risk aversions—that subjects these results to much debate. However, observable market data do reveal important information about the range of equity return expectations. In particular, we observe yields on corporate bonds for the same companies for which we desire the expected return on equity. Corporate bond yields—along with an estimate of the long-run expected loss on these bonds due to default—deliver reasonably accurate estimates of the expected return premium on corporate bonds. Since equity is a subordinated claim on the same assets of the firm, in equilibrium equity holders demand a premium above corporate bonds.

Using data from June 2002, we estimate the equity market capitalization weighted U.S. corporate bond yield above Treasuries is approximately 2.25 percent.[5] Using a rough estimate of historical default losses on U.S. corporate bonds of 0.75 percent, we arrive at an expected U.S. corporate bond risk premium of 1.5 percent. This provides, at a minimum, a lower bound on the current ERP. Considering that the volatility on equities is two to three times that on corporate bonds, we cautiously suggest that investors are currently demanding an ERP in the neighborhood of 3 percent or more. You might call this a casual empirical estimate!

THE EQUITY PREMIUM AND INVESTMENT POLICY

Why are investors so concerned about the level of the equity premium? The principal reason is very straightforward: Practically every important decision that an investor makes is driven by the equity premium assumption. Decisions like the split between equity and bond holdings, the allocation to alternative investments, and the level and structure of active risk taking all depend on the equity premium assumption. Given the importance of this assumption, it is not terribly surprising that so much time is spent in analyzing the historical record.

Unfortunately, however much time we spend analyzing the historical record, it will not be enough to estimate the equity premium with any level of certainty. For example, with 130 years of data from 1872 to 2001 and stock market volatility of 20 percent per year, the standard error in Fama and French's average return estimate is 1.75 percent. Therefore, an estimate of 3.5 percent is only two standard errors from zero. This permits us to reject the null hypothesis that the ERP is zero with a confidence level of 5 percent.

Let's turn the problem around, however, and test, at the same level, how different the equity premium is from 3.0 percent. For this test, we would need another 6,270 years of data! Thus, from a practical perspective, a significant level of uncertainty is bound to accompany any estimate of the long-run equity premium.

The equity premium clearly plays an important role in setting investment policy. The goal of this chapter has been to provide some guidance that investors can use to set their own equity premium assumptions. As the discussion has indicated,

[5]Using option-adjusted spreads over the U.S. Treasury curve on a broad portfolio of corporate bonds, including high-yield bonds.

an equity premium assumption will depend on a careful understanding of the past performance of equity markets, both in the United States and globally. This experience should be tempered by an appreciation of the limitations inherent in statistical analysis of equity returns. As well, the historical experience should be analyzed in the context of an underlying theory. Finally, the theory should be rich enough to provide some guidance as to the likely impact of changes in important external forces (e.g., the tax and regulatory environment) on asset markets.

CHAPTER 6

Global Equilibrium Expected Returns

Bob Litterman

The domestic Capital Asset Pricing Model (CAPM) is a very good starting point for a global equilibrium model. In fact, to the extent that all people around the globe share a common utility function the domestic CAPM extends quite naturally to the global context. We can think of individuals in a global economy investing in global assets and consuming a common global basket of goods and services. Just as in the domestic context, risk premiums should be proportional to the covariance of each asset's returns with the global market portfolio. In a 1977 discussion of this issue,[1] Richard Roll and Bruno Solnik summed it up this way: "If markets were perfect, or nearly so, and if the same consumption of goods were produced and consumed in the same proportions in all countries of the world; if anticipation were homogeneous and if transportation were costless and instantaneous; then the international asset pricing theory would be indeed a trivial extension of the standard domestic model."

There is nothing fundamentally wrong with this simple extension of the domestic model to the international sphere, but there is an immediate issue, which, over the years since the publication of the domestic CAPM, has led to many alternative, more complicated, global models being proposed. The unfortunate issue that leads to these complications is currency risk. The currency issue arises from the seemingly trivial question, "What units do we measure things in?" We might suppose that units shouldn't affect real quantities, and that is correct up to a point. We can suppose that everything be measured in U.S. dollars, or gold, or units of the common consumption basket—it doesn't really matter as long as everyone has a common utility function. In this simple world, the domestic CAPM functions as a global CAPM and all the results remain true. Roll and Solnik put it this way: "Under these circumstances [their idealized conditions quoted earlier], the fact that francs were used in one location and pounds, yen, or cuzeiros used in others would only constitute a multinational version of the 'veil of money.' Real interest rates would be equal everywhere as would the real price of risk, and capital asset pricing relations

[1]This reference appears in the paper, "A Pure Foreign Exchange Asset Pricing Model," in the *Journal of International Economics*, volume 7, pages 161–179.

would be identical for the residents of all countries. In such idealized circumstances, real exchange risk would be absent. . . ."

The problem, however, is that in the real world exchange risk is present, and the domestic CAPM does not address the issue of currency risk. In practice, people around the world don't have a common consumption basket, and people measure the utility of their wealth in different units. The fluctuating relative values of the different currency units that investors use to measure their wealth, and the real risk those fluctuations create, have led a number of academics, including Fischer Black, to work on global generalizations of the domestic CAPM that address the issue of currency risk. Black's 1989 paper, "Universal Hedging,"[2] is one of these generalizations. Unfortunately, as we will see, the global generalizations lead to a significant amount of complexity relative to the domestic CAPM.

Although the math is complex, we will nonetheless push forward. Our feeling is that these models do lead to some important insights, in particular into issues such as what is the optimal degree of currency hedging (which, of course, was exactly Black's original focus). But for our purposes, an even more important benefit is that the Universal Hedging equilibrium provides a starting point for managing global portfolios.

Black made a number of simplifying assumptions relative to earlier versions of what is known as the "international CAPM," and we will ultimately focus on his version of the global equilibrium model. Black was surprised, and delighted, when he realized that under a particular set of assumptions the global CAPM equilibrium included the surprisingly simple result that all investors in all countries around the world should hedge the same significant fraction of their foreign currency exposure.[3] It was because of this result that Black called his extension of the international CAPM "universal hedging." In Black's equilibrium, the degree of risk aversion of investors determines the fraction of the currency risk that should be hedged, and Black estimated that in equilibrium this fraction of currency that should be hedged is approximately 77 percent.

In the decade after Black developed his result it became clear that his international equilibrium asset pricing model has many applications, only one of which is its insights on currency hedging. In fact, since the world is not in equilibrium and most investors do not hold market capitalization weighted portfolios, the "universal" hedging percentage does not generally apply as a portfolio prescription. However, by simplifying the international CAPM model and taking it seriously as a reference for expected returns, Black provided the intellectual framework from which many other applications, including the Black-Litterman global asset allocation model, have emerged.

Black's international CAPM was certainly not the first globalization of the domestic CAPM (see, for example, Solnik (1974); Adler and Dumas (1983); Grauer,

---

[2]Black's paper, "Universal Hedging: Optimizing Currency Risk and Reward in International Equity Portfolios," appeared in the *Financial Analysts Journal*, July/August 1989, pages 16–22.

[3]For Black's reflections on his work, see "How I Discovered Universal Hedging," *Risk Management*, Winter 1990.

Litzenberger, and Stehle (1976); and Roll and Solnik (1977), among others[4]), but Black was the first to point out the universal hedging property, which arises when all investors have the same degree of risk aversion and when wealth in each country equals that country's market capitalization. Black's equilibrium is a simple special case of the more general equilibrium model.[5]

Before jumping into the math, it is perhaps best to clarify first what the international CAPM model addresses, and what it does not address. In most versions of the model, including Black's, the term "currency" refers to real rates of exchange between the consumption bundles of different groups of investors. Thus, the theory does not include inflation risk, a potential cause of changes in the exchange rates of the nominal currencies that we generally think about in the real world. Another set of complexities of the real world that the universal hedging equilibrium does not address is the distribution of ownership of wealth across different countries, and the heterogeneity of investors' risk tolerances across countries. The theory takes these characteristics as inputs, and as noted earlier, one of the simplifying assumptions of Black's equilibrium is that investors in each country have wealth equal to the market capitalization of the domestic assets of their country. Another simplifying assumption in Black's model, which we will see is easy to relax, is that investors in all countries have the same degree of risk tolerance. The standard international CAPM equilibrium models also assume that the usual efficient markets conditions hold; there are no barriers to trade; and there are no capital controls, information barriers, or other costs that make investors prefer domestic assets. Finally, as in the domestic CAPM, these models assume a single, infinitesimal time period. These one-period models do not address the intertemporal risks that arise in a dynamic economy. Other academics have, of course, extended the results described here by relaxing various of these assumptions.

As in Chapter 4, we consider first the simplest version of the model, a world in which there are only two currencies and two assets and investors solve a mean-variance portfolio optimization problem. We then address the general model.

Consider a two-country world in which there are two risky assets, domestic equity in each country. We will refer to the two countries as the United States and Japan and we will later work out an example with parameters reflective of them. Denote the exchange rate between the two countries—that is, the number of units of Japanese currency per unit of U.S. currency—by X. Without loss of generality, assume that at the beginning of the investment period X has the value 1. In other words, at the beginning of the period one unit of a Japanese consumption bundle trades for one unit of a U.S. consumption bundle. At the end of the period, X has an uncertain value that gives the rate of exchange between units of consumption in

---

[4]Roll and Solnik (1977) is referenced earlier. The additional references are as follows: Solnik, Bruno H., 1974, "An Equilibrium Model of the International Capital Market," *Journal of Economic Theory* 8, 500–524; Adler, M. and B. Dumas, 1983, "International Portfolio Choice and Corporation Finance: A Synthesis," *Journal of Finance* 38, 925–984; and Grauer, F., R. Litzenberger, and R. Stehle, 1976, "Sharing Rules and Equilibrium in an International Capital Market under Uncertainty," *Journal of Financial Economics* 3, 233–256.

[5]Some have argued that Black's is not a very interesting special case because we have no reason, for example, to believe that investors all have the same risk aversion. While this concern is legitimate, risk aversion is very difficult to estimate, and so one might also argue that in the absence of evidence to the contrary, Black's special case is a reasonable place to start.

the United States and Japan. Thus, the expected returns and risks of investors will have to take this additional uncertainty into account. Over a short period of time, the return to a U.S. investor from holding Japanese equity will have two components, the return on the equity earned by domestic Japanese investors plus the return earned by U.S. investors from holding yen-denominated assets. A U.S. investor holds portfolio weights d_U and d_J, respectively, in the equity of the United States and Japan, and may choose to hedge (or increase) the currency exposure of the Japanese equity such that there is an outstanding yen exposure in the amount d_X. These weights, d_U, d_J, and d_X, are all expressed as percentages of the wealth of the dollar investor.

The expected excess return over the risk-free rate, denominated in dollars, for an investor in the United States holding these weights is given by:

$$\mu_P^\$ = \mu_U^\$ \cdot d_U + \mu_J^\$ \cdot d_J + \mu_X^\$ \cdot d_X \tag{6.1}$$

where $\mu_U^\$$ = Expected excess return for a dollar-based investor holding U.S. equity
$\mu_J^\$$ = Expected excess return for a dollar-based investor holding currency hedged Japanese equity[6]
$\mu_X^\$$ = Expected excess return on holding yen for a U.S. dollar–based investor

As we shall see, it turns out that even when the currency risk is hedged, the expected excess return on Japanese equity for a dollar-based investor will generally differ from that of a yen-based investor because the investors in different countries measure their expected returns in terms of different units (currencies).

The risk of this portfolio for the U.S. dollar–based investor is given by the volatility, $\sigma_P^\$$, determined as follows by the variances and covariances of dollar-based risky assets:

$$\left(\sigma_P^\$\right)^2 = \Sigma_{a=\{U,J,X\}} \Sigma_{b=\{U,J,X\}} \left(d_a d_b \sigma_{ab}^\$\right) \tag{6.2}$$

where $\sigma_{ab}^\$$ is the covariance (or variance if $a = b$) of returns of asset a with asset b from a dollar investor's point of view.

Similarly, the expected return, denominated in yen, for an investor in Japan holding weights y_J and y_U, respectively, in the equities of Japan and the United States, and hedging the currency exposure on U.S. equity such that there is a net dollar exposure of an amount, y_X, is given by:

---

[6]The excess return on foreign currency exposures is given by $r_x = (F_t^{t+1} - X_{t+1})/X_t$, where F_t^{t+1} is the one-period forward exchange rate at time t, that is, the forward rate at time t at which you can contract to exchange yen for dollars at time $t + 1$. In terms of short-term deposit rates in the United States and Japan, $R_\$$ and R_Y, covered interest parity requires that $F_t^{t+1} = (1 + R_Y) \cdot X_t/(1 + R_\$)$. The currency hedged excess return on Japanese equity from time t to $t + 1$ is given by $r_j = [(P_{t+1}/X_{t+1})/(P_t/X_t) - 1] - R_\$ - (1 - R_\$) \cdot r_x$ where P_t is the yen price of the Japanese equity at time t.

$$\mu_P^Y = \mu_J^Y \cdot y_J + \mu_U^Y \cdot y_U + \mu_X^Y \cdot y_X \tag{6.3}$$

where μ_J^Y = Expected excess return for a yen-based investor holding Japanese equity

μ_U^Y = Expected excess return for a yen-based investor holding currency hedged U.S. equity

μ_X^Y = Expected excess return on holding dollars for a yen-based investor

The risk of this yen-denominated portfolio is given by the volatility, σ_P^Y, determined as follows by the variances and covariances of yen-based risky assets:

$$\left(\sigma_P^Y\right)^2 = \Sigma_{a=\{U,J,X\}}\Sigma_{b=\{U,J,X\}}\left(y_a y_b \sigma_{ab}^Y\right) \tag{6.4}$$

where σ_{ab}^Y is the covariance (or variance if $a = b$) of returns of asset a with asset b from a yen investor's point of view. Note that for the dollar-based investor the foreign exchange asset represented by the subscript X is a yen exposure; for the yen-based investor, the asset represented by the subscript X is a dollar exposure.

The equilibrium for this model is a set of expected excess returns that clear markets. The markets that need to clear are equities and short-term borrowing. Note that in the context of the domestic CAPM we did not explicitly require equilibrium for short-term borrowing. In that context if wealth equals market capitalization, then the net demand for cash must be zero. In the international context there is more than one source of cash or short-term borrowing; we will refer to these alternative supplies as "bills." The supply of equities is taken to be the fixed market capitalization. The net supply of borrowing (i.e., bills) in each currency is assumed to be zero. Demands are generated from the optimization of investors' utility, which is assumed to have the same form as in the domestic CAPM. Investors maximize a utility function: Utility of investors in country c (either \$ or Y) is given by

$$U = \mu_P^c - .5 \cdot \lambda \cdot \left(\sigma_P^c\right)^2 \tag{6.5}$$

where λ is the risk aversion parameter.

In the global example we consider here, we differentiate U.S. investors from Japanese investors, and we solve each of their optimization problems separately. We sum the demands of each type of investor for U.S. equities and for Japanese equities, and we sum the demands for short-term lending in each country. Finally, we search for equilibrium values of expected excess returns, which are defined as those for which the total demand for each type of equity equals the supply and such that the net demand for short-term lending is zero. The zero net demand condition requires that U.S. investors are comfortable lending to Japanese investors the amount of dollars that they want to borrow, and vice versa.

Before we can solve for the equilibrium expected excess returns, though, we have to recognize that there are relationships between the dollar-based expected excess returns, $\mu_U^\$$, $\mu_J^\$$, $\mu_X^\$$, and the yen-based expected excess returns, μ_U^Y, μ_J^Y, μ_X^Y. Unfortunately, now we must confront head-on some of the complexity that comes with foreign exchange risk.

Consideration of foreign exchange risk adds a number of complexities in the real world, most of which we will safely ignore, but some of which we must address. We will ignore the complexity associated with different securities that can be used to add or hedge foreign exchange risk. One could use forward contracts, swaps, futures, or simply short-term borrowing and lending. We will also ignore the risk of depreciation of the profits earned during a finite period of time, a small effect sometimes referred to as the "cross product." If the time period is sufficiently short, the profit is arbitrarily small relative to the exposure, and so the risk of depreciation of the profit can be ignored. Finally, we will ignore the effects of inflation.

We can think most simply of a foreign exchange hedge as any position that benefits when a foreign currency depreciates, but does not create any other risk exposures. One obvious such position is a forward contract. Another is a short-term loan denominated in the foreign currency and invested in domestic short rates. Think of the currency hedge as the amount of such a loan. If a dollar-based investor borrows in yen, exchanges the yen for dollars at the beginning of the period, and invests the dollars in the U.S. short-term deposits, then depreciation of the yen allows the investor to repay the loan with fewer dollars, and thus benefit from the depreciation. The profit on the loan would exactly offset the loss from currency depreciation of a similarly sized yen-denominated investment.

Expected returns on such currency positions cause much confusion. Many investors have heard that currency is a zero-sum game, and thus assume the expected return on currency exposures is zero. This is not true, even in equilibrium. Currencies can have positive or negative expected returns. Consider the expected returns on currencies in our simple two-country world and focus on the relationship between $\mu_X^\$$ and μ_X^Y. The first term is the expected return to a dollar investor of holding yen. The second term is the expected return to a yen investor of holding dollars. Clearly, in a rational, efficient equilibrium these two different expectations should be consistent with each other. If one exchange rate is expected to go up, it would seem intuitive that the other must be expected to go down. The most natural intuition might seem to be that

$$\mu_X^Y = -\mu_X^\$ \tag{6.6}$$

Interestingly, the relationship is not quite that simple. Consider that if the exchange rate for \$/yen goes from 1 to 1.1, then there is a 10 percent appreciation of the yen from a dollar perspective and a .1/1.1 = 9.09% depreciation of the dollar from the yen perspective. Conversely, a move from 1 to .9—that is, a 10 percent depreciation of the yen from a dollar perspective—implies an appreciation of 11.1 percent of the dollar from a yen perspective.

More generally, the percentage appreciation of one currency relative to another is always larger than the percentage depreciation of the second currency relative to the first. If one currency appreciates by x from a second currency perspective, then the second currency depreciates by $x/(1 + x)$ from the perspective of the first. This bias of appreciation relative to depreciation of returns from the two different perspectives is given the name "Siegel's paradox."[7] One consequence is that $\mu_X^\$$ and μ_X^Y are not simply equal but opposite in sign as in equation (6.6). In fact, it is very possible for both $\mu_X^\$$ and μ_X^Y to be positive at the same time.

This strange behavior of currency expected returns makes many people uncomfortable. It feels like a magic trick. How can investors in both countries rationally expect their foreign currency holdings to appreciate? In order to understand this phenomenon, consider a simple world in which the \$/yen exchange rate starts at 1. At the end of a period a coin is flipped: If it comes up heads, the \$/yen exchange rate is 2; if it comes up tails, the \$/yen exchange rate is .5. From a dollar perspective, a person holding yen has two outcomes with equal probability, a return of 100 percent or a return of –50 percent. The expected return is positive, in fact is 25 percent. But consider the symmetry of the situation. The expected return to someone viewing the world from a yen perspective holding dollars is also positive 25 percent.

How can this be? How can individuals from both perspectives and identical information and expectations have positive expected return from holding each other's currency? The simplest answer is that they could not both rationally expect to be better off if all wealth was measured in the same units—but as long as they each measure their wealth from their own different currency perspective, they can both expect to be better off holding some of the other's currency—at least as measured in their own units. The more volatility there is to the exchange rate, the more these currency expected returns are biased upward relative to each other.

The relationship that must be true between $\mu_X^\$$ and μ_X^Y is as follows:

$$\mu_X^\$ = -\mu_X^Y + \sigma_X^2 \tag{6.7}$$

where σ_X is the volatility of the exchange rate.[8]

Why do we care about this curiosity of exchange rates? After all, we assume the time of our period is arbitrarily short so that the actual returns on yen and dollar during this period are arbitrarily close to equal, but of opposite sign. The answer to why we care is that this variance term in the expected excess returns relationship pins down the equilibrium returns on all assets in a world with multiple currencies.

Consider again the portfolio optimization problem discussed earlier. In addition to the volatilities and correlation of the equities, σ_U, σ_J, and ρ_{UJ}, and the

---

[7]The name Siegel's paradox" is widely used. The reference is to a paper: Siegel, J. J., 1972, "Risk, Interest Rates and the Foreign Exchange," *Quarterly Journal of Economics* 89, 173–175.

[8]The origin of this variance term is the positive curvature of the function, $1/x$, relating yen/\$ to \$/yen. The more variance there is in the distribution of potential outcomes, the more this curvature increases the expected value of the foreign exchange holding. The mathematical theorem required to show that this is the correct formula involves taking a limit as the length of the time period goes to zero and is known as Ito's lemma. An intuitive derivation of Ito's lemma can be found in Robert C. Merton's text, *Continuous-Time Finance* (Blackwell, 1990).

volatility, σ_X, of the exchange rate, we have two additional correlations to consider, $\rho^{\$}_{XU}$ and $\rho^{\$}_{XJ}$, between the exchange rate and the U.S. and Japanese equities, respectively, from a U.S. dollar perspective. Note that the correlations between each asset and the exchange rate from the Japanese yen perspective are simply –1 times the correlation from the U.S. dollar perspective; that is:

$$\rho^{Y}_{XJ} = -\rho^{\$}_{XJ} \tag{6.8}$$

Beyond Siegel's paradox, which relates expected excess returns on currencies from different country perspectives to the variance of the exchange rate, there are similarly derived relationships between the expected excess returns on investment assets and currencies from different currency perspectives that involve covariances. One example comes up only when there are more than two currencies. Consider the expected excess return on holding the euro from the perspective of a yen investor. It turns out that this expectation is equal to the sum of the expected excess return to holding dollars from a yen perspective and the expected excess return to holding euros from a dollar perspective, less the covariance of returns to holding yen and returns to holding euros from a dollar perspective. Of course, this covariance term doesn't enter our two-country example because we have only two currencies.

There is also a relationship between the expected excess returns on U.S. equity from a dollar versus a yen perspective, that is, between $\mu^{\$}_U$ and μ^{Y}_U. In this case again, it is not the variance of the exchange rate that relates the two expectations, but rather the covariance between the exchange rate and the stock return that comes into play. A similar relationship exists between $\mu^{\$}_J$ and μ^{Y}_J. Notice that we are considering currency-hedged stock returns in both cases, so the covariance that drives this expected return difference is not due to the currency effect directly entering one of the returns, but rather is a function of the expectation being taken from different currency perspectives.[9]

To gain an intuition about this covariance term in the expected return relationship, consider the hedged return on U.S. equity from a Japanese perspective. Suppose there is a positive correlation between currency hedged U.S. equity returns from a yen perspective and the returns to a yen investor holding dollars. When this correlation, ρ^{Y}_{XU} is positive, returns on U.S. equity will have a component that moves with the dollar when viewed from a yen perspective. Recall that expected returns on dollar holdings, from a yen perspective, have a positive component, σ^2_X, due to Siegel's paradox. To the extent U.S. equity returns mirror those of the dollar, this effect similarly increases the expected return on U.S. equity from a yen perspective relative to expected returns from a dollar perspective. If we form a projection of U.S. equity returns on dollar currency returns from a yen perspective, we can decompose the equity returns into a component that is a multiple of the dollar returns and an uncorrelated component. This projection on the dollar return has a coefficient that is the ratio of the above-mentioned covariance (between U.S. equity returns and returns on holding dollars from a yen perspective) and the variance to a

[9]The existence of these covariance terms in the expected excess return relationships can be derived using a multivariate version of Ito's lemma.

yen investor of dollar returns. The Siegel's paradox contribution to expected returns on the dollar is exactly this variance, so it makes sense that the contribution to expected excess returns of hedged U.S. equity from a yen perspective is this coefficient times the variance, which is simply the above-mentioned covariance. This covariance effect implies that the following two relationships hold:

$$\mu_U^Y = \mu_U^\$ + \sigma_{XU}^Y = \mu_U^\$ - \sigma_{XU}^\$ \tag{6.9}$$

$$\mu_J^Y = \mu_J^\$ + \sigma_{XJ}^Y = \mu_J^\$ - \sigma_{XJ}^\$ \tag{6.10}$$

We have now seen that there is a set of equations relating expected excess returns from a yen perspective to the expected returns from a dollar perspective (and, of course, vice versa). We can search over either the dollar-based or the yen-based expected excess returns, and the other set will be determined.

Let us now consider a simple example. The following inputs allow us to solve for a simple two-country "universal hedging" equilibrium:

U.S. market cap = 80
Japan market cap = 20
U.S. wealth = 80
Japan wealth = 20
U.S. risk aversion = Japan risk aversion = 2
U.S. equity volatility =15%
Japan equity volatility = 17%
Correlation between U.S. and Japan equity = .5
Dollar/yen volatility = 10%
Correlation between U.S. equity and yen = .06
Correlation between Japan equity and yen = .1

Given these inputs, the covariance matrix for a U.S. investor is as shown in Table 6.1.

The covariance matrix for a Japanese investor is only slightly different (see Table 6.2); the covariances between equity returns and the foreign currency have the opposite sign. If U.S. equity returns are positively correlated with returns on

TABLE 6.1 Covariance Matrix for a U.S. Investor

	U.S. Equity	Japan Equity	Yen
U.S. equity	.0225	.0128	.0009
Japan equity	.0128	.0289	.0017
Yen	.0009	.0017	.0100

TABLE 6.2 Covariance Matrix for a Japanese Investor

	U.S. Equity	Japan Equity	Dollar
U.S. equity	.0225	.0128	–.0009
Japan equity	.0128	.0289	–.0017
Dollar	–.0009	–.0017	.0100

holding yen, then clearly U.S. equity returns are negatively correlated with returns on holding dollars for yen-based investors.

As seen in Chapter 4, the inverses of these covariance matrixes are required to find the optimal portfolio weights. These inverse matrixes are shown in Tables 6.3 and 6.4.

Now the portfolio percentage allocations follow directly from the optimization of utility as in Chapter 4.

Portfolio Allocations from a U.S. Investor

U.S. equity: $d_U = .5 \cdot (59.27 \cdot \mu_U^{\$} - 26.09 \cdot \mu_J^{\$} - .90 \cdot \mu_X^{\$})$

Japan equity: $d_J = .5 \cdot (-26.09 \cdot \mu_U^{\$} + 46.44 \cdot \mu_J^{\$} - 5.55 \cdot \mu_X^{\$})$

Yen exposure: $d_X = .5 \cdot (-.90 \cdot \mu_U^{\$} - 5.55 \cdot \mu_J^{\$} + 101.02 \cdot \mu_X^{\$})$

Portfolio Allocations from a Japanese Investor

U.S. equity: $y_U = .5 \cdot (59.27 \cdot \mu_U^{y} - 26.09 \cdot \mu_J^{y} + .90 \cdot \mu_X^{y})$

Japan equity: $y_J = .5 \cdot (-26.09 \cdot \mu_U^{y} + 46.44 \cdot \mu_J^{\$} + 5.55 \cdot \mu_X^{y})$

Dollar exposure: $y_X = .5 \cdot (.90 \cdot \mu_U^{y} + 5.55 \cdot \mu_J^{y} + 101.02 \cdot \mu_X^{y})$

TABLE 6.3 U.S. Investor's Inverse Covariance Matrix

	U.S. Equity	Japan Equity	Yen
U.S. equity	59.27	–26.09	–.90
Japan equity	–26.09	46.44	–5.55
Yen	–.90	–5.55	101.02

TABLE 6.4 Japanese Investor's Inverse Covariance Matrix

	U.S. Equity	Japan Equity	Dollar
U.S. equity	59.27	–26.09	.90
Japan equity	–26.09	46.44	5.55
Dollar	.90	5.55	101.02

Total demand for U.S. equities is given by summing the two:

$$\text{U.S. equity demand} = \text{U.S. wealth} \cdot d_U + \text{Japan wealth} \cdot y_U \tag{6.11}$$

$$\text{Japan equity demand} = \text{U.S. wealth} \cdot d_J + \text{Japan wealth} \cdot y_J \tag{6.12}$$

Demand for borrowing in yen comes from U.S. investors who want to hedge some of their equity exposure. In particular, total yen exposure is the difference between the holdings of Japanese equity and the yen borrowing that hedges the currency exposure. To simplify notation, let us denote yen lending by dollar investors (yen lending is just –1 times yen borrowing) by d_Y. Then $d_X = d_J + d_Y$. Thus, yen lending by dollar-based investors is given by the equation $d_Y = d_X - d_J$. Similarly, dollar lending by yen investors, denoted $y_\$$, is given by the equation $y_\$ = y_X - y_U$.

Dollar lending by dollar-based investors is whatever is left after U.S. investors purchase U.S. equity, purchase Japanese equity, and participate in yen lending. Thus, dollar lending by dollar-based investors, denoted $d_\$$, is given by $d_\$ = (1 - d_U - d_J - d_Y)$. Similarly, yen lending by yen-based investors, denoted y_Y is given by $y_Y = (1 - y_U - y_J - y_\$)$.

These equations allow us to complete the demand functions:

$$\text{Demand for dollar lending} = \text{U.S. wealth} \cdot d_\$ + \text{Japan wealth} \cdot y_\$ \tag{6.13}$$

$$\text{Demand for yen lending} = \text{U.S. wealth} \cdot d_Y + \text{Japan wealth} \cdot y_Y \tag{6.14}$$

Equilibrium is the condition that demand equals supply; thus our equilibrium conditions are as follows:

$$\text{U.S. wealth} \cdot d_U + \text{Japan wealth} \cdot y_U = \text{Market cap of U.S. equity} = 80 \tag{6.15}$$

$$\text{U.S. wealth} \cdot d_J + \text{Japan wealth} \cdot y_J = \text{Market cap of Japan equity} = 20 \tag{6.16}$$

$$\text{U.S. wealth} \cdot d_\$ + \text{Japan wealth} \cdot y_\$ = \text{Net supply of dollar lending} = 0 \tag{6.17}$$

$$\text{U.S. wealth} \cdot d_y + \text{Japan wealth} \cdot y_y = \text{Net supply of yen lending} = 0 \tag{6.18}$$

In this simple economy, we can solve for the values of the dollar-based expected excess returns for which these equilibrium conditions are satisfied. The interested reader may verify that the equilibrium expected excess returns are:

$\mu_U^\$ = 4.128\%$
$\mu_J^\$ = 3.230\%$
$\mu_X^\$ = .412\%$

and that the resulting yen-based equilibrium expected excess returns are:

$\mu_U^Y = 4.038\%$
$\mu_J^Y = 3.060\%$
$\mu_X^Y = .588\%$

The optimal portfolio allocations for a U.S. investor are given by the following weights:

$d_U = 80\%$
$d_J = 20\%$
$d_X = 10\%$

implying that the foreign equity holding is 50 percent hedged. Note that these values suggest that the demand for lending in dollars and yen are as follows:

$d_\$ = 10\%$
$d_Y = -10\%$

Finally, the optimal portfolio allocations for a Japanese investor are given by the following weights:

$y_U = 80\%$
$y_J = 20\%$
$y_X = 40\%$

again implying that the foreign equity holding is 50 percent hedged. And note that these values imply that the demand for lending in dollars and yen are as follows:

$y_\$ = -40\%$
$y_Y = 40\%$

The reader may verify that the equilibrium conditions are satisfied. For example, the U.S. investors with 80 units of wealth demand 64 units of U.S. equities. Japanese investors with 20 units of wealth demand 16 units of U.S. equities, so that the total demand equals the total supply, a market capitalization weight of 80.

How can one find these equilibrium values for the expected excess returns? One way would be to set up a simple algorithm that equates supply and demand. For example, in a spreadsheet you can define certain cells to have the various demands as a function of the expected excess returns. Then you can set other cells to be the excess demands, the difference between the demands and the supply, and ask the solver function to search for values of the expected excess returns that minimize the sum of squared excess demands. Such an approach will work in a simple example such as this, but it does not highlight the conditions that define an equilibrium. In order to accomplish this, in the next section we use matrix notation to show a more general approach.

As should be clear from this simple two-country example, the international CAPM gets complicated very quickly. When we consider more than two countries, the notation and complexity of considering all the expected returns from various different points of view, the correlations and volatilities, and the relationships between them become cumbersome. In order to keep the notation as manageable as possible, in this section we use matrix algebra to simplify the presentation and develop the general approach.

PRELIMINARIES

Let there be n countries with each country having a risky equity asset.[10] Let r_1 be a $(2n - 1)$-vector of returns of risky assets from the perspective of country 1, which we will designate the home, or base currency, country.[11] We arrange to have the first element of r_1 be the return of the home country equity (which obviously has no currency risk), the next element be the currency-hedged return of the equity of country 2 (or, over a short time interval, equivalently the domestic return of the equity in country 2), and so on through the nth element, which is the return of the currency-hedged equity from country n. The $n + 1$st element is the return on holding currency from country 2, the $n + 2$nd element is the return on holding currency from country 3, and so on through the last element, which is the return on holding currency from country n.

Let Σ_1 be the $(2n - 1) \times (2n - 1)$ covariance matrix of r_1.

We define r_i similarly as the returns on risky assets from the perspective of country i. The first n elements are currency-hedged returns on the equities of countries 1 through n. The $n + 1$st element is the return on holding currency of country 1, the $n + 2$nd is the return on holding currency of country 2, and so on through the $n + (i - 1)$st element, which is the return on holding currency of country $i - 1$. The $n + i$th element is the return on holding currency of country $i + 1$, and so on through the last element, which is the return on holding currency of country n.

For example, in a four-country world including the United States, Japan, Europe, and the United Kingdom, the four return vectors, r_1, r_2, r_3, r_4, would include the following assets:

r_1 = U.S. equity, Japan equity, Europe equity, U.K. equity, yen, euro, pound
r_2 = U.S. equity, Japan equity, Europe equity, U.K. equity, dollar, euro, pound
r_3 = U.S. equity, Japan equity, Europe equity, U.K. equity, dollar, yen, pound
r_4 = U.S. equity, Japan equity, Europe equity, U.K. equity, dollar, yen, euro

Let Σ_i be the $(2n - 1) \times (2n - 1)$ covariance matrix of r_i.

We will find it convenient to define a matrix, I_i, which transforms r_1 into r_i. The elements of I_i are all 0's, 1's, and −1's, and it has a particularly simple structure. Of course, I_1 is simply the identity; it transforms r_1 into r_1. If we partition each of I_2 through I_n into four submatrices, an $n \times n$ upper-left corner, the $n \times (n - 1)$ upper-right corner, the $(n - 1) \times n$ lower-left corner, and the $(n - 1) \times (n - 1)$ lower-right corner, only the latter is interesting. The upper-left corner is always the identity; currency-hedged returns on equities are the same from each country perspective. The upper-right and lower-left corners are always identically 0.

The $(n - 1) \times (n - 1)$ lower-right submatrix has a column of −1's in the $(i - 1)$st

---

[10]The reader should think of our equity asset as an equity market index, or more generally as a market capitalization weighted basket of equities, bonds, and other assets. At the cost of slight notational complexity, one could easily include multiple assets in each country.

[11]There is nothing special about the home country except that it establishes a basis for defining notation.

column. The first row is all 0's except for the –1 in the $(i-1)$st column. If $i > 2$, then there is an $(i-2) \times (i-2)$ identity matrix starting in row 2, column 1. If $i < n$, then there is an $(n-i) \times (n-i)$ identity matrix starting in row i, column i. All other elements are 0.

Here is an illustration of I_4 for a six-country case:

$$\begin{matrix} 1 & 0 & 0 & 0 & 0 & 0 & 0 & 0 & 0 & 0 & 0 \\ 0 & 1 & 0 & 0 & 0 & 0 & 0 & 0 & 0 & 0 & 0 \\ 0 & 0 & 1 & 0 & 0 & 0 & 0 & 0 & 0 & 0 & 0 \\ 0 & 0 & 0 & 1 & 0 & 0 & 0 & 0 & 0 & 0 & 0 \\ 0 & 0 & 0 & 0 & 1 & 0 & 0 & 0 & 0 & 0 & 0 \\ 0 & 0 & 0 & 0 & 0 & 1 & 0 & 0 & 0 & 0 & 0 \\ 0 & 0 & 0 & 0 & 0 & 0 & 0 & 0 & -1 & 0 & 0 \\ 0 & 0 & 0 & 0 & 0 & 0 & 1 & 0 & -1 & 0 & 0 \\ 0 & 0 & 0 & 0 & 0 & 0 & 0 & 1 & -1 & 0 & 0 \\ 0 & 0 & 0 & 0 & 0 & 0 & 0 & 0 & -1 & 1 & 0 \\ 0 & 0 & 0 & 0 & 0 & 0 & 0 & 0 & -1 & 0 & 1 \end{matrix}$$

Also notice that since $r_i = I_i r_1$, it follows that $\Sigma_i = E(r_i r_i') = E(I_i r_1 r_1' I_i') = I_i \Sigma_1 I_i'$.

We will also find it convenient to define a $(2n) \times (2n-1)$ matrix, H_i, that transforms the $(2n-1)$-vector of portfolio allocations of risky assets—that is, equities and currencies—in country i, denoted w_i, into a $2n$-vector of demands for equities and lending (equivalently, holdings of bills) in each of the n countries, which we will denote d_i. Let 1^n_m be an n-vector with a 1 in the mth position and 0's elsewhere (1^{2n}_{n+i} is a $2n$-vector with a 1 in the $n+i$th position which corresponds to the demand for lending in country i). When H_i is defined as below, we will have:

$$d_i = 1^{2n}_{n+i} + \mathrm{H}_i w_i \tag{6.19}$$

In defining H_i again we consider four submatrices. The $n \times n$ upper-left matrix is the identity. The $n \times (n-1)$ upper-right matrix is identically 0. The $n \times n$ lower-left matrix is –1 times the identity. Only the lower-right submatrix changes with i. The $n \times (n-1)$ lower-right submatrix has a row of –1's in the ith row. For $i > 1$ there is a $(i-1) \times (i-1)$ identity matrix starting in row 1, column 1. For $i < n$ there is an $(n-\mathrm{i}) \times (n-1)$ identity matrix starting in row $i+1$, column i. All other elements are 0.

Here is an illustration of H_4 for a six-country case:

$$\begin{matrix} 1 & 0 & 0 & 0 & 0 & 0 & 0 & 0 & 0 & 0 & 0 \\ 0 & 1 & 0 & 0 & 0 & 0 & 0 & 0 & 0 & 0 & 0 \\ 0 & 0 & 1 & 0 & 0 & 0 & 0 & 0 & 0 & 0 & 0 \\ 0 & 0 & 0 & 1 & 0 & 0 & 0 & 0 & 0 & 0 & 0 \\ 0 & 0 & 0 & 0 & 1 & 0 & 0 & 0 & 0 & 0 & 0 \\ 0 & 0 & 0 & 0 & 0 & 1 & 0 & 0 & 0 & 0 & 0 \end{matrix}$$

$$
\begin{array}{rrrrrrrrrrr}
-1 & 0 & 0 & 0 & 0 & 0 & 1 & 0 & 0 & 0 & 0 \\
0 & -1 & 0 & 0 & 0 & 0 & 0 & 1 & 0 & 0 & 0 \\
0 & 0 & -1 & 0 & 0 & 0 & 0 & 0 & 1 & 0 & 0 \\
0 & 0 & 0 & -1 & 0 & 0 & -1 & -1 & -1 & -1 & -1 \\
0 & 0 & 0 & 0 & -1 & 0 & 0 & 0 & 0 & 1 & 0 \\
0 & 0 & 0 & 0 & 0 & -1 & 0 & 0 & 0 & 0 & 1
\end{array}
$$

The reader can verify that with H_i defined according to these rules the demands for equities are passed through and the demand for bills (lending) reflects the logic explained in the two-country case—namely that the demand for borrowing in foreign countries reflects currency hedging and the demand for lending domestically is 1 minus the sum of allocations to domestic equity and foreign lending.

It will also be useful to note that the $2n \times (2n - 1)$-dimensional matrix formed by taking the product, $H_i(I_i^{-1})'$, is a constant matrix for all i. We denote this matrix, which we use later in equation (6.22), J. The form of J for the six-country case is:

$$
\begin{array}{rrrrrrrrrrr}
1 & 0 & 0 & 0 & 0 & 0 & 0 & 0 & 0 & 0 & 0 \\
0 & 1 & 0 & 0 & 0 & 0 & 0 & 0 & 0 & 0 & 0 \\
0 & 0 & 1 & 0 & 0 & 0 & 0 & 0 & 0 & 0 & 0 \\
0 & 0 & 0 & 1 & 0 & 0 & 0 & 0 & 0 & 0 & 0 \\
0 & 0 & 0 & 0 & 1 & 0 & 0 & 0 & 0 & 0 & 0 \\
0 & 0 & 0 & 0 & 0 & 1 & 0 & 0 & 0 & 0 & 0 \\
-1 & 0 & 0 & 0 & 0 & 0 & -1 & -1 & -1 & -1 & -1 \\
0 & -1 & 0 & 0 & 0 & 0 & 1 & 0 & 0 & 0 & 0 \\
0 & 0 & -1 & 0 & 0 & 0 & 0 & 1 & 0 & 0 & 0 \\
0 & 0 & 0 & -1 & 0 & 0 & 0 & 0 & 1 & 0 & 0 \\
0 & 0 & 0 & 0 & -1 & 0 & 0 & 0 & 0 & 1 & 0 \\
0 & 0 & 0 & 0 & 0 & -1 & 0 & 0 & 0 & 0 & 1
\end{array}
$$

The next step in developing the general model is to put the relationships among expected excess returns into matrix notation. The expected excess returns for country i have two components corresponding to linear and nonlinear effects, respectively. The first component is the linear transformation of the expected excess return vector of the home country to the perspective of country i. The second component is the addition of a column from the covariance matrix of country i. As was discussed in the two-country example, the covariance component arises from the Siegel's paradox effect of the nonlinearity of the inverse function relating exchange rates. Normalizing on country 1 as the home country, then the covariance component is exactly the n + 1st column of the country i covariance matrix. We can pick off this column by postmultiplying the covariance matrix by the vector of 1's and 0's, 1^{2n-1}_{n+1}, defined earlier.

Thus, the formula for the expected excess return vector for country i is given by:

$$
\mu_i = I_i\mu_1 + (I_i\,\Sigma_1 I_i')1^{2n-1}_{n+1} \tag{6.20}
$$

The I_i matrix, defined earlier, transforms the expected return vector of the home country into the linear portion of the expected return vector from country *i*. The $(I_i\Sigma_1 I_i')$ is the formula for the covariance matrix of country *i*, as a function of the covariance matrix of the home country. Finally, the 1_{n+1}^{2n-1} vector picks off the column of the covariance matrix that corresponds to the home country currency covariance with each of the country *i* assets. This covariance is the appropriate numerator for the coefficient of the projection of that asset's return on the home country currency.

Next, we form the optimal portfolio weights for each country's optimal asset allocation. This portfolio weight vector, w_i, is the CAPM optimal portfolio. Thus, from Chapter 4 the vector of portfolio weights is given by the formula:

$$\begin{aligned} w_i &= \left(\frac{1}{\lambda_i}\right) \cdot \Sigma_i^{-1}\mu_i \\ &= \left(\frac{1}{\lambda_i}\right) \cdot \left(I_i^{-1}\right)' \Sigma_1^{-1} I_i^{-1}\left[I_i\mu_1 + \left(I_i\Sigma_1 I_i'\right)1_{n+1}^{2n-1}\right] \\ &= \left(\frac{1}{\lambda_i}\right) \cdot \left[\left(I_i^{-1}\right)' \Sigma_1^{-1}\mu_1 + 1_{n+1}^{2n-1}\right] \end{aligned} \tag{6.21}$$

Using the preceding formula we now form the country *i* *n*-dimensional demand vector for equities and lending:

$$\begin{aligned} d_i &= 1_{n+i}^{2n} + H_i w_i \\ &= 1_{n+i}^{2n} + \left(\frac{1}{\lambda_i}\right) \cdot H_i\left(I_i^{-1}\right)' \Sigma_1^{-1}\mu_1 + \left(\frac{1}{\lambda_i}\right) \cdot H_i 1_{n+1}^{2n-1} \\ &= 1_{n+i}^{2n} + \left(\frac{\lambda_1}{\lambda_i}\right) \cdot \left[H_i\left(I_i^{-1}\right)'\right]\left[\left(\frac{1}{\lambda_1}\right)\Sigma_1^{-1}\mu_1\right] + \left(\frac{1}{\lambda_i}\right) \cdot H_i 1_{n+1}^{2n-1} \\ &= 1_{n+i}^{2n} + \left(\frac{\lambda_1}{\lambda_i}\right) \cdot J w_1 + \left(\frac{1}{\lambda_i}\right) \cdot H_i 1_{n+1}^{2n-1} \end{aligned} \tag{6.22}$$

Finally, we solve for an equilibrium set of expected excess returns in the home country. Set total demand equal to the exogenously given supplies of equities and zero net lending.

EQUILIBRIUM CONDITION

$$\Sigma_{i=1,\ldots,n} W_i d_i = s \tag{6.23}$$

Where W_i is the proportion of wealth held in country *i*, and the vector of supply, *s*, is the 2*n*-dimensional vector whose first *n* elements are proportion of market capitalization weight held in each country and next *n* elements are zeros.

Substituting for the d_i we have:

$$\left[\Sigma_{i=1,\ldots,n} W_i 1_{n+i}^{2n}\right] + \left[\Sigma_{i=1,\ldots,n}\left(\frac{\lambda_1}{\lambda_i}\right) \cdot W_i\right] J w_1 + \left[\Sigma_{i=1,\ldots,n} W_i \cdot \left(\frac{1}{\lambda_i}\right) \cdot H_i 1_{n+1}^{2n-1}\right] = s \quad (6.24)$$

Substituting for w_1 we have:

$$\left[\Sigma_{i=1,\ldots,n} W_i 1_{n+i}^{2n}\right] + \left[\Sigma_{i=1,\ldots,n}\left(\frac{1}{\lambda_i}\right) \cdot W_i\right] J \Sigma_1^{-1} \mu_1 + \left[\Sigma_{i=1,\ldots,n} W_i \cdot \left(\frac{1}{\lambda_i}\right) \cdot H_i 1_{n+1}^{2n-1}\right] = s \quad (6.25)$$

Note that the $2n$-dimensional vector formed by taking the weighted sum, $[\Sigma_{i=1,\ldots,n} W_i \cdot (1/\lambda_i) \cdot H_i 1_{n+1}^{2n-1}]$, is a constant; we denote this vector j. We denote the risk tolerance weighted wealth, $[\Sigma_{i=1,\ldots,n}(1/\lambda_i) \cdot W_i]$, by the symbol τ.

Letting W be the $2n$-dimensional vector with 0's in the first n elements and country wealth in the second n elements, we have that:

$$W + \tau \cdot J \Sigma_1^{-1} \mu_1 + j = s \quad (6.26)$$

We now solve for the equilibrium values of the expected excess return vector, μ_1.

$$\tau \cdot J \Sigma_1^{-1} \mu_1 = (s - W - j) \quad (6.27)$$

We premultiply by J' and then by the inverse of the $(2n - 1) \times (2n - 1)$ matrix, $[J'J]$.

$$\tau \cdot \Sigma_1^{-1} \mu_1 = (J'J)^{-1} J'(s - W - j) \quad (6.28)$$

$$\mu_1 = \left(\frac{1}{\tau}\right) \cdot \Sigma_1 (J'J)^{-1} J'(s - W - j) \quad (6.29)$$

Here we have the equilibrium expected excess returns from the home currency perspective. Thus, the equilibrium portfolio weights are:

$$\begin{aligned} w_1 &= \left(\frac{1}{\lambda_1}\right) \cdot \Sigma_1^{-1} \mu_1 \\ &= \left(\frac{1}{\tau\lambda_1}\right) \cdot (J'J)^{-1} J'(s - W - j) \end{aligned} \quad (6.30)$$

and for i not equal to 1, using (6.21), we have:

$$
\begin{aligned}
w_i &= \left(\frac{1}{\lambda_i}\right) \cdot \left[\left(I_i^{-1}\right)' \Sigma_1^{-1} \mu_1 + 1_{n+1}^{2n-1}\right] \\
&= \left(\frac{1}{\lambda_i}\right) \cdot \left[\left(\frac{1}{\tau}\right)\left(I_i^{-1}\right)' (J'J)^{-1} J'(s - W - j) + 1_{n+1}^{2n-1}\right] \\
&= \left(\frac{\lambda_1}{\lambda_i}\right)\left(I_i^{-1}\right)' w_1 + \left(\frac{1}{\lambda_i}\right) 1_{n+1}^{2n-1}
\end{aligned}
\tag{6.31}
$$

And, using (6.22), the equilibrium portfolio demands are:

$$
\begin{aligned}
d_1 &= 1_{n+1}^{2n} + \left(\frac{1}{\lambda_1}\right) H_1 \Sigma_1^{-1} \mu_1 \\
&= 1_{n+1}^{2n} + \left(\frac{1}{\tau\lambda_1}\right) H_1 \Sigma_1^{-1} \Sigma_1 (J'J)^{-1} J'(s - W - j) \\
&= 1_{n+1}^{2n} + \left(\frac{1}{\tau\lambda_1}\right) H_1 (J'J)^{-1} J'(s - W - j)
\end{aligned}
\tag{6.32}
$$

and for i not equal to 1:

$$
\begin{aligned}
d_i &= 1_{n+i}^{2n} + \left(\frac{\lambda_1}{\lambda_i}\right) \cdot J\left(\frac{1}{\lambda_1}\right) \cdot \Sigma_1^{-1} \mu_1 + \left(\frac{1}{\lambda_i}\right) \cdot H_i 1_{n+1}^{2n-1} \\
&= 1_{n+i}^{2n} + \left(\frac{1}{\tau\lambda_i}\right) \cdot J\Sigma_1^{-1} \Sigma_1 (J'J)^{-1} J(s - W - j) + \left(\frac{1}{\lambda_i}\right) \cdot H_i 1_{n+1}^{2n-1} \\
&= 1_{n+1}^{2n} + \left(\frac{1}{\tau\lambda_i}\right) \cdot J(J'J)^{-1} J'(s - W - j) + \left(\frac{1}{\lambda_i}\right) \cdot H_i 1_{n+1}^{2n-1}
\end{aligned}
\tag{6.33}
$$

We now have equations that give the equilibrium expected excess returns, the optimal portfolio weights, and the portfolio demands for equities and bills, all as a function of the covariances of returns, and market capitalizations, wealth, and risk aversions of investors around the world. Fischer Black's universal hedging equilibrium is a special case that arises when market capitalizations equal wealth in each country and risk aversions are the same in all countries. To see this, let us use the notation λ for the common risk aversion, and look a little more closely at the demand equations:

$$
d_i = 1_{n+1}^{2n} + \left(\frac{1}{\tau\lambda}\right) \cdot J(J'J)^{-1} J'(s - W - j) + \left(\frac{1}{\lambda}\right) \cdot H_i 1_{n+1}^{2n-1} \tag{6.34}
$$

To examine the currency hedging in country i, we look at the demand vector, d_i. The currency hedging of the foreign equity held in country j is the negative of the ratio of the bill holding in country j to the equity holding in country j. Thus, we examine the negative of ratio of the $n + j$th element to the jth element. The universal hedging result is the statement that this ratio is the same from the perspective of all countries, i, and in each country, for all foreign holdings, that is for all j not equal to i.

As we see above, the demand from country i, d_i, is a sum of three vectors. We consider the first and third components first because they are straightforward. The first vector is just 100 percent weight in the domestic bill of the ith country, so this does not affect the universal hedging issue. The third vector is all zeros for the home country—that is, country 1—and for other countries is all zeros except two elements: the demand for the home country bill—element $n + 1$—is $(1/\lambda)$, the demand for the domestic bill of the ith country, element $n + i$, is $-(1/\lambda)$.

The second vector has three components, a scale factor, $(1/\tau\lambda)$; a matrix, $J(J'J)^{-1} J'$, which it turns out is the identity matrix minus a constant matrix; and a vector $(s - W - j)$. Recall that the vector s has proportion of market capitalization weights in the first n elements and zeros thereafter. The vector W has zeros in its first n elements and the proportion of wealth in each country thereafter. When wealth proportion equals market capitalization proportion, then the difference, $s - W$, has equal but opposite values in elements i and $n + i$. Premultiplication by $J(J'J)^{-1} J'$, because of its structure, preserves these values. Thus, consideration of only the contribution of $s - W$ would create 100 percent hedging. It is the contributions from other components that lead to less than 100 percent hedging. First consider the vector j. From its definition it turns out that the first n elements are zero. For elements $n + j$ that correspond to bills other than the domestic bill, the value is simply the product of the proportion of wealth in country j times $(-1/\lambda)$. The domestic bill is minus the sum of these values so that the sum of the elements is zero and thus premultiplication by $J(J'J)^{-1} J'$, because of its structure, preserves these values.

Now putting these results together, consider the demands for hedging from the home country. These hedging demands arise only in the second vector, and here the hedging demands are a constant proportion, $1 - (1/\lambda)$, of the wealth in each country.

Finally, consider the demands for hedging in any country i which is not the home country. The third vector affects only the demands for the bill of the home country and the domestic bill. Since the domestic bill does not affect foreign asset hedging, it suffices in considering hedging from the perspective of country i to consider only the demand for the home country bill. All other hedges will remain at the $1 - (1/\lambda)$ rate seen in the home country. The contribution to home country hedging demand in the third vector is $(1/\lambda)$. The contribution to hedging demand from the vector, j, is minus $(1/\lambda)$ times the sum of weights from the countries other than the home country. Thus, the total demand for hedging of the home country is $(1/\lambda)$ times (1 – Wealth outside the home country), which of course is just $(1/\lambda)$ times the wealth in the home country. Thus, once again the hedging demand is $1 - (1/\lambda)$ times the wealth in the country. Fischer Black's universal hedging result obtains, and the fraction hedged is the constant, $1 - (1/\lambda)$. Clearly, the greater λ, the risk aversion, is, the larger the fraction of currency risk that is hedged.

In practice, these equilibrium equations provide us estimates of risk premiums for various global assets. Let us now examine the risk premiums for a number of assets in an example of a universal hedging equilibrium. We take as assets the largest developed global equity and government bond markets, as well as the aggregate fixed income market in the United States. We also include as asset classes emerging equity, emerging fixed income, and U.S. high yield, just to give a sense of how these more risky assets fit into the equilibrium framework. In Chapter 8 we discuss many issues that arise in attempting to define the market portfolio, whereas here we simply try to capture the substance of the equilibrium without too much detail. The matrix computations needed to compute the equilibrium are easily handled in a spreadsheet.

In Table 6.5 we show for the global market capitalization weighted portfolio the asset classes, the market capitalization weights, the annualized volatilities, the correlation with the global portfolio, and the equilibrium risk premiums. The total market capitalization of these assets as of the end of June 2002 is $26.7 trillion. The volatilities and correlations are estimated using daily excess returns relative to one-month London InterBank Offer Rate (LIBOR) from January 1980 through

TABLE 6.5 Global Equilibrium

Asset	Market Capitalization Weight	Volatility	Correlation with Market	Risk Premium
Equity				
Australia	0.98%	16.00%	.64	2.73%
Canada	1.22	17.80	.77	3.66
France	2.23	20.43	.74	4.03
Germany	1.64	22.04	.70	4.16
Italy	0.87	24.91	.56	3.70
Japan	5.06	19.52	.56	2.91
Netherlands	1.39	18.48	.77	3.80
Spain	0.69	23.46	.66	4.17
Switzerland	1.87	18.36	.74	3.62
United Kingdom	6.16	15.99	.79	3.37
United States	30.10	15.82	.94	4.00
Emerging markets	2.13	25.27	.70	4.71
Government Bonds				
Canada	0.69%	5.27%	.24	0.33%
Europe	8.22	3.53	.19	0.18
Japan	6.21	4.14	.05	0.05
United Kingdom	1.15	6.06	.22	0.36
U.S. aggregate	27.46	4.49	.28	0.33
U.S. high yield	1.32	7.81	.57	1.19
Emerging debt markets	0.73	15.52	.61	2.52
Currency Exposures				
Australia	0.30%	10.00%	.28	0.75%
Canada	0.56	4.66	.29	0.37
Europe	4.66	10.80	–.08	–0.22
Japan	3.50	12.13	.12	0.40
Switzerland	0.58	11.54	–.14	–0.43
United Kingdom	2.27	9.24	–.04	–0.11

June 2002.[12] We calibrate the risk aversion of the global equilibrium to achieve a U.S. equity risk premium of 4 percent, as discussed in Chapter 5. This requires a risk aversion parameter, λ, of 3.22, implying a degree of currency hedging of 69.0 percent. The resulting currency exposures are shown in the table as well. The annualized volatility of the portfolio is 8.30 percent. The annualized equilibrium risk premium of the global portfolio is 2.22 percent. Thus, the expected Sharpe ratio of the global portfolio is .268.

Risk premiums are clearly a function of correlations with the market portfolio as well as volatilities. The Japanese equity market, for example, has a significantly higher volatility than does the U.S. equity market, but has a significantly lower risk premium reflecting its lower correlation with the global market portfolio. The highest risk premium belongs to the emerging markets equity asset class, which has both a high volatility and a relatively high correlation with the market portfolio.

Finally, we should reiterate the point made earlier that we do not treat the risk premiums as forecasts or expectations, but rather as reference points or hurdle rates. In other words, we find the equilibrium framework interesting even though we do not treat it as necessarily being an accurate reflection of the current expectations built into market prices. We expect to have expectations that are at odds with the equilibrium risk premiums, and we will treat those situations as opportunities.

[12] Except in the case of emerging markets and high-yield assets in which data begins later. See Chapter 16 for a description of how we treat missing data and why we put more weight on more recent observations. In this example the half-life of our data decay is 6.5 years. Also, we treat the emerging markets equity and debt as dollar denominated; that is, we do not hedge their currency exposures.

CHAPTER 7

Beyond Equilibrium, the Black-Litterman Approach

Bob Litterman

The Black-Litterman global asset allocation model provides a framework for combining market equilibrium with tactical views about investment opportunities. In order to understand the benefits of the model, it should be recognized that its development was motivated not at all by a belief that equilibrium provides useful short-term forecasts of returns. Rather, it was developed as a solution to a practical problem associated with portfolio optimization. As is well known, the standard mean-variance portfolio optimization discussed in Chapter 4 is not well behaved. Optimal portfolio weights are very sensitive to small changes in expected excess returns. Thus, the historical development of the Black-Litterman model began with a financial engineering question—"How can we make the standard portfolio optimizer better behaved?"—rather than, as developed in this book, as a natural extension of the global CAPM equilibrium.

The problem faced in 1989 in the fixed income research function at Goldman Sachs was a particularly badly behaved optimization exercise. We were advising investors with global bond portfolios, typically with some currency exposures. Many currencies, and most of the yield changes in bonds in the developed fixed income markets, have high correlations to each other. Changes in the forecasts of yields well below the precision with which any forecaster had confidence (for example, on the order of only a few basis points over a period of as much as six months into the future) would create major swings in optimal portfolio allocations. Moreover, it was virtually impossible, without significant constraints on both maximum and minimum holdings, to get portfolios that looked at all reasonable.

At the same time these portfolio optimization issues were being faced, Fischer Black had just finished his "Universal Hedging" paper on the global CAPM equilibrium. It was his suggestion that incorporation of the CAPM equilibrium into the mean-variance optimizer might make it better behaved. In retrospect, the suggestion perhaps seems obvious. It is well known that the properties of many statistical estimators can be improved by some shrinkage toward a neutral point that acts as a kind of center of gravity.[1] The more reasonable that point, the better the properties of the estimator. In the Black-Litterman model, the global CAPM equilibrium provides this center of gravity. At the time of Fischer Black's suggestion, though, despite the fact that mean-variance optimization and versions of the CAPM equilibrium had both been well understood for more than 20 years, it was not at all obvious that what the portfolio optimizer needed was the incorporation of such an equilibrium.

In fact, our first naive attempt to use the global equilibrium failed rather miserably. Rather than focus on expected excess returns as unknown quantities to be estimated, we simply tried to take a weighted average of investor-specified expected excess returns with the equilibrium values. We found, as we will show by example, that simply moving away from the equilibrium risk premiums in a naive manner quickly leads to portfolio weights that don't make sense. Further reflection on the nature of the problem led us to think about the uncertainty in the equilibrium risk premiums as well as the nature of information that the investors are trying to incorporate through their views. We also realized that it is essential to take into account the likely correlations among the expected returns of different assets. The estimator that we developed to take these issues into account eliminates the bad behavior of the optimization exercise and provides a robust framework for managing global portfolios.

What we discovered, however, was not simply a better optimizer, but rather a reformulation of the investor's problem. In the context of Black-Litterman, the investor is not asked to specify a vector of expected excess returns, one for each asset. Rather, the investor focuses on one or more views, each of which is an expectation of the return to a portfolio of his or her choosing. We refer to each of these portfolios for which an investor specifies an expected return as a "view portfolio." In the Black-Litterman model, the investor is asked to specify not only a return expectation for each of the view portfolios, but also a degree of confidence, which is a standard deviation around the expectation. This reformulation of the problem can be applied more generally, and among other benefits has greatly facilitated the use of quantitative return forecasting models in asset management.

In an unconstrained optimization context, the Black-Litterman model produces a very simple and intuitive result. The optimal portfolio is a weighted combination of the market capitalization equilibrium portfolio and the view portfolios.[2] The sizes of the tilts toward the view portfolios are a function of both the magnitude and the confidence expressed in the expected returns embedded in the investor-specified views. In fact, the solution is so straightforward one might question whether the model is actually adding value. The answer is that most portfolio optimizations are not so simple. When there are benchmarks, constraints, transactions costs to consider, or other complications, the optimal portfolios are not so obvious

---

[1]See, for example, the literature on Bayes-Stein estimation, including C. Stein, "Inadmissability of the Usual Estimator for the Mean of a Multivariate Normal Distribution," Proceedings of the Third Berkeley Symposium on Probability and Statistics (Berkeley, CA: University of California Press, 1955), and Jorion, Philippe, "Bayes-Stein Estimation for Portfolio Analysis," *Journal of Financial and Quantitative Analysis*, September 1986.

[2]The mathematical derivation of these results is included in "The Intuition behind Black-Litterman Model Portfolios," by Guangliang He and Robert Litterman, Goldman Sachs Investment Management Research paper, December 1999.

or easily interpreted. In these contexts the model provides the expected excess returns needed to drive the optimization process.

Let us now illustrate some of the difficulties in using standard portfolio optimizers to create optimal portfolios. One Wall Street prognosticator recently provided us with a nice set of inputs for our example by publishing a set of long-term expected returns for major asset classes. The forecasts and our estimated volatilities are shown in Table 7.1. We suspect our colleague used what he felt was informed judgment to create this outlook, but that he did not try to run the expected returns through an optimizer.

We proceeded to do exactly that, not to criticize our colleague (whose anonymity we shall respect), but rather to illustrate first how an optimizer looks for small inconsistencies in a set of forecasts and forms portfolios based on those inconsistencies, and second how difficult it is to specify a portfolio optimization problem in a way that leads to what might seem to be a reasonable solution. We formed a covariance matrix using historical returns for these various assets classes (and where necessary, as for private equity, used our best proxy). We then created two optimal portfolios, one completely unconstrained except that the weights were normalized to sum to 100 percent, and the other with the addition of no shorting constraints. These optimal portfolios are shown in Table 7.2. What we see in the completely unconstrained portfolio is that indeed the optimizer found some rather interesting opportunities—to create a hugely levered exposure to the global fixed income index while shorting offsetting weights in most of its components. Similarly, the unconstrained optimal portfolio forms a large overweight to the EAFE equity index, while shorting offsetting weights in several of its components. The constrained portfolio cannot take advantage of these long/short opportunities, so it simply chooses to hold large weights in hedge funds and high yield, and a smaller weight in real estate. Notice that the constrained portfolio has a much lower return per unit of volatility. Both portfolios seem quite unreasonable, despite the fact that

TABLE 7.1 A Sample Long-Term Outlook in Early 2002

Asset Class	Return	Volatility
Japanese government bonds	4.7%	4.2%
European government bonds	5.1	3.6
U.S. government bonds	5.2	4.6
U.S. equities	5.4	15.5
Global fixed income	6.0	3.6
European equities	6.1	16.6
U.S. high-grade corporate bonds	6.3	5.4
EAFE	8.0	15.3
Hedge fund portfolio	8.0	5.2
U.S. high yield	8.9	7.3
Private equity	9.0	28.9
Emerging debt	9.0	17.6
REITs	9.0	13.0
Japanese equities	9.5	19.6
Emerging market equities	11.8	23.4

TABLE 7.2 Optimal Portfolio Weights

Asset Class	Unconstrained Portfolio	Portfolio with No Shorting Constraint
Japanese government bonds	–202.7%	0.0%
European government bonds	–321.1	0.0
U.S. government bonds	–484.4	0.0
U.S. equities	–11.3	0.0
Global fixed income	1493.2	0.0
European equities	–258.0	0.0
U.S. high-grade corporate bonds	–385.8	0.0
EAFE	314.3	0.0
Hedge fund portfolio	58.1	55.3
U.S. high yield	–9.9	36.3
Private equity	0.5	0.0
Emerging debt	–28.8	0.0
REITs	4.3	7.7
Japanese equities	–71.7	0.7
Emerging market equities	3.1	0.0
Portfolio volatility	4.9%	5.1%
Portfolio expected return	18.2	8.4

from a mathematical point of view they each optimize the problem that was posed. Given the input forecasts, a large number of relatively tight minimum and maximum holdings would have to be specified (indeed, this is the usual approach) in order to get reasonable-looking answers out of the optimizer. In this situation the optimizer is obviously not adding a lot of value.

In the Black-Litterman approach we don't start with a set of expected returns for all asset classes. Instead, we start with equilibrium expected returns, which lead to the optimal portfolio having market capitalization weights. Though perhaps reasonable looking, this market capitalization portfolio doesn't change very much over time, and the obvious question is how to use an optimizer to tilt away from this portfolio in order to take advantage of perceived opportunities.

We create a simple equity-only example in order to illustrate how sensitive the optimized portfolio is to small changes in expected returns. Equity markets are not as highly correlated as fixed income markets and currencies; if we were to use a more complete set of assets it would only compound the problem. The equity-only equilibrium expected excess returns, shown in Table 7.3 along with market capitalization, differ slightly from those shown for the more complete global market portfolio in Table 6.5. However, since equities dominate the risk of the market portfolio the differences are not that great.

Consider a hypothetical situation in which an investor believes that over the next three months the German economic growth will be slightly weaker than expected and German equity will underperform relative to equilibrium expectations. We suppose that the investor quantifies this view as a 20 basis point lower than equilibrium expected return on the German equity market over the next three

TABLE 7.3 Global Equity Market Portfolio

Country	Market Capitalization	Equilibrium Expected Return	Equilibrium Excess Return
United States	53.98%	8.50%	4.00%
United Kingdom	10.60	7.47	2.97
Japan	9.85	7.07	2.57
France	4.44	8.39	3.89
Switzerland	3.49	7.32	2.82
Germany	3.27	9.11	4.61
Netherlands	2.58	8.19	3.69
Canada	2.28	7.71	3.21
Italy	1.78	8.01	3.51
Australia	1.73	5.99	1.49
Spain	1.37	8.26	3.76
Sweden	0.87	9.59	5.09
Hong Kong	0.83	7.29	2.79
Finland	0.67	11.48	6.98
Belgium	0.48	6.71	2.21
Singapore	0.40	7.05	2.55
Denmark	0.36	6.69	2.19
Ireland	0.30	7.02	2.52
Norway	0.24	6.82	2.32
Portugal	0.19	6.40	1.90
Greece	0.14	6.82	2.32
Austria	0.07	5.20	0.70
New Zealand	0.06	5.35	0.85

months. The investor holds all other expected returns unchanged at their equilibrium values. Given this slight alteration in expected returns, in Table 7.4 we show two new optimal portfolios together with the deviations of these two portfolios from the market capitalization weights. The first portfolio is optimized with no constraints except that weights sum to 100 percent; the second portfolio includes constraints against shorting.

When the portfolio is optimized without constraints the optimizer quickly recognizes a slight inconsistency between the expected return for Germany and the other equity markets and treats this inconsistency as an opportunity. It suggests a 54 percent short position in Germany offset by overweight positions in most of the other equity markets. Notice also, though, the odd short positions in Japan, Finland, Australia, Norway, and New Zealand. When no shorting constraints are imposed the opportunity is significantly reduced. The German equity position is zero and other deviations from market capitalization weights are reduced proportionately.

This unconstrained optimal portfolio has an expected return of 8.1 percent and an annualized volatility of 15.2 percent. These compare to the equilibrium portfolio values of 8.1 percent and 16.2 percent, respectively. The view of a slightly lower expected return on German stocks has provided an opportunity to reduce risk,

TABLE 7.4 Optimal Portfolio Given Bearish View on German Equity

Country	Unconstrained	Change from Market Cap	No Shorting	Change from Market Cap
United States	57.6%	3.6%	54.2%	0.2%
United Kingdom	11.7	1.1	10.6	0.1
Japan	8.4	–1.4	9.8	–0.1
France	18.9	14.4	5.3	0.9
Switzerland	9.2	5.7	3.8	0.3
Germany	–53.7	–57.0	0.0	–3.3
Netherlands	11.5	8.9	3.1	0.5
Canada	2.9	0.6	2.3	0.0
Italy	14.6	12.9	2.5	0.7
Australia	–2.7	–4.4	1.5	–0.2
Spain	3.8	2.4	1.5	0.1
Sweden	8.1	7.3	1.3	0.4
Hong Kong	3.0	2.2	1.0	0.1
Finland	0.1	–0.6	0.6	0.0
Belgium	1.9	1.4	0.6	0.1
Singapore	1.0	0.6	0.4	0.0
Denmark	1.1	0.7	0.4	0.0
Ireland	2.2	1.9	0.4	0.1
Norway	–3.7	–3.9	0.0	–0.2
Portugal	2.8	2.6	0.4	0.2
Greece	0.7	0.5	0.2	0.0
Austria	1.2	1.1	0.1	0.1
New Zealand	–0.4	–0.4	0.0	0.0
Volatility	15.2		16.2	
Expected return	8.1		8.1	

while holding expected return essentially unchanged. In this sense the optimizer is working as it should.

If we compare the portfolio weights in the new unconstrained optimal portfolio with those of the global market capitalization weighted portfolio, however, the changes in country weights are very large, and in some cases inexplicable. This type of behavior is typical of an unconstrained mean-variance optimization. For this reason portfolio optimizations are usually run with many tight constraints on asset weights.

Black-Litterman addresses this excessive sensitivity of portfolio optimizations without adding constraints. The Black-Litterman approach assumes there are two distinct sources of information about future excess returns: investor views and market equilibrium. Both sources of information are assumed to be uncertain and are expressed in terms of probability distributions. The expected excess returns that are used to drive the portfolio optimization are estimates that combine both sources of information.

In the Black-Litterman model a view is a statement about the expected return of any portfolio together with a degree of confidence. Mathematically, a view is expressed as follows:

$$p\mu = q + \varepsilon \tag{7.1}$$

where p = n-vector of weights in the view portfolio, one for each of the n assets
μ = n-vector of expected excess returns on underlying assets
q = Expected excess return of the portfolio
ε = Normally distributed random variable

The confidence in the view is $1/\omega$ where ω is the variance of ε.

As an example, in order to express a bearish view on German equity, let p have weights reflecting a portfolio long 1 percent of German equities, in other words all zeros except a value of .01 for German equity. We let q reflect the 80 basis points less than equilibrium annualized performance suggested above. We specify a degree of confidence of 4 to reflect a one standard deviation uncertainty around q of 50 basis points. The Black-Litterman optimal portfolio, shown in Table 7.5, is simply

TABLE 7.5 Black-Litterman Portfolio Reflecting a Bearish View on German Equity

Country	Unconstrained	Change from Market Cap	Percent Change from Market Cap
United States	58.7%	4.7%	8.8%
United Kingdom	11.5	0.9	8.8
Japan	10.7	0.9	8.8
France	4.8	0.4	8.8
Switzerland	3.8	0.3	8.8
Germany	–5.2	–8.5	–259.6
Netherlands	2.8	0.2	8.8
Canada	2.5	0.2	8.8
Italy	1.9	0.2	8.8
Australia	1.9	0.2	8.8
Spain	1.5	0.1	8.8
Sweden	0.9	0.1	8.8
Hong Kong	0.9	0.1	8.8
Finland	0.7	0.1	8.8
Belgium	0.5	0.0	8.8
Singapore	0.4	0.0	8.8
Denmark	0.4	0.0	8.8
Ireland	0.3	0.0	8.8
Norway	0.3	0.0	8.8
Portugal	0.2	0.0	8.8
Greece	0.2	0.0	8.8
Austria	0.1	0.0	8.8
New Zealand	0.1	0.0	8.8
Volatility	15.9		
Expected return	7.7		

a set of deviations from market capitalization weights in the direction of the view portfolio—that is, a proportional increase in the market portfolio offset by a short position in German equities. The model provides the appropriate weights on the view portfolio, given the stated expected return on the portfolio and the degree of confidence in that view. The model balances the contributions to expected return of the view portfolio and the market portfolio against their contributions to overall portfolio risk. The result is transparent and intuitive.

How does this approach differ from the badly behaved approach of the standard optimizer? In both cases the unconstrained optimal portfolio, w^*, is given by the same matrix equation:

$$w^* = \kappa\Sigma^{-1}\mu^* \tag{7.2}$$

where κ = Risk aversion parameter
Σ = Covariance matrix of excess returns
μ^* = Vector of expected excess returns

The difference between the Black-Litterman approach and the previous approach is that rather than specifying the expected excess returns directly, we define view portfolios, specify expected returns and degrees of confidence in the view portfolios, and apply the following Black-Litterman formula:[3]

$$\mu^* = [(\tau\Sigma)^{-1} + P'\Omega^{-1} P]^{-1}[(\tau\Sigma)^{-1}\Pi + P'\Omega^{-1}Q] \tag{7.3}$$

This formula creates an expected excess return vector, μ^*, from the information in k views:

$$P\mu = Q + \varepsilon \tag{7.4}$$

and in a prior reflecting equilibrium:

$$\mu = \Pi + \varepsilon^e \tag{7.5}$$

In these formulas P is a $k \times n$ matrix specifying k view portfolios in terms of their weights on the n assets. Q is a k-vector expressing the expected excess returns on the k view portfolios. Ω is the covariance matrix of the random variables representing the uncertainty in the views. Π is the n-vector of equilibrium risk premiums. Finally, τ scales the covariance matrix of returns in order to specify the covariance matrix of the zero-mean distribution for ε^e.

Let us look at the Black-Litterman expected excess returns. These expected excess returns and their deviations from equilibrium are given in Table 7.6. In

---

[3]This formula was derived in the paper "Global Portfolio Optimization," by Fischer Black and Robert Litterman, *Financial Analysts Journal*, September–October 1992, pages 28–43. In a subsequent paper, "A Demystification of the Black-Litterman Model: Managing Quantitative and Traditional Portfolio Construction," published in the *Journal of Asset Management*, 2000, vol. 1, no. 2, pages 138–150, Stephen Satchell and Alan Scowcroft extend the analysis.

TABLE 7.6 Black-Litterman Expected Excess Returns

Country	Excess Returns	Deviation from Equilibrium
United States	3.64%	–0.36%
United Kingdom	2.61	–0.36
Japan	2.34	–0.23
France	3.38	–0.51
Switzerland	2.46	–0.37
Germany	3.93	–0.68
Netherlands	3.20	–0.49
Canada	2.88	–0.32
Italy	3.02	–0.49
Australia	1.34	–0.15
Spain	3.27	–0.50
Sweden	4.46	–0.63
Hong Kong	2.47	–0.33
Finland	6.17	–0.81
Belgium	1.91	–0.30
Singapore	2.26	–0.30
Denmark	1.93	–0.26
Ireland	2.20	–0.32
Norway	2.04	–0.28
Portugal	1.63	–0.27
Greece	2.03	–0.29
Austria	0.60	–0.10
New Zealand	0.75	–0.10

contrast to the traditional approach, the Black-Litterman model adjusts all of the expected returns away from their starting values in a manner consistent with the views being expressed. Because the view expressed here is bearish on German equities, the expected returns on German equities decline. The total adjustment away from equilibrium is 68 basis points, less than the 80 basis points expressed in the view. This result reflects the assumption that the view has some uncertainty associated with it. The equilibrium is given some weight as well and acts as a center of gravity, pulling the Black-Litterman expected returns away from the view itself, back toward the equilibrium values.

Suppose we add another view. This time let us specify that a portfolio long 100 percent of Japanese equity and short 100 percent of U.K. equity will have a positive expected excess return of 100 basis points. We also give this view a confidence of 4 and assume that its error is uncorrelated with that of the previous view.

The unconstrained Black-Litterman optimal portfolio given these two views is shown in Table 7.7. We can see that the deviations of the optimal portfolio from equilibrium weights are exactly proportional to the sum of the two view portfolios. This result illustrates a very important general property of the Black-Litterman model. In general, the unconstrained optimal portfolio from the Black-Litterman

TABLE 7.7 Optimal Portfolio Given Two Views

Country	Excess Returns	Deviation from Equilibrium	Portfolio Weights	Percent Deviation from Market Cap
United States	3.71%	–0.29%	53.98%	0.00%
United Kingdom	2.59	–0.38	3.96	–6.64
Japan	2.72	0.14	16.49	6.64
France	3.44	–0.46	4.44	0.00
Switzerland	2.48	–0.34	3.49	0.00
Germany	4.04	–0.57	–2.27	–5.54
Netherlands	3.25	–0.45	2.58	0.00
Canada	2.94	–0.26	2.28	0.00
Italy	3.09	–0.42	1.78	0.00
Australia	1.41	–0.09	1.73	0.00
Spain	3.33	–0.43	1.37	0.00
Sweden	4.56	–0.53	0.87	0.00
Hong Kong	2.58	–0.22	0.83	0.00
Finland	6.27	–0.71	0.67	0.00
Belgium	1.93	–0.28	0.48	0.00
Singapore	2.40	–0.15	0.40	0.00
Denmark	1.98	–0.22	0.36	0.00
Ireland	2.25	–0.26	0.30	0.00
Norway	2.08	–0.24	0.24	0.00
Portugal	1.70	–0.21	0.19	0.00
Greece	2.10	–0.23	0.14	0.00
Austria	0.60	–0.10	0.07	0.00
New Zealand	0.79	–0.06	0.06	0.00

model is the market equilibrium portfolio plus a weighted sum of the portfolios about which the investor has views.

We will now investigate how changes in some of the Black-Litterman parameters affect the optimal portfolio tilts. In this simple unconstrained optimization environment,[4] we can characterize the deviations of the optimal portfolios from the market capitalization portfolio by the weights, w_1 and w_2, on the two view portfolios. For example, in Table 7.7, $w_1 = 5.54$ and $w_2 = 6.64$. In Table 7.8 we show how these weights vary with changes in the expected excess returns of the view portfolios (q_1 and q_2), the degrees of confidence ($1/\omega_1$ and $1/\omega_2$), and the correlation between the views. Notice that a view portfolio is given zero weight not when it has zero expected return, but rather when it has a return equal to that implied by a combination of equilibrium and all other views. Thus, adding a view creates a positive tilt toward that view portfolio only when the view is more bullish than the expected return implied by the Black-Litterman model without this particular view.

In an unconstrained optimization environment the Black-Litterman model is, in some respects, a complex tool for solving a relatively straightforward problem.

[4]See He and Litterman (1999).

TABLE 7.8 Effect of Parameter Changes on View Weights

	Expected Return		Confidence			Weights on Views	
Scenario	View 1	View 2	View 1	View 2	Correlation	View 1	View 2
Equilibrium	0.80%	0.40%	0	0	0	0.00%	0.00%
Base case	0.80	0.40	4	4	0	5.54	6.64
Weaker view 1	0.40	0.40	4	4	0	2.28	7.13
Stronger view 1	1.60	0.40	4	4	0	12.07	5.65
More confidence in view 1	0.80	0.40	16	4	0	7.40	6.36
Less confidence in view 1	0.80	0.40	1	4	0	2.77	7.06
No confidence in view 1	0.80	0.40	0	4	0	0.00	7.47
Zero expected return on view 1	0.00	0.40	4	4	0	–0.99	7.62
12 bps expected return on view 1	0.12	0.40	4	4	0	0.00	7.48
Weaker view 2	0.80	0.25	4	4	0	5.73	5.21
Stronger view 2	0.80	1.00	4	4	0	4.80	12.34
More confidence in view 2	0.80	0.40	4	16	0	5.19	9.38
Less confidence in view 2	0.80	0.40	4	1	0	6.01	3.06
No confidence in view 2	0.80	0.40	4	0	0	6.40	0.00
Zero expected return on view 2	0.80	0.00	4	4	0	6.04	2.83
–20 bps expected return on view 2	0.80	–0.20	4	4	0	6.28	0.93
–30 bps expected return on view 2	0.80	–0.30	4	4	0	6.41	–0.02
–40 bps expected return on view 2	0.80	–0.40	4	4	0	6.53	–0.97
Positively correlated views	0.80	0.40	4	4	0.5	6.67	7.74
Negatively correlated views	0.80	0.40	4	4	–0.5	4.68	5.87
Positively colinear views	0.80	0.40	4	4	1	8.26	9.38
Negatively colinear views	0.80	0.40	4	4	–1	3.94	5.37

Once one recognizes that view portfolios provide a flexible format for formulating views, and that the optimal portfolio is simply one that tilts with some set of weights on the view portfolios, it is probably easier to specify weights on those tilt portfolios directly rather than to specify expected returns, degrees of confidence, and correlations between views. There are, however, at least two reasons why the Black-Litterman model is necessary.

First, if one simply specifies weights on view portfolios, one loses the insights that Black-Litterman brings concerning the effects of the different parameters on the optimal weights. Of course that loss has to be balanced against the difficulty of knowing how to set those parameters in the first place. Since the original Black-Litterman paper was written, I have often received the question, "How do you determine the omega matrix?" There is no simple or universal answer. We know what these parameters represent—the expected excess returns on the view portfolios, the degree of uncertainty in the views, and the correlations between views—but the right way to specify such information is certainly context dependent. When the views are the product of quantitative modeling, for example, the expected returns might be a function of historical performance, the degree of confidence might be set proportional to the amount of data supporting the view, and correlations between views might be assumed to be equal to the historical correlations between view portfolio returns.

Other direct approaches to specifying weights on view portfolios can generally be mapped into particular assumptions on the expected excess returns and the omega matrix of Black-Litterman. At least in the context of Black-Litterman, the portfolio manager knows what these parameters represent, and can thus address the issue of whether those specifications make sense.

The second, and perhaps more important, reason that the Black-Litterman framework really is necessary is because in the real world one hardly ever optimizes in an unconstrained environment. The real power of the Black-Litterman model arises when there is a benchmark, a risk or beta target, or other constraints, or when transaction costs are taken into account. In these more complex contexts, the optimal weights are no longer obvious or intuitive. The optimal portfolio is certainly not simply a set of tilts on view portfolios. Nonetheless, the manager can be confident that when the optimizer goes to work using the Black-Litterman expected excess returns, the same trade-off of risk and return—which leads to intuitive results that match the manager's intended views in the unconstrained case—remains operative when there are constraints or other considerations.

Having made this point, it is nonetheless worth noting that, as shown in He and Litterman (1999), in a few special cases the optimal portfolios given constraints retain some intuitive properties. In our paper we consider in turn the case of a risk constraint, a leverage constraint, and a market exposure constraint. In the case of optimizing relative to a specified level of risk, the optimal portfolio is just a linearly scaled version of the solution of the unconstrained optimization problem. However, because of the scaling, the view portfolio deviations no longer tilt away from the market portfolio, but rather from a scaled market portfolio. Otherwise the intuition of the unconstrained portfolio remains.

In the case of a fully invested, no-leverage constraint, a constraint where the portfolio weights sum to 1, another portfolio enters the picture. There exists a "global minimum-variance portfolio" that minimizes the risk of all portfolios that are fully invested in risky assets. When portfolios are optimized subject to being fully invested, the optimal portfolio is a weighted average of the unconstrained optimal portfolio and the global minimum-variance portfolio.

Finally, a common constraint on portfolios is that their market exposure is 1, meaning that the coefficient or beta in a projection on the market portfolio is 1. In this case, the Black-Litterman optimal portfolio is a linear combination of the unconstrained optimal portfolio, the global minimum-variance portfolio, and the equilibrium portfolio.

PART Two

Institutional Funds

CHAPTER 8

The Market Portfolio

Ripsy Bandourian and Kurt Winkelmann

Throughout our presentation of the Capital Asset Pricing Model (CAPM), we often refer to the market portfolio, which includes all risky assets. Most of the original research on the CAPM was conducted using the U.S. stock market with the S&P 500 index representing the market portfolio. However, the actual market portfolio is not limited either geographically or in the scope of the asset classes. In later research, U.S. government and corporate bonds were often added to the market portfolio. This expanded the universe of securities covered by the market portfolio but by no means made it exhaustive. Other markets grew and developed, especially non-U.S. bonds and equity. As a result, investors were forced to expand their definition of the market portfolio. The market portfolio came to consist of global bonds and global equity. In addition, as the investable markets grew globally, many practitioners thought about how to include foreign currencies as part of the analysis. Indeed, any global investor is forced to consider currencies as an additional source of risk, potentially with either a positive or a negative expected return. This discussion is addressed in greater detail in Chapters 6 and 11. In this chapter we will address two basic questions: What does the market portfolio look like? What issues are associated with its construction?

GLOBAL EQUITY

Institutional investors use a variety of benchmarks for the global equity portion of their portfolios. These include the Morgan Stanley Capital International (MSCI) All Country World Index (ACWI) and its regional components; the Salomon Smith Barney (SSB) Global Equity Index (GEI) and its regional components; and the Financial Times Stock Exchange (FTSE) All World global family of indexes. Note, however, that the FTSE All World is mostly used by European investors. The presence of these different global index groups and their varied use across the world imply that although indexes have many applications, not all indexes should be used with all applications. In light of our objective, which is to determine the best way to represent the global equity portion of the market portfolio, we outline in Table 8.1 several characteristics that are important to us.

Since our objective is to find an efficient and manageable way to represent the

TABLE 8.1 Desirable and Undesirable Characteristics of Indexes

Desirable	Undesirable
Rule based	Ad hoc revisions
Broad	Narrow
Float weighted	Market cap weighted
Consistent data availability	Poor data availability
Comparable across countries	Different methodologies for each country index
Widely used by investors	Not used by investors

investable global equity portfolio, we seek indexes that provide consistent data across countries, have sufficiently long price history, and are widely used by global investors. In addition, we believe that having an index that is constructed in a systematic manner with the same set of rules and principles applied to all countries is beneficial. Consistency and comparability of data are lost if security inclusion rules are different for each country index. It is also imperative that security weights be adjusted to reflect the true, free floated market capitalization that is available to global investors. In addition, we seek an index that has a broad rather than narrow representation of each equity market.

We can apply these characteristics in evaluating three alternatives that we have identified to represent the global equity portion of the market portfolio. These alternatives are either to use MSCI ACWI or SSBGEI index families, or to construct a portfolio of local indexes (such as the Russell 3000 for the United States, Nikkei 225 for Japan, and FTSE 300 for the United Kingdom). Note that since the FTSE All World indexes are mostly used by European investors and we have a global investor in mind, we are focusing our attention on the MSCI ACWI and SSBGEI.

Salomon Smith Barney Global Equity Index

According to its creators, the objective of the SSBGEI is "to provide the definitive global equity benchmark."[1] The index does so by implementing a top-down index methodology, which is based on a set of simple rules and leads to a complete and unbiased construction. The main rule, which dictates company inclusion in the index, states that *all* companies with total available market capitalization greater than $100 million will be included. This methodology assures an objective representation and eliminates unintended biases and distortions that may be caused by stock selection. Also, the proportion of each

[1]See Nadbielny, Thomas S., Michael Sullivan, and Marc De Luise, "Introducing the Salomon Brothers World Equity Index," Salomon Brothers, June 1994, and Sullivan, Michael, Marc De Luise, Kevin Sung, and Patrick A. Kerr, "Global Stock Market Review: May 2002," Salomon Smith Barney Equity Research: Global Equity Index, June 13, 2002.

company's total market capitalization that is available to a foreign investor determines its weight in the index.

SSBGEI covers 50 developed and emerging markets. Countries are chosen for inclusion if the available float capital of index-eligible companies within a country is equal to or greater than $1 billion. Countries are removed from the SSBGEI if their total float capitalization falls below $750 million. This assures a lower turnover or that countries are eliminated from an index less frequently. In order to be classified as part of the developed index, the country's GDP per capita (adjusted for purchasing parity) must exceed $10,000 for the most recent calendar year, and there must have been no widespread restrictions against foreign investment. Although it is not very often that countries become excluded from the Global Equity Index, countries can migrate between the Developed World and Emerging Composite indexes. For instance, the Czech Republic and South Korea became part of the Developed World index during the 2001 index reconstitution. The current index composition is presented in Table 8.2.

MSCI Equity Indexes

MSCI All Country World Index (ACWI) covers 24 developed economies and 27 emerging markets. The developed portion of the ACWI is referred to as the MSCI World, and the emerging markets index is referred to as MSCI EMF. The individual market weights in the index are based on relative market capitalization of each country. MSCI continues to expand its universal coverage. For instance, MSCI Egypt and MSCI Morocco were added to MSCI EMF effective May 31, 2001. Also, individual country indexes may be reclassified as developed or emerging markets. For example, MSCI Greece index was reclassified as a developed market as of May 31, 2001.

According to MSCI, the objective for its Equity Index Series is to serve as

TABLE 8.2 Current Global Equity Index Composition

Country	Weight in Index	Country	Weight in Index
Australia	1.61%	Japan	8.75%
Austria	0.07	Netherlands	2.25
Belgium	0.52	New Zealand	0.05
Canada	2.28	Norway	0.18
Czech Republic	0.01	Portugal	0.15
Denmark	0.29	Singapore	0.34
Finland	0.64	South Korea	0.82
France	3.75	Spain	1.20
Germany	2.74	Sweden	0.77
Greece	0.17	Switzerland	3.05
Hong Kong	0.83	United Kingdom	10.33
Iceland	0.01	United States	54.06
Ireland	0.31	Emerging markets	3.28
Italy	1.54		

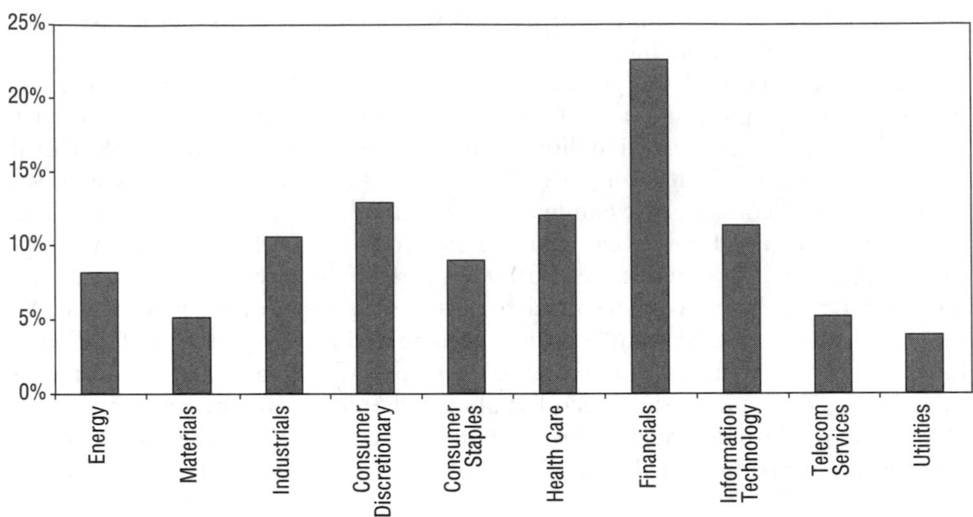

FIGURE 8.1 Sector Weights in the MSCI World Index

"global benchmark indexes that contribute to the investment process by serving as relevant and accurate performance benchmarks and effective research tools."[2]

In light of this objective, MSCI indexes are constructed in such a manner as to provide a "broad and fair market representation," which MSCI defines as an accurate reflection of business activities across and within industries, accessible to international investors. Unlike SSBGEI, which is based on simple rules, MSCI index construction is a four-step iterative process. First, MSCI identifies the equity universe in a given country, which includes all listed securities that can be characterized as equities, except investment trusts, mutual funds, and equity derivatives (99 percent of the world's total equity market capitalization). Second, market capitalization is adjusted to reflect the free float available to a nondomiciled investor. Third, securities are classified into one of the industries defined by the Global Industry Classification Standard. And as a fourth and final step, securities in each industry are analyzed to determine their inclusion in the index. Factors that affect the inclusion of a company in the index are the size of the company, its liquidity, and the level of market concentration. Although MSCI targets an 85 percent industry representation within each sector within each country, sector weights for the World index depend on both industry representation and the country relative market capitalization. Currently, sector weights in the MSCI World vary between 4 percent and 22 percent (see Figure 8.1).

Index composition (as of June 28, 2002) is presented in Table 8.3, where relative index weights for all developed countries included in the MSCI World are listed.

[2]See Morgan Stanley Capital International, "MSCI Enhanced Methodology: Index Construction Objectives, Guiding Principles and Methodology for the MSCI Provisional Equity Index Series," May 2001.

TABLE 8.3 Relative MSCI ACWI Weights

Country	Weight in Index	Country	Weight in Index
Austria	0.05%	Spain	1.22%
Belgium	0.43	Sweden	0.76
Denmark	0.32	Switzerland	3.31
Finland	0.70	United Kingdom	10.87
France	3.93	Hong Kong	0.64
Germany	2.90	Japan	8.94
Greece	0.15	Singapore	0.33
Ireland	0.33	Australia	1.73
Italy	1.49	New Zealand	0.06
Netherlands	2.45	Canada	2.16
Norway	0.20	United States	53.15
Portugal	0.14	Emerging markets	3.76

It is interesting to examine regional composition of the MSCI World index and how it changes over time. If any given region significantly outperforms others, that portion of the index will grow. Note in Figure 8.2 that in the late 1980s Australasia and the Far East constituted nearly 50 percent of the index, whereas the current weight is only 13 percent.

Basket of Local Indexes

In addition to using a family of global equity indexes such as SSBGEI or MSCI ACWI, we can consider using a basket of market capitalization weighted local indexes. Table 8.4 shows a list of countries that are included in the SSBGEI and MSCI World (developed), and their corresponding local indexes.

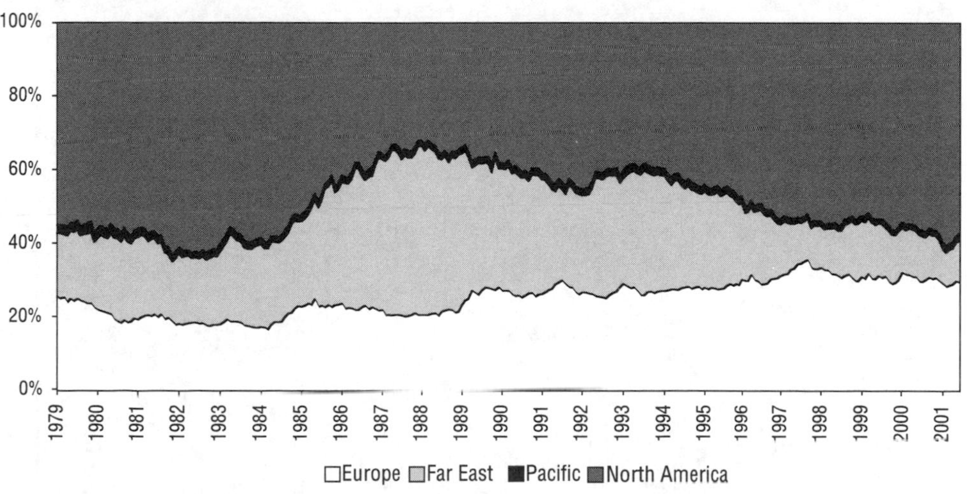

FIGURE 8.2 Regional Composition of the MSCI World Index

TABLE 8.4 Countries in the MSCI World and SSBGEI, and Their Local Indexes

	MSCI		SSBGEI		Local Index		
	Market Value	Number of Securities	Market Value	Number of Securities	Index	Market Value	Number of Securities
Austria	7.3	12	12.3	30	Austrian Traded ATX Index	22.24	40
Belgium	64.2	17	93.3	46	BEL 20	100.22	20
Denmark	47.7	25	53.2	49	KFX Copenhagen Index Share	67.78	20
Finland	106.1	20	116.2	51	HEX General Index		
France	593.4	55	676.7	215	CAC 40	651.21	40
Germany	438.2	51	493.6	158	DAX	547.03	100
Greece	22.9	22	31.3	68	Greece ASE Composite Index	55.24	60
Ireland	49.8	14	55.6	34	Irish Overall Index	58.86	63
Italy	224.6	43	278.7	134	Milan MIB 30	349.67	30
Netherlands	369.8	24	406.1	94	Amsterdam Exchanges Index	341.53	24
Norway	29.3	25	32.1	50	OBX Stock Index	51.43	25
Portugal	21.1	10	27.3	20	PSI 20	35.80	20
Spain	183.9	29	216.0	82	IBEX 35	259.77	35
Sweden	114.3	37	139.4	90	Stockholm Options Market Index	118.18	30
Switzerland	499.9	36	549.6	133	Swiss Market Index	414.74	27
United Kingdom	1,641.6	134	1,863.8	547	FTSE 100	1,457.68	101
Hong Kong	97.1	28	150.1	150	Hang Seng	365.39	33
Japan	1,350.3	321	1,579.6	1194	Nikkei 225	1,588.71	225
Singapore	50.3	35	61.2	63	SES All Share	117.07	310
Australia	261.0	70	290.0	118	ASX All Ordinary Stocks	364.97	490
New Zealand	8.5	13	8.9	21	NZSE All Ordinary Stocks		
Canada	326.1	80	412.2	296	S&P/TSE 60	298.64	60
United States	8,028.0	413	9,756.2	2,966	S&P 500	7,270.00	500
Total	14,536.7	1,514	17,303.81	6,609		14,536.18	2,253

In addition, we have analyzed the performance of MSCI indexes relative to the local ones and have found that they are very similar. In fact, as shown in Table 8.5, a regression of MSCI country indexes on their local counterparts indicates that almost all variation in the local indexes can be explained by the MSCI indexes. On the other hand, both the annualized tracking error and the average difference in annual returns shown in Table 8.6 are significantly different from zero.

One explanation for this difference is the variety of methodologies employed in constructing local market indexes. Most local indexes are capitalization weighted; however, not all are adjusted for free float. In addition, security selection methodology for inclusion in the index is different between countries. In several instances, for example, the index represents a couple dozen of the most often traded stocks on the local stock exchange.

Now that we have discussed all three alternative ways of representing global equity in the market portfolio, we can turn back to Table 8.1, which outlines characteristics we consider desirable. Consider the following characteristics: consistent index methodology across countries, historical availability, and total market representation. Most of the commonly used local indexes do not satisfy these criteria. Take, for instance, the S&P 500 for the United States. The S&P 500 is a capitalization-weighted index that includes 500 stocks chosen based on their liquidity, market size, and industry group to represent the U.S. equity market. However, stock inclusion in the S&P 500 is determined by a committee rather than by a set of well-defined rules and hence has been a topic of debate. Also, the index methodology

TABLE 8.5 Variation in Local Indexes in Relation to MSCI Indexes

Country	Local Index	Beta*	Intercept*	R-Squared
United States	S&P 500	1.00	0.00	1.00
United Kingdom	FTSE 100	0.99	0.00	0.99
Germany	DAX Xetra	0.98	0.00	0.97
Japan	Nikkei 225	0.97	0.00	0.87
France	CAC 40	1.06	0.00	0.98

*Beta is statistically significant on a 1 percent level, whereas the hypothesis that the intercept is equal to zero could not be rejected.

TABLE 8.6 Annualized Tracking Error and Average Difference in Annual Returns

Country	Local Index	Tracking Error (bps)	Average Difference
United States	S&P 500	105	–3.1%
United Kingdom	FTSE 100	196	–2.7
Germany	DAX Xetra	361	–1.0
Japan	Nikkei 225	731	–3.1
France	CAC 40	305	–1.1

does not allow for free float adjustment, thus introducing an upward bias in individual index weights for certain companies. Since similar reasoning can be applied to a number of the local indexes, we suggest that rather than choosing a basket of local indexes for global indexes we use a global index family.

The choice then lies between the MSCI ACWI and the SSBGEI index groups. Although both indexes satisfy most of the desirable characteristics outlined in Table 8.1, we favor using the MSCI indexes for the following reasons. First of all, MSCI data for individual countries is available going back to 1970, whereas Salomon indexes were originated in 1989. For most time series analyses, longer time series are more desirable as they may provide more insight into the events of the past and give us more confidence in our predictions for the future. Second, MSCI ACWI or World is the index most widely used by global investors. In fact, 93 percent of total active international equity accounts are managed against MSCI indexes. Likewise, 95 percent of total global equity accounts are managed against MSCI.[3] Third, although SSB's top-down methodology may seem appealing, in practice the GEI is difficult to use as a benchmark as it holds a very large proportion of small and illiquid securities, which global investors may not be able to reflect in their portfolios. Based on these arguments, we suggest using the MSCI ACWI index family to represent the global equity portion of the market portfolio.

GLOBAL BONDS

Whereas the issuers in the equity market all have at least one thing in common, the fact that they are public corporations, issuers in the bond capital markets are very diverse. They vary among governments, agencies, and corporations. Table 8.7 lists the major types of bonds that are included in global fixed income indexes. The securities issued by them also vary in nature: They may be backed by the credit of the issuer (be it corporation or government) or by collateral (pools of car loans, credit card debt, etc.). In fact, the Lehman Global Aggregate index contains a variety of bonds, and its composition is broken down by issuer type in Table 8.7.

Lehman Global Aggregate

The Lehman Global Aggregate index is a relatively new index, but has become fairly popular with international bond investors for several reasons. First, the majority of global bond indexes are based on government securities only, but for a growing number of investors these indexes are becoming unsatisfactory. For instance, Japanese government bonds currently form about 18 percent of the index. If no credit is added, and more governments (including the U.S. and European) shrink their debt while Japan continues to finance its fiscal deficit with debt, the Japanese share of a global treasury index could grow to as high as 50 percent.[4]

[3] Source: Intersec.

[4] See Berkley, Steve, and Nick Gendron, "A Guide to the Lehman Global Family of Fixed Income Indices," Lehman Brothers Fixed Income Research, February 2002.

TABLE 8.7 Universe of Fixed Income Securities

Type of Security	Issuer
Government bonds (Treasuries)	Federal government
Government agency bonds	Government-sponsored organizations and agencies
Municipal bonds	Local authorities (states, counties, cities, etc.)
Corporate bonds	Corporations
Mortgage-backed securities	Agencies, corporations
Asset-backed securities	Agencies, corporations
High-yield bonds	Corporations
Supranational bonds	Organizations such as World Bank, International Monetary Fund
Sovereign bonds	Government bonds issued in foreign markets

Lehman indexes are rule-based. This top-down approach to index construction tends to produce indexes that are unbiased and very representative of their respective markets. Country weights in the Lehman index are presented in Table 8.8.

Second, bonds, unlike common stock, are issued by a variety of entities such as governments, corporations, or agencies. They can be securities or not, and can have different provisions. For instance, Lehman Global Aggregate index consists of nearly 46 percent government bonds, about 17 percent corporate credit, and approximately 22 percent mortgage-backed securities. It also contains agency bonds, local authority and local agency bonds, and sovereign bonds. (See Figure 8.3.) Its average duration is 4.83 and its average maturity is 7.26 (as of May 31, 2002).

TABLE 8.8 Country Weights in Lehman Global Aggregate Index

Country	Weight in Index	Country	Weight in Index
Austria	0.83%	Spain	1.96%
Belgium	1.21	Sweden	0.66
Denmark	0.50	Switzerland	0.13
Finland	0.37	United Kingdom	3.46
France	5.26	Hong Kong	0.08
Germany	9.17	Japan	18.35
Greece	0.64	Singapore	0.18
Ireland	0.15	Australia	0.41
Italy	4.66	New Zealand	0.07
Luxembourg	0.15	Canada	1.77
Netherlands	1.92	United States	44.26
Norway	0.15	Supranational	1.75
Portugal	0.37	Emerging markets	1.52

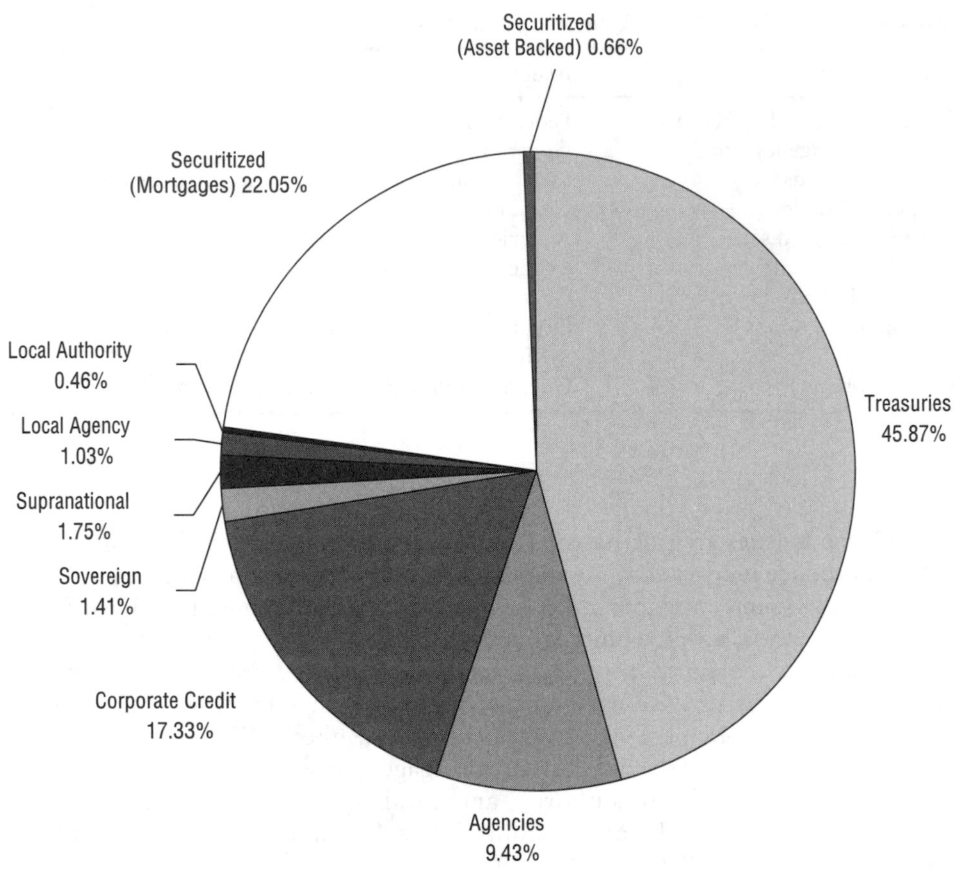

FIGURE 8.3 Lehman Global Aggregate Index

CONSTRUCTING THE MARKET PORTFOLIO

As mentioned earlier, due to prevailing globalization the market portfolio today should at least contain global equities and global bonds. As shown in Figure 8.4, the equity/bond split of the market portfolio has varied substantially throughout the years. In the past decade, the equity portion of the portfolio hit a minimum of 47 percent in October 1992 and a maximum of 63 percent in March 2000.

However, would a combination of these two asset classes suffice as a market portfolio? Currently, an average investor holds about 30 percent of his or her wealth in real estate. How would one replicate this portfolio and represent it in an aggregate state? The very fact that the market portfolio is indeed intangible and cannot be easily estimated served as the main premise of Richard Roll's paper published in 1977.[5] In his argument, also known as Roll's critique, Roll suggests that it is nearly impossible to empirically test the CAPM. Indeed, the linear relationship between

[5]See Roll, Richard, 1977, "A Critique of the Asset Pricing Theory's Tests; Part I: On Past and Potential Testability of the Theory," *Journal of Financial Economics* 4, 129–176.

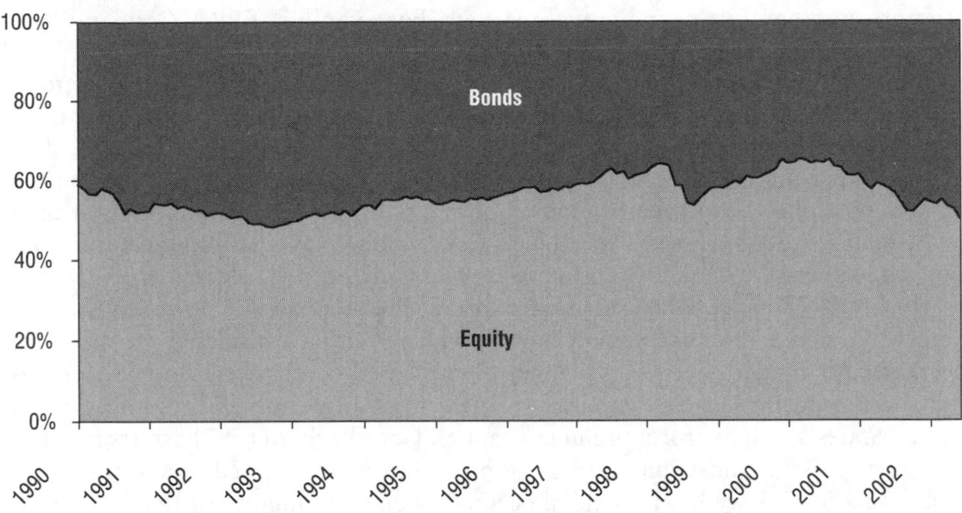

FIGURE 8.4 The Equity/Bond Split of the Market

expected return and beta follows directly from the efficiency of the market portfolio. Thus, if the market portfolio were misspecified, CAPM would produce biased betas. In addition, any test that attempted to validate the CAPM would be fully dependent on how efficient the "market" portfolio is. This in turn implies that the theory is testable only when every individual asset is included in the market portfolio. Some asset classes that come to mind immediately as being difficult to measure include private equity, commodities, real estate, and human capital.

Other Assets in the Market Portfolio

Publicly traded real estate could be easily added to the market portfolio in the form of the Wilshire REIT index. This index is comprised of companies whose main business activity involves ownership and operation of commercial real estate, and that derive at least 75 percent of revenue from these activities. There are 93 stocks included in the index, selected based on their source of revenue, liquidity, and market capitalization. These stocks are classified into sectors, which include factory outlets, hotels, industrial, local and regional retail, office, storage, apartments, and offices. The total market capitalization for the index is $144.8 billion (as of June 28, 2002).

However, there are two issues associated with adding the Wilshire REIT index to the market portfolio as a proxy for real estate. First, the Wilshire REIT index represents publicly traded real estate only in the United States. Adding this index alone to the market portfolio would lead to a distorted regional representation in the market portfolio, as the relative portion of U.S. in the market portfolio will be higher than it is in reality. This may lead to overstating correlations between U.S. asset classes and the market portfolio, subsequently resulting in higher CAPM expected returns. Although there are indexes representing publicly traded real estate in Europe (European Public Real Estate Association, or EPRA) and in Japan (Topixx), they do not regularly provide market capitalizations and often are not representative of individual markets. For example, EPRA Germany contains only eight stocks.

Second, publicly traded commercial real estate is only a small portion of total real estate in any economy, especially in the United States. In fact, owner-occupied housing is often one of the largest investments that an average investor holds during his or her lifetime. It is thus natural that one would suggest including it in the market portfolio. Unfortunately, most housing is owner occupied, and as such is not a readily tradable asset. Due to high transaction costs and imperfect information, consumers are unlikely to trade their primary residence frequently.

In his 1977 paper, Roll had suggested that the true market portfolio was not observable mainly because human capital, which is often considered the most important part of aggregate assets, cannot be measured or observed. In fact, Jorgenson and Fraumeni[6] suggest that nearly 93 percent of all wealth and resources of the United States are in the form of human capital. Gary Becker (1997) asserts that human capital is the most important type of wealth in the United States and other modern nations. Since human capital occupies such a dominant position in average investors' portfolios, it is impossible to ignore it when discussing the market portfolio. However, it is important to note that the market portfolio consists of assets that are divisible and can be freely sold in the marketplace. Human capital possesses neither of these characteristics. In addition, modeling human capital for inclusion in the model portfolio is impeded by the lack of a generalized measure. Although a number of measures (such as growth rate in labor income along with a term that depends on future expected returns) have been proposed, they are hard to implement. While it is clearly very difficult to measure the value of human capital, most economists would agree that the fluctuations in its aggregate value must correlate highly with the aggregate returns on the public equity markets. Thus, although we know that human capital is important and difficult to measure, one might hope that its absence from a market portfolio does not significantly alter the risk characteristics of that portfolio.

Private equity, discussed in detail in Chapter 28, usually refers to investments in companies that are not quoted on a public exchange. In spite of its many complexities (illiquidity, unpredictability, and increased liability), the demand for institutional investments in private equity has been rising. In fact, in 2001 the top 1,000 defined benefit plans held 3.8 percent in private equity (up from 3.4 percent in 2000).[7] According to Venture Economics/Thomson Financial's 2001 Investment Benchmarks Reports, $170 billion was committed to private equity that year.

Given that private equity represents securities or agreements that are claims on real assets, one may suggest that it should be included in the market portfolio. Its illiquid nature, though, would lead one to think that private equity is not readily tradable. In addition, due to the limited partnership nature of private equity investments, there are no indexes that document their historical performance or total

---

[6]See Jorgenson, D. W., and B. Fraumeni, 1989, "The Accumulation of Human and Non-Human Capital, 1948–84," in *The Measurement of Saving, Investment, and Wealth*, edited by R. E. Lipsey and H. S. Tice, NBER Studies in Income and Wealth, 52, 227–282.

[7]Source: *Pensions & Investments*, "The *P&I* 1000: Our Annual Look at the Largest Pension Funds," January 21, 2002.

market capitalization. It is only due to these data limitations that we exclude private equity from the market portfolio.

One alternative asset class that has become very popular with institutional investors recently is hedge funds. Although very interesting and a great portfolio diversifier, there is little doubt that hedge funds should not be included in the market portfolio. Hedge funds utilize strategies that capitalize on opportunistic trading positions and benefit from market inefficiencies. Just like mutual funds, hedge funds do not create new assets. Thus, if we were to include hedge funds, we would be double counting and inflating the value of the market portfolio.

Two other asset classes that need to be considered for inclusion in the market portfolio are commodities and natural resources. One may safely assert that a large portion of wealth is attributable to commodities and natural resources. However, just like hedge funds, if we were to include all commodities and raw materials in the market portfolio, we would be double counting. For instance, a good portion of the Goldman Sachs Commodities index consists of oil. However, some of this oil is already accounted for in the total market capitalization of such petroleum firms as BP Amoco, Chevron, and others. On the other hand, much oil is owned by governments and is not part of the public equity markets. We think a good argument can be made that oil is a very significant resource that is underweighted in the usual definitions of the market portfolio.

Although some of the asset classes discussed in this section may indeed be part of the true theoretical market portfolio, it may not be necessary to include them all in one while testing or implementing the CAPM. Stambaugh (1982) tested this exact hypothesis and showed that CAPM results are not sensitive to the choice of the market portfolio. Thus, an approximation of the market portfolio that includes all publicly traded assets may very well suffice for both testing and implementing the CAPM.

CHAPTER 9

Issues in Strategic Asset Allocation

Kurt Winkelmann

Most investment professionals would agree that the most important decision an investor makes is the asset allocation decision. Often, investors distinguish between two types of asset allocation decisions: a strategic asset allocation and a tactical asset allocation. A useful way to tell the two types apart is by focusing on the time horizon. Usually, investors regard a strategic asset allocation as a portfolio designed to reflect their long-term investment objectives (10 years or longer), while a tactical asset allocation reflects shorter-term investment objectives (perhaps as short as the next month).

The focus of this chapter is on strategic asset allocation. First, we'll review the key decision points in strategic asset allocation. Second, we'll review the shortcomings with the standard approaches to asset allocation. Third, we'll show how an equilibrium approach can resolve many of these issues. Finally, we'll use the discussion of an equilibrium approach and the key decision points to provide a guide to three subsequent chapters.

DECISION POINTS IN STRATEGIC ASSET ALLOCATION

Practitioners often regard asset allocation analysis with a mixture of awe and trepidation. Both reactions, as it turns out, are a result of the computational effort that seems to be required to derive optimal portfolios. Computational effort notwithstanding, a useful way to think about asset allocation is to identify the key decisions necessary to do it successfully. From our perspective, there are five distinct decision points in strategic asset allocation: (1) the bond/equity split, (2) the level of diversification across publicly traded equity and fixed income securities, (3) the level of currency hedging, (4) the level and structure of active risk, and (5) the allocation to alternative asset classes such as hedge funds, private equity, or real estate. The impact of each of these decisions has important consequences for the risk and return characteristics of an investor's ultimate portfolio.

The split between fixed income and equities generally turns out to be the most important driver of the total level of portfolio risk. Investors who are not comfortable with high risk levels in their portfolios would naturally be expected to have higher fixed income allocations, and vice versa. This decision is often usefully analyzed in the context of an asset/liability study (Chapter 10 has a longer discussion of the impact of liabilities on asset allocation).

Further risk reductions can be easily achieved through international diversification of the equity and fixed income portions of the portfolio. Each of these decisions has the impact of reducing total portfolio volatility and correspondingly increasing the total portfolio Sharpe ratio (to a point). A portfolio's Sharpe ratio is simply its excess return divided by its volatility.

While international diversification has the benefit of reducing portfolio volatility, it also exposes the portfolio to currency fluctuations. These fluctuations in turn mean that the portfolio has another risk exposure. Consequently, investors need to formulate a long-term currency hedging policy. This policy should clearly balance the level of currency risk in the portfolio with the risk exposure from other asset classes. Note that since this policy is the strategic currency hedging policy, it should not reflect any short-term views on currency movements. These views are best expressed as part of an active management process.

Exposure to active management represents a fourth policy decision. In our view, active risk represents exposure to both another source of risk and, correspondingly, another source of potential performance. Investors can improve their Sharpe ratios by including allocations to active risk. The basic issues are to balance the allocation to active risk against other portfolio exposures, and to structure an active portfolio so that active risk is being taken where it is most likely to be rewarded.

The final strategic issue that investors must consider is the allocation to alternative asset classes such as hedge funds, private equity, real estate, and natural resources. Exposures to these asset classes can provide important sources of portfolio performance. Thorough portfolio analysis, however, is made more difficult due to the generally poor quality of data.

Each of these decisions deserves careful consideration. In addition to a thorough analysis of each component, investors would be well advised to consider how each decision interacts with all other decisions. To our minds, the best analytical structure to consider these decisions is an equilibrium approach. This approach, as best we can tell, is the only one that lets investors consider all trade-offs in a theoretically consistent manner. It is relatively easy to implement, identifies the key trade-offs, is portable across clientele types, and is free of the limitations of standard approaches to asset allocation.

ISSUES WITH STANDARD FRAMEWORK AS USUALLY APPLIED

Asset allocation analysis has played an important role in the management of institutional assets for at least the past 20 years. As computer costs dropped, it became increasingly easy for institutional investors to implement the textbook approaches to asset allocation. Figure 9.1 gives a paradigm for finding a strategic asset allocation based on applications of standard tools.

The approach outlined in Figure 9.1 begins with an assessment of the available asset classes. Moving clockwise, in the next step an investor assesses the volatility and correlation of excess returns for each of the asset classes. The following step is to define expected returns over the investment horizon for each of the asset classes.

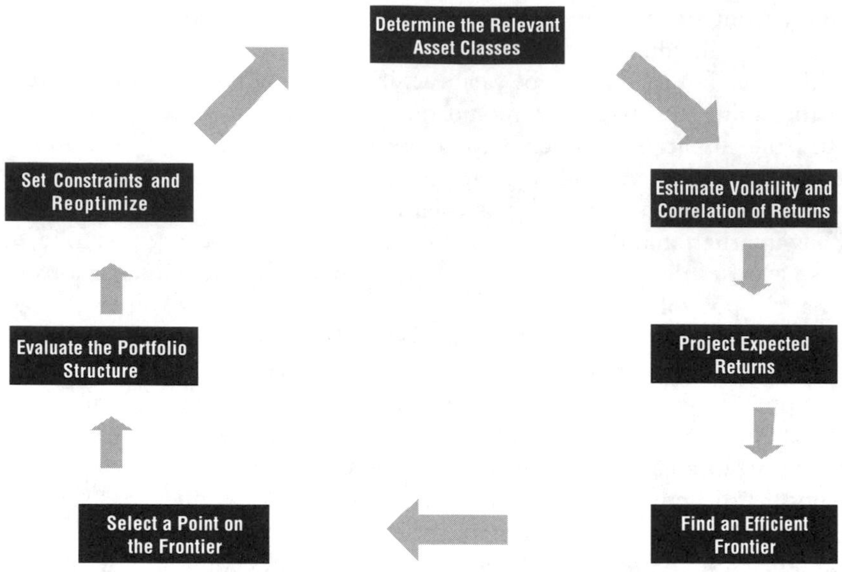

FIGURE 9.1 Asset Allocation Paradigm

Once the risk and return characteristics for each asset class have been defined, the investor then develops an efficient frontier, and selects a point on the efficient frontier that corresponds to his or her desired risk level. After analyzing the portfolio structure, and judging it to be inadequate, the investor imposes constraints and reoptimizes. The circle of constraints and reoptimization continues until the investor finds a portfolio that is judged to be satisfactory.

Why do investors feel the need to impose constraints and reoptimize? The principal reason is because the optimal portfolio weights appear to be too extreme. Viewed differently, the investor believes that the optimal asset allocation should not make the aggressive switches between asset classes that are favored by the optimizer.

The principal reason that the optimal portfolio weights may appear to be too extreme is because optimal asset allocations are quite sensitive to small changes in expected return assumptions. (This concern was crucial in the development of the Black-Litterman global asset allocation model.) A second, and related, issue is that historical average returns are quite sensitive to the choice of historical time period. Thus, we have a perplexing problem: Investors form views about expected future performance by calculating historical averages. These averages are quite sensitive to the choice of historical time period. The historical averages are then used in an optimizer, whose output (optimal portfolio weights) is quite sensitive to expected return assumptions. Little wonder, then, that practitioners are not completely satisfied with the standard methodology.

A simple example may help to clarify some of these issues. Table 9.1 shows the historical average returns for three principal equity regions over two distinct time periods. The chosen equity regions are the United States, Japan, and Europe, while the time periods are the decade of the 1980s and the decade of the

TABLE 9.1 Average Returns and Volatilities

	1980–1990			
	MSCI World	MSCI Europe	MSCI U.S.	MSCI Japan
Average return	19.2%	18.1%	16.9%	24.3%
Volatility	14.4	17.7	15.9	21.7
	1991–2001			
	MSCI World	MSCI Europe	MSCI U.S.	MSCI Japan
Average return	6.5%	8.7%	12.5%	–5.6%
Volatility	14.6	15.3	14.5	25.2

1990s. Also shown in the table are the historical standard deviations of returns. Both statistics (historical average return and historical volatility) were calculated using monthly excess return data. As the table clearly illustrates, the historical average returns are quite sensitive to the choice of time period. For example, in the 1980s the best-performing of these three equity markets was the Japanese market, while in the 1990s the U.S. market showed the best performance. Notice that while historical averages seem to be quite sensitive to the choice of time period, the historical volatilities appear to be less so. This is an important point to which we will return.

Now, suppose that an investor decided to construct optimal portfolios on the basis of the average returns shown in Table 9.1. In other words, suppose that an investor used the average returns (and risk characteristics) of the 1980s and built an optimal portfolio, and then did the same using the data from the 1990s. How would these portfolios compare?

Figure 9.2 shows the two sets of optimal asset allocations, with the very loose constraint that the portfolio weights must sum to 100 percent. As we can see, the choice of time period used for estimating returns has dramatic consequences for the portfolio weights. Using the data from the 1980s, the optimal portfolio has a long position in Japanese equity. By contrast, a short position in Japanese equity is implied when the sample is restricted to the data from the 1990s. In any event, the portfolio weights are so extreme that no prudent investor would actually implement them as a strategic asset allocation.

The technical issues associated with standard approaches to strategic asset allocation give rise to two practical issues. First, because of the potential for extreme portfolio positions, practitioners often find it hard to develop an intuition behind the portfolio. Second, because it is unlikely that investors will implement the extreme portfolio positions, it is hard to develop an approach to portfolio advice that can be used across clientele types: Each clientele type is likely to need their own set of constraints. Thus, the standard approach to strategic asset allocation fails on two grounds: It gives extreme portfolios, and does not allow for consistent advice giving. Each of these issues can be addressed by using an equilibrium approach.

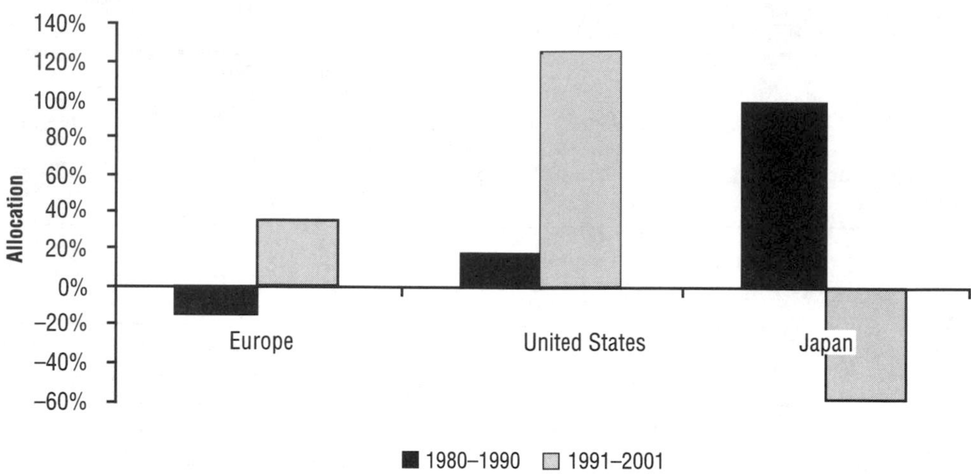

FIGURE 9.2 Optimal Portfolio Weights

BENEFITS OF AN EQUILIBRIUM APPROACH

An equilibrium approach gives investors three specific advantages over standard approaches to strategic asset allocation. First, it provides a more theoretically correct neutral point. Second, an equilibrium approach relies on more easily observable and estimable information. Finally, an equilibrium approach enables investors to more easily identify and understand the key trade-offs.

As discussed in previous chapters, the predictions of asset-pricing theory are quite clear: When capital markets are in equilibrium, investors should hold a portion of their wealth in the market portfolio. The remaining portion of an investor's wealth should be held in either cash or debt. Investors would hold cash if they were not willing to tolerate portfolio risk at the level of the market portfolio. They would issue debt (i.e., become levered) if they were willing to take more risk than the market portfolio. These predictions are independent of the investor's geographic region or industry type. Thus, the market portfolio provides a meaningful starting point for portfolio analysis: Differences between investor types (geographic region or clientele type) can be understood in terms of deviations from the market portfolio.

Applying an equilibrium approach in practice is relatively straightforward. As a first step, investors must identify a suitable market portfolio. That is, investors must determine the market value of all assets, and perhaps express these values as percentages of the total value of all assets. As discussed in Chapter 8, for most publicly traded securities markets this step is relatively straightforward. Most of the world's publicly traded equity markets are valued daily. Similarly, daily valuations are available on most government bond markets. For other asset classes, valuations are likely to occur less frequently. That caveat notwithstanding, it is feasible for investors to get assessments of the value of the market portfolio on a regular basis.

A second ingredient that is necessary for investors to apply an equilibrium approach is some notion of the risk characteristics of each of the asset classes. Volatility and correlation of asset returns are important because investors must judge whether they would like their portfolios to have more or less risk than the market portfolio. These characteristics must be estimated on the basis of available data, as they cannot be directly observed. Fortunately (and as discussed in Chapter 16), volatility and correlation estimation do not suffer from the same issues as expected return estimation. Historical data can be used to provide quite robust estimates of future volatility and correlation. As seen in Table 9.1, while the historical volatility figures were different in each of the decades, they were not nearly as sensitive as the average return estimates.

Of course, investors would also like to know portfolio return in addition to portfolio risk. Fortunately, an equilibrium approach helps investors in this dimension as well. Chapter 6 discussed the linkage between portfolio weights, risk characteristics, and expected returns. To pin down the third from the first two, investors must assess the overall level of risk aversion. In turn, there is a mapping from the level of risk aversion to the market equity risk premium. Thus, an assessment of the equity premium (discussed in Chapter 5) gives investors a view on the level of risk aversion, which in turn drives expected returns on all other asset classes.

The true benefit of an equilibrium approach is that it gives an internally consistent platform for portfolio analysis. On an *ex post* basis, an equilibrium approach helps us understand differences in investor behavior. On an *ex ante* basis, strategic asset allocations can be formed as deviations from the equilibrium portfolio. Investors will naturally deviate from the equilibrium portfolio if they believe that they can be adequately compensated for doing so.

How would an investor analyze a deviation from equilibrium? One way is to follow the approach outlined in Chapter 7—that is, to specify a set of views and to apply the Black-Litterman model. If specific views are not well defined, then an alternative approach is to recognize that there is a mapping between views and optimal portfolios and to start with the latter; that is, propose a portfolio that represents a deviation from equilibrium. Using the same risk characteristics and equity risk premium, work backward to find the expected asset returns associated with the proposed portfolio. Next, calculate the difference between the new expected returns and the equilibrium returns. Finally, assess (on the basis of data analysis and financial economic theory) whether the differences seem reasonable. If so, then the proposed portfolio should be implemented. If not, then a new portfolio should be proposed.

In the next several chapters, we show how an equilibrium approach can be applied to each of the key decisions in strategic asset allocation. The level of the bond/equity split, and its relation to liabilities, is discussed in Chapter 10. The impact of international diversification and currency hedging are discussed in Chapter 11. The application of an equilibrium approach to uncorrelated asset classes is addressed in Chapter 12.

CHAPTER 10

Strategic Asset Allocation in the Presence of Uncertain Liabilities

Ronald Howard and Yoel Lax

Most strategic asset allocation analysis considers only the dynamics of asset values and abstracts from the presence of any liabilities. Thirty-five years of academic and applied research have developed a more or less unified theory of investing assets for the long run and capital market equilibria resulting from the optimal investment behavior of individuals. For many investors, this type of analysis is reasonably appropriate. For example, a retired homeowner who has no mortgage and no children can be assumed to have no liabilities, and his or her asset allocation can be analyzed using classical methods. For other types of investors, the abstraction from the presence of liabilities is more troublesome. Pension funds in particular exist for the sole purpose of paying out pensions in the present and future. Ignoring their liability stream can lead to suboptimal asset allocations.

In this chapter we investigate the strategic asset allocation process in the presence of liabilities. The presence of liabilities introduces an interesting complexity into the asset allocation problem. Rather than investing to get "the biggest bang for the buck," investors may forgo higher expected returns in order to allocate to an asset that is highly correlated with liabilities. By investing in this manner, they ensure that the value of their assets increases when the value of liabilities does, thereby protecting the surplus.

The issues we investigate in the context of our framework are the three drivers of long-term performance: the bond/equity split, the level of diversification, and the duration of the bond portfolio. Our numerical results show that there is a dichotomy between the optimal asset allocations for over- and underfunded plans. The latter must take a large amount of equity risk in order to improve their funding status, while the former may actually be better off with lower equity allocations. Similarly, overfunded plans benefit from global equity diversification, while underfunded plans do not. Finally, the benefit from duration matching the bond portfolio with liabilities is much greater for underfunded than for overfunded plans.

From the outset, we outline our approach to modeling liabilities. Subsequently, we analyze the asset allocation decision, where we initially focus on a single-period setup. This framework is a simple extension of the setup without liabilities often studied, in which investments are evaluated by their Sharpe ratios. Subsequently, we investigate the asset allocation problem in a multiperiod simulation framework that allows us to study the impact of payouts.

MODELING LIABILITIES

Put simply, the liability stream of a typical pension fund is a series of future payments that are unknown as of today. Although actuaries project future payments, they cannot do so with certainty since the actual payments will depend on a number of factors that are unknown as of the projection date.

One source of uncertainty is due to mortality rates. Although actuarial mortality tables can be used to predict the life span of the average pensioner, and a fund with many beneficiaries may experience a mortality rate quite like the actuarially assumed average, a random element remains nevertheless. In addition, if the average life expectancy increases due to trends in lifestyle and/or health care, the current mortality table may understate the present value of the benefit obligation.

Another source of uncertainty relates to future salary growth. For a benefit plan with a career-pay or final-pay provision, the future benefit obligation will depend on career-average pay or the average pay over the final few years of employment, respectively. When actual salary growth differs from the actuarial assumed growth rates, the projected benefit obligation will require an adjustment. Furthermore, there may be one-time benefit increases that are not reflected in the actuarial salary growth assumptions. For example, many union plans experience periodic increases in the benefit obligation due to collective bargaining.

Finally, there may be uncertainty about employee demographics. If the industry or company undergoes structural change, such as increased competition or an acquisition/merger, the company may decide to offer incentives for early retirement or may be forced to terminate a portion of the workforce. Any such change could have a significant impact on the benefit obligation of the pension plan.

If the payments were known with certainty, the liability stream would resemble a bond (or portfolio of bonds) that could be priced using the current term structure of interest rates. In the presence of uncertainty about future payments, one can still use this approach, keeping in mind that the value of liabilities calculated in this way is "noisy."

This insight leads to an intuitive way for modeling liabilities. We assume the value of liabilities consists of two parts—a bond, which reflects the best guess about future obligations, and a noise term, which reflects the uncertainty of the future payments. The return on the bond as well as its correlation with other assets can be calculated by discounting projected obligations by the current term structure. Alternatively, a publicly traded bond index can be used as a proxy, where the index is levered to match the duration of the liability stream. Mathematically,

$$R_{L,t} - R_{f,t} = \beta(R_{B,t} - R_{f,t}) + \varepsilon_t \tag{10.1}$$

where $R_{L,t}$ = Total return on the liability index at time t

$R_{f,t}$ = Risk-free rate of return

$R_{B,t}$ = Total return on a bond index

ε_t = Noise term

The parameter β is used to duration-match the liability and bond indexes. The noise term is assumed to have volatility σ_ε and to be uncorrelated with the bond index, but it may be correlated with other returns.

When the current cash flow projections reflect all available information (and therefore represent a best guess as to future benefit payouts), the expected change in the benefit obligation due to changes in projected payouts is zero. Since the noise term reflects uncertainty about future payouts, we can assume that the noise term has a zero mean as long as the current projected payouts are equal to their expected values.

The appendix contains a numerical example of how to pin down the parameters β and σ_ε from the balance sheet of a pension fund.

EVALUATING INVESTMENT DECISIONS IN THE PRESENCE OF LIABILITIES

In the absence of liabilities, alternative investment structures are often compared on the basis of their Sharpe ratios. The Sharpe ratio measures how much return in excess of a risk-free rate an investment offers for each unit of volatility:

$$SR_i = \frac{\mu_i - R_f}{\sigma_i} \tag{10.2}$$

where μ_i and σ_i are the mean and volatility, respectively, of investment structure i. In other words, the risk and return of investments are evaluated relative to cash. The objective of maximizing the portfolio Sharpe ratio in an asset-only framework is theoretically well-founded. As was shown in Chapter 4, in a one-period model an investor who maximizes his or her utility over end-of-period wealth will choose the portfolio with the highest Sharpe ratio if the investor's utility function is quadratic (irrespective of the distribution of returns) or if returns are multivariately normally distributed (irrespective of the investor's utility function).

In the context of an asset-liability framework, there are two shortcomings to measuring the trade-off between risk and return using the Sharpe ratio. First, the Sharpe ratio considers only the risk and return of assets and ignores the presence of any liability stream. As we will see, some investment structures are better suited to hedge against changes in the value of liabilities than others. This ability to hedge should be taken into account when evaluating an investment, but it is ignored by the Sharpe ratio.

A second shortcoming of the Sharpe ratio in the present context is that it is really only a theoretically well-founded concept in a one-period model. The solution of the maximum Sharpe ratio portfolio to the optimization problem with quadratic utility does not obtain when the investor derives utility from intermediate consumption as well as from final wealth, even when the period utility function is of the quadratic form.

Assuming that a pension fund cares only about the distribution of assets (or the surplus) at one future point in time seems inappropriate for at least two reasons. First, it is unclear how to choose the future date given that pension funds generally expect to remain in business indefinitely. Second, a pension fund will care about funding characteristics in intermediate periods as well to ensure being able to pay its liabilities in every period.

The remainder of this chapter focuses on both a static (one-period) setup, as well as a dynamic setup. In our static analysis, we extend the notion of a risk/return trade-off in the form of a Sharpe ratio to accommodate the presence of a liability stream. In the dynamic analysis, we investigate the effect of payouts on overall funding characteristics of a pension plan.

STATIC ANALYSIS

In the absence of any liabilities, investors care about the characteristics of the distribution of the returns on their assets. In the presence of liabilities, investors care about returns on both assets and liabilities, and on how they are correlated. In order to develop a measure to compare asset allocations in the presence of liabilities, let's first define a few quantities. Let us denote by A_t and L_t the value of assets and liabilities, respectively, at time t. The surplus is given by

$$S_t \equiv A_t - L_t \tag{10.3}$$

and the funding ratio is given by

$$F_t \equiv \frac{A_t}{L_t} \tag{10.4}$$

Thinking of a pension plan as a company, the surplus measure is the equivalent of the market value of equity of a public company: It is the value that would be left for the shareholders if the company used all of its assets to pay off all of its liabilities. The important caveat in this comparison is that while owners of public companies are subject to limited liability and therefore the market value of their equity cannot be negative, the surplus of a pension plan can be negative. Of course, a deficit cannot be carried on forever, since otherwise the plan will become insolvent at some point in time. This will be mitigated either by a contribution from the sponsor to the plan or by asset returns that exceed the returns on the liabilities.

In this section, we assume that pension plans care about the return on the surplus instead of the return on assets alone. This assumption nicely fits the analogy of a pension plan with a public company whose managers are entrusted with maximizing the value of shareholder equity. Talking about the percentage return on the surplus is slightly tricky, however, because the surplus can be zero, and hence any change in the surplus would lead to an infinite return. Therefore, instead of focusing on the percentage return, we consider the dollar change in the surplus as the primary concern of a pension fund.

When a pension fund cares about the change in the surplus, what are some of the quantities it may be interested in? For one thing, the fund will be interested in the expected change in the surplus, and whether it is positive (surplus is expected to grow or deficit is expected to decline) or negative (surplus is expected to decline or deficit is expected to grow). The fund may also be interested in the uncertainty in the change in the surplus. Finally, a pension fund may be interested in the risk/return trade-off—that is, how much risk it has to accept in the surplus change in order to achieve a certain expected change.

The last measure of interest leads us to generalize the notion of the Sharpe ratio to the asset-liability framework. We define the risk-adjusted change in surplus (RACS) as

$$RACS_t \equiv \frac{E_t\left[S_{t+1} - S_t\left(1+R_f\right)\right]}{\sigma_t\left[S_{t+1} - S_t\left(1+R_f\right)\right]} = \frac{E_t\left[S_{t+1} - S_t\left(1+R_f\right)\right]}{\sigma_t\left[S_{t+1}\right]} \quad (10.5)$$

where the second equality follows from the fact that S_t is known at time t. Here we assume the risk-free rate is constant through time, $R_{f,t} \equiv R_f$. We claim that the RACS is the natural extension of the Sharpe ratio to an asset-liability framework. To see this, let $R_{A,t}$ denote the return at time t on the asset portfolio and rewrite the last expression as

$$RACS_t = \frac{E_t\left[A_t\left(1+R_{A,t+1}\right) - L_t\left(1+R_{L,t+1}\right) - \left(A_t - L_t\right)\left(1+R_f\right)\right]}{\sigma_t\left[A_t\left(1+R_{A,t+1}\right) - L_t\left(1+R_{L,t+1}\right)\right]} \quad (10.6)$$

and note that in the absence of any liabilities ($L_t = 0$), the RACS becomes

$$RACS_t = \frac{E_t\left[A_t\left(R_{A,t+1} - R_f\right)\right]}{\sigma_t\left[A_t\left(1+R_{A,t+1}\right)\right]} = \frac{E_t\left[R_{A,t+1}\right] - R_f}{\sigma_t\left[R_{A,t+1}\right]} \quad (10.7)$$

The last expression is the Sharpe ratio of the asset portfolio. Our new measure, the RACS, therefore has the nice property that it simplifies to the Sharpe ratio in the absence of liabilities. For this reason, it is a natural extension of the Sharpe ratio to the asset-liability framework. Whereas the Sharpe ratio evaluates investments relative to cash, the RACS evaluates them relative to liabilities.

How does one interpret the RACS? The numerator measures the dollar return on the surplus that is expected in excess of the risk-free rate of return. The denominator measures the risk in the same quantity. Consider a fund with positive surplus and a perfectly known liability stream (i.e., no noise in the liabilities). One possible investment strategy for the fund is to purchase a portfolio of bonds to exactly match its future liabilities and to invest the remaining surplus into a risk-free asset. This strategy is completely risk-free and will produce a return of $(1 + R_f)$ on the surplus with no volatility. If the fund undertakes any other investment strategy, the RACS measures how much the fund is being compensated for taking risk relative to the risk-free strategy.

Next consider a fund with a deficit but whose liabilities are also known with certainty. If we assume that the fund can borrow at the risk-free rate, the fund can borrow the amount of its deficit at the rate R_f and purchase a portfolio of bonds to exactly match its future liabilities. This strategy produces no volatility in the deficit and locks in a proportional increase of R_f in the deficit. For this fund, the RACS also measures how much it is being compensated for taking risk relative to the risk-free strategy of locking in an increase of R_f in the deficit.

In general a fund does not know exactly its future liabilities, giving rise to the noise term discussed earlier. For such a fund there is no risk-free strategy in the sense that no asset allocation exists that will lock in a certain rate of return on the surplus. The least risky strategy for this fund is to purchase a portfolio of bonds that represents the best guess about future liabilities and to invest the remainder into the risk-free asset. This strategy will yield the lowest surplus volatility of all possible strategies, and this volatility will equal the noise volatility.[1] Therefore it is natural to evaluate other investment strategies relative to this least volatile of all strategies in terms of their risk/reward trade-off. This is precisely what the RACS does.

At this point in the discussion, we find it helpful to consider a concrete example in order to illustrate how a fund may want to think about asset allocation. The example will allow us to put to use the theoretical concepts we have developed thus far. We will now introduce the return and risk assumptions at the foundation of the example to follow.

ILLUSTRATION OF STATIC MODEL

For the purpose of the calculations to follow, we use equilibrium return assumptions derived from the Black-Litterman model with no views based on historically estimated volatilities and correlations. It is important to note, however, that the calculations to follow can be performed with any return assumptions desired. In fact, sometimes it is useful to see how sensitive the results are to the specific assumptions used.

For the present analysis, we choose to model liabilities with respect to the Lehman Long Government and Credit Index and noise. As of June 30, 2002, the duration of this index was about 10.5. We hypothetically consider a pension fund with a duration of liabilities of 12. This dictates the choice of $\beta = {}^{12}/_{10.5} = 1.14$. For our basic scenario, we arbitrarily consider a noise return of zero and a volatility of 2 percent. This number is perhaps easier to interpret in terms of a confidence interval: If the noise is normally distributed, a noise volatility of 2 percent implies that in each given period the (excess) return on the liability index is within ±4 percent of the (excess) return of the levered Lehman Long Government and Credit Index with a probability of 95 percent. For the liability index with a duration of 12, the ±4 percent interval on returns translates into a ±4%/12 = ±33 bps interval on the yield on the liability index.

Table 10.1 summarizes the risk/return assumptions used in the analysis to follow. All numbers reflect an annual horizon.

For now, let us focus only on U.S. equity (represented by the S&P 500 index), the Lehman Long Government and Credit Index, and the liability index. First, because the duration of the liability index was assumed to be larger than that of the Lehman index, its excess return is also higher. This implies that even for a fund with a surplus, an all-bond allocation is a losing strategy in the long run, since the

[1]This is true as long as there is no asset that is negatively correlated with the noise. If such an asset exists, the fund can achieve a surplus volatility lower than the noise volatility.

TABLE 10.1 Risk and Return Assumptions

				Correlation					
Asset Class	Excess Return	Volatility	Sharpe Ratio	U.S. Equity	Global Equity	Lehman Long Government and Credit Index	Lehman Aggregate Index	Global Fixed Income	Liability Index
U.S. equity	4.02%	15.63%	0.26	1					
Global equity	3.89	14.54	0.27	0.96	1				
Lehman Long Government and Credit Index	0.57	8.07	0.07	0.17	0.12	1			
Lehman Aggregate Index	0.30	4.52	0.07	0.16	0.10	0.95	1		
Global fixed income	0.21	7.12	0.03	0.06	–0.02	0.85	0.83	1	
Liability index	0.65	9.42	0.07	0.17	0.12	0.98	0.93	0.83	1

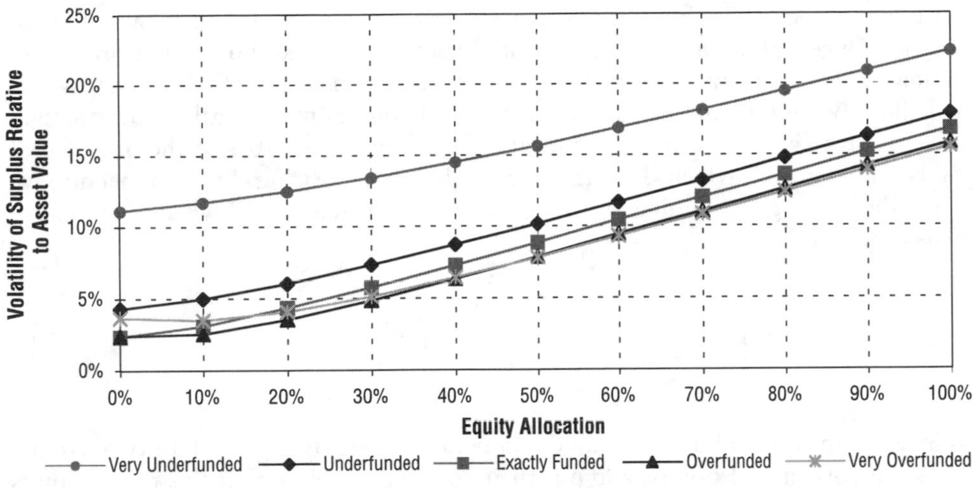

FIGURE 10.1 Surplus Risk

asset portfolio will grow more slowly than the liability index on average.[2] Equities appear more attractive from this perspective.

A second observation relates to the correlations between the series. Note that the liability index is more highly correlated with the Lehman Long Government and Credit Index than with equities. Therefore, bonds appear to be a better hedge against changes in the value of liabilities than equities. We will now examine this trade-off arising from higher allocations to equity more closely.

Example: Surplus Risk, Expected Change, and the RACS

Let us begin by looking at the surplus risk. Figure 10.1 plots the surplus risk as a fraction of asset value:

$$\frac{\sigma_t\left[S_{t+1}\right]}{A_t} \tag{10.8}$$

Along the horizontal axis we plot different equity allocations, ranging from 0 percent to 100 percent, with the remainder of the assets invested in the Lehman Long Government and Credit Index. Each line in the graph represents a different initial funding ratio.[3] In order to interpret this graph, let's again compare the present case to the one without liabilities. In this case, the surplus simply equals the assets, and the quantity plotted would be the volatility of asset returns. Since equities are more

[2]As long as there are no payouts, an average return on assets that is lower than that on liabilities will lead to a decrease in the funding ratio. In the presence of payouts an overfunded plan can accept a lower return on assets than on liabilities and still maintain or grow its surplus and/or funding ratio. We will show this later in the chapter when we incorporate payouts into our setup.

[3]The funding ratios are 0.5, 0.8, 1, 1.5, and 2, respectively.

volatile than bonds, it should come as no surprise to see the lines generally upward sloping. Since equities and bonds are not perfectly correlated, however, a small allocation to equity in an otherwise all-bond portfolio may actually decrease overall volatility. When the funding ratio is very large, liabilities matter little in determining the surplus risk. We see this diversification effect in Figure 10.1 in the line labeled "very overfunded," which decreases initially before increasing. In the appendix, we show that for a given funding ratio the surplus risk is minimized when a fraction of assets equal to

$$\frac{\left(1-\beta\frac{L_t}{A_t}\right)\left(\sigma_B^2-\rho\sigma_B\sigma_E\right)}{\sigma_E^2+\sigma_B^2-2\rho\sigma_B\sigma_E} \tag{10.9}$$

is invested in equity and the remainder in bonds, where σ_E is the volatility of equity, σ_B is the volatility of bonds, and ρ is their correlation. Note that this expression is independent of the noise volatility. This should be intuitive since in the present setup neither bonds nor equity can be used to diversify away the uncorrelated noise. Furthermore, this expression is increasing in the initial funding ratio.[4] A fund with a deficit is better off investing in bonds, because they offer a better hedge against changes in the value of liabilities, leading to a lower surplus volatility. A fund with a surplus, however, may want to invest in bonds up to a point so as to duration match the liabilities, which offers the best possible hedge against changes in the liability value. Beyond that point, the fund may be better off (in terms of minimizing surplus volatility) by investing an incremental dollar in equities rather than bonds due to the diversification effect between equities and bonds mentioned earlier. To understand this effect, consider the case in which the fund can actually invest in its liability index. An overfunded plan will then minimize its surplus volatility by investing an amount equal to the value of liabilities into the liability index (thereby eliminating liabilities completely from the asset allocation problem) and investing the remaining surplus into the volatility-minimizing portfolio of equities and bonds. So why do the other lines in the above graph show the smallest risk for an equity allocation equal to zero? The answer is simply that the graph shows only the range of equity allocations from 0 percent to 100 percent, and the smallest risk for the other funding ratios actually occurs for *negative* equity allocations.

Finally, let us look at the line labeled "very underfunded." The surplus risk for this plan is very large, as should be intuitive. Furthermore, compared to the other lines in the graph this line is flatter (i.e., it varies less with the equity allocation). When the value of the assets is very small compared to the liabilities, exactly how these assets are invested matters less from a risk perspective.

Having inspected the surplus risk emanating from various equity allocations, let us now turn to analyzing the expected change in surplus for the various plans in our example. Figure 10.2 shows the expected change in surplus relative to initial asset value as a function of the equity allocation.

Two interesting facts emerge from this picture. First, for a given funding ratio

[4]This is true as long as $\sigma_b > \rho\sigma_e$, which holds for the values in the example. If this inequality is reversed, the expression will be decreasing in the funding ratio.

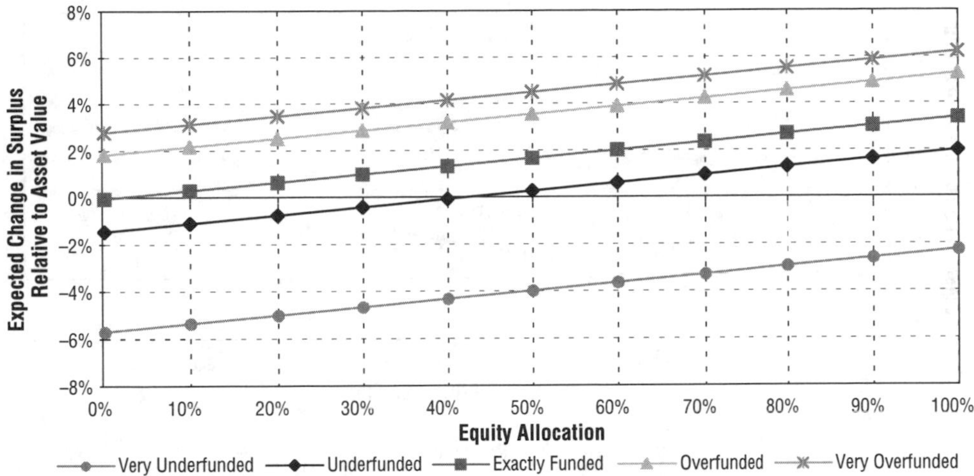

FIGURE 10.2 Surplus "Return"

the expected change in surplus is linearly increasing in the equity allocation. It is easy to show that this is the case whenever the expected return on equity is larger than that on bonds, and it should be quite intuitive as well. The other interesting result shown here is the minimum equity allocation needed for a fund to prevent the surplus from shrinking. In the appendix this is shown to be

$$\frac{\mu_B\left(\beta\frac{L_t}{A_t}-1\right)+\frac{L_t}{A_t}R_f\left(1-\beta\right)}{\mu_E-\mu_B} \tag{10.10}$$

where μ_B and μ_E are the total expected return on bonds and equity, respectively. Given our present assumptions, for an underfunded plan (funding ratio 0.8) the minimum equity allocation is a little over 40 percent; at lower equity allocations the deficit will grow on average. Overfunded plans, on the contrary, will see their surplus grow even for a zero equity allocation. The important thing to remember in interpreting these results is, of course, that we have so far abstracted from any payouts. For an underfunded plan, the presence of payouts will further increase the required equity allocation to prevent the surplus from shrinking. We will come back to this point later in the dynamic analysis.

Up to this point, we have shown that higher equity allocations lead to (usually) higher funding risk as well as higher expected changes in the surplus. This trade-off between risk and return can be illustrated by plotting both quantities in the same graph. The resulting picture very much resembles an efficient frontier and is shown in Figure 10.3. To facilitate the following interpretation, we have not normalized by the current asset value in this figure. We consider three funds with liabilities of \$100 and assets of \$80, \$100, and \$120, respectively.

Along each line plotted, the solid markers represent equity allocations ranging from 0 percent at the left to 100 percent at the right. Let's look at the line labeled "underfunded," which corresponds to a funding ratio of 0.8, in a little more detail. Again, we see that a minimum equity allocation of over 40 percent is needed for

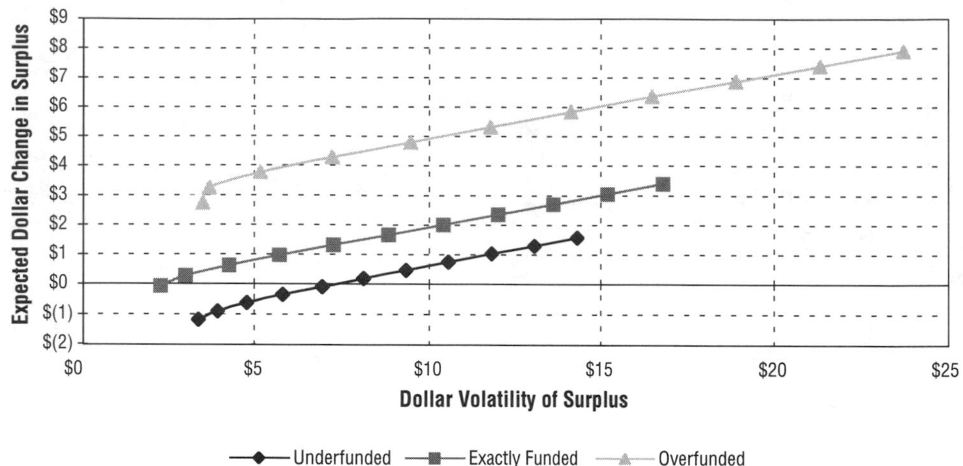

FIGURE 10.3 Surplus Risk and Return Trade-Off

this plan to prevent the deficit from growing. But we also see that at this level of equity allocation, the risk versus the liabilities is about \$7. In other words, a one standard deviation event would lead to an increase in the deficit of \$7 to \$27. The new funding ratio would be 0.73. Similarly, a two standard deviation event would lead to a funding ratio of 0.66. These numbers show the considerable risk underfunded plans face in attempting to reach fully funded status.

The concept of risk-adjusted change in surplus (RACS) introduced earlier can be used to shed more light on how much a fund is earning in excess return for each unit of risk taken. Figure 10.4 graphs the RACS for the plans we have been discussing.

Figure 10.4 clearly shows that for the underfunded and exactly funded plans the RACS is strictly increasing in the equity allocation, although for the underfunded plan the slope is steeper, implying that this plan is rewarded more for taking additional equity risk on a risk-adjusted basis. For the overfunded plan the story is quite different. The RACS increases very steeply early on but reaches its maximum at an equity allocation of around 30 percent. In order to understand this result, let's for a moment abstract from the presence of any noise. In this case, what strategy maximizes the RACS? A plan with sufficient funds can invest βL_t in the bond index, perfectly hedging any future change in liabilities. Having thus basically eliminated liabilities from the asset allocation problem, the fund may use its remaining assets to purchase the portfolio that maximizes the Sharpe ratio of these assets.[5] This case is illustrated in Figure 10.5, which plots the RACS for an overfunded plan (funding ratio 1.5) for different noise levels.

What happens when we introduce noise? In this case, the ability of bonds to hedge changes in the liabilities is negatively impacted, and equity, with its higher Sharpe ratio, looks relatively more attractive. We therefore expect the optimal equity allocation (i.e., the allocation that maximizes the RACS) to increase. This can

[5]In the context of the numbers presented here, the portfolio of U.S. equity and the Lehman Long Government and Credit Index that maximizes the Sharpe ratio has an 83/17 bond/equity split.

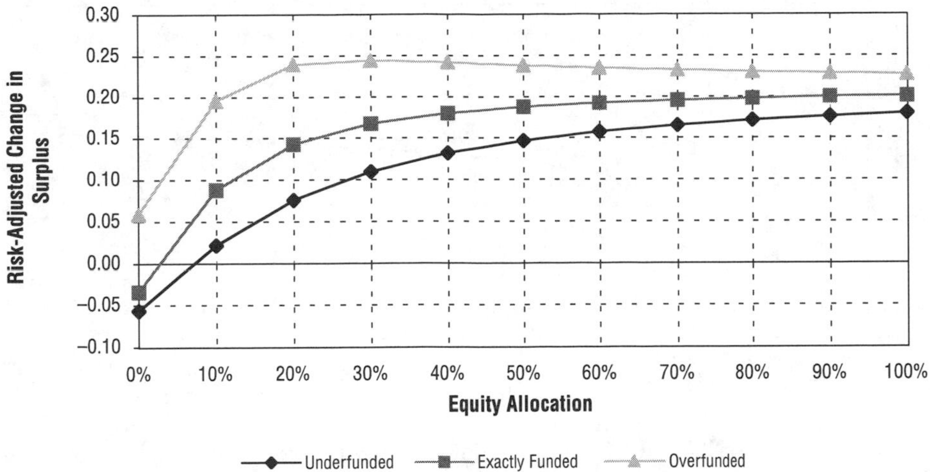

FIGURE 10.4 Risk-Adjusted Change in Surplus (RACS): Different Funding Levels

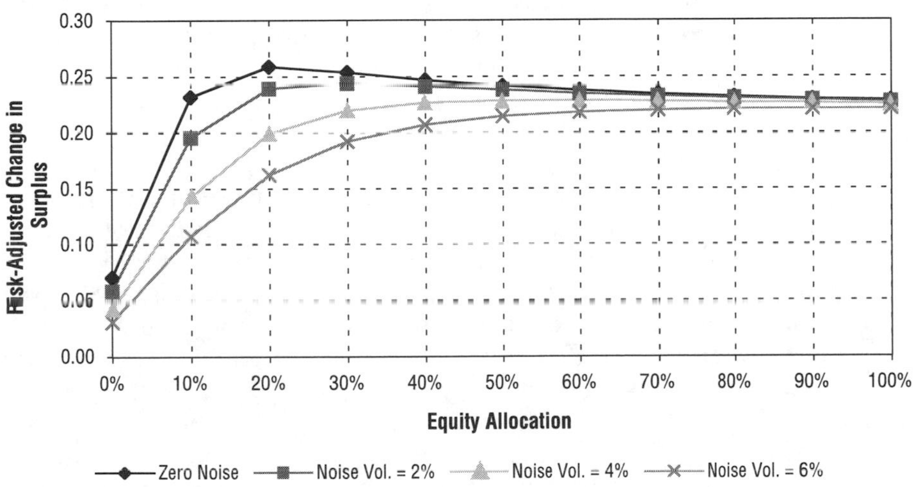

FIGURE 10.5 Risk-Adjusted Change in Surplus (RACS) for Overfunded Plan: Different Noise Levels

be seen in Figure 10.5: As the noise increases from zero to 2 percent to 4 percent to 6 percent, the optimal equity allocation increases from 20 percent to 30 percent to 50 percent to 100 percent. The bottom line of this analysis is that *the more underfunded a plan is, and the more uncertain future liabilities are, the more attractive equity appears relative to fixed income.*

Even though the analysis in this section is strictly static, the figures and accompanying discussion shed some light on dynamic asset allocation as well. Ceteris paribus, when the funding ratio decreases (perhaps due to dismal asset returns), a fund that is trying to maximize its RACS ought to invest more in equities. Similarly, if the noise in liabilities increases (perhaps due to legislative uncertainty), a fund ought to increase its equity allocation as well.

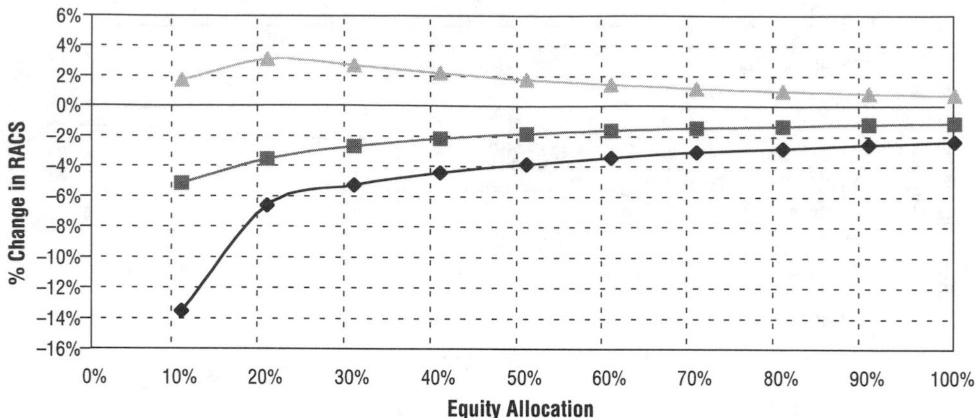

FIGURE 10.6 Effect of Global Equity Diversification

Our present setup also allows us to analyze the effects of global diversification in equity and bond portfolios, as well as the effect of investing in a bond portfolio with a different duration. We now turn to these issues.

Example: Global Diversification

Is a fund better off investing only in domestic assets or should it diversify globally? In answering this question we first look at global equity diversification and then turn to the issue of fixed income diversification.

Our return assumptions clearly show that global equity has a higher Sharpe ratio than domestic equity, but also a lower correlation with the liability index. We therefore face the same trade-off as before when we were deciding between allocating to domestic equity or bonds.

Figure 10.6 shows the percentage change in the RACS from investing in global rather than domestic equity. The pattern emerging from this picture is that while the overfunded plan benefits from investing globally rather than domestically, the other two plans are better off with domestic equity. The intuition for this pattern is actually quite simple when we abstract from the presence of noise once again.

The overfunded plan can, at low equity allocations, match the duration of its liabilities with bonds. In the absence of noise, the plan thus basically eliminates the liabilities from the asset allocation problem. With the remaining funds, the plan faces a choice of domestic versus global equity. Since the Sharpe ratio of global equity is higher than that of domestic equity, the fund finds it optimal to choose global equity. Now, at higher equity allocations, the fund is no longer exactly eliminating liabilities from the asset allocation problem, and therefore the correlation of equity with the liability index matters in determining the RACS. Since global equity is less highly correlated with liabilities than domestic equity, it should come as no surprise that at high equity allocations the benefit from global diversification is diminished.

Finally, the presence of noise also diminishes the ability of the plan to eliminate li-

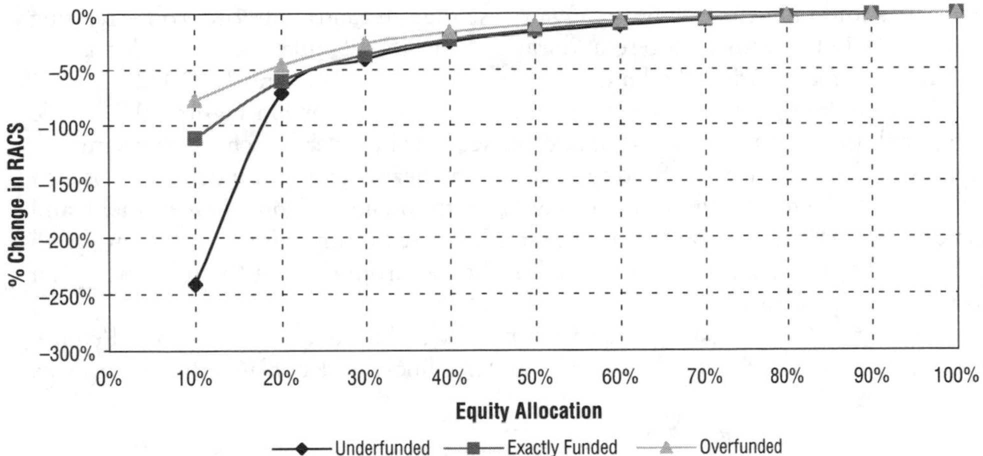

FIGURE 10.7 Effect of Global Fixed Income Diversification

abilities by allocating to bonds. Thus, the correlation of equities with liabilities matters once more. It can be verified that for higher noise levels the overfunded plan actually experiences a decrease in the RACS when switching from domestic to global equity.

After this discussion, it should be easy to see why the exactly funded and underfunded plans may want to stick with domestic equity. Due to a lack of funds, they cannot eliminate (in the absence of noise) or nearly eliminate (otherwise) liabilities from the asset allocation problem. For these funds, the correlation of domestic equity with liabilities is crucial. Hence these funds do not gain from diversification.[6]

Now let us briefly turn to the issue of global fixed income diversification. The discussion centering on equity diversification provides some insights here as well. In the present context bonds are attractive because they hedge against changes in liabilities. Since we modeled liabilities with respect to a domestic bond index (as seems reasonable for most pension plans), global bonds will generally not be an attractive asset class since they correlate with liabilities to a lower extent *by construction*. Figure 10.7 shows that our conjecture is correct, with all funds experiencing a decrease in the RACS.

Example: Choosing the Right Duration of the Bond Portfolio

The last topic in the static analysis is choosing the duration of the bond portfolio. Of course, the more closely the duration of the asset portfolio matches that of the liability index the better, since it leads to better immunization against changes in liability

[6]Here we only considered the cases of no and full diversification. It can be shown that slightly underfunded plans may benefit from a small level of equity diversification at high equity allocations. In other words, these plans may see a small increase in the RACS by investing *part* of their equity outside the home country.

value. It should therefore come as no surprise that all funds will lose from investing in a bond index with a different duration. The bond index we consider is the Lehman Aggregate, which had a duration of about 4.3 as of June 30, 2002.

Figure 10.8 shows an efficient frontier graph like the one in Figure 10.3. In the top panel, the funding ratio is 0.8, and we see that in order to achieve the same return as in the base case, the fund must accept higher surplus risk when it chooses to invest in the Lehman Aggregate rather than the Lehman Long Government and Credit, against which liabilities are modeled. In the bottom panel the funding ratio is 1.5, and the same conclusion holds, but the loss from moving to an index with a lower duration is smaller.

These results are easiest to understand if we choose a particular bond/equity split (one of the highlighted points along the lines) and consider what happens

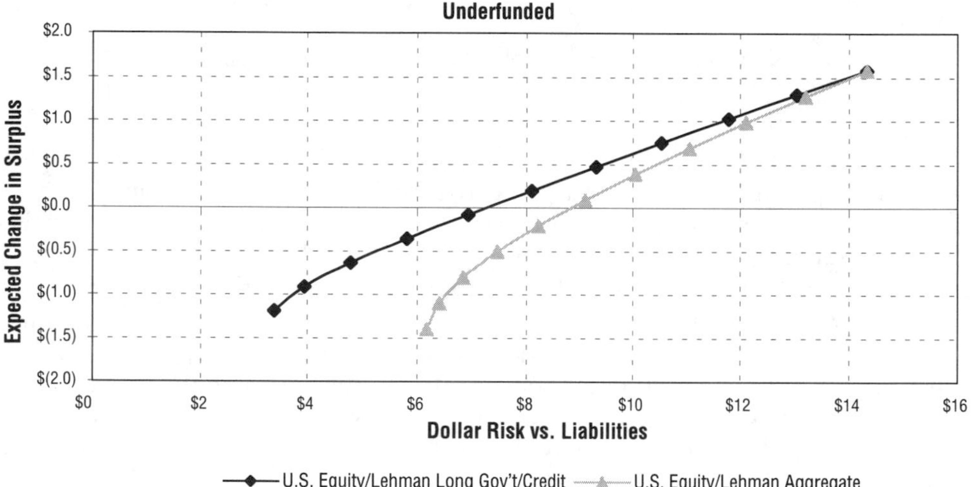

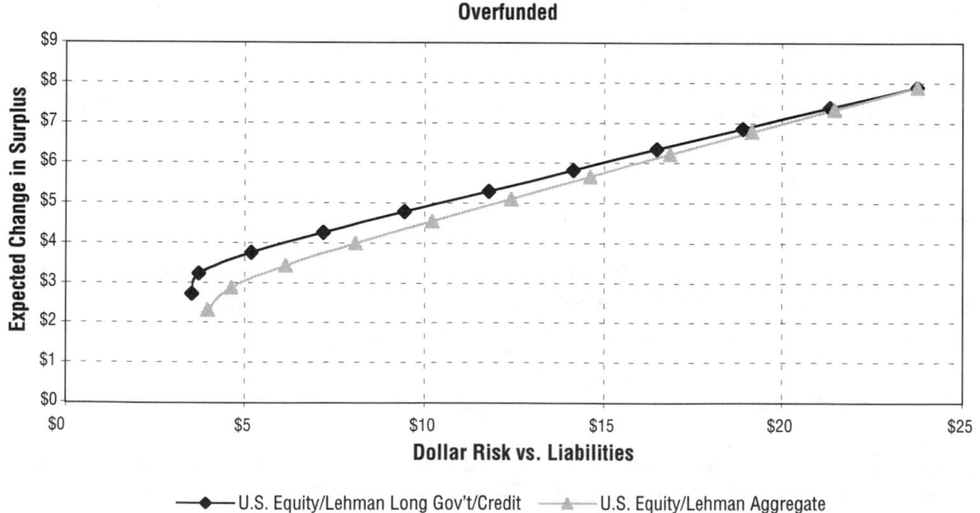

FIGURE 10.8 Effect of Shortening Duration of Bond Portfolio

when we change the fixed income benchmark from the Lehman Long Government and Credit Index to the Lehman Aggregate Index with a lower duration.

First, since the expected return on the Lehman Aggregate is lower than that on the longer-duration index, the expected change in surplus will decrease, marked by a vertical downward shift in the graph. Second, since the Lehman Aggregate is a poor hedge for changes in liability value when compared with the Lehman Long Government and Credit, the surplus risk will increase. This is expressed by a horizontal shift to the right in Figure 10.8. The combined outcome of these two effects is, of course, a shift to the bottom right of each point along the line. For the overfunded plan, the vertical shift is higher than for the underfunded plan because there are simply more dollars changing benchmark, and the fund receives a lower expected return on each dollar. The horizontal shift, on the contrary, is larger the closer the fund is to fully funded status. When the fund is very underfunded, the hedging ability of the fixed income benchmark matters much less for surplus volatility than the absolute volatility of liabilities. When the fund is very overfunded, the presence of liabilities can almost be ignored, and what matters most is the absolute volatility of assets. In Figure 10.8, the fund on the top is closer to fully funded than the one on the bottom, and hence experiences the larger increase in volatility of the two.

The above discussion implies that a fund is well served to invest in a bond index that is similar in duration to its liabilities. An additional issue that must be given consideration, however, is the difference in liquidity between short- and long-duration bonds. Large pension plans with long-duration liabilities will often find it impracticable to invest heavily in long-duration bonds, since the relatively low liquidity of these bonds impedes active trading. This issue is obviously more important the larger the pension fund, and it must be weighed with any return and hedging benefits from investing in long-duration bonds.

DYNAMIC ANALYSIS

Up to this point, we have investigated the asset allocation decision of a pension fund from a static point of view. We pretended that the fund had to make no payouts, and that it was concerned only with what happens to its surplus over one period, arbitrarily chosen to be one year. The setup was well suited to address many important issues like international diversification and the duration of the bond index to choose in the benchmark, but it leaves unanswered many important questions that affect pension funds in the long run.

In this section we will look at a dynamic setup that will allow us to investigate the long-run impact of payouts. For analytical convenience we assume that the pension fund pays out a fixed fraction p of the value of liabilities at the end of each period.[7] Mathematically, asset and liability values are assumed to evolve according to

[7]Some of the expressions we derive will not have closed-form solutions if we assume that the payout was made at the beginning of the period. We have performed various simulation exercises to gauge the quantitative impact of our assumption and have found that the numerical results are not at all sensitive to whether payouts are made at the beginning or end of the period. For this reason we have decided to stick with the more convenient setup.

$$\begin{aligned} A_{t+1} &= A_t\left(1+R_{A,t+1}\right) - pL_t\left(1+R_{L,t+1}\right) \\ L_{t+1} &= L_t\left(1+R_{L,t+1}\right)(1-p) \end{aligned} \tag{10.11}$$

where we make the same assumptions about the liability return as before: that it consists of a (possibly levered) position in a long bond index and uncorrelated noise. Furthermore, we shall assume that returns are independently lognormally distributed through time with the means, volatilities, and correlations shown in the beginning of this chapter.

Using the above expressions for the dynamics of assets and liabilities, it is easy to see that the surplus is not affected by the payout structure p. This should be intuitive, since a payout reduces assets and liabilities by the same amount. In a multiperiod setup, however, the surplus is less useful a measure than in a single-period setup, since the absolute value of assets and liabilities can fluctuate widely. A \$10 million surplus is a comfortable cushion for a plan with a \$50 million liability, but will not evoke the same comfort if the value of liabilities grows to \$100 million. For this reason we will focus on the funding ratio as the measure of interest in this section. The funding ratio, as will become apparent soon, does depend on the payout structure.

Using our setup, we shall attempt to answer the following questions:

- For an underfunded plan, what return on assets in excess of the return on liabilities is necessary to (1) retain the original funding ratio and (2) reach fully funded status over a given horizon?
- For a given initial funding ratio, payout policy, and bond/equity split, how does the probability of being underfunded vary with the horizon?

Required Returns

Given a payout structure p, what return will keep the funding ratio constant on average? Letting $F_t = A_t/L_t$, we can write

$$E_t\left[F_{t+1}\right] = F_t E_t\left[\frac{1+R_{A,t+1}}{1+R_{L,t+a}}\right]\frac{1}{1-p} - \frac{p}{1-p} \tag{10.12}$$

and defining $R_{x,t} = (1 + R_{A,t})/(1 + R_{L,t}) - 1$ as the return on assets in excess of the return on liabilities, we find that

$$E_t\left[R_{x,t+1}\right] = \frac{E_t\left[F_{t+1}\right](1-p)+p}{F_t} \tag{10.13}$$

To keep the funding ratio constant on average we require $E_t[F_{t+1}]=F_t$. Using the last expression we can easily calculate the required average return as a function of the initial funding ratio for a given payout policy. Figure 10.9 shows the results.

A plan that is 80 percent funded and pays out 7.5 percent of its liability value in a given year must achieve a 2 percent return on assets in excess of the return on liabilities in order to keep its funding ratio constant. A return lower than that will

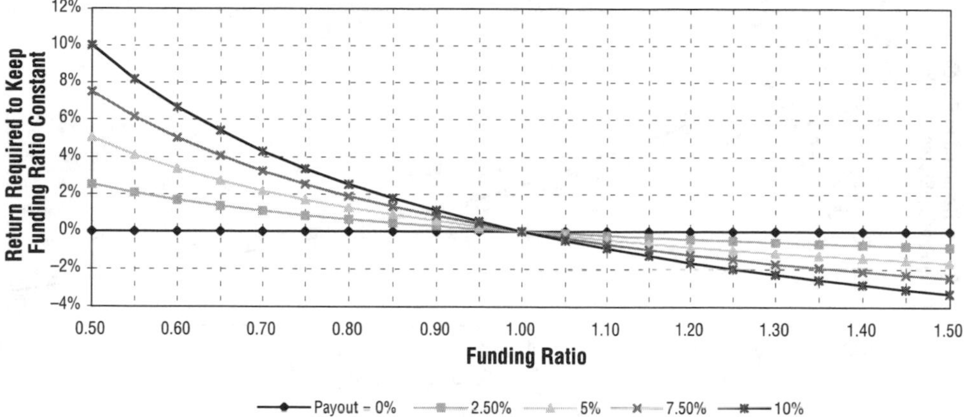

FIGURE 10.9 Required Returns for Maintaining Funding Status

lead to a decrease in the funding ratio. The larger the payout and the lower the funding ratio, the larger the required return.

The results highlight the need for large equity allocations (or allocations to bond indexes that have a higher duration than the liability index) for underfunded plans. Overfunded plans, on the contrary, can tolerate negative returns and still maintain their funding status. Actually, for overfunded plans the higher the payout ratio, the larger the negative return they can tolerate. This is true because a given payout decreases assets by a smaller percentage than liabilities when the plan is overfunded.

While maintaining current funding status is a plausible objective for overfunded plans, underfunded plans will need to try to improve their funding ratios unless they can count on a contribution from the plan sponsor. We next look at the returns required to reach fully funded status for underfunded plans. In the appendix, we show that given an initial value for the funding ratio F_0, the expected funding ratio at any time t is given by

$$E_0\left[F_t\right]=\left[\frac{1+E\left[R_x\right]}{1-p}\right]^t F_0+p\frac{1-\left[\frac{1+E\left[R_x\right]}{1-p}\right]^t}{E\left[R_x\right]+p} \qquad (10.14)$$

Note that the expected funding ratio depends only on the average return, not on its volatility.

In order to calculate the return required to reach fully funded status over a given horizon, we set the left-hand side in the above expression equal to 1, fix the horizon t, and find the value for $E[R_x]$ that satisfies the equality.[8] Figure 10.10 shows the results for $t = 10$.

For the underfunded plans, the required return to reach fully funded status in 10 years is obviously larger than the return required to maintain current funding status. The difference between these two rates of return is larger the lower the payout policy.

---

[8]Since there is no analytical solution we use a numerical algorithm.

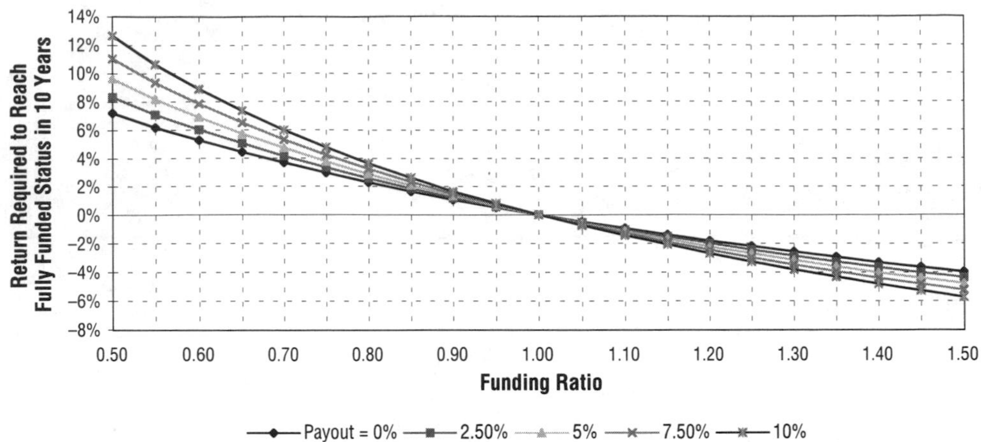

FIGURE 10.10 Required Return to Reach Fully Funded Status in 10 Years

To pick out a number again, a plan that is 80 percent funded and pays out 7.5 percent of the liability value must achieve an average return of 3.2 percent per year in excess of the return on liabilities in order to reach a funding ratio of 1 in 10 years. It is clear that such return targets are realistic only with large equity allocations. Unfortunately, there is no free lunch here since higher equity allocations also increase the risk. This is the issue to which we turn next.

Funding Probabilities

In order to assess the probability of being underfunded at any given horizon we resort to a Monte Carlo simulation. Figure 10.11 shows the results.

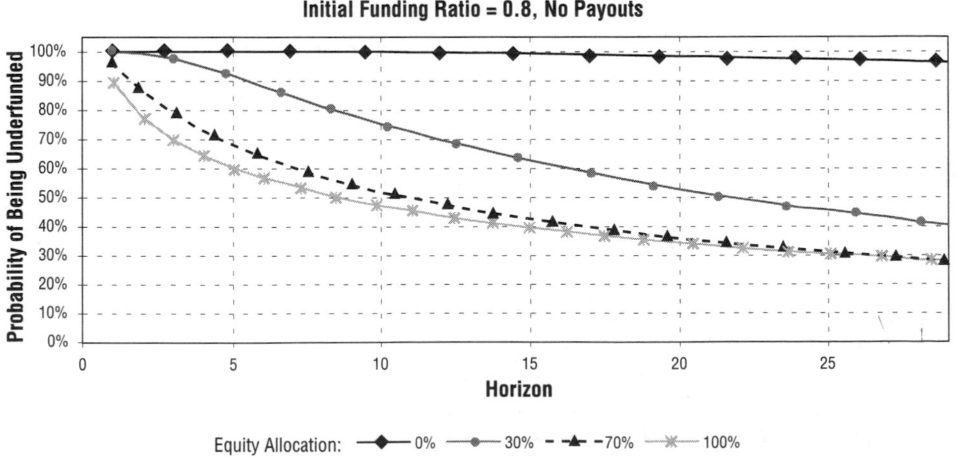

FIGURE 10.11 Simulated Probabilities of Being Underfunded, Different Funding Levels and Payout Ratios

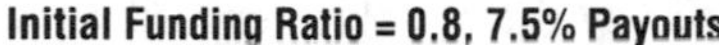

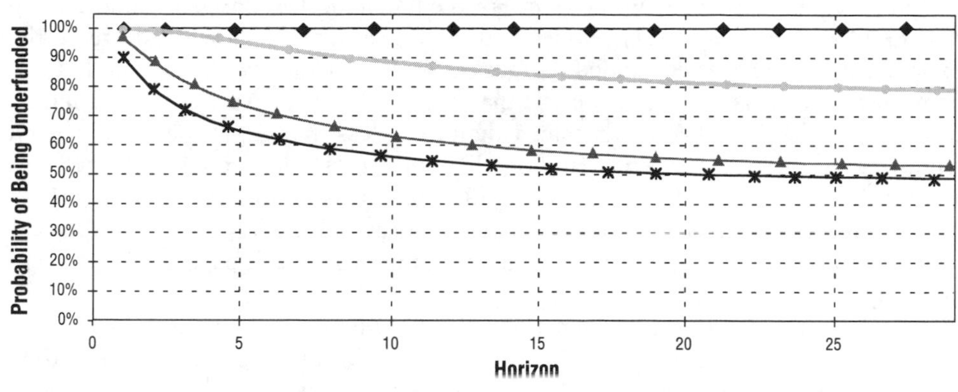

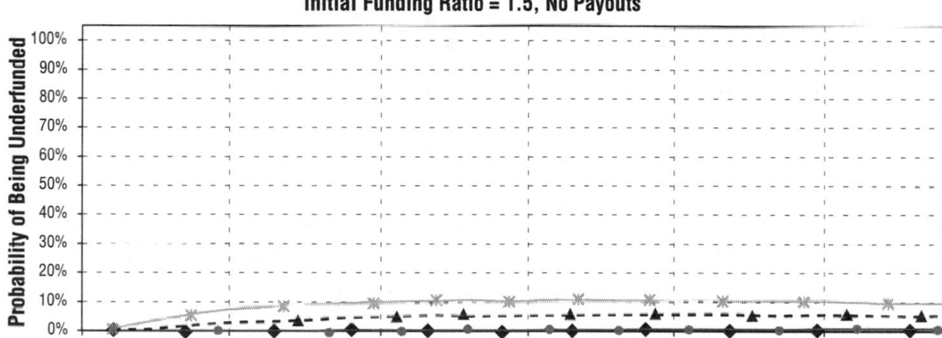

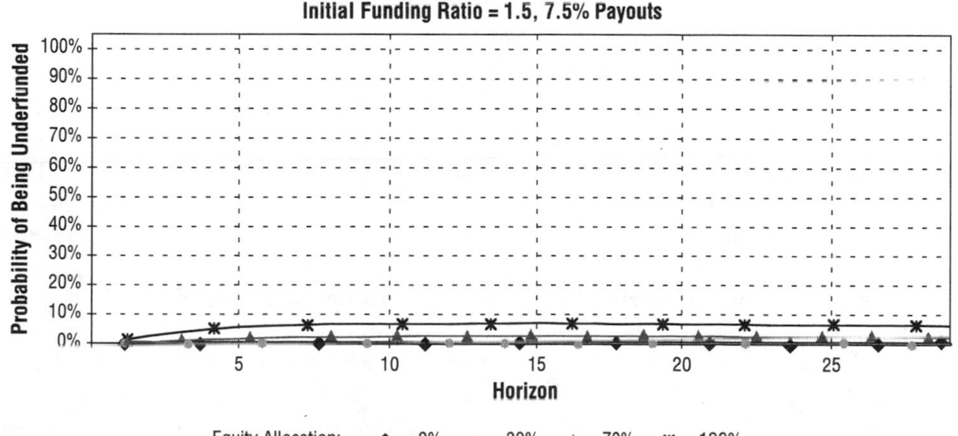

FIGURE 10.11 *(Continued)*

Each of the four lines within a plot represents a different equity allocation, ranging from 0 percent to 100 percent. For the underfunded plan (shown in the top two graphs of Figure 10.11), modest equity allocations can greatly decrease the probability of being underfunded. Larger equity allocations yield only modest improvement. What is also interesting is the time necessary to wait until the funding ratio is more likely to be greater than 1 than to be less than 1. This can be inferred from finding the point at which any one line intersects a horizontal line drawn at 50 percent on the vertical axis, and finding the corresponding horizon along the horizontal axis. With a 100 percent equity allocation, a plan that is 80 percent funded and makes no payouts must wait about nine years; if it pays out 7.5 percent annually, it must wait 21 years!

Overfunded plans actually increase the probability of losing their surplus by allocating to more equities. This conclusion fits in with all of our results regarding overfunded plans—namely, that the risk from large equity allocations may actually outweigh the benefits.

CONCLUSIONS

We set out to investigate the asset allocation decision process in the presence of liabilities. We defined three important decision points in this context, the equity/bond split, the duration of the bond portfolio, and international diversification. In our initial setup, we abstracted from payouts and focused on a single-period problem in which we generalized the familiar concept of a Sharpe ratio to account for the presence of liabilities. Our new measure, the risk-adjusted change in surplus (RACS), enabled us to investigate the trade-offs faced by pension plans in addressing the three important decision points. Our main findings were:

- Underfunded plans benefit more from higher equity allocations than do overfunded plans for which the RACS often decreases after a certain equity allocation is reached.
- Matching the duration of the bond portfolio to that of liabilities is important for all plans, with underfunded plans benefiting the most.
- Global equity diversification is an attractive opportunity for overfunded plans, which can benefit from the higher Sharpe ratio of global equity. Underfunded plans are better off investing domestically in order to benefit from the higher correlation of liabilities with domestic assets.
- Fixed income diversification is not attractive for any of the plans studied. The effect of increase in Sharpe ratio of assets from moving to global fixed income is more than offset by the lower correlation of liabilities with nondomestic assets.

Subsequently, we analyzed the asset allocation decision in a dynamic framework that also incorporates payouts. We calculated returns required by underfunded plans to reach fully funded status over a given horizon and found that large equity allocations are necessitated by the need to become fully funded. We also investigated the risks associated with such allocations. Just as in the single-period setup, the main finding was that underfunded plans must take more equity risk to improve their funding status.

SUMMARY

The concepts of mean-variance optimization in a one-period model can be extended to a setup that also includes liabilities by focusing on the surplus instead of on assets alone.

When the quantity of interest is the surplus, the notion of a Sharpe ratio can be extended to that of a risk-adjusted change in surplus (RACS).

Using the RACS as the measure of optimality, we find that underfunded plans, those for whom the value of liabilities exceeds the value of assets, gain most from higher equity allocations, whereas diversification of the equity portfolio is most beneficial to overfunded plans.

In a dynamic model with payouts it can be shown once again that underfunded plans must take on large equity allocations in order to improve their funding status.

APPENDIX
Choice of Parameters for Liability Modeling

In the preceding discussion, we have modeled the value of liabilities as a sum of two parts—a bond, which reflects the best guess about future obligations, and a noise term, which reflects the uncertainty of the future payments. The return on the bond as well as its correlation with other assets can be calculated by discounting projected obligations by the current term structure. Alternatively, a publicly traded bond index can be used as a proxy, where the index is levered to match the duration of the liability stream.

Mathematically,

$$R_{L,t} - R_{f,t} = \beta(R_{B,t} - R_{f,t}) + \varepsilon_t \tag{10A.1}$$

where $R_{L,t}$ = Total return on the liability index at time t
$R_{f,t}$ = Risk-free rate of return
$R_{B,t}$ = Total return on a bond index
ε_t = Noise term

The parameter β reflects the duration of the liability relative to the specified bond index. As such, it reflects uncertainty in the value of liabilities due to changes in interest rates. The noise term (with assumed mean return η, and volatility σ_ε) reflects uncertainty in future payouts and is assumed to be uncorrelated with the bond index, although it may be correlated with other returns.

To illustrate a methodology for choosing parameters, we consider the case of modeling the projected benefit obligation (PBO) for a corporate defined benefit pension plan. For a pension plan, the PBO reflects the actuarial present value of benefits attributed to employees to date. As such, the PBO is an actuarial measure of the pension liability that is based on a number of assumptions, including mortality rates, future salary growth, early retirement, lump sum payouts, and an actuarial discount rate. The changes in the PBO are typically disclosed in the company's 10-K filing in the section "Pensions and Other Postretirement Benefits."

As a simplified case, one can evaluate the situation where the pension plan has a single benefit payment in year T. The present value V of the projected benefit payment as of time t will be given by the following equation:

$$V = Ce^{-r(T-t)} \tag{10A.2}$$

where C = Projected benefit payment as of time t
r = Discount rate as of time t

Over a short period of time, we can evaluate changes in the value of the benefit obligation due to changes in our projected benefit, changes in the discount rate, and the passage of time:

$$\begin{aligned} dV &= \frac{\partial V}{\partial C}dC + \frac{\partial V}{\partial r}dr + \frac{\partial V}{\partial t}dt \\ &= V\frac{dC}{C} - (T-t)Vdr + rVdt \end{aligned} \tag{10A.3}$$

As a consequence, we have that

$$\frac{dV}{V} = \frac{dC}{C} - (T-t)dr + rdt \tag{10A.4}$$

Put another way, the incremental percentage change in the value of the liability is a sum of three terms. The first term, dC/C, is the percentage change in the projected benefit payout and therefore represents our uncertainty in the benefit cash flow. The second term, $-(T-t)dr$, reflects the uncertainty in the value due to uncertainty in discount rates (the term $-(T-t)$ is the duration of the cash flow as of time t), whereas the final term, rdt, reflects change in value due to passage of time.

In the context of a pension plan, the first term could be interpreted as changes in the PBO due to changes in the actuarial cash flow projections resulting from, for example, different mortality assumptions, early terminations, lump sums, plan amendments, and acquisition/divestiture activity. The second term could be interpreted as the actuarial gain/loss due to a change in the discount rate, whereas the final term could be interpreted as the interest cost for the pension plan.

More generally, one could consider a pension plan with a steady rate of projected benefit payments C_T, in which case the value of the liability as of time t would be given by

$$V = \int_t^{\infty} C_T e^{-r_T(T-t)} dT \tag{10A.5}$$

As before, we can evaluate the incremental changes in the value of the benefit obligation due to changes in projected cash flows, changes in the term structure of discount rates, and the passage of time:

$$dV = -C_t dt + \int_t^{\infty} \left[dC_T - (T-t)C_T + r_T C_T \right] e^{-r_T(T-t)} dT \tag{10A.6}$$

Again, each of the terms in equation (10A.6) has a natural interpretation in economic terms. The first term, $-C_t dt$, corresponds to benefits paid during the incremental time interval dt. As for the integrands, the first term corresponds to a change in the benefit obligation due to adjustments in projected benefit payouts. The second integrand corresponds to a change in the benefit obligation due to changes in interest rates, whereas the final integrand corresponds to interest cost.

Although the preceding model is simplified by looking only at incremental changes in value, it provides a connection to our methodology for modeling the noise term. In particular, the noise term is given by the expression

$$d\varepsilon_t = \frac{\int_t^\infty dC_T e^{-r_T(T-t)} dT}{\int_t^\infty C_T e^{-r_T(T-t)} dT} \tag{10A.7}$$

When the current cash flow projections reflect all available information (and therefore represent a best guess as to future benefit payouts), we have that the expected change in the benefit obligation due to change in projected payouts is zero; that is,

$$E_t[d\varepsilon_i] = 0 \tag{10A.8}$$

Also, if we assume that the process ε_t has independent increments that are identically normally distributed, we have that

$$E_t[d\varepsilon_t^2] = \sigma_\varepsilon^2 dt \tag{10A.9}$$

where σ_ε is the instantaneous volatility of the noise process.

MINIMIZING SURPLUS RISK FOR A GIVEN FUNDING RATIO

Denoting the returns on equity and fixed income at time t as $R_{E,t}$ and $R_{B,t}$, respectively, and the fraction of the surplus invested in equity as α, we write the surplus as

$$S_{t+1} = A_t\left[\alpha\left(1 + R_{E,t+1}\right) + (1-\alpha)\left(1 + R_{B,t+1}\right)\right] - L_t\left[1 + R_f + \beta\left(R_{B,t+1} - R_f\right) + \varepsilon_{t+1}\right] \tag{10A.10}$$

where we have used our model of the liability return. Dividing by the asset value A_t we obtain

$$\frac{S_{t+1}}{A_t} = \alpha\left(1 + R_{E,t+1}\right) + R_{B,t+1}\left(1 - \alpha - \frac{L_t}{A_t}\beta\right) - \frac{L_t}{A_t}\varepsilon_{t+1} + 1 - \alpha - \frac{L_t}{A_t}\left[1 + (1-\beta)R_f\right] \tag{10A.11}$$

Our objective is to minimize the variance of this expression, or

$$\begin{aligned} \min_{\alpha} Var_t\left(\frac{S_{t+1}}{A_t}\right) &= \alpha^2\sigma_E^2 + \left(1 - \alpha - \beta\frac{L_t}{A_t}\right)^2 \sigma_B^2 + \left(\frac{L_t}{A_t}\right)^2 \sigma_\varepsilon^2 \\ &+ 2\alpha\left(1 - \alpha - \beta\frac{L_t}{A_t}\right)\rho\sigma_E\sigma_B \end{aligned} \tag{10A.12}$$

The first-order condition is given by

$$\alpha\sigma_E^2 + \left(\alpha - 1 + \beta\frac{L_t}{A_t}\right)\sigma_B^2 + \left(1 - 2\alpha - \beta\frac{L_t}{A_t}\right)\rho\sigma_E\sigma_B = 0 \tag{10A.13}$$

which can be rearranged to give

$$\alpha = \frac{\left(1 - \beta\frac{L_t}{A_t}\right)\left(\sigma_B^2 - \rho\sigma_E\sigma_B\right)}{\sigma_E^2 + \sigma_B^2 - 2\rho\sigma_E\sigma_B} \bullet QED \tag{10A.14}$$

MINIMAL EQUITY ALLOCATION NEEDED TO PREVENT DECREASE IN SURPLUS

The expected future surplus is given by

$$E_t\left(S_{t+1}\right) = E_t\left\{A_t\left[\alpha R_{E,t+1} + (1-\alpha)R_{B,t+1}\right] - L_t\left[R_f + \beta\left(R_{B,t+1} - R_f\right) + \varepsilon_{t+1}\right]\right\} \tag{10A.15}$$

Setting the left-hand side equal to zero and solving for α we obtain

$$\alpha = \frac{\mu_B\left(\beta\frac{L_t}{A_t} - 1\right) + \frac{L_t}{A_t}\left[R_f(1-\beta) + \eta\right]}{\mu_E - \mu_B} \bullet QED \tag{10A.16}$$

EXPECTED FUTURE FUNDING RATIO GIVEN INITIAL FUNDING RATIO

Using the definition of the funding ratio and the evolution of assets and liabilities shown in (10.11) we can write for the funding ratio at time 1

$$\begin{aligned} F_1 &= \frac{1}{1-p}F_0\left(1 + R_{x,1}\right) - \frac{p}{1-p} \\ &= aF_0\left(1 + R_{x,1}\right) + b \end{aligned} \tag{10A.17}$$

where we have defined $a = 1/(1 - p)$ and $b = -p/(1 - p)$. Similarly, the funding ratio at time 2 equals

$$\begin{aligned} F_2 &= aF_1\left(1 + R_{x,2}\right) + b \\ &= a\left[aF_0\left(1 + R_{x,1}\right) + b\right]\left(1 + R_{x,2}\right) + b \\ &= a^2F_0\left(1 + R_{x,1}\right)\left(1 + R_{x,2}\right) + ab\left(1 + R_{x,2}\right) + b \end{aligned} \tag{10A.18}$$

More generally, the funding ratio for any time $t > 0$ is given by

$$F_t = a^t F_0 \prod_{\substack{1 \le s \le t \\ s \in N}} \left(1 + R_{x,s}\right) + b \sum_{i=0}^{t-1} a^i \prod_{\substack{1 \le j \le i \\ j \in N}} \left(1 + R_{x,t-(j-1)}\right) \tag{10A.19}$$

where Π denotes the product operator, the product over an empty set is defined to equal 1, and N denotes the set of all integers.

Now we take expectations of both sides:

$$\begin{aligned} E_0\left(F_t\right) &= a^t F_0 E_0\left[\prod_{\substack{1 \le s \le t \\ s \in N}} \left(1 + R_{x,s}\right)\right] + b \sum_{i=0}^{t-1} a^i E_0\left[\prod_{\substack{1 \le j \le i \\ j \in N}} \left(1 + R_{x,t-(j-1)}\right)\right] \\ &= a^t F_0 \left(1 + \mu_x\right)^t + b \sum_{i=0}^{t-1} a^i \left(1 + \mu_x\right)^i \end{aligned} \tag{10A.20}$$

where we have used our assumptions that returns are identically and independently distributed (iid) to conclude that

$$E_0\left[\prod_{\substack{1 \le s \le t \\ s \in N}} \left(1 + R_{x,s}\right)\right] = \prod_{\substack{1 \le s \le t \\ s \in N}} E_0\left[1 + R_{x,s}\right] = \left(1 + \mu_x\right)^t \tag{10A.21}$$

Using the properties of a geometric series we write

$$E_0\left[F_t\right] = \left(\frac{1 + \mu_x}{1 - p}\right)^t F_0 + p \frac{1 - \left(\frac{1 + \mu_x}{1 - p}\right)^t}{\mu_x + p} \bullet QED \tag{10A.22}$$

CHAPTER 11

International Diversification and Currency Hedging

Kurt Winkelmann

Many investors have begun to diversify their portfolios by moving some holdings to international equity and fixed income markets. This strategy can enhance a portfolio's risk-adjusted performance, but it also exposes investors to exchange rate fluctuations. Consequently, investors not only must choose strategic (or long-term) foreign asset allocations, they also must decide on a policy for managing currency exposure. An equilibrium approach to strategic asset allocation provides investors with key insights regarding both the level of international diversification and the corresponding level of currency hedging. For example, as we have seen, in equilibrium all investors would hold global assets in their capitalization weight proportions. In reality, while investors have been increasing their international holdings over time, it is still the case that on average most investors globally are overweight domestic securities.

Thus, it becomes more important to understand what are rational reasons for deviating from holding the market portfolio and what are the potential costs of doing so. In this chapter, we'll first explore the issue of international diversification. Judged from a different perspective, we'll discuss the introduction of home bias in an investor's portfolio. (Home bias is the tendency for investors to hold a disproportionate level of their investments in the domestic market.)

After discussing home bias, we'll turn our attention to the issue of strategic currency hedging. We'll start by looking at the impact of currency hedging on individual asset classes, and then consider what an equilibrium currency hedge ratio should look like. After developing the equilibrium hedge ratio, we'll explore the impact of home bias on the currency hedge ratio.

Our results are very straightforward and make intuitive sense. First, we find that a moderate degree of home bias is not particularly costly in terms of the risk it creates. Second, we find that investors should distinguish between asset classes when making currency hedging decisions: Basically, foreign bond holdings should be hedged at the 100 percent level, while the hedge ratio for foreign equities depends on the level of home bias in the portfolio.

TABLE 11.1 Fixed Income Home Bias

	Global Capitalization Weighted	United States	European Monetary Union	United Kingdom	Japan
Equilibrium excess return	3.98%	4.03%	3.93%	4.02%	3.81%
Volatility	9.33%	9.48%	9.29%	9.65%	9.05%
Sharpe ratio	0.426	0.425	0.424	0.417	0.421

INTERNATIONAL DIVERSIFICATION AND HOME BIAS

Few investors' holdings actually reflect global capitalization weights; most portfolios have disproportionately large domestic exposure. This tendency to concentrate assets domestically—referred to as home bias—influences the currency hedging policy because fewer underlying assets are invested abroad. Is there an underlying economic rationale for home bias? Are there rules of thumb to help determine a suitable home bias level and how does the home bias affect the currency hedging policy?

Let's look first at how home bias affects the Sharpe ratio of the strategic, or long-term, asset allocation.[1] Using equilibrium returns (discussed in Chapter 6), we can calculate a global capitalization weighted portfolio's risk-adjusted performance and then compare it to the risk-adjusted performance of a portfolio whose fixed income or equity portion is invested solely in domestic assets.

Table 11.1 shows how fixed income home bias affects the Sharpe ratio. It compares the expected excess return, volatility, and Sharpe ratio for the global capitalization weighted portfolio of marketable securities (discussed in Chapter 8) to the same elements of portfolios with global equity investments and domestic-only fixed income holdings. The capitalization weight split is held constant—32 percent fixed income and 68 percent global equities (held in their capitalization weights)—and all assets are assumed to be currency hedged. Domestic portfolios are shown for euro-, sterling-, U.S. dollar-, and yen-based investors. To facilitate the analysis, all portfolios are held on a currency-hedged basis.

The figures suggest that global diversification in the fixed income portion of a portfolio does not materially affect the Sharpe ratio (at least when equilibrium returns are used). For example, a euro-based investor's Sharpe ratio declines from 0.426 to 0.424 when bonds are held in the Euroland fixed income market only. Similarly modest changes in the Sharpe ratio occur from the other three currency perspectives.

Although Table 11.1 seems to suggest that there's no benefit from diversifying into international bonds, there are a couple of important caveats. First, a portfolio's equity allocation greatly affects the impact of international fixed income exposure. Consider Figure 11.1, which plots portfolio Sharpe ratios (with and without international bonds) against equity allocations. When equity allocations

[1]The Sharpe ratio is just a portfolio's excess return (i.e., total return less the cash rate) divided by the portfolio volatility.

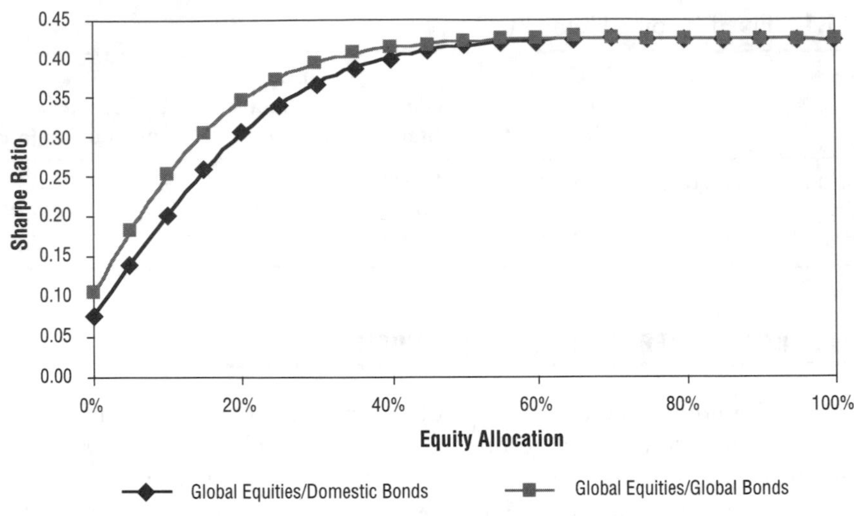

FIGURE 11.1 Impact of Fixed Income Diversification

exceed 50 percent, diversifying into international fixed income has little effect on the Sharpe ratio. When equity allocations are less than 50 percent, however, adding international bonds significantly improves risk-adjusted performance. The reason is simple: The Sharpe ratios for equities are typically higher than those for bonds, so when equity allocations are high, the effects of the equity portfolio swamp the impact of diversifying the bond portfolio.

Second, strategic allocations to foreign fixed income can add another source of potential outperformance. For example, suppose that an investor had a 65 percent allocation to equity. On the basis of the figures in Table 11.1 and Figure 11.1, the investor should be indifferent between holding all bonds domestically or holding bonds in their global capitalization weights. However, by holding bonds domestically, the investor gives up the opportunity to add value through an active management program in international fixed income. Many investors have attempted to add the active component of international fixed income by structuring opportunistic mandates versus domestic fixed income benchmarks. However, unless these mandates also give the manager the ability to take short positions in foreign bonds, they do not have the same ability to generate outperformance that an actively managed strategic allocation to foreign bonds has. The role and structure of active management will be discussed in more detail in Chapter 13.

Next consider how home bias affects equity allocations. Table 11.2 compares the Sharpe ratios of global capitalization weighted portfolios with those of portfolios whose equities are all domestic. As in Table 11.1, all portfolios are assumed to be currency hedged. It shows that the benefits of international diversification can be substantial. For example, the Sharpe ratio of yen-based investors can improve from 0.256 when equities are held domestically to 0.426 when equities mirror global capitalization weights. Even the risk-adjusted performance of U.S. dollar investors improves by almost 10 percent when equities include international holdings.

Although many investors have already begun to internationalize their holdings, few hold equities in global capitalization weighted proportions—most retain a

TABLE 11.2 Impact of Equity Home Bias

	Global Capitalization Weighted	United States	European Monetary Union	United Kingdom	Japan
Equilibrium excess return	3.98%	3.98%	4.40%	3.82%	3.39%
Volatility	9.33%	10.21%	12.15%	11.25%	13.25%
Sharpe ratio	0.426	0.390	0.362	0.339	0.256

home bias. At what point do diversification gains begin to taper off? Consider first the incremental impact of international equity allocations on the Sharpe ratio. In the first 10 percent step toward a global capitalization weighted portfolio, the Sharpe ratio increases. The second 10 percent step also improves, but not as dramatically as the first, and the incremental impact of each succeeding 10 percent step is smaller than that of the preceding steps. Figure 11.2 shows, in percentage terms, this effect on euro-, sterling-, U.S. dollar-, and yen-based investors. According to the graph, a 20 percent step toward a global capitalization weighted portfolio produces, on balance, a 25 percent improvement in the Sharpe ratio. For example, the Sharpe ratio of a euro-based investor who makes a 20 percent step toward a fully diversified portfolio increases from 0.362 to 0.377. The Sharpe ratio improvement of .015 represents around 23 percent of the total potential improvement (i.e., from .362 to .426).

The similarity of incremental diversification benefits is striking: Regardless of base currency, the benefits begin to taper off after potential equity diversification reaches 60 percent. And the impact on the Sharpe ratio correspondingly wanes when approximately 75 percent of the potential benefit has been achieved, irrespective of the base currency. For example, sterling-based investors who moved 60

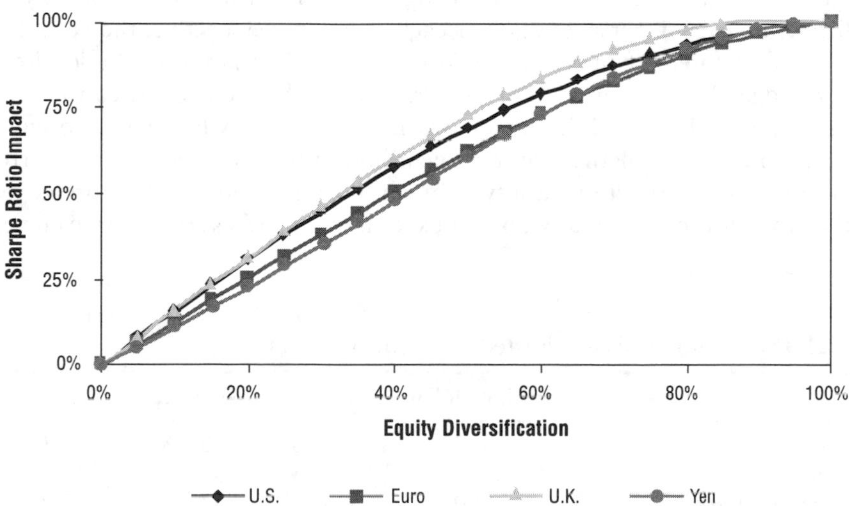

FIGURE 11.2 Incremental Impact of Diversifying Equity Exposure

percent of the way toward a fully diversified portfolio would see the Sharpe ratio increase from .339 to .404.

This approach to international diversification can be insightful because it approximates actual investor behavior. When the benefits of diversification are great, investors are motivated to reallocate assets. When the benefits are small, however, investors weigh the incremental benefits of continuing the diversification program against alternative investment opportunities. This may explain, at least partially, much of the recent interest in alternative assets such as private equity.

Suppose an investor decides to move 60 percent of the way toward full diversification. Table 11.3, which pegs the corresponding portfolio weights for euro, sterling, U.S. dollar, and yen investors, shows that the proportion of total equity allocated to international equity depends on domestic equity's proportion of the global capitalization weighted portfolio: The smaller the domestic market's capitalization weight, the larger the fraction invested internationally. For example, a U.S. dollar-based investor who follows our general rule would hold 68 percent of total equity domestically (and 32 percent internationally). By contrast, a like-minded sterling-based investor would invest 45 percent of total equity domestically (and 55 percent internationally).

IMPACT OF CURRENCY HEDGING ON INDIVIDUAL ASSET CLASSES

Having established that the benefits of global diversification significantly decline when investors move around 60 percent of the way toward market capitalization weights in international markets, we can now turn our attention to setting currency hedging policy. We'll approach this issue in three steps: First, we'll assess the impact of currency hedging on individual asset classes. Second, we'll see what the impact of currency hedging is when all investors hold the market portfolio. Finally, we'll see what happens when investors hold our home bias–adjusted portfolios.

Figure 11.3 shows how alternative hedge ratios affect portfolio volatility from four different currency perspectives. For each currency perspective, the volatility of foreign bond or foreign equity investments is plotted in relation to the level of the currency hedge. Two conclusions, irrespective of the base currency, can be drawn from the graphs in Figure 11.3. First, at any level of currency hedging, a foreign equity portfolio is more volatile than a foreign bond portfolio. Second, the currency hedge's impact on portfolio volatility is much more pronounced for foreign bond portfolios than for foreign equity portfolios. In fact, regardless of the base currency,

TABLE 11.3 Home Bias–Adjusted Portfolio Weights

	U.S. Dollar	Euro	Sterling	Yen
Domestic equity	46.0%	34.3%	30.8%	32.3%
Foreign equity	22.0	33.7	37.2	35.6
Domestic fixed income	32.0	32.0	32.0	32.0
Domestic equity/total equity	67.7	50.5	45.3	47.6

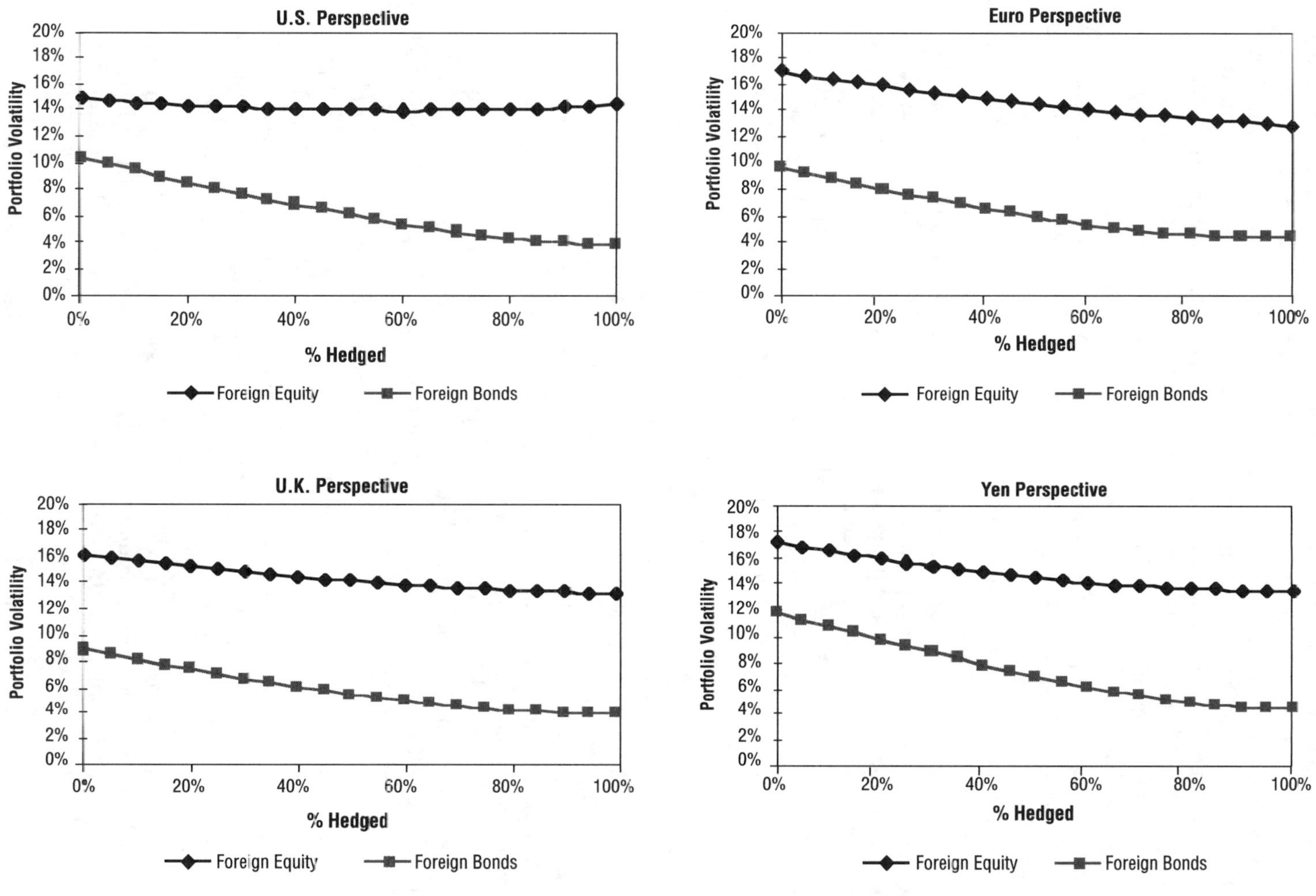

FIGURE 11.3 Foreign Asset Volatility and Currency Hedging

foreign bond portfolio volatility at least doubles as the portfolio shifts from being completely hedged to being completely unhedged. For example, a euro investor's foreign bond volatility increases from about 4 percent to almost 10 percent when the portfolio shifts from being completely hedged to being completely unhedged.

The same point can be made using a portfolio risk decomposition, or *hot spots*, analysis (see Chapter 3). Rather than focus on portfolio volatility, this method looks at the marginal contribution to risk (expressed in percentage terms) of currency positions at different levels of currency hedging. The results are illustrated in Figure 11.4, which uses the same portfolio volatility levels, alternative currency perspectives, and separate foreign equity and foreign bond portfolio analyses as Figure 11.3.

Figure 11.4 shows that *open currency positions contribute (at the margin) significantly larger portfolio risk to foreign bond portfolios than to foreign equity portfolios, irrespective of base currency.* In fact, currency accounts for more than 80 percent of the risk in a completely unhedged foreign bond portfolio, regardless of base currency, but no more than 40 percent of portfolio volatility (at the margin) in a completely unhedged foreign equity portfolio.

How can investors use the information in Figure 11.4? Suppose an investor wants no more than 20 percent of a foreign asset portfolio's volatility to be associated with currency. An investor would need to hedge at least 75 percent of the currency exposure in their foreign bond portfolio (irrespective of base currency) but no more than 50 percent in their foreign equity portfolio. *Because currency dramatically affects foreign fixed income, we recommend that investors hedge 100 percent of the currency exposure in their foreign bond portfolios.*

Figure 11.4 also suggests that currency hedging affects foreign equity portfolio risk much more dramatically for euro-, sterling-, and yen-based investors than it does for investors using U.S. dollars. In fact, currency contributes little risk to a U.S. investor's foreign equity portfolio, which may explain why many U.S. investors set unhedged global equity benchmarks.

Figures 11.3 and 11.4 gauge currency hedging's impact on portfolios that have foreign equity and foreign bond holdings only. Most investors, of course, hold domestic as well as foreign assets. How does currency hedging affect a portfolio that includes both domestic and foreign assets?

To answer this question, let's first look at a portfolio such as the portfolio of global equities and global bonds held in their global capitalization weighted proportions. As shown in Chapter 8, most of the value of global asset markets is concentrated in U.S. dollar-denominated assets. Although most investors' assets don't mirror global capitalization weights, these allocations can provide a useful neutral reference point for portfolio analysis. Our objective is to isolate a neutral reference point hedge ratio.

Suppose investors in each region hold their assets according to their global capitalization weighted proportions. We could easily assess how different levels of currency hedging affect portfolio volatility. And we could quickly measure currency's contribution, at the margin, to overall portfolio risk at different currency hedging levels.

The four graphs in Figure 11.5 show how currency hedge levels affect portfolio volatility (assuming that all investors are holding their assets according to global capitalization weights). For each currency hedge level, the graphs plot portfolio

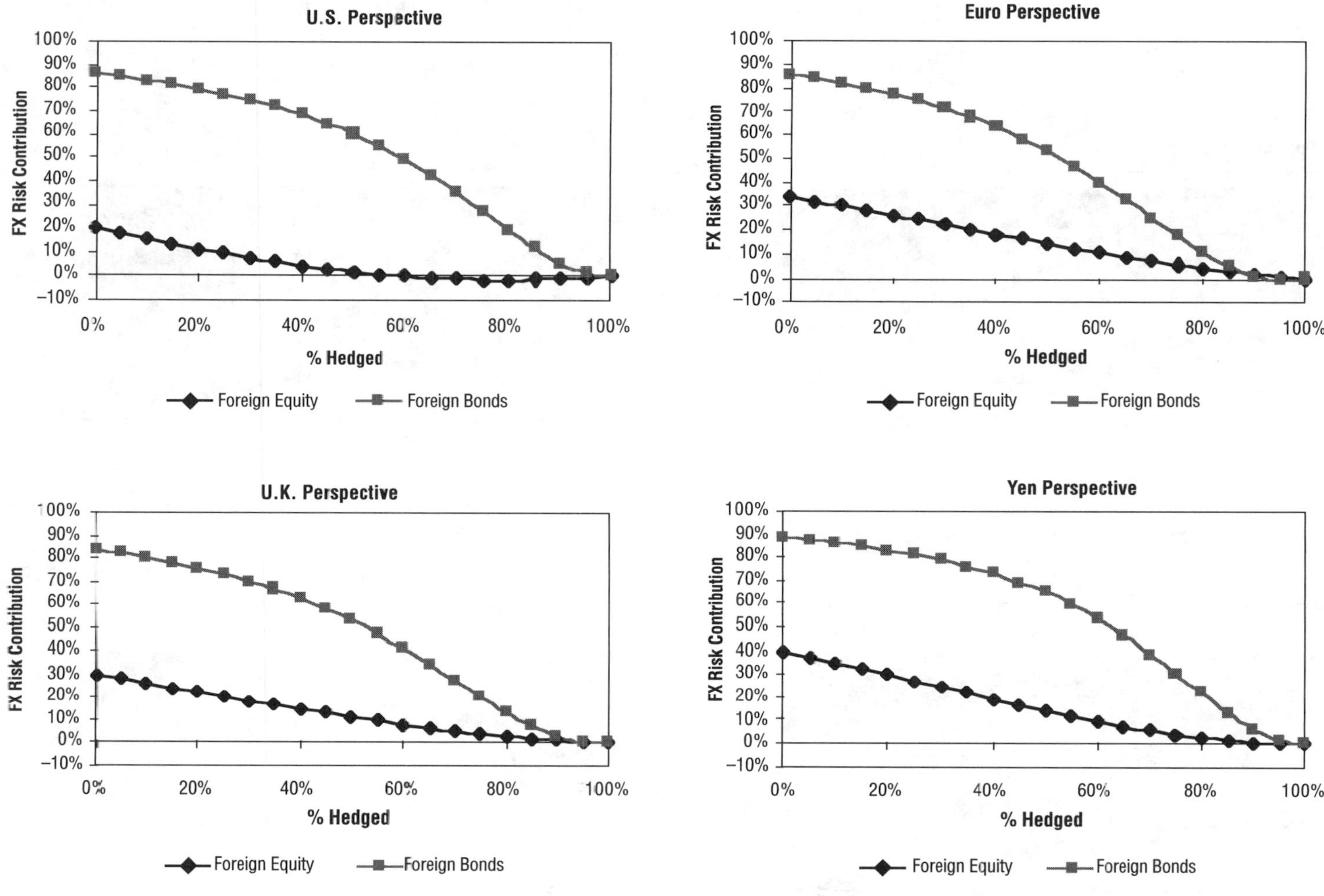

FIGURE 11.4 Currency's Contribution to Portfolio Risk

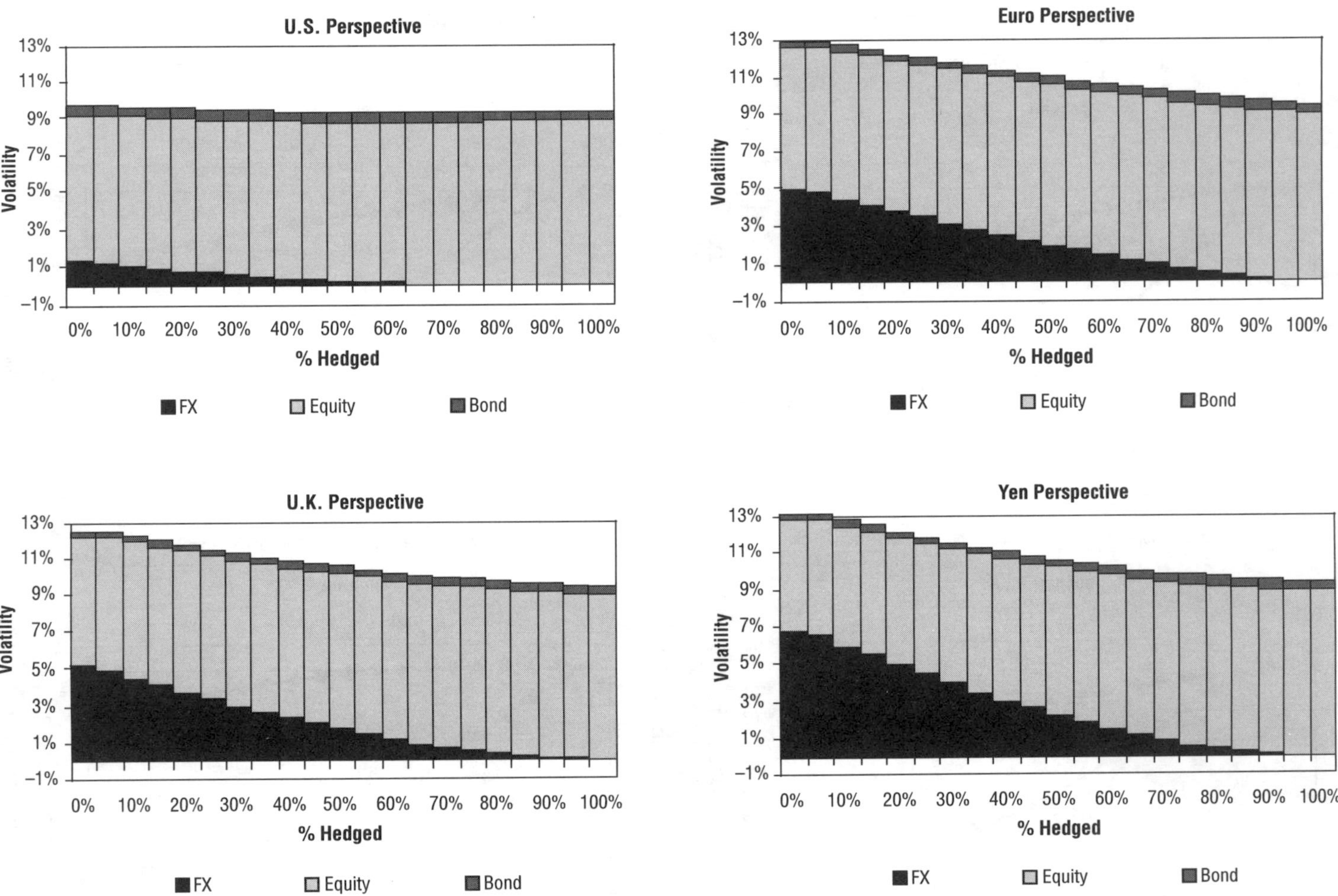

FIGURE 11.5 Global Capitalization Weight Volatility and Risk Decomposition

volatility and the decomposition of portfolio volatility, showing how much of portfolio volatility can be attributed, at the margin, to fixed income, equity, and foreign exchange (FX) positions.

The graphs reveal clear patterns. First, when currency exposure is fully hedged, all portfolios have volatility of roughly 9 percent, with most of the risk attributable (at the margin) to the equity positions. Second, when none of the currency exposure is hedged, the fixed income positions contribute least to portfolio risk. Finally, currency positions are the greatest source of portfolio volatility for yen investors without currency hedging.

Figure 11.5 suggests some flexibility across regions in setting currency hedging policies. For example, suppose that all investors want currency to contribute least to portfolio volatility (at the margin). According to Figure 11.5, U.S. dollar-based investors would hedge 40 percent of their currency exposure, while euro-based investors would hedge 80 percent.

Now, how does home bias influence the currency hedging decision? Figure 11.6 plots currency's contribution to portfolio risk depending on the level of the currency hedge, the reference currency, and the degree of home bias (assuming that holdings are 32 percent fixed income and 68 percent equity). Each graph corresponds to a different reference currency, while one line reflects market capitalization weights and the other corresponds to a moderate, 60 percent diversified, "representative" degree of home bias. As a general rule, the greater the home bias, the lower the currency contribution to portfolio risk at each level of currency hedging.

Clearly the risk associated with currency varies depending on the base currency and the degree of home bias. As a general rule, however, a 50 percent currency hedging policy will be sufficient to make currency a relatively small source of risk in the portfolio.

Up to this point, we've focused on the risk associated with strategic currency positions. Viewed differently, we've specified allocations to domestic and international assets and levels of currency hedging, and then calculated portfolio volatility and the contribution to portfolio volatility of open foreign exchange positions. Little has been said about the *returns* associated with open currency positions. Because we're discussing currency in a portfolio context, our exploration of how hedging affects currency returns naturally focuses on the *excess* returns to currency—the returns an investor would receive above the returns embedded in the interest rate differentials (or currency forwards).

We think implied returns analysis is a useful way to approach the issue of currency returns. Rather than assume explicit views on asset and currency returns to determine optimal portfolio weights, this method starts with a set of portfolio weights and determines what returns would optimize the portfolios.[2]

---

[2]Let x be an $N \times 1$ vector of portfolio weights, Ω be an $N \times N$ covariance matrix of asset returns (excess), and λ a scalar risk aversion parameter. Then the $N \times 1$ vector of returns R implied by the portfolio weights x is given by $R = \lambda\Omega x$. When x is the global capitalization weighted portfolio, then R is the vector of equilibrium returns. Notice that λ can be calibrated so that portfolio excess returns are consistent with very-long-run historical experience.

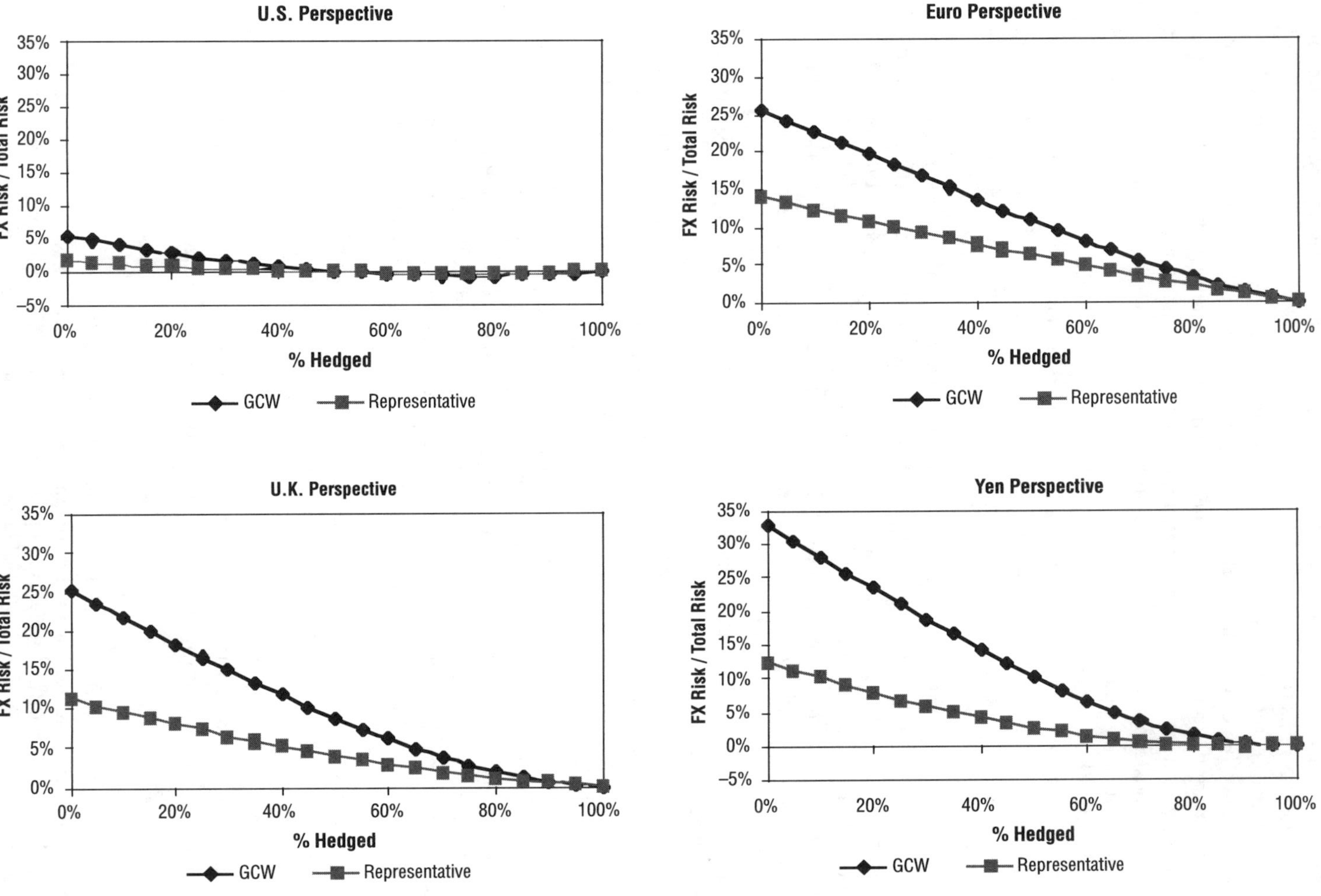

FIGURE 11.6 Risk Decomposition and Home Bias

We prefer to look at implied returns rather than historical averages for two reasons. First, assuming you want to optimize returns, implied returns analysis indicates what the return of an asset or currency must be before you'd be willing to bear the additional risk of taking a position in it. As a result, implied returns on assets and currencies are computed directly from the marginal contribution to risk analysis.

Second, historical averages are notoriously poor predictors of expected returns, in part because estimates vary widely depending on which historical period is used. For example, the expected return on the yen/dollar exchange rate differs markedly if you use 1980–1990, rather than 1990–2000, as the basis for the historical average.

Implied returns analysis can assess the currency returns of different hedging levels. In other words, working backward from a set of portfolio weights and an assumption about the currency hedging level, we can find the corresponding implied currency return.

Assume that all investors hold a global capitalization weighted portfolio. The asset "weight" applied to currency is the unhedged currency position. For example, a yen investor who holds 20 percent of his or her portfolio in U.S. equities and hedges 50 percent of currency exposure would have an open U.S. dollar position of 10 percent.

Figure 11.7 plots the relationship between implied currency returns and the level of currency hedging, from euro, sterling, U.S. dollar, and yen perspectives. The graphs show that *the greater the currency hedging, the lower the implied currency return*. For example, when euro-based investors leave all currency positions completely open, the implied return (excess) on the U.S. dollar is 3.3 percent. When all positions are hedged at the 50 percent level, however, the implied U.S. dollar return is approximately 2.1 percent.

The relationship between implied currency returns and the level of currency hedging is not really surprising. Remember, Figure 11.6's risk decomposition analysis suggests that higher levels of currency hedging mean lower levels of portfolio risk attributable to currency. Thus, in order for it to be optimal for investors to hedge at higher levels, they must also believe that currency will have lower expected excess returns.

The graphs in Figure 11.7 also indicate that at higher currency hedging levels, the implied excess return of some currencies actually becomes negative. For example, U.S. dollar investors who hedge 100 percent of their open currency positions are implying that returns to the yen will be negative. Although counterintuitive, this result can be explained by a negative correlation between excess currency returns and excess asset returns. Given this surprising result, a more detailed analysis of the historical correlation between currency and asset returns is warranted. Furthermore, if we assume that excess currency returns and excess asset returns are uncorrelated, how is implied currency return affected?

Figure 11.8 looks at the long-term correlation between currency and asset returns. It plots a beta time series from a regression of a basket of G-7 currency returns on a portfolio of G-7 asset returns. (The G-7 countries include Canada, France, Germany, Italy, Japan, the United Kingdom, and the United States.) The regression was estimated on 90-day rolling windows over a 20-year period. The graph reveals two interesting features about the time series: First, the beta coefficients are

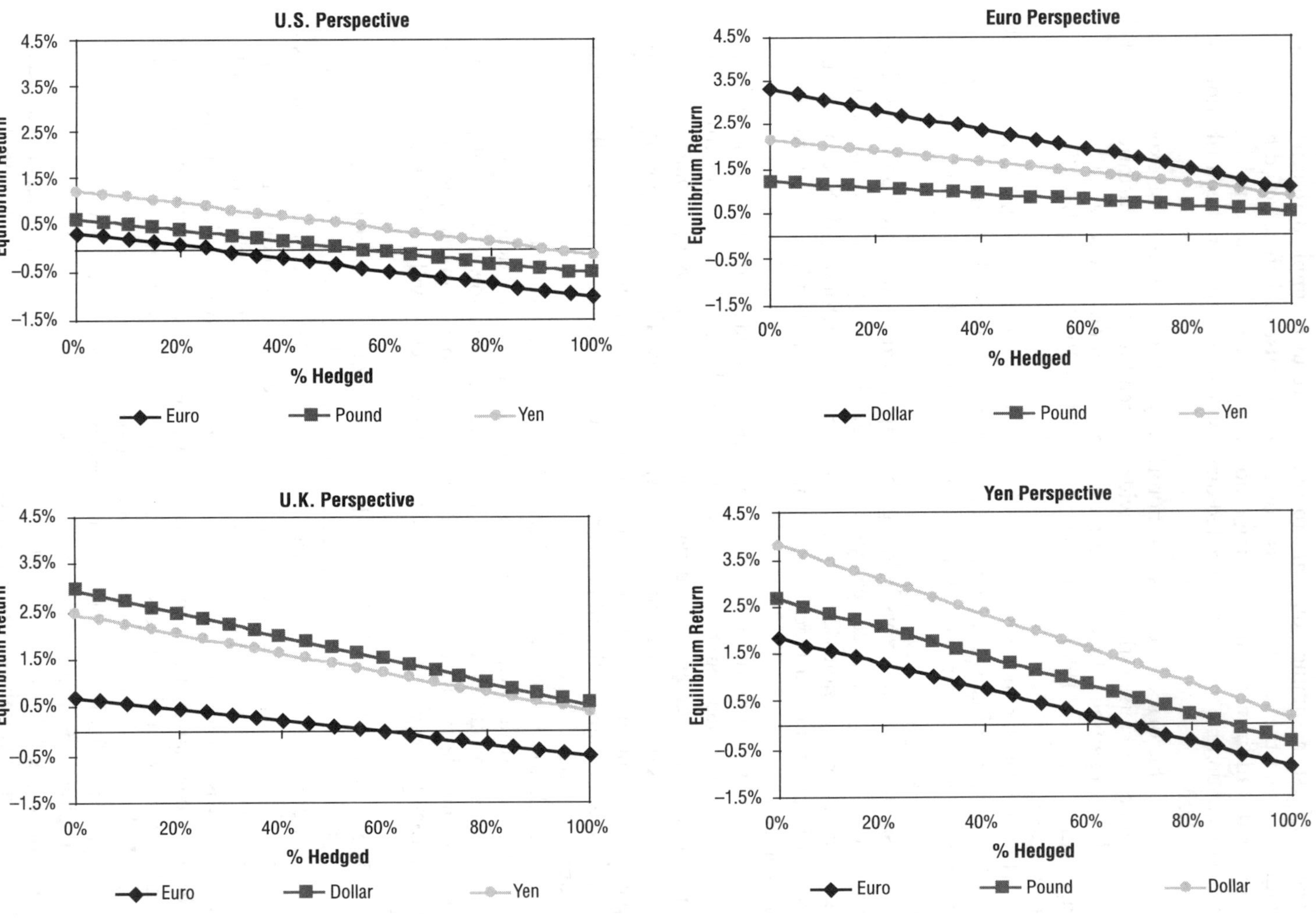

FIGURE 11.7 Implied Currency Returns

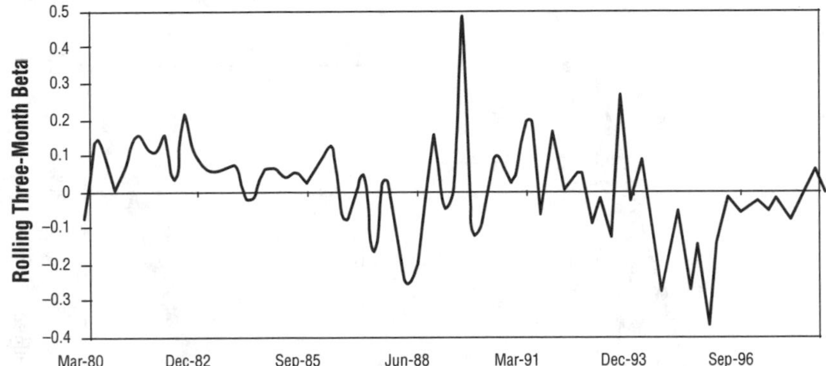

FIGURE 11.8 Beta of Currency against Hedged Assets (G–7 Portfolio, U.S. Perspective)

both positive and negative (and, on occasion, extremely so). Second, while the beta coefficients vary depending on the time, the central tendency seems to be zero.

To explore this issue further, we broke the sample into several discrete pieces and calculated the beta coefficients and correlations for each segment. Table 11.4 illustrates that over long periods of time (e.g., 10 or 20 years), the beta coefficients and correlation levels are close to zero. Over shorter time intervals, however, both elements can deviate dramatically from zero.

The data in Table 11.4 have two important implications for portfolio strategy. First, given that the correlation figures are quite low over long time horizons, *little is lost by assuming, for strategic asset allocation purposes, that the correlation between currency and asset excess returns is zero*. Second, the observation that correlations change sign, and for prolonged periods, can be viewed as providing a rationale for active currency management.

How does the assumption that the long-term correlation between currency and asset excess returns is zero affect implied currency returns? Figure 11.9 plots the relationship between the implied currency return and the currency hedge ratio. Similar to the results shown in Figure 11.7, the implied return to currency decreases as the percentage of currency hedged increases. As currency's marginal contribution to risk decreases, the implied return associated with open currency positions also decreases (under the assumption of optimality). In contrast with

TABLE 11.4 Beta Coefficients by Period

Period	Beta	Correlation	T-Statistic*
Past 10 years	−0.02	−0.05	−2.52
Past 20 years	−0.01	−0.03	−1.87
1/1/78–12/31/85	0.05	0.16	7.00
1/1/86–12/31/88	−0.06	−0.16	−4.43
1/1/89–12/31/93	0.05	0.10	3.65
1/1/94–12/31/97	−0.09	−0.24	−8.03

*The t-statistic is a measure of statistical significance.

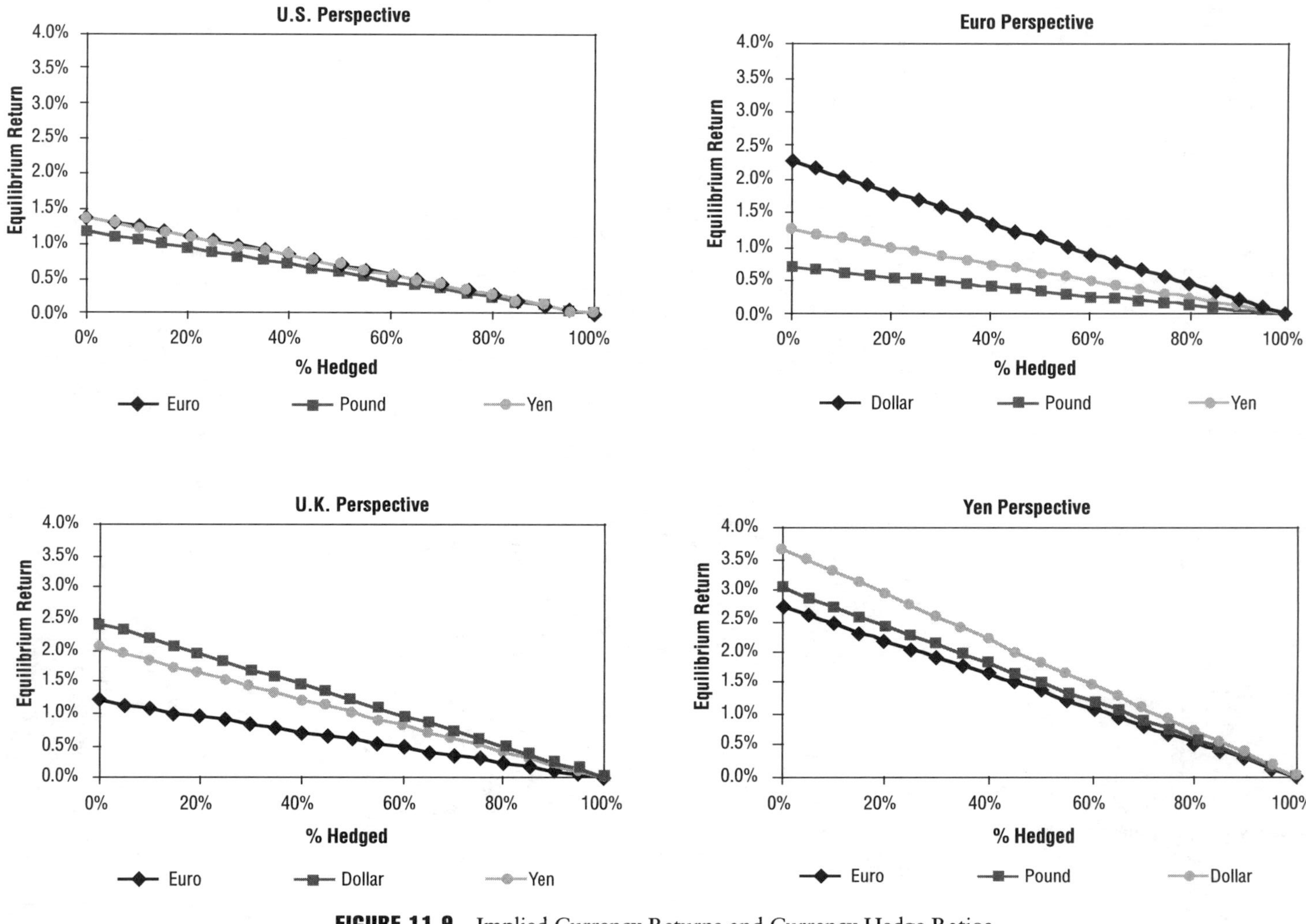

FIGURE 11.9 Implied Currency Returns and Currency Hedge Ratios

Figure 11.7, however, all implied currency returns are non-negative. When we assume that the correlation between currency and asset returns is zero, the implied currency return for a 100 percent currency-hedged portfolio is also zero, while open currency positions lead to positive implied currency returns.

CONCLUSIONS

What's the best strategic (or long-term) currency hedging policy? Our approach to this issue has focused on assessing the risk budget associated with alternative levels of currency hedging. Additionally, to make our advice as universal as possible, we've applied our analysis to euro-, sterling-, U.S. dollar-, and yen-based portfolios.

Our conclusions? First, currency hedging affects equity and fixed income assets differently. Since currency accounts for a disproportionate amount of the risk in unhedged foreign fixed income portfolios, we recommend a 100 percent currency hedge.

Second, the appropriate currency hedge level changes with the home bias level. Assuming you want currency to be the smallest source of portfolio risk, a currency hedge of 80 percent is appropriate for a global capitalization weighted portfolio. As home bias increases, the appropriate currency hedging level decreases (assuming you want currency exposure to be your portfolio's smallest source of risk).

Third, irrespective of base currency, investors achieve 75 percent of the potential Sharpe ratio improvement (based on equilibrium returns) when they move 60 percent of the way from a purely domestic portfolio toward a global capitalization weighted portfolio. This suggests appropriate currency hedge ratios of about 40 percent (again, assuming you want open currency positions to be your portfolio's smallest source of risk).

Finally, when a global capitalization weighted portfolio is 80 percent hedged, the implied currency excess returns approximate 50 basis points.

CHAPTER 12

The Value of Uncorrelated Sources of Return

Bob Litterman

When do uncorrelated assets add value to a portfolio? In the CAPM equilibrium, assets whose returns are not correlated with the market portfolio have zero expected excess return. This result, which was shown in Chapter 4, should give pause to those, such as ourselves, who hope to use uncorrelated assets to add value to portfolios. The CAPM theory implies that in equilibrium uncorrelated assets have no particular value in portfolio construction. Uncorrelated assets can diversify portfolios, but if one reduces risk by switching from assets that have positive expected return into assets that do not, then the diversification has not improved the characteristics of the portfolio.

Risk reduction is not an end in itself. Investors can most easily lower or raise portfolio risk by choosing to hold more or less cash. The value of uncorrelated assets is not their ability to reduce risk, but rather their potential to increase expected returns while at the same time reducing, or at least not increasing, risk. Uncorrelated assets that do provide a positive expected return can play, depending on the size of the expected return, a very valuable role in portfolios, but this capability depends crucially on the existence of some deviation from equilibrium.

Active risk, the risk created by active management relative to a benchmark, suffers from a similar conundrum. Active risk almost always has zero expected correlation to the market, has no expected excess return in equilibrium, and thus does not contribute value to a portfolio. Any role for active risk in portfolio construction must reflect a deviation from equilibrium.

In this chapter we will attempt to highlight two results: first, how important and valuable active risk and other sources of uncorrelated returns are in portfolio construction, and second, how the equilibrium approach guides and informs the search for positive returns associated with uncorrelated risks, returns that the theory itself suggests should not exist.

The fact that an equilibrium approach does not provide a role for uncorrelated assets in a portfolio does not mean that an equilibrium approach is wrong or uninteresting. What the equilibrium does provide is a framework in which to identify opportunities. In other words, an equilibrium framework allows us to identify when it is the case that assets with various characteristics, such as being uncorrelated with the market, have expected returns that are not consistent with equilibrium, and can therefore be especially attractive. The equilibrium framework provides a reference for expected excess returns such that returns greater than that reference are attractive. In particular, as we will show in this chapter, assets with uncorrelated returns that also have a positive expected excess return will add significant value to a portfolio that otherwise is structured to create returns through exposures to equilibrium risk premiums.

The investment management industry has developed an unfortunate terminology for discussing uncorrelated assets and other sources of active risk. What is unfortunate is that the defining characteristic of being statistically uncorrelated with the market portfolio is often unclear in the description of investment products. Moreover, many products whose returns are manifestly positively correlated with the market are nonetheless marketed as being either uncorrelated or market neutral.

Because uncorrelated assets are not part of the set of standard asset classes, they are generally included in a category that is referred to as "alternative" assets. But the alternative asset class also includes many other assets that are highly correlated with the market portfolio. "Alternative" generally refers to the fact that an asset is not part of a standard asset class; it does not imply low correlation with the market. Examples of alternative assets with significant positive correlations with the market include private equity, real estate, and many hedge funds. On the other hand, many other alternative assets are indeed basically uncorrelated with the market portfolio. Examples of these would include commodities, managed futures accounts, and many truly market-neutral hedge funds. The best way to identify uncorrelated returns is to gather data and compute correlations with market returns.

In addition to these alternative assets, there are many other potential sources of uncorrelated returns with positive expected returns. For example, the active risks coupled with benchmarks in the form of active management assignments are generally uncorrelated with the underlying asset classes. Finally, the active returns in many types of overlay strategies, such as active currency management and global tactical asset allocation, are generally uncorrelated with the market.

The difference between correlated and uncorrelated alternative assets is significant. Uncorrelated assets add very little risk to the portfolio, at least at the margin. In most contexts where investors are contemplating investments in alternative assets, there is an implicit assumption that the asset has a positive expected excess return. Adding positive expected return and not adding risk always improves the risk/return characteristics of a portfolio. In this sense, uncorrelated investments have a relatively low hurdle rate—the expected return only has to be positive.

For assets positively correlated with the market, an assumption of a positive expected excess return makes sense. For positively correlated assets, a positive return is an equilibrium phenomenon: It is a risk premium that ought to exist. The problem with assets that are correlated with the market is that they generally add risk to the portfolio, even at the margin. The question for investors in this context is whether the risk premium is large enough to justify the added risk to the portfolio.

For uncorrelated assets, on the other hand, there should be no such presumption of a positive expected excess return. The assumption of a positive expected excess return for an uncorrelated asset per se represents a deviation from equilibrium and, if it exists, represents an opportunity.

Investors should take the following general approach to evaluating sources of risk in their portfolios: All sources of risk should be divided into two components, market risk and uncorrelated risk. This division is conceptually simple—project the returns of each investment on the returns of the market and estimate the beta, the coefficient that estimates the multiple of the market return that is to be expected from that investment. The market risk of the investment is contributed by the estimated beta times the market return; the uncorrelated risk of the investment is contributed by what is left—that is, by the volatility of the investment return minus the market return times the investment beta. The return associated with this residual component, called alpha, is the holy grail of active investment management.

This division is interesting for a number of reasons. First, the market component of risk should be expected to earn a market-determined risk premium. As emphasized earlier, such a premium is available essentially for free in the market—that is, without an investment management fee. The cost of the market risk premium is not a fee, but rather its usage of a scarce resource, the investor's limited appetite for exposure to market risk. Uncorrelated risk is just the opposite. The uncorrelated risk does not create additional exposure to market risk. In most portfolios it therefore contributes very little to portfolio risk. Sources of uncorrelated risk, on the other hand, generally require an active management fee. The challenge highlighted by the equilibrium theory is whether an investment manager can actually create a positive alpha, that is, an expected return greater than the fee the manager charges for uncorrelated risk. The only way an investor can rationally determine whether the fees charged by a manager are reasonable, and whether the returns are adequate, is to separately identify the market risk and the uncorrelated risk components of the investment.

We have opened this chapter with the question, when do uncorrelated assets add value to a portfolio? This question is interesting because it immediately highlights the fact that adding value to a portfolio is a function not of risk characteristics per se, but rather of the relationship between expected excess return and risk. In equilibrium, there is no special value to uncorrelated assets; in fact, they do not deserve an expected excess return. However, as we will show, the issues raised by considering uncorrelated assets are of more general interest. The circumstances that can make uncorrelated assets attractive, an expected excess return greater than the equilibrium value, can also apply to assets with positive correlations. Thus, this discussion leads naturally to a consideration of when, at the margin, adding any investment activity adds value to a portfolio. And finally, we will see that the same risk and return trade-offs apply not only at the margin, but also to the more general problem of how to optimally size all positions in a portfolio.

Perhaps someday the world will be such that all investors will understand the distinction between market risk and uncorrelated risk, they will monitor the divisions of these components of risk in their investments, and their behavior will force prices to adjust so that there is no excess return, no alpha, left to be found in sources of uncorrelated risk. If that happens, investing will become less interesting and there will be fewer avenues through which to add value to portfolios. Our view is that such a world has not yet arrived, and our search for alpha continues.

We do find it interesting, however, to think about how close we are to such a world by quantifying the Sharpe ratio—that is, the ratio of expected return to volatility—in sources of uncorrelated risk. In equilibrium, of course, this ratio is zero. More generally, the larger this ratio, the more value uncorrelated risk has in portfolio construction. Our view is that while markets are generally very efficient today, there is, nonetheless, still significant opportunity to create investment products with uncorrelated risk having Sharpe ratios of .25 and higher, often much higher, after fees. As we will show, at such levels of the ratio of expected return per unit of risk the value of such products in portfolios is much greater than is generally understood, and the amount of uncorrelated risk that is optimal is much greater than that which is generally taken.

Since, as we have highlighted, such an expectation for positive returns, much less returns greater than fees, is not an equilibrium phenomenon, perhaps we should explain why we think it exists. First, we believe most investors do not understand the distinction between market risk and uncorrelated risk. An important implication is that most investors have an aversion to uncorrelated risk that is not justified in equilibrium. This lack of understanding can create opportunities for investors willing to take advantage of them. A simple example of this phenomenon is provided by value stocks. Value stocks, those with low price-to-book and price-to-earnings ratios, tend to have lower than average betas, which in equilibrium would imply lower than average expected returns. Historically such stocks have actually provided higher than average returns. Second, we believe that not all information is public and fully digested by investors—the processing of information about relative values of assets is an expensive activity that requires resources, the allocation of capital, and exposure to risk. Those who initiate the purchases and sales that drive prices to fair value should be, and we believe are, compensated for their efforts. Third, there are noneconomic players in the marketplace, such as governments and central banks, which provide opportunities for profit-maximizing investors. Finally, there are many structural inefficiencies that prevent investors from driving risk premiums to their equilibrium values. These inefficiencies, such as higher than justified risk premiums in markets with barriers to foreign investors, again provide opportunities for those willing and able to take advantage of them.

If these deviations from rationality and inefficiencies exist, then how does the CAPM help us to identify value? As we have seen in previous chapters, despite the fact that the "PM" in the acronym "CAPM" stands for "Pricing Model," in fact the CAPM does not price securities in the sense that it provides a level against which one can measure richness or cheapness. Rather, what the CAPM provides is a framework in which we can identify the equilibrium expected excess return for a security as a function of the risk characteristics of that security. In particular, the equilibrium expected excess return is a multiple of the beta of a security with the market portfolio.

The equilibrium expected excess return should be interpreted as an economy-wide fair value for the degree of risk embedded in a security. It is not a function of the particular portfolio or situation of an individual investor. Even if the market does not cause all investments to yield an equilibrium risk premium, it is still useful to have such a neutral starting point from which an investor can then think about portfolio construction.

If the equilibrium provides an "external" measure of value, one independent of the particular situation of the investor, then the investor's portfolio itself provides an "internal" measure of value—that is, one specific to that portfolio. As noted in Chapter 2, all one needs to have in order to solve for this internal measure of value is the expected excess return for one asset class. One suggestion is to normalize on the expected excess return of the market portfolio. In any case, given one reference for an expected excess return, we can solve for the implied views—that is, the set of expected excess returns for every other asset class in the portfolio such that the existing portfolio is optimal relative to those expected excess returns. As mentioned in Chapter 2, the implied views provide a natural set of hurdle rates against which to gauge whether the positions in the portfolio are sized appropriately.

As a first step in analyzing a portfolio, it makes sense to compare the implied views with the equilibrium expected excess returns. When implied views differ from equilibrium values, the implication is that the investor has identified an opportunity, a situation where an asset is expected to return more or less than the equilibrium risk premium consistent with its risk characteristics. The investor may want to compare the deviations of expected excess returns imbedded in the implied views against the equilibrium values as a way to identify any inconsistencies or opportunities embedded in the portfolio.

Just as an asset that is uncorrelated with the market portfolio has an equilibrium risk premium of zero, an asset whose returns are uncorrelated with the returns of a particular portfolio has an implied view of zero expected excess return. In this situation the investor may often want to ask, does the size of this exposure really make sense? When an investor has a positive weight in an asset, it usually exists because the investor has a positive outlook for the returns of that asset. If, in this situation, the implied view is zero or negative, that usually is associated with a circumstance in which the investor would be better off increasing the size of the position to more accurately reflect a positive outlook.

The second step in portfolio analysis is to understand the risk contributions of each asset to the overall portfolio and to know what is the risk-minimizing position for each asset. The risk contributions are useful in sizing positions appropriately given the investor's views. Most investors find it hard to give with any confidence an estimate of the expected excess return for an asset. They can with much more confidence suggest a percentage of the portfolio risk that they would feel comfortable with coming from that asset. One drawback of looking only at risk contributions, however, is that it's not always obvious how to change a position if one wants to increase or decrease its risk contribution. Understanding where the risk-minimizing position is located is important in this regard.

The risk-minimizing position is the position in a particular asset for which the portfolio risk is minimized, holding all other positions unchanged. The risk-minimizing position is also the position for which the returns of an asset would be uncorrelated with those of the portfolio, and, as noted earlier, this position has an implied view of zero expected excess return. If the current position is greater than the risk-minimizing position, then the current position represents a positive expected excess return, and adding to the position increases risk and increases expected return. Similarly, if the current position is less than the risk-minimizing position, then the current position represents a negative expected excess return, and selling the position increases risk and increases expected return.

There is no reason for the risk-minimizing position to be a zero weight. One can easily have a positive weight in an asset, or an overweight position relative to a benchmark, and still have the weight be less than the risk-minimizing position. In such a case adding to the asset reduces risk. Moreover, we refer to such positions as having counterintuitive implied views—counterintuitive because such positions have positive weight, but negative implied views. Investors constructing portfolios without the benefit of risk tools can easily mistakenly create such a position while intending to create a portfolio representing a positive outlook. When such circumstances are found, the investor can improve the portfolio risk and return by increasing the exposure. In fact, in such a context the optimal portfolio weight would typically be a point well beyond the risk-minimizing position.

Analyzing portfolios from both a return perspective and a risk perspective allows the investor to ask and answer two basic questions. First, "What is my best estimate at what is a reasonable expected excess return on each asset and is it consistent with the implied views of the portfolio?" Second, "What is my desired risk contribution from each asset and is it consistent with the current portfolio weights?" It is often easier for investors to think about the latter issue, how much risk is desired for various assets to contribute to a portfolio, rather than to specify with enough precision what are the appropriate expected excess returns. As we shall see, the optimal portfolio weights are often wildly sensitive to small changes in the expected excess returns, whereas risk contributions generally are not sensitive to small changes in portfolio weights.[1]

We now consider three examples. In the first example we will create a very simple problem in order to highlight the value of uncorrelated risk. We assume that there are only two investment decisions to make, the quantity of market risk and the quantity of uncorrelated risk to include in the portfolio. We then investigate how the optimal quantity of uncorrelated risk varies as a function of the Sharpe ratio of the uncorrelated risk. The optimal quantity of uncorrelated risk grows very quickly to levels not usually seen in institutional portfolios as the Sharpe ratio of the uncorrelated risk increases above zero. In the second example we investigate the sensitivity of optimal asset allocations to small changes in expected returns for various asset classes. We suggest that investors may want to think about asset allocations in terms of risk allocations directly, rather than first specifying expected returns and running an optimizer. Finally, in the third example we contrast the expected returns that justify typical strategic asset allocations to equity markets versus the expected returns that justify tactical deviations from those allocations. For typical-sized exposures, the implied views justifying tactical deviations are an order of magnitude smaller than those that justify strategic asset allocations. In the conclusion we will comment on the implications of these results for the process by which asset allocations should be established in institutional portfolios.

Our first example is simple, but illuminating. We consider an investor trying to maximize expected return for a given level of risk in which the only two decisions

---

[1]This lack of sensitivity is not always the case. When two assets are highly correlated and have opposite exposures, the risk contribution of one asset can change significantly with small changes in its position. As an example, consider a basis trade, a deliverable bond hedged against the corresponding future contract. If the future is sized to minimize the risk of the trade it will have a risk contribution of zero. In that context, a small increase in its position will cause it to dominate the risk of the joint position.

are the levels of exposure to market risk and to uncorrelated risk. We assume both types of risk are available in unlimited supply (in other words, there is no constraint on borrowing). We don't worry about the sources of the two types of risk, but simply assume an equilibrium risk premium on the market risk and investigate the optimal allocations as a function of the assumed Sharpe ratio of the uncorrelated risk.

By construction, the portfolio risk is given by $\sigma_p = SQRT(M^2 + U^2)$ where M and U are the allocations, measured in terms of volatility, to market risk and uncorrelated risk, respectively. The investor wants to maximize expected return, given by $\mu_p = M \cdot S_m + U \cdot S_u$ where S_m and S_u are the Sharpe ratios on market risk and uncorrelated risk, respectively. We assume S_m is equal to .268, the market Sharpe ratio reported in Chapter 6, which arises from an equilibrium risk premium of 2.22 percent per annum together with the annual volatility of 8.3 percent.

Suppose we set the risk appetite of the investor at 8.3 percent, the volatility of the market portfolio. If S_u, the Sharpe ratio on uncorrelated risk, is equal to the equilibrium value of zero, then the optimal allocations to market and uncorrelated risk are clearly 8.3 and 0, respectively. When S_u is greater than zero the optimization requires reduction in market risk and an allocation to uncorrelated risk such that the total risk is unchanged and the expected return of the portfolio is maximized. Figure 12.1 shows how these quantities vary as a function of the assumed Sharpe ratio for uncorrelated risk.

This figure illustrates how the optimal allocation of uncorrelated risk rises dramatically as the Sharpe ratio increases. A Sharpe ratio of only .05 on uncorrelated risk justifies an allocation of over 150 basis points, an allocation typical of large pension plans. A Sharpe ratio of only .15 justifies over 400 basis points of uncorrelated risk, an allocation larger than the tracking error of most large funds relative to their strategic benchmarks. Why is the optimal allocation to uncorrelated risk so large for relatively low levels of expected return? The answer is that uncorrelated risk contributes very little to portfolio risk. At the margin the hurdle rate to justify allocations to uncorrelated risk is quite low.

One point this figure does not highlight is that the total expected return of the fund increases with higher Sharpe ratios on uncorrelated risk. Whereas the fund generates only an equilibrium expected excess return of 2.22 percent when the un-

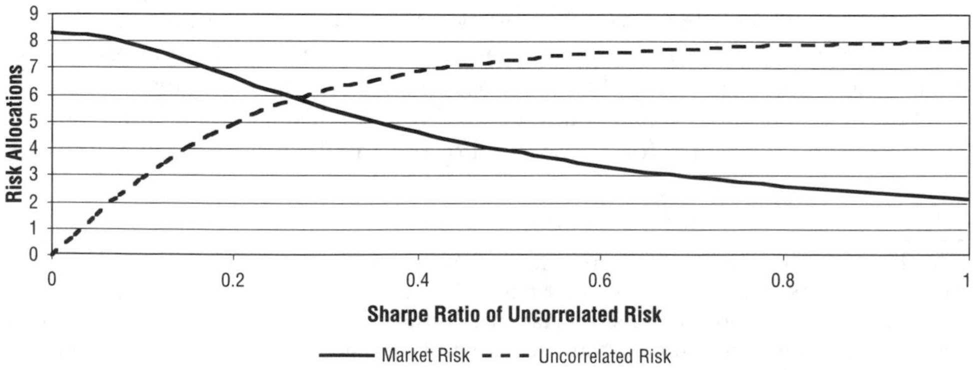

FIGURE 12.1 Optimal Allocations to Market and Uncorrelated Risk

correlated risk has no expected return, the expected excess return of optimal allocations of risk rises by 15 percent to 2.55 when the Sharpe ratio is .15. If the Sharpe ratio is .3, then the excess return reaches 3.34, a 50 percent increase. A Sharpe ratio of .5 allows a more than doubling, to 4.71 percent, of the expected excess return of the fund.

Looked at another way, the alpha associated with uncorrelated risk is the source of return that can allow funds to hit return targets that are otherwise unachievable with standard risk allocations. Rather than ask what is the highest return achievable for a portfolio with 8.3 percent volatility, we can ask how much market risk and uncorrelated risk is optimal in order to achieve a particular return target. For example, Figure 12.2 shows these optimal risk allocations and the total portfolio risk required to achieve a total return of 8 percent—that is, an excess return of 4 percent plus an assumed 4 percent risk-free rate.

In Figure 12.2 the targeted expected return is held constant and the benefit of higher Sharpe ratios on uncorrelated risk is the ability to hit the target with reasonable levels of total portfolio volatility. Given the 4 percent excess return target, market risk premium alone requires almost 15 percent annualized volatility. In this example, in order to keep the analysis simple we assume the market portfolio can be leveraged; when leverage is not practical this level of risk and return could be achieved through an almost 100 percent allocation to equity. When the Sharpe ratio increases to .05 the optimal allocation to uncorrelated risk reaches 2.7 percent. At a Sharpe ratio of .15, the optimal allocation to uncorrelated risk reaches 6.4 percent, the optimal market risk is 11.4 percent (which would imply an equity asset weight of approximately 75 percent), and the total required portfolio risk declines to 13 percent. At a Sharpe ratio of .2, the optimal allocation to uncorrelated risk is 7.2 percent, the optimal market risk is 9.6 percent (which implies an equity asset weight of approximately 63 percent), and the total required portfolio risk declines to 12 percent. Again we see that even at very modest assumed Sharpe ratios the optimal levels of uncorrelated risk are far larger than is typical of institutional funds.

In our second example we consider a U.S. investor trying to create a global equity asset allocation and contrast the sensitivity of optimal allocations based on

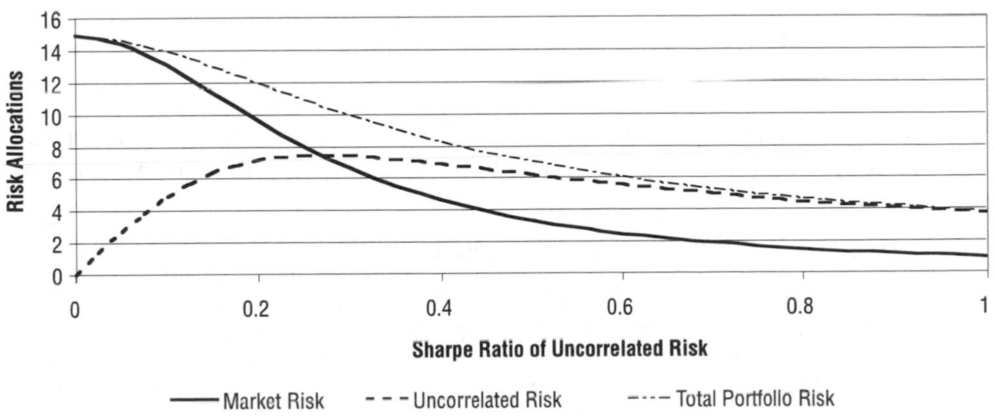

FIGURE 12.2 Optimal Allocations of Market and Uncorrelated Risk Required to Hit an 8 Percent Return Target

specifying expected returns with allocations based on specifying a risk decomposition. To keep the context simple, consider only allocations to the United States, Europe, Japan, and emerging markets and let us assume we do not hedge the currency exposures. Suppose the investor starts with a portfolio that has allocations of 40 percent in the United States, 40 percent in Europe, 20 percent in Japan, and zero weight in emerging markets. As shown in Table 12.1, the equilibrium risk premiums for these assets are 4.00 percent, 3.97 percent, 3.02 percent, and 4.97 percent, respectively. The weighted average risk premium (using the portfolio weights) is 3.79 percent.

These weights differ from the market capitalization weights in being overweight Europe and Japan, and underweight the United States and emerging markets. We compute the implied views by using as the normalization that the weighted average risk premium for the portfolio is equal to that using equilibrium values—that is, 3.79 percent. Using this approach, the implied views for the United States, Europe, Japan, and emerging markets are 3.74 percent, 4.00 percent, 3.48 percent, and 4.83 percent, respectively. Relative to equilibrium risk premiums, the portfolio is bearish on the United States by 26 basis points, bullish on Europe by 3 basis points, bullish on Japan by 46 basis points, and bearish on emerging markets by 14 basis points.

Before reflecting further on whether these views might accurately reflect those of the investor, let's recognize that these are extremely small differences from equilibrium and instead analyze the risk contributions. Given the allocations, 39.5 percent of the risk is coming from the U.S. equity, 42.2 percent of the risk is coming from Europe equity, and 18.3 percent of the risk is coming from the Japanese position. Suppose an asset allocation study has recommended increased diversification and, in particular, an allocation to emerging markets. One proposal is to create weights such that the risk contributions are 40 percent United States, 30 percent Europe, 20 percent Japan, and 10 percent emerging markets.

Recall from Chapter 2 that the formula for marginal contribution to risk is as follows, letting $(\Sigma)_i$ represent the ith row of the covariance matrix, w the portfolio weight vector, with ith element w_i, and σ_p^2 the portfolio variance, which equals $w\Sigma w'$:

$$\text{Percent contribution to risk for asset } i = w_i \cdot (\Sigma)_i \frac{w'}{\sigma_p^2}$$

We can attempt to solve for the weights, w, that create a particular contribution to risk, but notice that this is a quadratic equation and solutions may or may

TABLE 12.1 Risk Premiums and Weights

Asset Class	Market Weight	Portfolio Weight	Equilibrium Risk Premium	Implied View
U.S. equity	55.9%	40%	4.00%	3.74%
European equity	30.7	40	3.97	4.00
Japanese equity	9.4	20	3.02	3.48
Emerging markets equity	4.0	0	4.97	4.83

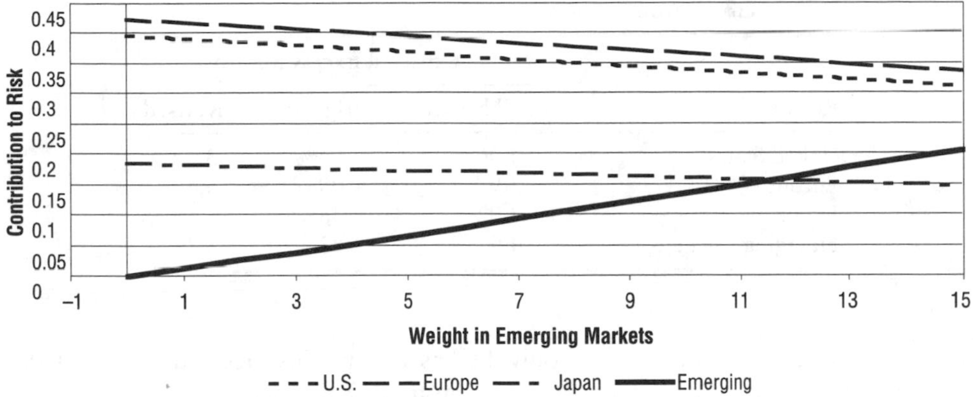

FIGURE 12.3 Marginal Contributions to Risk

not exist. In Figure 12.3, we graph the contribution to risk as a function of the weight in emerging markets, where we reduce the weights to each other asset proportionally. More generally, solving for weights that create specific contributions to risk such as described earlier entails a set of nonlinear equations. Solutions can be obtained, for example, by setting up an optimization in a spreadsheet.

Using this approach, we find that if we desire the above risk decomposition, then we require that the weights be given as in Table 12.2. Now, these weights would require increasing the allocation to the United States by 1.4 percent, decreasing the allocation to Europe by 10.3 percent, increasing the allocation to Japan by 1.4 percent, and adding a 7.4 percent allocation to emerging markets.

Do these changes make sense? One quick check is whether the implied views for which this allocation is optimal seem reasonable. The implied views (normalizing as above such that the expected return equals that in equilibrium) are found in Table 12.3.

Anyone who has used portfolio optimization software has observed that optimal portfolio weights are sensitive to small changes in expected returns. Here, we see the other side of that relationship—the expected excess returns, which represent the implied views, are not very sensitive to changes in optimal portfolio weights. A relatively small change in the expected return on emerging markets, just 35 basis points (together with similar small changes in the expected returns in the other asset classes), justifies an increase in portfolio weight from 0 percent to 7.4 percent.

TABLE 12.2 Weights Required for Desired Risk Decomposition

Region	Weight	Contribution to Risk
United States	41.4%	40.0%
Europe	29.7	30.0
Japan	21.4	20.0
Emerging markets	7.4	10.0

TABLE 12.3 Implied Views

	Expected Excess Returns		
Region	Equilibrium	Original	Revised
United States	4.00%	3.74%	3.72%
Europe	3.97	4.00	3.89
Japan	3.02	3.48	3.59
Emerging markets	4.97	4.83	5.18

At the same time, the decrease of only 11 basis points justifies a decrease of the weight in European equities from 40.0 percent to 29.7 percent.

Because of this sensitivity of optimal portfolio weights to small changes in expected excess returns, we prefer to focus on targeted contributions to risk and to the changes in excess return implied by different portfolios, rather than the usual approach, which focuses on formulating expected excess returns first and then relies on an optimizer to construct an optimal portfolio subject to constraints.

Let's now change gears and consider a final example in which we focus on tactical deviations from a strategic benchmark given by the portfolio in the previous example with risk contributions of 40, 30, 20, and 10 percent respectively to the United States, Europe, Japan, and emerging markets. In this example let us suppose that the investor wants to express a bullish view on the Japanese equity market so that the objective is to tactically overweight Japanese equity and tactically to underweight the United States and Europe. To be precise, let us suppose the objective is to create an exposure that generates 100 basis points of tracking error and to set the underweight positions in the U.S. and European regions such that the portfolio is dollar neutral (the underweight in the United States plus Europe equal the overweight of Japan) and the two underweight regions contribute equally to the portfolio risk.

Setting this optimization problem up in an Excel spreadsheet is relatively straightforward. Using the solver function in Excel we find that the weights for which these conditions are met are an overweight in Japan of 5.53 percent and underweights of 2.6 percent in the United States and 2.9 percent in Europe. The risk contributions to the portfolio are 74.2 percent coming from Japan and 12.9 percent each coming from the United States and Europe.

The purpose of this example is to contrast the magnitude of expected returns that are required to increase market risk against the magnitude of expected returns that justify adding uncorrelated risk. Note that the risk of this portfolio of tactical deviations is approximately market neutral. If we want to find the implied views of this portfolio, a natural normalization is that the position has a particular Sharpe ratio, the ratio of expected excess return per unit of volatility. In this case the volatility was set to 100 basis points. Let's assume the position has an expected ratio of return per unit of volatility of .2. Given these assumptions, the expected return of the portfolio must be 20 basis points per annum, and we can solve for the expected excess returns: 2.68 percent for Japan, –.99 percent for the United States, and –.90 percent for Europe.

We have intentionally chosen in this example to focus on a ratio of expected return to risk that might be seen as relatively conservative. Most active equity managers target a Sharpe ratio of .5. Hedge fund managers generally target higher ratios, often greater than 1. Of course, this is just one position. We might imagine that a typical hedge fund manager has a portfolio of at least six independent positions with similar risk and return characteristics in a portfolio at any point in time. Clearly, the Sharpe ratio of such a portfolio is higher than that of any individual position. In fact, six independent positions, each with a volatility of 100 basis points and a Sharpe ratio of .2, will have a combined volatility of 245 basis points, the square root of 6; and the total portfolio will have an expected excess return of 120 basis points. Thus, assuming six positions of the type described here with a Sharpe ratio of .2 and with maximum diversification leads to a portfolio with a Sharpe ratio of .49. What we shall see is that a Sharpe ratio of .2 is not conservative. In fact, a Sharpe ratio of .2 would justify holding much more than 100 basis points of risk.

To see this, let us compare the implied views of the tactical asset allocation deviations with the implied views of the strategic asset allocation portfolio. Clearly they are inconsistent. For the United States, for example, the strategic asset allocation portfolio implies expected excess returns of 3.72 percent, whereas the tactical portfolio implies –.99 percent. How can we make sense of the differences? Suppose we overlay the tactical deviations on the strategic asset allocation portfolio and compute the implied views of the combined portfolio. We might expect that these implied views would combine the implied views of the two portfolios. In fact, we compare the implied views in Table 12.4.

The differences in the implied views between the original strategic portfolio and the combined portfolio have the same pattern in terms of sign and relative magnitude as do the implied views of the tactical portfolio by itself, but their absolute magnitude is only about one-tenth as big. Of course, these differences are sensitive to the normalization of the implied views, but we have chosen that normalization to match the expected returns of the portfolio with the returns of the portfolio using equilibrium expected returns. In other words, we have set the risk aversion to match the level of implied views of the tactical portfolio as closely as

TABLE 12.4 Comparison of Implied Views

	Portfolio Weights		
Region	Strategic	Tactical	Combined
United States	41.4%	–2.6%	38.8%
Europe	29.7	–2.9	26.9
Japan	21.4	5.5	27.0
Emerging markets	7.4	0.0	7.4

	Implied Views Expected Excess Returns (bps)			
Region	Strategic	Tactical	Combined	Difference
United States	372	–99	364	–8.5
Europe	389	–90	381	–7.7
Japan	359	268	382	23.1
Emerging markets	518	–9	517	–0.7

possible to that of the strategic portfolio. Given that we have matched the level, the only way to make the tactical views consistent with the expected excess returns from the strategic asset allocation is to shrink the magnitude of the tactical views by a factor of approximately 11.6. Having done so, we can match them exactly.

What are these incredibly small implied views in the tactical portfolio telling us? These implied views are the changes in expected excess returns for which it is optimal to move from the original strategic portfolio to the new portfolio with the tactical deviations as we specified. The condition for optimality is that the return per unit of portfolio risk is the same across all assets. In this case, we can think of the portfolio of tactical deviations as one asset, and what the factor of 11.6 is telling us is that if the Sharpe ratio of these positions is really .2 then we ought to significantly increase the size of the deviations. Conversely, given the size of the positions (the size of which was set to create 100 basis points of risk) the Sharpe ratio can't be .2; it can only be .008. We might think of this result as suggesting that tactical exposures that contribute relatively small amounts of uncorrelated risk to a portfolio have implied Sharpe ratios that are quite small—in fact, incredibly small.

There is a very important message for investors hidden in these calculations. Let's put into simple words what we have just shown. First, we examined a very simple global portfolio of equity exposures. We called this the strategic asset allocation portfolio, and we think of it as a crude proxy for the basic risk faced by almost all investors, the risk of the global equity markets. We then considered a portfolio of tactical deviations. We think of this portfolio as an example of an asset with positive expected returns and which has returns that are uncorrelated with the market portfolio. In fact, in our particular example, the historical returns of the tactical portfolio happen to have been slightly negatively correlated with those of the market portfolio. We then chose to add a small amount of this essentially uncorrelated asset to the strategic portfolio. We chose the amount of tracking error, 100 basis points, to approximate the amount of tactical asset allocation risk that many institutional investors tend to look at. We then made what we thought was a conservative assumption about the expected returns of that tactical portfolio, and the implied views told us that either our return assumption was over 10 times too big, or the risk of our position was much too small.

Let's boil this observation down to its essential components. We started with a strategic global equity portfolio with expected excess return of 385 basis points per year and with a volatility of 14.8 percent. We think these are realistic values for a global equity portfolio. Many investors in recent years have significantly reduced their return estimates, and might think the expected excess return we use to be relatively optimistic. (If so, their pessimism just strengthens our argument.) Suppose there is an uncorrelated asset with an unknown Sharpe ratio. We investigate the optimal amounts of this uncorrelated risk to add to the strategic portfolio as a function of the assumed Sharpe ratio of the uncorrelated risk. The surprising results are shown in Table 12.5, which parallels Figure 12.1. For each Sharpe ratio assumption, we solve for the optimal combination of the uncorrelated asset risk from the tactical asset allocation portfolio and market risk holding fixed the total portfolio volatility. We report the risk decomposition, the portfolio Sharpe ratio, the additional basis points of excess return that are added, and the percentage increase in portfolio excess return.

We can read from Table 12.5 that if there is an uncorrelated asset with a Sharpe ratio of .5, we should optimally put over 80 percent of our risk into that asset and take only 20 percent of our risk in exposure to the market. Even if the Sharpe ratio of the active risk is only .2, we should still take over one-third of our risk there rather than in the market. The last column can be viewed as the increase in efficiency of the overall portfolio. An uncorrelated asset with a Sharpe ratio of .2 adds 27 percent more return to the overall portfolio holding the portfolio's total volatility constant. Uncorrelated active risk with a Sharpe ratio of .5 adds 118 percent more return at the same level of risk.

In order to highlight what is so special about uncorrelated assets, we repeat the exercise with one slight modification. Rather than considering the portfolio long Japan and short the United States and Europe, we examine what happens when we consider a tactical asset allocation portfolio for which the only position is long Japan. First, we find that a position long 5.11 percent in Japan creates 100 basis points of risk. It doesn't make so much sense to think about the implied views of this portfolio because there are no relative returns. The entire issue is the normalization, but following the previous example we could assume a Sharpe ratio of .2 on this trade. This assumption requires an expected excess return of 3.91 percent for the Japanese equity market. This return assumption is below the implied view for Japan of the strategic benchmark, however, so it doesn't make sense to think of this level of excess return as justifying an overweight position. Rather than make an assumption about Sharpe ratios, let's turn to the implied views of the combined portfolio.

We next look at the implied views of the combined portfolio where we overweight the Japanese equity market by 5.11 percent relative to the strategic benchmark. In practice, we might have to sell some other assets to fund this position, but for the purpose of this exercise, let's suppose that we can create the exposure from cash or through the use of derivative markets while holding other positions unchanged. As above, the normalization that we take is to match the deviations of implied views of the combined portfolio versus those of the strategic benchmark to a scaled set of implied views from the deviation portfolio. This exercise leads to an expected excess return of Japanese equity of 3.95 percent, 36 basis points greater than the implied views of the strategic benchmark. This expected excess return implies a Sharpe ratio on the Japanese equity overweight of just over .2.

Notice how the result of this exercise differs from the result of the previous exercise. When we looked at the approximately uncorrelated portfolio consisting of overweight Japan and underweight United States and Europe, the implied Sharpe ratio that justified adding 100 basis points of risk was .008. When we look at the same exercise for a portfolio overweight Japan alone, and no longer uncorrelated, the implied Sharpe ratio is above .2. The bottom line is that the hurdle rate for adding assets that are correlated with the market portfolio is much higher than that for adding uncorrelated assets.

As we did earlier, let's investigate how much overweight we should be to an asset in order to create an optimal portfolio as a function of our assumption of Sharpe ratio. In this context, instead of looking at a Sharpe ratio assumption for an uncorrelated asset, we look at a Sharpe ratio assumption for a correlated asset. Japanese equity has a correlation of .71 with the strategic benchmark portfolio.

Again, we solve for the optimal combination of a deviation portfolio and the strategic benchmark. In this context, we will refer to the risk as timing risk because it is significantly positively correlated with the benchmark portfolio. Again, start with the same assumptions about the benchmark portfolio: that it has expected excess return of 385 basis points and a volatility of 14.8 percent. We will hold the total portfolio volatility constant as we combine timing risk with market risk. As before, we report the risk decomposition, the portfolio Sharpe ratio, the additional basis points of excess return that are added, and the percentage increase in portfolio excess return (see Table 12.6). However, here we add a new column showing the multiple of the 100 basis point timing exposure that has been added. We do this because at smaller Sharpe ratio assumptions the optimal strategy is actually to reduce the exposure to the Japanese market.

The first thing we notice about these results is the strange outcomes for portfolio efficiency for Sharpe ratios below .2. These cases represent opportunities to sell the correlated asset in order to hedge the portfolio. In the first case, where the expected excess return is zero, the optimal portfolio is one that is leveraged long the market portfolio and hedged by being short the correlated, zero-returning asset. The case of a Sharpe ratio of .2 represents the situation in which the correlated asset earns an expected return only slightly above the implied return of the portfolio. In this case, the asset contributes very little value; the portfolio efficiency rises by only 5 percent. Compare this increase with that of the uncorrelated asset which produces an efficiency gain of 27 percent at a Sharpe ratio of .2.

What we have seen in this chapter is that uncorrelated assets that contribute positive return have a significant opportunity to improve portfolio return and return per unit of risk. Correlated assets have a much higher hurdle and need to have significantly higher expected returns in order to add value to portfolios.

These results illuminate the source of the sensitivity seen in asset allocation optimizations. Small changes in expected returns create opportunities to benefit from uncorrelated risks that provide positive excess return. Optimizers seeing such opportunities will allocate significant exposures and risk toward taking advantage of them.

Taken together, these observations suggest a two-step approach to how asset allocations should be determined. Rather than trying to specify expected returns and optimize allocations directly, in step 1 a strategic allocation should simply be made to market capitalization or alternative strategic weights based on long-term, equilibrium expected returns. In step 2 a risk budget should then be utilized to allocate uncorrelated risk to various sources including active risk, uncorrelated assets, and tactical deviations from the strategic asset allocation. The risk budgeting should reflect the assumed Sharpe ratios of these various activities in order to optimize the total expected returns on the uncorrelated risk. Finally, to the extent the tactical deviations from the strategic asset allocation are relative value opportunities and are somewhat uncorrelated with the market, they represent great opportunities to add value and should be sized based on the optimal allocation of the overall budget for uncorrelated risk. The results in Figure 12.1 and Table 12.5 may provide guidance. To the extent that the tactical views are more correlated with the market and therefore represent timing rather than rela-

TABLE 12.5 Optimal Risk Allocations to Tactical (Uncorrelated) Exposures

Sharpe Ratio of the Tactical Deviations	Optimal Basis Points of Tactical Tracking Error	Portfolio Risk Portfolio Risk Decomposition % from Tactical Deviations	Decomposition % Market Risk	Optimal Portfolio Sharpe Ratio	Added Value Basis Points of Excess Return	Percentage Increase
0.008	100	0%	100%	0.26	0	0%
0.1	585	14	86	0.28	28	7
0.2	949	39	61	0.33	102	27
0.3	1,156	59	41	0.40	206	53
0.4	1,272	72	28	0.48	326	85
0.5	1,338	81	19	0.57	456	118
0.6	1,379	86	14	0.66	591	154

TABLE 12.6 Optimal Risk Allocations to Timing (Correlated) Risk

Sharpe Ratio of the Timing Exposure	Multiple of the 100 bps Timing Exposure	Optimal Basis Points of Timing Tracking Error	Portfolio Risk Decomposition % from Timing Deviations	Portfolio Risk Decomposition % Market Risk	Optimal Portfolio Sharpe Ratio	Added Value Basis Points of Excess Return	Percentage Increase
0	−14.7	1,472	0%	100%	0.18	−112	−29%
0.1	−5.9	589	−19	119	0.21	−75	−19
0.2	0.9	89	4	96	0.27	18	5
0.3	4.9	489	28	72	0.35	136	35
0.4	7.3	726	45	55	0.44	267	69
0.5	8.8	877	56	44	0.53	404	105
0.6	9.8	980	63	37	0.63	544	141

tive value exposures, the opportunities are much less, and the results in Table 12.6 may be more instructive.

The preceding discussion assumes that there are no constraints on the ability to generate market or active risk in the portfolio. In practice, market and active risk are generally packaged together in investment products, and the ability to add active risk is complicated by capital constraints, fees, risk management concerns, and other implementation details. Many of the later chapters in this text are designed to help investors address these practical implementation issues.

PART Three

Risk Budgeting

CHAPTER 13

Developing an Optimal Active Risk Budget

Kurt Winkelmann

INTRODUCTION

Previous chapters have discussed the development of a strategic asset allocation, and shown how an equilibrium approach can be used to develop it. The strategic asset allocation can be viewed as the first step in the development of an investment policy. At some point, though, institutional investors generally begin to implement their strategic asset allocations by hiring investment managers.

The process of hiring external investment managers forces investors to focus on formulating investment policies about the active risk in their portfolios. A partial list of issues on which policies should be developed would include:

- The total level of active risk in the portfolio.
- The weight given to active managers versus passive managers.
- The allocation of active risk across various asset classes.
- The allocation of active risk to specific investment managers within each asset class:
  - According to substyles such as growth or value.
  - According to risk levels such as structured or concentrated.
- The frequency of portfolio rebalancing.
- The allocation of active risk to active overlay strategies.

Each of these is an example of investment decisions that deserve the same focus and attention as the strategic asset allocation.

Setting the total level of active risk was discussed in Chapter 12. In particular, that chapter showed that active risk deserves special consideration in portfolio construction, principally because it is uncorrelated with market risk. It is because of the uncorrelated nature of active risk that there is a natural reason for investors to demand more of it. Chapter 12 also showed that although investors have a natural demand for more active risk, they may also be frustrated in their ability to increase the active risk levels in their portfolios.

The focus of this chapter is on the efficient allocation of active risk, conditioned on the investor having selected an active risk level. That is, we are interested in exploring what questions investors should answer in deciding whether an allocation of active risk is consistent with their investment objectives.

Developing policies on the allocation of active risk also has important implications for manager monitoring. An allocation of active risk necessarily depends on assumptions about the active risk levels of individual managers. Thus, the realized risk characteristics of the total portfolio and individual managers should be carefully monitored (see Chapter 15 for a more extensive discussion of manager monitoring). By comparing *ex post* behavior with *ex ante* assumptions, investors can identify and correct problems, and gain a better understanding of the impact of each investment decision and policy.

In a world without constraints, the ingredients that investors might use to develop policies on active risk taking are reasonably straightforward. In point of fact, it is easy to imagine a world where investors would start with a set of assumptions about the risk premiums for each asset class and the skill level for individual managers. They would then measure the levels of active risk for individual managers and across asset classes. Finally, they would optimize, thereby finding the allocations of active risk to each individual manager and across asset classes.

There are, however, three drawbacks with this approach. First, the optimal allocations are not likely to be credible, as they are driven by assumptions about expected active returns and, as shown in Chapter 12, are likely to be very sensitive to small changes in those assumptions. Second, by applying the approach outlined earlier, investors would be ignoring any notion of equilibrium, and would consequently be avoiding a careful analysis of the sources of active returns. Third, in practice there are many practical constraints and costs that would be difficult to include in an optimization: The presence of transaction costs means that in actual fact most investors make marginal changes to their portfolios rather than wholesale reoptimizations.

Rather than trying to apply traditional portfolio optimization to this complex problem, we suggest an alternative approach. Start with an existing risk allocation. Recognize the marginal condition required for the allocation to be optimal—that the expected excess return contributed by each allocation should be proportional to its contribution to portfolio risk.

The contributions to portfolio risk can be measured; thus the portfolio implies a set of expected excess returns for each allocation of active and market risk. As in Chapter 12, we pin down the level of the expected returns by setting the market risk premium (discussed in Chapter 5) equal to an equilibrium value. Opportunities to improve the active risk allocation will be identified as differences between the implied views and the investor's actual views about skill levels of managers and risk premiums for underlying asset classes.

There are a variety of ways to express views about skill levels, but we like the approach followed in the Black-Litterman model described in Chapter 7. The implied views in the portfolio can be compared to the expected excess returns created by the Black-Litterman model, which are in turn driven by specific sets of views about the skills of active managers. An important part of the model is that it explicitly forces investors to consider equilibrium conditions and correlations in thinking about expected returns.

The Black-Litterman model allows a decomposition of views into states about relative as well as absolute expected excess returns, as well as about relative degrees of confidence. This decomposition is important to investors, as it allows them to focus on inputs that may be more intuitive, rather than only about specific point estimates of active returns. Understanding the active risk budget in this way allows investors to identify the asset classes where they are more (or less) confident in the ability of active managers to add value (relative to the current allocations). That information is important to the development of investment policy, as it can be used to improve the risk/return profile of the portfolio.

OPTIMALITY AND RISK BUDGETING

Chapter 12 discussed the relationship between expected returns and optimal portfolio weights. An important condition for portfolio optimality was described in that chapter. In particular, it was shown that portfolio weights are optimal when the ratio of the expected excess return to the marginal contribution to risk is the same for all assets.

Before proceeding, let's make the following distinctions: a *risk budget* is simply a particular allocation of portfolio risk. An *optimal risk budget* is simply the allocation of risk such that the first order conditions for portfolio optimization are satisfied. The *risk budgeting process* is the process of finding an optimal risk budget. These terms apply to both the process of finding an optimal allocation of risk in the strategic asset allocation as well as the active risk budget. The focus of this chapter is on the application to the active risk budget. Of course, understanding the active risk budgeting process requires a further understanding of the sources of risk and return to active managers. This topic is addressed in the next section.

RISK BUDGETING AND ACTIVE RISK

To apply risk budgeting to active managers, we need first to understand their sources of risk and return. As discussed in Chapter 4, the Capital Asset Pricing Model suggests that the return on any security can be described in terms of its exposure to the market portfolio, measured through the beta.

We can easily apply the same basic insight to individual portfolio managers; that is, each individual manager's performance should depend on exposure to the market, or beta. In addition, a manager's performance will depend on other investment decisions that are independent of the market. These decisions will also have a distribution, presumably with an expected value that is positive.

This description of a manager's performance can be written algebraically as shown in equation (13.1):

$$R_i - r_f = \alpha_i + \beta_i(R_I - r_f) + \varepsilon_i \tag{13.1}$$

In equation (13.1), the ith manager's return versus a risk-free rate (or excess return) is written as $(R_i - r_f)$. As described earlier, the manager's excess return depends on two components. The first is the impact of market movements. Market movements can be measured by an index, whose return will be denoted R_I. The impact of market movements on a specific manager's returns is measured by the product of the excess return on the index ($R_I - r_f$) and the manager's exposure to the index (β_i).

The second component of a manager's excess return is idiosyncratic to the manager, and is meant to capture the impact of the investment strategies that the manager is following to add value. The long-run expected value of the manager's strategies is measured by the term α_i, while the randomness in the manager's strategies is captured by the term ε_i, or the *residual return*. The randomness in the manager's strategies is uncorrelated with market returns; any correlation would be incorporated in the manager's beta.

By squaring both sides of equation (13.1), taking the expected value and taking the square root, we arrive at a simple expression that describes the risk of any particular manager, shown in equation (13.2). In the equation, the volatility of excess returns for any particular manager depends on the volatility of the returns on the index, the manager's exposure to the index, and the volatility of the manager's residual return. As any of these increases, the manager's risk also increases.

$$\sigma_i = \sqrt{\left(\beta_i^2 \sigma_I^2 + \sigma_{\varepsilon i}^2\right)} \tag{13.2}$$

Now, let's subtract the excess return on the benchmark from each side of equation (13.1) to produce the excess return of the manager relative to the benchmark, or the manager's *active return*. Using equation (13.1), we can see that the manager's active return depends on the alpha, the exposure to the market (or beta), and the residual. This relationship is shown in equation (13.3):

$$R_i - R_I = \alpha_i + (\beta_i - 1)(R_I - r_f) + \varepsilon_i \tag{13.3}$$

Squaring both sides of equation (13.1), taking the expected value and taking the square root, we arrive at a description of the manager's risk relative to the benchmark. This quantity is the manager's *tracking error*, and is shown in equation (13.4):

$$TE_i = \sqrt{\left[(1-\beta_i)^2 \sigma_I^2 + \sigma_{\varepsilon i}^2\right]} \tag{13.4}$$

As is evident from equation (13.4), the manager's tracking error, or *active risk*, increases when the beta deviates from 1.0, increases when the volatility of the index increases (if β_i does not equal 1.0), and increases when the residual risk increases. It is also evident from equation (13.4) that there are two risk characteristics that managers can control, and one that they cannot. Specifically, managers can control their market exposure (β_i) and the amount of residual risk (ε_i) they take. They cannot, however, control the level of market volatility (σ_I). Thus, managers who want to reduce the impact of market volatility on portfolio risk should seek to keep β_i close to 1.0.

Clearly, we can describe portfolio level returns by simply multiplying the exposure of each manager times the description of their returns. That is, if X_{ij} represents the portfolio weight allocated to manager i in asset class j, and R_{ij} denotes the return of manager i in asset class j, then the total portfolio return, R_p, is simply:

$$R_p = \Sigma_i \Sigma_j X_{ij} R_{ij} \tag{13.5}$$

By subtracting the risk-free rate and substituting equation (13.1) for each manager, we get:

$$R_p - r_f = \Sigma_i \Sigma_j X_{ij} \left[\alpha_{ij} + \beta_{ij} \left(R_I^j - r_f \right) + \varepsilon_{ij} \right] \tag{13.6}$$

Now, consider the return to a portfolio of managers within an asset class j, denoted R_j. The total portfolio weight in asset class j, denoted X_j, is simply $X_j = \Sigma_j X_{ij}$. The return of the portfolio of managers within asset class j is given as:

$$\begin{aligned} R_j &= \Sigma_i X_{ij} R_{ij} \\ &= \Sigma_i X_{ij} \left[\alpha_{ij} + \beta_{ij} \left(R_I^j - r_f \right) + \varepsilon_{ij} \right] \\ &= \Sigma_i X_{ij} \alpha_{ij} + \Sigma_i X_{ij} \beta_{ij} \left(R_I^j - r_f \right) + \Sigma_i X_{ij} \varepsilon_{ij} \\ &= X_j \alpha_j + X_j \beta_j \left(R_I^j - r_f \right) + X_j \varepsilon_j \end{aligned} \tag{13.7}$$

In equation (13.7), α_j, β_j, and ε_j represent the average alpha, beta, and error term respectively of all of the managers in asset class j, and R_I^j represents the return on the index for the jth asset class.

Now let's look at the strategic benchmark. In this case, let X_j^I represent the long-term allocation to the jth asset class, whose return is represented as R_I^j. With this notation, the excess return of the strategic benchmark relative to cash is given by:

$$R_B - r_f = \Sigma_j X_j^I R_I^j - r_f \tag{13.8}$$

By subtracting equation (13.8) from equation (13.6), we arrive at an easy description of the portfolio return relative to the strategic benchmark. This difference is shown in equation (13.9):

$$\begin{aligned} R_p - R_B &= \Sigma_i \Sigma_j X_{ij} \left[\alpha_{ij} + \beta_{ij} \left(R_I^j - r_f \right) + \varepsilon_{ij} \right] - \Sigma_j X_j^I \left(R_j^I - r_f \right) \\ &= \Sigma_i \Sigma_j X_{ij} \alpha_{ij} + \Sigma_i \Sigma_j X_{ij} \varepsilon_{ij} + \Sigma_i \Sigma_j X_{ij} \beta_{ij} \left(R_I^j - r_f \right) - \Sigma_j X_j^I \left(R_j^I - r_f \right) \\ &= \Sigma_i \Sigma_j X_{ij} \alpha_{ij} + \Sigma_i \Sigma_j X_{ij} \varepsilon_{ij} + \Sigma_j \left[X_j \beta_j \left(R_j^I - r_f \right) - X_j^I \left(R_j^I - r_f \right) \right] \\ &= \Sigma_i \Sigma_j X_{ij} \alpha_{ij} + \Sigma_i \Sigma_j X_{ij} \varepsilon_{ij} + \Sigma_j \left[\left(X_j \beta_j - X_j^I \right) \left(R_j^I - r_f \right) \right] \\ &= \Sigma_i \Sigma_j X_{ij} \alpha_{ij} + \Sigma_i \Sigma_j X_{ij} \varepsilon_{ij} + \Sigma_j \left[X_j \left(\beta_j - 1 \right) - \left(X_j - X_j^I \right) \left(R_j^I - r_f \right) \right] \\ &= \Sigma_i \Sigma_j X_{ij} \alpha_{ij} + \Sigma_i \Sigma_j X_{ij} \varepsilon_{ij} + \Sigma_j X_j \left(\beta_j - 1 \right) \left(R_j^I - r_f \right) \\ &\quad + \Sigma_j \left(X_j - X_j^I \right) \left(R_j^I - r_f \right) \end{aligned} \tag{13.9}$$

We can see from equation (13.9) that the excess return on the portfolio relative to the strategic benchmark has four pieces. The first ($\Sigma_i \Sigma_j X_{ij} \alpha_{ij}$) is the weighted average of each manager's expected alpha, while the second ($\Sigma_i \Sigma_j X_{ij} \varepsilon_{ij}$) is the random element of each manager's return generating process. The third $[\Sigma_j X_j(\beta_j - 1)(R_j^I - r_f)]$ reflects the directional bias (as measured by the beta) of each portfolio of managers in each asset class. The final component $[\Sigma_j(X_j - X_j^I)(R_j^I - r_f)]$ reflects the asset allocation mismatch of the portfolio versus its strategic benchmark.

Substitution of equation (13.7) into equation (13.9) means that we can describe the differences between the portfolio and benchmark returns in terms of the average alpha, beta, and residual at the asset class level. This distinction is important, because it influences the types of questions that we want to pose. More specifically, we are interested in answering questions about the sources of alpha at the asset class level, and interested in the relative ability of managers within each asset class to exploit those sources. Because the questions are different, it makes sense to differentiate between risk budgeting exercises. The first is an active risk budgeting exercise across asset classes, while the second is a risk budgeting exercise across managers within an asset class.

Clearly we can use equation (13.8) to find the *ex ante* total fund active risk.[1] The *ex ante* active risk will then reflect five principal decisions: (1) the overall level of active risk in the total portfolio; (2) the allocation of residual risk across asset classes, that is, the allocation of total residual risk $\Sigma_i\Sigma_j X_{ij}\varepsilon_{ij}$ across the j asset classes (e.g., how much active risk is allocated to a portfolio of U.S. large cap managers versus a portfolio of U.S. small cap managers); (3) the allocation of residual risk within each asset class to individual managers, that is, the allocation of $\Sigma_i\Sigma_j X_{ij}\varepsilon_i$ across the I managers within an asset class; (4) the directional bias of each asset class, that is, the deviation of the average beta from one in $\Sigma_j X_j[(\beta_j - 1)(R_j^I - r_f)]$; and (5) the asset allocation mismatch, that is, the deviation of the portfolio weights from the benchmark allocations in $\Sigma_j(X_j - X_j^I)(R_j^I - r_f)$. Each of these is clearly a risk budgeting decision. For our purposes, though, we will focus on those decisions that relate to the allocation of residual risk, both across asset classes and to managers within an asset class.

What process do we use to decide how much of the residual risk should be allocated to each manager, or to each asset class? Active risk budgeting provides a framework for answering these questions. Ideally, an active risk budgeting process would help us reconcile historical performance characteristics for asset classes and managers with notions of capital market equilibrium. To do this, though, we need to understand the historical risk and return characteristics of active managers in the principal asset classes. This topic is addressed in the next section.

DATA ANALYSIS

There are several statistics about the historical performance of active managers that are of interest. Some important statistics are:

- The median alpha for each asset class.
- The median tracking error for each asset class.

[1]This would be done by simply subtracting from equation (13.7) its expected value, squaring the difference, taking the expected value, and then taking the square root.

TABLE 13.1 Historical Active Performance

	Gross Alpha	Tracking Error (bps)			Information Ratio		
		1 Mgr	2 Mgr	4 Mgr	1 Mgr	2 Mgr	4 Mgr
Enhanced Index	75	150	145	120	0.59	0.61	0.66
U.S. Large Cap Growth	230	720	583	510	0.36	0.45	0.54
U.S. Large Cap Value	50	580	460	410	0.12	0.17	0.21
U.S. Small Cap Growth	720	1,090	880	775	0.69	0.88	1.08
U.S. Small Cap Value	275	880	710	640	0.33	0.41	0.49
International Equity—EAFE	335	600	460	415	0.57	0.73	0.93
Emerging Markets Equity	340	715	610	545	0.39	0.53	0.64
Core+ Fixed Income	25	90	75	65	0.35	0.39	0.42
High Yield	255	270	225	200	0.92	1.08	1.24

- The median correlation of excess returns for each asset class.
- The median correlation of excess returns across asset classes.

Because many investors hold portfolios of managers within each asset class rather than individual managers, we would like these statistics at the portfolio level as well as the individual manager level.

Table 13.1 summarizes the results of such an analysis. The table shows the median gross (unadjusted for fees) alpha, median tracking error, and median information ratio for randomly selected portfolios of managers. The tracking error figure shown in the table is adjusted for market directionality; in other words, it is the residual volatility. The raw performance data on monthly composite returns[2] were taken from the Nelsons Database. Our study covered the period October 1992 through September 2002.

The figures in the table show interesting historical performance patterns. For example, the historical information ratios for the median manager were substantially higher in high yield than in Core+ fixed income.[3] For another example, the historical information ratio for EAFE is larger than either of the traditional active U.S. large cap styles (growth and value). Finally, we can see that the information ratios increase as we increase the number of managers, suggesting that historically, increasing the number of managers provided diversification benefits.[4]

Table 13.2 explores the pattern of correlation in somewhat more detail. The table shows the average correlation both within an asset class and across asset

[2]A manager's composite return represents the performance of a representative institutional separate account.

[3]Core+ fixed income managers operate relatively low tracking error portfolios that are managed against an investment grade bond index such as the Lehman Aggregate or Salomon Smith Barney Broad Investment Grade Index.

[4]Fee breaks and transaction costs put a practical limit on the number of managers in any asset class.

TABLE 13.2 Historical Correlation of Active Returns: Two-Manager Portfolios

	US LC-G	US LC-V	US SC-G	US SC-V	IE-EAFE	EME	Core+	HY
U.S. Large Cap Growth	0.33	−0.09	0.07	−0.04	0.06	0.00	0.11	0.03
U.S. Large Cap Value	−0.09	0.28	0.01	0.07	0.05	0.08	0.07	0.05
U.S. Small Cap Growth	0.07	0.01	0.30	0.10	−0.01	0.08	0.00	0.08
U.S. Small Cap Value	−0.04	0.07	0.10	0.40	−0.02	0.08	0.06	0.03
International Equity—EAFE	0.06	0.05	−0.01	−0.02	0.38	0.15	0.15	0.05
Emerging Markets Equity	0.00	0.08	0.08	0.08	0.15	0.41	0.06	0.06
Core+ Fixed Income	0.11	0.07	0.00	0.06	0.15	0.06	0.40	0.12
High Yield	0.03	0.05	0.08	0.03	0.05	0.06	0.12	0.28

classes for portfolios of two managers, again after adjusting for market directionality. The numbers on the main diagonal in the table show the average correlation within an asset class, while the off-diagonal figures are the correlation of excess returns across asset classes. Since we have adjusted for the beta impact, these correlations are the correlation of residual returns.

What is interesting about the figures in Table 13.2 is that, on balance, the correlation of excess returns appears to be close to zero across asset classes, but nonzero within an asset class. For example, the average correlation of excess returns of two U.S. large cap growth managers was .33, while the correlation of a portfolio of two U.S. large cap value managers with a portfolio of two Core+ fixed income managers was around .07.

Previous chapters (e.g., Chapters 7, 9, and 12) have discussed the difficulties involved in using optimizers to find portfolio weights. The general issues associated with optimizers are also relevant when we consider allocations of active risk, and would lead us away from simply taking the historical alpha and tracking error figures from Table 13.1 and optimizing allocations. In particular, we need to be careful about the limitations of the data analysis summarized in Table 13.1, and the inconsistency of positive alphas with capital market theory.

Looking first at the limitations of data analysis, three observations can be made. First, the data in Nelsons Database are not free from survivorship bias. Although attempts can be (and have been) made to correct for survivorship bias, nonetheless survivorship bias persists principally because the database is a self-reporting database: Managers are in the database because they choose to report. Thus, we could be ignoring the poor returns of managers who simply choose not to report.

Second, the historical median performance figures suffer from the same issue that historical average asset returns do (as discussed in Chapter 9). That is, historical averages (and medians) are notoriously poor predictors of future performance, simply because they are time period dependent. This issue is compounded when we look at historical performance across a short time period for a large number of managers. In fact, we do not have sufficient data to tell whether a manager's historical performance is meaningfully different from zero.

Third, even if the median performance figures were statistically meaningful, the tables are silent about the persistence of returns. Unfortunately, the academic literature is not comforting on this topic. Indeed, the empirical research seems to suggest that there is very limited evidence of persistence in active returns. (See Brown and Harlow 2001 and Carhart 1997).

Now let's look at consistency with capital market theory. Capital asset pricing theory quite clearly predicts that in equilibrium the expected alpha is zero, both in the aggregate and for any specific manager. Thus, an important part of formulating a policy about active risk is reconciling observed alphas with equilibrium. Investors avoid these issues when they use historical alphas (such as Table 13.1) in an optimizer. Approaching investment policy from a risk budgeting perspective, however, forces us to confront these issues.

We believe that data analyses such as Tables 13.1 and 13.2 are an important component of the active risk budgeting process. The data on the correlation of active returns in Table 13.2 are important because they help us estimate total residual volatility and the risk budget. Data such as shown in Table 13.1 provide an established source of a "view" about active returns. The issue that investors must confront is how much weight to give to these data, or any other source of a view, relative to equilibrium. The next two sections will show how investors can approach the allocation of active risk from a risk budgeting perspective.

IMPLIED RETURNS

Rather than start with a set of expected returns and optimize, our preferred approach is to begin with an existing portfolio and ask what changes could bring about an efficiency improvement. To do this, we exploit the portfolio optimality conditions discussed in Chapter 3. That is, we know that for a given set of portfolio weights, there is a set of expected return assumptions for which the weights are optimal. We can call this set of expected returns the *implied returns*.[5] Clearly, if the implied returns are found by assuming that the portfolio weights are optimal, then the associated risk budget is also optimal. Thus, there is a very clear connection between the implied returns and the risk budget.

Implied returns analysis can be easily applied to the active portfolio by exploiting equation (13.6). What we are looking for now are the implied returns for both the asset classes and the active risks for each asset class j, implied by a portfolio of managers. To apply the analysis of Chapter 12, we simply expand the structure of the covariance matrix to include active risk, and use equation (13.6) to define the active exposures. To complete the picture, we need to specify the long-term expected return on an anchor asset class (i.e., calibrate the risk aversion parameter).

[5]The implied returns are given by $R = \lambda \Sigma x$.

TABLE 13.3 Portfolio Allocations and Risk Characteristics

	Portfolio Weight	Asset Class Volatility	Active Allocation	Residual Risk (bps)
U.S. Large Cap Equity	39.6%	17.2%	39.6%	250
U.S. Small Cap Equity	4.4	20.7	4.4	560
International Equity	19.8	16.1	19.8	460
Emerging Markets Equity	2.2	25.1	2.2	610
Core+ Fixed Income	30.0	4.5	30.0	70
High Yield	4.0	8.1	4.0	230
Overlay			10.0	250

Clearly, the higher we set the long-term return on the anchor asset class, the higher the implied returns for all other asset classes, including the implied alphas. Our preferred method is to calibrate the implied returns to our assumption about the long-term U.S. equity premium. We prefer calibrating the implied returns to a long-term equity premium assumption because it provides a specific link to equilibrium.

For example, suppose we calibrate the U.S. equity premium to 350 basis points. The implied return on any other asset class (including active risk) would be driven by the U.S. equity return assumption of 350 basis points and its covariance with total portfolio returns.

To see this, let's work through a simple example. Table 13.3 shows the allocations in a hypothetical portfolio, as well as each asset's volatility. Six asset classes have been chosen: U.S. Large Cap, U.S. Small Cap, International Equity, Emerging Markets Equity, Investment Grade Fixed Income, and High Yield. The second column of the table shows the portfolio holdings, and the third column shows the asset class volatility. Active allocations are shown in the table's fourth column, while the final column shows the active risk levels, as measured by the residual risk, for each asset class. The residual risk figures are the same as those for a two-manager portfolio in Table 13.1, and thus carry with them the assumption of market neutrality (i.e., the average beta equals one). We have also added a row for another active strategy called "Overlay."[6] Thus, we have 13 possible sources of risk, or risk exposures.

Table 13.4 shows the overall risk characteristics for the portfolio. As the table illustrates, the total portfolio tracking error is around 140 basis points. In the aggregate, active risk is contributing around 1.6 percent of the total portfolio volatility of 11.1 percent.

We can focus on the attribution of active risk in somewhat more detail. Table 13.5 shows the allocation of the 140 basis points of active risk across the seven active strategies, or the active risk budget. As we can see, there are two principal sources of active risk in the portfolio: Around 50 percent of the active risk in this

[6]By design, returns on active overlay strategies are uncorrelated with market risk. An additional benefit of the strategy is that it requires very small commitments of capital.

TABLE 13.4 Portfolio Risk Characteristics

	Risk Level	Contribution to Risk
Asset class exposures	11.0%	98.4%
Active exposures	1.4	1.6
Total portfolio	11.1	100.0

TABLE 13.5 Active Risk Budget

	Contribution to Active Risk
U.S. Large Cap Equity	50.7%
U.S. Small Cap Equity	2.9
International Equity	39.9
Emerging Markets Equity	0.9
Core+ Fixed Income	2.2
High Yield	0.4
Overlay	3.0

portfolio is being budgeted to active U.S. Large Cap managers, and just under 40 percent is allocated to International Equity managers. What are the portfolio allocations and the risk budget implying about returns?

The implied returns associated with this portfolio under three assumptions about the U.S. equity premium are shown in Table 13.6. As we can see, increasing the U.S. equity premium increases the implied returns for both asset classes and the implied alphas associated with active risk taking in each asset class. It is important to remember that because we have assumed market neutrality, each of the alphas represents the implied return from taking residual risk. For discussion, let's focus on the implied returns associated with an implied U.S. equity premium of 350 basis points.

A natural interpretation of the figures is as "hurdle rates." That is, we can view the alphas (or information ratios) as the minimum acceptable performance level associated with each active management in each asset class. Clearly, as we increase the U.S. equity premium assumption, we will also increase the implied hurdle rates for active management.

It is interesting to compare the implied alphas from this portfolio with the historical alphas from Table 13.1. The reason we want to make this comparison is because we would like to use the historical alphas as a view about the expected alpha for each asset class. Since the historical alphas in Table 13.1 are gross, we must first correct for fees. It is also worthwhile applying a simple correction for survivorship bias.

Survivorship bias is important, because it will bias upward the historical averages. For example, suppose that a fraction of the worst-performing managers is dropped every year. The time series of returns that we are left with will include only

TABLE 13.6 Implied Returns (in Basis Points)

	U.S. Equity Premium Assumption		
Asset Class	**250**	**350**	**450**
U.S. Large Cap Equity	250	350	450
U.S. Small Cap Equity	260	365	465
International Equity	215	300	385
Emerging Markets Equity	270	380	485
Core+ Fixed Income	8	12	15
High Yield	72	100	130
Active Allocations			
U.S. Large Cap Equity	4	6	7
U.S. Small Cap Equity	4	6	7
International Equity	7	10	13
Emerging Markets Equity	3	5	6
Core+ Fixed Income	1	1	1
High Yield	1	2	2
Overlay	2	3	3

the better-performing managers. In computing the sample average performance, we should include all managers. However, since we have omitted the poorest-performing managers, the sample average that we compute will exceed the average that we should compute.

The impact of survivorship bias could vary by asset class. For illustrative purposes, we'll apply a very simple adjustment for survivorship bias. In particular, we'll assume that the impact of survivorship bias is to overstate the sample average by 5.25 percent. Consequently, we'll scale each net-of-fee alpha by a constant fraction, or 95 percent.

Table 13.7 shows an example of these types of adjustments, under hypothetical assumptions about fee levels and the impact of survivorship bias.

After adjusting the historical alphas for fees and survivorship bias, we can compare them with the alphas implied by the portfolio weights. These figures are

TABLE 13.7 Adjusted Historical Alphas

	Historical Alpha (bps)	Historical IR	Fees (bps)	Adjusted Alpha (bps)	Adjusted IR
U.S. Large Cap Equity	120	0.47	40	76	0.30
U.S. Small Cap Equity	465	0.83	60	385	0.71
International Equity	335	0.73	50	271	0.58
Emerging Markets Equity	340	0.53	60	266	0.44
Core+ Fixed Income	25	0.39	17	5	0.06
High Yield	255	1.08	50	195	0.86
Overlay	200	0.80	50	143	0.57

shown in Table 13.8. As is quite evident from Table 13.8, the implied alphas are substantially lower than their historical counterparts, even after adjustments.

A resolution to the large discrepancy between the implied historical alphas is to simply increase the assumed equity premium until the differences are minimal. The drawback to this approach is that we will have to assume implausible levels of the equity premium in order to get the implied alphas close to the historical alphas. For example, to get the implied alphas in our example to be consistent with the historical alphas, we need to assume an equity premium in excess of 50 percent, which is clearly significantly out of the range of plausible alternatives. Since our objective is to analyze active risk in the context of equilibrium, this approach hardly seems like a viable option.

Some analysts have concluded that the real issue is not the level of the equity premium, but rather the structure of investor preferences (see, for instance, Grinold and Kahn, 1999). They have proposed that investor preferences can be segmented such that a lower risk premium is assigned to market risk (for example, in the form of the strategic asset allocation) than to active risk.

It is easy to see the flaws in this approach. Suppose that an investor can add exposure to another asset class, with the same volatility and expected return assumptions as the active risk component, and uncorrelated with market risk. Suppose that the Sharpe ratio on market risk is .2, and that the information ratio on the active component is .5. Clearly, if the new asset class has the same Sharpe ratio as the information ratio on the active component, and the expected returns are expected to persist, then the allocation to the new asset class will be significant, and investor utility will increase.

Rather than account for the difference between implied and historical alphas by changing investor preferences, we prefer to reverse the problem and ask what observed investor behavior is actually telling us. The key issue to confront relates to the assumption that the expected active return is anticipated to persist. We know that in equilibrium there is a fundamental difference between active returns and asset class returns: Asset classes have positive returns, while active risk (in the form of purely uncorrelated risk) does not. This is the issue that must be considered in portfolio construction and investment policy design. In the next two sections, we'll exploit the insights of the Black-Litterman model and outline a framework that can be used to incorporate an assumption about the equilibrium properties of active

TABLE 13.8 Implied versus Adjusted Historical Alphas and Information Ratios

	Implied Alpha (bps)	Implied IR	Adjusted Alpha (bps)	Adjusted IR
U.S. Large Cap Equity	6	0.02	76	0.30
U.S. Small Cap Equity	6	0.02	385	0.71
International Equity	10	0.01	271	0.58
Emerging Markets Equity	5	0.02	266	0.44
Core+ Fixed Income	1	0.02	5	0.06
High Yield	2	0.01	195	0.86
Overlay	3	0.01	143	0.57

risk. In particular, this framework will help us begin to understand the differences shown in Table 13.8.

ACTIVE RISK AND BLACK-LITTERMAN

Chapter 7 introduced the Black-Litterman model. This model provides a very elegant framework for combining equilibrium returns with investor-specific views about asset class returns. In particular, the Black-Litterman model tells us that for a given set of asset classes, the vector of expected returns depends on four factors: The first is the vector of equilibrium returns; the second is the vector of investor-specific views; the third is the weight ($1/\tau$) the investor places on equilibrium; and the fourth is the confidence level that the investor places on each view.[7]

Equation (13.10) shows the Black-Litterman expected returns for active risk, under the assumption that the portfolio is market-neutral and has no asset allocation deviations. In the Black-Litterman framework, and under these assumptions, we can consider the expected active returns separately from the expected asset class returns because the two are uncorrelated.

$$ER_A = \left[\left(\tau\Sigma_A\right)^{-1} + P'\Omega_A^{-1}P\right]^{-1}\left[\left(\tau\Sigma_A\right)^{-1}\Pi_A + P'\Omega_A^{-1}Q_A\right] \tag{13.10}$$

In equation (13.10), Σ_A is the covariance matrix of active returns, Ω_A is the (diagonal) matrix of confidence levels on active returns, Π_A is the vector of equilibrium active returns, and Q_A is the vector of views about active returns.

Equation (13.10) can be simplified further. Suppose that we have a separate view on each source of active returns. In this case, P is an identity matrix, so the dimensions of Σ_A and Ω_A are the same. We also know that in equilibrium, active returns are zero. Consequently, every element of Π_A is zero. Thus, we have:

$$ER_A = \left[\left(\tau\Sigma_A\right)^{-1} + \Omega_A^{-1}\right]^{-1}\left(\Omega_A^{-1}Q_A\right) \tag{13.11}$$

Equation (13.11) relates expected active returns to views about active returns, equilibrium returns (which are assumed to be zero), the weight placed on equilibrium, and the confidence expressed in any particular view. Notice, though, that equation (13.11) can be worked in reverse: That is, if we are given a set of views

[7]Suppose that we have N asset classes. Let ER be the $N \times 1$ vector of expected returns, let Π be the $N \times 1$ vector of equilibrium returns, and let Q be an $M \times 1$ vector of views. We'll denote by Σ the $N \times N$ covariance matrix of asset returns. Views will be related to expected returns by the $N \times M$ matrix P, with each row corresponding to a view. Confidences will be reflected with the diagonal matrix Ω, and τ will represent the weight on views. In this model, the investor specifies Q, P, Ω and τ. The Black-Litterman model relates ER to Π and Q as follows:

$$ER = [(\tau\Sigma)^{-1} + P'\Omega^{-1}P]^{-1}[(\tau\Sigma)^{-1}\Pi + P'\Omega^{-1}Q]$$

and a set of expected returns, then we can find the confidence assigned to any particular view. Doing this, we have:

$$\left[\left(\tau\Sigma_A\right)^{-1} + \Omega_A^{-1}\right]ER_A = \left[\Omega_A^{-1}Q_A\right] \tag{13.12}$$

which simplifies to:

$$\left(\tau\Sigma_A\right)^{-1} ER_A = \Omega_A^{-1}\left(Q_A - ER_A\right) \tag{13.13}$$

Denote the *i*th element of the left-hand side of (13.13) as $er\_\sigma_i^A$. Since Ω_A is diagonal, we know that:

$$er\_\sigma_i^A = \frac{q_i - er_i^A}{o_{ii}} \tag{13.14}$$

where q_i is the *i*th element of Q_A, er_i^A is the *i*th element of ER_A, and o_{ii} is the *ii*th element of Ω_A. Thus, we have a very simple way to "back out" the confidence levels implied by any set of expected returns and a particular set of views. The next section gives an example of how this insight can be applied to a portfolio, and relates it to the active risk budget.

VIEWS, IMPLIED CONFIDENCE LEVELS, AND INVESTMENT POLICY

How can we apply the insights outlined in the preceding section to portfolio design? The key is to work backwards from a set of expected returns implied by a portfolio to find a set of confidences implied by a set of views. To be more specific, we can work backwards from a set of portfolio weights, and the associated risk budget, to find the implied returns. These implied returns are then treated as the expected returns. For a given set of views, we can then work backwards again to find the implied confidence levels. Thus, we have a clear link between the confidence levels and the risk budget, conditioned on a set of views.

What complicates our analysis on the one hand, but opens up opportunities for additional insight into the investment process on the other hand, is that the implied confidence levels will depend on the initial set of views. The following example illustrates this point.

Suppose that we have two sets of views on alphas. The first is a very simple view that the net information ratio is constant across active strategies. The second source of views is the adjusted alphas (and information ratios) shown in Table 13.8. We might choose to use a table such as 13.8 because the data are readily available and well researched, and are widely shared across institutional investors.

By applying equation (13.14) to both sets of views, we can find the implied confidence level for every source of active risk, and relate these to the active risk budget. These confidence levels are shown in Table 13.9, normalized to the confidence of

TABLE 13.9 Normalized Active Confidence Levels and Active Risk Budget

	Confidence Relative to U.S. Large Cap		Active
	Historical IR	Equal Net IR	Risk Budget
U.S. Large Cap Equity	1.00	1.00	50.7
U.S. Small Cap Equity	0.10	0.23	2.9
International Equity	0.40	0.88	39.9
Emerging Markets Equity	0.10	0.13	0.9
Core+ Fixed Income	1.25	0.20	2.2
High Yield	0.03	0.09	0.4
Overlay	0.12	0.24	3.0

U.S. Large Cap. For reference, the normalized confidence levels are contrasted in Table 13.9 with the active risk budget.

What is striking about Table 13.9 is the impact of switching the set of views. When we assume that the net information ratio is constant, then there is a very close qualitative ordering between the risk budget and the relative confidence levels. This ordering breaks down when we use the historical information ratios.

For a simple example, let's look at Core+ Fixed Income. The allocation to Core+ Fixed Income is only 2.2 percent of the active risk budget. When we assume that the net information ratio is the same across all active strategies, the active risk budget implies that we are 25 percent more confident in our view on U.S. Large Cap than in our view on Core+ Fixed Income.

Alternatively, when we use the adjusted historical information ratios, the relationship between the two sources of active risk is reversed. In fact, the allocation to Core+ Fixed Income is now implying a confidence level that is 25 percent larger than that of U.S. Large Cap. Given that we believe that historical averages are poor predictors of future returns, we might be inclined to use an assumption of a constant net information ratio as a starting view, and then adjust this view depending on the policy question.

How can our analysis be applied to investment policy choices, and what do those choices imply about how we think about views and confidence levels? There are three distinct investment policy decisions that investors must make. Each of these is a risk budgeting choice. The first choice is the split between asset class risk and active risk. This is a decision about the efficient allocation of total portfolio risk between active and asset class risk. Once an active risk level has been selected, the second choice is the efficient allocation of active risk across asset classes. The final choice is the efficient allocation of risk to individual managers within an asset class.

Let's look first at the implications of changing the split between asset class risk and active risk. An easy way to do this in the context of our example is to assume that the asset allocation is fixed at the allocations of Table 13.3 and scale up each asset class's active risk level. Doing so will increase the total tracking error, increase the total portfolio risk, and increase the contribution of active risk to the total risk budget. Table 13.10 shows the results of this analysis for our example.

The table also shows the implied returns for each level of active risk. As the fig-

TABLE 13.10 Impact of Increasing Active Risk

Scaling Factor	Total Tracking Error (bps)	Total Portfolio Volatility	Contribution of Active Risk	Implied Alpha (bps)	Implied IR
0.5	70	11.0	0.4%	1	0.01
1	140	11.1	1.6	4	0.03
2	280	11.3	6.2	15	0.05
5	700	13.0	29.1	95	0.14
10	1,400	17.8	62.2	380	0.27

ures in the table indicate, scaling up the level of active risk increases the associated implied return. In fact, at roughly 1,400 basis points of tracking error, the implied information ratio for the active portfolio exceeds the Sharpe ratio for the underlying asset classes.[8]

Of course, investors cannot simply scale up the active risk in each asset class linearly. In active strategies such as U.S. Large Cap, constraints such as the no net short constraint become binding at higher risk levels. By contrast, strategies such as active overlay are typically not subject to the same constraint. The implication is that at higher risk levels, we should start to anticipate some deterioration in the information ratio for more constrained strategies. Consequently, at higher risk levels we would want to analyze confidence levels on the basis of differences in the net information ratio.[9]

In addition to the overall level of active risk, investors are also interested in the efficient allocation of active risk (i.e., an optimal active risk budget). To see the impact on the risk budget and associated implied confidence levels, let's work through the following example.

Suppose that we triple the allocation of active risk to the Overlay strategies, and shift 10 percent of the portfolio from active U.S. Large Cap to U.S. Small Cap. The results of these shifts are shown in Table 13.11. As we can see, the confidence on active U.S. Small Cap and Overlay strategies relative to U.S. Large Cap has increased. As well, the allocation of active risk has shifted away from U.S. Large Cap and into the other two strategies (as illustrated by the change in the relative risk allocation columns). In fact, the rebalanced active risk budget appears to be more diversified. This example illustrates a basic idea, which is that there is a very close correspondence between the allocation of active risk and the relative confidence placed on views.

Why would an investor choose to assign more confidence to the active returns in one asset class versus another? Given that most investors have access to the same data and would share the same basic ranking of the historical information ratios,

[8]Assuming that we hold the relative confidence levels roughly fixed, improving the Sharpe ratio by increasing the level of active risk relative to the risk on the underlying asset classes means, as a first approximation, that the investor is also increasing the implied level of τ, or the weight on views. One interpretation would be that the investor believes that markets take a long time to correct to equilibrium.

[9]Higher costs at higher risk levels could also cause information ratio deterioriation.

TABLE 13.11 Implied Confidence Levels after Rebalancing

	Confidence Relative to U.S. Large Cap		Active
	Historical IR	Constant IR	Risk Budget
U.S. Large Cap Equity	1.00	1.00	21.7
U.S. Small Cap Equity	0.47	1.05	24.0
International Equity	0.55	1.19	30.6
Emerging Markets Equity	0.14	0.17	0.7
Core+ Fixed Income	46.59	0.27	1.7
High Yield	0.04	0.12	0.3
Overlay	0.48	0.98	21.0

our view is that investors gain more insight into the investment process by focusing on factors that would set their relative confidence levels. Here is a partial list of factors that could guide setting relative confidence levels for active risk at the asset class level.

- *Is the source of the historical alpha a one-time event that all market participants shared?* If the historical alpha represents a one-time event that is not likely to repeat itself, then the confidence level should be lowered relative to other sources of active risk. Consequently, less of the active risk budget would be allocated to these strategies. An example of such a phenomenon is the historical performance of international managers relative to EAFE, where most managers were underweight Japan.
- *Is the source of the historical alpha a function of benchmark anomalies?* Poor benchmark construction (e.g., benchmarks where index arbitrage is difficult) give rise to an embedded ability for active managers to add value. To the extent that the investor thought that benchmark construction was unlikely to change, a higher relative confidence could be assigned to the active strategies, and more of the active risk budget allocated to them. Two examples of such sources of alpha include the EAFE benchmark and the Russell 2000 benchmark.
- *Does the source of the historical alpha represent a structural inefficiency?* Structural inefficiencies can occur when one (or more) market participant has an objective function that is other than mean-variance optimization. In these cases, mean-variance optimizers have the ability to generate alpha. Consequently, relatively more confidence could be placed in these strategies, and more of the risk budget allocated to them. An example of a structural inefficiency is the currency market, where central banks have macroeconomic policy objectives that cannot be easily represented in a mean-variance framework.

So far, we've focused on the allocation of portfolio risk between active and asset class risk, and on allocating active risk across portfolios of active strategies (e.g., a portfolio of active U.S. Large Cap managers versus a portfolio of active U.S. Small Cap managers. The same analysis can be easily extended to the manager-specific level. In that case, we would be calculating the allocation of active risk assigned to a specific manager, the implied alpha to that manager, and the confidence in that manager relative to a numeraire manager.

For example, suppose that we have a portfolio of three International Equity managers. Furthermore, suppose that the correlation of excess returns between the managers is .38 (from Table 13.2), and that the tracking error target for the portfolio of managers is 460 basis points (from Table 13.3). Table 13.12 shows the tracking error targets for each manager, their allocations, and the risk budget for this portfolio of managers.

In Table 13.5, International Equity was allocated roughly 40 percent of the total active risk budget, under the assumption that the portfolio of managers had a target tracking error of 460 basis points. Implicit in this decision was the view that in the aggregate, International Equity managers were more likely to add value in line with the historical performance than managers in other asset classes.

Table 13.12 is telling us that the third manager has been allocated around 50 percent of the active risk in International Equity. Now our question is, what does this allocation of risk imply about our confidence in any particular manager's ability to deliver alpha?

The confidence levels for each manager, normalized to manager 2, are shown in Table 13.13. These have been calculated using two sets of views. The first view is that the information ratio for each manager is the median information ratio. The second view is that managers have different information ratios. More specifically, we've assumed that the first manager's expected information ratio is .25, while expected information ratios for the second and third managers are .57 and .75 respectively.

As expected, the risk budget reveals quite different information about our confidence in each manager's ability to deliver alpha, depending on the view. When we assume an equal information ratio for each manager, then the risk budget is effectively

TABLE 13.12 International Manager Weights

	Allocation	Tracking Error (bps)	Risk Budget
Manager 1	20.0%	500	14.4%
Manager 2	35.0	575	35.3
Manager 3	45.0	675	50.3
Total	100.0	450	100.0

TABLE 13.13 Relative Confidence Levels

	Confidence Relative to Manager 2	
	Constant IR	Differential IR
Manager 1	0.5	1.6
Manager 2	1.0	1.0
Manager 3	1.5	1.1

telling us that we are 50 percent as confident in the ability of the first manager to achieve the median information ratio as the second manager.

From a practical perspective, if we truly believed that we could not differentiate between managers, then the lower confidence on manager 1 and higher confidence on manager 3 is indicating that we should reallocate risk away from manager 3 and into manager 1.

Now let's look at the case when we have views that the information ratios differ by manager. In this example, the confidence levels are the same across managers. More specifically, in this example we are confident in the ability of each manager to hit its respective expected alphas.

Separating out the impact of confidence levels and views is an important step to take in understanding the risk budget. Just as in the previous example, where we allocated active risk at the asset class level (e.g., U.S. Large Cap equity versus Core+ Fixed Income), we can start to identify factors that affect views, and those that affect confidence levels at the individual manager level.

For example, suppose that we take as our starting view that each manager in an asset class will earn the median information ratio. We would change that view for a particular manager if there were structural factors that made us believe that they could outperform the median. An example would be the impact of no net short constraints: Lower tracking error managers are usually less susceptible to these constraints, suggesting that their expected information ratios should be higher.

What would influence our choice of confidence in one manager versus another? One factor that we could consider is the length of the track record. All else being equal, we might be more confident in managers with longer track records than those with shorter histories. We might then believe that more risk should be allocated to those managers with longer track records.

A second factor that might influence our confidence in one manager versus another is the stability of the team. Investment managers with less stable teams might cause us to dampen the degree of confidence, and consequently take more risk with other, more stable teams.

Third, we might consider the risk "footprint" of one manager versus another. Consider, for example, two managers with the same information ratios and historical tracking errors. However, suppose that one manager seems to switch (for no apparent reason) between low and high tracking error regimes, while the other does not. Because the reasons for the switch between regimes are not evident, we might be less confident in the first manager.

CONCLUSIONS

Developing an allocation of active risk is an important part of the design of any investment policy. The allocation of active risk across strategies sets the framework for the ongoing evaluation of specific active strategies and specific investment managers. In this chapter, we have illustrated how active risk budgeting can be used to approach this issue.

The predictions of asset pricing theory are quite clear about the return to active risk: in equilibrium it is zero. Nonetheless, because active risk is uncorrelated with market risk and because markets over the short term are not in equilibrium, investors have a natural demand for active risk. Thus, the real issue is how to efficiently structure an active portfolio.

In this chapter, we have shown how risk budgeting can be used to approach this problem. We have focused on risk budgeting because we believe that risk characteristics are more easily estimated than expected returns. By exploiting the properties of portfolio optimality, we have shown that risk budgets can be interpreted as return expectations.

By using the Black-Litterman model and the assumption that active returns are zero in equilibrium, we have shown that any active risk budget maps into a set of views about active returns and confidences in those views. Furthermore, we have shown how investors can begin to apply this framework to their portfolios. More specifically, we have shown that investors need to focus on whether issues relate to their views or to their confidences in those views.

CHAPTER 14

Budgeting Risk along the Active Risk Spectrum

Andrew Alford, Robert Jones, and Kurt Winkelmann

The preceding chapter introduced the idea of an active risk budget, and showed how investors could develop such a risk budget at the asset class level. That chapter also briefly discussed how risk budgeting could be applied to develop a roster of specific investment managers. At some point in the implementation process, most investors must eventually face the following issue: What is the best blend of active and passive managers in their equity portfolios? Some investors implement fully passive portfolios. Others use the passive alternative to dilute the risk in their active program by "barbelling"—that is, hiring a roster of traditional active managers at one end of the risk spectrum, and mixing in index funds at the other, to hit an active risk target that lies somewhere in the middle.

We believe that investors who follow a barbell strategy are missing a valuable opportunity to put their passive exposure to work. This lost opportunity is analogous to the opportunity that investors miss when they include cash in their strategic asset allocations. In our view, investors can improve the expected risk-adjusted performance of their active portfolios by substituting structured equity managers for their passive positions.

It is now commonplace to categorize active managers by their level of active risk, with *structured* managers usually taking less active risk than *traditional* managers.[1] In our view, most investors should allocate risk across the *entire* active risk spectrum—that is, most equity programs should contain a blend of passive, structured, and traditional equity management. We call this approach the "spectrum strategy."

Why are investors better off using a spectrum strategy rather than a barbell? We believe there are four principal reasons. First, on average, the historical risk-adjusted performance of structured managers has exceeded that of traditional managers. Second, we believe these performance differences are the result of inherent methodolog-

[1]In this chapter, *structured* refers to low tracking error managers, who are often called *enhanced-index* or *benchmark-sensitive* managers. *Traditional* refers to concentrated active managers who usually have higher tracking errors and are less benchmark sensitive.

ical differences. Third, to the extent that active management can add value, investors with significant passive exposures are effectively creating drag on their overall portfolio performance. Finally, because the spectrum strategy diversifies the active risk budget, we believe that investors can achieve a higher return per unit of active risk by including structured equity products in their portfolios.

These themes will be explored in detail. We'll first examine the historical track records of structured and traditional active equity managers. We'll then explore the methodological differences that drive these performance differences. Later, we'll show how investors can apply these findings, together with active risk budgeting techniques, to their large-cap U.S. equity portfolios and reach some more general conclusions.

COMPARING STRUCTURED AND TRADITIONAL MANAGERS

Many investors implement their long-term asset allocations to large-cap U.S. equities by combining passive and traditional active management. Because we believe that investors should also include structured equity in the mix, let's review the historical risk and performance characteristics of traditional and structured managers. Viewing these historical results will motivate further discussion of the methodological differences that distinguish these two management styles.

For our analysis, we will use historical tracking errors to segregate managers, classifying lower tracking error managers as structured, and higher tracking error managers as traditional. Market conventions place structured equity managers in a target tracking error range of 100 to 250 basis points. Given that realized (or historical) tracking errors could exceed targets, we identify structured managers as those with realized tracking error levels between 100 and 300 basis points.

Market convention also suggests that traditional (or concentrated) managers have tracking error targets—to the extent they are benchmark sensitive and *have* tracking error targets—in excess of 600 basis points. Of course, realized tracking error levels can also undershoot targets. Hence, we define traditional managers as those with realized tracking errors in excess of 500 basis points, but below 1,500 basis points. (The upper bound is meant to exclude managers who may have significant holdings in other asset classes, such as small-cap equities, international equities, or bonds.) We judged it too difficult to classify managers with realized tracking errors between 300 and 500 basis points; such managers were thus omitted from further analysis. However, our results are not sensitive to omitting these managers.

Table 14.1 summarizes our results. Using the Plan Sponsor Network (PSN) database,[2] we constructed a set of quarterly time-series returns for 1,052 large-cap U.S. equity managers. The returns, which are gross of fees, cover the period 1989 to

[2]The Plan Sponsor Network is a database of institutional manager returns. These returns are gross of fees and contain both self-selection and survivor bias. That is, only managers who choose to submit are included (presumably those with better returns), and managers who fail or merge are dropped. Thus, our median results may actually be closer to the 55th percentile results. Nonetheless, despite these biases (which affect both manager styles), we believe the comparisons between structured and traditional managers are valid.

TABLE 14.1 Historical Performance (1989–2001)

	Average	Median	Top Quartile	Bottom Quartile
Structured Managers (64 Managers)				
Active return (bps)	43	52	92	–4
Tracking error (bps)	209	221	266	147
Information ratio	0.26	0.28	0.44	–0.02
Pairwise correlation	0.08	0.08	0.27	–0.1
Traditional Managers (561 Managers)				
Active return (bps)	53	53	201	–120
Tracking error (bps)	821	769	971	619
Information ratio	0.05	0.07	0.27	–0.16
Pairwise correlation	0.13	0.14	0.36	–0.1

2001, inclusive. We included all managers with at least 24 quarters of performance history. As discussed earlier, we reduced the number of managers in our database further by restricting our attention to low and high tracking error managers.

Of course, our methodology might misclassify some managers. For example, a manager could intentionally switch between low and high tracking error regimes as part of the active decision-making process. If the tracking error levels in each regime are sufficiently different, and the manager spends an insufficient amount of time in the high tracking error regime, then we could mistakenly classify the manager as "structured." Unfortunately, we do not have sufficient data to easily discern such regime-switching behavior. This caveat notwithstanding, we do feel that our database is rich enough both to classify managers and to produce historical differences that are sufficiently interesting for further discussion.

Table 14.1 shows the summary performance and risk characteristics for each group of managers. The table shows the historical average, median, top-quartile, and bottom-quartile figures for four performance and risk characteristics: active return, tracking error, information ratio, and pairwise correlation. We independently calculated these quartile cutoff points for each risk or performance characteristic. For example, the structured manager with the median active return may not be the same as the manager with the median tracking error.

The performance and risk figures in Table 14.1 are quite revealing, and indicate why selection among different types of managers is such a challenge for institutional investors. Let's look at the performance record first, and then consider the differences in risk.

Historically, the average active return was quite similar for structured and traditional managers. On average, traditional managers had an active return of 53 basis points, while the active return for structured managers was slightly smaller at 43 basis points. The median active returns were even closer at 52 basis points for structured managers and 53 basis points for traditional managers—despite significantly lower risk of the structured managers. Given that traditional managers usually charge higher fees, it would be hard to argue that, on average, traditional managers have provided higher risk-adjusted excess returns net of fees.

More interesting, though, is the dispersion in performance. The top-quartile structured manager had an active return of 92 basis points, while the bottom-quartile manager had an active return of negative 4 basis points. Consistent with the differences in risk taking, the top-quartile traditional manager had an active return of 201 basis points, while the bottom-quartile manager underperformed the benchmark by 120 basis points. Thus, the historical performance record seems to indicate that, on average, structured and traditional managers outperformed by roughly the same amount. However, manager selection is much more important for traditional managers because the spread in results is much wider.

Historical returns alone provide an incomplete comparison between manager styles; to complete the picture, we should also look at risk. For this reason, Table 14.1 also includes a summary of the distribution of historical tracking errors for structured and traditional managers.

Given that we intentionally classified managers using realized tracking errors, we shouldn't be surprised that the tracking errors for structured managers are lower than those for traditional managers. For example, the median tracking errors are 221 and 769 basis points, respectively, for the structured and traditional managers. At the extremes, the top-quartile structured manager had an historical tracking error of 266 basis points, while the bottom-quartile manager had a realized tracking error of 147 basis points. By contrast, the top-quartile traditional manager had a tracking error of 971 basis points, while the bottom-quartile manager had a tracking error of 619 basis points. Thus, consistent with the way we've defined our sample, investors were likely to see higher realized active risk levels from their traditional managers than from their structured managers.

A useful way to assess the risk/reward trade-off is with the information ratio, defined as active return per unit of active risk (or active return divided by tracking error). Table 14.1 also shows information ratios. These figures are perhaps the most interesting, as they suggest significant differences between these active management styles. That is, the historical information ratios for structured managers are higher than those for traditional managers at all skill levels. For example, the median structured manager had an information ratio of 0.28, while the median traditional manager had a realized information ratio of 0.07.

Table 14.1 also shows that the *dispersion* of information ratios was more pronounced for traditional managers. The top-quartile information ratio for traditional managers was almost four times greater than the median. For structured managers, the top-quartile information ratio is only 57 percent higher than the median. Taken together, these figures suggest that structured managers added more active return per unit of active risk,[3] and further that manager selection would have been incredibly important in developing a portfolio of traditional managers.

Table 14.1 also explores the level of pairwise correlations between active returns. For the most part, these figures show no difference by active management style. The median correlation between structured managers was 0.08, while for

[3]These results are consistent with the study of mutual funds by Brown and Harlow (2002), which shows a clear connection between consistency of investment style, active risk levels, and persistence of performance. Generally, a high level of consistency corresponds to lower active risk levels and more persistent benchmark outperformance.

traditional managers the median correlation was 0.14. These figures are comforting, since they suggest that, within each management style, managers are not loading up on the same risks. In other words, managers seem to be expressing different views or using different portfolio construction techniques (or both!) in their active decisions.

The figures in Table 14.1 provide evidence on the *ex post* performance of *individual* managers. On the basis of this evidence, investors may wonder whether it makes sense to include traditional managers in the mix at all. The reason for including traditional managers is straightforward: Most institutional investors hold *portfolios* of managers. Thus, the *choice is not between a structured manager and a traditional manager, but between alternative portfolios of managers.* What happens if we view the historical experience in this light?

To assess the differences between structured and traditional strategies at the portfolio level, we created composites of structured and traditional active managers for the period between 1992 and 2001. As with our earlier analysis, we distinguished between the different manager types using realized tracking errors—but this time we used the prior three years to classify managers for the next three-year holding period (i.e., an investable strategy). We continue to measure performance against the S&P 500.

For each three-year time period, we filtered the data into two groups: structured equity managers (1 to 3 percent tracking error) and traditional active managers (5 to 15 percent tracking error). Within each group, we next created 100 randomly selected composite portfolios of two and four managers (equally weighted), and then calculated average buy-and-hold returns for each subsequent three-year period.

In Table 14.2, we show the active returns, tracking errors, and information ratios for various cutoff points in the sample. For example, the top quartile represents the 25th best portfolio of managers in the sample according to the indicated statistic. Thus, we can think of these cutoff points as representing an investor's skill level in developing a portfolio of managers.

The results in Table 14.2 are consistent with those in Table 14.1: Compared to portfolios of traditional managers, the portfolios of structured managers have higher median excess returns (with less risk), and higher information ratios at all levels. For example, comparing the results with four managers, the median information ratio for portfolios of structured managers is 0.24 compared to –0.12 for portfolios of traditional managers. Not surprisingly, the portfolios of structured managers also have lower average tracking errors and less dispersion in tracking errors and excess returns. Thus, skill at manager selection is much more important when developing a portfolio of traditional managers.

While this is a compelling first cut at an investable strategy, comparing core S&P structured and traditional managers may be a naive way of approaching the issue of optimal manager combinations. Many institutional investors choose traditional managers on the basis of a particular expertise: for example, growth and value. How would the results look if we created portfolios of growth and value managers? Table 14.3 shows the results achieved by composite portfolios of growth and value managers over the period from 1992 through 2001, where active returns, tracking errors, and information ratios are measured relative to the S&P 500.

TABLE 14.2 Results of S&P 500 Managers (1992–2001)

	Two Managers			Four Managers		
	AR (bps)	TE (bps)	IR	AR (bps)	TE (bps)	IR
Structured Managers						
Bottom quartile	–54	178	–0.26	–29	141	–0.21
Median	61	234	0.21	49	176	0.24
Top quartile	155	297	0.66	123	217	0.63
Traditional Managers						
Bottom quartile	–247	430	–0.51	–180	366	–0.46
Median	–23	572	–0.09	–14	461	–0.12
Top quartile	240	784	0.37	170	589	0.28

AR—Active return.
TE—Tracking error.
IR—Information ratio.

TABLE 14.3 Results of Growth/Value Traditional Active Managers (1992–2001)

	Two Managers			Four Managers		
	AR (bps)	TE (bps)	IR	AR (bps)	TE (bps)	IR
Traditional Growth Managers						
Bottom quartile	39	635	–0.05	82	639	0.02
Median	246	800	0.22	253	775	0.24
Top quartile	481	1,010	0.50	438	932	0.44
Traditional Value Managers						
Bottom quartile	–200	512	–0.36	–163	486	–0.29
Median	–32	605	–0.05	–50	567	–0.05
Top quartile	121	714	0.25	64	647	0.18

AR—Active return.
TE—Tracking error.
IR—Information ratio.

Clearly, taking style into account makes a difference: The median information ratio for a portfolio of traditional growth managers is slightly higher than that for the portfolio of structured managers, while the relation is reversed for traditional value managers. We believe, however, that this result is time period dependent: Growth managers did quite well, on average, over the latter part of the 1990s. Thus, we are still left with a puzzle: Why did structured managers perform so well (on a risk-adjusted basis) relative to their traditional counterparts? To answer this question, we must dig deeper into the underlying investment methodologies of structured and traditional managers.

STRUCTURED AND TRADITIONAL APPROACHES TO INVESTING

The primary difference between structured and traditional managers lies in their approach to risk and benchmarks. Structured managers are highly benchmark sensitive and tend to target relatively low levels of tracking error. Further, structured managers usually attempt to hit their lower targets by relying on a relatively large number of small active deviations (i.e., overweights and underweights).

By contrast, traditional active managers usually target high *ex ante* excess returns. Although most do not explicitly target tracking error, their quest for excess returns often results in high *ex post* active risk. This is because traditional managers usually restrict their active decision making to a small number of relatively large positions. *The difference in the magnitude of active positions is key to understanding the risk and performance differences between traditional and structured managers.*

One major consequence is that traditional managers are less able to achieve symmetry between their bullish and bearish views. Why? Because of the no-short constraint that most institutional investors face. That is, managers can generally overweight a stock by as much as they'd like, but they can only underweight a stock up to its weight in the benchmark. Since traditional managers usually want to implement relatively large active deviations, this constraint is often binding. Whereas they can theoretically overweight their favorite names by as much as they'd like, they can only fully underweight their least favorite names in a few cases (i.e., those where the benchmark weight is large enough to accommodate the desired underweighting). As a result, because overweights and underweights must sum to zero, the no-short constraint effectively hinders a manager's ability to express bullish views. Consequently, the no-short constraint and related lack of symmetry will reduce a traditional manager's potential information ratio.

Structured managers, in contrast, can take greater advantage of both their bullish and bearish views. They are able to more fully exploit their views because of their relatively low tracking error targets and their propensity to take a large number of relatively small active deviations. Thus, the no-short constraint is less binding because their desired underweights exceed the benchmark weights less often.

A second difference between structured and traditional managers is the emphasis on risk management. With tight tracking error targets, structured managers spend a great deal of time and effort managing risk and eliminating unintended bets—just as a household on a tight budget will be more frugal. Traditional managers, in contrast, feel less constrained by tracking error concerns and spend commensurately less time on risk management. As a result, unintended and uncompensated risks can creep into their portfolios.

For example, many traditional managers roughly equal-weight the names in their portfolios. This can produce large overweights in small-cap names and smaller overweights (or even underweights) in large-cap names. The resulting small-cap bias adds uncompensated risk to the portfolio. That is, the overweight in smaller names is driven by the manager's inattention to risk rather than a strong belief that small-cap stocks (as a class) will outperform large-cap stocks. By adding noise to the denominator (tracking error) without increasing the numerator (alpha), this practice reduces the information ratios of traditional managers.

In summary, the empirical information ratio advantage for structured managers reflects two methodological advantages: (1) their relative freedom from the no-short constraint (due to smaller intended active deviations) and (2) their greater focus on risk management (and the related reduction in noise in the information ratio's denominator). *If these conventions persist in the future, then we would expect the information ratio advantage to persist as well.*

Given the historical information ratio advantage of structured managers, investors might conclude from our discussion that they should allocate little, if any, of their active risk budgets to traditional active strategies. This is not necessarily the case. There are at least two good reasons to include traditional managers in the mix.

First, despite the reasons noted, the information ratio advantage for structured managers may not persist. Historical information ratios are poor predictors of future performance, and especially so for comparatively small samples such as ours. Our sample uses quarterly data and has a relatively small number of structured managers. Consequently, we should regard our statistical results as suggestive rather than definitive.[4] Prudent diversification, then, argues for using managers at both ends of the active risk spectrum.

Second, at least *some* traditional managers have added value historically, and their performances were relatively uncorrelated with structured managers, suggesting that investors can improve their expected information ratios by allocating at least some of their active risk budgets to traditional strategies. *Thus, the real issue is the size of the allocation to each active strategy, both relative to one another and relative to the passive allocation.*

FINDING THE RIGHT MANAGER MIX

How should investors allocate assets between active and passive strategies? Should they adopt a barbell approach or take risk across the entire active risk spectrum? Whatever approach they ultimately adopt, investors should carefully evaluate the trade-offs that accompany each key decision. As discussed in the preceding chapter, we believe the best way to assess these trade-offs is through an analysis of the *active risk budget.*[5]

There are three important concepts to clarify about active risk budgeting: (1) the active risk budget, (2) the optimal active risk budget, and (3) the active risk budgeting process. An active risk budget is simply an attribution of active risk to its constituent parts. Suppose, for example, that an investor has six domestic equity managers with different levels of active risk. Armed with estimates of the correlations between managers, it is quite straightforward to calculate the tracking error of the portfolio of managers relative to the combined benchmark, and then attribute the total equity tracking error to each of the six managers. This decomposition is the active risk budget.

[4]The t-statistic on the difference between median information ratios for portfolios of four structured and traditional managers is 1.72, which is significant at the 11 percent level.
[5]The active risk budget analyzes the effects of deviations from the strategic benchmark.

Because the active risk budget identifies the sources of active risk, it also provides important information about the structure of an investor's active equity portfolio. In fact, there is a direct relation between the active risk budget and an investor's views about active returns: In the absence of constraints, the total portfolio information ratio is maximized when active risk is allocated so that the marginal contribution to active performance equals the marginal contribution to active risk for all active investments. Constraints can alter this ideal relation, but any allocation of active risk that maximizes the information ratio (for a given level of active risk) is called an optimal active risk budget.[6] The process of finding this optimal active risk budget is the risk budgeting process.

A simple example may help illustrate these points. Suppose an investor has two sources of active performance: a portfolio of two structured managers and a portfolio of four traditional managers. To simplify our discussion, we'll assume that active returns—the returns over the benchmark—are uncorrelated across all managers, an assumption that we'll relax later on. (As shown in Table 14.1, traditional and structured managers are unlikely to have completely uncorrelated excess returns.) Reflecting the results of our historical analysis, we'll also assume that each structured manager has a tracking error of 215 basis points, while each traditional manager has a tracking error of 800 basis points. Finally, we'll assume that each manager is equally weighted within its type—namely, each structured manager invests 50 percent of the structured portfolio and each traditional manager invests 25 percent of the traditional portfolio. In this simple example, risk budgeting means deciding how much of the active risk budget to allocate to each group of managers.

To make this decision, we must first calculate the active risk level for each portfolio of managers. Under our simple assumptions, the tracking error for the portfolio of structured managers is around 150 basis points, while the tracking error for the portfolio of traditional managers is 400 basis points.[7] (These calculations assume each portfolio of managers has a beta of 1.0 relative to the benchmark index.)

Recall that when there are no constraints, we should allocate active risk such that the marginal contribution to active risk equals the marginal contribution to active return for all investments (or managers). Thus, the next step is to estimate active returns for groups of managers.

For simplicity, let's assume that structured managers have expected information ratios of 0.45, while traditional managers have expected information ratios of 0.30. These assumptions roughly correspond to the top or first-quartile figures in Table 14.1, and imply that the investor has some skill in manager selection. Using these assumptions, the expected information ratio and active return for the group

---

[6]Of course, this works only if we assume that active risk is uncorrelated with the underlying strategic asset allocation. If the active returns are negatively correlated with the underlying assets, then the total portfolio information ratio could be improved by using a suboptimal active portfolio. In practice, the correlation between active risk and the strategic asset allocation is quite low.

[7]The tracking error of 150 basis points for the portfolio of two structured managers is calculated as the square root of the following sum: $(\frac{1}{2} \times 215)^2 + 2 \times \frac{1}{2} \times \frac{1}{2} \times 0 \times 215 \times 215 + (\frac{1}{2} \times 215)^2$. The zero in the middle term represents the correlation assumption. A similar approach applies to the portfolio of four traditional managers.

TABLE 14.4 Illustrative Risk and Return Assumptions

	Number of Managers	Information Ratio	Active Return (bps)	Tracking Error (bps)
Structured equity	2	0.64	97	152
Traditional equity	4	0.60	240	400

TABLE 14.5 Information Ratios and Tracking Errors

Traditional Allocation	Structured Allocation	Active Return (bps)	Tracking Error (bps)	Information Ratio
0%	100%	97	152	0.64
10	90	111	143	0.78
20	80	125	146	0.86
30	**70**	**140**	**160**	**0.87**
40	60	154	184	0.84
50	50	168	214	0.79
60	40	183	248	0.74
70	30	197	284	0.69
80	20	211	321	0.66
90	10	226	360	0.63
100	0	240	400	0.60

of two structured managers are 0.64 and 97 basis points, while the expected information ratio and active return for the group of four traditional active managers are 0.60 and 240 basis points.[8] The information ratios for the portfolios of managers are higher than for any individual manager because we've assumed the excess returns are uncorrelated.[9] Table 14.4 summarizes our assumptions.

How should we build a portfolio that combines the structured and traditional equity products? A simple way to approach this problem is to vary the proportion invested with the two equity programs and assess the impact on the total information ratio and tracking error, as shown in Table 14.5.

An interesting pattern emerges in Table 14.5: The information ratio hits its maximum when the investor blends structured and traditional managers. Under our assumptions, the optimal portfolio allocates 70 percent to structured managers and 30 percent to traditional strategies.[10] Of course, the optimal proportions will

[8]These information ratios differ from the top-quartile information ratios in Table 14.2 because here we are building a portfolio of top-quartile managers, whereas in Table 14.2 we are analyzing a top-quartile portfolio of managers. Thus, here we are assuming considerably more skill at manager selection.

[9]The median correlation between excess returns for the structured and traditional portfolios is 0.07.

[10]Table 14.5 assumes the allocation of active risk is being considered independently from the strategic asset allocation. Put differently, Table 14.5 assumes the investor first develops a target for total active risk in the U.S. equity portfolio and then optimizes the manager structure.

vary depending on the underlying information ratio assumptions. However, the central point remains the same: *As long as the expected information ratios for each strategy are positive and uncorrelated, investors achieve a higher information ratio by combining strategies rather than relying on either strategy exclusively.*

So far, we have focused on the split between structured and active equity products, without discussing passive management. The reason is that, in active risk budgeting, passive management is both a risk-free and return-free strategy, while we have been focused on the allocation of active risk between the two active return-generating (i.e., risk-taking) strategies. How does passive management fit into the mix?

The risk-free nature of passive management means that investors can use it to dampen the total active risk of their equity portfolios. As discussed in the preceding chapter, the first step is to decide on an appropriate level of total active risk (expressed in tracking error terms), and then to blend the optimal portfolio of active strategies with passive management to hit this target.

For example, suppose an investor decides that the tracking error target for a domestic equity program should be 200 basis points. Suppose further that the investor estimates that the portfolio of traditional managers has a tracking error of 400 basis points (as shown earlier) and an information ratio of 0.60. If the investor allocates 50 percent of the total portfolio to a passive manager and 50 percent to the portfolio of traditional managers, the combined tracking error would hit its target of 200 basis points. Under our assumptions, the expected information ratio for the total domestic equity portfolio would be 0.60. This, in essence, is the barbell strategy.

With a spectrum strategy, however, investors can do better. In Table 14.5, a 70/30 mix of structured and traditional managers achieves the highest information ratio (0.87). However, the tracking error of this mix is 160 basis points, which is less than the target of 200 basis points. Assuming the investor can't lever the optimal information ratio portfolio, the next best solution is to pick the mix in Table 14.5 that has a tracking error closest to the target. This portfolio has roughly 55 percent invested in structured strategies and the remaining 45 percent invested with traditional managers. The new information ratio of 0.81 is almost 7 percent lower than the optimal information ratio. This shortfall amounts to about 12 basis points in expected excess return,[11] which equals the efficiency cost of the no-leverage constraint.

Relative to the barbell strategy, however, this new mix represents a 35 percent improvement in efficiency (i.e., 0.81 versus 0.60), and an improvement in expected excess return of 42 basis points. *Importantly, the source of this efficiency gain is moving from passive to structured management.* In fact, in this example, for any tracking error target above 160 basis points, investors should have no passive exposure, and should instead allocate all of their equity assets to the structured and traditional programs.

Next, let's look at an active risk target that is below 160 basis points. Suppose the targeted tracking error is 100 basis points for the total U.S. equity portfolio. We know from Table 14.5 that a mix of 70 percent invested in structured equity and 30

[11]Or 200 bps times (0.87 – 0.81).

percent invested with traditional managers has the highest information ratio. This portfolio has a tracking error of 160 basis points. If we construct a portfolio that has 38 percent invested passively and 62 percent invested in the optimal blend portfolio, the total portfolio will hit the tracking error target of 100 basis points. Thus, the passive position effectively dilutes the active risk in the optimal blend portfolio *without reducing the total portfolio's information ratio.* The total portfolio now has an information ratio of 0.87 and an expected excess return of 87 basis points, with 38 percent invested passively, 43 percent invested with structured managers, and 19 percent invested in traditional strategies. Thus, this portfolio clearly takes risk across the spectrum.

How does this optimal portfolio compare to the barbell strategy? To achieve a targeted tracking error of 100 basis points in the barbell strategy, the investor would need to allocate 25 percent to the traditional portfolio and 75 percent to the passive portfolio. This portfolio would have an information ratio of 0.60. *Moreover, we can easily see that the structured equity allocation comes almost entirely from the passive position: By putting more of the passive assets to work in a structured equity program, the information ratio for the total U.S. equity portfolio increases from 0.60 to 0.87, or almost 45 percent!*

Table 14.6 summarizes these two examples and provides the strategy split and information ratios for other tracking error targets. This table contrasts these figures with the barbell strategy: The information ratio increases as risk is taken along the active risk spectrum. *What is more striking, though, is that for the most part funding for the structured equity position comes out of the passive allocation.*

So far, our analysis has assumed that excess returns are uncorrelated across managers within an active management type, and across active management types. This assumption has been roughly consistent with the observed median correlation, as shown in Table 14.6. What happens to the information ratio if we assume the correlations are higher?

For example, suppose the pairwise correlations are close to the first quartile level in Table 14.6. That is, the average excess return correlation among structured managers is 0.25, and the average correlation among traditional managers is 0.35. We'll continue to assume that each prospective manager in each strategy can generate first quartile risk-adjusted performance.

In the two-manager structured equity program, the tracking error increases by about 12 percent, going from 152 basis points to 170 basis points. This increase in tracking error reduces the information ratio for the structured portfolio from 0.64 to 0.57. For the traditional equity program, the higher correlations increase the overall tracking error by 44 percent, from 400 basis points (with four managers) to around 575 basis points. As with the structured program, the information ratio declines, going from 0.60 to 0.42. *Thus, the larger increase in correlation among traditional managers produces more significant deterioration in their total tracking error and information ratio.*

Suppose an investor decides to improve the efficiency of the traditional program by doubling the number of managers. The tracking error for the traditional program would fall from 575 to 525 basis points. Correspondingly, the information ratio would increase from 0.42 to 0.46. Thus, the higher correlation of excess returns among traditional managers may produce an incentive to hold more

TABLE 14.6 Strategy Mix and Total U.S. Equity Tracking Error

	Spectrum				Barbell		
U.S. Equity Target Risk	Passive Allocation	Structured Allocation	Traditional Allocation	Information Ratio	Passive Allocation	Traditional Allocation	Information Ratio
0%	100%	0%	0%	0.00	100%	0%	0.00
50	68	22	10	0.87	88	12	0.60
100	38	43	19	0.87	75	25	0.60
150	6	66	28	0.87	63	37	0.60
200	0	55	45	0.81	50	50	0.60
250	0	40	60	0.74	38	62	0.60
300	0	26	74	0.68	25	75	0.60
350	0	13	87	0.84	12	88	0.60
400	0	0	100	0.60	0	100	0.60

TABLE 14.7 Equity Allocations and Correlation Levels

Structured Manager Correlation	Traditional Manager Correlation	Number of Structured Managers	Number of Traditional Managers	Structured Allocation	Traditional Allocation	Information Ratio
0.00	0.00	2	4	55%	45%	0.81
0.25	0.35	2	4	70	30	0.67
0.25	0.35	2	8	70	30	0.71

traditional managers in a portfolio.[12] This higher correlation does not mean, however, that investors should allocate more assets to traditional managers. *In fact, the opposite is true: When the correlations among traditional managers increase, investors should allocate more assets (i.e., more of the active risk budget) to the structured equity program.*

We can see the impact on the active risk budget as follows. Suppose an investor has a tracking error target for the overall active program of 200 basis points. When the correlation of excess returns is zero, we determined that a 55/45 blend of structured and traditional managers achieved the target tracking error. This blend has an expected information ratio of 0.81, as shown in Table 14.7.

Now let's consider what happens when we assume higher correlations among excess returns. Table 14.7 shows the results. All else being equal, higher correlations mean higher tracking errors and lower information ratios for both active programs. Because the correlation increases more for the traditional program, however, its tracking error also increases more (and its information ratio falls more). Consequently, investors should allocate more assets to the structured program in order to neutralize the impact of higher active risk in the traditional program. In fact, it now takes a 70/30 mix to hit the risk target of 200 basis points. The information ratio for the combined program is now 0.67, which amounts to a decline in expected return of 28 basis points relative to the zero-correlation case. *This example highlights the importance of finding managers with independent and uncorrelated sources of excess return.*

Of course, the expected information ratio for the U.S. equity program will also vary with the investor's views about manager performance. Since we have used first-quartile information ratios for both structured and traditional managers, our examples have implicitly assumed skill in manager selection. Suppose that we are less confident in our ability to pick managers, and instead decide to use median information ratios in our analysis. What happens to the mix of passive, structured, and traditional managers?

Clearly, the information ratio for the total U.S. equity portfolio will decline at all tracking error levels. Table 14.8 illustrates this point by showing the active re-

[12]Of course, the diversification benefit of adding more managers must be balanced against the real cost of potentially higher fees. Adding more managers at what are likely to be lower allocations per manager makes it likely that investors will be unable to achieve fee breaks. Selection and monitoring costs are also likely to rise as the investor adds more managers.

TABLE 14.8 Strategy Split with Median Information Ratios

Traditional Allocation	Structured Allocation	Active Return (bps)	Tracking Error (bps)	Information Ratio
0%	100%	65	152	0.42
10	90	66	143	0.46
20	80	68	146	0.46
30	70	69	160	0.43
40	60	71	184	0.38
50	50	72	214	0.34
60	40	74	248	0.30
70	30	75	284	0.27
80	20	77	321	0.24
90	10	78	360	0.22
100	0	80	400	0.20

turn, tracking error, and information ratio at alternative splits between structured and traditional active managers. As with Table 14.5, we have assumed portfolios of two structured managers and four active managers.

Consistent with the median values in Table 14.1, we have assumed that each structured manager has an expected information ratio of 0.30, and each traditional manager has an expected information ratio of 0.10. If we further assume that there is no correlation between manager alphas, then the portfolio of two structured managers has an expected information ratio of 0.42, while the portfolio of four traditional managers has an expected information ratio of 0.20.

Notice in Table 14.8 that the maximum information ratio is achieved when the portfolio has between 80 percent and 90 percent allocated to structured equities and 10 percent to 20 percent allocated to traditional strategies. This portfolio has an expected information ratio around 0.46, and a tracking error between 143 basis points and 146 basis points. In comparison with Table 14.5, the tracking error for the optimal mix is lower, while the allocation to structured equity strategies is higher. This result should not be surprising given the relative declines in information ratios (from top-quartile to median) for the two strategies.

Now, let's suppose the tracking error target for the total U.S. equity program is 200 basis points. Since this target is greater than the tracking error for the optimal portfolio, we know that risk considerations will determine the optimal split between structured and traditional strategies. That is, the allocation to structured strategies will be exactly the same as when we used first-quartile manager information ratios. As Table 14.8 suggests, we will still allocate 55 percent to structured equities and 45 percent to traditional strategies. However, the expected information ratio is now much lower at 0.36, versus 0.81 when we assumed greater skill at manager selection.

For a more interesting case, suppose the tracking error target is 100 basis points. Since this target is less than the tracking error of the optimal blend portfolio, we know that we will need to dilute the active risk with passive managers. Table 14.9 contrasts the mix among passive, structured, and traditional managers

TABLE 14.9 Strategy Split for Median and Top-Quartile Information Ratios

Manager Information Ratio Assumption	Passive Allocation	Structured Allocation	Traditional Allocation	Tracking Error (bps)	Active Return (bps)	Information Ratio
Top quartile	38%	44%	18%	100	87	0.87
Median	32	54	14	100	46	0.46

at the 100 basis point tracking error target under our two assumptions for manager information ratios.

The results in Table 14.9 are quite interesting. When investors use the median information ratios (i.e., no particular skill in manager selection), the allocation to structured equity increases. *Moreover, while the allocation to structured equity is funded out of both the passive and traditional strategies, the impact is more pronounced on the passive program.*

The assumptions underlying the analysis of Tables 14.5 and 14.6 are that there are differences between structured and traditional managers, and that investors are skilled in manager selection. In Tables 14.8 and 14.9, we assumed that investors are neutral in their abilities to pick managers, but that the differences between structured and traditional managers are expected to continue. The implication for portfolio strategy in both cases is that investors should move away from a barbell strategy and take active risk across the active risk spectrum. They should do so by reducing their passive positions and adding structured active equity programs. There is a final possibility that deserves consideration: Suppose investors believe there are no long-term performance differences between structured and traditional managers and that they are not skilled in manager selection.

An easy way to reflect the assumption of no difference between structured and traditional managers is to assume that the median information ratio for all managers is 0.20—that is, approximately halfway between the median information ratios shown in Table 14.1. (Of course, we could have taken a value-weighted average, but the portfolio structuring implication would be the same.) Under this assumption, portfolios of two structured managers and four traditional managers will have information ratios of 0.28 and 0.40, respectively. The optimal information ratio portfolio has 60 percent allocated to the structured program and 40 percent allocated to the traditional program, with an overall tracking error of 184 basis points and an overall information ratio of 0.49.

Suppose the total tracking error target is 200 basis points. As in our earlier examples, the allocations to each strategy are driven by risk rather than information ratio considerations. Consequently, 55 percent of the portfolio is allocated to the portfolio of structured strategies and 45 percent is allocated to the portfolio of traditional strategies.

Now, let's see what happens at a lower tracking error target. Continuing with our previous examples, suppose the tracking error target is 100 basis points. In this case, the proper strategy is to make allocations to the optimal information ratio portfolio and the passive strategy. The optimal blend is now 46 percent allocated to passive, 32 percent allocated to the structured portfolio, and 22 percent allocated to traditional strategies. This allocation produces an expected information ratio of 0.49. *So, even when investors believe that they are unable to differentiate between the structured and traditional strategies and are neutral in their manager selection abilities, it is still optimal to follow the spectrum strategy.*

So far, we have developed allocations to hypothetical managers whose expected outperformance (as measured by the information ratio) resembles that of the top-quartile manager in each strategy, and whose tracking error resembles that of the median manager. Additionally, we have explored the investment implications of changing assumptions about the correlations among managers (Table 14.7) and the assumed information ratios (Tables 14.8 and 14.9). To complete the analysis, we will now develop optimal active risk budgets using results from the composite portfolio analysis shown in Tables 14.2 and 14.3. Table 14.10 shows these allocations.

In Table 14.10, we continue to assume some skill in manager selection, but the bar is a bit lower. That is, we assume that the investor can develop a top-quartile portfolio of managers, rather than a portfolio consisting of only top-quartile managers. We also include growth and value managers in the analysis. We will abstract from style effects by assuming that the two style benchmarks have the same expected returns, and that the investor can select a top-quartile portfolio of managers (as measured by the information ratio) in each style group. As in our earlier analysis, we again see that it is always beneficial to include a healthy allocation to structured equity managers.

For ease of comparison, let's focus on the 200 basis point tracking error target. Table 14.10 shows that an investor can hit this tracking error target with an allocation of 58 percent to structured managers and 42 percent to traditional managers. These allocations compare quite favorably with the figures in Table 14.6.

Irrespective of whether our analysis develops optimal portfolios using historical results from individual managers or uses results from composite portfolios, the conclusions are the same: *As long as the expected information ratios are positive,*

TABLE 14.10 Optimal Strategy Mix at Various Tracking Error Targets (1992–2001)

Tracking Error Level	Passive	Structured	Traditional Large Cap	Traditional Growth	Traditional Value	Active Return (bps)	Information Ratio
0.0%	100.0%	0.0%	0.0%	0.0%	0.0%	0	N/A
0.5	72.0	21.0	0.0	5.2	1.8	60	1.20
1.0	43.9	42.1	0.0	10.5	3.5	120	1.20
1.5	15.9	63.1	0.0	15.7	5.3	180	1.20
1.8	0.0	75.0	0.0	18.7	6.3	214	1.20
2.0	**0.0**	**58.2**	**0.7**	**26.4**	**14.7**	**234**	**1.17**
2.5	0.0	31.6	10.4	33.7	24.3	269	1.08
3.0	0.0	9.6	17.4	41.4	31.6	300	1.00
3.2	0.0	0.0	23.1	41.9	35.0	312	0.98
3.5	0.0	0.0	34.1	40.6	25.3	328	0.93
4.0	0.0	0.0	45.2	39.1	15.7	344	0.86
4.5	0.0	0.0	56.2	37.8	6.0	360	0.80

every institutional U.S. equity portfolio should include structured equities, with the allocation coming primarily from the passive portfolio. Investors should allocate significant amounts to passive products only when their tracking error targets are quite low. In our examples, a large allocation to passive management is appropriate only when the tracking error target for the entire U.S. equity portfolio is less than 100 basis points.[13]

CONCLUSIONS

A basic issue that most institutional investors face is how to allocate assets between active and passive strategies. Many investors adopt a barbell approach in which they achieve their active risk targets by blending traditional, high-tracking-error active managers with passive index funds. However, by including passive management, investors are forgoing excess returns on what may be a significant portion of their portfolios.

Most investors would benefit from putting this capital to work in structured equity programs; that is, most investors can achieve potentially significant improvements in excess returns and information ratios by reducing their passive allocations and replacing them with allocations to structured equity. By allocating risk across the active risk spectrum, investors can significantly enhance the expected active performance of their U.S. equity portfolios.

The actual optimal risk allocations will depend on investor assumptions about the ability of active managers to outperform their benchmarks.[14] Using historical separate account data, we have shown that the median and top-quartile information ratios for structured managers have exceeded those of traditional managers. This result is not surprising: Given their lower tracking error objectives and relative freedom from the no-short constraint, we *expect* realized information ratios to be higher for structured managers. (This result is consistent with the emerging literature that explores performance differences in mutual funds.)

Thus, investors should not be alarmed by the relative differences in historical information ratios. If these differences persist, then the practical implication is that investors will continue to need traditional managers within their active manager rosters—although possibly with somewhat smaller allocations. Our analysis also shows that manager selection is extremely important among traditional managers. Thus, when developing a portfolio of traditional managers, investors should balance the benefits of diversification against the higher fees and monitoring costs that come with manager proliferation.

Our main conclusion, however, is that investors should allocate risks across the entire active risk spectrum. Moreover, when moving from a barbell approach to a spectrum strategy, the allocation to structured managers is more likely to come

[13]Note that 100 basis points of tracking error should have little impact on the risk of the overall plan, given the small amount of active risk vis-à-vis the total risk in equities.

[14]Software has been developed that can help clients determine optimal risk allocations based on their own assumptions for risks, correlations, and expected returns across various managers and management styles.

from the passive side than from the traditional active side. Finally, this conclusion is reasonably insensitive to different assumptions about manager information ratios and correlations. Given reasonable expectations based on historical experience, most investors can benefit from adding a healthy percentage of structured management to their active equity programs.

SUMMARY

We believe investors can achieve better results by including low-tracking-error structured managers (also known as enhanced-index or benchmark-sensitive managers) in their mix of managers. We call this approach the "spectrum strategy" because it allocates risk across the entire active risk spectrum.

Historical analysis shows structured managers have generally achieved higher risk-adjusted returns (that is, information ratios) than traditional managers. We believe the relative performance advantage of structured managers is due to their focus on risk management and their relative freedom from the no-short constraint.

Importantly, and perhaps surprisingly, given the expected information ratio advantage, we find that allocations to structured managers should come primarily from the plan's passive allocation rather than from traditional managers.

CHAPTER 15

Risk Management and Risk Budgeting at the Total Fund Level

Jason Gottlieb

Plan sponsors are often faced with the challenges of evaluating the efficacy of their investment programs. A common methodology centers on the excess returns of their investment managers. However, there are inherent problems with focusing solely on performance. First, the mean is a very imprecise statistic and it can potentially take several years before any distinction between luck and skill of an investment manager can be made. Second, it is widely recognized that what matters to investors is not simply return, but risk-adjusted return, as measured, for example, by the information ratio.

Knowing investment programs have a limited capacity for active risk helps crystallize the importance of generating as much return per unit of risk as possible. Good practices of plan management require not only constructing diagnostic risk tools but also effective and careful monitoring. This chapter will highlight, among other things: the importance of risk and risk-adjusted measures, the setting of tracking error targets for monitoring purposes, the process around monitoring plan risk, and how to use the Green Sheet and risk budget as tools in an effective risk monitoring program. These tools are paramount in determining whether an investment program is being adequately compensated for the associated risks.

Chapter 13 explained the process of building a risk budget and Chapter 21 deals with the subject of manager selection. The focus of this chapter, rather, is on building a framework to monitor whether a plan is on track. The building of a risk-monitoring framework also means incorporating a set of assumptions about returns and volatility behavior, among other things. The task of monitoring is partly verifying that these assumptions are consistent with publicly available data. Should this not be the case, the deviations will have to be investigated. This feedback process is critical to measuring the efficacy of the investment program.

Chapter 3 on risk measurement highlighted the important choices that need to be made as part of risk budgeting implementation. It is important from this to recognize that there isn't a one-size-fits-all active risk budget that plan sponsors can implement. Rather, plan sponsors need to answer several questions before determining the appropriate level of active risk to be taken. Most appropriately, plan sponsors need to fully understand what their appetite for risk is and to know at what level of active risk the total plan volatility becomes unacceptably high. A plan's appetite for active risk must be weighed against several factors, including its ability to sustain losses in excess of its strategic benchmark. Just as a household needs to impose a budget that constrains spending to levels not exceeding income earned, so does a plan sponsor need to budget a realistic level of active risk commensurate with its ability to tolerate persistent active manager underperformance.

Once a level of active risk at each asset class and at the plan level has been agreed upon and managers have been selected to implement their strategies, it is then up to the risk oversight team to ensure effective implementation of the risk program. Effectiveness begins with understanding both individual manager and asset class level active risk characteristics and setting targets commensurate with expectations. Implementation of a risk program at the total fund can be a simple yet effective way of determining the efficacy of the investment program. The tools and techniques described in this chapter will provide insights into how a risk program can be executed.

Clearly, the goal of an active investment manager is to outperform a benchmark. However, we suggest that there is an additional dimension that ought to be used to measure investment manager skill. Investment managers should also be managing to a targeted level of risk, and in particular, managing the range within which the tracking error of their portfolio fluctuates.[1] It is our belief that most investment managers look to produce consistent, risk-adjusted performance relative to a benchmark. What this suggests is that investment managers must first develop the skills necessary to understand and manage their tracking error.

For example, just because a domestic equity manager is able to beat the Russell 3000 index, we shouldn't automatically assume that a plan sponsor should want to continue to retain the manager's services. Suppose the manager's outperformance is being derived with unacceptably high levels of tracking error, thus degrading the manager's realized information ratio. Clearly, not knowing how much risk is being taken at the manager level unduly handicaps a plan sponsor's ability to make sound investment decisions. These manager-specific issues can also exaggerate the amount and quality of risk[2] being taken at the total plan level.

An effective risk monitoring program is simple to put in place, however, and empowers the plan sponsor to evaluate not only the level of active risk at the manager and plan levels, but also the sources and the quality of active risk being generated in the investment program.

Fortunately, for plan sponsors there are alternatives as to how their investment plans can be implemented. First and foremost, a plan sponsor can choose to implement a strategic asset allocation through low-cost passive index alternatives that attempt to replicate the return and risk characteristics of an asset class. In doing so, plan sponsors would be making a determination that active managers do not have the skills required to beat the relevant asset class benchmark by enough to cover their fees and transaction costs (implicit and explicit) plus the costs associated with

[1]For more information, please see "The Green Zone . . . Assessing the Quality of Returns" (March 2000) by Robert Litterman et al. of Goldman Sachs & Co.

[2]We typically think of quality of risk as the percentage of active variance not explained via systematic factors, such as market, style, industry, or sector factors.

managing and monitoring an active program. Alternatively, plan sponsors can choose to allocate capital across both active and passive strategies, thus implementing their views where they believe value in excess of the benchmark can be added. The addition of active managers to the plan creates the need to manage and monitor the associated risks.

However, before allocating active risk, a plan sponsor will need to better understand the return, risk, and diversification characteristics of active managers within each asset class. These characteristics are essential in defining in what areas of the market it pays to have assets actively managed. We would suggest the usage of a robust universe of institutional manager data.

Peer universe data provides key insights into determining the potential for excess returns above respective benchmarks, associated tracking errors, and diversification or correlation benefits present in the asset class. Table 15.1 highlights the characteristics for various asset classes. We can draw some easy conclusions from the analysis. First, historically international developed and small-cap growth managers have been able to achieve superior risk-adjusted performance, as evidenced by their high information ratios. Second, domestic large-cap equities have historically had difficulty adding value above their benchmark and have been experiencing approximately 600 to 700 basis points of tracking error. Last, it is clear from the correlation analysis that in the international developed and emerging markets active

TABLE 15.1 Peer Universe Data for Different Asset Classes

	Annualized 10-Year Median		
Peer Universe Statistics	**ER (bps)**	**TE (bps)**	**IR**
U.S. Large Cap Growth (LCG)	113	715	0.16
U.S. Large Cap Value (LCV)	124	628	0.20
U.S. Small Cap Growth (SCG)	805	1,280	0.63
U.S. Small Cap Value (SCV)	282	918	0.31
International Equities (EAFE)	346	661	0.52
Emerging Equities (EMER)	425	832	0.48
Core Plus (CORE+)	57	126	0.43

ER—Excess return.
TE—Tracking error.
IR—Information ratio.

Correlation Matrix	**LCG**	**LCV**	**SCG**	**SCV**	**EAFE**	**EMER**	**CORE+**
LCG	0.07						
LCV	0.01	0.24					
SCG	0.00	0.05	0.27				
SCV	0.01	0.01	0.00	0.25			
EAFE	0.00	0.05	0.06	0.10	0.30		
EMER	0.05	0.00	0.07	0.11	0.04	0.32	
CORE+	0.02	0.06	0.00	0.03	0.03	0.08	0.22

managers tend to show similar characteristics. Thus, it is more difficult to diversify within the asset class as exhibited by the higher intra–asset class correlation.

It should be clear that the ability of investment managers to understand and manage the risk in their portfolios is of direct benefit to the client. Arguably managers' ability to quantify portfolio risks is a strong indication of skill and should positively correlate with their ability to consistently outperform the market. The foundation of successful portfolio construction is predicated on a manager's ability to understand and quantify sources of risk in a portfolio, to size intended exposures appropriately, and to avoid unintended exposures.

Risk managers can implement a simple approach to measuring the success or failure of their investment manager's ability to size their risk appropriately. We call this approach the "green zone." The idea is to define three levels of outcomes for tracking error. The first range of outcomes represents those that are close enough to a manager's targeted realized tracking error to be considered a successful event. This is the green zone. The second range of outcomes, the yellow zone, represents outcomes that are not successful, but that are close enough to target to be expected to happen on occasion. While the yellow zone is deemed to be unsuccessful, we should nonetheless expect even the most skilled investment managers to operate occasionally in the yellow zone simply because realized tracking error isn't fully controllable. Yellow zone outcomes should be viewed as warning signals to the risk manager. However, there may be a reasonable explanation for the event. Finally, we will define bad tracking error outcomes as the red zone. Events in this zone should occur rarely, if at all, for an investment manager who understands the sources of risk in their portfolio. Red zone events should be thought of not only as warnings, but as likely indications of a lack of control in the portfolio construction process.

This green zone discussion brings us back to our earlier example of the domestic equity manager who was able to beat the Russell 3000 index. Clearly, we are delighted that one of our managers is able to generate performance in excess of the benchmark. However, the manager was using higher levels of risk than we expected in order to generate positive performance. These unsuccessful tracking error outcomes not only are warnings for the risk manager but are likely indications of a lack of control in the manager's portfolio construction process. A thorough review of this manager should be conducted to ensure that inclusion in the total plan is wise. The manager analysis should also take into account not only the amount of risk being taken by the manager, but the manager's impact at the asset class and plan level as well. We say this because if our manager is taking on larger unintended exposures in the portfolio, it will typically mean that our domestic equity asset class will have a higher tracking error and contribution to total plan risk than budgeted.

It's worthwhile to spend time describing the process of setting manager level tracking error targets. The process entails the use of a manager's performance history or track record and the benchmark to which our manager's portfolio is compared. It is not uncommon for managers to have daily track records in the case of mutual funds; however, some institutional managers produce composite performance only on a monthly basis. In either case, data frequency should not present a major hurdle as long as the managers with monthly performance data have long enough track records. The objective is to compute rolling tracking error over various periods of time (i.e., rolling 20- and 60-day with daily performance data and

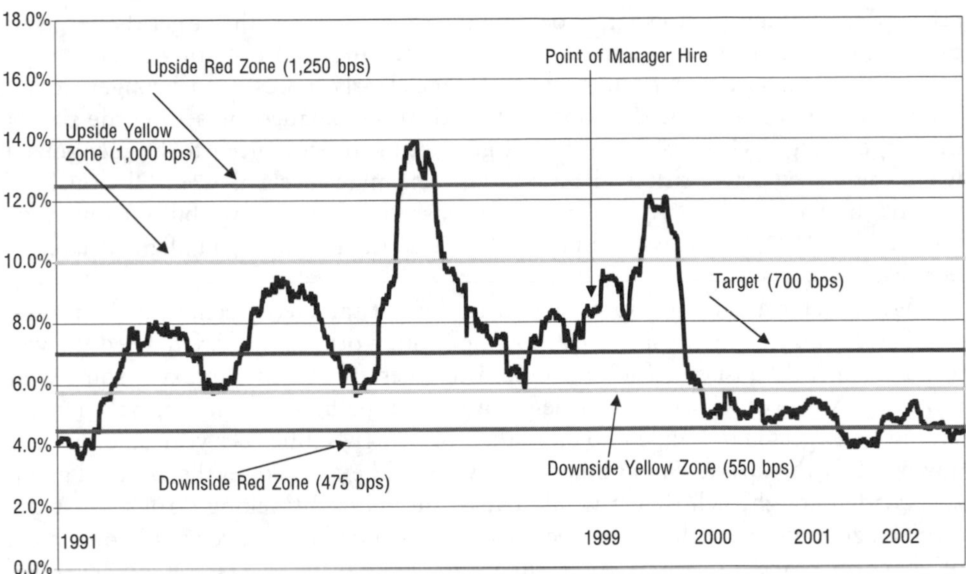

FIGURE 15.1 Rolling 60-Day Tracking Error (Annualized) International Manager O

rolling 24- and 36-month with monthly performance data). The tracking error of a manager can be computed as:[3]

$$\sigma_r = \sqrt{\frac{n \cdot \sum_{t=1}^{n} (r_{t,P} - r_{t,B})^2 - \left[\sum_{t=1}^{n} (r_{t,P} - r_{t,B}) \right]^2}{n^2}} \tag{15.1}$$

where n = Number of observations
$r_{t,P}$ = Return of the portfolio at time t
$r_{t,B}$ = Return of the benchmark at time t

Once the rolling analysis (Figure 15.1) has been completed, we can draw conclusions from the data with the use of simple statistics. By calculating the mean of our rolling tracking error analysis, we can see that on average our international manager has achieved 700 basis points of tracking error over the respective benchmark prior to hiring. We should reasonably expect that future tracking error observations should fall somewhere near the mean. By plotting the rolling analysis, we can graphically see our manager's historical "risk footprint." The graphical analysis should serve as the basis for discussing tracking error expectations with managers.

One of the most difficult questions that arises when attempting to set a range of

[3]There are other measures of tracking error, such as residual tracking error, which aims at removing directional or beta biases embedded in a manager's return series.

acceptable outcomes is how large to make the range. Clearly, the larger the targeted range, the easier it is for the manager to stay within it. Also, with a larger target range or green zone, a departure from the range clearly represents a stronger signal. Thus, there will always be a tension that needs to be balanced in setting the size of the target range. These issues in the target setting process need to be recognized when budgeting active risk at the asset class and plan levels as well. Obviously, if we give managers a longer tracking error leash, it impacts our ability to manage targeted levels of asset class and plan risk. These issues will be highlighted later in our discussion.

When determining the exact boundaries for the targeted green, yellow, and red zones, we would suggest using the following framework. Earlier, we defined the yellow zone as an "unsuccessful" outcome. Unsuccessful in this context is somewhat arbitrary, however, so we suggest defining it as something that in normal markets should be expected to happen no more than one or two times per year on either the downside or the upside. Put another way, we would expect to set the targeted green zone wide enough such that it would cause the realized tracking error to exit the targeted zone no more than twice per year. We also defined the red zone to be a set of "bad" or "rare" outcomes. Again, in a somewhat arbitrary fashion, however, we can build the red zones by appropriately setting the upper and lower boundaries for our yellow zones. In the case of the red zone, we define "rare" as an event that goes beyond the yellow zone on the upside or the downside no more than one or two times in five years.

It is important to note that while we are introducing a relatively simple color-coded approach to managing tracking error, we also recognize that the simplicity of this approach may be deceiving. The random influences of environmental factors in different markets, as well as the complexities of portfolio construction, statistical estimation, and so on, lead quickly to a thicket of complicated issues when one attempts to apply this approach in practice. Nonetheless, as yellow and red warnings occur, such issues are very relevant to the risk manager in interpreting the cause and implications of the signal.

While the use of either daily or monthly data in the target-setting process is appropriate, we would strongly advocate the use of daily data for tracking error computations after managers are hired for an assignment. Daily performance data coming in the form of manager feeds or performance attribution systems will help investors in identifying tracking error issues before they impact performance. Understandably, rolling 20-day and 60-day tracking error estimates can at times be noisy, yet they provide a reasonably accurate depiction of what is going on in the portfolio at the time. Therefore, we believe that shorter estimation periods can also be a leading indicator and highlight potential issues in a manager's portfolio. Finding out relatively quickly allows a risk manager to react equally as fast. For example, if our international equity manager's targeted tracking error is 550 to 1,000 basis points and we compute the most recent 60-day tracking error of his portfolio to be 400 basis points, then clearly this is an indication to the risk manager that further analysis is required to better understand the associated exposures that are leading to the unexpectedly low tracking error. Low tracking error is of as much concern as high tracking error because it makes achieving return targets more difficult.

If we were constrained by the frequency of monthly data for our risk analysis, we would have the unavoidable disadvantage of not being able to react as quickly to changes in realized tracking error as we are able to do with daily estimation. Potentially, two years would have to elapse before we had a reasonable estimate of the portfolio's realized tracking error. Needless to say, a lot can happen in two years. Let's say for argument's sake that monthly data was all we had access to. If we ran a rolling analysis after two years and found the realized tracking error to be well in excess of our expectation of 550 to 1,000 basis points, chances are it would be too late to react to the signals. Potential unidentified flaws in the investment process would be caught too late and could have the unfortunate ability to detract from plan value.

The framework of setting tracking error bands is a combination of both art and science. In areas of the market where the valuation transparency is low and market liquidity constrains a manager's ability to react, there needs to be an even greater emphasis on judgment. Emerging equity and high-yield debt markets are two examples that readily come to mind. High-yield markets are typically illiquid, which at times makes the costs of trading prohibitively expensive. If market conditions were such that managers could not trade their portfolios efficiently, then we would expect larger, uncontrolled deviations from the benchmarks. In these cases, we would suggest using wider bands to accommodate the need for a smooth portfolio transition when market volatilities are changing.

GREEN SHEET

One of the tools risk managers can deploy when managing a large portfolio of investment managers is what we call the "Green Sheet." The Green Sheet is a diagnostic tool developed to help risk managers better understand the active performance and risk drivers at the total plan level. In doing so the Green Sheet allows risk managers to focus their attention on managers and asset classes that are exhibiting performance or risk out of line with expectations.

In looking at the sample Green Sheet shown in Table 15.2, we notice that ABC pension fund's tracking error over the past 60 days is 128 basis points, which is far in excess of its 65 to 110 basis point target. As expected, this puts the plan's tracking error in the upper yellow zone. On a stand-alone basis, knowing that ABC's plan has exceeded risk expectations doesn't shed much light for the risk manager about what the potential risk drivers may be. However, the Green Sheet is quick to highlight for the risk manager that most active large and small cap managers are experiencing tracking errors that exceed expectations. For example, small cap growth manager G has a 60-day tracking error two times expectations.

In fact, at the asset class level both large caps and small caps are exhibiting large deviations from their targets. Further investigation through the use of a second tool, the risk budget (Table 15.3), shows that our large cap managers are exhibiting higher correlations to one another than expected. We will be talking more about the practical applications of the risk budget in the next section.

It is the risk manager's responsibility to spend time understanding the market and portfolio dynamics before initiating a conversation with a portfolio manager. Many times the risk management team will be able to attribute the deviations in active risk away from targets without manager discussions. Factors such as changes

TABLE 15.2 ABC Pension Plan Green Sheet

		Normalized Return			Annualized Tracking Error						Month to Date		
Portfolio	Benchmark	MTD	YTD	SI	Last 20D (bps)	Last 60D (bps)	Last 12M (bps)	Last 20D/ Target	Last 60D/ Target	Last 12M/ Target	P (%)	B (%)	ER (bps)
US Equity—Total LC	R1000				95	130[1]	101	1.06	1.44[1]	1.12	4.22	4.11	11
Passive	R1000				0	0	12				4.11	4.11	(0)
US Equity—Active LC	R1000				221	185	178				4.27	4.11	16
Manager A	R1000V	(0.58)	(1.69)	(0.11)	227[2]	233[2]	241[2]	0.65[2]	0.66[2]	0.69[2]	4.32	4.73	(41)
Manager B	R1000G	1.08	0.26	1.02	1,235	1,302[1]	1,162	1.30	1.37[1]	1.22	6.71	3.46	325
Manager C	R1000G	0.41	(0.85)	0.23	580[1]	956	919	0.77[1]	1.27	1.23	4.60	3.46	114
Manager D	R1000G	1.01	(0.59)	(1.38)	1,745[2]	1,654[2]	1,501[1]	1.94[2]	1.84[2]	1.67[1]	6.33	3.46	288
Manager E	R1000	(1.40)	(0.62)	(0.21)	162	175	-	0.81	0.88	-	3.45	4.11	(66)
Manager F	S&P 500	0.58	0.60	(0.09)	85	90	-	0.85	0.90	-	4.00	3.76	24
US Equity—Total SC	R2000				692[1]	851[2]	556	1.49[1]	1.83[2]	1.20	11.13	8.03	310
US Equity—SCG	R2000G				987	1,013	911				10.78	8.69	209
Manager G	R2000G	0.52	(0.69)	0.26	1,350	1,890[2]	1,100	1.50	2.10[2]	1.22	10.34	8.69	165
Manager K	R2000G	0.76	-	(0.87)	936	1,500[1]	925	0.94	1.50[1]	0.93	11.22	8.69	252
US Equity—SCV	R2000V				544	580	503				11.32	7.48	384
Manager L	R2000V	1.57	(0.26)	0.64	319[2]	405[2]	425[1]	0.53[2]	0.68[2]	0.71[1]	10.33	7.48	285
Manager M	R2000V	2.23	1.37	0.75	1,423[1]	1,350	-	1.42[1]	1.35	-	14.04	7.48	656
Int'l—Total Dev	EAFE 50% Hdgd				271	265	248	0.96	0.94	0.88	4.76	4.94	(19)
Passive	EAFE				-	28	69				5.35	5.41	(6)
Int'l—Active Dev	EAFE				302	304	332				5.46	5.41	6
Manager N	EAFE	(0.46)	(0.66)	(0.40)	560	575	675	1.02	1.05	1.23	4.96	5.41	(45)
Manager O	EAFE	0.28	0.65	(0.51)	385[2]	390[2]	386[2]	0.55[2]	0.56[2]	0.55[2]	6.01	5.41	60
Manager P	EAFE	(0.09)	0.19	1.01	456	650	587	0.91	1.30	1.17	5.52	5.41	11
Non-US—Emerg	EMF				385[1]	409	564	0.76[1]	0.81	1.11	6.39	6.01	39
Manager Q	EMF	0.14	0.38	0.20	402	415	424	0.80	0.83	0.85	6.37	6.01	36
Manager R	EMF	0.02	(0.16)	(1.63)	725	800	896	0.81	0.89	1.00	6.46	6.01	45
Global FI	Leh Agg				78	71	85	1.13	1.03	1.23	(1.73)	(1.66)	(7)
Manager S	Leh Agg	(0.96)	(0.60)	(0.58)	110	95[1]	120	0.88	0.76[1]	0.96	(1.92)	(1.66)	(26)
Manager T	Leh Agg	(1.62)	(0.79)	(0.72)	152[1]	135	140	1.52[1]	1.35	1.40	(2.05)	(1.66)	(39)
Passive	Leh Agg				-	3	12				(1.56)	(1.66)	10
Total Fund	Strategic	0.37	(0.17)	(0.16)	100	128[1]	105	1.25	1.60[1]	1.31	2.99	2.78	21

[1]Yellow zone.
[2]Red zone.

in market volatility or changing correlations and volatilities of the stocks within the portfolio or benchmark can often help explain a manager's deviation from target. Other times there will be clear signals within the portfolio such as significant active over- or underweights that largely contribute to the sizable deviation. If it is determined through internal analysis and research that systematic or market factors aren't sufficient in helping explain a portfolio's deviations from target, then we would suggest immediately initiating contact with the portfolio manager.

Manager conversations should focus on two specific areas: (1) gaining a better understanding of what decision factors and exposures have led to the deviations from target and (2) gaining a clear understanding of near-term and long-term expectations regarding the portfolio's tracking error.

The decisions that led to the deviation from target help us to better evaluate whether the portfolio manager's exposures are intended exposures, which are more

YTD Thru March 28, 2002			SI Thru March 28, 2002			Annualized Gross Targets			Downside Zone		Upside Zone	
P (%)	B (%)	ER (bps)	P (%)	B (%)	ER (bps)	ER (bps)	TE (bps)	IR	Red TE[2] (bps)	Yellow TE[1] (bps)	Yellow TE[1] (bps)	Red TE[2] (bps)
0.38	0.74	(36)	(3.82)	(4.48)	66	45	90	0.50	63	72	126	162
0.78	0.74	4	(4.41)	(4.48)	7							
0.08	0.74	(65)	(0.57)	(3.51)	294							
1.62	4.09	(248)	4.79	3.16	163	200	350	0.57	245	280	500	650
(0.21)	(2.59)	238	0.79	(13.42)	1,421	450	950	0.47	665	760	1,250	1,500
(4.90)	(2.59)	(232)	(8.22)	(13.42)	519	350	750	0.47	525	600	1,050	1,600
(4.27)	(2.59)	(168)	(26.98)	(18.60)	(838)	400	900	0.44	630	720	1,250	1,600
0.52	0.74	(22)	(4.26)	(5.11)	85	160	200	0.80	140	160	300	400
0.83	0.27	56	(3.00)	(3.64)	64	100	100	1.00	70	80	150	200
5.39	3.98	141	14.29	8.58	571	232	465	0.50	326	372	652	838
(4.46)	(1.96)	(250)	0.89	(4.38)	527							
(4.04)	(1.96)	(208)	2.14	(4.38)	652	415	900	0.40	630	720	1,350	1,600
			(1.02)	1.66	(267)	500	1,000	0.50	700	800	1,400	1,700
11.47	9.58	189	23.42	21.25	217							
9.40	9.58	(18)	27.48	21.25	623	240	600	0.40	420	480	850	1,050
17.36	9.58	778	21.94	13.39	856	350	1,000	0.35	700	800	1,400	1,650
1.87	1.23	64	(5.69)	(8.53)	284	141	283	0.50	198	226	396	509
0.49	0.51	(1)	(10.28)	(10.65)	37							
1.37	0.51	86	(4.85)	(8.98)	413							
(0.51)	0.51	(102)	(7.92)	(8.98)	106	325	550	0.59	385	440	750	950
2.78	0.51	227	(9.04)	(8.98)	(6)	350	700	0.50	475	550	1,000	1,250
2.08	0.51	157	1.60	(8.98)	1,057	250	500	0.50	350	400	700	950
13.00	11.81	119	(6.56)	(3.11)	(346)	254	508	0.50	356	407	711	915
13.27	11.81	147	(3.72)	(6.72)	301	200	500	0.40	350	400	700	800
12.33	11.81	52	(1.19)	8.49	(967)	500	900	0.56	630	720	1,300	1,600
0.22	0.10	13	7.78	7.89	(11)	35	69	0.50	48	55	97	124
(0.02)	0.10	(12)	8.16	7.89	27	100	125	0.80	88	100	165	200
(0.10)	0.10	(20)	8.46	8.39	8	80	100	0.80	70	80	150	200
0.36	0.10	26	10.19	9.18	101							
1.82	1.53	29	3.03	1.74	130	145	80	1.81	55	65	110	140

palatable than unintended exposures. This brings us back to a point made earlier regarding the correlation between managers' ability to quantify risks in their portfolios and their ability to generate returns in excess of their benchmarks. Managers who don't fully understand the risks in their portfolios will over time find it more difficult to add value after fees for their clients.

Setting near-term expectations is also important because it allows for more effective ongoing oversight of the portfolio. Risk managers can monitor the specific decisions and milestones that should ultimately bring the portfolio manager's risk back in line with expectations. For example, suppose that through conversations it is determined that the portfolio manager believes several near-term catalysts in the technology sector will significantly enhance the prices of stocks in the portfolio. Further, suppose the portfolio manager states the intent to reduce exposure to those stocks as the rise occurs, or subsequently, if the sector's news isn't as posi-

TABLE 15.3 ABC Pension Plan Risk Budget

Asset Class	Tracking Error							Active Risk % Decomposition				
	Current Tracking Error	Target Zone (.7×)	Target Zone (.8×)	Tracking Error	Target Zone (1.4×)	Target Zone (1.8×)	Current Beta	Asset Allocation	Beta	Manager-Specific	Current % Risk*	Target % Risk*
U.S. large cap equity	**130**[1]	63	72	90	126	162	**0.99**	2.3%	–0.5%	16.1%	**18.0%**[1]	15.0%
U.S. small cap equity	**851**[2]	326	372	465	652	838	**0.99**	–0.3	–0.2	24.2	**23.7**[1]	20.7
International equity	**265**[3]	198	226	283	396	509	**0.98**	–0.2	–0.1	41.3	**40.9**[3]	41.7
Emerging markets equity	**409**[3]	356	407	508	711	915	**1.06**	4.1	1.4	4.4	**9.9**[3]	12.7
Global fixed income	**71**[3]	48	55	69	97	124	**1.00**	0.4	0.0	7.1	**7.5**[3]	9.9
Plan	**128**[1]	55	65	80	110	140	**1.00**	6.3	0.7	70.4	**100.0**	100.0

Asset Class	Asset Allocation		
	Current Allocation	Target Allocation	Delta Current–Target
U.S. large cap equity	**34.1%**	32.5%	1.6%
U.S. small cap equity	**7.4**	8.3	–0.9
International equity	**20.4**	21.6	–1.2
Emerging markets equity	**4.6**	4.8	–0.1
Global fixed income	**33.4**	32.8	0.6
Plan	**100.0**	100	

Top 10 Risk Contributors (% Plan Risk)		
Manager	Current	Budget
Manager M	**15.5%**	22.5%
Manager G	**16.2**	2.2
Manager L	**9.6**	12.8
Manager N	**8.0**	5.1
Manager R	**7.0**	3.2
Manager Q	**6.5**	–0.1
Manager K	**5.1**	3.7
Manager P	**4.8**	0.0
Manager H	**2.9**	4.9
Manager C	**2.9**	4.9
	78.5	59.2

*Current risk – Target risk: if between +/– 3 and 7%: yellow; if greater than +/– 7%: red.

[1] Yellow zone.

[2] Red zone.

[3] Green zone.

tive, to reduce exposures as well. This is powerful information for the risk manager. Now, based on the specific information gleaned from conversations with the portfolio manager, the risk manager can more effectively monitor changes and risk levels in the portfolio.

RISK BUDGET

Understanding the nature and the sources of risks taken in the investment program is essential. Ultimately, intelligent placing of portfolio exposures will result in a more consistent alpha generation process. The risk budget (Table 15.3) is the diagnostic tool of risk decomposition: Its aim is to identify the sources and magnitudes of risk taken in the aggregate portfolio. Before plan sponsors prescribe changes to the composition or implementation of the investment program, they can make use of the risk budget to obtain a diagnosis of the situation.

Suppose that when risk targets are set, it is with the paradigm in mind that the bulk of active plan risk should come from security selection rather than other deviations from the given benchmark. Security selection resulting from in-depth investment research is typically considered an area where active managers can add value. If we think of risk management as resource allocation in a scarce or budgeted environment, the risk budget will hopefully streamline that process by giving the sponsors signals about realized risks. If these signals are not congruent to expectations, this tool allows tracing the misalignment to three areas: asset allocation, beta or market leverage, and individual security selection. Furthermore, the risk budgeting tool provides relevant information at the manager, asset class, and fund level.

At the asset class or manager level, plan sponsors will have a target allocation set as a percentage of the total fund. To the extent managers are over/underfunded an asset allocation risk is generated: The fund is over/underexposed to this asset class. This can occur, for example, as a result of market drifts between asset classes. In the example summarized in Table 15.3, the U.S. equity asset class is above target weight, and this accounts for 2.3 percent of the total plan risk. U.S. equities have outperformed their international counterpart, which has created a 1.6 percent overweight in U.S. equities. In order to correct this situation, plan sponsors often employ completion strategies. Completion managers will utilize futures, long and short, to bring the asset class over/underweights back to strategic targets. Completion strategies are discussed further in Chapter 25. Completion strategies remove the need to frequently move capital in and out of active strategies, thus alleviating undue transaction costs for the aggregate portfolio.

An additional source of risk can come from the sensitivity of a manager's portfolio to the swings of its underlying benchmark. The statistical measure of this sensitivity is known as beta. When beta is greater than 1.0, the portfolio exhibits a form of market leverage: It can be expected to outperform in up markets and underperform in down markets. In Table 15.3, the international equity asset class has a beta of 0.98. This implies that the intended asset allocation is somewhat distorted. The low beta can translate into the fund being underexposed to international equity. In this particular case, one of the managers in the international roster is systematically tilted toward the value side of the benchmark, investing in undervalued stocks. This results in a low beta against the benchmark. Note, however, that being underexposed due to a low beta and being overexposed due to overallocation can run counter to one another.

Finally, the stock selection risk represents the tracking error incurred after adjusting for beta effects in the relative movements of the portfolio vis-à-vis the benchmark, sector, and style exposures. A high ratio of security selection risk to total risk is typically a sign of high-quality risk taking. The underlying presumption is that managers can add value in security selection but that timing markets or making substantial sector or style bets is a much harder game to play. Therefore, high beta risk, sector, or style exposures can often bode ill for the plan's performance.

The assumptions underlying the risk budget will invariably be tested and reanalyzed during the life of a plan. Understanding the differences in return and risk characteristics of the individual managers and how these compare with outside peers is also a key component of the process. Plans have a only finite capacity to take active risk. Given that active risk is seen as a scarce resource, the importance of monitoring the budget should not be underestimated.

We highlighted throughout this discussion the need for plan sponsors to focus more attention on risk-adjusted measures as we believe risk-adjusted measures provide a much more robust framework than a performance-only based analysis. Also, a well defined and carefully thought out risk monitoring program predicated on risk-adjusted measures is a simple yet highly effective way to determine the efficacy of an investment program. While tools such as the Green Sheet and risk budget are samples of many available, the two combined can provide a powerful framework for monitoring aggregate plan risks.

SUMMARY

Plan risk should be thought of as a finite commodity to be used or spent intelligently across the spectrum of managers in the investment program as a means to maximizing expected return.

The importance of risk-adjusted returns becomes more relevant in a risk budgeting framework since its underlying tools help us understand whether a program is being adequately rewarded for its active risks.

These tools include the setting of tracking error zones for each manager and/or asset class in the program. This approach, known as the Green Zone, represents an alternative to monitor relative risk behavior, market conditions, and the level of control in the portfolio construction process.

A related approach, known as the Green Sheet, summarizes tracking error and performance outcomes at the manager, asset class, and plan level on a 20-day, 60-day, and 12-month basis. These tools will unearth areas of risk taking that need further analysis or exploration while potentially triggering conversations with portfolio managers. They will also provide indirect feedback to the validity and soundness of the initial target-setting process.

In a third approach, the risk budget decomposes the active risk incurred in the program, tracing it to mainly three sources: asset allocation, beta, and manager-specific risk. This tool streamlines the process of risk allocation by contrasting targets against realized risks. The attribution of risk is important given the paradigm that most of the active risk should come from security selection as opposed to market timing and asset class bets. Like the other tools, an indirect feedback emerges from the risk budget, as the assumptions associated with the budget will invariably be tested once the investment program is implemented.

The array of risk monitoring tools presented in this chapter highlights the importance of focusing more time and resources on risk-adjusted measures, as we believe they provide a more robust framework to determine the efficacy of an investment program.

CHAPTER 16

Covariance Matrix Estimation

Giorgio De Santis, Bob Litterman,
Adrien Vesval, and Kurt Winkelmann

INTRODUCTION

A large number of applications in finance require measures of volatilities and correlations. A well-known example is the portfolio optimization problem originally developed by Markowitz (1952), in which an investor forms a portfolio of assets from a given universe by maximizing the expected return on the portfolio subject to a risk constraint. Risk in this case is measured by a weighted sum of the variances and covariances of all assets. More generally, risk measures are needed to solve problems such as optimal hedging, pricing of derivative securities, decomposition of risk for a given portfolio, and so on.

When dealing with multiple assets, measures of risk are typically organized in a variance-covariance matrix, which is a square array of numbers that contains variances along its main diagonal and covariances between all pairs of assets in the off-diagonal positions. Unfortunately, although it is a necessary input to many problems in finance, the true covariance matrix of asset returns is not observed and, therefore, must be estimated using statistical techniques.

Having established the need for estimation, one may still be skeptical about the need for an entire chapter on this topic. After all, variances and covariances can often be estimated using fairly basic methods. For example, suppose that our objective is to estimate the variance-covariance matrix of monthly returns for a given set of assets, and assume that we have access to 10 years of monthly data (120 monthly observations). We could estimate variances and covariances using the well-known formulas for sample moments:

$$\mathrm{var}\left[r_i(m)\right] = \frac{\sum_{t=1}^{120}\left[r_{i,t}(m) - \bar{r}_i(m)\right]^2}{120}$$

and

$$\operatorname{cov}\left[r_i(m), r_j(m)\right] = \frac{\sum_{t=1}^{120}\left[r_{i,t}(m) - \bar{r}_i(m)\right]\left[r_{j,t}(m) - \bar{r}_j(m)\right]}{120}$$

where $r_{i,t}(m)$ denotes the return on asset i between month $t - 1$ and month t, and $\bar{r}_i(m)$ indicates its sample mean.

This estimator is easy to compute and update at the end of each month. Unfortunately, it also has a number of limitations. For example, it assigns the same weight to all the observations in the sample. This makes sense if the distribution that generates the monthly returns does not change over the 10-year period. However, if market volatility increased (decreased) significantly over the last part of the sample, this simple estimator would take a long time (often too long) to capture this change, because each new observation added to the sample has a small weight. In addition, the estimator uses only monthly data and, therefore, is not able to accommodate changes in market conditions that may be reflected in data at higher frequency, for example daily. The natural question to ask at this point is whether these limitations are relevant in practice. More specifically, are we likely to change our investment decisions due to the choice of a particular covariance matrix estimator? To answer this question, we present two scenarios in which the covariance matrix estimator plays an important role, and discuss the sensitivity of our conclusions to the use of two alternative estimators.

In the first example, we consider two specifications of a $100 million portfolio invested in 18 developed equity markets: a market capitalization weighted portfolio, with the weights measured at the end of May 2002, and an equally weighted portfolio. For each portfolio, we want to estimate the risk contribution from each individual position, and the Value at Risk (VaR), which we identify with the amount of capital that would be expected to be lost once in 100 months. The two covariance matrix estimators that we use are both based on standard techniques followed by investment professionals.[1] The first estimator (risk model A) uses 10 years of daily data and assigns a larger weight to more recent observations, starting from a weight of 1 and reducing it by approximately 25 percent on a monthly basis. The second estimator (risk model B) uses nine years of monthly data and assigns the same weight to all observations.

The left part of Table 16.1 shows that the two estimators generate different values in the risk decomposition of the value-weighted portfolio. Not surprisingly, the differences are more pronounced for the largest positions in the portfolio (United States, United Kingdom, and Japan). The estimated VaR also increases by more than 7 percent when using estimator A instead of B.

The right part of Table 16.1 contains similar statistics for the equally weighted portfolio. The effect on risk decomposition is even more striking. For example, Hong Kong and Singapore are among the bottom contributors to risk when using

[1]At this point, we do not discuss which estimator is more desirable. We leave that analysis for the main section of this chapter.

TABLE 16.1 Risk Decomposition and Value at Risk Sensitivity to Different Covariance Matrix Estimators

	Market Capitalization Weights (May 2002)			Equal Weights		
	Weights	Risk Model A Risk	Risk Model B Risk	Weights	Risk Model A Risk	Risk Model B Risk
Australia	1.75%	0.28%	1.18%	5.56%	1.45%	3.68%
Austria	0.07	0.01	0.05	5.56	1.65	4.76
Belgium	0.49	0.28	0.35	5.56	4.74	3.97
Canada	2.31	1.87	2.46	5.56	4.86	5.13
Denmark	0.36	0.16	0.32	5.56	4.23	5.15
France	4.51	4.35	5.09	5.56	8.01	6.23
Germany	3.31	3.94	3.95	5.56	8.90	6.57
Hong Kong	0.85	0.23	1.21	5.56	3.40	8.02
Italy	1.80	1.59	1.86	5.56	7.23	6.17
Japan	9.99	5.56	7.89	5.56	3.88	3.82
Netherlands	2.62	2.51	2.83	5.56	8.15	5.90
Norway	0.24	0.12	0.25	5.56	4.58	6.10
Singapore	0.41	0.17	0.50	5.56	4.23	6.75
Spain	1.39	1.40	1.68	5.56	8.35	6.84
Sweden	0.88	1.01	1.19	5.56	9.78	7.49
Switzerland	3.54	2.18	3.31	5.56	5.43	5.02
United Kingdom	10.74	7.55	8.46	5.56	5.60	4.07
United States	54.73	66.80	57.43	5.56	5.50	4.33
Sum/VaR	100.00%	$9.06 million	$8.44 million	100.00%	$7.37 million	$9.36 million

estimator A, but become two of the top four contributors when using estimator B. In this case, the estimated VaR declines by more than 21 percent when switching from estimator B to estimator A.

Another typical problem that uses the covariance matrix as an input is the asset allocation problem. We focus on this example because it is often argued that the main driver behind the construction of an optimal portfolio is a good set of expected returns, and that the risk model plays only a secondary role. The evidence from our examples suggests that this is clearly a misconception.

We consider two portfolio managers who rebalance their assets at the end of each quarter, and attempt to maximize their expected returns subject to a tracking error constraint of 1 percent per quarter, relative to the same cash benchmark. We follow both managers from the first quarter of 1982 to the first quarter of 2002, for a total of 81 quarters. As in the previous example, the managers can form their optimal portfolios from a menu of 18 developed equity markets. They share the same views on the market in terms of expected returns, but use different models to estimate the covariance matrix.

To provide direct evidence on the claim that a good forecasting model is likely to overcome any weakness of the risk model, we assume that the expected returns for each quarter are equal to the realized returns for that quarter. This is a model with perfect foresight and, therefore, superior to any realistic forecasting model that uses only available data at any point in time. The two covariance matrices are estimated as follows: Portfolio manager A uses only daily data from the upcoming quarter, whereas manager B uses daily data from a rolling window of 10 years. Obviously, the risk forecasts for manager A are based on information that would not be available at the time of rebalancing. However, this risk model is a good benchmark because it is updated frequently and captures, by construction, any changes in volatilities and correlations that occur in the quarter following each rebalance. The risk model used by manager B, on the other hand, is updated very slowly. If market risk varies over time, this model may capture volatilities and correlations correctly on average, but is likely to underestimate/overestimate risk over shorter periods. Based on this setup, we should expect both managers to do equally well if their performance is mostly driven by their forecasting model for expected returns. If, though, the risk model is also relevant, then we may expect manager A to outperform manager B, due to the superiority of manager A's risk model.

Over the 20 years in the sample, manager A's average excess return is equal to 5.52 percent per quarter, whereas manager B outperforms the cash benchmark by an average of 4.97 percent per quarter.[2] In terms of realized risk, both managers experience a higher risk relative to their target. However, the quarterly volatility for manager A is equal to 1.78 percent, which is considerably lower than the 2.59 percent realized by manager B. Since investors like excess returns and dislike volatility, manager A outperforms manager B in both dimensions. In fact, the information ratio (the annualized excess return per unit of risk) of manager A is 60 percent higher than that of manager B. This result is quite striking, considering that it is driven only by differences in the covariance matrix estimators used by the two managers.

Our two examples indicate that investment decisions and performance may be significantly affected by the choice of the covariance matrix estimator. Therefore, in the remainder of this chapter we discuss estimation techniques that can be used to produce covariance matrices with desirable statistical properties. Given the extensive literature on this topic, any attempt to provide a complete summary of the various methodologies proposed over the past few decades would be doomed to fail. We prefer to take a more practical approach. First, we identify some empirical regularities of financial data that should be captured by any covariance matrix estimator. Next, we discuss some relatively simple techniques that can be used to produce covariance matrix estimators with desirable statistical properties. Third, we discuss some data problems that are often faced by practitioners when building risk models, and we provide solutions for those problems. Finally, we discuss potential extensions and alternatives to our approach.

SOME INTERESTING PROPERTIES OF FINANCIAL DATA

The normal distribution is often used to characterize the uncertain outcome of an experiment. Finance is no exception to this tendency, and therefore in many applications the returns on sets of financial assets are assumed to follow a multivariate

[2]These numbers are considerably higher than those observed for actual portfolio managers. This is because our forecasting model uses data that are not observable at the time of rebalancing.

normal distribution. Sometimes, it is also assumed that this distribution is stationary over time, which implies that means, volatilities, and correlations do not change over time. Here, we argue that these assumptions are usually incorrect and, therefore, should not be maintained when constructing a covariance matrix estimator.

As a first step, we analyze the distribution of realized daily returns for the equity indexes of four of the largest markets in the MSCI universe: the United States, Japan, the United Kingdom, and Germany. We focus on daily returns from January 1997 to December 2001, for a total of 1,935 observations. A well-known property of the normal distribution is that, relative to its mean, 95.4 percent of the observations are within a two standard deviation interval, and 68.3 percent of the observations are within a one standard deviation interval. Given the size of our sample, if the returns for each market were normally distributed, then we should expect only 89 observations to fall outside a two standard deviation range relative to the long-term average return, and 1,322 observations to be within one standard deviation of that average. Table 16.2 shows that neither condition is satisfied by the data. In fact, for all the countries in our set, we find that the number of observations outside the two standard deviation range is considerably larger than what is predicted by a normal distribution, and so is the number of observations concentrated around the long-term average. Although this is not a formal test of the hypothesis of normality, the consistency of the evidence across the four markets suggests that daily returns follow a distribution with heavier tails than the normal (so-called leptokurtic distribution).

Next, we address the issue of stationarity. Again, we use daily data for the United States, Japan, the United Kingdom, and Germany. The sample starts in January 1980 and ends in May 2002, for a total of 5,850 observations. We use two different estimators for the covariance matrix. The first estimator assumes that the moments of the distribution are constant throughout the sample, and therefore uses the entire history of data and assigns the same weight to each observation. The second estimator is based on a popular technique used by many practitioners to capture time variation in second moments. At each point in time, volatilities and correlations are estimated using only the most recent data, contained in a moving window of prespecified length. In our case, the window contains the most recent 100 observations. Each day, we update the estimates by adding the most recent return observations and deleting the observations that are now 101 days old.

We start with an analysis of the volatilities. Figure 16.1 displays the estimates obtained from the two methodologies for each of the four equity markets. Visual inspection suggests that the estimates obtained from a rolling window of data oscil-

TABLE 16.2 Empirical Distribution of Daily Equity Returns

Sample Period: January 1997 to December 2001
Sample Size: 1,935

	N(0,1)	Germany	Japan	U.K.	U.S.
Number of returns > 2std	89	162	132	127	128
Number of returns < 1std	1,322	1,330	1,375	1,407	1,404

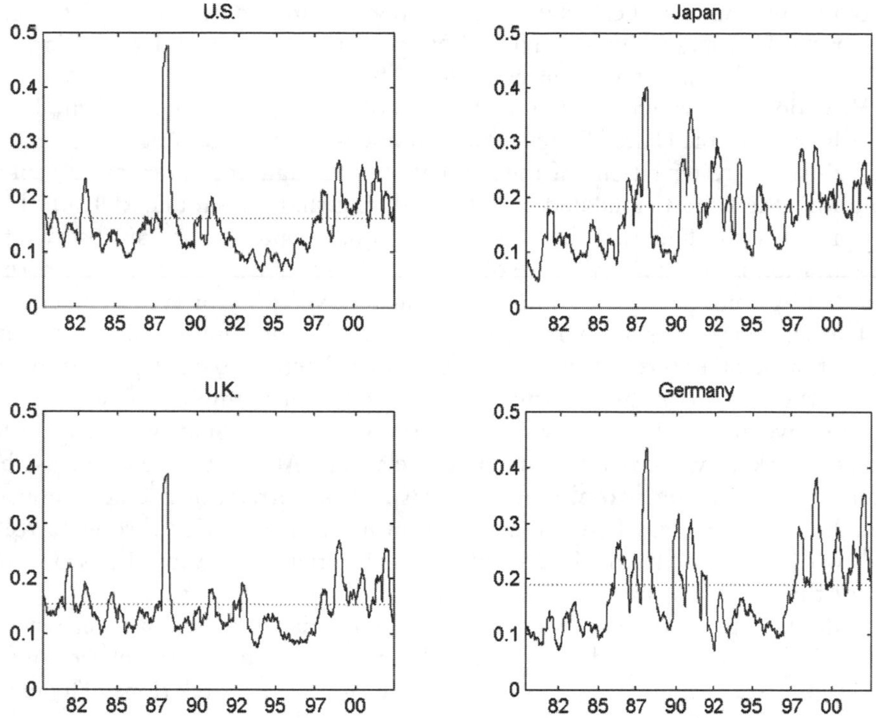

FIGURE 16.1 Annualized Volatilities: Comparison between Constant and Time-Varying Estimates

late significantly around the constant estimate. For example, the annualized constant volatility for the U.S. equity market is equal to 16.06 percent in our sample. However, over the same period, the time-varying estimate oscillates between a maximum of 48.49 percent and a minimum of 6.51 percent. The evidence is similar for the other three markets.

The question is whether the fluctuations generated by the second estimator reflect actual variations in market volatility or are the consequence of noise in the data. In fact, one could argue that the rolling window is too short and, therefore, too sensitive to the addition/deletion of a single large observation. To address this issue, we perform a simple exercise based on a technique known as Monte Carlo simulation.

A typical Monte Carlo simulation is performed as follows. Start by postulating a null hypothesis to be tested. In our case, we postulate that the annual volatility of the U.S. market between 1980 and 2002 is constant and equal to 16.06 percent. Second, generate a large number of histories (time series of data) assuming that the null hypothesis is true. For our exercise, we generated 1,000 histories, each containing 5,850 observations, assuming that the data were drawn from a normal distribution with an annual volatility of 16.06 percent. For each history, we constructed the time series of volatilities based on the rolling window technique, and computed the average absolute deviation (aad) between those volatilities and the postulated true volatility. Since we generated 1,000 histories, we were able to compute 1,000 aad's and calculate their mean and standard deviation. The average aad for the U.S. market was equal to 0.91 percent, with a standard deviation of 0.07 percent. The largest aad was equal to 1.18 percent.

How does the evidence from the observed data compare to the simulated histories? The aad for the United States in our sample is equal to 4.46 percent, well outside two standard deviations of the simulated mean aad and, even more striking, well above the largest simulated aad. Considering that we simulated 1,000 histories, one must conclude that there is less than a 0.001 probability of observing the time variation in volatilities that we observe in our sample, if the data were actually generated by a normal distribution with a constant volatility of 16.06 percent.

The summary statistics in Table 16.3 confirm that our findings are just as convincing for the other three countries in the sample. Therefore, it is hard not to reject the hypothesis of a constant volatility, at least within our sampling period.

Next, we analyze the history of correlations over time. Since we focus on four different markets, we have a total of six correlations. Also in this case, we use both estimators to compute two alternative measures of correlations: One is constant throughout the sample, whereas the other captures time variation through a rolling window of 100 days. Figure 16.2 displays the differences between the two estimators for the six correlations.

Following the same approach as in the volatility analysis, we performed a Monte Carlo simulation to determine whether the observed aad's from the constant correlations are a legitimate sign of time-variation in the correlations. The experiment reveals that the observed aad's are larger than the maximum aad's simulated in 1,000 Monte Carlo histories assuming a constant correlation. The summary statistics for this experiment are reported in Table 16.4.

To summarize, the evidence from our sample suggests that:

- Daily returns appear to be generated by a distribution with heavier tails (a higher probability of extreme events) than the normal distribution.
- Volatilities and correlations vary over time.

These properties of the distribution of daily returns must be kept in mind as we embark in our main task: the identification of a desirable estimator of the covariance matrix. The next challenge is to find an estimator that strikes a balanced compromise between statistical sophistication and parsimony. In fact, on one hand we

TABLE 16.3 Test of Time Variation in Volatilities

	Observed Data			Monte Carlo Data		
	Constant Volatility Estimate	Observed aad	Standard Deviation of Time Varying Estimates	Average aad	Standard Deviation of aad	Maximum aad
United States	16.1%	4.46%	4.30%	0.91%	0.07%	1.18%
Japan	18.4	5.63	4.03	1.04	0.08	1.36
United Kingdom	15.4	3.53	3.35	0.87	0.07	1.14
Germany	18.9	6.29	4.11	1.07	0.08	1.40

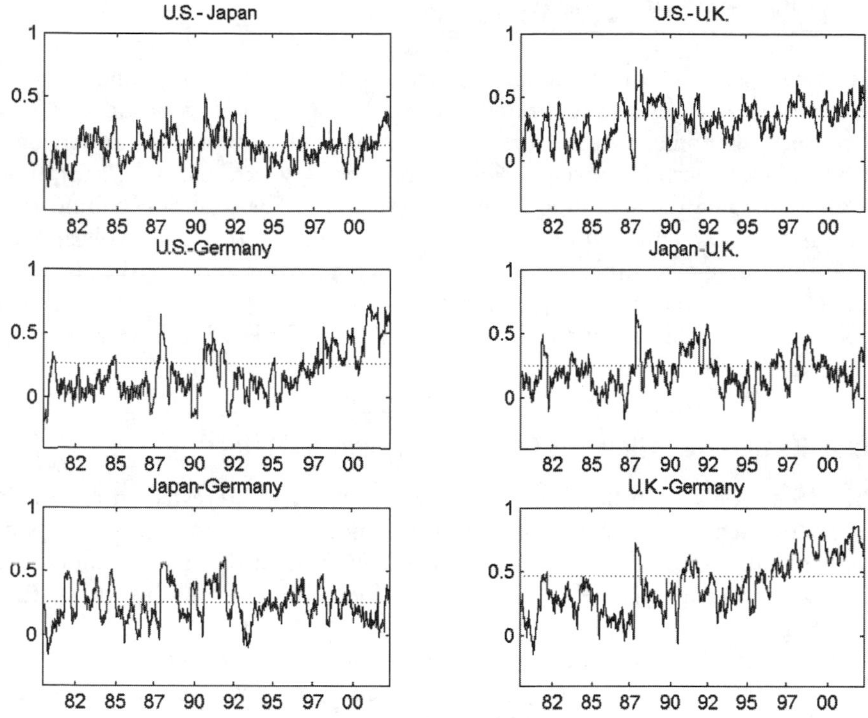

FIGURE 16.2 Correlations: Comparison between Constant and Time-Varying Estimates

want to construct an estimator that can capture as many empirical regularities as possible. On the other hand, we must keep in mind that most practitioners need to estimate covariance matrices of large dimensions, for hundreds or even thousands of assets. A model that is excessively parameterized may be impossible to estimate when applied to large sets of assets, and therefore its flexibility may become the cause of its practical irrelevance.

TABLE 16.4 Test of Time Variation in Correlations

	Observed Data			Monte Carlo Data		
	Constant Volatility Estimate	Observed aad	Standard Deviation of Time Varying Estimates	Average aad	Standard Deviation of aad	Maximum aad
U.S.-Japan	0.1150	0.0965	0.0729	0.0788	0.0062	0.1033
U.S.-U.K.	0.3514	0.1201	0.0907	0.0703	0.0056	0.0883
U.S.-Germany	0.2654	0.1728	0.1080	0.0744	0.0057	0.0919
Japan-U.K.	0.2478	0.1184	0.0859	0.0753	0.0059	0.0956
Japan-Germany	0.2569	0.1196	0.0813	0.0747	0.0056	0.0986
U.K.-Germany	0.4684	0.1927	0.1221	0.0627	0.0048	0.0771

COVARIANCE MATRIX ESTIMATION: THEORY

We start this section by quoting an important result for anybody interested in the estimation of variances and covariances. Under rather general conditions, the accuracy of second moment estimators improves with the ability to sample data at higher frequency within a given period, rather than by extending the sampling period while keeping the sampling frequency constant. The intuition behind this result, unlike its mathematical derivation, is rather simple. If market volatilities and correlations move over time, focusing on shorter horizons and high-frequency data increases the probability of using observations from the same volatility regime. Going too far back in history would contaminate the sample with data from a different regime, thus biasing the risk estimates.[3]

Using Daily Data to Estimate a Monthly Covariance Matrix

In the discussion that follows, we assume that we are interested in estimating a covariance matrix to forecast risk with a one-month horizon, and we propose an estimator that uses daily returns. Obviously, our estimator can be generalized to any horizon (quarter, year, etc.), but we will focus on one month to keep the notation simple.

Let $r_{i,t}(d)$ be the daily return on asset i computed from the close of day $t - 1$ to the close of day t. If returns are continuously compounded, then time aggregation for any horizon can be performed by simply adding returns at higher frequency. For example, if a month contains p business days, then the monthly return on asset i, which we denote with $r_i(m)$, can be computed by adding the daily returns for that month:

$$r_i(m) = \sum_{t=1}^{p} r_{i,t}(d) \tag{16.1}$$

Since the covariance between two sums of random variables is equal to the sum of the covariances between each pair of random variables in the sums, the covariance between the monthly returns on two generic assets i and j can be computed as:[4]

$$\text{cov}\left[r_i(m), r_j(m)\right] = \sum_{t=1}^{p} \sum_{s=1}^{p} \text{cov}\left[r_{i,t}(d), r_{j,s}(d)\right] \tag{16.2}$$

It is useful to rewrite equation (16.2) in a more disaggregate form, to better understand all the components involved in the calculation of the monthly covariance:

---

[3]See Merton (1980) for a formal discussion of this result.

[4]In our discussion, we focus on the covariance between two generic assets. However, the same arguments apply to variances. In fact, the variance of the return on any asset can be obtained as a special case in which $i = j$.

$$\begin{aligned}\text{cov}\left[r_i(m), r_j(m)\right] = {} & p \cdot \text{cov}\left[r_{i,t}(d), r_{j,t}(d)\right] \\ & +(p-1) \cdot \left\{\text{cov}\left[r_{i,t+1}(d), r_{j,t}(d)\right] + \text{cov}\left[r_{i,t}(d), r_{j,t+1}(d)\right]\right\} \\ & +(p-2) \cdot \left\{\text{cov}\left[r_{i,t+2}(d), r_{j,t}(d)\right] + \text{cov}\left[r_{i,t}(d), r_{j,t+2}(d)\right]\right\} + \\ & \ldots \\ & +\left\{\text{cov}\left[r_{i,t+p-1}(d), r_{j,t}(d)\right] + \text{cov}\left[r_{i,t}(d), r_{j,t+p-1}(d)\right]\right\}\end{aligned} \quad (16.2')$$

The expression in equation (16.2′) is more intuitive than it looks. To compute the monthly covariance between the two assets, one must estimate several covariances between daily returns, including the covariances between returns that occur on different days within the month. The covariances between returns that occur on the same day have a larger weight, because we observe p simultaneous daily returns each month. Returns that are farther apart within the month are observed less often, and therefore their covariances have a smaller weight.

To use a slightly more technical terminology, equation (16.2′) indicates that when dealing with high-frequency data (e.g., daily data), one must take into account the serial correlation between returns to construct a covariance estimator for a longer horizon (e.g., one month). This is an interesting result, because it warns us against the temptation to estimate the monthly covariance by simply multiplying the daily covariance between the two assets by the number of business days within a month. Such a procedure is correct only when daily returns are identically and independently distributed (iid) because, in this case, all the covariances between returns observed on different days are equal to zero.

The natural question at this point is: What degree of serial correlation should one assume when dealing with daily data? Unfortunately, there is not a simple answer that fits all scenarios. If we had a very large sample of data, then we could simply apply equation (16.2′). For example, if the true covariance between returns with two or more day lags were zero, the sample covariances of those returns would probably be very close to zero as well. However, if the sample of available data is not sufficiently large, then the estimated sample covariances are likely to reflect noise (spurious correlation) rather than a real statistical link between returns.

To get a sense of how serious the role of noise can be in small samples, we performed a simple experiment. We generated 1,000 observations from a bivariate distribution, assuming zero correlation between the two random variables. Next, we tested how the sample estimates of the correlation change when using only a subset of the observations. To do this, we constructed two different estimators: The first one used only 50 random observations from the sample; the second one used 100 random observations. We computed each estimator 100 times. Not surprisingly, both estimators were on average very close to zero. However, as documented in Table 16.5, the dispersion around the mean (standard deviation) for the first estimator was almost double the dispersion for the second estimator. The largest estimated correlation when using 50 observations was equal to 0.48, and the smallest was –0.36—quite a large variation when one is trying to estimate the risk of a portfolio. The extreme values were reduced to half the size when we used 100 observations.

TABLE 16.5 Correlation Estimation in Small Samples

	Observations Used in Estimation	
	50	100
Mean	0.006	–0.009
Standard deviation	0.154	0.087
Maximum	0.477	0.240
Minimum	–0.364	–0.189

In practice, it is advisable to use a parsimonious version of the estimator by including only as many lags as suggested by economic intuition and/or empirical evidence. For example, daily returns in international equity markets are likely to display some form of serial correlation because markets in different countries are open at different times. Suppose that new information becomes available at time t, when the U.S. market is open and the Japanese market is closed. Also assume that the news is expected to have a positive effect on all equity markets around the globe. The U.S. market will presumably incorporate the new information at time t, whereas prices in Japan can adjust only at time $t + 1$. This suggests that one should expect to observe nonnegligible correlation between returns that are one day apart. Of course, if the information is not immediately incorporated into prices (for example, because of lack of liquidity in parts of the market) then one may have to incorporate a higher order of serial correlation into the estimator. A formal analysis of the serial correlation of daily data can be useful at this stage.[5]

Estimation is performed by replacing the covariances in equation (16.2′) with their sample counterparts:[6]

$$\begin{aligned} \hat{\text{cov}}_T\left[r_i(d), r_j(d)\right] &= \frac{1}{T}\sum_{t=1}^{T} r_{i,t}(d) r_{j,t}(d) \\ \hat{\text{cov}}_T\left[r_i(d), r_{j,+k}(d)\right] &= \frac{1}{T}\sum_{t=1}^{T-k} r_{i,t}(d) r_{j,t+k}(d) \end{aligned} \tag{16.3}$$

At this point, it is convenient to introduce some matrix algebra to write the estimator in a more compact form. If T daily return observations are available for N assets, then we can organize them in a matrix $R(d)$. Each column in the matrix con-

[5] A description of techniques for the detection of serial correlation is beyond the scope of this chapter. The interested reader can find a discussion of this topic in any time-series textbook. Hamilton (1994) is a very thorough reference.

[6] In the formulas we assume that daily returns have a mean equal to zero. Although this is not necessarily the case, Merton (1980) points out that this approximation is often innocuous when dealing with high-frequency data, considering the amount of estimation error that characterizes average returns. If necessary the formula is easily generalized to incorporate the estimated mean of the returns.

tains T returns for one of the assets, and the matrix contains N columns. Applying the rules of matrix multiplication, it is easy to verify that the daily covariance matrix of asset returns can be computed as $S_0(d)=R(d)'R(d)/T$. However, as we know from our earlier discussion, in order to compute the monthly covariance matrix we must also estimate the covariances between returns observed on different days. This can easily be done in matrix form by introducing a new matrix $R_{-k}(d)$ which contains zeros in the first k rows, and the first $T - k$ rows of $R(d)$ in its last $T - k$ rows. Again, one can verify that the matrix product $S_k(d) = R(d)'R_{-k}(d)/T$ provides sample estimates of the daily covariances between returns observed k days apart. If daily returns display a serial correlation of order q, the monthly covariance matrix estimator can be written as:

$$S(m) = p \cdot S_0(d) + \sum_{k=1}^{q} (p-k)\left[S_k(d) + S_k(d)'\right] \qquad (16.3')$$

The more technically inclined reader will note that this estimator has the desirable feature of generating a monthly covariance matrix that is guaranteed to be positive semidefinite. Loosely speaking, this is the matrix equivalent of requiring that an estimator of the variance should be non-negative. In practice, this property guarantees that whenever it is used to estimate the risk of a portfolio, this estimator will generate a non-negative value.[7]

Weighting the Observations

A common criticism of the estimator discussed in the previous section is that it assigns the same weight to each observation, no matter when the observation occurred. Obviously, this would not be a problem if daily returns were iid, because in that case all returns would be drawn from the same distribution. However, when the iid assumption becomes questionable, it might be desirable to associate a larger weight with recent observations. In the discussion that follows, we propose a simple way of incorporating this feature within the estimation framework developed so far.

An intuitive weighting scheme assigns a weight of 1 to the most recent observation and discounts previous observations at a prespecified rate δ. Formally, if w_t is the weight assigned to the observation at time t, then the sequence of weights can be computed in a recursive fashion from $w_{t-1} = (1 - \delta)w_t$. Intuitively, the larger the rate δ, the faster the decay process, or equivalently, the larger the relative weight assigned to recent observations.

[7] De Santis and Tavel (1999) provide a more technical discussion of this estimator. They show that the same estimator would be obtained by estimating a daily covariance matrix using the serial correlation correction proposed by Newey and West (1987), and then scaling the daily covariance matrix by the number of trading days in one month. They also show that this estimator provides a formal justification for the common practice of adjusting for serial correlation by averaging returns over several days (so-called overlapping).

Typically, a specific weighting scheme is identified by the decay rate applied on a monthly basis and the half-life associated with it. The half-life is an interesting measure because it identifies how many months one must go back in the history of the data to find an observation with a weight equal to 0.5. For example, assume 21 business days in a month and a daily decay rate of 0.5 percent. Applying the recursive weighting formula, it is easy to verify that this corresponds to a monthly decay rate of approximately 10 percent and a half-life of 6.6 months.

Since we are working with second moments, our weights will be assigned to squared returns and cross products between returns on different assets, so that the standard covariance formula is modified as:[8]

$$\hat{\mathrm{cov}}_T\left[r_i(d), r_j(d)\right] = \frac{\sum_{t=1}^{T} w_t^{1/2} r_{i,t}(d) w_t^{1/2} r_{j,t}(d)}{\sum_{t=1}^{T} w_t} \tag{16.4}$$

More generally, to incorporate a weighting scheme into the monthly covariance estimator defined in equation (16.3′), we can proceed in steps: First, assign weights to the original return data; then apply the expression in (16.3′) to the modified data. Formally, define the matrix of weighted daily returns as:

$$\hat{R}(d) = w^{1/2} * R(d)$$

$$= \begin{bmatrix} (1-\delta)^{\frac{T-1}{2}} r_{1,1}(d) & (1-\delta)^{\frac{T-1}{2}} r_{1,2}(d) & \cdots & (1-\delta)^{\frac{T-1}{2}} r_{1,N}(d) \\ \vdots & \vdots & \ddots & \vdots \\ (1-\delta)^{\frac{1}{2}} r_{T-1,1}(d) & (1-\delta)^{\frac{1}{2}} r_{T-1,2}(d) & \cdots & (1-\delta)^{\frac{1}{2}} r_{T-1,N}(d) \\ r_{T,1}(d) & r_{T,2}(d) & \cdots & r_{T,N}(d) \end{bmatrix} \tag{16.5}$$

where the symbol * indicates that each element in the vector of weights w must be multiplied by all the elements in the corresponding row of $R(d)$. Once the daily returns have been adjusted by the weighting scheme, the modified formula for the covariance matrix estimator is

$$\hat{S}(m) = p \cdot \hat{S}_0(d) + \sum_{k=1}^{q} (p-k)\left[\hat{S}_k(d) + \hat{S}_k(d)'\right] \tag{16.6}$$

where

[8]Obviously assigning a weight w_t to the cross product is equivalent to assigning the square root of that weight to each of the components of the cross product. As it will become clear later, the latter specification is easier to implement when working with matrices.

$$\hat{S}_0(d) = \frac{\hat{R}(d)'\hat{R}(d)}{\sum_{t=1}^{T} w_t} \quad \text{and} \quad \hat{S}_k(d) = \frac{\hat{R}(d)'\hat{R}_{-k}(d)}{\sum_{t=1}^{T} w_t}$$

This estimator has the three features that we identified earlier as desirable properties of a covariance matrix estimator:

1. It uses high-frequency data (daily) to estimate volatilities and covariances over a longer horizon (monthly).
2. It accommodates a correction for the existence of serial correlation in high-frequency data.
3. It accommodates a weighting scheme that assigns a larger weight to recent observations.

The estimator that we have developed is very general. In fact, the interested reader can verify that simple estimators that assume that daily returns are iid (and therefore do not adjust for correlation in daily data, and do assign equal weight to all observations) can be obtained as a special case from (16.6) by setting $q = 0$ and all the elements in w equal to 1.

COVARIANCE MATRIX ESTIMATION: PRACTICE

So far we have identified some important regularities of financial data and provided a theoretical framework to take those regularities into account when building a risk model. In this section, we discuss how to approach the problem of covariance matrix estimation in practice.

Assuming that the researcher has access to a complete set of daily returns for a sufficiently long period,[9] there are at least two parameters that must be estimated to produce a covariance matrix: the order of serial correlation (q in our notation) and the decay parameter for the weighting scheme (δ in our notation).

As mentioned earlier, a thorough analysis of the correlation structure of the data is probably the best way to identify the appropriate value of q. However, a discussion of the time-series methodologies that accomplish this task is beyond the scope of this chapter and the interested reader should refer to a more specialized treatment of this topic.[10] Here, we want to focus on the intuition behind the choice of q. How are the serial correlation components going to affect the estimated volatility? To get an insight, let us look at a special case of equation (16.2′) in which the variance of the returns on asset i is estimated assuming $q = 1$:

$$\text{var}\left[r_i(m)\right] = p \cdot \text{var}\left[r_{i,t}(d)\right] + 2(p-1) \cdot \text{cov}\left[r_{i,t+1}(d), r_{i,t}(d)\right] \tag{16.7}$$

[9]A scenario in which a shorter history is available for some of the data is an important one. For this reason, we dedicate an entire section to that problem later in this chapter.

[10]See, for example, Hamilton (1994).

If daily returns were iid, then we would simply estimate the daily variance and scale it by the number of business days in the month (p in our notation). However, suppose that positive returns tend to be followed by negative returns (and vice versa), so that daily returns display first order negative correlation. Equation (16.7) suggests that our monthly volatility estimate would be lower than the estimate obtained assuming iid returns. On the other hand, if positive (negative) daily returns tend to be followed by more positive (negative) returns, so that they display first order positive correlation, then equation (16.7) indicates that our monthly volatility estimate would be higher than the estimate under the iid assumption.

In Figure 16.3, we plot estimates of the (annualized) monthly volatility for the U.S. equity market using a five-year window of daily data. We consider three alternative estimators that assume a serial correlation correction of 0, 10, and 21 respectively. The plots indicate that the three estimators follow very similar dynamics. However, for the past 15 years in the sample, including a significant correction for serial correlation would have reduced the volatility estimates. Interestingly, as the value of q increases, the estimates display more oscillations around their trends. This is due to the fact that the covariances between returns that are 21 days apart are based on a relatively small number of observations (only approximately 60 observations in a five-year window) and, therefore, are more sensitive to a few extreme observations. As argued earlier, these oscillations often reflect noise rather than real economic signals, and therefore parsimonious corrections for serial correlation are preferable.

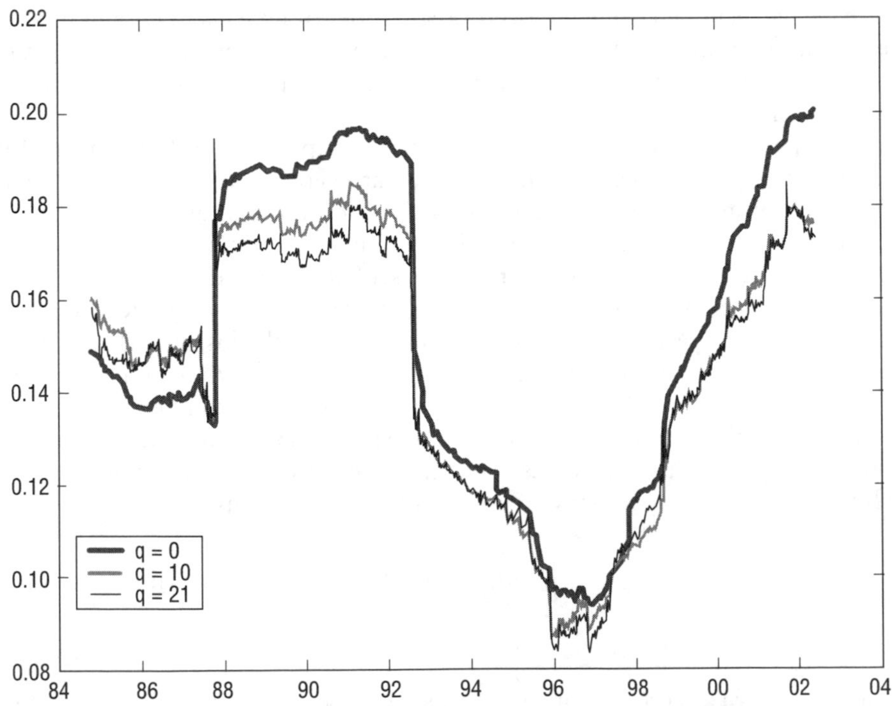

FIGURE 16.3 Annualized U.S. Equity Volatility with Different Corrections for Serial Correlation

For our purposes, we have found that when dealing with daily data on international equity markets, a correction for serial correlation of relatively low order (one or two) is often sufficient. This is in line with our expectations, given the way information is likely to be transmitted across markets that are open at different times during the day. In the discussion that follows, we maintain the hypothesis that $q = 2$ and proceed to estimating the *optimal* decay rate.

For a decay rate to be considered optimal, we must define an objective function whose value changes as δ changes, and then select a value of δ that maximizes that function. This is a standard technique in econometrics known as maximum likelihood estimation. In our case, the problem can be approached as follows. The returns in our sample are generated by some distribution. Assume for the moment that the distribution is a multivariate normal with mean zero and unknown covariance matrix, which is fully characterized by the decay parameter δ.[11] The likelihood function measures the probability that the data in our sample are generated by a multivariate normal distribution with mean zero and a covariance matrix that varies with δ. Our objective is to find the value of δ that maximizes the likelihood function or, equivalently, the probability of observing the data in our sample.

In performing the optimization of the likelihood function, we use daily data from January 1980 through May 2002. The sample includes 18 equity markets: Australia, Austria, Belgium, Canada, Denmark, France, Germany, Hong Kong, Italy, Japan, Netherlands, Norway, Singapore, Spain, Sweden, Switzerland, United Kingdom, and United States. Therefore, the covariance matrix contains a total of 18 variances and 153 different covariances.[12] Our results indicate that, when assuming a serial correlation of order two, the estimated optimal decay rate is 0.10 per month, which implies a half-life of slightly more than six months.

Figures 16.4 shows how the maximum likelihood estimates of the U.S. volatility and U.S.-Japan correlation compare to their constant counterparts. Not surprisingly, our findings indicate that there exists significant variation in both volatilities and correlations.

COVARIANCE MATRIX ESTIMATION: GENERALIZATIONS

The covariance matrix estimator discussed so far has many desirable properties. However, it still fails to address a number of relevant issues. First, it assumes multivariate normality for the joint distribution of international equity returns. As we have argued earlier, this assumption does not appear to be supported by the data. Second, it imposes the same decay rate to all assets and to both volatilities and correlations. One can easily envision scenarios when this assumption is too

[11]Later in this section we relax the assumption of normality. The assumption of zero mean can also be relaxed, and the unknown means can be estimated using maximum likelihood. However, in our case this assumption is fairly innocuous since we are working with daily data.

[12]The covariance matrix contains all the variances along its main diagonal. The covariances are located off the main diagonal and, since $\text{cov}(x,y) = \text{cov}(y,x)$, the total number of different covariances in our example is equal to $(18 \times 17)/2 = 153$.

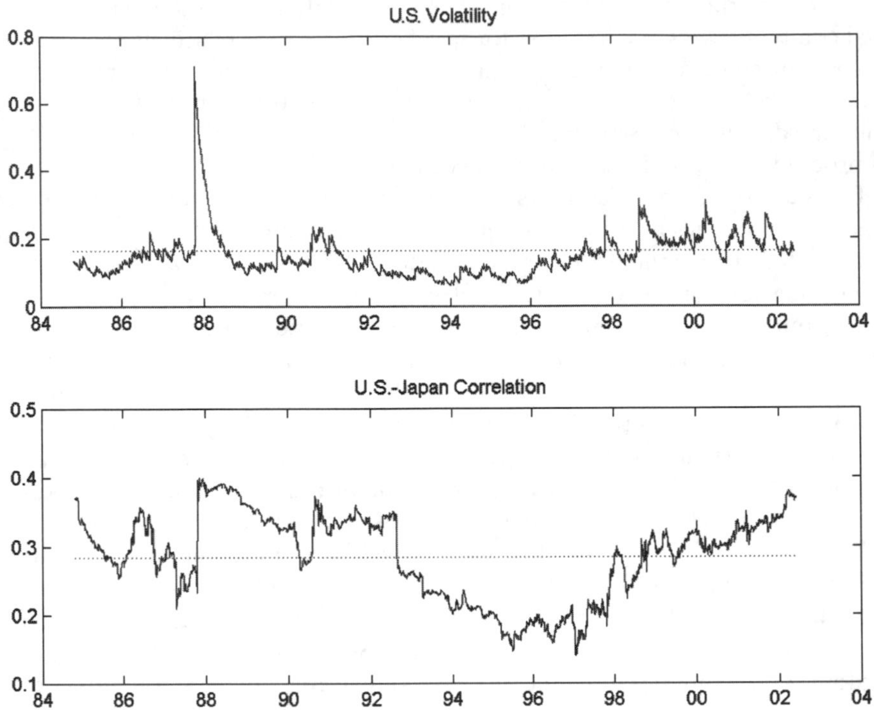

FIGURE 16.4 Volatility and Correlations: Comparison betweem Constant and Maximum Likelihood

restrictive. For example, when building covariance matrices that include different asset classes (e.g., equity and fixed income) it may be desirable to allow for a different weighting scheme for each asset class. In addition, even when working with a single asset class, it may be desirable to use different decay rates for volatilities and correlations. In fact, it is often argued that although volatilities tend to change quickly, correlations are more likely to move slowly over time. In this section, we discuss how to generalize our covariance matrix estimator to incorporate these desirable features.

Mixture of Normal Distributions

The evidence of heavy tails in the return distribution suggests that extremely large (positive or negative) returns occur more often than predicted by a multivariate normal distribution. Therefore, assuming normality when writing the likelihood function can be problematic. In fact, the maximum likelihood approach tries to find a value of the decay parameter that maximizes the probability of observing the data in our sample, while maintaining the hypothesis that the data are generated by a normal distribution. If the sample contains enough extreme observations, the estimate of the decay parameter will be affected by the need to *accommodate* those extreme observations within a normal distribution.

To capture the heavy tails, we assume that at each point in time returns can be drawn from one of two different normal distributions. The two distributions have the same mean and correlation structure, but different volatilities.[13] Most of the time returns are associated with a low-volatility regime, but every so often volatilities spike up and returns are drawn from a high-volatility regime. Variances in the high-volatility regime are a constant multiple of the variances in the low-volatility regime.

In this case, the likelihood function measures the probability of our data being generated by a mixture of normal distributions. In addition to the decay rate, we now need to estimate the ratio between the volatilities in the two regimes, and the probability of being in one of the two volatility regimes. Using our sample, we find that with a mixture of normal distributions the optimal decay rate on a monthly basis is equal to 9 percent, which corresponds to a half-life of 7.3 months. We also find that the ratio between volatilities in the high and low regimes is equal to 3.23, and that the probability of being in the low-volatility regime is equal to 84 percent.

One may ask whether the difference in decay rates between the likelihood that assumes normality (10 percent) and the likelihood that assumes a mixture of normal distributions (9 percent) is actually meaningful or, to use a more technical term, statistically significant. Econometricians use a simple technique to answer this question. They measure the likelihood function in the more general case (mixture of normal distributions in our exercise) and in the restricted case (normal distribution in our exercise) and then ask whether the change in the value of the likelihood function is sufficiently large to claim that the difference in the estimated parameters is significant from a statistical point of view. The intuition behind this procedure is relatively simple. The model with a normal distribution is obviously a special case of the model with a mixture of normal distributions. In fact, if the data were generated by a single volatility regime, then the estimated parameters when using a mixture of normal distributions would indicate that the ratio between volatilities in the two regimes is one and that the probability of being in the low-volatility regime is one. In other words, the likelihood functions in the two different specifications would coincide. However, if the model with two regimes is a better description of the data generating process, then the value of the likelihood function associated with it will be higher. In our case, the difference between the two likelihood functions leads to a strong rejection of the hypothesis that the data are generated by a normal distribution with a single volatility regime.

Do Volatilities and Correlations Move at a Different Speed?

Although there is a widespread consensus among academics and practitioners that volatilities and correlations change over time, opinions are less uniform when looking at the speed at which volatilities and correlations change through time. More specifically, volatility displays interesting regularities: First, it changes rather quickly in response to market shocks; second, it occurs in clusters so that periods of high (low) volatility tend to be followed by more periods of high (low)

[13]Clearly, these assumptions can be relaxed to accommodate even richer scenarios. We leave those extensions to future research.

volatility.[14] The evidence on correlations is arguably different. In fact, although correlations may spike during periods of extreme market distress, they appear to move considerably more slowly than volatilities over time.[15] Therefore, it would be useful to construct a covariance matrix estimator that can accommodate the different dynamics in volatilities and correlations. Luckily, this task is easily accomplished within our framework.

We start from the relationship between covariance and correlation for a generic pair of daily returns:

$$\text{cov}[r_i(d),r_j(d)] = \text{corr}[r_i(d),r_j(d)] \times \text{std}[r_i(d)] \times \text{std}[r_j(d)]$$

In words, the covariance between the two daily returns is equal to the correlation between those returns, multiplied by the product of their volatilities, as measured by the standard deviations. Since a covariance matrix is nothing else than a collection of covariances and variances (squared volatilities), we can apply the same decomposition to the entire covariance matrix. If Σ is a covariance matrix for a set of N assets, then we can write:

$$\Sigma = D\Omega D' \tag{16.8}$$

where D is a diagonal matrix of return volatilities (and so is D'), and Ω is a correlation matrix with 1s along its main diagonal, and all pairs of return correlations off the diagonal.

The covariance matrix decomposition in equation (16.8) may appear obvious. However, it has a powerful implication for our task: One can estimate volatilities and correlations using different assumptions on their dynamics, and still preserve the positive semidefinite nature of the covariance matrix. For example, the following specification allows for a different weighting scheme (decay rate) for volatilities relative to correlations:

$$\hat{\text{var}}_T\left[r_i(d)\right] = \frac{\sum_{t=1}^{T} w_t r_{i,t}^2(d)}{\sum_{t=1}^{T} w_t}$$

and

$$\tilde{\text{corr}}_T\left[r_i(d),r_j(d)\right] = \frac{\left[\sum_{t=1}^{T} \text{v}_t^{1/2} r_{i,t}(d)\text{v}_t^{1/2} r_{j,t}(d)\right] / \sum_{t=1}^{T} \text{v}_t}{\tilde{\text{std}}_T\left[r_i(d)\right] \times \tilde{\text{std}}_T\left[r_j(d)\right]}$$

[14]These features of volatility have been extensively documented since the work of Engle (1982).

[15]See, for example, De Santis and Gerard (1997).

where the weights w and v indicate that different decay rates are used when estimating volatilities and correlations.[16]

We applied this approach to our sample of 18 equity markets and found interesting results. Assuming, as before, a correction of order two for the serial correlation in the data, and a mixture of normal distributions, the maximum likelihood estimates for the decay parameters are equal to 47 percent for volatilities and 4 percent for correlations. This suggests that volatilities are mostly affected by very recent observations, since the half-life of the volatility estimator is only slightly longer than one month. However, correlation estimates use a considerably longer history of data, with a half-life of almost 17 months. Since individual observations have a much larger weight in the estimation of volatilities relative to correlations, the implication is that volatilities tend to respond much faster than correlations to market surprises.

Next, we compare the values of the likelihood functions for the two different specifications of the risk model. Clearly, the model with two different decay parameters is less constrained. If the evidence supported the model with a single decay parameter, then we should expect the two likelihood functions to be very close in value. Otherwise, the model with two different decay parameters should generate a larger value of the likelihood. The difference in our case leads to a strong rejection of the model with a single decay parameter.

We conclude this section by pointing out the strong potential of this last specification of the covariance matrix estimator. For example, when working with different asset classes, as we do, one can accommodate different decay rates for the volatilities in different asset classes, and a different decay rate for the correlation matrix. Even more generally, one could specify a different volatility process for each asset, and estimate those processes separately, and then estimate the correlation matrix for all the assets using a different model.[17]

ESTIMATING COVARIANCE MATRICES WITH HISTORIES OF DIFFERENT LENGTHS

So far we have worked in a fairly ideal scenario in terms of data availability. In fact, in all our examples we assume that daily data are available for the entire sampling period for all the assets in our universe. Although this may be true in some applications, most practitioners know too well that this is not usually the case. Even for such widely used data as daily equity returns in developed markets, the available history can be considerably shorter for some of the smaller markets. The problem becomes even more extreme when dealing with data from emerging markets.

How should we deal with histories of different lengths?[18] One easy but definitely suboptimal answer is to disregard part of the longer series and start the analysis at a

---

[16]We use the symbol ^ to identify estimators that use the weights w, and the symbol ~ to identify estimators that use the weight v.

[17]For some interesting applications of this approach, see Engle (2002).

[18]This section requires familiarity with regression analysis and some tolerance for rather heavy formal notation. However, in our opinion, the benefits for the researcher who faces this kind of problem outweigh the cost of reading through this section.

date when a long enough history is available for all the assets of interest (so-called truncated-sample estimation). A more appealing alternative was proposed in a paper by Stambaugh (1997). Since his approach requires several technical steps, we start by describing the method in words and then proceed to a formal description:

1. Estimate the truncated-sample moments for both sets of assets.
2. Estimate a regression of each of the assets with a shorter history on all the assets with a longer history (use the truncated sample for this step). The regression coefficients identify the statistical relationship between the two sets of data.
3. For the assets with a longer history:
   a. Estimate the moments for the entire sample.
   b. Measure the difference between the moments computed over the entire sample and the moments computed using the truncated sample. If the difference is positive, this means that the moments computed over the shorter sample underestimate the more precise estimates obtained using the entire sample (and vice versa).
4. Using the results from the regressions and the measures from step 3b, adjust the moment estimates for the series with a shorter history.

The method proposed by Stambaugh was not originally developed to accommodate some of the features that we have incorporated into our estimator (serial correlation correction and a weighting scheme that assigns more weight to more recent observations). However, since the case of no serial correlation and constant weight is a special case of our estimator, we proceed to a formal presentation of Stambaugh's method using our notation, which is more general.

Start by defining two sets of assets, and group them into two matrices $\hat{R}_A(d)$ and $\hat{R}_B(d)$. The first matrix contains T observations on N_A assets, whereas the second matrix contains S observations on N_B assets. If $S < T$, then the second matrix contains the assets with a shorter history. Assuming that the assets have already been premultiplied by a vector of weights, we proceed according to the steps described earlier.

First, estimate the truncated-sample moments for both groups of assets using the estimator in equation (16.6). Let $\hat{S}_{AA,S}(m)$ and $\hat{S}_{BB,S}(m)$ be the covariance matrices for the two sets of data, based on the truncated sample.

Second, run a regression for each of the assets in $\hat{R}_B(d)$ on the entire set of assets in $\hat{R}_A(d)$. For each regression, use the truncated sample (i.e., the last S observations). Since the parameters of a regression can be estimated using variances and covariances, this is easily accomplished using the covariance matrix estimator proposed in (16.6) and selecting the appropriate components:

$$B_S = \hat{S}_{AA,S}(m)^{-1}\hat{S}_{AB,S}(m) \tag{16.9}$$

where $\hat{S}_{AB,S}(m)$ is the covariance matrix between the returns in $\hat{R}_A(d)$ and the returns in $\hat{R}_B(d)$, estimated using the last S observations.

In addition, compute the covariance matrix of the regression residuals from the truncated sample:

$$V_S = \hat{S}_{BB,S}(m) - B_S'\hat{S}_{AA,S}(m)B_S$$

Third, compute the covariance matrix for the assets with the longer history, using their entire history. Again, this can be done by applying equation (16.6) to the first set of assets. Let $\hat{S}_{AA,T}(m)$ indicate the estimator that uses the entire history.

Fourth, construct all the covariance estimates by exploiting the information collected so far:

$$\begin{aligned}
\hat{S}_{AA}(m) &= \hat{S}_{AA,T}(m) \\
\hat{S}_{BA}(m) &= \hat{S}_{BA,S}(m) - B_S'\left[\hat{S}_{AA,S}(m) - \hat{S}_{AA}(m)\right] \\
\hat{S}_{BB}(m) &= \hat{S}_{BB,S}(m) - B_S'\left[\hat{S}_{AA,S}(m) - \hat{S}_{AA}(m)\right]B_S
\end{aligned} \tag{16.10}$$

When the researcher faces more than two subsets of assets with histories of different lengths, the same methodology can be applied recursively, starting from the shortest history common to all assets and moving back in steps until the entire set of available data is used.

ALTERNATIVE COVARIANCE MATRIX ESTIMATION METHODS

The estimation technique that we have described in the previous sections has the appealing feature of capturing most of the empirical regularities of financial data, while being easy to implement when applied to large sets of assets. In this section, we briefly review some alternative covariance matrix estimators that have been proposed in the literature and discuss how they relate to our framework.

GARCH Processes

Since the work of Engle (1982) and Bollerslev (1986), generalized autoregressive conditionally heteroscedastic (GARCH) processes have become one of the most popular methods to estimate volatility in financial markets. These processes were originally designed to capture the tendency for volatility to cluster over time: Periods of high (low) volatility tend to be followed by more periods of high (low) volatility. Formally, a univariate GARCH(1,1) process for the daily volatility on a generic asset can be written as:

$$\text{var}_{T+1}\left[r(d)\right] = \omega + \alpha\,\text{var}_T\left[r(d)\right] + \beta r_T^2 \tag{16.11}$$

In words, the volatility for the asset at time $T + 1$ depends on the volatility of the asset at time T and on the squared return on the asset at time T. The coefficient α captures persistence in volatility; the closer α is to 1, the larger the persistence. The coefficient β reflects the tendency for volatility to adjust in reaction to market surprises. If β is positive, then a large market return at time T induces an upward revision in the forecast of volatility for time $T + 1$.

Does the GARCH estimator share any similarities with our variance estimator, which uses a set of decaying weights on the return data? The answer to this question is easily found by rearranging equation (16.4) as follows:[19]

$$\text{var}_{T+1}\left[r(d)\right] = (1 - w_T)\,\text{var}_T\left[r(d)\right] + w_T r_T^2 \tag{16.11'}$$

Clearly, our estimator is a restricted version of a GARCH(1,1) process, in which the parameter ω is set equal to zero, and α and β are restricted to add up to 1 (so-called integrated GARCH process). At first one may conclude that our specification, although more parsimonious, is too restrictive. In practice, the benefit of parsimony becomes apparent when dealing with multiple assets. In fact, the proliferation of parameters in a multivariate GARCH process without restrictions makes it often very hard if not impossible to estimate.

The covariance matrix decomposition in equation (16.8) provides a great opportunity to use relatively unrestricted GARCH processes even when dealing with large sets of assets. In fact, as long as the specification of the correlation matrix is kept simple (e.g., a slow-moving correlation matrix like the one proposed earlier in this chapter), the volatility process for each asset can be modeled separately and estimated as a univariate process, without altering the positive semidefinite nature of the covariance matrix.

Implied Volatilities

In recent years, with the increasing popularity of derivatives markets, researchers have focused their interest on volatility measures implied by traded options. This is essentially an exercise in reverse engineering. Since volatility is one of the key inputs into the Black-Scholes option pricing model (and its variations), one can infer the volatility perceived by market participants by using option prices and recovering the implied volatility from a standard option pricing model. These estimates are based on prevailing market prices rather than on the past history of returns and, therefore, they are forward-looking measures of volatility.

Unfortunately, although the idea sounds appealing, this approach has some limitations. First, the number of liquid markets on derivatives products is still very limited compared to the number of assets for which we may be interested in building a risk model. Second, most derivatives can be used to infer implied volatilities, but very few products exist whose price depends on the correlation between two assets. This means that, for most assets, we are still far from being able to estimate implied correlations from observed market prices.

For the time being, we believe that the evidence from implied volatilities can be used in a productive way under special circumstances. For example, in the presence of extreme events, one may want to measure the change in implied

[19]Although equation (16.4) defines the covariance between two assets, the formula for the variance is obtained by assuming that assets i and j coincide.

volatilities on some of the major market indexes. This information can then be used to update volatility estimates that use only historical data. In fact, traditional volatility estimators may be too slow in incorporating extreme events. Once again, the covariance matrix decomposition in (16.8) provides an ideal ground to implement these variations.

Factor Models

Linear factor models are an appealing alternative to the risk models described so far. In addition to providing economic intuition on the forces that drive volatilities and correlations for asset returns, they simplify the estimation process when dealing with large sets of assets. For example, risk models for individual securities, which often include thousands of assets, are often specified as factor models.

The basic assumption behind a factor model is that returns are driven by a number of systematic factors common to all assets in the economy, plus an idiosyncratic factor that reflects a random component specific to each asset. Formally, the return on a generic asset i can be described as follows:

$$r_{i,t}(d) = a_i + \sum_{k=1}^{K} b_{ik} f_{k,t} + \varepsilon_{i,t} \tag{16.12}$$

The idiosyncratic term $\varepsilon_{i,t}$ has a mean of zero because, by assumption, it reflects unpredictable changes in the return on asset i. The K systematic factors reflect economic forces that are likely to affect all asset returns, and the coefficients $b_{i,k}$, which are often referred to as factor loadings, capture the effect of the common factors on a specific asset. For example, in the case of equity markets the common factors may represent measures of economic growth for the economy, indicators of future expected inflation, measures of recent market performance, and so on. Since the idiosyncratic factor is asset specific, we assume that ε_i is uncorrelated with the systematic factors, and with the idiosyncratic factor of any other asset.

Given a set of N assets, we can stack their returns at time t in a vector $R_t(d)$ and rewrite the factor model in matrix form:

$$R_t(d) = a + BF_t + \varepsilon_t \tag{16.12$'$}$$

where a is a vector of constants with N elements, B is a matrix with N rows and K columns (each row corresponds to the factor loadings for a specific asset), F_t is a vector that contains the values of the K factors at time t, and ε_t is a vector that contains the idiosyncratic factors for the N assets. If we indicate with Σ_R the covariance matrix for the N assets, then equation (16.12′) combined with our assumptions on the lack of correlation between systematic and idiosyncratic factors implies the following covariance matrix decomposition:

$$\Sigma_R = B\Sigma_F B' + \Sigma_\varepsilon \tag{16.13}$$

where Σ_F is a $K \times K$ covariance matrix for the K factors, and Σ_ε is a diagonal matrix whose elements represent the variances of the idiosyncratic components.

In practice, the risk model can be estimated in stages. First, the factor loadings in B are obtained from time-series regressions of the linear factor model in equation (16.12). Then an estimator is constructed for the covariance matrix of the factors and for the idiosyncratic variances. Finally, the entire covariance matrix for the N assets is estimated using equation (16.13).

The parsimonious nature of this approach becomes apparent with an example. Suppose we want to estimate a covariance matrix for the returns in the Russell 3000 universe. Given the symmetric nature of the variance-covariance matrix, we would need to estimate a total of $(3{,}000 \times 3{,}001)/2 = 4{,}501{,}500$ different parameters. Assume, however, that a linear factor model with 50 factors satisfactorily describes the returns on the Russell 3000 universe. In this case, once we have estimated the factor loadings in B, we have to estimate a covariance matrix with $(50 \times 51)/2 = 1{,}275$ different parameters, and the 3,000 volatilities in $\Sigma_{\varepsilon.}$ Clearly this is a much easier task. In fact, one can apply the techniques described in this chapter to estimate Σ_F and Σ_ε, and then construct the appropriate estimator for Σ_R.

SUMMARY

Covariance matrices are a necessary input to many problems in finance, such as construction of optimal portfolios, optimal hedging, monitoring and decomposition of portfolio risk, and pricing of derivative securities.

Investment decisions can be significantly affected by a choice of a particular covariance matrix estimator. Therefore, it is important to identify the main features of financial data that should be taken into account when selecting a covariance matrix estimator:

- Volatilities and correlations vary over time. In addition, volatilities and correlations may react with different speed to market news and may follow different trends.
- Given the time-varying nature of second moments, it is preferable to use data sampled at high frequency over a given period of time, rather than data sampled at low frequency over a longer period of time.
- When working with data at relatively high frequencies, such as daily data, it is important to take into account the potential for autocorrelation in returns, due to different liquidity across assets and asynchroneity across markets.
- Daily returns appear to be generated by a distribution with heavier tails than the normal distribution. A mixture of normal distributions often provides a better description of the data-generating process.

CHAPTER 17

Risk Monitoring and Performance Measurement

Jacob Rosengarten and Peter Zangari

OVERVIEW

The *Oxford English Dictionary* describes risk as:

> *a) the chance or hazard of commercial loss; also . . .*
> *b) . . . the chance that is accepted in economic enterprise and considered the source of (an entrepreneur's) profit.*

This definition asserts that risk reveals itself in the form of uncertainty. This uncertainty of loss, which risk professionals quantify using the laws of probability, represents the cost that businesses accept to produce profit. Loss potential (i.e., "risk") represents the "shadow price" behind profit expectations. A willingness to accept loss in order to generate profit suggests that a cost benefit process is present. For a return to be deemed desirable, it should attain levels that compensate for the risks incurred.

There are typically policy limits that constrain an organization's willingness to assume risk in order to generate profit. To manage this constraint, many organizations formally budget risk usage through asset allocation policies and methods (e.g., mean-variance optimization techniques). The result yields a blend of assets that will produce a level of expected returns and risk consistent with policy guidelines.

Risk, in financial institutions, is frequently defined as Value at Risk (VaR). VaR refers to the maximum dollar earnings/loss potential associated with a given level of statistical confidence over a given period of time. VaR is alternatively expressed as the number of standard deviations associated with a particular dollar earnings/loss potential over a given period of time. If an asset's returns (or those of an asset class) are normally distributed, 67 percent of all outcomes lie within the asset's average returns plus or minus one standard deviation.

Asset managers use a concept analogous to VaR—called tracking error—to gauge their risk profile relative to a benchmark. In the case of asset managers, clients typically assign a benchmark and a projected risk and return target vis à vis that benchmark for all monies assigned to the asset manager's stewardship. The risk budget is often referred to as tracking error, which is defined as the standard deviation of excess returns (the difference between the portfolio's returns and the benchmark's returns). If excess returns are normally distributed, 67 percent of all outcomes lie within the benchmark's returns plus or minus one standard deviation.

VaR is sometimes expressed as dollar value at risk by multiplying the VaR by assets under management. In this manner, the owner of the capital is able to estimate the dollar impact of losses that could be incurred over a given period of time and with a given confidence level. To achieve targeted levels of dollar VaR, owners of capital allocate capital among asset classes (each of which has its own VaR). An owner of capital who wishes to incur only the risks and returns of a particular asset class might invest in an index fund type product that is designed to replicate a particular index with precision. To the extent that the owner wishes to enjoy some discretion around the composition of the index, he or she allows the investment managers to hold views and positions that are somewhat different than the index. The ability to take risks away from the index is often referred to as active management. Tracking error is used to describe the extent to which the investment manager is allowed latitude to differ from the index. For the owner of capital, the VaR associated with any given asset class is based on the combination of the risks associated with the asset class and the risks associated with active management.[1] The same premise holds for the VaR associated with any combination of asset classes and active management related to such asset classes.

By now it is apparent that risk—whether expressed as VaR or tracking error—is a scarce resource in the sense that individuals and organizations place limits on their willingness to accept loss. For any given level of risk assumed, the objective is to engage into as many intelligent profit-making opportunities as possible. If risk is squandered or used unwisely, the ability of the organization to achieve its profit objectives is put at risk. If excessive levels of risk are taken vis à vis budget, the organization is risking unacceptably large losses in order to produce returns that it neither expects nor desires. If too little risk is taken vis à vis budgeted levels, return expectations will likely fall short of budget. The point here is that the ability of an organization to achieve its risk and return targets may be put at risk anytime that risk capital is used wastefully or in amounts inconsistent with the policies established by such organization.

With the above as context, we now delve into the concepts and methods be-

---

[1]More formally, the return of the portfolio (R_p) invested in a particular asset class can be described as follows:

$$R_p = (R_p - R_a) + R_a$$

where R_a refers to the return of the index or benchmark. The term in parenthesis is often referred to as active or excess return. From this expression, one can see that the variance of the portfolio's return (V_p) can be reduced to:

$$V_p = \text{Variance(Excess return)} + \text{Variance(Benchmark)} \\ + 2\text{(Covariance between excess return and benchmark return)}$$

The standard deviation of the portfolio is of course the square root of the variance.

hind risk monitoring and performance measurement in greater depth. The chapter is organized along five themes:

1. We emphasize that risk monitoring is a fundamental part of the internal control environment. It helps ensure that the organization is entering into transactions that are authorized and properly scaled; it helps distinguish between events that are unusual and those that should have been anticipated.
2. We show that there are three fundamental dimensions behind risk management—planning, budgeting, and monitoring. We observe that these three dimensions are intimately related and that they can be more completely understood by looking at their commonly used counterparts in the world of financial accounting controls. We posit that there is a direct correspondence between financial planning, financial budgeting, and financial variance monitoring and their risk management counterparts—namely, risk planning, risk budgeting, and risk monitoring.
3. We introduce the concept of a risk management unit (RMU) and describe its role and placement within the organization. We discuss its objectives as well as the need for it to remain independent of portfolio management activities. As we will see, the existence of an independent RMU is a "best practice" for all types of investors, including asset managers, pension funds, and corporations.
4. We describe techniques the RMU uses to monitor exposures in portfolios and provide samples of reports that might be used to deliver such information.
5. Last, we introduce tools that are commonly used in the world of performance measurement. We observe that there is a duality between risk monitoring and performance measurement. Risk monitoring reports on risk that is possible, whereas performance measurement reports on performance (and so risk) that has materialized. We posit that performance measurement is a form of model validation.

We would be remiss if we did not briefly observe that because the sources of risk are many, the modern organization must have a multidisciplinary approach to risk management. In their book, *The Practice of Risk Management*, Robert Litterman and Robert Gumerlock identify at least six distinct sources of risk.[2] These include market, credit, liquidity, settlement, operational, and legal risk. Professional standards, quantitative tools, preemptive actions, internal control systems, and dedicated management teams exist in the modern organization to address each of these. Frequently, these risks overlap and various professional disciplines are required to work together to creatively craft solutions. While in this paper, our primary focus will be management and measurement of market risk and performance, these other risks are ever present and material. Often, stresses in market factors make these other risks more apparent and costly.

[2]*The Practice of Risk Management*, by Robert Litterman and Robert Gumerlock, Euromoney Publications PLC, 1998, page 32.

For this reason, all of these sources of risk are worthy of separate study and investigation.

THE THREE LEGS OF FINANCIAL ACCOUNTING CONTROL: PLANNING, BUDGETING, AND VARIANCE MONITORING

In the world of financial accounting controls, the concepts of planning, budgeting, and variance monitoring are intimately related. Each is one of the legs of a three-legged stool that defines organizational structure and control. Each leg is fundamental to the success of the organization's raison d'être.

As we will see, the risk management process also can be described as a three-legged stool. Effective risk management processes also have planning, budgeting, and variance monitoring dimensions. It is intuitive that there should exist such a close correspondence between the models that support risk management and those that support financial accounting controls. Remember that risk is the cost of returns—the shadow price of returns. Hence, behind every number in a financial plan or budget there must exist a corresponding risk dimension. This duality suggests that risk management can be described, organized, and implemented using an approach that is already commonly used in the world of financial controls—namely, planning, budgeting, and monitoring.

For a moment, let's focus on the world of financial accounting to explore this point further. Consider how the "financial controls stool" is constructed. The first leg of this stool is a strategic plan or vision that describes earnings targets (e.g., return on equity, earnings per share, etc.) and other goals for the organization (e.g., revenue diversification objectives, geographic location, new product development, market penetration standards, etc.). The strategic plan is a policy statement that broadly articulates bright lines that define points of organizational success or failure.

Once a plan exists, the second leg of the financial controls stool—a financial budget—is created to give form to the plan. The financial budget articulates how assets are to be expended to achieve earnings and other objectives of the plan. The budget represents a financial asset allocation plan that, in the opinion of management, should be followed to best position the organization to achieve the goals laid out in the strategic plan. The budget—a statement of expected revenues and expenses by activity—is a numeric blueprint that quantifies how the strategic plan's broad vision is to be implemented.

The strategic plan and financial budget both presuppose scarcity. In a world of unlimited resources, there is clearly no need for either a budget or a plan. Any mistake could easily be rectified. In a world of scarcity, however, it is apparent that a variance monitoring process—the third leg of the stool—helps ensure that scarce resources are spent wisely in accordance with the guidance offered by the plan and the budget. Monitoring exists because material variances from financial budget put the long-term strategic plan at risk.

In the world of risk management, these same three elements of control—planning, budgeting, and monitoring—apply as well. Although this paper focuses primarily on risk monitoring, it is useful to step back and provide a more complete context for risk monitoring.

BUILDING THE THREE-LEGGED RISK MANAGEMENT STOOL: THE RISK PLAN, THE RISK BUDGET, AND THE RISK MONITORING PROCESS

The Risk Plan

The following discussion of what constitutes a risk plan may at first blush seem highly theoretical. But upon closer review, the reader will see that sound financial planning standards already incorporate many of the elements that are discussed. We expect many of the ideas referred to here already exist within the body of a comprehensive strategic planning document. For example, most strategic plans include a strengths, weaknesses, opportunities, and threats (SWOT) section in which major risks to the organization are discussed. By introducing the concept of a separate risk plan, however, we are proposing an even greater degree of formality for discussion of risk themes and issues.

We believe that the risk plan should be incorporated as a separate section of the organization's strategic planning document. As such, it should receive all of the vetting and discussion that any other part of the planning document would receive. When in final form, its main themes should be capable of being articulated to analysts, auditors, boards, actuaries, management teams, suppliers of capital, and other interested constituencies.

The risk plan should include five guideposts:

1. The risk plan should set expected return and volatility (e.g., VaR and tracking error) goals for the relevant time period and establish mileposts which would let oversight bodies recognize points of success or failure. The risk plan should use scenario analysis to explore those kinds of factors that could cause the business plan to fail (e.g., identify unaffordable loss scenarios) and strategic responses in the event these factors actually occur. The risk plan helps ensure that responses to events—be they probable or improbable—are planned and not driven by emotion. Difficult business climates have happened before and they will happen again. The planning process should explore the many "paths to the long term" and prepare the organization, and its owners and managers, for the bumps[3] along the way. If any of these bumps are material, concrete contingency plans should be developed and approved by the organization's owners and managers.[4]
2. The risk plan should define points of success or failure. Examples are acceptable levels of return on equity (ROE) or returns on risk capital (RORC). For the purposes of the planning document, risk capital might be defined using Value at Risk (VaR) methods. Since organizations typically report and budget results over various time horizons (monthly, quarterly, annually), separate VaR measures for each time interval should be explored. The VaR (or risk capital)

[3]In statistical terms, a "bump" might be defined as a three or greater standard deviation event in a relatively short period of time.

[4]Note that scenario analysis can be explored qualitatively as well as quantitatively. In fact, many extreme events lend themselves more to qualitative analysis than quantitative methods.

allocated to any activity should be sized in such a way that the exposures and upside associated with the activity are at levels that are deemed appropriate by the organization's owners and managers. A second benefit of attempting to measure the risk capital associated with each activity is that the process helps management understand the uncertainty levels associated with each activity in the plan. The greater the amount of uncertainty and the greater the cost associated with the downside of the VaR estimate actually materializing, the more intensive must be the quality of contingency and remedial planning.

3. The risk plan should paint a vision of how risk capital will be deployed to meet the organization's objectives. For example, the plan should define minimum acceptable RORCs for each allocation of risk capital. In so doing, it helps ensure that the return per unit of risk meets minimum standards for any activity pursued by the organization. The plan should also explore the correlations among each of these RORCs as well to ensure that the consolidated RORC yields an expected ROE, and variability around such expectation, that is at acceptable levels. Finally, the plan should also have a diversification or risk decomposition policy. This policy should address how much of the organization's risk capital should be spent on any one theme.[5]
4. A risk plan helps organizations define the bright line between those events that are merely disappointing and those that inflict serious damage. Strategic responses should exist for any franchise-threatening event—*even if* such events are low-probability situations. The risk plan should identify those types of losses that are so severe that insurance coverage (e.g., asset class puts) should be sought to cover the downside. For example, every organization pays fire insurance premiums to insure against the unaffordable costs of a fire. Fire is one of those events that are so potentially devastating that there is universal agreement on the need to carry insurance protection. Now, consider a more complex example from the world of investment portfolio policy. From an investment standpoint, there may be losses of such magnitude—even if they are infrequent and improbable—that they endanger the long-term viability of the investment plan. For example, firms or plans with large equity holdings[6] could face material loss and earnings variability in the event of protracted and substantial stock market losses. In this case, the risk plan should explore the potential merits of financial insurance (e.g., options on broad market indexes). At a minimum, if such insurance is not purchased, the decision to self-insure should be formally discussed and agreed upon by the organization's owners and management.
5. The risk plan should identify critical dependencies that exist inside and outside the organization. The plan should describe the nature of the responses to be followed if there are breakdowns in such dependencies. Examples of critical de-

[5]Diversification policies are routinely included in strategic planning. Such policies take the form of geographic diversification, product diversification, customer base diversification, and so on. Just as organizations produce standards on how much revenue should come from any one source, so too should they examine how much risk originates from any one theme (asset class, portfolio manager, individual security, etc.).

[6]In this context, a "large" holding refers to one that can generate earnings exposures that are deemed material vis à vis the business plan.

pendencies include reliance on key employees and important sources of financing capacity.

The risk plan should explore how key dependencies behave in good and bad environments.[7] Frequently, very good and or very bad events don't occur in a vacuum; they occur simultaneously with other material events. For example, consider a possible challenge faced by a pension plan. It is conceivable that periods of economic downturn could coincide with lower investment performance, acceleration of liabilities, and a decreased capacity of the contributing organization to fund the plan. For this reason, scenario planning for the pension plan should explore what other factors affect the pension plan's business model in both good and bad environments and develop appropriate steps to help the plan succeed.

An effective risk plan requires the active involvement of the organization's most senior leadership. This involvement creates a mechanism by which risk and return issues are addressed, understood, and articulated to suppliers of capital (owners or beneficiaries), management, and oversight boards. It helps describe the philosophical context for allocations of risk and financial capital and helps organizations ensure that such allocations reflect organizational strengths and underpinnings. It helps organizations discuss and understand the shadow price that must be accepted in order to generate returns.

The existence of a risk plan makes an important statement about how business activities are to be managed. It indicates that owners and managers understand that risk is the fuel that drives returns. It suggests that a higher standard of business maturity is present. Indeed, its very existence demonstrates an understanding that the downside consequences of risk—loss and disappointment—are not unusual. These consequences are directly related to the chance that management and owners accept in seeking profit. This indicates that management aspires to understand the source of profit. The risk plan also promotes an organizational risk awareness and the development of a common language of risk. It demonstrates an intolerance for mistakes/losses that are material, predictable, and avoidable.

The Risk Budget

The risk budget—often called asset allocation—should *quantify* the vision of the plan. Once a plan is put into place, a formal budgeting process should exist to express exactly how risk capital will be allocated such that the organization's strategic vision is likely to be realized. The budget helps the organization stay on course with respect to its risk plan. For each allocation of risk budget, there should be a corresponding (and acceptable) return expectation. For each return expectation, some sense of expected variability around that expectation should be explored. When all of the expected returns, risks, and covariations among risk budgets are considered, the expected return streams, and the variability of such, should be consistent with the organization's strategic objectives and risk tolerances.

[7]Once again, examining correlations among critical business dependencies in periods of stress may be done in a qualitative or quantitative manner.

As noted earlier, there are many similarities between financial budgets and risk budgets. Financial budgets calculate net income as the difference between revenue and expenses. ROE is then estimated as net income divided by capital invested. In the case of risk budgets, a risk "charge"—defined as VaR or some other proxy for "risk expense"—can be associated with each line item of projected revenue and expense. Hence, a RORC can be associated with each activity as well as for the aggregation of all activities.

In the case of both financial and risk budgets, presumably ROE and RORC must exceed some minimum levels for them to be deemed acceptable. Both statistics are concerned with whether the organization is sufficiently compensated—in cost/benefit terms—for the expenses and/or risks associated with generating revenues. Just as the financial budget allocates revenue and expense amounts across activities to determine their profitability, so too should a risk budget exist for each activity in order to estimate the *risk-adjusted* profitability of the activity. Just as financial budgets show a contribution to ROE by activity, so too can risk budgets show a contribution to overall risk capital usage by activity. For example, standard mean-variance optimization methods produce estimates of weights to be assigned to each asset class, in addition to overall estimates of portfolio standard deviation and the marginal contribution to risk[8] from each allocation.

Note that both RORC and ROE can and should be estimated over all time intervals that are deemed relevant. For example, if investment boards meet monthly and are likely to react to short-term performance, monthly RORC is relevant. Hence, management must define the time horizons over which risk budget allocations are to be spent and over which RORC should be measured.[9]

An example at this point might be helpful. Assume that an organization has a material investment portfolio. The organization is concerned about the impact of the earnings volatility of this portfolio on reported earnings and, therefore, share price. In constructing a risk budget for this portfolio, the organization might:

- From the risk and business plan, identify acceptable levels of RORC and ROE over various time horizons.
- Using mean variance optimization or other techniques, determine appropriate weights for each investment class.
- Simulate the performance of a portfolio (including the behavior of related liabilities, if relevant) constructed with these weights over various time horizons, and test the sensitivity of this performance to changes in return and covariance assumptions.

[8]The marginal contribution to risk from any asset is defined as the change in risk associated with a small change in the underlying weight of that asset in the portfolio.

[9]We know that risk across different time dimensions does not simply scale by the square root of time. The path to the long term may be much bumpier than a simple scaling might imply. In fact, the long-term result may be entirely consistent with a fair number of short-term anomalies. If so, management must ensure that risk allocations are sized in such a manner that losses associated with short-term market difficulties can be negotiated effectively. Hence, in a manner analogous to financial budgeting, the risk budget helps managers size the bets in each revenue-producing area.

- Ensure that the levels of risk assumed at the individual asset class level as well as for the portfolio taken as a whole are at appropriate levels vis à vis the business and risk plan.
- Ensure that the expected variability around expected RORC is at acceptable levels. If there is too much variability vis à vis a competitor's ROE and RORC, the earnings profile might be deemed to be low quality by the marketplace. Accordingly the risk budgeting process must concern itself with not only the absolute magnitude of the RORC at the strategy and overall portfolio levels, but also the variability in such magnitude.
- Explore the downside scenarios associated with each allocation over various time horizons. Ensure that the plan's owners and managers identify such downside as merely disappointing and not unacceptably large (i.e., lethal) given the plan's objectives.
- In each significant downside scenario, loop back to the planning process and ensure that contingency steps exist to bring about a logical and measured response. Ensure that owners, managers, and other outside constituencies (e.g., suppliers of capital) are aware and supportive of these responses.

Clearly, risk budgeting incorporates elements of mathematical modeling. At this point, some readers may assert that quantitative models are prone to failure at the worst possible moments and, as such, are not sufficiently reliable to be used as a control tool. We do not agree. The reality is that budget variances are a fact of life *in both* financial budgeting and risk budgeting. Variances from budget can result from organization-specific factors (e.g., inefficiency) or completely unforeseen anomalies (e.g., macroeconomic events, wars, weather, etc.). Even though such unforeseen events cause ROE variances, some of which may even be large, most managers still find value in the process of financial budgeting. The existence of a variance from budget, per se, is not a reason to condemn the financial budgeting exercise.

So, too, we believe that the existence of variances from risk budget by unforeseen factors does not mean that the risk budgeting process is irrelevant. To the contrary. Frequently the greatest value of the risk budget derives from the budgeting *process* itself—from the discussions, vetting, arguments, and harmonies that are a natural part of whatever budget is ultimately agreed to. Managers who perform risk budgeting understand that variances from budget are a fact of life and are unavoidable, but are not a reason to avoid a formal risk budgeting process. To the contrary, understanding the causes and extent of such variances and ensuring that appropriate remedial responses exist make the budgeting and planning process even more valuable.

Risk Monitoring

Variance monitoring is a basic financial control tool. Since revenue and expense dollars are scarce, monitoring teams are established to identify material deviations from target. Unusual deviations from target are routinely investigated and explained as part of this process.

If we accept the premise that risk capital is a scarce commodity, it follows that monitoring controls should exist to ensure that risk capital is used in a manner consistent with the risk budget. Material variances from risk budget are threats to the investment vehicle's ability to meet its ROE and RORC targets. If excessive risk is used, unacceptable levels of loss may result. If too little risk is spent, unacceptable shortfalls in earnings may result. Risk monitoring is required to ensure that material deviations from risk budget are detected and addressed in a timely fashion.

RISK MONITORING—RATIONALE AND ACTIVITIES

There is an increasing sense of risk consciousness among and within organizations. This risk consciousness derives from several sources:

- Banks that lend to investors increasingly care about where assets are placed.
- Boards of investment clients, senior management, investors, and plan sponsors are more knowledgeable of risk matters and have a greater awareness of their oversight responsibilities. Especially as investments become more complicated, there is an increasing focus to ensure that there is effective oversight over asset management activities—whether such activities are managed directly by an organization or delegated to an outside asset manager.
- Investors themselves are expected to have more firsthand knowledge about their investment choices. Perhaps this has been driven, in part, by the notoriety of losses incurred by Procter & Gamble, Unilever, Gibson Greeting Cards, Orange County (California), the Common Fund, and others. After these events, organizations have become interested in stresses and the portfolio's behavior in more unusual environments. Further, in the asset management world, asset managers increasingly must be able to explain, ex ante, how their products will fare in stressful environments. This enhanced client dialogue disclosure is beneficial from two perspectives: First, it raises the level of client confidence in the manager. Second, it reduces the risk of return litigation arising from types of events that were predictable on an ex ante basis.

In response to this heightened level of risk consciousness, many organizations and asset managers have formed independent risk management units (RMUs) that oversee the risk exposures of portfolios and ensure that such exposures are authorized and in line with risk budgets. This trend was definitely spurred on by a highly influential paper authored by the Working Group[10] in 1996.

[10]The Working Group was established in April 1996 by 11 individuals from the institutional investment community. Its mission was: "To create a set of risk standards for institutional investment managers and institutional investors." In drafting the final standards, opinions were solicited from a wide range of participants in the financial community including asset managers, academics, plan sponsors, custodians, and regulators. More recently, Paul Myners, in his report (dated March 6, 2001) addressed to the Chancellor of the Exchequer of the United Kingdom entitled *Institutional Investment in the United Kingdom—A Review*, argued persuasively for the increased need for professional development and product understanding of those individuals charged with overseeing pension plans.

The Working Group suggested that the RMU's reporting line should incorporate a segregation of duties—a fundamental element of an effective internal controls environment. To be effective, the RMU should be independent in both fact and appearance. This assertion is ratified by industry and professional guidance. For example, the Third Standard produced by the Working Group reads in part:

> *Where possible, an independent internal group . . . should perform oversight. . . . Functions checked independently should include:*
>
> - *Oversight of investment activity*
> - *Limits, monitoring, exception reports and action plans relating to exception reports*
> - *Stress tests and back tests*
> - *. . . Fiduciaries should verify that Managers conduct independent risk oversight of their employees and activities.*

In their book, *The Practice of Risk Management*, Robert Gumerlock and Robert Litterman ratify this Standard by stating:

> *It is essential that the risk management function itself must be established independently from the business areas and operate as a controlling or monitoring function. The role of the risk management function is to provide assurance to senior management and the Board that the firm is assessing its risk effectively, and is complying with its own risk management standards. This means that the risk management function has to have an independent reporting line to senior management.*

The risk monitoring unit is a necessary part of the process that ensures best practices and consistency of approach across the firm. It helps ensure that a process exists by which risks are identified, measured, and reported to senior management in a timely fashion. The function is part of an internal control framework designed to safeguard assets and ensure that such assets are managed in accordance with each organization's expectations and management direction.

Objectives of an Independent Risk Management Unit

The objectives of the RMU are:

- The RMU gathers, monitors, analyzes, and distributes risk data to managers, clients, and senior management in order to better understand and control risk. This mission requires that the RMU deliver the right information to the right constituency at the right time.
- The RMU helps the organization develop a disciplined process and framework by which risk topics are identified and addressed. The RMU is part of the process that ensures the adoption and implementation of best risk practices and consistency/comparability of approach and risk consciousness across the firm. As such it is a key promoter of an organization's risk culture and internal control environment.

- To be vibrant, the RMU must be more than a publisher of periodic VaR information. It must also proactively pursue topics and have a topical vein. The RMU should be actively involved in setting and implementing the risk agenda and related initiatives.
- The RMU watches trends in risk as they occur and identifies unusual events to management in a timely fashion. While it is helpful to identify a risk once it is present, it is more meaningful to identify a trend before it becomes a large problem.
- The RMU is a catalyst for a *comprehensive* discussion of risk-related matters, including those matters that do not easily lend themselves to measurement. For example, the RMU should be actively involved in the identification of and organizational response to low-probability yet high-damage events. It should promote discussion throughout the organization and encourage development of a context by which risk data and issues are discussed and internalized.
- The RMU is an element of the risk culture. It should represent one of the nodes of managerial convergence—a locus where risk topics are identified, discussed, and disseminated across the organization and clients. In so doing, it helps promote enhanced risk awareness together with a common risk culture and vocabulary.
- As a part of the internal control environment, the RMU helps ensure that transactions are authorized in accordance with management direction and client expectations. For example, the RMU should measure a portfolio's *potential* (i.e., ex ante) tracking error and ensure that the risk profile is in consonance with expectations.[11]
- Together with portfolio managers and senior management, the RMU identifies and develops risk measurement and performance attribution analytical tools. The RMU also assesses the quality of models used to measure risk. This task involves back testing of models and proactive research into "model risk."
- The RMU develops an inventory of risk data for use in evaluating portfolio managers and market environments. This data, and the methodologies used to create it, must be of a quality and credibility that it is both useful to and accepted by the portfolio managers. This risk data should be synthesized, and routinely circulated to the appropriate decision makers and members of senior management.
- The RMU provides tools for both senior management and individual portfolio management to better understand risk in individual portfolios and the source of performance. It establishes risk reporting and performance attribution systems to portfolio managers and senior management. In the process, the RMU promotes transparency of risk information.

[11]For asset management firms, this oversight spans a different dimension of risk than the function currently performed by compliance departments. In fact, the RMU forms a natural complement to the efforts of the compliance department within asset management firms. By definition, the matching of actual positions with guidelines by the compliance department involves examining events that have already happened. In contrast, by stressing data and exploring both common and uncommon scenarios, the RMU explores the implications of what *might* happen in the future.

- The RMU should not manage risk, which is the responsibility of the individual portfolio managers, but rather *measure* risk for use by those with a vested interest in the process. The RMU cannot reduce or replace the decision methods and responsibilities of portfolio managers. It also cannot replace the activities of quantitative and risk support professionals currently working for the portfolio managers. Trading decisions and the related software and research that support these decisions should remain the responsibility of the portfolio managers and their support staffs. The RMU measures the extent to which portfolio managers trade in consonance with product objectives, management expectations, and client mandates. If the RMU finds what it deems to be unusual activities or risk profiles, it should be charged with bringing these to the attention of the portfolio managers and senior management so that an appropriate response can be developed and implemented.

Examples of the Risk Management Unit in Action

An effective internal control environment requires timely, meaningful, and accurate information flows between senior management and the rest of the organization. Information flows allow management to ask questions. Questions and the ability to probe into the process by which the business operates are fundamental to loss avoidance and profit maximization.

Risk monitoring is principally concerned with whether investment activities are behaving as expected. This suggests that there should be clear direction as to what results and risk profiles should be deemed normal versus abnormal. It is our experience that the very best managers in the world achieve success in no small part because they have a time-tested conviction and a philosophy that has a stable footprint. For example, the best growth managers do not invest in value themes; the best U.S. fixed income managers do not take most of their risk in non-U.S. instruments; and so on. In fact, the premier managers remain true to their time-tested convictions, styles, and philosophies. Further, the best managers apply well-defined limits—expressed both in absolute terms as well as in marginal contribution to risk terms—on how they spend any given amount of risk budget. The result of this discipline is a portfolio that produces a return distribution that meets the following world-class standards:

- It is consistent with client expectations. The risk capital consumed by the manager approximates the amount of risk budget the client authorized the manager to spend.
- It is derived from organizational or individual strengths (e.g., stock selection, sectors of the market like growth or value, portfolio construction techniques, etc.).
- It is high-quality in the sense that it is not the result of luck, but rather of sound organizational plans and decisions that have been executed in accordance with philosophy and conviction.
- It is the result of a well-articulated and well-defined process and risk culture whose major elements are understood and embodied by the organization.
- It is stable, consistent, and controlled. It produces results that can be explained and repeated across time with a high degree of confidence.

The RMU helps create systems to report risk information to interested constituencies (senior management, control nodes, portfolio managers, etc.). This information should reveal several broad themes. In particular, it should allow the user to be conclusive concerning:

- Whether the manager is generating a forecasted level of tracking error that is consistent with the target established by the mandate.
- Whether, for each portfolio taken, individually and for the sum of all portfolios taken as a whole, risk capital is spent in the expected themes.
- Whether the risk forecasting model is behaving as predicted.

Is the Forecasted Tracking Error Consistent with the Target? The forecasted tracking error is an estimate of the potential risk that can be inferred from the positions held by the portfolio derived from statistical or other forward-looking estimation techniques. An effective risk process requires that portfolio managers take an appropriate level of risk (i.e., neither too high nor too low) vis à vis client expectations. This forecast should be run for each individual portfolio as well as for the sum of all portfolios owned by the client. Tracking error forecasts should be compared to tracking error budgets[12] for reasonableness. Policy standards should determine what magnitude of variance from target should be deemed so unusual as to prompt a question and what magnitude is so material as to prompt immediate corrective action. In this manner, unusual deviations across accounts will be easier to identify.

Figure 17.1 is an example of a tracking error forecast report for a sample U.S. equity fund produced by Goldman Sachs Asset Management (GSAM) on its proprietary portfolio analysis and construction environment (PACE) platform. PACE is a risk and return attribution system that we use to forecast risk across the spectrum of equities managed by GSAM. Observe from the header of this report that the forecasted tracking error for this account, as estimated by the PACE model, is 3.68 percent per annum. A second equity factor risk model, Barra, projects a tracking error forecast of 2.57 percent. Since each model uses different assumptions to forecast risk, it is not surprising that two different models would produce different results. What is comforting in this case is that both measures of risk are comparable to the targeted risk level of 3.25 percent per annum.

This same report should be produced for each account that is supposed to be managed in a parallel manner to ensure consistency of overall risk levels.

Is Risk Capital Spent in the Expected Themes for Each Portfolio? In financial variance monitoring, it is insufficient to know *only* that the overall expense levels are in line with expectations. Each line item that makes up the total must also correspond to expectations. If there are material variances among line items that tend to offset each other, the person monitoring variances should be on notice that unusual activity may be present. As an example, if a department meets its overall ex-

[12]Tracking error budgets should exist for each portfolio and be determined as part of the organization's asset allocation process.

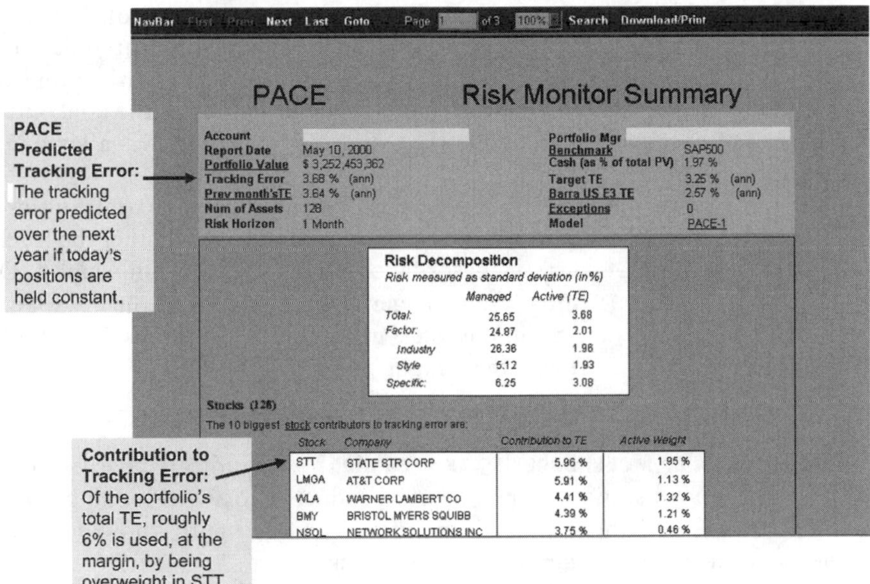

FIGURE 17.1 Risk Report for a U.S. Equity Fund

pense budget but is materially over budget in legal fees (with favorable offsets in other areas), the reviewer might conclude that an event is present that might put future returns at risk.

The same principle holds for risk monitoring. Managers should be able not only to articulate overall tracking error expectations, but also to identify how such tracking error is decomposed into its constituent parts. This will let the risk manager opine on whether risk is being incurred in accordance with expectations both in total as well as at the constituent level. If the risk decomposition is not in keeping with expectations, the manager may not be investing in accordance with the stated philosophy. This type of situation is often referred to as "style drift." An example of this might be a growth manager who is investing in consonance with the correct overall tracking error target, but who is placing most of the risk in value themes. In this case, the investor is acquiring the correct level of overall risk, but the wrong style decomposition.

Examples of risk decomposition that a manager should be able to articulate and which the RMU should monitor might include:

- The range of acceptable active weights (portfolio holdings less benchmark holdings) at the stock, industry, sector, and country levels.
- The range of acceptable marginal contributions to risk at the stock, industry, sector, and country levels.

Refer again to Figure 17.1. For this particular portfolio, we observe that State Street Corp. represents an active weight of 1.95 percent of the total portfolio and that its marginal contribution to tracking error is 5.96 percent. The risk monitoring function should conclude as to whether this active weight and risk decomposition—which may alternatively be described as the portfolio's diversification footprint—is in line with expectations. What is being measured here is the extent to which the manager is investing capital in accordance with stated policies. This report should be run at the manager level as well as at the consolidated portfolio level to ensure that no undue (i.e., unacceptably large vis à vis budget) concentrations of risk are present.

Figure 17.2 shows the largest active exposures and marginal contributions at the industry level. The risk monitor should be able to opine on whether the levels of risk concentration observed are in accordance with manager philosophy. Once again, this report should be run at the manager level as well as at the consolidated portfolio level to ensure that no undue (i.e., unacceptably large vis à vis budget) concentrations of risk are present that might put either a strategy or the overall plan at risk.

Is the Risk Forecasting Model Behaving as Predicted? As indicated earlier, the risk forecasting model uses statistical methods to produce a forward-looking estimate of tracking error. Accordingly, the risk monitor is charged with knowing whether the model is producing meaningful estimates of risk.

For example, GSAM's PACE tabulates the number of times that a portfolio's actual return is materially different from its risk forecasts. As an example of this test, please refer to Figure 17.3. Note that if the model is behaving as expected, the portfolio's actual returns should exceed the tracking error forecast by approximately one day per month. Over the four months ended April 30, one therefore expects that there should be four occurrences where actual returns exceed forecast. In fact, there are three. The risk monitor can conclude that the model is behaving appropriately over the period. Had this result not been reached, some of the model's assumptions might have needed to be revisited.

Note from Figure 17.3 that this technique gives no guidance as to how much the model might underestimate risk in the event that the actual result exceeds forecast. It only explores the frequency with which this result occurs. The risk monitor-

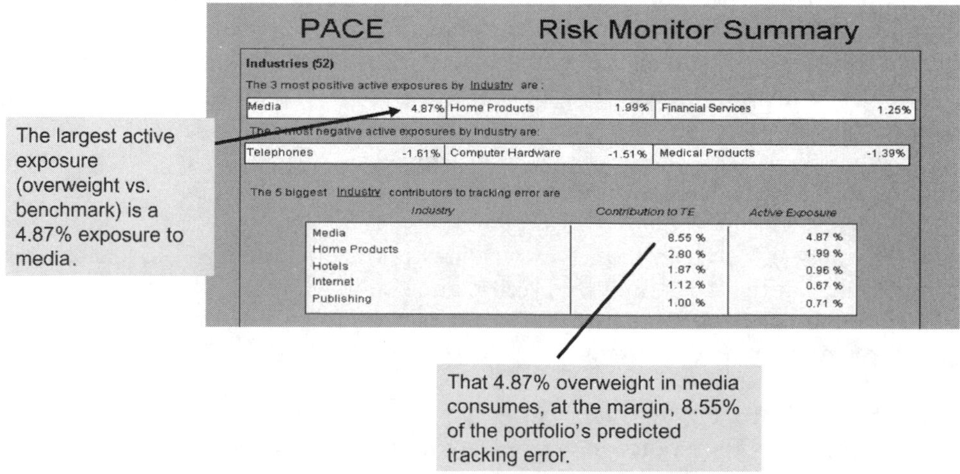

FIGURE 17.2 Industry-Level Exposures and Marginal Contributions

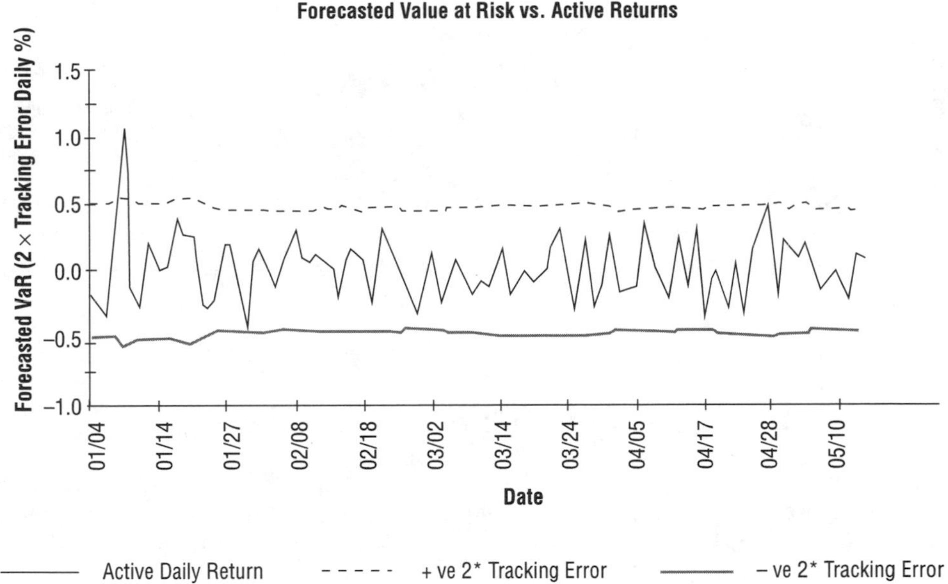

FIGURE 17.3 Model Validation

ing professional should also explore how tracking error might behave in more unusual circumstances.[13]

There are many ways to examine how a portfolio might behave during periods of stress. One technique is historical simulation. To apply this approach, one takes today's positions and applies historical price changes to them to see what the earnings impact would have been had such positions been held fixed over a period of time. A shortfall of this method is that observed history produces only one set of realized outcomes. A more robust approach would allow us to examine the myriad outcomes that are probabilistically implied by the one set of outcomes that actually occurred. To examine these implied paths, Monte Carlo methods are commonly applied.

Figure 17.4 graphs the results of a Monte Carlo simulation for a sample equity portfolio that was prepared to study how tracking error forecasts fluctuate depending on the environment used to estimate the risk forecast.[14] Note that as of April 26, 2002, for this portfolio, the PACE risk model projected a tracking error of 5.08 percent per annum. The tracking error target for this portfolio was 5 percent. So, at

[13]It is often true that a three standard deviation scenario is more draconian than that value that is implied by multiplying a one standard deviation loss by three. This result occurs for two reasons: (1) Many products have nonlinear payoff structures (i.e., embedded options); and (2) the global stresses that are present in a three standard deviation scenario are qualitatively different than those which are present in a one standard deviation scenario. As an example, counterparty credit risk increases in more unusual environments.

[14]It is beyond the scope of this chapter to delve in depth into the calculation methodology behind Monte Carlo methods. Rather we present an output of a Monte Carlo analysis to give the reader a sense as to the types of insights it might provide.

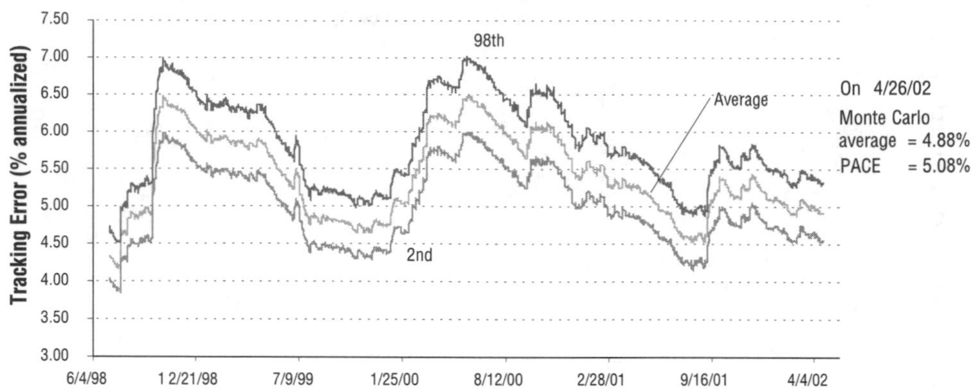

FIGURE 17.4 Example of Monte Carlo Methods to Explore Tracking Error Stresses

first blush, it seems as though the portfolio has an overall risk profile that is closely aligned with the risk target. Common sense tells us, however, that the particular combination of assets held in the portfolio might exhibit quite different tracking error characteristics in different environments.

The PACE forecast is derived by assuming that the underlying data have a half-life of about half a year. When estimating the covariance matrix[15] that is at the heart of the risk forecast, data that are six months old are weighted half as much as current data, and data that are one year old are weighted about one-quarter of current data, and so on. So, more import is given to recent data than to aged data in forecasting risk. This key assumption means that the covariance matrix itself fluctuates over time not only because different data are used to estimate its components but also because the passage of time causes the import of any particular element in the matrix to have an ever smaller weight.

To examine how a tracking error forecast might fluctuate over time, Figure 17.4 simulates the frequency distribution of the tracking error of the positions held at April 26, 2002, over the period from June 1998 until April 26, 2002. These positions, when introduced into the Monte Carlo engine, would have yielded an average tracking error forecast that would have peaked at 6.5 percent in late 1998 and mid-2000. At these times, the 98th percentile risk forecast reached levels of 7 percent.

The risk monitoring professional should consider whether these ranges of tracking error that might occur during periods of stress fall within acceptable levels vis à vis the long-term target of 5 percent. If these levels of tracking error are deemed unacceptably large, an appropriate response might be to run the portfolio at a lower risk profile (say, 4 percent) such that there is reason to believe that the tracking error is less likely to reach unacceptably large levels during periods of stress.[16]

---

[15]Recall that the standard deviation (or tracking error) is calculated by the formula: Tracking error = $[W^T \Sigma W]^{1/2}$ where W is an $N \times 1$ matrix of weights applied to particular factors (e.g., risk factors, or market value of stock holdings, etc.) and Σ represents the $N \times N$ covariance matrix associated with the returns of these factors.

[16]Recall that tracking error is shorthand for the magnitude of earnings variability associated with a certain degree of statistical confidence. If this variability is unacceptably large, it may place the organization's overall strategic plan and goals at risk.

Quantifying Illiquidity Concerns

Since a portfolio's liquidity profile can change dramatically during difficult market environments, tools that measure portfolio liquidity are an essential element of the stress analysis. For example, investors must be aware if a partial redemption could cause an illiquid asset to exceed some guideline.[17] Since redemption risk can correlate with difficult markets, some illiquid situations (e.g., 144A securities, position concentrations, etc.) can coincide with unanticipated redemptions of capital.[18] The risks associated with many of these situations are often apparent only if large stresses are assumed. A tool we use at GSAM to assess the potential implications of illiquidity is the "liquidity duration" statistic.

To calculate this statistic, begin by estimating the average number of days required to liquidate a portfolio assuming that the firm does not wish to exceed a specified percent of the daily volume in any given security. The point here is that we wish to estimate how long it would take to liquidate a portfolio's holdings in an orderly fashion—that is, without material market impact. For example, suppose that we do not wish to exceed more than 15 percent of the daily volume in any given security holding. The number of days required to liquidate any given security we term the liquidity duration for that security. More precisely, the liquidity duration for security *i* can be defined as:

$$LD_i = Q_i/(.15 \cdot V_i)$$

where LD_i = Liquidity duration statistic for security *i*, assuming that we do not wish to exceed 15% of the daily volume in that security
Q_i = Number of shares held in security *i*
V_i = Daily volume of security *i*

An estimate of liquidity duration for the portfolio taken as a whole can be derived by weighting each security's liquidity duration by that security's weight in the portfolio.

Liquidity duration is readily calculated for equity holdings, as volume data are easily available. In the case of fixed income securities, where volume information is not available, the estimate of the number of days required to liquidate a position—and an overall portfolio—in an orderly fashion (i.e., without a material adverse earnings impact) will likely result from discussions with portfolio managers.

Credit Risk Monitoring

For the purposes of this discussion, we assume that the credit risk of each instrument is researched and understood by the portfolio manager. We further assume

[17]As an example, a U.S. mutual fund cannot hold more than 15 percent of its assets in illiquid securities.

[18]An example of this statement is the acceleration of liabilities in a pension plan due to increases in early retirements in periods of recession.

that through factor models or other techniques, the RMU professional can estimate the VaR or tracking error consequences of credit exposures imbedded in the securities held by the portfolio.

In addition to quantifying security-specific and overall portfolio credit exposure, it is important that the RMU understand the credit consequences of dealing with brokers, custodians, execution counterparties, and the like. It is a truism that credit risk is frequently the other side of the coin of market risk. Discussions on market risk are often, at their heart, driven by credit matters. In certain asset classes (e.g., emerging markets) credit risk and market risk may be virtually inseparable. Further, since credit risk is an attribute of performance, it should also be an element of the risk process. As an example, many global indexes (e.g., IFC) now include emerging market countries. To the extent that financial systems in such countries (e.g., Egypt and Russia) are evolving and immature, institutions face credit risk when settling trades. The expected return on such transactions is a function not only of issuer-specific risk, but of credit/settlement risk as well. For this reason, the RMU should ensure that all counterparties used to execute and settle trades meet credit policy criteria.

PERFORMANCE MEASUREMENT—TOOLS AND THEORY

Until now, we have largely focused our attention on measuring potential risk—an estimate of the risk and return that is possible. The other side of this coin is measurement of realized outcomes. In theory, if the ex ante forecasts are meaningful, they should be validated by the actual outcomes experienced. In this sense, performance measurement might be thought of as a form of risk model validation.

In general, the objectives of performance measurement tools are:

- To determine whether a manager generates consistent excess risk-adjusted performance vis à vis a benchmark.
- To determine whether a manager generates superior risk-adjusted performance vis à vis the peer group.
- To determine whether the returns achieved are sufficient to compensate for the risk assumed in cost/benefit terms.
- To provide a basis for identifying those managers whose processes generate high-quality excess risk-adjusted returns. We believe that consistently superior risk-adjusted performance results suggest that a manager's processes, and the resulting performance, can be replicated in the future, making the returns high-quality.

Reasons That Support Using Multiple Performance Measurement Tools

To calculate a risk-adjusted performance measure, two items must be known:

1. Returns over the relevant time period.[19]
2. Risk incurred to achieve such returns.

Risk is ultimately a very human concept comprised of many human dimensions (e.g., emotion, psychological response to uncertainty, fear of underperformance, etc.). Since no two human beings are identical, no two risk assessments are identical. To measure risk and return most comprehensively, we have seen that a panoply of tools (e.g., historical simulations, liquidity awareness, Monte Carlo methods, etc.) can be helpful in order to gain the most complete understanding of the risk present in a portfolio. If the tools yield materially different forecasts, the onus is on the risk professional, working together with senior management and portfolio managers, to apply judgment to determine the most appropriate forecast under the circumstances.

How to Improve the Meaningfulness of Performance Measurement Tools

Performance tools are especially robust when they confirm a priori expectations regarding the quality of returns. If we can identify a disciplined and effective process, we should expect that the process will generate superior risk-adjusted returns. The tools provide a means of measuring the extent of the process's effectiveness. The tools should confirm our belief that the process is indeed functioning the way it was designed to. For example, risk decomposition analysis should show that small cap managers are in fact taking most of their risk in small cap themes. Similarly, a manager with a particular industry specialization should be able to demonstrate that most of that risk budget is spent in securities in that industry. And so on.

For a process to be present, one must be able to define "normal behavior." If normalcy is not identified, the process is likely to be too amorphous to be quantified. Simply put, a process cannot exist without well-defined expectations and decision rules.

Normal behavior suggests that behavior should be predictable. If a process is effective, continued normal behavior (i.e., trading in a manner consistent with the established process) should give us reason to conclude that high-quality returns observed in the past are likely to replicate themselves in the future.

Later on in this chapter, we will introduce some commonly used performance tools. Before discussing these, however, it is worth noting that performance tools, while necessary, are not a substitute for timely management intervention when there is an indication of abnormal behavior. By the time that abnormal behavior manifests itself in the form of poor performance statistics, the damage might al-

[19]In cases where a portfolio holds illiquid assets, returns are the product of human judgment to some degree. It is conceivable that two individuals looking at the same positions could arrive at materially different valuations—this phenomenon occurs because there can be a material divergence between value and price in illiquid markets. In contrast, for liquid securities, the low bid/ask spread is an indication that price is a good approximation of value.

ready be irreversible. For this reason, we believe that performance tools must be supplemented with:

- A clear articulation of management philosophy from each portfolio manager. This philosophy statement should identify how the manager expects to extract returns from the market. It should identify ways of knowing when the manager's process is successful and when it is unsuccessful.
- A routine position and style monitoring process designed to identify deviations from philosophy or process. This is a type of early warning system.

Appendix A at the end of this chapter gives examples of the kinds of information that might be obtained from each manager to help the RMU define and understand each manager's investment philosophy more completely. This list is not meant to be exhaustive, nor is it appropriate for every organization and manager. We provide it here as an example of techniques used in identifying and monitoring "normalcy."

For quantitative portfolio measurement tools to be effective, we must have a sufficient number of data points to form a conclusion with a certain level of statistical confidence. For the purposes of the remainder this chapter, we will assume away this issue. In practice, however, the dearth of performance data often hinders the effectiveness of performance measurement tools. In such cases, the organization will be even more dependent on measuring compliance with manager philosophy.[20]

At this point, we turn our focus to identifying some commonly used performance tools and techniques. (Appendix B, for the reader's reference, is a more mathematical treatment of performance calculation methodologies.)

Tool #1—The Green Zone

Each portfolio manager should be evaluated not only on the basis of ability to produce a portfolio with potential (i.e., forecasted) risk characteristics comparable to target, but also on the basis of being able to *achieve* actual risk levels that approximate target. A manager who can accomplish this task, and earn excess returns in the process, has demonstrated the ability to anticipate, react to, and profit from changing economic circumstances.

---

[20]Even though an organization lacks sufficient data to measure the effectiveness of many managers based on their historical results, it still has sufficient information to conclude whether:

- A manager's philosophy and practices meet commonsense criteria and are likely to extract risk-adjusted performance from the market.
- Each manager's portfolio is consistent with stated philosophy. For example, the RMU should be able to determine that the current portfolio has overall risk levels and risk decomposition characteristics that conform to the manager's philosophy.

An administrative process that measures congruence between manager philosophy and actual trades, money management behavior, loss control, position sizing, and so on is also a form of performance measurement, although not one that we intend to deal with in this paper. If the manager cannot articulate his portfolio management techniques effectively, and if adherence to stated techniques cannot be measured, it is difficult to conclude that a process exists which can be replicated successfully in the future.

At GSAM, we have pioneered a concept called the green zone[21] to identify instances of performance or achieved tracking error that are outside of normal expectations. The green zone concept embodies the following elements:

1. For the prior week, month, and rolling 12 months, we calculate the portfolio's *normalized returns*, which are defined as excess returns over the period minus budgeted excess returns over such period, all divided by target tracking error scaled for time.[22] This statistic might be viewed as a test of the null hypothesis that the achieved levels of excess returns are statistically different from the targeted/budgeted excess returns.
2. For the prior 20- and 60-day periods, we calculate the ratio of annualized tracking error to targeted tracking error. In this test, we examine whether the variability in excess returns is statistically comparable to what was expected.[23] Note that there is no one correct period of time over which to measure tracking error. While for the purposes of this chapter we have selected a shorter-term horizon, strong arguments can be made for including longer-term horizons as well. The point here is that unusual blips in volatility may serve as filters for identifying anomalous environments in which underlying risk dimensions may be undergoing profound change. This tool is designed to help management and portfolio managers ask better and timelier questions.

   As an example of this point, consider Figure 17.5, which shows the time series of predicted tracking errors juxtaposed against rolling 20- and 60-day tracking errors. Not surprisingly, the 20-day measure is more volatile than the 60-day measure and is therefore more responsive to changes in market behavior. The challenge for the risk monitoring professional is to ascertain whether the signal is anomalous or whether it carries information content that should be acted upon. At GSAM, we use this signal as a basis for initiating dialogue between the RMU and portfolio managers to better understand the causes behind these two signals and their consequences.
3. For each of the calculations in (1) and (2) above, we form policy decisions about what type of deviation from expectation is large enough, from a statistical standpoint, to say that it does not fall in the zone of reasonable expectations that we call the green zone. If an event is unusual, but still is expected to occur with some regularity, we term it a yellow zone event. Finally, red zone events are defined as truly unusual and requiring immediate follow-up. The definition of when one zone ends and a second begins is a policy consideration that is a function of how certain we would like to be that all truly unusual events are detected in a timely fashion. For example, if the cost of an unusual

---

[21]Refer to an article entitled: "The Green Zone . . . Assessing the Quality of Returns," by Robert Litterman, Jacques Longerstaey, Jacob Rosengarten, and Kurt Winkelmann of Goldman Sachs & Co. (March 2000).

[22]For example, in calculating the monthly normalized return, the denominator consists of the annual tracking error target divided by the square root of 12.

[23]This test is analogous to ANOVA techniques (e.g., the "F" test) in which one looks at the ratio of variances to determine whether they are statistically comparable. In this case, we are examining the ratio of standard deviations.

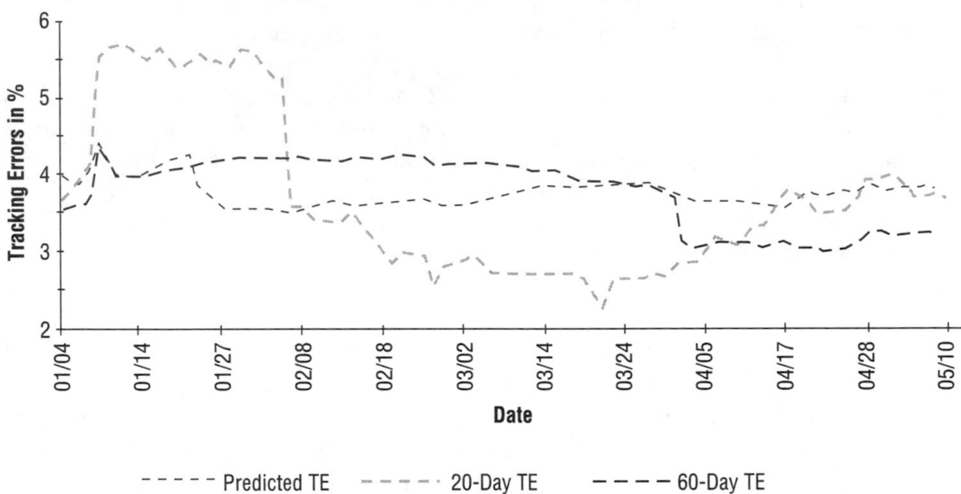

FIGURE 17.5 Example of Rolling 20- and 60-Day Tracking Errors (Annualized)

event is very high, one would expect a very narrow green zone and quite wide yellow and red zones. In this case, one would expect to find more false positives, which are by-products of the policy's conservatism.

4. The results of the green zone analysis are summarized in a document of the form shown in Figure 17.6. What follows is a brief description of this document excerpted from the article entitled *The Green Zone . . . Assessing the Quality of Returns.*

> [*In Figure 17.6*] *we show an example of a portion of one of our weekly performance reports (using hypothetical products). This report, known internally as the "green sheet," has columns that are color-coded for easy recognition of signals of tracking error concerns. For example, we have defined the green zone for a hypothetical set of U.S. equity portfolios, including all ratios of realized 20-day tracking error to target between .7 and 1.4, and have defined the red zone as ratios below .6 or above 2. For the 60-day*

Net Performance		Normalized Return vs. Target					Annualized Tracking Error										
							Last	Last	Last20D	Last60D	Target	Prior Week			Month To Dat		
		Week	MTD	YTD	3Mo	12Mo	20D	60D	/Target	/Target	TE	P	B	D	P	B	
Portfolio	Benchmark																
U.S. Equity Portfolios																	
Portfolio 1	S&P 500	-1.21	-0.22	-0.16	-0.19	0.45	263	260	1.05	1.04	250	0.76	1.18	-0.42	-1.02	-0.91	-(
Portfolio 2	R 1000 Growth	0.37	0.91	1.70	3.14	0.91	526	390	1.75	1.30	300	2.13	1.98	0.15	0.62	0.06	(
Portfolio 3	R 1000 Value	0.26	0.85	1.44	1.22	1.36	226	240	0.90	0.96	250	1.32	1.23	0.09	-0.39	-0.83	(
Portfolio 4	R 2000	0.28	-0.12	0.37	-0.07	-0.68	300	288	0.86	0.82	350	4.39	4.25	0.14	1.68	1.76	-(

FIGURE 17.6 Representative Green Sheet

Note: This chart is to be used for illustrative purposes only. These are not, and should not be viewed as, predictions or projections of future returns of those classes of assets or any investments, including any fund or separate account managed by GSAM, Goldman Sachs & Co., or any other brokerage account.

tracking error we define the green zone as the range between .8 and 1.3. The red zone is defined as ratios below .7 or above 1.8.

. . . the predefined green, yellow, and red zones provide clear expectations for the asset management division portfolio managers. When portfolios move into the yellow or red zone, which will happen every so often, it may be time for a discussion of what is going on. We never expect portfolio management, or risk monitoring, to be reduced to a formula, but these types of quantitative tools have proved to be useful in setting expectations and in providing useful feedback which can foster better quality control of the investment management process.

Tool #2—Attribution of Returns

A commonly used tool to measure the quality of returns is performance attribution. This technique attributes the source of returns to individual securities and/or common factors. Recall that when analyzing the risk profile of a portfolio, we discussed techniques (e.g., risk decomposition) to measure the extent to which the implied risks in a portfolio are consistent with expectations and manager philosophy. So, too, when examining the actual returns of a portfolio, we are concerned that the returns were sourced from those themes where the manager intended to take risk and that such returns are consistent with the risks implied by the *ex ante* risk analysis.

One form of attribution, commonly called variance analysis, shows the contribution to overall performance for each security in the portfolio. Figure 17.7 is an excerpt of this kind of analysis for a stock portfolio. This same kind of analysis can be performed at the industry, sector, and country levels, essentially by combining the performance of individual securities into the correct groupings. The RMU professional can use this analysis to ascertain whether the portfolio tended to earn returns in those securities, industries, sectors, and countries where the risk model indicated that the risk budget was being spent.

To the extent that the manager thinks of risk in factor space as opposed to security-specific space, the attribution process can be performed on this basis. Namely, the attribution process captures the weightings in various risk factors on a periodic basis and also accumulates the returns to such factors in order to produce a variance analysis expressed in factor terms.

As a general rule, it is most meaningful to attribute returns on the same basis that *ex ante* risk for such returns is measured. For managers who think in factor terms, factor risk analysis and factor attribution will likely be more meaningful. For managers who think about risk in terms of individual securities, risk forecasting and attribution at the security level will likely be more relevant. This is not to say that risk should not be measured using a range of models. The point here is that portfolio managers will likely find most meaningful those techniques that measure and describe risk in the same manner that they internalize these issues. Once again, this argues for having a range of risk and attribution models in order to achieve the most robust understanding.

Tool #3—The Sharpe and Information Ratios

The Sharpe ratio divides a portfolio's return in excess of the risk-free rate by the portfolio's standard deviation. The information ratio divides a portfolio's excess

PACE

Multi Period Attribution

Contributors to Active Return by Asset ***(All entries in %)***

Top 30 *(Ranked from highest to lowest Active Contrib.)*

Stock	Company	Contribution	Avg. Active Wgt.
INTC	INTEL CORP	1.45	-3.70
INTU	INTUIT INC	0.88	4.97
JNJ	JOHNSON & JOHNSON	0.46	-3.05
HD	HOME DEPOT INC	0.41	-2.11
GE	GENERAL ELECTRIC CO	0.34	-6.73
CSCO	CISCO SYSTEMS INC	0.27	-2.50
ABT	ABBOTT LABS	0.25	-0.89
IBM	INTERNATIONAL BUSINESS	0.25	-2.06
ENR	ENERGIZER HOLDINGS INC	0.23	2.20
MO	PHILIP MORRIS COS INC	0.23	-1.08
TXN	TEXAS INSTRUMENTS INC	0.23	-1.06
AMAT	APPLIED MATERIALS INC	0.21	-0.81
OMC	OMNICOM GROUP INC	0.17	-0.30
MRK	MERCK & CO INC	0.16	-1.69
WYE	WYETH	0.16	-1.60

Bottom 30 *(Ranked from lowest to highest Active Contrib.)*

Stock	Company	Contribution	Avg. Active Wgt.
CVC	CABLEVISION SYSTEMS CORP	-0.86	1.30
CCU	CLEAR CHANNEL	-0.81	2.45
UVN	UNIVISION COMMUNICATIONS	-0.78	3.78
RMG	Rainbow Media Group	-0.66	0.88
VIA.B	VIACOM INC	-0.61	8.59
DISH	ECHOSTAR COMMUNICATIONS	-0.60	2.52
HET	HARRAHS ENTERTAINMENT	-0.56	7.65
EVC	ENTRAVISION	-0.47	2.03
MGM	METRO GOLDWYN MAYER INC	-0.45	1.68
WON	WESTWOOD ONE INC	-0.41	3.88
FRE	FEDERAL HOME LOAN	-0.41	5.32
FNM	FEDERAL NATIONAL	-0.40	5.78
PCS	SPRINT CORP	-0.35	0.51
CD	CENDANT CORP	-0.34	3.03
TSG	SABRE GROUP HOLDINGS INC	-0.33	3.37

FIGURE 17.7 Sample Variance Analysis

returns (vis à vis the benchmark) by the portfolio's tracking error. Both of these tools are designed to produce estimates of risk-adjusted returns, where risk is defined in standard deviation or tracking error space.

In theory, two different estimates of standard deviation (or tracking error) could be used for these ratios—actual levels of standard deviation as well as forecasted levels. In our judgment, both are relevant. There are occasions where the realized risk—the risk actually observed by the investor—is materially different from the potential risk forecasted by a risk model.[24] In the Monte Carlo analysis in Figure 17.4 we saw how stress tests can be used to provide a picture of how identical holdings can have quite different return and risk characteristics depending on the environment. If the estimates of potential risk capture these stressed scenarios, potential risk might well exceed realized risk. A favorable Sharpe or information ratio calculated using *realized* risk might be much less attractive when expressed in *potential* risk space. Over time, if the risk model is accurate, the realized risk will center on the potential risk.

The Sharpe and information ratios incorporate the following strengths:

- They can be used to measure relative performance vis à vis the competition by identifying managers who generate superior risk-adjusted excess returns vis à vis a relevant peer group. RMUs and investors might specify some minimum rate of acceptable risk-adjusted return when evaluating manager performance.
- They test whether the manager has generated sufficient excess returns to compensate for the risk assumed.
- The statistics can be applied both at the portfolio level as well as for individual industrial sectors and countries. For example, they can help determine which managers have excess risk-adjusted performance at the sector or country level.

The Sharpe and information ratios incorporate the following weaknesses:

- They may require data that may not be available for either the manager or many of his competitors. Often an insufficient history is present for one to be conclusive about the attractiveness of the risk-adjusted returns.
- When one calculates the statistic based on achieved risk instead of potential risk, the statistic's relevance depends, to some degree, on whether the environment is friendly to the manager.

Tool #4—Alpha versus the Benchmark

This tool regresses the excess returns of the fund against the excess returns of the benchmark.

The outputs of this regression are:

- An intercept, often referred to as "alpha," or skill.
- A slope coefficient against the excess returns of the benchmark, often referred to as "beta."

---

[24]Risk models attempt to measure potential risk. Ultimately, the true potential risk is not knowable. We only see its footprints over time in the form of realized risk. Still, even this realized risk is only one outcome of an infinite number of outcomes that were in theory possible.

Standard confidence tests can be applied to the regression's outputs. The alpha term can be tested for statistical significance to see if it is both positive and statistically different from zero.

This performance tool incorporates the following strengths:

- It allows management to opine whether skill is truly present or excess returns are happenstance. It tests whether the manager has generated excess returns vis à vis the benchmark.
- It allows management to distinguish between excess returns due to leverage and excess returns due to skill.
- The alpha and beta statistics, and tests of significance, are easy to calculate.
- The beta statistic shows if an element of the manager's returns are derived from being overweight or underweight the market (occurs if the beta is statistically different from 1.0).

This performance tool incorporates the following weakness:

- There may not be a sufficient number of data points to permit a satisfactory conclusion about the statistical significance of alpha.

Tool #5—Alpha versus the Peer Group

This tool regresses the manager's excess returns against the excess returns of the manager's peer group. It is used to determine whether the manager demonstrates skill over and above what is found in the peer group.

The peer group's return is the capital-weighted average return of all managers who trade comparable strategies. The peer group is basically the manager's competitors in his strategy.

The outputs of this regression are:

- An intercept, often referred to as "alpha," or skill.
- A slope coefficient against the excess returns of peer group, often referred to as "beta."

The alpha term represents the manager's excess return against the peer group. The beta term measures the extent to which the manager employs greater or lesser amounts of leverage than do competitors.

Standard confidence tests can be applied to the regression's outputs. The alpha term can be tested for statistical significance to see if it is both positive and statistically different from zero.

This performance tool incorporates the following strengths:

- It allows management to opine whether skill is truly present or excess returns are happenstance. It tests whether the manager has generated excess returns vis à vis the peer group.
- It allows management to distinguish between excess returns due to leverage and excess returns due to skill.
- The alpha and beta statistics, and tests of significance, are easy to calculate.

This performance tool incorporates the following weaknesses:

- There may not be a sufficient number of data points to permit a satisfactory conclusion about the statistical significance of alpha or beta.
- Returns of the peer group are biased due to the existence of survivorship biases.
- There is often a wide divergence in the amount of money under management among the peers. It is often easier to make larger risk-adjusted excess returns with smaller sums under management than with larger sums.

SUMMARY

Risk represents a shadow cost that businesses accept in order to produce profit. For a return to be deemed acceptable, expected returns must be adequate to compensate for the risk assumed. Risk management therefore implies that cost benefit process is at work.

Risk is a scarce resource in the sense that organizations place limits on their willingness to accept loss. For any given level of risk assumed, the objective is to engage into as many intelligent profit-making opportunities as possible. If risk is squandered or used unwisely, the ability of the organization to achieve its profit objectives is put at risk. If excessive levels of risk are taken vis à vis budget, the organization is risking unacceptably large losses in order to produce returns that it neither expects nor desires. If too little risk is taken vis à vis budgeted levels, return expectations will likely fall short of budget. The ability of an organization to achieve its risk and return targets is put at risk anytime that risk capital is used wastefully or in amounts inconsistent with the policies established by such organization.

There are three fundamental dimensions behind risk management—planning, budgeting, and monitoring. We observe that these three dimensions are intimately related and that they can be more completely understood by looking at their commonly used counterparts in the world of financial accounting controls. We posit that there is a direct correspondence between financial planning, financial budgeting, and financial variance monitoring and their risk management counterparts—namely, risk planning, risk budgeting, and risk monitoring. This conclusion follows from the assertion that risk is the shadow cost behind returns. Hence behind every line item in a financial plan or budget must lie a corresponding risk dimension. Financial plans and budgets can therefore be alternatively expressed using risk management vocabulary.

The risk plan should set points of success or failure for the organization (e.g., return and volatility expectations, VaR policies, risk diversification standards, minimum acceptable levels of return on risk capital, etc.). The risk plan should be well vetted and discussed among the organization's senior leadership and oversight bodies. Its main themes should be capable of being articulated to analysts, boards, actuaries, management teams, and so on. For example, strategic plans have ROE targets and business diversification policies that are well known. The risk plan should describe how risk capital is to be allocated such that the expected returns on such risk capital yield the financial outcomes sought with a high degree of certainty.

The risk budget—often called asset allocation—quantifies the vision of the risk plan. The risk budget is a numeric blueprint that gives shape and form to the risk plan. There are many similarities between financial budgets and risk budgets. Financial budgets calculate net income as the difference between revenue and expenses. ROE is then estimated as net income divided by capital invested. In the case of risk budgets, a risk "charge"—defined as VaR or some other proxy for "risk expense"—can be associated with each line item of projected revenue and expense. Hence, a RORC (return on risk capital) can be associated with each activity as well as for the aggregation of all activities. In the case of both financial and risk budgets, ROE and RORC must exceed some minimum levels for them to be deemed acceptable. Both statistics are concerned with whether the organization is sufficiently compensated—in cost/benefit terms—for the expenses and/or risks associated with generating revenues. Finally, both RORC and ROE can and should be estimated over all time intervals that are deemed relevant.

If we accept the premise that risk capital is a scarce commodity, it follows that monitoring controls should exist to ensure that risk capital is used in a manner consistent with the risk budget. Material variances from risk budget are threats to the investment vehicle's ability to meet its ROE and RORC targets. If excessive risk is used, unacceptable levels of loss may result. If too little risk is spent, unacceptable shortfalls in earnings may result. Risk monitoring is required to ensure that material deviations from risk budget are detected and addressed in a timely fashion. The chapter introduces the concept of an independent risk management unit (RMU) as a best practice in risk monitoring space. It discusses its objectives and provides examples of how it might operate in practice.

The final part of the chapter deals with performance measurement tools and related theory. Performance tools are especially robust when they confirm a priori expectations regarding the quality of returns. Among the objectives of these tools are:

- To determine whether a manager generates consistent excess risk-adjusted performance vis à vis a benchmark.
- To determine whether a manager generates superior risk-adjusted performance vis à vis the peer group.
- To determine whether the returns achieved are sufficient to compensate for the risk assumed in cost/benefit terms.
- To provide a basis for identifying those managers whose processes generate high-quality excess risk-adjusted returns. We believe that consistently superior risk-adjusted performance results suggest that a manager's processes, and the resulting performance, can be replicated in the future, making the returns high-quality.

The chapter then describes tools to measure the nature of performance. Unusual volatility and performance results can be identified by categorizing each outcome as statistically expected (a green zone outcome), somewhat unusual (a yellow zone outcome), and statistically improbable (a red zone outcome). Other performance tools that are explored include return attribution, the Sharpe and information ratios, and portfolio manager alpha versus the benchmark and versus a peer group. In each case, strengths and weaknesses of the performance measurement tool are briefly discussed.

Appendix B provides a more mathematical treatment of account performance measurement.

APPENDIX A
Representative Questions to Help Define Manager Philosophies/Processes

1. What sectors do you trade?
2. What countries and regions do you trade?
3. What products do you trade (equities, over-the counter (OTC) foreign exchange (FX), fixed income, etc.)?
4. If you trade OTC, do ISDA, FX Netting agreements, and so on exist?
5. How many accounts do you trade?
6. Define your assets under management.
7. Are you able to produce a historical track record?
8. Does your strategy require a minimum amount of money under management in order for you to trade your entire portfolio?
9. Is your process capacity constrained? Can you estimate at what point it might be?
10. Describe the process by which you know that you are trading in accordance with client guidelines.
11. Do you believe that your process is volume sensitive in terms of the number of accounts under management? If so, discuss.
12. Describe how your process generates profits. That is, what is the source of your excess returns (e.g., superior stock selection, superior quantitative modeling, superior fundamental research, etc.)?
13. Define the list of your benchmarks. Are all of them easily calculated or are some nonstandard? For nonstandard benchmarks, describe how you manage risk in your portfolio. Would you prefer standard benchmarks if that option was available to you?
14. What risk system do you use to measure risk and build portfolios?
15. Have you found weaknesses or problems with these systems from time to time? To the extent that these systems can be inadequate, how do you compensate?
16. Define the following on a daily, monthly, quarterly, and annual basis both in terms of active weights vis à vis a benchmark as well as in terms of marginal contribution to risk: maximum exposure by security; maximum exposure by sector; maximum exposure by country; maximum exposure at the portfolio level.
    a. For each of the above, define exposure at the one and three standard deviation levels.
    b. When will you liquidate a position? Does this answer correlate to the answers given at (a) above?
    c. At what point are losses vis à vis the benchmark so large that you would conclude that your process is no longer working?
17. Describe those environments that are harmful for you.
18. Describe those environments that are favorable for you.
19. Is any part of your book vulnerable to market illiquidity? That is, does the genre of products you trade have evidence of becoming much less illiquid (based on historical observation)?

20. Do you have risk limits in terms of:
    - Maximum percentage of the security outstanding
    - Maximum percentage of daily volume (alternatively, how many days to liquidate if you never want to be more than, say, 15 percent of the daily volume).

    Describe how these limits are applied. Are they applied on an account-by-account basis as well as on an overall basis (i.e., the sum total of all accounts under your direction)?
21. Define the risk factors that drive your returns. Does your risk software follow all of these factors? If not, how do you compensate?
22. Describe the process by which you review your daily results. What reports do you look at?
23. What process exists to ensure that accounts are traded in a parallel fashion?
24. Of the various fundamental factors followed by your risk system, define a normal band around each one.
25. Does redemption risk enter into your portfolio management? If so, how?
26. Have you had any material trading errors over the past year? If so, what were the circumstances?
27. At year-end, how would you define successful portfolio management? What statistics should we look to as guidance for measuring the quality of risk-adjusted performance?
28. Describe controls over valuation of your portfolio.
29. Describe the nature of the credit review you perform for custodians and executing brokers.

APPENDIX B
Calculation of Account Performance

Performance measurement provides an objective, quantitative assessment of the change in value of a portfolio or portfolio segment over an evaluation period, including the impact of any cash flows during that period. The calculation of total return in the absence of cash flows for a period is based on the formula

$$r_p(t) = \frac{MVE - MVB}{MVB} \tag{17B.1}$$

where $r_p(t)$ = Portfolio return
MVE = Market value of portfolio at end of period, including all accrued income
MVB = Portfolio's market value at beginning of period, including all income accrued up to end of previous period

This definition of a portfolio's return is valid only if there are no intraperiod cash flows. In practice, this condition is often violated as cash flows frequently occur due to capital allocated to or removed from the portfolio (client's account) or through transactions from buying and selling securities.

If cash flows do occur over the period in which returns are calculated, we need to do the following:

- Compute the market value of the cash flows at the date/time at which they occur.
- Calculate the interim rate of return for the subperiod according to equation (17B.1).
- Link the subperiod returns to get the return for the entire period.

In equity markets, the primary drivers of performance include the shares held of each asset and its market price as well as accrued income from dividends. Dividends ex-not-paid affect a stock's price whereas cash dividends on the pay date do not.

When cash flows occur, there are two proposed methods for measuring a portfolio's return. The first is a *dollar-weighted return* and the second is a *time-weighted return.*

DOLLAR-WEIGHTED RETURN

There are two methods for computing a dollar-weighted return. The first is the internal rate of return and the second is the modified Dietz method. To compute the internal rate of return of a portfolio we assume that the portfolio has I ($I = 1, \ldots, I$) cash flows over some period (e.g., one day, one month, one quarter) and solve for the internal rate of return, *IRRATE*, such that the following relationship holds

$$MVE = \sum_{i=1}^{I} FLOW_i \times (1 + IRRATE_i)^{\overline{w}_i} \tag{17B.2}$$

where $FLOW_i$ = ith cash flow over the return period, in the form of either a deposit (cash or security) or a withdrawal

$\overline{w}_i$ = Proportion of the total number of days in period that $FLOW_i$ has been in (or out of) portfolio. The formula for $\overline{w}_i$ assuming cash flows occur at end of day, is

$$\overline{w}_i = \frac{(CD - D_i)}{CD}$$

where CD = Total number of days in return period

D_i = Number of days since beginning of period when the flow, $FLOW_i$, occurred

Equation (17B.2) is also known as the modified Bank Administration Institute method (modified BAI). It is an acceptable approximation to the time-weighted return (discussed in the next section) when the results are calculated at least quarterly and geometrically linked over time.

A portfolio's return based on the Modified Dietz method is given by

$$R_{\text{Dietz}} = \frac{MVE - MVB - F}{MVB + FW} \tag{17B.3}$$

where F = Sum of cash flows within period

FW = Sum of cash flows each multiplied by its weight

$$\left(\text{i.e., } FW = \sum_{i=1}^{I} FLOW_i \times \overline{w}_i\right)$$

TIME-WEIGHTED RETURN

Ideally, we would want to compute a portfolio's return in such a way as to incorporate the precise time when the cash flows occur. To this end, the time-weighted rate of return (also known as the daily valuation method) for a portfolio is given by

$$R_{RWR} = (S_1 \times S_2 \times \ldots \times S_P) - 1 \tag{17B.4}$$

where P ($p = 1, \ldots, P$) is the number of subperiods that are defined within the period's return and

$$S_P = \frac{MVE_p}{MVB_p} \tag{17B.5}$$

where MVE_p is the market value of the portfolio at the end of the pth subperiod, before any cash flows in period p but including accrued income for the period, and MVB_p is the market value at the end of the previous subperiod (i.e., beginning of this subperiod), including any cash flows at the end of the previous subperiod and including accrued income up to the end of the previous period.This method is the most exact of the three explained here.

Note that the main difference between the dollar-weighted return and the time-weighted return is that the former assumes the same rate of return over the whole period. The time-weighted return, on the other hand, uses the geometric average of returns from each individual period.

A good way to understand the methods described is to look at a numerical example. Suppose that on January 1, 2002, we invested \$100 in the Nasdaq Composite index. On March 1, 2002, we invest another \$100. The total return on the Nasdaq from January 1, 2002, through February 28, 2002, was –11.22 percent. Hence our initial investment of \$100 is now worth \$88.78. However, since we invested another \$100, the total value of our investment is \$188.78. By March 28, 2002, the total value of our investment has grown to \$201.20 and we sell \$100. The Nasdaq then declines until finally, on May 10, 2002, we are left with \$87.79.

We compute our return on this investment as of May 10, 2002, under the different methods presented above.

- The ideal time-weighted return is

$$[(88.78/100) \times (201.20/188.78) \times (87.79/101.20)] - 1 = -17.92\%$$

- The dollar-weighted annualized return based on the BAI method is

$$\begin{aligned} 87.79 &= 100(1 + IRRATE)^{90/252} + 100(1 + IRRATE)^{50/252} \\ &\quad - 100(1 + IRRATE)^{30/252} \\ IRRATE &= -25.50\% \end{aligned}$$

■ According to the modified Dietz method, the annualized return is

$$\frac{87.79-100-(100-100)}{100+7.94}=-11.31\%$$

Clearly, the dollar-weighted return calculation takes into account the timing of the decisions to sell or buy as reflected by the –25.50 percent return.

COMPUTING RETURNS

Let $R_n^\ell(t)$ represent the local return on the nth asset as measured in percent:

$$R_n^\ell(t)=\frac{P_n^\ell(t)+d_n(t-h,t)-P_n^\ell(t-1)}{P_n^\ell(t-1)} \tag{17B.6}$$

$P_n^\ell(t)$ = Time t local price of security or asset
$d_n(t-h,t)$ = Dividend (per share) paid out at time t for period $t-h$ through t

In a global framework we need to incorporate exchange rates into the return calculations. We define exchange rates as the reporting currency over the local currency (reporting/local). The local currency is sometimes referred to as the risk currency. For example, USD/GBP would be the exchange rate where the reporting currency is the U.S. dollar and the risk currency is the British pound. A USD-based investor with holdings in U.K. equities would use the USD/GBP rate to convert the value of the stock to U.S. dollars.

Suppose a portfolio with U.S. dollars as its reporting currency has holdings in German, Australian, and Japanese equities. The local and/or risk currencies are EUR, AUD, and JPY, respectively. The total return of each equity position consists of the local return on equity and the return on the currency expressed in reporting/local.

We assume that a generic portfolio contains N assets ($n = 1, \ldots, N$). Let $P_n^\ell(t)$ represent the price, in euros, of one share of Siemens stock. $X_{ij}(t)$ is the exchange rate expressed as the ith currency per unit of currency j. For example, with USD as the reporting currency, the exchange rate where $X_{ij}(t)$ = USD/EUR (i is USD and j is EUR) is used to convert Siemens equity (expressed in euros) to U.S. dollars. In general, the exchange rate is expressed in reporting over local currency.

It follows from these definitions that the price of the nth asset expressed in reporting currency is

$$P_n(t)=P_n^\ell(t)X_{ij}(t) \tag{17B.7}$$

We use (17B.7) as a basis for defining total return, local return, and exchange rate return. The total return of an asset or portfolio is simply the return that incorporates both the local return and exchange rate return. Depending on how returns are defined—continuous or discrete (percent)—we get different equations for how returns are calculated. Following directly from (17B.7), an asset's total return, using percent returns, is defined as

$$\begin{aligned} R_n(t) &= \left[1 + R_n^{\ell}(t)\right]\left[1 + E_{ij}(t)\right] - 1 \\ &= R_n^{\ell}(t) + E_{ij}(t) + R_n^{\ell}(t) \times E_{ij}(t) \end{aligned} \tag{17B.8}$$

where $R_n(t)$ = One-period total return on the nth asset

R_n^{ℓ} = One-period percent return on the equity positions expressed in local currency (i.e., the local return)

$E_{ij}(t)$ = One-period percent return on the ith currency per unit of currency j

$$E_{ij}(t) = X_{ij}(t)/X_{ij}(t-1) - 1$$

For example, suppose that the nth position is a position in the DAX equity index. In this case, $R_n^{\ell}(t)$ is the local return on DAX and $E_{ij}(t)$ is the return in the USD/EUR exchange rate. When the euro strengthens, USD/EUR increases and $E_{ij}(t) > 0$. Holding all other things constant, this increases the total return on the equity position.

CHAPTER 18

The Need for Independent Valuation

Jean-Pierre Mittaz

Reliable and accurate securities valuations are a cornerstone of the investment management industry and represent a significant day-to-day responsibility for asset management. This is especially important for pooled investment vehicles (such as mutual funds, hedge funds, etc.) where the accurate valuation of the pool's assets forms the basis of investment transactions among existing, new, and departing investors. Inaccurate valuations expose investment management institutions to both financial and reputation risk. For example, in a high-profile case in the United Kingdom, British regulators in 1997 fined Morgan Grenfell Asset Management $3.3 million after the fund manager overstated the value of unlisted stocks in the firm's funds. Or, in 1998, a former manager of a PaineWebber bond fund settled Securities and Exchange Commission (SEC) charges that he inflated the fund's net asset value (NAV) by frequently valuing some holdings at prices much higher than those suggested by the fund's custodian.

While certain markets have good price transparency (e.g., listed equities during trading hours), others do not (e.g., many fixed income and derivative instruments, and even equities markets at particular times[1]). Furthermore, even in transparent and liquid markets, unforeseen events such as market closures, trading halts, or other events can affect the ability to adequately price portfolios at fair valuations. For example, how should a manager value portfolio holdings in Taiwanese securities when the Taiwan stock exchange unexpectedly gets closed for days following a local earthquake? Or what is the fair value of a security that ceases trading due to a trading halt on the stock exchange?

This chapter focuses on the functions performed by an independent valuation oversight group that is increasingly a feature of a state-of-the-art control environment for an asset manager. The organization of the chapter is:

- We suggest that a *valuation oversight philosophy* should be incorporated as a part of the risk management and control framework of an investment manager.

[1]For example, the price transparency for Asian equities held in a U.S.-domiciled mutual fund to be priced at 4:00 P.M. Eastern time is not clear given that the last data point from liquid trading activity might be as "stale" as 11 to 15 hours.

- We discuss some key responsibilities and activities of an independent *valuation oversight group*. We briefly list and describe some *valuation verification tools and techniques* that a valuation oversight group should make use of.
- We offer a few words about a supervisory body, the *valuation committee*, that should determine and ratify appropriate valuation policies and procedures.
- Finally, we illustrate some potential *consequences of mispricings* in the context of mutual funds to underscore the significance of the valuation process.

VALUATION OVERSIGHT PHILOSOPHY: SOME CONCEPTUAL CORNERSTONES

The principal objective of the pricing function is to ensure that assets are priced fairly. Fair pricing should reflect those pricing levels where, at a particular point in time, assets could be liquidated in the normal course of business. Proper valuations and pricing are not only important information content for various reporting functions such as client reporting, performance measurement, and risk analysis. They can be even more critical where they become the basis of contractual financial transactions between investing parties. As an example, open-end pooled vehicles such as mutual funds or hedge funds allow investors to join or leave the investment pool by transacting at the pool's NAV per share.[2] Needless to say, any inaccurate valuations would lead to an unfair and inappropriate wealth transfer between transacting parties. In other words, valuations need to be fair to all—purchasing, redeeming, and remaining investors.[3]

Let us begin with some high-level themes and principles to describe the framework and objectives in which a valuation oversight function should be positioned.

Statutory Valuation Guidelines

It is important to distinguish between price and value. These two concepts do not always have to agree. For example, an investor purchasing an asset believes that the asset's value exceeds its current price. The converse holds for an investor selling an asset. For liquid markets, prices reflect the current market consensus view regarding value. Since the bid/ask spread for liquid assets is typically small, there is a narrow confidence interval around the market consensus of economic value.

For less liquid markets, this condition does not hold. These markets are characterized by wide bid/ask spreads, suggesting less market consensus regarding economic value. A statistician would describe this situation as being one in which there is a wide confidence interval around the true economic mark. By definition, every point on this wide interval is possible. Hence, if a subsequent transaction takes

[2]In the case of mutual funds, the proper fair value of the assets (often hundreds of security positions), as represented by the NAV, needs to be determined on a daily basis within a few hours, which creates operational and logistical challenges. As we will see, to get this right, the devil is—as is often the case—in the details.

[3]For example, if a fund's NAV is understated and a new investor joins the investment pool, existing investors are inadvertently forced to give up a part of their wealth to the new investor. The same is true when a fund investor redeems and the NAV happens to be overstated.

place at a price that is different from the established mark, it does not necessarily follow that the mark was "wrong." In fact, given the width of the confidence interval, the mark may still have been appropriate.

The policy issues raised here are how to appropriately price an asset that has a fuzzy market consensus view as to its value. For liquid markets, price and value tend to converge on the same number. Hence, pricing feeds received from numerous vendors should yield the same result. This condition does not hold for less liquid markets which are characterized by a divergence between price and value. In such cases, there is a need for judgment to determine the most appropriate pricing given all relevant factors. As we will show later, such judgments are most credible when they are applied by professionals who are independent of the portfolio management process in both fact and appearance.

In establishing valuation and pricing policies, it is important to review best industry practices, industry regulation, and government regulation. The long established and highly regulated mutual fund arena is a very good starting point for reviewing valuation policies. Even if for other market segments such as hedge funds and institutional separate accounts there is less formal guidance, the mutual fund–related rules could help define the general framework of best practices across all investment management products.

The fundamental rules governing valuation of portfolio securities for mutual funds are set forth in Section 2(a)(41) of the Investment Company Act of 1940 (the 1940 Act), which defines the "value" of fund assets in terms of a simple dichotomy:

- Securities "for which market quotations are readily available" are to be valued at such quotations or prices.
- All other securities are to be priced at "fair value as determined in good faith by the board of directors."

Various SEC regulations reiterate these statutory standards. In 1969 and 1970, the SEC became concerned about the appropriateness of fund valuation practices and issued accounting releases that offer guidance on proper valuations. ASR 113[4] principally addresses valuation practices with respect to restricted securities, but also offers guidance on certain other aspects of the valuation process. Then, ASR 118 deals with the use of fair value methodologies to price securities and sets forth the general principle that the fair value of securities "would appear to be the amount which the reasonable expect to receive upon their current sale." Under ASR 118, funds were instructed "generally" to use the last quoted sales price at the time of valuation. For securities that are listed on more than one exchange, ASR 118 indicates that funds should use the last sales price from the exchange on which the security is principally traded and that the last sales information from the other exchanges should be used only when there are no trades reported on the primary exchange on that date. When there is no quoted sales information, ASR 118 contemplates the use of bid and ask prices quoted by broker-dealers. Best practice is to obtain quotes from multiple dealers "particularly if quotations are available only

[4]Accounting Series Release No. 113, Investment Company Act Rel. No. 5,847 (1937–1982 Accounting Series Release Transfer Binder), Fed. Sec. L. Rep. (CCH).

from broker-dealers not known to be established market makers in that security." Securities laws put the onus on fund directors to ensure that funds price their holdings properly. ASRs 113 and 118 remain the primary SEC authority on permissible valuation practices.

Recent SEC staff guidance in 1999 and 2001 has focused on funds' obligations to monitor for "significant events" and to determine when market quotations are not "readily available," thereby triggering the obligation to employ fair valuation procedures in determining the value of portfolio securities.

Documented and Ratified Valuation Procedures and Valuation Authorizations

At first blush, it would seem to be a relatively simple matter to determine a security's price value at a given point in time. In practice, this process is often quite complex and subjective, however. Valuation determinations frequently involve a significant amount of judgment, ranging from the selection of pricing sources to decisions as to when, and on what basis, to override pricing data obtained from those sources.

Having formalized documented policies and procedures in place is a fundamental aspect of any consistently applied high-quality valuation process. These policies and procedures help ensure that controls exist around judgments applied to pricing and that the proper control and supervisory structure over such judgments is in place. For example, during examinations of mutual funds, the SEC staff often reviews funds' valuation policies and procedures to validate the presence of this kind of control environment. The importance of adequate supervision and control was highlighted, for example, by the SEC censure of an investment advisor for failing to adequately supervise the pricing practices of one of its portfolio managers. The SEC's order indicated that the advisor

> *had no written procedures to implement the Fund's policy to use bid side market value prices for valuing securities. The firm's practices concerning the daily pricing were insufficient in that they, among other things, gave too much control over the pricing process with little or no oversight by anyone in a supervisory capacity. In addition, there was no procedure in place to alert [the advisor] when bid side market prices were not available. [The advisor] did not independently verify the daily prices provided to [the advisor's] accounting department with the pricing source or any secondary sources.*[5]

Valuation procedures need to cover various dimensions that should be considered in defining the "right" price. Among these are:

- The parameters for data collection and computation. For example, such procedures should establish criteria for determining when securities are considered to have readily available market quotations and when fair value is required.

[5]Van Kampen American Capital Asset Management, Inc., Investment Advisers Act Rel. No. 1,525, 60 SEC Docket 1,045 (September 29, 1995).

- Identification of acceptable sources of pricing information and methodologies for each asset type held by a portfolio.

  Pricing date and time (e.g., 4:00 P.M. Eastern time, close of New York Stock Exchange, 4:00 P.M. Central time, previous day close, etc.).

  Pricing type (e.g., bid versus ask versus mean versus close versus last sale; pricing location (e.g., price from exchange where principally traded, global listings, etc.).

  Pricing methodologies for over-the-counter (OTC) or illiquid securities with no current price transparency (e.g., matrix pricing, broker quotes, model valuations, etc.).

  Pricing override/manual price procedures.
- Specification of the types of reports, automated flagging systems and other controls to be applied to the initial pricing information in order to ensure accuracy and reliability. Further, pricing override and manual pricing procedures should be documented.
- Determination of the portfolio management/senior management to whom valuation issues should be reported, as well as specification of the circumstances under which supervisory approval and/or board action is required.
- Finally, fair valuation policies, which determine under what circumstances an obtained price still reflects fair value, or whether an alternative pricing mechanism is to be used.

Positions Marked by Independent Accounting Agents

Valuations are, among other things, used to determine asset manager compensation. Valuations affect both the size of assets under management on which fixed fees are paid as well as reported portfolio performance on which incentive fees may be earned. In order to avoid conflicts of interest in either fact or appearance, pricing responsibility should lie with a team that is removed from and independent of portfolio management and the investment process. In general, segregation of duties in valuation matters is a clear best practice and a necessary but not sufficient condition for an effective internal control environment.

Parties that are independent of the investment process such as operations or investment accounting departments, or possibly even outsourced accounting agents, are examples of professional teams that can provide this necessary independent oversight of pricing. It is, of course, critical for the valuation process to have appropriately qualified staff that exhibits a sound knowledge of the financial products to be priced. Commercially available accounting agents with their own internal controls[6] can act as the first line of defense for the verification of pricing data. Comparisons of prices across sources, tolerance levels for day-to-day price movements, and comparisons to related securities from the same issuer are some of the sanity checks that can be built into the pricing process of an accounting agent. As we will see in

[6]Often documented in Statement on Auditing Standards No. 70 (SAS 70)/Financial Reporting and Auditing Group (SAS70/FRAG21)—Reviews.

greater detail, the work of these agents can and should be further supplemented by professionals within the firm ultimately responsible for the investment product.

Wherever possible, prices should be sourced from independent parties like pricing vendors or stock exchanges. For some products such as OTC derivatives, broker quotes might get sourced from the trades' counterparties in addition to unrelated counterparties. Where fully independent price sources aren't available, separate price verification will be required to help mitigate any risks of mispricing.

Separate Valuation Oversight and Price Verification

It is a best practice to establish an independent (i.e., independent of portfolio management) and separate valuation oversight function that monitors the various aspects of the valuation policies and procedures and ensures continuous focus. This team should coordinate the valuation processes across different functions, perform an oversight of the pricing processes, and regularly assess the quality of the pricing used (price verification). If, as an exception,[7] portfolio valuations need to be generated or obtained by the investment advisor, the independent valuation oversight team should play an active role in ensuring that such valuations are reasonable and appropriate. When all is said and done, this team should be deemed as ultimately and solely responsible for the fairness of pricing used.

In an enforcement procedure involving a bank serving as a fund accountant for a money market fund, the SEC alleged that the bank lacked adequate controls because an employee improperly treated a significant drop in securities prices as a transmission error and manually overrode it. The SEC order indicated that, among other things, there was no oversight or review of pricing deviations by senior management, and no control or "flags" were put in place to alert senior management.[8]

Management Reporting and Valuation Committee

The establishment of a valuation committee with senior management representation emphasizes the importance of the valuation control function. In addition to being a senior supervisory body, the valuation committee acts as a discussion forum and decision maker on any related topics. Representation should cover control functions such as risk management, legal, compliance, and controllers, as well as senior management. It should ensure that policies and procedures exist for reliable and accurate pricing, that an independent valuation oversight group exists to execute these procedures and policies, and that such group is independent of portfolio management and is adequately trained and funded. Finally, this committee should ensure that it is informed in a timely manner of all material judgments involving valuation practices.

Reporting to this committee should be the valuation oversight group comprised of professionals charged with the responsibility of executing the policies and stan-

---

[7]For example, for the case where no external quote could be obtained or the obtained price was deemed no longer accurate.

[8]In the Matter of the Bank of California, N.A., Investment Company Act Rel. No. 19,545, 54 SEC Docket 989 (June 28, 1993).

dards of the valuation committee. We now explore the valuation oversight group in greater detail.

RESPONSIBILITIES OF AN INDEPENDENT VALUATION OVERSIGHT GROUP

The mission statement of an independent valuation oversight group should include the need to:

> *Establish, monitor, and address valuation practices and issues across the investment management division's products, globally, with particular focus on pooled investment vehicles.*

Responsibilities of a valuation oversight area include the following objectives:

- Maintain and monitor formalized valuation procedures and valuation authorizations for various products.
- Monitor pricing data sources for coverage and quality aspects.
- Prepare and analyze periodic price verification reports that compare prices obtained from different sources, and manage any pricing exceptions.
- Coordinate any necessary fair valuation adjustments.
- Organize activities of the valuation committee.
- Provide timely and value-added management and board reporting.

Valuation Verification Tools

Controls need to be incorporated at every level of the valuation process, starting at the operational (primary pricing group) and then continuing through the supervisory structure. Various techniques and tools can be employed for valuation verification. The objective is to use various forms of independent data points that help validate the accuracy or valuations used. It is the combination of the tools that increases the control level around pricing, as one technique alone is often not able to validate all aspects. Here are some techniques that are typically employed.

Transaction Prices versus Valuation Prices With this technique, actual transaction prices for securities purchased or sold are used to validate end-of-day valuation levels. Actual transaction prices (in an orderly market) are probably the strongest indicator of what fair market valuation of a security may be, given that two independent counterparties contractually agreed to purchase and sell a security at a price. So, for example, if a fairly liquid bond position changes hands at a price of 105 today, and during previous and subsequent days the pricing service provides a price of, let's say, 110, the valuation oversight process should challenge the latter's appropriateness for daily valuations. This technique may also be applied for similar and comparable securities when an actual transaction price is known.

Price Comparisons between Various Pricing Sources This control tool encompasses periodic cross checks of prices received from pricing services or brokers either against other pricing vendors or against broker quotes from market makers. Each alternative price or an average thereof may be used for comparative purposes, and asset-class-specific thresholds are set to define tolerable deviation. (See Figure 18.1.) These cross checks are performed after the fact as a means of confirming that the valuation process is working. There can be significant differences between matrix-pricing vendors, especially in the areas of less liquid bonds. This type of control would have avoided the Heartland High Yield Muni Bond and Heartland Short Duration High Yield Muni fund pricing misfortune in October 2000, where the funds' NAVs tumbled 70 percent and 44 percent respectively in a single day when the funds slashed the values of certain bonds in the portfolios. The valuations for the bonds were provided by an external pricing service.

Price Comparisons against Independent Model Prices If independent broker quotes are not available, another source of an independent price for validation may be derived from an internal pricing model. For products like interest rate swaps, cross-currency swaps, options, and variance swaps, independent models can be used to capture the terms, and fair valuation can be derived based on independent market data input (such as interest rate curves, volatilities, foreign exchange rates, etc.). A prerequisite to using models for price comparisons is the testing of the model itself. Ideally, all such models should be independently validated by a third-party source such as an audit firm or a model oversight group. Further controls should be established to ensure that changes to such model's assumptions are authorized.

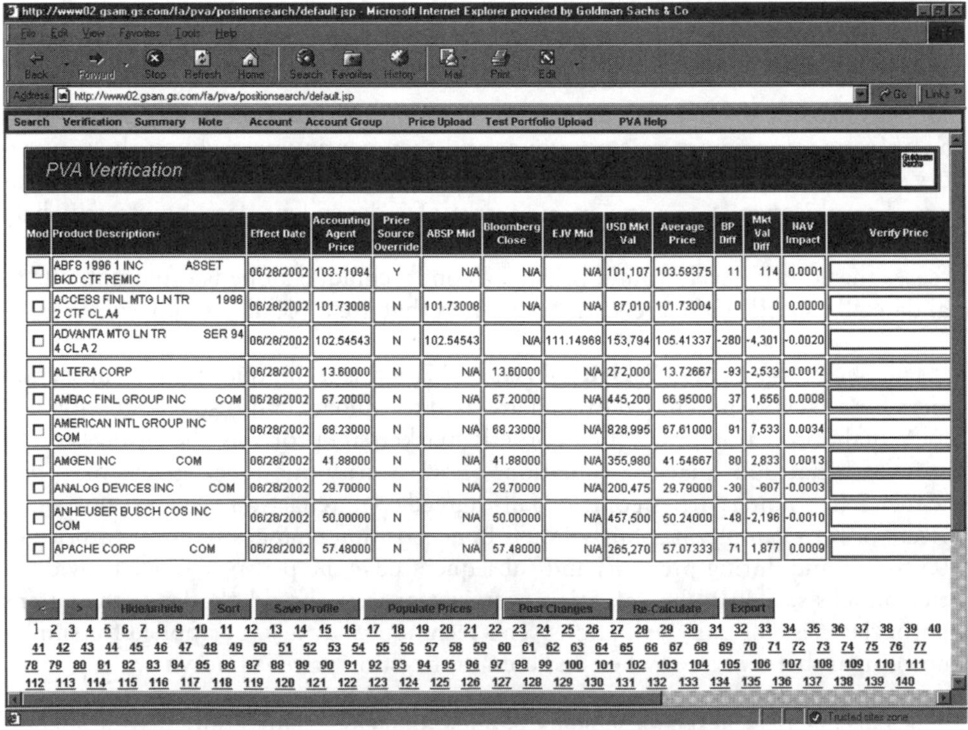

Mod	Product Description+	Effect Date	Accounting Agent Price	Price Source Override	ABSP Mid	Bloomberg Close	EJV Mid	USD Mkt Val	Average Price	BP Diff	Mkt Val Diff	NAV Impact	Verify Price
☐	ABFS 1996 1 INC ASSET BKD CTF REMIC	06/28/2002	103.71094	Y	N/A	N/A	N/A	101,107	103.59375	11	114	0.0001	
☐	ACCESS FINL MTG LN TR 1996 2 CTF CL A4	06/28/2002	101.73008	N	101.73008	N/A	N/A	87,010	101.73004	0	0	0.0000	
☐	ADVANTA MTG LN TR SER 94 4 CL A 2	06/28/2002	102.54543	N	102.54543	N/A	111.14968	153,794	105.41337	-280	-4,301	-0.0020	
☐	ALTERA CORP	06/28/2002	13.60000	N	N/A	13.60000	N/A	272,000	13.72667	-93	-2,533	-0.0012	
☐	AMBAC FINL GROUP INC COM	06/28/2002	67.20000	N	N/A	67.20000	N/A	445,200	66.95000	37	1,656	0.0008	
☐	AMERICAN INTL GROUP INC COM	06/28/2002	68.23000	N	N/A	68.23000	N/A	828,995	67.61000	91	7,533	0.0034	
☐	AMGEN INC COM	06/28/2002	41.88000	N	N/A	41.88000	N/A	355,980	41.54667	80	2,833	0.0013	
☐	ANALOG DEVICES INC COM	06/28/2002	29.70000	N	N/A	29.70000	N/A	200,475	29.79000	-30	-607	-0.0003	
☐	ANHEUSER BUSCH COS INC COM	06/28/2002	50.00000	N	N/A	50.00000	N/A	457,500	50.24000	-48	-2,196	-0.0010	
☐	APACHE CORP COM	06/28/2002	57.48000	N	N/A	57.48000	N/A	265,270	57.07333	71	1,877	0.0009	

FIGURE 18.1 Price Verification Application (PVA)

Figure 18.2 gives an example of a swap model used at Goldman Sachs Asset Management to value certain swap contracts.

Other Auditing Tools There are many other techniques used to assess and monitor the ongoing quality of the pricing. Examples include:

- *Stale pricing exception reports*, whereby we can look at any position where the price has not changed over a defined period of time (especially when the general market did move), create other items for attention, and follow up.
- *Cross-portfolio pricing comparisons* are possible when different accounting agents (or custodians), with processes independent of each other, are used to administer portfolios with similar holdings.
- *Periodic reviews of the portfolio valuations* by the portfolio manager, although not an independent party, can be a useful addition to the set of independent controls mentioned earlier. After all, the portfolio manager who follows his securities on a daily basis is often the most knowledgeable party to bring warnings about potentially inaccurate pricing levels to the attention of the valuation oversight area.

As employing all these tools can lead to quite an extensive workload, it might be practical to perform them not all on a daily basis, but rather on a periodic and/or sample basis (e.g., once per month). Automation is useful to achieve scalability, and

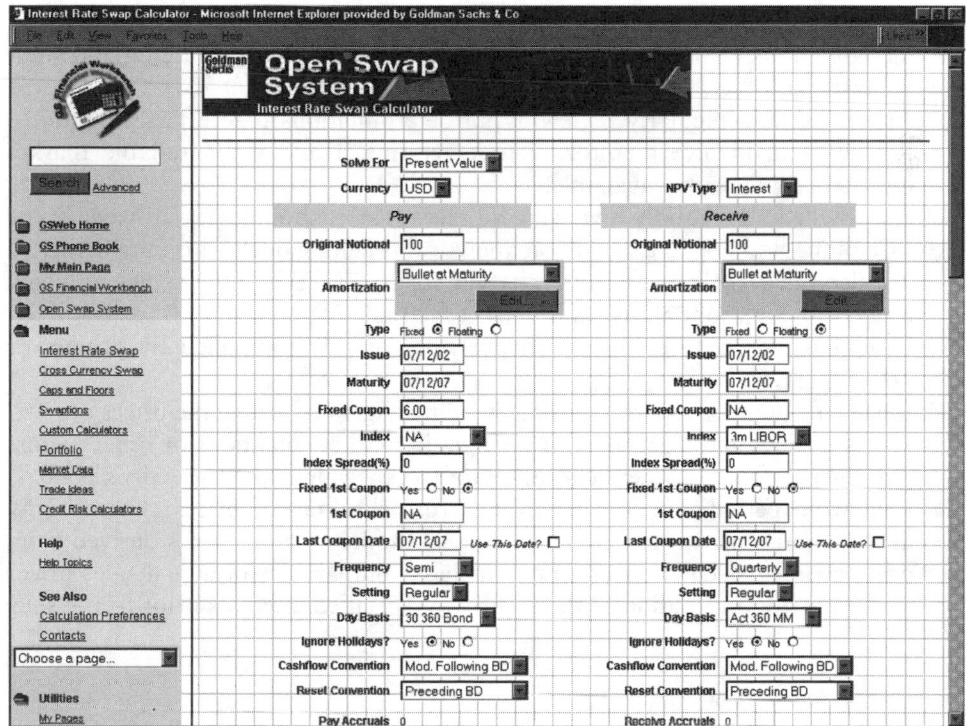

FIGURE 18.2 Swap Valuation Model

it allows for increased valuation verification frequency. It should be noted that all these control measures can and do provide for substantial protection of accurate pricing processes. When discrepancies are identified, corrective steps should be taken not only to handle the current situation at hand, but also to avoid allowing the same error to occur in the future.

VALUATION COMMITTEE

As part of the supervisory oversight of valuation, a senior-positioned valuation committee helps to create strategic direction, senior management buy-in, and an additional layer of oversight control. Designated supervisory personnel across an asset management division may be organized as a valuation committee to supervise the activities of the valuation oversight area. The functions and level of detailed involvement can vary from firm to firm, and therefore also the committee's membership. In our experience, the valuation committee combines various control areas such as representatives from risk management, legal, compliance, portfolio administration, and fund administration as well as senior management. We would say that typically, for independence purposes, representatives from portfolio management are not on the committee. However, at regular occasions, portfolio managers are invited to present certain valuation aspects of their business to the valuation committee.

Possible functions of a valuation committee may include the following:[9]

- Approving and regularly reviewing the methodologies used by pricing services, including the extent of and basis for their reliance on matrix pricing and similar systems.
- Approving and regularly reviewing all determinations to use fair valuations. Reviews can involve monitoring to determine if and when reliable market quotes become readily available.
- Approving and regularly reviewing all fair value methodologies utilized. In the case of methodologies that rely on analytical pricing models, this may involve a detailed review of the basis and reliability of the model and the extent to which it takes into account all relevant market factors.
- Developing procedures to govern overrides of prices supplied by dealers or pricing services.
- Reviewing periodic reports from portfolio managers regarding the prices of portfolio securities and regarding any changes in market conditions or other factors that the portfolio manager believes may affect the validity of a security's price.
- Reviewing periodic reports regarding cross checking of prices generated by dealer quotes, matrix pricing, or analytical models against prices derived from other sources. Such checks also can include comparisons of actual sales prices to the portfolio valuation of the security at specified intervals prior to the sale.

[9]See Investment Company Institute, 1997, "Valuation and Liquidity Issues for Mutual Funds," February, page 28.

FAIR VALUATION AND THE POTENTIAL CONSEQUENCES OF MISPRICING—MUTUAL FUNDS

Just how important correct valuations are can be illustrated by the particular examples of mutual funds that invest in global markets. For example, let's think of a U.S.-domiciled mutual fund that invests in Asian securities: The mutual fund is required to calculate a daily NAV, which would typically be done at 4:00 P.M. Eastern time (ET), when the New York Stock Exchange closes. At this time, the readily available price quotes for Asian stocks are the respective closing prices in the respective local exchanges. However, let's note that these local closing prices at this point are anywhere between 11 to 15 hours old ("stale"). Do they still reflect fair value, 11 to 15 hours later at 4:00 P.M. ET? Significant market moves in the United States are known to affect prices in other time zones.

Why does it matter? The problem arises when there is additional information available, disseminated after the local markets close, that—had the local markets been open—would have affected the local share prices. Analyzing this type of subsequent information, an investor has the opportunity to draw the conclusion that the price as of the local close would have changed in a certain direction had the local markets still been open. So, equipped with this conclusion, our investor now has an arbitrage opportunity to buy or sell a mutual fund, priced based on local closing prices, at a discount or premium respectively versus the estimated fair valuation, based on the subsequent information. Such activity implicitly leads to a transfer of value from the fund (and therefore all existing shareholders) to our investor; let's call this the "dilution effect." Academic studies have shown that arbitrage trading in internationally invested funds can earn annualized excess returns of 40 to 70 percent. Evidence from a sample of funds suggests that long-term shareholders may be losing up to 2 percent of assets per year to dilution effects (Zitzewitz 2002).

> ***Example: October 28, 1997***[10]
>
> *Asian markets were down, following a 9% prior day drop in the S&P 500, but after Asian markets closed, the U.S. market rallied by 10% from its morning lows. Most U.S. based Asian funds used local closes, allowing arbitrageurs to earn one-day returns of 8–10%. [See Table 18.1.]*
>
> *On Day 1, the Asian market closes (at 3:00 A.M. Eastern time) significantly lower causing the value of the securities held in the fund to decrease by 10%. During Day 1, U.S. trading in other instruments indicates . . . the prevailing increase in value of approximately 10%, which strongly suggests that stock prices in the Asian market when it opens will increase to a similar level as before the previous day's decrease. Knowing this, investors buy $10 million worth of shares to try to take advantage of the arbitrage opportunity. At the end of Day 1, using the share prices at the close of the Asian market, [the fund] calculates its NAV at $9 per share. This is the price at which investors buy shares of the fund.*

---

[10]Letter to Craig S. Tyle, general counsel, Investment Company Institute, from Douglas Scheidt, associate director and chief counsel, Division of Investment, U.S. Securities and Exchange Commission, dated April 30, 2001, Exhibit 1.

TABLE 18.1 Example of Dilution Effect, October 28, 1997

Closing Market Prices	Beginning	Day 1	Day 2	After Redemption by Investors
Total assets	$50 million	$45 million	$60 million	$49.09 million
Number of fund shares	5 million	5 million	6.11 million	5 million
Net asset value	$10/share	$9/share	$9.82/share	$9.82/share
Profit taken by investors				$911,110
Loss to long-term investors				$911,110

On Day 2, the Asian market rebounds to equal to the original level before Day 1. The market closes on Day 2 at this level. The valuation of the securities in the fund increases and offsets the losses from the previous day.

The end result is that investors who bought fund shares on Day 1 redeem their shares on Day 2 [and] have a profit of $911,110, which reflects their purchase of undervalued shares at $9 per share on Day 1. This profit is at the expense of long term shareholders, whose share value is reduced by $0.18 per share. This $0.18 represents profit taken by the short term redeeming investors.

In the United States, the Securities and Exchange Commission (SEC) has warned fund firms that relying on stale securities prices can lead to misleading fund prices.[11] Furthermore, it appears that a growing number of investors are taking advantage of the price differences between local market closes and the time funds' NAVs get calculated. To avoid these activities, and therefore to protect the existing mutual fund investors, the funds' holdings need to be priced at fair values as per the time the NAV gets calculated, at prices/values that would likely prevail if the local markets indeed were open at this same time. The SEC notes:

If a fund determines that a significant event has occurred after the foreign market has closed, but before the NAV calculation, then the closing price for that security would be considered a "not readily available" market quotation, and the fund must value the security pursuant to a fair value pricing methodology.[12]

There are various techniques and models that can be set up by fund firms to monitor for such significant events. For example, factor models as described in Chapter 20 might also be used as a tool for the generation of fair value prices. We will not get into the details of valuing with factor models at this point; however, it is fair to highlight that a dedicated and independent valuation oversight group is best placed to organize and coordinate these aspects of mutual fund pricing.

[11]SEC letter 2001.
[12]Ibid.

CHAPTER 19

Return Attribution

Peter Zangari

Return attribution is the process in which sources of a portfolio's return are identified and measured. Attribution is a critical component of the quality control process within investment management and must be closely aligned with risk measurement. Optimal portfolio construction requires that exposures are created with risk proportional to the available opportunities to add value. Return attribution looks back and attempts to identify where and to what extent the exposures were successful. In order for this feedback process to be useful returns should be attributed as closely as possible to factors that fit into the portfolio manager's way of organizing and sizing risk exposures.

Managers may rely on return attribution reports developed in-house or from commercially available systems. As for commercially available software, each system typically employs its own particular brand of attribution. Differences across systems can vary in certain ways, from the algorithms applied to the terminology used to describe the sources of return. The differences in algorithms and terminology can lead to confusion and make it difficult for managers to understand their portfolio's sources of return. Unfortunately, in many cases the return attribution system is a completely separate system from that used in risk measurement. When this is the case it may be difficult for the organization to make effective use of the information provided by the return attribution system.

Suppose, for example, that a portfolio manager wants to invest in high-quality companies that have both growth potential and reasonable valuations. Suppose further that the manager has proprietary approaches to ranking companies along these dimensions. It would clearly be desirable to be able to measure to what extent the portfolio has exposure to these factors, and to monitor how much risk these exposures create and how much return these exposures have provided historically. Return attribution should answer this last question, and in order to do so, like a good risk system, it should be customizable to the process of the portfolio manager.

This chapter presents a comprehensive review of some of the most commonly used methods for performing return attribution. Our focus is on equity portfolios although the results we present generalize to other asset classes. We explain the various methods that are employed by commercially available systems within a framework that uses common terminology and notation. The purpose of this chapter is threefold: to increase the transparency of return attribution computations, to provide a unified framework for understanding attribution, and to identify and explain important practical issues related to conducting return attribution.

The rest of the chapter is organized as follows:

- First we review the usefulness of attribution to various market participants, from portfolio managers to clients of an asset management organization.
- Then we provide a review of return computations that are critical components to the return attribution calculation.
- The third section presents two return attribution methods[1] in the context of a single region (e.g., U.S.) framework. These methodologies are:

  1. ***Factor model.*** This approach is based on a linear factor model of returns and assumes that a cross section of returns can be explained by a set of common factors. Portfolio returns are decomposed into returns from systematic (factor) and stock-specific components. Typically, quantitatively oriented portfolio managers subscribe to this approach as it relies on a formal model of asset returns.
  2. ***Asset grouping.*** According to this methodology, stocks are grouped by some criterion such as industry, sector, or investment style classification. Returns from each of these groups are then computed. This approach, which generates so-called variance analysis reports, does not depend on a model of asset returns and, therefore, it is more ad hoc than the factor model–based methodology. We find that fundamental equity portfolio managers who do not rely heavily on a quantitative portfolio construction process subscribe to the asset grouping approach.

  The last part of this section explains *multiperiod attribution*. When going from single-period to multiperiod attribution, we need to "link" sources of return in order to get consistency among the sources and cumulative portfolio returns.

  We illustrate these methodologies using reports from Goldman Sachs' portfolio analysis and construction environment (PACE) on specific accounts.
- The next section presents return attribution on international equity portfolios. We present and explain how to calculate sources of return from countries and currencies not previously included in the single region model.
- Finally, we explain the potential differences between sources of performance and sources of return. This is an important practical matter and involves the residual term that arises when performance and return—which is based on a simple buy-and-hold strategy—differ.

WHY RETURN ATTRIBUTION MATTERS

Return attribution is the *ex post* complement to *ex ante* risk decomposition. It allows both portfolio managers and their clients to identify the sources of return and

[1]For a review of performance measurement and background on differentiating between performance attribution and return attribution, see Chapter 17.

ensure that these are consistent with the mandates they have entered into and the risks that were taken to generate these returns.

First of all, let us clarify the language we will use in this chapter. Return attribution is often referred to as performance attribution or performance contribution. These terms are frequently used interchangeably, but we have in practice clarified their use as follows:

- *Performance contribution* concerns the decomposition of officially reported[2] *total* returns. It therefore answers questions of the following type: "What factors have contributed to my portfolio's 10 percent return over the past year?"
- *Performance attribution* concerns the decomposition of officially reported *excess* returns over an assigned benchmark (such as the S&P 500, for example). It therefore answers questions of the following type: "Why has my portfolio outperformed the S&P 500 by 3 percent over the past year?"
- *Return attribution* is the same as performance attribution except that it involves estimated return (e.g., return estimated from assuming a buy-and-hold strategy over a one-day period). In practice, it is common to find sources of return based on a portfolio's estimate rather than the officially reported return.

The rest of this chapter is dedicated to outlining methods for return attribution, since in the investment management business we focus primarily on generating excess performance against an agreed-to benchmark or index.

Return attribution is important because investment returns are not, or should not be, the result of chance. Returns should be generated by a well-articulated investment process agreed to at the inception of a mandate. Active investment managers are typically hired because they have demonstrated a particular skill set. Return attribution allows both portfolio managers and clients to identify and measure these skills and ensure consistency between the portrayal of skill and its implementation.

Assume an equity portfolio manager has been hired because of his or her ability to pick stocks within the U.S. value market as defined by the Russell 2000 Value index (R2000V). Return attribution will allow the client to ensure that the portfolio manager's returns are consistent with the plan. If it appears that all of the excess performance versus the R2000V results from market timing (the portfolio may have held a significant amount of cash in a declining equity market), and if the portfolio manager did not claim to be able to time the market, then the client could argue that the portfolio manager has not been true to his or her investment style or philosophy.

Similarly, in the fixed income world, a client generally would want to know if a manager, hired because of an ability to forecast changes in interest rates, was outperforming his or her benchmark because of loading up on lower-credit-rated bonds instead of deviating in terms of duration or yield curve exposure.

Why is it important for managers to be true to their style?

First of all, clients have the right to get what they pay for. If a particular active

[2]The term "officially reported" means the reconciled performance numbers that have been either reported by a custodian or derived from the official books and records.

manager is generating excess returns from market timing when claiming his or her skill is stock selection, then there is clear deception going on. The client may not believe in market timing, or if it was desired could probably implement a market timing strategy more cost-effectively using a combination of cash and futures contracts than by hiring an active equity manager.

The other reason for managers to be true to their style is that a particular portfolio manager is most likely but one component of a broader strategy implemented by the client. The performance of the client's overall portfolio is highly dependent on each investment mandate adhering to its guidelines. Deviating from one's assigned mandate would have the same impact on performance as a concert pianist switching to the drums in a Mozart piano sonata!

COMPUTING RETURNS

Portfolio and asset returns are a cornerstone of return attribution. In this section we define one-period asset returns that are used in the calculation of domestic and international portfolio returns. Let $R_n^\ell(t)$ represent the local return on the nth asset as measured in percent format:

$$R_n^\ell(t) = \frac{P_n^\ell(t) + d_n(t-h,t) - P_n^\ell(t-1)}{P_n^\ell(t-1)} \tag{19.1}$$

where $P_n^\ell(t)$ = Time t local price of the security or asset
$d_n(t-h,t)$ = Dividend (per share) paid out at time t for period $t-h$ through t

In a global framework we need to incorporate exchange rates into the return calculations. We define exchange rates as the reporting currency over the local currency (reporting/local). The local currency is sometimes referred to as the risk currency. For example, USD/GBP would be the exchange rate where the reporting currency is the U.S. dollar and the risk currency is the British pound. A USD-based investor with holdings in U.K. equities would use the USD/GBP rate to convert the value of the U.K. stock to U.S. dollars.

Suppose a portfolio with U.S. dollars as its reporting currency has holdings in German, Australian, and Japanese equities. The local and/or risk currencies are EUR, AUD, and JPY, respectively. The total return of each equity position consists of the local return on equity and the return on the currency expressed in reporting/local.

We assume that a generic portfolio contains N assets ($n = 1, \ldots, N$). Suppose that $P_n^\ell(t)$ represents the price, in euros, of one share of Siemens stock (traded in Germany). $X_{ij}(t)$ is the exchange rate expressed as the ith currency per unit of currency j. For example, with USD as the reporting currency, the exchange rate where $X_{ij}(t)$ = USD/EUR (i is USD and j is EUR) is used to convert Siemens equity (expressed in euros) to U.S. dollars. In general, the exchange rate is expressed in reporting over local currency.

It follows from these definitions that the price of the nth asset expressed in reporting currency is

$$P_n(t) = P_n^{\ell}(t)X_{ij}(t) \tag{19.2}$$

We use (19.2) as a basis for defining total return, local return, and exchange rate (currency) return. The total return of an asset or portfolio is simply the return that incorporates both the local return and exchange rate return. Depending on how returns are defined—continuous or discrete (percent)—we get different equations for how returns are calculated. Following directly from (19.2), an asset's total return, using percent returns, is defined as

$$\begin{aligned} R_n(t) &= \left[1 + R_n^{\ell}(t)\right]\left[1 + E_{ij}(t)\right] - 1 \\ &= R_n^{\ell}(t) + E_{ij}(t) + R_n^{\ell}(t) \times E_{ij}(t) \end{aligned} \tag{19.3}$$

where $R_n(t)$ = One-period percent total return on the nth asset
$R_n^{\ell}(t)$ = One-period percent return on the equity positions expressed in local currency (i.e., the local return)
$E_{ij}(t)$ = One-period percent return on the ith currency per unit of currency j

$$E_{ij}(t) = \frac{X_{ij}(t)}{X_{ij}(t-1)} - 1$$

For example, suppose that the nth position is one that represents the DAX equity index. In this case, $R_n^{\ell}(t)$ is the local return on DAX and $E_{ij}(t)$ is the return on the USD/EUR exchange rate. When the euro strengthens, USD/EUR increases and $E_{ij}(t) > 0$. Holding all other things constant, this increases the total return on the equity position.

SINGLE REGION (LOCAL MODEL) RETURN ATTRIBUTION

In this section we explain return attribution based on a single region (e.g., U.S.) framework. We present two methods—factor model–based and asset grouping—for computing a portfolio's sources of return. In terms of defining portfolios, we refer to managed, benchmark, and active portfolios. The managed portfolio is directed by the portfolio manager. The benchmark portfolio, on the other hand, is some representative, passive portfolio (e.g., S&P 500). The active portfolio is the difference between the managed and benchmark portfolios.

Factor Model–Based Approach

Factor return attribution decomposes a portfolio's return into factor and specific components. There are three principal sources of return in the factor model–based approach.

1. *Common factors:* return due to factors.
2. *Market timing:* return due to active beta exposure.
3. *Stock selection:* return due to a portfolio manager's ability to select stocks.

Return attribution is based on the cross-sectional model of returns:

$$R^{\ell}(t) = B^{\ell}(t-1)F^{\ell}(t) + u^{\ell}(t) \tag{19.4}$$

where $R^{\ell}(t)$ is an N-vector of local excess returns (over the local risk-free rate) from time $t - 1$ to t; $B^{\ell}(t-1)$ is an $N \times K$ matrix of exposures to factors that are available as of $t - 1$. These factors include investment styles such as growth or momentum and industry classifications. In the case where we may want to attribute return to sources that are contemporaneous (unlike a risk model), the information contained in the exposures matrix will be as of time t. $F^{\ell}(t)$ is a $K \times 1$ vector of returns to factors, and $u^{\ell}(t)$ is an N-vector of mean-zero-specific returns from $t - 1$ to t.

There are three steps involved in the return attribution computation based on a factor model. (In the following discussion, we focus on the managed portfolio. However, our results generalize to any portfolio type.)

Step 1: Define a set of exposures to factors and estimate the cross-sectional return model specified by (19.4). This gives estimates of one-period returns to factors, that is, factor returns from period $t - 1$ to t.

Step 2: Compute the local return on the managed portfolio.

Letting $w^p(t - 1)$ represent an N-vector of managed portfolio weights at time $t - 1$, the return on the managed portfolio is given by

$$r_p^{\ell}(t) = w^p(t-1)^T R^{\ell}(t) = b^p(t-1)^T F^{\ell}(t) + u_p^{\ell}(t) \tag{19.5}$$

where $r_p^{\ell}(t)$ = Managed local excess portfolio return from period $t - 1$ to t
$b^p(t - 1)$ = K-vector of managed portfolio exposures
$F^{\ell}(t)$ = K-vector of factor returns
$u_p^{\ell}(t)$ = Specific local portfolio return

Step 3: Quantify the sources of local return. For example, a managed portfolio with N assets has $K + N$ sources of return—K sources from factor returns and N sources from specific returns (one for each asset).

The **source of return from the kth factor** is given by the component

$$S_k^{\ell}(t) = b_k^p(t-1)F_k(t) \qquad \text{for } k = 1, \ldots, K \tag{19.6}$$

The **specific return contribution** from the nth asset is simply the return on that asset's specific return times its portfolio weight.

$$S_n^{\ell}(t) = w_n^p(t-1)u_n(t) \qquad n = 1, \ldots, N \tag{19.7}$$

Hence, the portfolio return is the sum of $K + N$ sources of return and can be written as

$$r_p^\ell(t) = w^p(t-1)^T R^\ell(t) = \sum_{k=1}^{K} S_k^\ell(t) + \sum_{n=1}^{N} S_n^\ell(t) \qquad n = 1, \ldots, N \tag{19.8}$$

Equation (19.8) is a decomposition of the return on the managed portfolio. Decompositions of active, benchmark, market, or other types of portfolio returns are derived in an analogous fashion. The only difference is that different portfolio weights are used.

Consider an example with an active portfolio consisting of three assets and a linear factor model with two common factors. In this case, $K = 2$, $N = 3$, and the decomposition of the portfolio's active return can be written as:

$$\begin{aligned} r_a^\ell(t) &= w_1^a(t-1)R_1^\ell(t) + w_2^a(t-1)R_2^\ell(t) + w_3^a(t-1)R_3^\ell(t) \\ &= \underbrace{S_1^\ell(t) + S_2^\ell(t)}_{\text{Factor contribution}} + \underbrace{w_1^a(t-1)u_1^\ell(t) + w_2^a(t-1)u_2^\ell(t) + w_3^a(t-1)u_3^\ell(t)}_{\text{Specific contribution}} \end{aligned} \tag{19.9}$$

In the above discussion we provide a simple decomposition of return. That is, assuming a linear factor model, the total return on an arbitrary portfolio can be attributed to exposures to factors such as investment styles, industries, and countries, and to returns specific to individual assets. Within the factor model–based approach, a more sophisticated decomposition of total return first separates out the expected market-related exposure. This approach works as follows.[3] Start with an estimate of the portfolio's total return in excess of the local risk-free rate. A portfolio's local excess return can be written as $r_p^\ell(t) - r_f^\ell(t)$. It is the sum of the benchmark portfolio's excess return, $r_b^\ell(t) - r_f^\ell(t)$, and the active portfolio return, $r_p^\ell(t) - r_b^\ell(t)$. Alternatively expressed,

$$r_p^\ell(t) - r_f^\ell(t) = \left[r_p^\ell(t) - r_b^\ell(t)\right] + \left[r_b^\ell(t) - r_f^\ell(t)\right] \tag{19.10}$$

The total active return can be written as the sum of (1) the expected active return and (2) the exceptional active return. The *expected active return* is defined as the product of the active beta and the expected long-run return on the relevant market. Mathematically, the expected active return is written as $\beta_{\text{active}}(t) \times r_m^{\text{long-run}}(t)$ where $\beta_{\text{active}}(t)$ is defined as the difference between the managed portfolio's beta and the benchmark portfolio's beta. When the benchmark is the same as the market portfolio, the benchmark portfolio's beta is 1. The long-run expected return on the relevant market may be based on history or fixed at some annualized amount such as 10 percent.

Expected active return is the part of active return that is consistent with the market. For example, suppose that the portfolio manager's active beta (difference between managed beta and benchmark beta) is zero. In this case, the portfolio manager would not expect to out- or underperform the market in the long run.

---

[3]Reference: R. C. Grinold and R. N. Kahn, 1999, *Active Portfolio Management: A Quantitative Approach for Producing Superior Returns and Selecting Superior Returns and Controlling Risk*, 2nd Edition, New York: McGraw-Hill.

The *exceptional active return* is defined as the difference between the active portfolio return and the expected active return. It is written as $r_a(t) - \beta_{\text{active}}(t) \times r_m^{\text{long-run}}(t)$.

The exceptional active return is one way that a portfolio manager adds value since it measures the performance of the active portfolio relative to what would be expected under normal market conditions. Since it is a measure of value-added performance, we are interested in finding sources of exceptional active return. To this end, we decompose this return into (1) market timing, (2) factor return contributions, and (3) stock selection (which is not the same as specific return contribution).

Market timing is defined as the active beta, $\beta_{\text{active}}(t)$, times the difference between the realized market portfolio return over some historical period (e.g., prior six months), and the long-run expected return on the market, $r_m(t) - r_m^{\text{long-run}}(t)$.

Factor contributions were defined previously in equation (19.6).

Stock selection refers to a portfolio manager's ability to choose stocks. Within the context of a factor model, stock selection may be defined as the exceptional active return minus the sum of (1) factor return contributions and (2) market timing. Note that stock selection is not the same as the contribution from specific return, which was defined in equation (19.7).

Mathematically, we derive the decomposition of stock selection as follows (assuming the market return is the same as the benchmark return). First, rewrite the active return as

$$\begin{aligned} r_a^\ell(t) &= r_p^\ell(t) - r_m^\ell(t) \\ &= \beta_{\text{active}}(t) r_m^{\text{long-run}}(t) + r_a^\ell(t) - \beta_{\text{active}}(t) r_m^{\text{long-run}}(t) \end{aligned} \tag{19.11}$$

Equation (19.11) shows that the active local portfolio return is the sum of the expected and exceptional return. Stock selection is defined as

$$\begin{aligned} \text{Stock selection} = {} & r_a^\ell(t) - \beta_{\text{active}}(t) r_m^{\text{long-run}}(t) - \beta_{\text{active}}(t)\left[r_m(t) - r_m^{\text{long-run}}(t)\right] \\ & - \text{Factor contribution} \end{aligned} \tag{19.12}$$

The term *stock selection* should be used with caution, as it may not necessarily measure a portfolio manager's ability to select stocks. To better understand this point, note that stock selection is a function of factor contribution. Therefore, stock selection can vary depending on which factor model is used to measure return. As a result, what may be interpreted as stock selection may, in fact, simply measure a factor model's ability to explain portfolio returns.

In review of this section, we started with a linear cross-sectional local factor model. This model explains the cross-section of returns in terms of a set of common factors. For a set of portfolio weights, the return on the active portfolio consists of the sum of factor and specific contributions. We decompose a portfolio's local return into an expected and exceptional return. The exceptional return is the sum of market timing, factor contribution, and stock selection. Stock selection is defined as the difference between exceptional return and the sum of market timing and factor contributions.

Example Using PACE The various concepts outlined in the preceding section are illustrated in the following example using PACE (see Figure 19.1).

Account	XYZ	Portfolio Mgr	
Report Date	Sep 30, 2002	Benchmark	SAP500
Attribution Period	07/01/02-09/30/02	Model	PACE_US_D

Return Decomposition

	PACE	Published	Difference
Managed Return	-16.07 %	-16.07 %	0bp
Benchmark Return	-17.28 %	-17.28 %	-0bp
Active Return	1.21 %	1.21 %	0bp
Expected Active Return	0.10 %		
Exceptional Active	1.11 %		
Market Timing	-1.17 %		
Stock Selection	1.74 %		
Factor Contrib	0.54 %		
Industry	0.30 %		
Style	0.24 %		
Currency	0.00 %		
Country	0.00 %		

Active Return (1.21 %) = Factor Contrib (0.54 %) + Specific Return Contrib (0.67 %)

Contributors to Specific Return *(All entries in %)*

Top 10 *(see last page of report for Top and Bottom 30)*

Stock		Contribution	Avg. Active Wgt.
QCOM	QUALCOMM INC	0.43	1.10
HET	HARRAHS ENTERTAINMENT INC	0.34	1.99
JPM	JP MORGAN CHASE & CO	0.20	-0.60
FRE	FREDDIE MAC	0.20	2.03
BLS	BELLSOUTH CORP	0.18	-0.57
ENR	ENERGIZER HOLDINGS INC	0.18	0.95
VCI	VALASSIS COMMUNICATIONS INC	0.16	0.99
KRB	MBNA CORP	0.14	1.15
CL	COLGATE-PALMOLIVE CO	0.13	1.21
CCU	CLEAR CHANNEL COMMUNICATIONS	0.12	0.44

Bottom 10

Stock		Contribution	Avg. Active Wgt.
TSG	SABRE HOLDINGS CORP	-0.22	0.62
T	AT&T CORP	-0.22	-0.50
PEP	PEPSICO INC	-0.21	1.62
UVN	UNIVISION COMMUNICATIONS-A	-0.19	0.86
WYE	WYETH	-0.16	0.47
CD	CENDANT CORP	-0.15	1.20
HOT	STARWOOD HOTELS & RESORTS	-0.14	0.76
L	LIBERTY MEDIA CORP-A	-0.14	0.76
ABK	AMBAC FINANCIAL GROUP INC	-0.13	1.86
TMPW	TMP WORLDWIDE INC	-0.12	0.29

Contributors to Active Return by Sector *(All entries in %)*

	Contrib	Avg. Act Exp.	HR	IR
Utilities	0.40	-2.37	57.03	13.62
Telecommunications	0.35	-1.79	55.47	14.28
Consumer cyclicals	0.22	-1.11	55.08	39.26
Energy	0.21	-0.58	50.00	26.18
Transport	0.17	-1.44	54.17	16.42
Health care	0.14	-2.81	50.39	7.33
Basic Materials	0.14	-0.71	52.73	15.35

	Contrib	Avg. Act Exp.	HR	IR
Industrials	0.08	-0.38	53.52	26.95
Consumer Noncyclicals	-0.06	2.22	53.13	-4.02
Technology	-0.08	0.49	52.81	-5.54
Financial	-0.08	-1.65	51.56	-2.27
Commercial services	-0.28	1.21	47.92	-27.98
Consumer services	-0.91	8.42	47.66	-22.72

Daily Return Attribution   Previous Month Attribution   Previous Quarter Attribution   Previous Year Attribution

Contributors to Active Return by Style *(All entries in %)*

Top 5	Contrib	Avg. Active Exp. in SD	HR	IR
Dividend-to-Price	0.17	-0.19	59.38	4.20
Price Momentum	0.13	0.04	60.94	13.03
Earnings-to-Price	0.10	-0.11	51.56	3.29
Book-to-Price	0.06	-0.09	54.69	3.01
Debt Sensitivity	0.04	0.10	53.13	2.25

Bottom 5	Contrib	Avg. Active Exp. in SD	HR	IR
Volatility	-0.12	0.03	43.75	-6.94
Market Cap	-0.06	0.17	46.88	-1.53
FX Sensitivity	-0.03	0.04	45.31	-4.13
Earnings Variability	-0.02	0.03	50.00	-6.31
Liquidity	-0.02	-0.01	54.69	-4.73

Contributors to Active Return by Industry *(All entries in %)*

Top 5	Contrib	Avg. Active	HR	IR
Banks	0.51	-3.73	59.38	6.56
Electric utilities	0.36	-1.96	60.94	7.17
Telephones	0.30	-1.32	57.81	8.59
Energy Reserves &	0.20	-0.31	50.00	16.75
Chemicals	0.17	-0.84	60.94	9.42

Bottom 5	Contrib	Avg. Active	HR	IR
Financial services	-0.83	3.71	39.06	-10.02
Hotels	-0.48	3.68	39.06	-5.60
Computer software	-0.37	1.78	39.06	-10.13
Media	-0.28	2.59	50.00	-3.58
Information services	-0.25	1.05	45.31	-9.74

FIGURE 19.1 PACE Factor Attribution

For the period from July 1, 2002, to September 30, 2002, account XYZ, which is benchmarked to the S&P 500 index, outperformed by 121 basis points. Given our definition of active return, its exceptional active return was 111 basis points. Of that, 174 basis points came from stock selection and 54 basis points from factors, while market timing actually detracted 117 basis points from the account's performance.

If you look at factor contributions, both the industry and style exposures added value, 30 basis points for industries and 24 basis points for styles. Currency and country contributions were nil since this is a single country portfolio.

The report also provides a more detailed breakdown of attribution at the stock (specific), sector, style, and industry levels. Contributors to specific return are computed by taking each stock's active weight and multiplying it by the difference between the stock's total return and the return attributed to factors (excluding market timing). This difference is what forms specific return. Taking a look at the "Contributors to Specific Return" section of the table, we find that the majority of the top and bottom 10 contributors over this period are made up of positive active weights (i.e., higher weight in the portfolio than in the benchmark). If we consider positive active weights as representing stocks that the portfolio manager prefers, then we can see that many of his or her preferred stocks are some of the biggest contributors and detractors of specific return over this period.

Next, we explain an alternative return attribution methodology—asset grouping—that forms the basis of variance analysis.

Asset Grouping Methodology

Portfolio managers want to view their portfolios' sources of return in a simple and relatively straightforward manner. Some prefer not to use a factor model at all, as they do not view their portfolio construction process as being driven by some predefined, quantifiable set of factors. These managers usually rely on commercially available systems that employ an asset grouping methodology to generate so-called variance analysis reports. This methodology consists of three steps:

1. *Group assets.* For each time period (e.g., a day) we group assets according to the value of some factor. For example, we may group stocks by their industry classification or by their exposure to a particular investment style. In the case where we group assets by their style exposure, we may first generate deciles of the distribution of all exposures[4] to a particular style and then group assets into deciles based on their particular exposures.
2. *Compute the return of each group.* Once assets have been grouped, we compute their one-period returns. The return for the group is computed by taking a weighted average of all returns in the group where the weights are based on the group's total market value.
3. *Compute the contribution of each group to the total return.* The contribution of each group is computed by taking a weighted average of all returns in the

[4]A popular way to define all exposures is to use the exposures corresponding to the assets in the benchmark portfolio.

group where the weights are based on the entire portfolio's total market value. Note that the sum of contributions across all groups is equal to the portfolio's total return. In practice, we can compute group returns and group contributions for the managed, benchmark, and active portfolios. Examples of groups include: assets, industries, sectors, and percentiles of the distribution of a particular investment style. An "asset group" simply means that each asset is treated as a separate group. In this way the return to an asset group is that asset's total return, and the asset's contribution is the contribution of the individual asset to the entire portfolio return.

In the asset grouping approach, one-period active returns are defined in terms of stock selection, allocation effect (also known as group weight), and a so-called interaction effect. Mathematically, the asset grouping model for an active portfolio can be written as:

$$r_a(t) = S(t) + A(t) + I(t) \tag{19.13}$$

where $S(t)$ represents the one-period total stock selection component at time t. For a given group of stocks, stock selection is defined as follows. First, compute the difference between the group's return as defined by stocks in the managed portfolio and the (same) group's return as defined by stocks in the benchmark. An industry or sector is an example of a group. Second, multiply this difference by the group's benchmark weight. Mathematically, the stock selection component for the ith group of stocks at time t is

$$S_i(t) = w_i^b(t-1)\left[r_{i,p}(t) - r_{i,b}(t)\right] \tag{19.14}$$

where $r_{i,b}(t)$ = Return on stocks in the benchmark portfolio that belong to the ith group. For example, $r_{i,b}(t)$ might represent the return to all telecom stocks in the benchmark portfolio.

$r_{i,p}(t)$ = Return on stocks in the managed portfolio that belong to the ith group

$w_i^b(t-1)$ = Weight of the ith group in the benchmark portfolio

Summing over all i ($i = 1, \ldots, I$) groups gives us the total stock selection component

$$S(t) = \sum_{i=1}^{I} w_i^b(t-1)\left[r_{i,p}(t) - r_{i,b}(t)\right] \tag{19.15}$$

$A(t)$ is the allocation effect (also known as group weight) and measures the impact of over- or underweighting a particular group of stocks. The allocation effect for the ith group of stocks is defined as

$$A(t) = \sum_{i=1}^{I} A_i(t) \tag{19.16}$$

where $$A_i(t) = \left[w_i^p(t-1) - w_i^b(t-1)\right]\left[r_{i,b}(t) - r_b(t)\right]$$

$[w_i^p(t-1) - w_i^b(t-1)]$ = Difference between the *i*th group's weight in the managed $[w_i^p(t-1)]$ and benchmark $[w_i^b(t-1)]$ portfolios. For example, if $[w_i^p(t-1) - w_i^b(t-1)]$ is positive, then the managed portfolio is overweight relative to the benchmark portfolio.

$[r_{i,b}(t) - r_b(t)]$ = Difference between the return of the *i*th group in the benchmark portfolio and the benchmark portfolio's total return.

$I(t)$ = Interaction effect. This term has no intuitive content. Its only purpose is to make the right-hand side of equation (19.13) add up to the total active return. The interaction effect of the *i*th group is defined as

$$I(t) = \sum_{i=1}^{I} I_i(t) \tag{19.17}$$

where $I_i(t) = \left[w_i^p(t-1) - w_i^b(t-1)\right]\left[r_{i,p}(t) - r_{i,b}(t)\right]$

To summarize the results, the stock selection and allocation effects are measures of specific levels of return attribution. The allocation effect measures a portfolio manager's ability to select different groups of stock. Stock selection, on the other hand, measures how well a portfolio manager selects stocks within a particular group. In this calculation, more weight is given to groups that have a higher weight in the benchmark portfolio.

Why introduce the interaction effect? In order to get meaningful results it is important that the stock selection and allocation effects sum to the total active return. Unfortunately, stock selection plus allocation do not equal the total active return. To address this issue, the new term—the interaction effect—is created so that stock selection, allocation, and interaction sum to the total active return. In effect, the interaction term is a residual measure of performance. It captures what's left over after we account for stock selection and allocation.

Is there any way to get rid of the interaction effect? There is. But we have to forfeit some intuition in terms of how we define stock selection. In some commercial attribution systems, stock selection is defined using the managed portfolio weight in place of the benchmark portfolio weight; that is,

$$S_i(t) = w_i^p(t-1)\left[r_{i,p}(t) - r_{i,b}(t)\right] \tag{19.18}$$

Given this definition, the sum of the stock selection and allocation (or group weight) effects is now equal to the active portfolio return.

$$r_a(t) = S(t) + A(t) \tag{19.19}$$

Which definition of stock selection is more appropriate? For managers who actively manage a portfolio against a benchmark, the stock selection measure that uses the benchmark weight is clearly a more relevant measure. That is to say, more importance should be given to groups of stocks that make up a larger part of the benchmark rather than less. If this does not hold, then an inaccurate measure of attribution may result.

Additional terms and definitions that appear on variance analysis reports relate to asset-specific contributions. These terms include: *relative versus group*, *relative versus total*, *absolute versus group*, and *absolute verus total*.

For the nth asset at time t, these terms are defined as follows:

Relative versus group: Active weight × (Security return – Total return on the ith group based on benchmark)

$$w_n^a(t-1)\left[R_n(t)-r_{i,b}(t)\right] \tag{19.20}$$

Relative versus total: Active weight × (Security return – Benchmark total return)

$$w_n^a(t-1)\left[R_n(t)-r_b(t)\right] \tag{19.21}$$

Absolute versus group: Managed weight × (Security return – Total return on the ith group based on benchmark)

$$w_n^p(t-1)\left[R_n(t)-r_{i,b}(t)\right] \tag{19.22}$$

Absolute versus total: Managed weight × (Security return – Benchmark total return)

$$w_n^p(t-1)\left[R_n(t)-r_b(t)\right] \tag{19.23}$$

In the preceding two sections, we presented methods for return attribution. The first method is based on a linear factor model and decomposes return into factor and specific components. In this section, an asset grouping methodology was introduced. According to this approach, no model is assumed. All that is required is a set of mappings that tell us how to classify assets. An example of a mapping would be an industry classification scheme.

Also, in the previous two parts we defined and explained one-period return attribution procedures. Various issues arise when we need to compute attribution over multiple periods. For example, one-period attribution may be one-day attribution. When we compute attribution over, say, a quarter, we need to "link"[5] the daily sources of return so that the compounded quarterly portfolio return is consistent with the compounded sources of return.

Finally, we note an important difference between the asset grouping and factor model–based methodologies. In the factor model approach, at each point in time the returns to factors are estimated simultaneously. These estimates are the result of cross-sectional regressions[6] using equation (19.4). This process captures

[5]Linking is the process by which individual stocks, groups, or factors are compounded over time in such a way that the sum of the individual linked contributions is equal to the compounded total return on the portfolio.

[6]See Chapter 20 for details on how factor returns are estimated via cross-sectional regression.

Account		Period	07/01/02-09/30/02
Benchmark	SAP500	Report Date	Sep 30, 2002
Model	PACE_US_	Published	Applied
Style Report	Industry Details Report		Download to Excel

Return Summary

	Managed	Benchmark	Active	Contribution	
PACE:	-16.07 %	-17.28 %	1.21 %	Over Weight	-7.13%
Published:	-16.07 %	-17.28 %	1.21 %	Under Weight	8.34%
Difference:	0bp	0bp	0bp	Sum :	1.21 %

IR (Information Ratio) is active contribution divided by its standard deviation over the attribution period.
HR (HitRate) is the percentage of times active contribution is positive in the attribution period.

(sorted by Act. Contrib. -ve Act Weight is in grey color)

	Sector	Avg Mgd Wt	Managed Contrib	Avg Bench Wt	Benchmark Contrib	Avg Active Wt	Active Contrib	IR	HR (%)
1	Media & Communication	11.96%	-1.99%	6.91%	-1.52%	5.05%	-0.51%	-3.08	48.44
2	Consumer Discretionary	12.60%	-2.14%	9.18%	-1.70%	3.43%	-0.43%	-5.05	46.31
3	Health Care	11.44%	-1.07%	14.06%	-0.80%	-2.63%	-0.22%	-3.36	51.56
4	Producer Goods & Services	3.75%	-0.96%	4.56%	-0.79%	-0.81%	-0.15%	-4.84	48.44
5	Consumer Staples	12.59%	-0.93%	10.03%	-0.98%	2.56%	0.02%	0.44	43.75
6	Energy	6.13%	-1.40%	6.37%	-1.55%	-0.24%	0.15%	7.56	51.56
7	Technology	15.04%	-3.23%	14.20%	-3.72%	0.84%	0.48%	9.19	48.44
8	Finance	18.59%	-2.83%	20.35%	-3.43%	-1.76%	0.59%	6.08	48.44
9	Utilities	0.00%	0.00%	2.80%	-0.65%	-2.80%	0.63%	9.59	59.38
10	Cyclicals	7.40%	-1.51%	11.52%	-2.14%	-4.12%	0.64%	9.35	56.25
	Total	99.60%	-16.07%	99.97%	-17.28%	-0.48%	1.21%		

FIGURE 19.2 PACE Variance Analysis

any interaction among the factor returns. Conversely, in the asset grouping methodology, each group's return is estimated separately and, therefore, any interaction between groups is excluded.

Example Using PACE Using the same portfolio and date range as in the factor attribution report in Figure 19.1, we can generate a variance analysis report using the PACE infrastructure. A screen shot of the first page of the actual report is shown in Figure 19.2.[7]

As outlined in the methodology section, there is no model associated with attribution by industry grouping. The only required input is the industry and sector classification. These classifications may be provided by vendors such as Russell or Standard & Poor's, or they may be proprietary to the portfolio management team.

In this analysis, the 121 basis point outperformance over the review period is comprised of –713 basis points of underperformance related to overweight stocks and 834 basis points of outperformance related to underweight stocks. This particular portfolio manager was helped more by the stocks he or she underweighted performing even worse than the stocks he or she overweighted in a down market—the total return on the benchmark over the period was down 17.28 percent.

The section below the return summary shows the contributions for various sectors over the period. Finance, for example, had an average active weight of –1.76 percent over the period. Given that the sector had a negative total return, this contributed 59 basis points to the overall excess return of the account versus its benchmark.

[7]For illustration purposes we do not show the full report, which provides attribution at the stock level for both securities held in the portfolio and those which are not but are components of the benchmark portfolio.

Finance					Benchmark Contrib -3.43%		Active Weight -1.76%	Active Contrib 0.59%		
Symbol	**Company**	**Stock Return**	**Avg Act Wt**	**Active Contrib**	**Stock Selection Rel**	**Abs**	**Avg Mgd Wt**	**Mgd Ctrb**	**IR**	**HR (%)**
ABK	AMBAC FINANCIAL GROUP INC	-19.68%	1.86%	-0.35%	-0.08	-0.09	1.93	-0.38	-8.76	43.75
FNM	FANNIE MAE	-18.91%	1.78%	-0.31%	-0.07	-0.10	2.65	-0.49	-9.23	43.75
KRB	MBNA CORP	-16.34%	1.15%	-0.19%	0.04	0.05	1.46	-0.23	-4.04	46.31
FRE	FREDDIE MAC	-8.34%	2.03%	-0.16%	0.16	0.20	2.54	-0.20	-4.07	50.00
SCH	SCHWAB (CHARLES) CORP	-22.21%	0.58%	-0.15%	-0.03	-0.04	0.74	-0.19	-7.20	43.75
STT	STATE STREET CORP	-13.29%	0.90%	-0.13%	0.05	0.05	1.07	-0.14	-5.44	48.44
C	CITIGROUP INC	-17.66%	0.15%	-0.03%	0.01	0.03	2.19	-0.42	-4.59	43.75
BAC	BANK OF AMERICA CORP	-8.52%	0.15%	-0.01%	0.01	0.13	1.39	-0.12	-4.73	46.31
UPC	UNION PLANTERS CORP	-14.22%	-0.07%	0.01%	-0.00	0.00	0.00	0.00	7.76	56.25
JP	JEFFERSON-PILOT CORP	-14.08%	-0.08%	0.01%	-0.00	0.00	0.00	0.00	7.89	56.25
CF	CHARTER ONE FIN INC	-12.96%	-0.09%	0.01%	-0.00	0.00	0.00	0.00	5.47	56.25
TROW	T ROWE PRICE GROUP INC	-24.09%	-0.04%	0.01%	0.00	0.00	0.00	0.00	9.65	59.38
GDW	GOLDEN WEST FINANCIAL CORP	-9.50%	-0.12%	0.01%	-0.01	0.00	0.00	0.00	4.99	54.69
ALL	ALLSTATE CORP	-3.32%	-0.31%	0.01%	-0.04	0.00	0.00	0.00	2.62	54.69
EQR	EQUITY RESIDENTIAL	-16.31%	-0.09%	0.01%	-0.00	0.00	0.00	0.00	10.41	56.25
UNM	UNUMPROVIDENT CORP	-19.41%	-0.06%	0.01%	0.00	0.00	0.00	0.00	9.83	57.81
JNS	JANUS CAPITAL GROUP INC	-33.52%	-0.04%	0.01%	0.01	0.00	0.00	0.00	12.70	57.81
XL	X L CAPITAL LTD	-12.66%	-0.12%	0.02%	-0.01	0.00	0.00	0.00	5.30	56.25
NTRS	NORTHERN TRUST CORP	-14.08%	-0.11%	0.02%	-0.00	0.00	0.00	0.00	5.42	56.25
EOP	EQUITY OFFICE PROPERTIES TR	-12.59%	-0.14%	0.02%	-0.00	0.00	0.00	0.00	9.72	57.81
PGR	PROGRESSIVE CORP	-12.44%	-0.14%	0.02%	-0.01	0.00	0.00	0.00	7.37	63.13
BBT	BB&T CORPORATION	-8.50%	-0.21%	0.02%	-0.02	0.00	0.00	0.00	4.93	59.38
ONE	BANK ONE CORP	-2.30%	-0.54%	0.02%	-0.09	0.00	0.00	0.00	1.43	46.88
CINF	CINCINNATI FINANCIAL CORP	-23.06%	-0.08%	0.02%	0.01	0.00	0.00	0.00	13.04	67.19
STI	SUNTRUST BANKS INC	-8.63%	-0.22%	0.02%	-0.02	0.00	0.00	0.00	4.79	50.00
AET	AETNA INC	-25.36%	-0.07%	0.02%	0.01	0.00	0.00	0.00	10.67	57.81
SNV	SYNOVUS FINANCIAL CORP	-24.57%	-0.08%	0.02%	0.01	0.00	0.00	0.00	10.59	60.94
SPC	ST. PAUL COMPANIES	-25.50%	-0.08%	0.02%	0.01	0.00	0.00	0.00	10.38	54.69
LNC	LINCOLN NATIONAL CORP	-26.68%	-0.08%	0.02%	0.01	0.00	0.00	0.00	12.43	64.06
JHF	JOHN HANCOCK FINANCIAL SRVCS	-21.02%	-0.11%	0.02%	0.01	0.00	0.00	0.00	9.90	57.81
WM	WASHINGTON MUTUAL INC	-14.58%	-0.18%	0.02%	-0.00	0.00	0.24	-0.03	6.43	50.00
CMA	COMERICA INC	-20.79%	-0.12%	0.02%	0.01	0.00	0.00	0.00	10.17	51.56
AOC	AON CORP	-29.83%	-0.07%	0.03%	0.01	0.00	0.00	0.00	8.40	53.13

FIGURE 19.3 Breakdown of Contributions from Finance

More detail is of course available. Figure 19.3 shows the breakdown at the stock level of the contributions from finance, providing for each stock the return and average active weight over the period that contributed to the overall performance versus benchmark.

Next, we explain the issue of linking daily returns in multiperiod return attribution.

Multiperiod Attribution

Return attribution begins with calculating sources of return over a single time period (e.g., one day). Single period sources are then compounded, or linked, so that returns are computed over multiple periods (e.g., one month). Multiperiod attribution requires that we compound each group's (or factor's) contributions so that the sum of the compounded group contributions is equal to the compounded total return. In the following section, we use the linear factor model to describe linking. Note, however, that all results directly carry over to the case where the asset grouping methodology is applied.

Linking Returns Consider the one-period portfolio return written in terms of the linear factor model. We know from our earlier discussion that the return on the managed portfolio is given by:[8]

$$r_p(t) = b^p(t-1)F(t) + u_p(t) \tag{19.24}$$

[8]In order to avoid cluttering notation, we drop the local superscript when writing returns.

Let $S_k(t)$ represent the one-period source of return from the kth factor for $k = 1, \ldots, K$. $S_k(t)$ is equal to the kth element of $b^p(t-1)F(t)$. Let $S_0(t)$ represent the contribution from the total specific return.[9] This implies that there are $K + 1$ sources of return. Using these definitions we write equation (19.24) as

$$r_p(t) = \sum_{k=1}^{K} S_k(t) + S_0(t) \tag{19.25}$$

where the returns in (19.25) are defined in terms of percent changes. The T-period ($T > 0$) portfolio total return (cumulative return over T periods) is defined as

$$r_p^{t+T-1}(t) = \prod_{h=1}^{T}\left[1 + r_p(t+h-1)\right] - 1 = \prod_{h=1}^{T}\left[1 + \sum_{k=0}^{K} S_k(t+h-1)\right] - 1 \tag{19.26}$$

When $h = 1$, the one-period return is $r_p^t(t) = r_p(t)$, by definition.

Our goal is to determine the multiperiod attribution from a particular source. A natural definition of the T-period attribution from the kth source is the cumulative return from that source, i.e.,

$$S_k^{t+T-1}(t) = \prod_{h=1}^{T}\left[1 + S_k(t+h-1)\right] \tag{19.27}$$

Note that the definition of portfolio return in (19.26) and source of return in (19.27) are incompatible—that is, you cannot identify (19.27) by using (19.26) due to the presence of cross terms between sources.

Upon closer inspection, (19.26) shows that the multiperiod portfolio return is the product of sums of sources of return. This product of sums results in cross terms, which makes it impossible to isolate the source of any one return. For example, suppose that $T = 2$ (two periods) and $K = 2$ (two sources). In this case, the two-period return (from $t - 1$ to $t + 1$) is

$$\begin{aligned}
1 + r_p^{t+1}(t) &= \left[1 + r_p^t(t)\right]\left[1 + r_p^{t+1}(t+1)\right] = \left[1 + S_0(t) + S_1(t) + S_2(t)\right] \\
&\quad \times\left[1 + S_0(t+1) + S_1(t+1) + S_2(t+1)\right] \\
&= 1 + S_0(t) + S_1(t) + S_2(t) + S_0(t+1) + S_1(t+1) + S_2(t+1) \\
&\quad + S_0(t)S_0(t+1) + S_0(t)S_1(t+1) + S_0(t)S_2(t+1) \\
&\quad + S_1(t)S_0(t+1) + S_1(t)S_1(t+1) + S_1(t)S_2(t+1) \\
&\quad + S_2(t)S_0(t+1) + S_2(t)S_1(t+1) + S_2(t)S_2(t+1)
\end{aligned} \tag{19.28}$$

[9]Earlier we decomposed the specific return into N components.

What is the two-period return of source 1 (subscript 1)? If we want to have a consistent definition of a compounded return, the answer is $[1 + S_1(t)][1 + S_1(t + 1)]$. According to (19.28), however, the answer is not straightforward due to the cross terms between the first and other sources. All the terms in (19.28) containing the first source are:

$$\begin{aligned} &1 + S_1(t) + S_1(t + 1) + S_0(t)S_1(t + 1) + S_1(t)S_0(t + 1) \\ &+ S_1(t)S_1(t + 1) + S_1(t)S_2(t + 1) + S_2(t)S_1(t + 1) \end{aligned} \tag{19.29}$$

which does not equal $[1 + S_1(t)][1 + S_1(t + 1)]$. Quickly, one can see that the problem of isolating sources of return becomes unwieldy as the compounding period (T) increases along with the number of factors (K).

Developers of commercially available software that generates performance attribution reports appreciate the problems associated with computing multiperiod attribution and employ methods for handling this issue. Most vendors have their own proprietary methods for computing multiperiod return attribution (i.e., linking sources of return over time). Next, we present two methodologies to link sources of return. The first methodology presented was proposed by the Frank Russell Company. An advantage of the methodology that we present is that it is relatively simple and, therefore, it facilitates the explanation of the numerous issues associated with linking returns.

Methodology for Linking Sources of Return There are quite a few different methods for combining attribution effects over time. A recent summary of these methods can be found in Mirabelli (2000/2001). Among them is a simple yet effective methodology proposed by the Frank Russell Company.[10] This methodology is based on the differences between so-called continuously compounded (log) returns and discretely compounded (percent) returns. Before we explain this methodology we review the differences between percent and continuous returns.

Earlier, we defined the one-period local return for the nth asset as

$$R_n^\ell(t) = \frac{P_n^\ell(t) + d_n(t - h, t) - P_n^\ell(t - 1)}{P_n^\ell(t - 1)} \tag{19.30}$$

and its total return (including currency) as

$$R_n(t) = R_n^\ell(t) + E_{ij}(t) + R_n^\ell(t) \times E_{ij}(t) \tag{19.31}$$

where $E_{ij}(t)$ is the exchange rate return. The returns in (19.30) and (19.31) are in percent format. The continuous-time counterpart of (19.30) is the one-period log return, which is given by

[10]For details, see David R. Carino, of Frank Russell Company, Inc., 1999, "Combining Attribution Effects over Time," *Journal of Performance Measurement*, Summer, 5–14.

$$R^{\ell}_{\log,n}(t) = \log\left[\frac{P^{\ell}_n(t) + d_n(t-h,t)}{P^{\ell}_n(t-1)}\right] \tag{19.32}$$

The total log return, including currency, is given by

$$R_{\log,n}(t) = R^{\ell}_{\log,n}(t) + E_{\log,ij}(t) \tag{19.33}$$

Now, we consider cumulative returns. The T + 1–period percent return, denoted by $R^{t+T}_n(t)$—from t to t + T—is the product of T + 1 one-period returns, that is,

$$R^{t+T}_n(t) = \prod_{j=0}^{T}\left[1 + R_n(t+j)\right] - 1 \tag{19.34}$$

The T + 1 period cumulative log return, $R^{t+T}_{\log,n}(t)$—again, from t to t + T—is the sum of T + 1 one-period log returns, that is,

$$R^{t+T}_{\log,n}(t) = \sum_{j=0}^{T} R_{\log,n}(t+j) \tag{19.35}$$

Equation (19.35) shows the time aggregation property of log returns. Namely, the sum of one-period returns is equal to the multiperiod return. This is a very convenient property that is not shared by percent returns.

Suppose that instead of using percent returns, we assume that all returns are computed using log returns. In this case, we write the portfolio log return as a function of K + 1 sources of return.

$$r_{\log,p}(t) = \sum_{k=0}^{N} S_k(t) \tag{19.36}$$

Since log returns are additive over time, one may think that we should work with log returns since time aggregation would be easier (i.e., additive and, therefore, no cross terms to worry about). However, at a particular point in time log returns are not additive across assets. That is to say, when using log returns on individual assets, the return on the portfolio is no longer equal to the weighted average of individual asset returns. This leads to an obvious dilemma about how to compute returns.

We can summarize our dilemma of choosing log versus percent returns as follows:

- Percent returns are additive when dealing with cross sections. That is, a one-period portfolio return using percent returns is a weighted average of one-period asset level percent returns. Multiperiod percent returns are multiplicative.
- Log returns are additive across time but not in cross sections. That is, multiperiod log returns are the sum of successive one-period returns. However, one-

period portfolio log returns are not equal to the sum of one-period weighted asset level returns.

To compute multiperiod attribution, we begin with percent returns and convert these to log returns. Sources of return are defined in terms of log returns. The sources of return and the total portfolio return are then converted back to percent returns. Specifically, the approach works as follows.

Step 1: Define portfolio returns in terms of percent returns and estimate the one-period sources of return. This allows us to write the portfolio percent return as the sum of $K + 1$ sources of returns.

$$r_p(t) = \sum_{k=0}^{K} S_k(t) \tag{19.37}$$

Step 2: Convert each one-period portfolio percent return into a continuous portfolio return by multiplying equation (19.37) by the ratio of the portfolio log return to the percent return. This is done in two steps.

First, create the adjustment factor:

$$\kappa(t+j) = \frac{\text{Portfolio log return}}{\text{Portfolio percent return}} = \frac{r_{\log,p}(t+j)}{r_p(t+j)} \qquad j = 0, \ldots, T \tag{19.38}$$

Second, multiply each source of return by the adjustment factor so as to convert the portfolio percent return into a portfolio log return. Multiply equation (19.37) by $\kappa(t + j)$ to get

$$r_{\log,p}(t+j) = \sum_{k=0}^{K} \kappa(t+j) S_k(t+j) \tag{19.39}$$

Equation (19.39) is the continuous time counterpart to the discrete portfolio return (19.37). The element $\kappa(t + j)S_k(t + j)$ is the continuously compounded form of the source $S_k(t + j)$. From our earlier discussion, we know that one-period log returns sum to multiperiod returns, that is,

$$r_{\log,p}^{t+T}(t) = \sum_{j=0}^{T} r_{\log,p}(t+j) \tag{19.40}$$

Substituting (19.39) into (19.40) we have

$$r_{\log,p}^{t+T}(t) = \sum_{j=0}^{T}\sum_{k=0}^{K} \kappa(t+j) S_k(t+j) = S_{\kappa,0}^{t+T}(t) + S_{\kappa,1}^{t+T}(t) + \cdots + S_{\kappa,K}^{t+T}(t) \tag{19.41}$$

Equation (19.41) shows that we can write the compounded portfolio return, $r_{\log,p}^{t+T}(t)$, as the sum of $K + 1$ compounded sources of returns where each source of return, $S_{\kappa,k}^{t+T}(t)$, is defined in terms of log returns. The key to generating multiperiod sources of return that are additive was the conversion of percent returns to log returns.

Step 3: Transform (19.41) back to percent returns. Originally, we defined all returns as percent returns. Therefore, step 3 is to transform (19.41) back to percent returns. To do this, define the new adjustment factor:

$$\kappa^{t+T}(t) = \frac{\text{Multiperiod portfolio percent return}}{\text{Multiperiod portfolio log return}} = \frac{r^{t+T}(t+j)}{r_{\log,p}^{t+T}(t+j)} = \frac{\prod_{j=0}^{T}\left[1 + r^{t+T}(t+j)\right] - 1}{\sum_{j=0}^{T} r_{\log,p}(t+j)} \tag{19.42}$$

The $T + 1$ period cumulative attribution effect for the kth source, based on percent returns, is given by

$$S_k^{t+T}(t) = \frac{\sum_{j=0}^{T} \kappa(t+j) S_k(t+j)}{\kappa^{t+T}(t)} = \frac{S_{\kappa,k}^{t+T}(t)}{\kappa^{t+T}(t)} \tag{19.43}$$

Applying these transformations to (19.43) we are left with the result for cumulative percent returns:

$$\prod_{j=0}^{T}\left[1 + r_p(t+j)\right] - 1 = \frac{r_{\log,p}^{t+T}}{\kappa^{t+T}(t)} = \frac{S_{\kappa,0}^{t+T}(t)}{\kappa^{t+T}(t)} + \frac{S_{\kappa,1}^{t+T}(t)}{\kappa^{t+T}(t)} + \cdots + \frac{S_{\kappa,K}^{t+T}(t)}{\kappa^{t+T}(t)} \tag{19.44}$$

which yields

$$\prod_{j=0}^{T}\left[1 + r_p(t+j)\right] - 1 = \sum_{k=0}^{K} S_k^{t+T}(t) \tag{19.45}$$

Note that all we have done in the preceding analysis is convert log returns back to percent returns.

Equation (19.45) shows that the cumulative, multiperiod percent return is equal to the sum of cumulative, multiperiod sources of return (defined as percent returns). These results extend directly to the case where our focus is on active returns. In this case, the multiperiod active return is

$$\prod_{j=0}^{T}\left[1 + r_p(t+j)\right] - \prod_{j=0}^{T}\left[1 + r_b(t+j)\right] = \sum_{k=0}^{K} S_k^{t+T}(t) \tag{19.46}$$

Alternative Methodology for Linking Sources of Return Mirabelli (2000/2001) proposed an alternative methodology for linking sources of return that is described as "simply additive, yet formally exact." We present this methodology in three parts. First, we show that the geometrically compounded returns can be written as the sum of variables that are functions of the portfolio returns. We refer to the values of these variables at time t as diff(t), which are defined as follows:

$$\begin{aligned}
\text{diff}(1) &= [1+R(1)] \\
\text{diff}(2) &= [1+R(1)]\times[1+R(2)]-[1+R(1)] \\
\text{diff}(3) &= [1+R(1)]\times[1+R(2)]\times[1+R(3)]-[1+R(1)]\times[1+R(2)] \\
\text{diff}(4) &= [1+R(1)]\times[1+R(2)]\times[1+R(3)]\times[1+R(4)]-[1+R(1)]\times[1+R(2)]\times[1+R(3)]
\end{aligned}$$

and so on. In general we can write

$$\text{diff}(t) = \prod_{j=1}^{t}[1+R(j)] - \prod_{j=1}^{t-1}[1+R(j)] \tag{19.47}$$

It follows from these definitions that the geometric return can be written as the sum of diffs, that is,

$$\prod_{j=1}^{t}[1+R_{(j)}]-1 = \sum_{j=1}^{t}\text{diff}(j)-1 \tag{19.48}$$

Equation (19.48) is important because it allows us to write the geometric return as a sum.

Second, we rewrite the diffs as follows. Consider diff(2). Let's expand it so that we have

$$\begin{aligned}
\text{diff}(2) &= [1+R(1)]\times[1+R(2)]-[1+R(1)] \\
&= 1+R(2)+R(1)+R(1)\times R(2)-1-R(1) \\
&= [1+R(1)]\times R(2)
\end{aligned}$$

Similarly, working with diff(4), we get

$$\begin{aligned}
\text{diff}(4) &= [1+R(1)]\times[1+R(2)]\times[1+R(3)]\times[1+R(4)]-[1+R(1)]\times[1+R(2)]\times[1+R(3)] \\
&= [1+R(1)]\times[1+R(2)]\times[1+R(3)]+[1+R(1)]\times[1+R(2)]\times[1+R(3)]\times R(4) \\
&\quad -[1+R(1)]\times[1+R(2)]\times[1+R(3)] \\
&= \{[1+R(1)]\times[1+R(2)]\times[1+R(3)]\}\times R(4)
\end{aligned}$$

Generally, we have

$$\text{diff}(t) = \prod_{j=0}^{t-1} \left[1 + R(j)\right] \times R(t) \tag{19.49}$$

Let $r(t)$ represent the one-period (time t) return on a portfolio. The geometric return over T periods can now be written as

$$\prod_{j=1}^{T} \left[1 + r(j)\right] - 1 = \sum_{t=1}^{T} \left\{ \prod_{j=0}^{t-1} \left[1 + r(j)\right] \times r(t) \right\} - 1 \tag{19.50}$$

where we define $r(0) = 0$.

Equation (19.50) allows us to write the T-period geometric return as the sum of T one-period returns—the $R(t)$'s—which are scaled by one plus the geometric portfolio return from time 0 through time $t - 1$.

Consider the example where we compute a portfolio's return over four periods. In this case we have

$$\prod_{j=1}^{4} \left[1 + r(j)\right] = r(1) + \left[1 + r(1)\right] \times r(2) + \left[1 + r(2)\right] \times r(3) + \left[1 + r(3)\right] \times r(4) \tag{19.51}$$

The third part of the methodology involves writing the one-period portfolio return (at time t) in terms of its constituent level weights and returns. That is,

$$r(t) = \sum_{n=1}^{N} w_n R_n(t)$$

where we assume there are N assets in the portfolio and w_n represents the weight on the nth asset. Substituting the expression for the portfolio return into (19.50) yields

$$\prod_{j=1}^{T} \left[1 + r(j)\right] = \sum_{t=1}^{T} \left\{ \prod_{j=0}^{t-1} \left[1 + r(j)\right] \times \sum_{n=1}^{N} w_n R_n(t) \right\} \tag{19.52}$$

Equation (19.52) forms the basis for return attribution and linking sources of return at the asset (and any subsequent grouping) level. To see this, let's take the example where we have a portfolio with three assets ($N = 3$) and the portfolio's return is computed over four periods ($T = 4$).

$$\begin{aligned} \prod_{j=1}^{4} \left[1 + r(j)\right] - 1 = &\sum_{n=1}^{3} w_n R_n(1) + \left[1 + r(1)\right] \times \sum_{n=1}^{3} w_n R_n(2) + \left[1 + r(1)\right] \times \left[1 + r(2)\right] \\ &\times \sum_{n=1}^{3} w_n R_n(3) + \left[1 + r(1)\right] \times \left[1 + r(2)\right] \times \left[1 + r(2)\right] \\ &\times \sum_{n=1}^{3} w_n R_n(4) - 1 \end{aligned} \tag{19.53}$$

Let's break (19.53) down period by period (and ignore the minus ones).

At time $t = 1$:

Contribution to geometric return = $w_1R_1(1) + w_2R_2(1) + w_3R_3(1)$

At time $t = 2$:

Contribution to geometric return = $[1 + r(1)] \times [w_1R_1(2) + w_2R_2(2) + w_3R_3(2)]$

At time $t = 3$:

Contribution to geometric return = $[1 + r(1)] \times [1 + r(2)] \times [w_1R_1(3) + w_2R_2(3) + w_3R_3(3)]$

At time $t = 4$:

Contribution to geometric return = $[1 + r(1)] \times [1 + r(2)] \times [1 + r(3)] \times [w_1R_1(4) + w_2R_2(4) + w_3R_3(4)]$

Next define

$$\gamma(t-1) = \prod_{j=1}^{t-1}\left[1 + r(j)\right]$$

where $\gamma(0) = 1$. Using this notation, we can write asset 1's contribution to the portfolio's geometric return as

$$w_1R_1(1) + \gamma(1)w_1R_1(2) + \gamma(2)w_1R_1(3) + \gamma(3)w_1R_1(4) \qquad (19.54)$$

Generally, the nth asset's contribution to the portfolio return is

$$\sum_{t=1}^{T} \gamma(t-1)w_nR_n(t)$$

We can now rewrite (19.52) so that the portfolio's geometric return is

$$\prod_{j=1}^{T}\left[1 + r(j)\right] - 1 = \sum_{n=1}^{N}\sum_{t=1}^{T} \gamma(t-1)w_nR_n(t) - 1 \qquad (19.55)$$

This concludes our description of Mirabelli's methodology. In summary, we've taken the cumulative product of returns (i.e., geometric returns) and expressed them as the sum of one-period returns. Each period's contribution to return (at time t) is scaled by the portfolio's geometric return from the start of the attribution period through $t - 1$. Finally, note that although we can write the geometric return as the sum of one-period returns without using any approximations, cross terms are still involved.

This completes our description of the computations behind multiperiod return attribution. The results on linking hold both of the methods for generating sources of return, the factor model–based approach and the asset grouping methodology. Next, we turn our attention to international equity portfolios.

RETURN ATTRIBUTION ON INTERNATIONAL PORTFOLIOS

In this section we explain return attribution in the context of international equity portfolios. We assume that such portfolios may hold currency and equity futures as well as forwards, American depositary receipts (ADRs), cash, and similar instruments.

Overview: Portfolio Contributions and Returns

For international equity portfolios, we identify and measure six sources of return to managed, benchmark, and active portfolios. The sources are:

1. Country.
2. Currency (including forwards).
3. Investment style.
4. Industry and sector.
5. Asset (including cash and futures positions).
6. Cross product (measures the interaction of currency and other sources).

We measure contributions from country, industry, sector, and asset to a portfolio's total and local return return, where the total return combines the currency (exchange rate) return and local return. When measuring multicurrency attribution we show sources of return two ways—including and excluding the impact of currency.

Compared to our single country attribution methodology, we now have three additional sources of return: (1) country, (2) currency, and (3) cross product.

1. The country effect measures contribution to return from country exposure. This is computed for both the total and local returns.
2. The currency effect measures the contribution to return from currency exposure. We separate the currency effect into two components—currency surprise and forward premium. The former is an uncertain quantity whereas the latter is known with certainty.
3. The cross-product term measures the interaction between the currency effect and the local return. Generally, the interaction effect is relatively small compared to the other sources described so far. However, if the portfolio weight (or return) is significantly more or less than the benchmark weight (or return), the interaction effect has a larger impact. For convenience, interaction is often combined with other sources.

Table 19.1 summarizes the six sources of return and the type of returns that are computed for each.

In the following analysis, we work with percent returns. Recall that the total (percent) return for a portfolio is

$$r_p(t) = \left[1 + r_p^{\ell}(t)\right]\left[1 + E_{ij}(t)\right] - 1 \tag{19.56}$$

Let $w^p(t-1)$ represent an N-vector of portfolio weights where the weights are constructed with respect to the reporting currency. That is, nominal amounts that go into constructing the weights are expressed in the respective portfolio's reporting currency. In the case where a portfolio's reporting currency is U.S. dollars, the weights would be constructed by first converting all positions to U.S. dollars.

TABLE 19.1 Sources of Return for International Equity Portfolios: Contributions and Returns Measured for Managed, Benchmark, and Active Portfolios

Source	Contribution To	Return	In Single Country Model?
Country	Total and local return	Total and local	Possibly
Currency	Total return	Currency	No
Investment style	Total return and local return	Total	Yes
Industry and sector	Total and local return	Total and local	Yes
Asset	Total and local return	Total and local	Yes
Cross product	Total return	Total	No

The managed portfolio's total return, $r_p(t)$, is written as (from 19.56):

$$\begin{aligned} r_p(t) &= \sum_{n=1}^{N} w_n^p(t-1)R_n(t) \\ &= \sum_{n=1}^{N} w_n^p(t-1)R_n^\ell(t) + \sum_{n=1}^{N} w_n^p(t-1)E_{ij,t} + \sum_{n=1}^{N} w_n^p(t-1)E_{ij}(t)R_n^\ell(t) \\ &= \ell^p(t) + \varepsilon^p(t) + xc^p(t) \end{aligned} \tag{19.57}$$

From equation (19.57), we see that the managed portfolio's total return is the sum of:

- Its local return, $\ell^p(t)$.
- The portfolio's exchange rate return, $\varepsilon^p(t)$.
- A cross term, which is the product of the exchange rate return and local returns, $xc^p(t)$.

The Global Factor Model

A global factor model expresses the cross section of total asset returns in terms of local factors, exchange rate returns, and cross terms. Mathematically, the model is

$$R(t) = B^\ell(t-1)F^\ell(t) + u^\ell(t) + E_{ij}(t) + xc(t) \tag{19.58}$$

Let $w^m(t-1)$ represent market portfolio weights. The portfolio return $w^m(t-1)^T R(t)$ may be decomposed into the following sources: country, currency, investment style, industry, sector, and specific contribution. The specific return contribution to total return is based on the term $w^m(t-1)^T u^\ell(t)$. Similarly, the currency contribution is given by $w^m(t-1)^T E_{ij}(t)$. This contribution can be decomposed into two parts—the forward premium and a surprise currency change.[11]

[11]References include: G. P. Brinson and N. Fachler, 1985, "Measuring Non-U.S. Equity Portfolio Performance," *Journal of Portfolio Management*, Spring; and E. M. Ankrim and C. H. Hensel, 1994, "Multicurrency Performance Attribution," *Financial Analysts Journal*, March–April, 29–35.

We incorporate the forward premium and currency surprise into the currency return as follows. First, recall from the section on computing returns that the return from holding a foreign currency from period $t - 1$ to t is $E_{ij}(t) = [X_{ij}(t) - X_{ij}(t - 1)]/X_{ij}(t - 1)$. Next, let $FR(t)$ represent the forward exchange rate (expressed as reporting over base currency) at time $t - 1$ for forward delivery at time t. Rewrite the currency return at $t - 1$ for t as

$$E_{ij}(t) = \frac{X_{ij}(t) - FR(t) + FR(t) - X_{ij}(t-1)}{X_{ij}(t-1)} \tag{19.59}$$

Since the return is computed at $t - 1$, $X_{ij}(t)$ is uncertain and, therefore, so is $E_{ij}(t)$. It follows from (19.59) that the uncertain currency return consists of two parts: currency surprise, $s(t)$, and forward premium, $fp(t)$:

$$E_{ij}(t) = \underbrace{s(t)}_{\text{Currency surprise}} + \underbrace{fp(t)}_{\text{Forward premium}} \tag{19.60}$$

where $s(t) = [X_{ij}(t) - FR(t)]/X_{ij}(t - 1)$
$fp(t) = [FR(t) - X_{ij}(t - 1)]/X_{ij}(t - 1)$

Note that the currency surprise is unknown at $t - 1$ whereas the forward premium is known. Therefore, return attribution that incorporates contributions from currency should clearly measure contributions from currency surprise only. One should not attribute a portion of currency return to something that is known beforehand. When computing contribution, we can simply substitute (19.60) into (19.58) and get the contribution from the currency surprise. Because the value of active management lies in its ability to forecast the uncertain sources of return, performance attribution should focus on the ability to capture positive returns due to currency surprise.

The term $w^m(t - 1)^T xc(t)$ captures the contribution to the portfolio's return from the interaction between exchange rates and the portfolio's local return.

Asset Grouping Methodology

In order to derive expressions for international equity portfolios based on the asset grouping methodology, we need the following definitions.

$w_c^b(t-1)$	cth country's weight in the benchmark portfolio
$w_c^p(t-1)$	cth country's weight in the managed portfolio
$r_b^c(t)$	cth country's total return as constructed in the benchmark portfolio
$\ell_b^c(t)$	cth country's local return as constructed in the benchmark portfolio
$\ell_p^c(t)$	cth country's local return as constructed in the managed portfolio
$\ell_b(t)$	local return as constructed in the benchmark portfolio

Using these definitions, we can construct contributions to a portfolio's return by country, currency, investment style, industry, sector, and asset. While the results presented later apply to the managed portfolio, they extend directly to the active and benchmark portfolios as well.

Country Contributions to Return For a given country, compute the exposures of each position to that country. For example, a position may have an exposure of one if it is exposed to a country, zero otherwise. Let $q_{n,c}(t)$ be the nth security's exposure to the cth country. The one-period contributions from the cth country are defined as follows.

The cth country's contribution to the managed portfolio's total return is

$$\sum_{n=1}^{N} q_{n,c}(t) w_n^p(t-1) R_n(t)$$

Its contribution to the portfolio's local return is

$$\sum_{n=1}^{N} q_{n,c}(t) w_n^p(t-1) R_n^{\ell}(t)$$

In addition to contributions, we compute returns:

- The cth country's total return as computed from the managed portfolio's holdings is

$$\sum_{n=1}^{N} q_{n,c}(t) w_n^p(t-1) R_n(t) \div \sum_{n=1}^{N} q_{n,c}(t) w_n^p(t-1)$$

- The cth country's local return as computed from the managed portfolio's holdings is

$$\sum_{n=1}^{N} q_{n,c}(t) w_n^p(t-1) R_n^{\ell}(t) \div \sum_{n=1}^{N} q_{n,c}(t) w_n^p(t-1)$$

In addition to the preceding computations, within each country we identify and measure four sources of return. These sources sum (over all countries) to the portfolio's total active return.

1. ***Country currency weight.*** This is a measure of how well a portfolio's currency exposure has been managed relative to the currency exposure in a benchmark portfolio. Country currency weight is approximately equal to the difference between the exchange rate return of the managed portfolio and the exchange rate return of the benchmark portfolio. The country currency weight consists of two parts: (1) relative currency weight and (2) currency performance effect.

   Relative currency weight measures the impact that currency exposure has on the active portfolio's total return that results from differences between managed country weights and benchmark country weights.

   Currency performance effect measures the impact that currency exposure has on the active portfolio's total return that results from the performance of different currencies.

2. ***Country allocation (market weight).*** This measures the impact on the active portfolio return from selecting different countries in proportions that are different from the benchmark.

3. ***Country stock selection.*** Within each country, this measures the impact that stock selection has on the active portfolio's total return. It provides a measure of a portfolio manager's ability to select stocks within a country.
4. ***Country sector weight.*** Within each country, this measures the impact of relative sector weightings on the active portfolio's total return. It provides a measure of a portfolio manager's ability to choose sectors within a country.

We now explain these computations in more detail.

The *country currency weight* is the sum of the relative currency weight effect and the currency performance effect. These are defined as follows (for the cth country):

Relative currency weight:

$$\left[w_c^p(t-1) - w_c^b(t-1)\right] \times \left\{\left[r_b^c(t) - \ell_b^c(t)\right] - \left[r_b(t) - \ell_b(t)\right]\right\} \tag{19.61}$$

Currency performance:

$$w_c^p(t-1) \times \left\{\left[r_p^c(t) - \ell_p^c(t)\right] - \left[r_b^c(t) - \ell_b^c(t)\right]\right\} \tag{19.62}$$

The country currency weight is equal to (19.61) plus (19.62) and then summing over all countries. This yields:

$$\left\{\left[r_p(t) - \ell_p(t)\right] - \left[r_b(t) - \ell_b(t)\right]\right\} \tag{19.63}$$

Country allocation (i.e., market weight) is computed as follows (for the cth country):

$$\left[w_c^p(t-1) - w_c^b(t-1)\right] \times \left[\ell_b^c(t) - \ell_b(t)\right] \tag{19.64}$$

In order to define country stock selection and country sector weight, we need to define additional variables. We assume that there are $J (j = 1, \ldots, J)$ sectors within each of the C countries.

$\ell_b^{S_c(j)}(t)$ = Local return of the jth sector in the cth country based on the benchmark portfolio.

$\ell_p^{S_c(j)}(t)$ = Local return of the jth sector in the cth country based on the managed portfolio.

$w_{S_c(j)}^b(t-1)$ = Benchmark portfolio weight of the jth sector in the cth country.

$w_{S_c(j)}^p(t-1)$ = Managed portfolio weight of the jth sector in the cth country.

Country stock selection is defined as (for the cth country)

$$w_c^p(t-1) \times \left\{\sum_{j=1}^{J} \frac{w_{S_c(j)}^p(t-1)}{w_c^p(t-1)}\left[\ell_p^{S_c(j)}(t) - \ell_b^{S_c(j)}(t)\right]\right\} \tag{19.65}$$

Country sector weight is defined as (for the cth country)

$$w_c^p(t-1)\times\left\{\sum_{j=1}^{J}\left(\frac{w_{S_c(j)}^p(t-1)}{w_c^p(t-1)}-\frac{w_{S_c(j)}^b(t-1)}{w_c^b(t-1)}\right)\left[\ell_p^{S_c(j)}(t)-\ell_b^c(t)\right]\right\} \tag{19.66}$$

In the asset grouping approach,[12] the forward premium effect is defined as: (Portfolio weight – Benchmark weight) × (Expected currency return – Average premium in benchmark portfolio). In this context (i.e., when measuring the forward premium effect), the currency management effect is defined as: [(Portfolio weight – Benchmark weight) × (Currency surprise – Total benchmark currency surprise)] + (Forward contract adjustment).

An approach that incorporates the currency management and forward premium effect such as this one will help investors measure more accurately the value added by active management of individual stocks, of countries, and of currency hedges in an international portfolio.

Currency Contributions to Return For a given currency, compute the exposure of each position to that currency. A position will have an exposure of one if it is exposed to a currency, zero otherwise. Let $y_{n,j}(t)$ be the nth security's exposure to the jth currency. The jth currency's contribution to the managed portfolio's total return is

$$\sum_{n=1}^{N} y_{n,j}(t)w_n^p(t-1)E_{nj}(t)$$

The jth currency's total return as computed from the managed portfolio's holdings is

$$\sum_{n=1}^{N} y_{n,j}(t)w_n^p(t-1)E_{nj}(t)\div\sum_{n=1}^{N} y_{n,j}(t)w_n^p(t-1)$$

Industry and Sector Contributions to Return Industry and sector contributions are computed in the same way as country contributions and returns. Let $I_{n,s}(t)$ represent the nth position's weight in the sth industry. Typically, $I_{n,s}(t)$ takes a value of one if the company associated with the nth position is in the sth industry, zero otherwise.

The sth industry's contribution to the managed portfolio's total return is

$$\sum_{n=1}^{N} I_{n,s}(t)w_n^p(t-1)R_n(t)$$

Its contribution to the portfolio's local return is

$$\sum_{n=1}^{N} I_{n,s}(t)w_n^p(t-1)R_n^\ell(t)$$

Industry returns are computed as follows:

[12]See Brinson and Fachler (1985) and Ankrim and Hensel (1994) for details.

- The sth industry's total return, as computed from the managed portfolio's holdings, is

$$\sum_{n=1}^{N} I_{n,s}(t) w_n^p(t-1) R_n(t) \div \sum_{n=1}^{N} I_{n,s}(t) w_n^p(t-1)$$

- The sth industry's local return, as computed from the managed portfolio's holdings, is

$$\sum_{n=1}^{N} I_{n,s}(t) w_n^p(t-1) R_n^{\ell}(t) \div \sum_{n=1}^{N} I_{n,s}(t) w_n^p(t-1)$$

The same calculations are performed on sectors where each sector represents the combination of one or more industries.

For each industry and sector we define a stock selection and group weight measure.

- *Stock selection* (in terms of total return) for the ith industry at a particular point in time is defined as Industry's managed weight(t – 1) × [Industry's total return based on managed portfolio(t) – Industry's total return based on benchmark portfolio(t)].
- *Group weight* (in terms of total return) for the ith industry at a particular point in time is defined as Industry's active weight(t – 1) × {Industry's total return based on benchmark portfolio(t) – [Benchmark's total return(t) – Cash(t)]}.

Total of stock selection and group weight across all industries is:

$$\begin{aligned}
\text{Total} &= \sum_{i=1}^{S} w_i^p(t-1) \times \left[r_{i,p}(t) - r_{i,b}(t)\right] + \sum_{i=1}^{S} w_i^a(t-1) \times \left[r_{i,b}(t) - r_b(t)\right] \\
&= \left[r_p(t) - \text{Return on cash}\right] - \sum_{i=1}^{S} w_i^p(t-1) r_{i,b}(t) + \sum_{i=1}^{S} w_i^p(t-1) r_{i,b}(t) \\
&\quad - \sum_{i=1}^{S} w_i^b(t-1) r_{i,b}(t) - \sum_{i=1}^{S} w_i^a(t-1) r_b(t)
\end{aligned}$$

which is equal to:

$$\text{Total} = \left[r_p(t) - \text{Return on cash}\right] - r_b(t) - \sum_{i=1}^{S} w_i^a(t-1) r_b(t)$$

Investment Style Contributions to Return Contributions and returns for investment styles are computed as follows:

1. Sort assets according to their exposures to a particular investment style (e.g., sort assets by market capitalization).
2. Group the sorted assets into, say, 10 buckets where the break points represent deciles (or some other quantile).

3. For each decile group compute their contributions to total and local returns. Note that for a given investment style, the sum of managed contributions across all groups is equal to the portfolio's managed return.
4. Calculate the total and local return of each decile group.

Asset-Level Contributions to Return There are four different types of asset level contributions that we define in addition to managed, benchmark, and active contribution. These are:

1. ***Relative vs. group.*** For the nth asset at time t, this is defined as: Active weight × (Security return – Total return on the ith group based on the benchmark).
2. ***Relative vs. total.*** For the nth asset at time t, this is defined as: Active weight × (Security return – Benchmark total return).
3. ***Absolute vs. group.*** For the nth asset at time t, this is defined as: Managed weight × (Security return – Total return on the ith group based on the benchmark).
4. ***Absolute vs. yotal.*** For the nth asset at time t, this is defined as: Managed weight × (Security return – Benchmark total return).

IMPORTANT PRACTICAL MATTERS

In this section we explain how to compute a portfolio's residual return that is the difference between the officially reported return and the estimated return. Under certain conditions where the residual return is small, an algorithm to minimize the residual, while simultaneously not impacting any single source of return in a substantial way, can be applied.

Performance Measurement and Return Attribution

As stated at the outset of the discussion on return attribution, for a given account and time period, the identified sources of return are not necessarily the sources of the officially reported return. Return attribution relies, instead, on an estimate of the portfolio's official return. This estimate is derived from time $t - 1$ portfolio weights and time t returns. When there are no intraday cash flows or trades, then the estimate and the official return should be identical if:

- The prices used to compute the portfolio weights in return attribution are the same prices used to compute the officially reported return.
- The holdings used to compute the portfolio weights in return attribution are the same holdings used to compute the officially reported return.
- The asset (constituent) level returns used in return attribution are derived from the same prices and cash flows (e.g., dividends) as those used to compute the officially reported return.

The difference between the officially reported portfolio return and the estimated portfolio return is called the residual. The sources of return become distorted whenever the residual is not zero. Naturally, the problem becomes bigger as the absolute value of the residual gets bigger. The reason is simple. When we do attribution, we are doing it on the estimated return—that is, we are finding sources of the estimated return. The bigger the difference is between the estimated return and the officially reported return, the less relevant the sources are for the official return.

In practice, we address the problem of a nonzero residual by first measuring the residual and then reporting it. If we think that the residual is small enough to tolerate, we distribute the residual across all the sources of return. In the next section we explain, briefly, an algorithm behind the distribution of the error.

An Algorithm to Align Official and Estimates of Portfolio Returns

Where applicable, managers should compute the residual term on as frequent a basis as possible. In the case of daily return attribution we would compute, each day, the difference between the portfolio's one-day officially reported return and the estimate of the one-day return that is generated from portfolio positions and constituent total returns. In general, the smaller the time period is over which a portfolio's return is computed, the smaller the residual term. The reason for this is that as the portfolio's return horizon grows, so does the likelihood that intraperiod trades and cash flows will occur.

Let RES(t) represent the residual term computed for the return period $t - 1$ through t. Our objective is to make the residual zero in such a way as to minimize any effect on the computed sources of return. If we are running return attribution based on a factor model, then sources of return are from K factors and 1 specific term. Since the specific term consists of the sum of N asset-level specific contributions, we have a total of $K + N$ sources. In variance analysis, sources of return start at the asset level and are then aggregated depending on whether we are interested in contributions by industry, sector, country, or other. The precise number of sources depends on whether we are running variance analysis on the managed, benchmark, or active portfolio. Our goal is to distribute the residual term to as many sources as possible.

Assume that an active portfolio has Q sources of return. In practice, the number of unique assets in the managed and benchmark portfolios usually drive the number of sources. For example, if we apply a three-factor model to a portfolio that is managed against the S&P 500, then we may have somewhere around 503 sources of return. Our algorithm works as follows:

1. Each day compute the portfolio's estimated return and obtain the officially reported return from the official books and records.
2. Compute RES(t), which is the difference between the official and estimated portfolio returns.
3. Compute d = RES(t)/Q. This is the maximum amount that we can change any one contribution.
4. Add d to each contribution such that the following do not change: (1) the sign of the original contributions and (2) the ranking of the original contributions.

Note that the algorithm assumes that the source of error is random and is not due to any particular factor or asset. If there is a systematic source of residual, then we expect this to be picked up by a daily monitoring process that measures and evaluates the one-day residual returns for each portfolio that is tracked. This daily monitoring process increases the likelihood that systematic sources of residuals are identified in a timely manner.

To better understand the impact that a residual can have on return attribution, suppose we are interested in computing return attribution on a portfolio over a six-month period (126 business days) and, each business day, the residual is 0.25 basis points. If we ran a one-day attribution on any day over the period, the residual would be too small to see since our reports show numbers in whole basis points and not fractions. However, assuming that the residual is constant over the period, the six-month compounded portfolio return would have a residual of about 32 basis points (126 • 0.25 bps).

In order to reduce the six-month residual, we apply the adjustment algorithm described, each day, to the sources of return. If we had 100 assets (sources of return) in the active portfolio, then we would be modifying the contribution of each asset by a maximum of .25/100 bps or 0.0025 bps per day. The compounded adjustment to each source of return over the six-month period is, on average, 0.32 basis points. Moreover, the original ranking of the sources is unaffected.

An algorithm such as the one described should be applied only if the magnitude of the residual is considered small enough as to not materially affect the results. Typically, it requires that we have daily, officially reported returns. **Without the official returns, the algorithm cannot be applied.**

Finally, we present an additional reason for computing the residual as frequently as possible. Suppose that a manager has a return attribution report and the residual on the managed portfolio's return for the particular month is 0.5 bps. The manager of an equity portfolio might view this error as small, particularly if the return on the portfolio is relatively big—say, 5 percent. The question that we pose is, is the error really small?

To answer this question, a manager might look at each day's residual during the month—that is, taking daily position files, compute the difference between the managed portfolio's return and the official return, each day, over the attribution period. Suppose the manager finds that each day's residual is negligible, except for two days out of the month. On those days, the residuals are 50 bps and –51 bps. Since the sum of the daily residuals is approximately equal to the monthly residual, we might feel uncomfortable concluding that the monthly residual is small. In fact, the monthly residual may very well be meaningless.

SUMMARY

Return attribution is the process in which sources of a portfolio's return are identified and measured. Managers may rely on return attribution reports developed inhouse or from commercially available systems. Differences across systems can vary in certain respects, from the algorithms applied to the terminology used to describe the sources of return. The differences in algorithms and terminology can lead to confusion and make it difficult for managers to understand their portfolio's sources of return.

This chapter reviewed some of the most commonly used methods for performing return attribution. We focused on equity portfolios, although the results we presented generalize to other asset classes. We explained various methods that are employed by commercially available systems within a framework that uses common terminology and notation.

We began our presentation with a discussion of performance measurement and return calculations. We then presented the single and international frameworks for computing return attribution, which included the factor model–based approach and the asset grouping methodology. Finally, we reviewed the practical issues related to return attribution. These issues involved computing the residual return and an algorithm to distribute the residual so as to align the estimated and official daily returns.

Tables 19.2 and 19.3 summarize the results presented in this chapter.

TABLE 19.2 Factor Model–Based Definitions of Contributions to Return

	Name	Definition	Formula
1	Contribution to active total return by:		
1a	Asset	The *n*th asset's contribution to total active return	$w_n^a(t)^T R_n(t)$
1b	Industry	The *i*th industry's contribution to total active return	$b_i^a(t-1)^T F_i(t)$
1c	Investment style	The *k*th investment style's contribution to total active return	$b_k^a(t-1)^T F_k(t)$
1d	Country	The *c*th country's contribution to total active return	$b_c^a(t-1)^T F_c(t)$
1e	Currency	The *g*th currency's contribution to total active return	$b_g^a(t-1)^T F_g(t)$
2	Contribution to active local return by:		
2a	Asset	The *n*th asset's contribution to local active return	$w^a(t)^T R^l(t)$
2b	Industry	The *i*th industry's contribution to local active return	same as 1b
2c	Investment style	The *k*th investment style's contribution to local active return	same as 1c
2d	Country	The *c*th country's contribution to local active return	same as 1d
3	Specific contribution	Contribution of specific return to the active return	$w^a(t)^T u(t)$
4	Factor contribution	Contribution of all factors to the active return (assume total of *k* factors)	$\sum_{k=1}^{K} b_k^a(t-1)^T F_k(t)$
5	Market timing	Active beta times the difference between the realized return on the market and the long-run market return	$\beta^a(t)\left[r_m(t)-\bar{r}_m(t)\right]$
6	Expected return	Active beta times the long-run market return	$\beta^a(t)\bar{r}_m(t)$
7	Exceptional return	Active return minus the expected return	$r^a(t)-\beta^a(t)\bar{r}_m(t)$
8	Stock selection	Exceptional return minus the sum of market timing and factor contribution	$r^a(t)-\beta^a(t)\bar{r}_m(t)-\beta^a(t)\left[r_m(t)-\bar{r}_m(t)\right]$ – Factor contribution

TABLE 19.3 Asset Grouping Definitions of Contributions to Return

	Name	Definition	Formula
1	Total stock selection	The total out-/underperformance of a stock or group of stocks, relative to a benchmark.	$S(t)=\sum_{i=1}^{I} w_i^b(t-1)\times\left[r_{i,p}(t)-r_{i,b}(t)\right]$
1a	Stock selection for *i*th group of stocks	The out-underperformance of a stock or a specific group, relative to a benchmark.	$S_i(t)=w_i^b(t-1)\times\left[r_{i,p}(t)-r_{i,b}(t)\right]$
2	Allocation effect (group weight)	A measure of total performance based on the relative weighting of one group vs. another.	$A(t)=\sum_{i=1}^{I} A_i(t)$
2a	Allocation effect for *i*th group of stocks	A measure of performance based on the relative weighting of one group vs. another.	$A_i(t)=[w_i^p(t-1)-w_i^b(t-1)]\times[r_{i,b}(t-r_b(t)]$
3	Interaction effect for *i*th group of stocks	A cross term that captures the interaction of the active weights and stock selection.	$I_i(t)=[w_i^p(t-1)-w_i^b(t-1)]\times[r_{i,p}(t)-r_{i,b}(t)]$
4	Relative vs. group (by asset)	The active weight times the difference between the asset's return and the return on the *i*th group as represented in the benchmark.	$w_n^a(t-1)\times[R_n(t)-r_{i,b}(t)]$
5	Relative vs. total (by asset)	The active weight times the difference between the asset's return and the total return on the benchmark.	$w_n^a(t-1)\times[R_n(t)-r_b(t)]$
6	Absolute vs. group (by asset)	The managed weight times the difference between the asset's return and the total return on the benchmark.	$w_n^p(t-1)\times[R_n(t)-r_{i,b}(t)]$
7	Absolute vs. total (by asset)	The managed weight times the difference between the asset's return and the total return on the benchmark.	$w_n^p(t-1)\times[R_n(t)-r_b(t)]$
8	Relative vs. group by group (e.g., industry)	Same as 4 but use industry/country/sector in place of asset.	Same as 4 but by group
9	Relative vs. total by group (e.g., industry)	Same as 5 but use industry/country/sectorin place of asset.	Same as 5 but by group
10	Absolute vs. group by group (e.g., industry)	Same as 6 but use industry/country/sector in place of asset.	Same as 6 but by group

11 Absolute vs. total by group (e.g., industry)	Same as 7 but use industry/country/sector in place of asset.	Same as 7 but by group
12 Relative currency weight	Measures the impact that currency exposure has on the active portfolio's total return, resulting from differences between managed country and benchmark country weights.	$\left[w_c^p(t-1)-w_c^b(t-1)\right]\times\left\{\left[r_b^c(t)-\ell_b^c(t)\right]-\left[r_b(t)-\ell_b(t)\right]\right\}$
13 Currency performance effect	Measures the impact that currency exposure has on the active portfolio's total return that results from the performance of different currencies.	$w_c^p(t-1)\times\left\{\left[r_p^c(t)-\ell_p^c(t)\right]-\left[r_b^c(t)-\ell_b^c(t)\right]\right\}$
14 Country currency weight	Measures how well a portfolio's currency exposure has been managed relative to the currency exposure in a benchmark portfolio.	12 + 13
15 Country allocation	Measures the impact on the active portfolio return from selecting different countries in proportions that are different from the benchmark.	$[w_c^p(t-1)-w_c^b(t-1)]\times[\ell_b^c(t)-\ell_b(t)]$
16 Country stock selection	Within each country, measures the impact that stock selection has on the active portfolio's total return. It provides a measure of a portfolio manager's ability to select stocks within a country.	$w_c^p(t-1)\times\left\{\sum_{j=1}^{J}\frac{w_{s(j)}^p(t-1)}{w_c^p(t-1)}\left[\ell_p^s c^{(j)}(t)-\ell_b^s c^{(j)}(t)\right]\right\}$
17 Country sector weight	Within each country, measures the impact of relative sector weightings on the active portfolio's total return.	$w_c^p(t-1)\times\left\{\sum_{j=1}^{J}\left[\frac{w_{s_c(j)}^p(t-1)}{w_c^p(t-1)}-\frac{w_{s_c(j)}^b(t-1)}{w_c^b(t-1)}\right]\left[\ell_{b\,(t)}^{s_c(j)}-\ell_b^c(t)\right]\right\}$
18 Currency contribution	Contribution to total return from currency exposure.	$\sum_{n=1}^{N}y_{n,j}(t)w_n(t-1)e_{nj}(t)$
19 Country contribution	Contribution to total return from country exposure.	$\sum_{n=1}^{N}q_{n,c}(t)w_n(t-1)R_n(t)\div\sum_{n=1}^{N}q_{n,c}(t)w_n(t-1)$

CHAPTER 20

Equity Risk Factor Models

Peter Zangari

INTRODUCTION

Factor models are pervasive in investment management practice. In this chapter we explain, in detail, the foundations of equity risk factor models. This chapter contributes to the general decision-making process, education, and research on factor models in three important ways:

1. We provide a taxonomy of the various types of factor models that are the focus of the investment management community. In so doing, we streamline a somewhat fragmented academic and industry literature on factor models and present a consistent terminology to study and understand factor models and their output.
2. This chapter serves as a blueprint for risk calculations that are based on linear cross-sectional factor models. Such models are widely used among equity investment professionals, and a detailed understanding is critical for practitioners who rely on this information. We provide exact formulas for many factor model–based risk measures.
3. We present some important empirical issues related to the practical implementation of factor models.

A thorough understanding of factor models requires an understanding of factors at both a theoretical and an empirical level. As a concept, factor models are simple and intuitive. They offer the researcher parsimony—the ability to describe a large set of security returns in terms of relatively few factors—and the capacity to identify common sources of correlations among security returns.[1] To the portfolio or risk manager, however, factor models are more than a theoretical construct. They offer such managers a way to quantify the risk and attribute return in their

[1]In addition, factor models allow managers to describe the variation of security returns in terms of a relatively small set of systematic components. So, instead of having to analyze potentially massive data sets, the goal of factor models is to allow managers to explain or describe the level of direction, variation, and covariation with other returns in terms of relatively few determinants.

portfolio construction process. Hence, the greatest strengths of factor models rest in their empirical applications.

Factor models have numerous applications. Investment management professionals use factor models to quantify a portfolio's return and risk characteristics. For example, factor models have been used in portfolio risk optimization, performance evaluation, performance attribution, and style analysis.

In addition to the variety of applications, factor models have served as a basis to estimate:

- Average, or unconditional returns—explaining differences in returns across a universe of stocks at a particular point in time.
- Expected, or conditional returns—forecasting the expected value of stock returns using historical information.
- Variances and covariances of returns—explaining the systematic variations and comovements among stock returns.

In this chapter, our focus is on applications of equity factor models for measuring risk. The rest of this chapter is organized as follows:

- We present a simple example of an equity factor model. This example sets the stage for a more formal introduction to factor models presented later.
- We present the basics of factor returns and exposures. We provide two examples of different types of exposure calculations.
- We provide a taxonomy of equity risk factor models. We organize factor models by observed and unobserved factor returns.
- We take a detailed look at the linear cross-sectional factor model. We present local and global factor models. Typically, global factor models incorporate country and currency factors whereas local factor models do not.
- We turn our attention to measuring and identifying sources of risk in a factor model. This section begins with definitions of various aspects of portfolios, then presents numerous formulas used in calculating contributions to risk, and concludes with an example from PACE, Goldman Sachs' proprietary risk and return attribution platform.
- Finally, we summarize the risk estimation process and show the various steps required to estimate a linear factor model in practice.

SIMPLE EQUITY FACTOR MODEL: AN EXAMPLE

What are factor models and what should managers know about them? We address these questions with an example that involves a particular application of a factor model. Specifically, we are interested in measuring the risk of a portfolio of stocks. The risk statistic that we calculate, whether it's standard deviation or some measure of Value at Risk (VaR), depends on the covariance matrix of stock returns. Hence, our focus is on estimating this covariance matrix.

Suppose that our current portfolio consists of four stocks and that all time is measured in months. To calculate the portfolio's covariance matrix for the following month, from t to $t + 1$, we would do the following:

1. Collect monthly excess returns[2] for each of the four stocks over the prior 60 months. The choice of 60 months is arbitrary and is used only for illustrative purposes.
2. Construct a 60 × 4 matrix of returns, $R(t)$, where each column of $R(t)$ corresponds to a historical time series of returns over the prior 60 months. For example, the first column of $R(t)$ represents the time series of mean-zero returns[3] for stock 1; the second column of $R(t)$ represents the time series of mean-zero returns for stock 2; and so on.
3. The one-month volatility forecast, at time t, is based on the simple covariance matrix estimator[4] $V(t)$:

$$\hat{V}(t) = \frac{1}{60} R(t)^T R(t) \tag{20.1}$$

where the superscript "T" represents the transpose of the return matrix.

The covariance matrix $V(t)$ has 10 elements (6 covariances and 4 variances). In general, if our portfolio consists of N stocks, then the covariance matrix consists of $N(N + 1)/2$ variances and covariances. Obviously, even moderate-sized portfolios require many variance and covariance estimates. In practice, it is not uncommon to have a portfolio consist of 100 stocks, in which case we would have to estimate 5,050 parameters (100 variances and 4,950 covariances). In order to have a proper covariance matrix (i.e., positive semidefinite), this would require that we have at least 100 historical returns (i.e., about eight years of data) for each asset. However, a stable covariance matrix[5] would require even more observations.

Factor models are of interest not only because they offer an intuitive understanding of the sources of risk and return, but also because they provide parsimony. And in covariance matrix estimation, parsimony is a virtue. Therefore, it should not be surprising that much work has gone into developing methods that provide a good estimate of $V(t)$ without requiring the estimation of a large number of parameters. The way that factor models provide parsimony should become clear in the following example.

Consider a factor model that describes four stock returns in terms of two factors. For the time being we treat factors as an abstract concept. A standard factor model, at time t, can be written as follows:

$$\begin{aligned}
r_1(t) &= B_{11}(t-1)F_1(t) + B_{12}(t-1)F_2(t) + u_1(t) \\
r_2(t) &= B_{21}(t-1)F_1(t) + B_{22}(t-1)F_2(t) + u_2(t) \\
r_3(t) &= B_{31}(t-1)F_1(t) + B_{32}(t-1)F_2(t) + u_3(t) \\
r_4(t) &= B_{41}(t-1)F_1(t) + B_{42}(t-1)F_2(t) + u_4(t)
\end{aligned} \tag{20.2}$$

[2]Briefly, excess returns are defined as the difference between total returns and the return on the one-month risk-free rate.

[3]We subtract the sample mean from these excess returns.

[4]We use the simple covariance matrix estimator just as an example. We could also employ an estimator of the covariance matrix that applies an exponential weighting scheme to the data.

[5]By "stable covariance matrix" we mean a covariance matrix with a low condition number.

where $r_n(t)$ = nth stock's monthly excess return from time $t-1$ to t ($n = 1, 2, 3, 4$)
$F_k(t)$ = Monthly factor returns from time $t-1$ to t ($k = 1, 2$)
$B_{nk}(t-1)$ = Factor loadings that are known at time $t-1$ (i.e., at the beginning of the tth month). These loadings measure the sensitivity between the factor returns and the original set of four returns ($n = 1, 2, 3, 4$; $k = 1, 2$)
$u_n(t)$ = nth stock's specific return from time $t-1$ to t

Using matrix notation, we can write (20.2) in a more condensed format:

$$R(t) = B(t-1)F(t) + u(t) \tag{20.3}$$

where $R(t)$ = 4×1 vector of excess stock returns from $t-1$ to t
$F(t)$ = 2×1 vector of factor returns from $t-1$ to t
$B(t-1)$ = 4×2 matrix of factor loadings that are known at time $t-1$
$u(t)$ = 4×1 vector of stock-specific returns from $t-1$ to t (it is assumed that these returns are uncorrelated with one another)

We use the factor model presented in (20.3) to write the covariance matrix of excess returns, $V(t)$, in terms of variances and covariances of the factor returns and the security-specific returns. Taking the variance of (20.3), we get

$$V(t) = B(t-1)\Sigma(t)B(t-1)^T + \Delta(t) \tag{20.4}$$

where $\Sigma(t)$ = 2×2 covariance matrix of factor returns
$\Delta(t)$ = 4×4 covariance matrix of specific returns (we assume that specific returns are uncorrelated; therefore, $\Delta(t)$ is a diagonal matrix with specific return variances as elements)

Equation (20.4) shows how the covariance matrix of stock returns can be written in terms of the covariance matrix of factor returns and the covariance matrix of stock-specific returns. Next, we describe how we can estimate $\Sigma(t)$, $\Delta(t)$, and the covariance matrix of stock returns.

Assume for the moment that the factor loadings matrix $B(t-1)$ is known at time $t-1$ and that we have 60 months of history on factor returns $F(t)$ ($t = 1, 2, \ldots, 60$). We can form an estimate of the stock return covariance matrix as follows.

1. Use the historical time series of factor returns over the past 60 months to estimate the factor return covariance matrix, $\hat{\Sigma}(t)$.
2. Use (20.3) to construct a time series of stock-specific returns that are defined as $u(t) = R(t) - B(t-1)F(t)$. This involves generating a 4×1 vector of specific returns, $u(t)$, each month (one month at a time) over the 60-month estimation period.
3. Use the time series of stock-specific returns to estimate the stock-specific covariance matrix $\hat{\Delta}(t)$. By assuming zero correlation among specific returns, this simply requires the estimation of stock-specific variances.
4. An estimate of the stock return covariance matrix is given by $\hat{V}(t) = B(t-1)\hat{\Sigma}(t)B(t-1)^T + \hat{\Delta}(t)$. Note that we are not restricted to estimate $\hat{\Sigma}(t)$ and $\hat{\Delta}(t)$ in any particular way.

FACTOR RETURNS AND EXPOSURES: THE BASICS

Thus far, factors and factor returns have been treated as abstract concepts. In this section we define factors and provide some examples of their practical application.

We begin with a definition. A factor is a random variable that, at a particular point in time, can explain or account for the variation among a set of security returns.[6] Put another way, a factor is a variable that is common to a set of security returns, influencing each return through its factor loading. There are five key points to remember about equity factors:

1. Their values take the form of factor returns. For example, if the market is a factor, then its value is the market return.
2. A factor is common to all stocks at a particular point in time.
3. Estimates of factor return covariance matrices are based on time series of factor returns.
4. Factor loadings *individualize* factor returns. Loadings measure the sensitivity of a stock's return to a factor return. Alternatively, we can say that a factor return measures the sensitivity of a stock's return over a period for a given change in the factor's exposure.
5. Stock-specific returns, $u(t)$, measure the difference between the nth stock's excess return and the factor return contribution (loadings times factor returns), $u(t) = R(t) - B(t-1)F(t)$.

Factors can be defined in a variety of ways. The definition of different factors leads us to consider different types of factor models. Some examples of factors include:

- Macroeconomic factors (e.g., gross domestic product and the default premium).
- Market factors (e.g., the capital-weighted market portfolio).
- Fundamental factors (e.g., price/earnings and price/book value).

Regardless of the type of factor, managers require a time series of their values (i.e., factor returns) so that we can estimate a factor return covariance matrix. For example, returns to macroeconomic factors, such as the U.S. default premium (measured as the difference between the return on a high-yield bond index and the return on long-term government bonds), are observed time series. And, at each point in time, one value of the default premium corresponds to all values of stock returns. While we know the value of the factor, we do not know its sensitivity (factor loading) to each stock return. Hence, we have to use time series information on stock returns and the default premium to estimate factor loadings. The loading on the default premium factor may appear as the coefficient in a regression of stock returns on the return to the default premium factor. Alternatively expressed, we estimate the loading from the time series model

[6] This set contains one or more security returns.

$$r_n(t) = B_{n,\text{default premium}} F_{\text{default premium}}(t) + u_n(t) \tag{20.5}$$

where $r_n(t)$ = Excess return on the nth stock at time t
$B_{n,\text{default premium}}$ = nth stock's loading on the default premium
$F_{\text{default premium}}(t)$ = Default premium at time t
$u_n(t)$ = nth stock's specific return

Numerical Example Suppose that the current (time t) one-period return on a stock is 3.0 percent. If the current default premium is 1.5 percent (i.e., $F_{\text{default premium}}(t)$ = 1.5%) and the factor's sensitivity or loading to this stock is 0.5 (i.e., $B_{n,\text{default premium}}$ = 0.5), then the stock's implied return due to the default premium is 0.75 percent (0.5 × 1.5%). The stock-specific return is 2.25 percent. Now, suppose that spreads are expected to widen over the forthcoming month by 50 basis points. Assuming a constant factor exposure, the expected change in the stock's return is 0.25 percent (0.5% × 0.5 = 0.25%). (We take the expected specific return to be zero.)

This simple example shows how, by using factor models, practitioners can address questions about the movement of different stocks by considering a change in the factor's return and exposure. Unfortunately, however, we do not always observe a time series of factor returns and, therefore, may be required to first estimate these returns.

Suppose that instead of using a macroeconomic factor we use a fundamental factor such as value. A common measure of a stock's exposure to the value factor is its ratio of net earnings to share price (E/P). In this case, we observe each stock's exposure to the value factor but not the factor itself—that is, we do not know the factor return. This is the complete opposite of the situation where we knew the default premium but not the exposure of each stock to the default premium.

Mathematically, this translates into observing each stock's factor loadings, $B_n(t-1)$, but not the factor return $F(t)$; that is, we know the value of the loading but not the factor return. Since we do not observe the factor return and we have information on a cross section of stocks, we estimate the return to the exposure to the value factor at a particular point in time, using a regression of N excess stock returns on N earnings-to-price exposures. Each time this regression is run, it produces one estimate of the value factor return. If we conduct these regressions over a period of time, say 60 consecutive months, then we can construct a time series of value factor returns. Once we have estimates of these factors, we can estimate the factor and stock-specific covariance matrix as described earlier. Note that the fundamental approach (value factor) is more computationally intensive than the time series method (macroeconomic factor) since we must first estimate the factor returns from a series of cross-sectional regressions.

We conclude this section by expounding on the notion of factor returns and exposures. The values of $F(t)$ in the cross-sectional approach are often referred to as factor returns. We offer two examples to help explain why the $F(t)$s in (20.2) are referred to as factor returns.

Example 1 Suppose that we have 100 stocks whose returns we want to explain in terms of one factor—the value factor. For a particular month, we collect returns for all 100 stocks as well as each stock's exposure to the value factor. Using these data, we estimate the factor return $F(t)$, which turns out to be 5 percent.[7] Suppose that, for a particular stock, its exposure to the value factor is measured to be two standard deviations[8] (2 std) above the mean of all stocks in some predefined universe of stocks; that is, $B(t - 1)$= 2 std for this stock. Using $F(t)$, we can determine the change in the *average* or expected stock return, given a change in exposure. In other words, we can address the question, what is the *return* to an increased exposure to stocks with high earnings-to-price values? It follows from Equation (20.2) that $\Delta E[r(t)] = \Delta B(t-1)E[F(t)]$ where $\Delta E[r(t)]$ and $E[F(t)]$ represent the expected change in stock return and the expected value of the factor return, respectively. If we expect a particular stock's exposure to the value factor to increase, say, 0.5 std—that is, the stock becomes more of a value play—then the expected change in its stock return, given this change, is

$$\begin{aligned} \Delta E[r(t)] &= \Delta B(t-1)F(t) \\ &= 0.5 \text{ std} \times 0.05 \\ &= 250 \text{ basis points} \end{aligned} \tag{20.6}$$

In this example, $F(t)$ represents the return from an increase in the exposure to value stocks. To see this, we can rewrite (20.6):

$$E[F(t)] = \frac{\Delta E[r(t)]}{\Delta B(t-1)} \tag{20.7}$$

So, $F(t)$ represents the change in the average excess return for an increase (decrease) in exposure to stocks with high earnings-to-price levels.

Example 2 Factor returns are sometimes defined by first constructing a so-called factor-mimicking portfolio (FMP). Simply put, an FMP is a portfolio whose returns mimic the behavior of some underlying factor. There is a variety of techniques available to construct FMPs. A simple way[9] to build a portfolio that mimics the behavior of, say, the value factor return works as follows.

1. First, sort all assets in your portfolio according to their E/P.
2. Split the sorted assets into two groups. The first group contains assets that fall in the top half of assets ranked by E/P. We refer to these assets collectively as

[7]An explanation of the factor return estimation procedures is provided in the section on cross-sectional regressions later in the chapter.

[8]Exposures are sometimes normalized so that they are comparable. This normalization process will be discussed in more detail in the section on standardizing exposures later in the chapter.

[9]The academic literature is replete with better ways to construct a factor-mimicking portfolio. Here, the example we provide is for expositional purposes only.

group H. The second group contains assets that fall in the bottom half of all assets ranked by E/P. We refer to these assets as group L.
3. Use the market values and returns on each asset to form group returns. That is, we compute the return on group H and group L, respectively.
4. The return to the value factor is defined as the difference between the return on group H and the return on group L.

The return *H* minus *L* represents a return on a zero investment strategy that is long the high E/P assets and short the low E/P assets. The return on this strategy is what is known as the factor return because it reflects movements in the underlying factor. A mimicking portfolio that exhibits large return volatility is consistent with the underlying factor contributing a substantial common component to return movements.

A TAXONOMY OF EQUITY FACTOR RISK MODELS

Equity risk factor models take a variety of forms. In this section we provide an overview of the different types of factor models that are used by practitioners. We categorize factor models based on whether the model assumes the factor returns are observed or unobserved. Factor models that rely on observed factor returns include the market model and the macroeconomic factor model. Alternatively, factor models that assume factor returns are unobserved and, therefore, require that we estimate their values include statistical, technical, and fundamental models.

Background

Understanding a factor model begins with understanding factors. Given the wide application of factor models and the different variables that factors attempt to explain, it should not be surprising that the term "factor" has come to mean almost anything. For example, Chan, Karceski, and Lakonishok (1998) offer the following categorization of factors:

- Macroeconomic
- Fundamental
- Technical
- Statistical
- Market

Within each of these sets of factors are different variables, each of which attempts to capture a particular feature of individual security returns. Figure 20.1 presents a classification of factors. In order to make this classification a bit less abstract, Table 20.1 presents examples of factors for each factor class.

In addition to the different types of factors, factor models are differentiated by the data and model estimation methods that are used to estimate factor returns. For the most part, this estimation process consists of a combination of cross section and time series modeling. Figure 20.2 shows the relationship between the type of factor

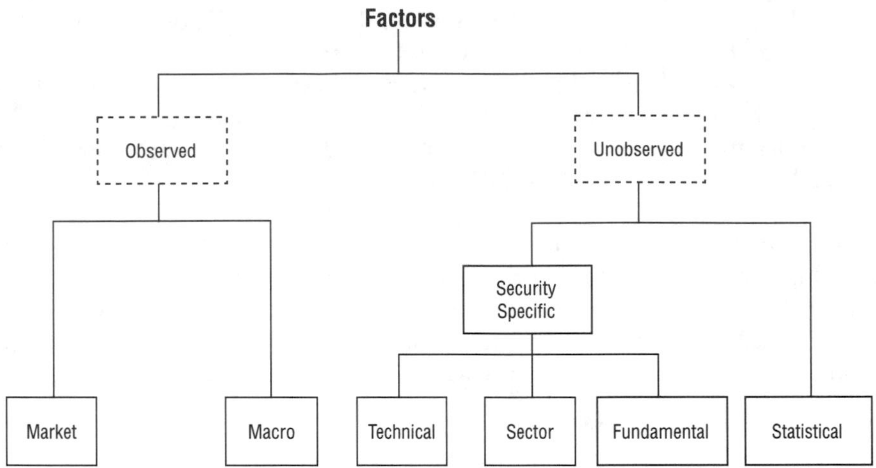

FIGURE 20.1 Hierarchy of Factors

and the data required to estimate the risk parameters of a factor model (i.e., factor return covariance matrix and specific variances).

In the next few sections, we explain the different methods shown in Figure 20.2. We introduce the reader to different types of factors so that the term "factor" becomes more precise. We begin by considering observed factors and then move on to factor models where the factor returns are unobserved.

It is important to note that in the factor models presented, factors are used to model the conditional mean of stock returns in equation (20.3). There are other types of factor models such as the one studied by King, Sentana, and Whadwani (1994) where factors are part of the conditional covariance matrix specification. We do not consider such factor models in this chapter.

Observed Factor Returns

The first class of factors that we consider is one that has observed factor returns. Two examples of factors that have observed returns are market factors and macroeconomic factors.

The Market The market model is probably the most common and simplest representation of a factor model. Suppose we want to model the relation between the ex-

TABLE 20.1 Examples of Factors

Factor Class	Examples
Market	S&P 500, Wilshire 5000, MSCI World indexes
Macroeconomic	Industrial production, unemployment rate, interest rates
Technical	Excess stock return on previous month, trading volumes
Sector	Energy, transportation, technology
Fundamental	Value, growth, return on equity
Statistical	Principal components

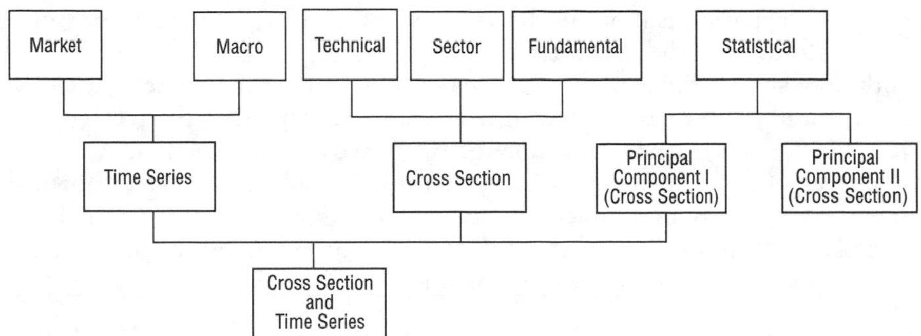

FIGURE 20.2 The Relationship between Factors, Data, and Model Estimation

cess return (over the risk-free rate) on a particular security and the return on the market portfolio. We assume that the number of securities totals *N*. The mathematical expression for the excess return on the *n*th security can be described by the following one-factor model:

$$r_n(t) - r^f(t) = \alpha_n(t) + \beta_n(t)[r^m(t) - r^f(t)] + e_n(t) \tag{20.8}$$

where $r_n(t)$ = Total return on the *n*th security at time *t*
$r^f(t)$ = Return on a risk-free security at time *t*
$\alpha_n(t)$ = Stock return's alpha for the *n*th return (alpha also represents the expected return on a stock that has zero correlation to the market)
$\beta_n(t)$ = Market beta (beta measures the covariation between the market and the security return)
$r^m(t)$ = Return on a market portfolio at time *t*
$e_n(t)$ = Mean-zero disturbance term at time *t*

Equation (20.8) describes how the excess return of the *n*th security varies over time with the return on the market portfolio, its uncorrelated expected value (alpha), and an idiosyncratic term. The factor return in this model is $r^m(t) - r^f(t)$ and it represents the systematic component of the *n*th stock's return. The idiosyncratic component of the *n*th stock's return is given by $\alpha_n(t) + e_n(t)$.

In practice, in order to estimate the risk of an asset or portfolio using the market model we must estimate the market beta. This is done via time series regression. For example, we may collect, say, monthly stock and market returns over the past five years. We then regress[10] 60 excess stock returns on a constant and 60 market portfolio returns (over the risk-free rate). This yields an estimate of alpha and the market beta. Beta measures the sensitivity between the *n*th stock's excess return and the market portfolio return over this five-year period. In addition to the estimates of alpha and the market beta, practitioners want to know how much of the variation in excess returns is explained by the variation in market returns. The R-squared statistic provides such a measure. Specifically, the R-squared provides a

[10]Due to the statistical properties of the stock's return and the market return, estimation may involve more than ordinary least squares.

measure of the linear relationship between excess returns and the return on the market portfolio (over the risk-free rate).

Although simple, the market model may not offer the practitioner a useful way to measure and explain risk. A manager may mistakenly select the wrong market portfolio in the analysis or may simply be interested in a richer model to help explain sources of risk and return. Also, Fama and French (1996) have shown that the market portfolio does a rather poor job at explaining movements in individual stock returns. The market return is not the only factor that may explain movements in excess stock returns, and therefore more factors are needed.

Macroeconomic Factors It is natural to think that stock returns reflect the state of the economy so that various measures of macroeconomic conditions serve as a basis for a set of additional factors. Chen, Roll, and Ross (1986) have investigated whether macroeconomic factors can explain stock returns. Examples of macroeconomic factors include: (1) the growth rate in monthly industrial production; (2) a measure of default premium (discussed earlier), measured as the difference between the monthly return on a high-yield bond index and the return on long-term government bonds; (3) the real interest rate; (4) the maturity premium, measured as the difference between return on the long-term government bond and the one-month Treasury bill return; and (5) the change in monthly expected inflation.

We incorporate macroeconomic factors into the market model as follows. Assume that, in addition to the market factor, there are $K - 1$ other factors that impact the nth security's excess return at time t. These additional factors enter into the market model through the residual or error, which for each security reflects the extent to which a stock's return is out of alignment with the expected relationship to the market portfolio return. Residual returns for common stocks arise in part from common factors that extend across many stocks, and in part from specific returns, which are unique to an individual company. Taking these issues into consideration, the market model now takes the following form:

$$r_n(t) - r^f(t) = \alpha_n(t) + \beta_n(t)[r^m(t) - r^f(t)] + e_n(t) \tag{20.9}$$

$$e_n(t) = \gamma_{n,1}(t)f_1(t) + \gamma_{n,2}(t)f_2(t) + \cdots + \gamma_{n,K-1}(t)f_{K-1}(t) + u_n(t) \tag{20.10}$$

where $f_k(t)$ = Return on the kth macroeconomic factor at time t
$\gamma_{n,k}(t)$ = Loading (exposure) of the kth factor on the nth asset
$u_n(t)$ = nth security's idiosyncratic return

Note that in (20.10) we no longer assume that the residual error term, $e_n(t)$, has a zero mean. In fact, its expected value will depend on the macroeconomic factor returns and factor loadings. Combining (20.9) and (20.10), we get the standard form of the so-called market model:

$$\begin{aligned} r_n(t) - r^f(t) = \alpha_n(t) &+ \beta_n(t)[r^m(t) - r^f(t)] + \gamma_{n,1}(t)f_1(t) \\ &+ \gamma_{n,2}(t)f_2(t) + \cdots + \gamma_{n,K-1}(t)f_{K-1}(t) + u_n(t) \end{aligned} \tag{20.11}$$

Time series regression methods can be used to estimate (20.11).

Unobserved Factor Returns

In the preceding section we briefly considered observed factors. Such factors appear as time series whose values are common to all stocks at a particular point in time. In this section we consider models where the values of factors are unobserved. Two examples of such factors are fundamental and industry factors.

Fundamental, Technical, and Industry (Sector) Factors When factor returns are unobserved, we need to estimate their values using information on their exposures and stock returns. This estimation is done using either a cross section of returns or their time series.

In the case where factors are unobserved and they are defined in terms of fundamental, technical, or industry designations, a popular factor model is a linear cross-sectional model.

$$R(t) = B(t-1)F(t) + u(t) \tag{20.12}$$

where $R(t)$ = N-vector of one-period asset (stock) returns
$B(t-1)$ = $N \times K$ matrix of asset exposures to factors as of time $t-1$
$F(t)$ = K-vector of one-period factor returns
$u(t)$ = N-vector of one-period specific returns

The columns of $B(t-1)$ represent exposures to a particular factor. The values of $F(t)$ are estimated, typically, by a cross-sectional regression of time t returns on time $t-1$ exposures. We explain the linear cross-sectional factor model in more detail later in this chapter.

Principal Components Principal component analysis (PCA) is often used to extract a number of unobserved factors from a set of returns. It is important to review principal component methods for two reasons. First, some commercially available risk systems use principal component analysis as part of their risk models. Second, for many practitioners principal components are what often come to mind when thinking about factors and factor models. We begin by reviewing the standard principal component method to estimate factors, and then discuss an alternative method to estimate principal components. This alternative method is known as the asymptotic principal component (APC) method.

A typical application of PCA to factor models[11] begins with the factor model (20.12) for $t = 1, \ldots, T$. We assume that the factor returns are orthogonal and specific returns are uncorrelated so that the variance of $R(t)$ is

$$V(t) = B(t-1)B(t-1)^T + \Delta(t) \tag{20.13}$$

where $\Delta(t)$ is diagonal. We can relax the assumption that security-specific returns are uncorrelated and allow for nonzero off-diagonal elements of $\Delta(t)$, in which case

[11]See, for example, Johnson & Wichern (1982). In this section we explain a very simple method to extract factors. There are other approaches that involve, for example, maximum likelihood estimation. For an application of maximum likelihood to estimate factors see Litterman, Knez, and Scheinkman (1994).

we will be working with a so-called approximate factor structure. However, for the following exposition we maintain the standard factor model.

We assume that $\Delta(t)$ is small enough to be ignored, so that

$$V(t) \cong B(t-1)B(t-1)^T \tag{20.14}$$

In the PCA approach, we first need to estimate the exposures matrix. A simple sample estimator of $V(t)$ is

$$\hat{V}(t) = \frac{1}{T}\sum_{j=0}^{T-1} R(t-j)R(t-j)^T \tag{20.15}$$

We find the exposures matrix, B, by decomposing $V(t)$ in terms of its eigensystem[12]

$$V(t) = P(t)\Theta(t)P(t)^T \tag{20.16}$$

where $P(t) = N \times N$ matrix of eigenvectors with each eigenvector stacked columnwise; that is, $P(t) = [p_1(t) \mid p_2(t) \mid \ldots \mid p_N(t)]$ and $p_n(t)$ represents the nth column of $P(t)$

$\Theta(t) = N \times N$ diagonal matrix with the eigenvalues $\theta_n(t)$ $(n = 1, \ldots, N)$ as its elements.

$$\Theta(t) = \begin{bmatrix} \theta_1(t) & 0 & 0 & 0 \\ 0 & \theta_2(t) & 0 & 0 \\ \vdots & \vdots & \ddots & \vdots \\ 0 & 0 & 0 & \theta_N(t) \end{bmatrix} \tag{20.17}$$

It follows from (20.14) and (20.16) that $BB^T = P(t)\Theta(t)P(t)^T$ and the factor loading matrix B is determined by the K largest eigenvalues and their corresponding eigenvectors; that is,

$$\hat{B} = P\Theta^{-1/2} = \left[\sqrt{\theta_1}\, p_1(t) \mid \sqrt{\theta_2}\, p_2(t) \mid \ldots \mid \sqrt{\theta_K}\, p_K(t)\right] \tag{20.18}$$

Equation (20.18) says that each column of the factor loading matrix, B, consists of an $N \times 1$ eigenvector scaled by its corresponding eigenvalue. Given our estimate of $B(t-1)$, we can estimate the factor returns, $F(t)$, by regressing $R(t)$ on $\hat{B}$. The regression yields:

[12]Factor models suffer from what can be referred to as "rotational indeterminacy," meaning that the parameters of the factor model are determined only up to some nonsingular matrix.

$$\hat{F}(t) = \left(\hat{B}^T\hat{B}\right)^{-1}\hat{B}^T R(t) \tag{20.19}$$

or, more specifically

$$\hat{F}(t) = \begin{bmatrix} \frac{1}{\sqrt{\theta_1(t)}} p_1(t)^T R(t) \\ \frac{1}{\sqrt{\theta_2(t)}} p_2(t)^T R(t) \\ \vdots \\ \frac{1}{\sqrt{\theta_K(t)}} p_K(t)^T R(t) \end{bmatrix} \tag{20.20}$$

The term $p_K(t)^T R(t)$ represents the kth principal component of returns. Equation (20.20) shows that each estimated factor return is a simple weighted average of the asset returns where the weights are given by its corresponding (scaled) eigenvector. In practice, estimating the principal components over time generates a time series of factor returns.

This concludes our discussion of standard PCA; next we explain the asymptotic principal component (APC) method developed by Connor and Koraczyk (1986).

Connor and Koraczyk (1986, 1988) apply an asymptotic principal component technique introduced by Chamberlain and Rothschild (1983) to estimate the factors influencing asset returns. The APC method is somewhat different from the typical Wall Street application of principal component analysis.

To motivate the asymptotic principal component approach, recall that factors are pervasive in that they relate to all N securities at a point in time. In practice, it is typical to have many more securities than historical observations; that is, N (number of assets) is much bigger than T (number of observations over time) and that the K market factors are not observed. We write the return process for each of the N assets over all T time periods—compare to Equation (20.12)—as

$$R = BF + u \tag{20.21}$$

where R = $N \times T$ matrix of excess returns; each row of R represents a time series of excess returns on the nth security
B = $N \times K$ matrix of factor loadings
F = $K \times T$ matrix of factor returns; each row of F represents a time series of factor returns
u = $N \times T$ matrix of specific returns

The asymptotic principal component method is similar to standard PCA except that it relies on large sample (asymptotic) results as the number of cross sections (N) grows large. From a practical perspective, standard PCA and APC differ in how we estimate $V(t)$. In APC we derive factors from the $T \times T$ cross product matrix

$$\hat{V} = \frac{1}{N} R^T R \tag{20.22}$$

$\hat{V}$ is the cross-sectional counterpart to $\hat{V}(t)$ given in (20.15). The K factors are given by the first K eigenvectors of $\hat{V}$. That is, each eigenvector represents a time series of a particular factor. Note, however, as in the case of standard principal components there is an indeterminacy issue. Connor and Koraczyk show that factors can be determined only up to some nonsingular linear transformation.

This concludes our discussion of principal component analysis.

A DETAILED LOOK AT THE LINEAR CROSS-SECTIONAL FACTOR MODEL

In this section we explain the linear cross-sectional factor model, which forms the basis of estimating risk. In order to estimate risk, we need to generate a time series of factor returns. Estimation of factor returns begins by assuming that each asset has an exposure to one or more factors. These exposures to factors are measurable and may be industry classifications, investment style exposures (e.g., book-to-price), or something else. Given the exposures, returns on individual securities are regressed, cross-sectionally, on the factor exposures. The estimates from this regression are the one-period factor returns. Repeating this process over time generates a time series of factor returns.

Local Framework

The *local* linear factor model posits a relationship between a cross section of returns and asset exposures, returns to factors, and specific returns. Specifically, the model describes the cross section of N ($n = 1, \ldots, N$) asset returns as a function of K ($k = 1, \ldots, K$) factors plus N specific returns. Mathematically, we have

$$R^{\ell}(t) = B^{\ell}(t-1)F^{\ell}(t) + u^{\ell}(t) \tag{20.23}$$

where $R^{\ell}(t)$ = N-vector of local excess asset returns (over the [local] risk-free rate) from time $t - 1$ to t. We take t as the current date.

$B^{\ell}(t-1)$ = $N \times K$ matrix of exposures that are available as of $t - 1$. In practice, the factor exposures may not be updated at the same frequency as the asset returns. In this case the information in the matrix B will be dated earlier than $t - 1$.

$F^{\ell}(t)$ = K-vector of factor returns. The return period is from $t - 1$ to t.

$u^{\ell}(t)$ = N-vector of mean-zero specific returns, from $t - 1$ to t, with covariance matrix $\sigma^2(t)I$ where $I = N \times N$ identity matrix

$\sigma^2(t)$ = Variance of $u^{\ell}(t)$ at time t

The security returns in (20.23) are computed as follows. Let $R^{\ell}_n(t)$ represent the nth asset of $R^{\ell}(t)$. $R^{\ell}_n(t)$ is defined as:

$$R_n^\ell(t) = \frac{P_n^\ell(t) + d_n(t-h,t) - P_n^\ell(t-1)}{P_n^\ell(t-1)} \tag{20.24}$$

where $P_n^\ell(t)$ = Time t local price of security or asset
$d_n(t-h,t)$ = Dividend (per share) paid out at time t for period $t-h$ through t

Global Framework

In the *global* framework we begin by defining exchange rates. Exchange rates are defined as the reporting currency over the base currency (reporting/base). The base currency is sometimes referred to as the risk currency. For example, USD/GBP would be the exchange rate where the reporting currency is the U.S. dollar and the base or risk currency is the British pound.

Suppose a portfolio with USD as its reporting currency has holdings in German, Australian, and Japanese equities. The base currencies in this example are EUR, AUD, and JPY, respectively. The total return of each equity position consists of the local return on equity and the return on base currency.

We assume that a generic portfolio contains N assets ($n = 1, \ldots, N$). Let $P_n^\ell(t)$ represent the local price of the nth asset at time t. For example, $P_n^\ell(t)$ represents the price, in euros, of one share of Siemens stock. $X_{ij}(t)$ is the exchange rate expressed as the ith currency per unit of currency j. For example, with USD as the reporting currency, the exchange rate $X_{ij}(t)$ = USD/EUR (i is USD and j is EUR) is used to convert Siemens equity (expressed in euros) into USD. In general, the exchange rate is expressed as reporting over base currency. Note that this may differ from the way currency is quoted in the foreign exchange market.

It follows from these definitions that the price of the nth asset expressed in reporting currency is

$$P_n(t) = P_n^\ell(t)X_{ij}(t) \tag{20.25}$$

We use equation (20.25) as a basis for defining the reporting return, local return, and exchange rate return. The total return of an asset or portfolio is simply the return that incorporates both the local return and the exchange rate return. Following directly from equation (20.25), an asset's reporting return, using percent returns, is defined as

$$\begin{aligned} R_n(t) &= \left[1 + R_n^\ell(t)\right]\left[1 + E_{ij}(t)\right] - 1 \\ &= R_n^\ell(t) + E_{ij}(t) + R_n^\ell(t) \times E_{ij}(t) \end{aligned} \tag{20.26}$$

where $R_n(t)$ = One-period total reporting return on the nth asset
$R_n^\ell(t)$ = One-period local return on the nth asset
$E_{ij}(t)$ = One-period return on the ith exchange rate per unit of currency j

$$E_{ij}(t) = X_{ij}(t)/X_{ij}(t-1) - 1$$

Combining the local factor model with equation (20.26), we can write the linear factor model in terms of total returns:

$$R(t) = B^{\ell}(t-1)F^{\ell}(t) + u^{\ell}(t) + E_{ij}(t) + xc(t) \qquad (20.27)$$

where $xc(t) = R_n^{\ell}(t) \times E_{ij}(t)$ is a cross term between local returns and exchange rate returns.

Equation (20.27) allows us to explain the cross section of international asset returns. So, for example, we can identify a set of factors that explain the cross-sectional dispersion of U.S., European, and Japanese stock returns.

Finally, note that in equation (20.27), $F^{\ell}(t)$ is not restricted exclusively to so-called local factor returns. As we show later, $F^{\ell}(t)$ may include returns to global factors such as the Global Industry Classification Standard (GICS) classifications.

Having explained the basic framework for the local and global models, we will now describe how the asset exposures in these models are constructed.

Asset Exposures

In the linear cross-sectional factor model, exposures are defined at the asset level and then aggregated to generate portfolio exposures. Each asset is related to (i.e., has exposure to) some factor. For example, an asset can have exposure to:

- Itself.
- A particular industry or sector.
- A country (local market).
- A currency.
- Investment styles and/or risk factors.

Examples of Asset Exposures An asset's exposure to a particular factor depends on the type of exposure we are dealing with. For example, typically an asset's exposure to an industry is either one (the asset belongs to an industry) or zero (the asset does not belong to an industry). On the other hand, consider the calculation of an asset's exposure to volatility. When computing this exposure, three steps are usually involved:

1. We compute some measure of historical volatility for each asset. This is known as the raw exposure.
2. We define an estimation universe and compute the average volatility exposure across all assets, as well as the standard deviation of volatility exposure (again, across all assets).
3. We standardize the value of each raw volatility exposure by subtracting the mean and then dividing by the standard deviation.

The next section discusses various types of exposures covering industries, investment styles, countries, and currencies.

Industry Exposures Probably the easiest set of exposures to understand is industry exposures. An asset's exposure to an industry is usually one if it is in that industry, zero otherwise. Some classification schemes allocate an asset's exposure to multiple industries. For example, rather than allocating a company 100 percent to computer hardware, a company may have an allocation 60 percent computer hardware and 40 percent electronic equipment. For a given asset, the sum of industry allocations across all industries is equal to one (or 100 percent).

Industry assignments are provided by various vendors; some of the more popular are presented in Table 20.2. The Global Industry Classification Standard, which has been developed by Standard & Poor's and Morgan Stanley Capital International, provides a consistent set of global sector and industry definitions. Note that each industry classification scheme has associated with it a set of sector definitions. Sectors are groups of industries and provide a coarser grouping of assets.

Investment Style/Risk Exposures Also known as risk exposures, investment style exposures capture an asset's sensitivity to a particular investment strategy. For example, a portfolio may have a high exposure to large-cap assets. This exposure would come about from either an overweight in large-cap stocks and/or an underweight of small-cap stocks, or some combination of both.

Table 20.3 provides some examples of investment style factors. We provide a brief description of each factor and an example of how we measure an asset's exposure to the factor.

Country or Local Market Exposures We present two ways in which to define an asset's country exposure. In the first approach, an asset exposure takes a value of one if it belongs to a country, zero otherwise. An important question is, what do we mean by the term *belongs*? To answer the question, we can think of two types of associations that a company can have with a country:

1. ***Country of domicile***—the country where a company has been registered.
2. ***Country of issuance***—the country where stock has been issued. This is the same location as the stock exchange. Note that certain stocks may be issued in

TABLE 20.2 Some Popular Industry Classification Vendors by Region

Market	Vendor
United States	Russell, Barra, Standard & Poor's (pre-GICS), GICS
Canada	MSCI (pre-GICS), GICS
Europe	FTSE, MSCI (pre-GICS), Dow Jones STOXX, GICS
Japan	Topix, GICS
Asia except Japan	GICS
Global	MSCI (pre-GICS), GICS

GICS—Global Industry Classification Standard.
MSCI—Morgan Stanley Capital International.
FTSE—Result of joint effort between the *Financial Times* and the London Stock Exchange.

TABLE 20.3 Examples of Investment Style Asset Exposures

Factor	Brief Description	How Calculated
Volatility	This factor is designed to capture the relative volatility of assets. Assets that have high (low) historical volatility have a high (low) exposure to the volatility factor.	An asset's exposure to volatility may be computed as the standard deviation of its historical returns.
Momentum	This factor captures the common variation in returns related to historical price behavior. Assets that had positive excess returns in the recent past are grouped separately from those that displayed negative excess returns. Assets that have high (low) excess returns over the risk-free rate have a high (low) exposure to the momentum factor.	An asset's exposure to the momentum factor may be computed as its cumulative return over the previous 12 months over the risk-free rate.
Market capitalization	Also known as the size factor, this factor distinguishes among assets on the basis of their company's market capitalization. Companies with large (small) market capitalization have high (low) exposure to the size factor.	An asset's exposure to this factor is defined as the observed market capitalization of the factor.
Value	This factor distinguishes among companies on the basis of their value orientations.	An asset's exposure to value may be defined as the ratio of its price to book value.

more than one location (e.g., Allied-Irish stock shares are traded in both Dublin and London).

In general, there can be problems with using the country of domicile as defining a country's exposure. A good example of this is companies that are domiciled in Bermuda. Clearly, a large part of their market risk may be independent of Bermuda's local economic effects.

An alternative approach to defining an asset's exposure is to use local market betas. For example, an asset's exposure to a particular country, using realized betas, may be computed as follows:

Step 1 Assign each asset to a country or countries.

Step 2 Identify the market portfolio corresponding to each country. This portfolio is referred to as the local market index.

Step 3 Regress the returns of the asset on the returns of the local market index to get the beta.

Step 4 The estimated value of beta is that asset's exposure to the country.

This four-step process applies to estimating multiple country exposures (i.e., multiple betas) for a particular asset. In this case, the regression in step 3 becomes a multivariate regression.

Within the context of the local model, we can estimate the return to the local market. In the case where the exposures matrix consists of a vector of ones—that is, a constant—the corresponding factor return may be interpreted as the return on the market after controlling for other local factors (such as industry and investment styles). Another way of deriving the return on the market is to use local market betas as each asset's exposure to the local market. In the case of the global model, if one of the columns of the exposures matrix is a vector of ones, then the corresponding factor return is the global factor return.

Currency Exposures An asset's currency exposure attempts to capture how sensitive its returns are to the returns on a particular currency. Currency exposure may be computed in the same way as country exposure. For example, if you hold IBM stock that trades in Germany, your country exposure is to United States and the currency exposure is to the euro.

Standardizing Exposures In practice, we standardize some asset exposures to investment style factors. A primary reason for doing so is to make exposures across different investment styles comparable. In other words, the values of different types of exposures can be very different, and, therefore, we need to rescale them in such a way as to make their comparisons useful. Take the example of comparing an asset's exposure to market size and volatility.

One measure of an asset's market size exposure is the square root of its current market capitalization. A company may have a market capitalization of $1 billion, which produces a market size exposure of $31,663. The same asset's exposure to volatility may be 24 percent (historical volatility annualized). Therefore, any such analysis comparing $31,663 and 24 percent would be more meaningful if these values were converted to some standardized units. After standardizing, we may find that the asset's market exposure and volatility exposure turn out to be 1.0 and 1.5 standard deviations, respectively. As explained in more detail later, we interpret these numbers as showing that this asset has a high exposure to the market size and volatility factors.

We discuss two methodologies for standardizing asset exposures. The first approach works as follows. For a particular exposure (e.g., market size), carry out the following steps.

Step 1 Define the universe of assets over which a particular group of exposures will be standardized.

Step 2 Compute the average exposure of this universe where the average is based on the market capitalization weights of each asset.

Step 3 Compute the simple standard deviation of exposures for this universe.

Step 4 An asset's standardized exposure is defined as the raw (original) exposure, centered around the mean (computed in step 2), all divided by the standard deviation of exposures.

$$\text{Standardized exposure} = \frac{\text{Raw exposure} - \text{Cap-weighted mean exposure}}{\text{Standard deviation of exposures}}$$

The resulting standardized exposures from this approach are measured in units of standard deviation. In practice, there are some variations to this methodology. For example, the universe used to standardize investment style exposures may be based on the individual assets industry classification. Suppose we were going to standardize the size factor according to this approach. In this case, we would first group all size exposures (measured by market capitalization) according to their respective companies' industry designations. So, the market caps of stocks belonging to the automotive industry would make up one group, all financial stocks would make up another group, and so on. Next, within each group we would compute the mean market capitalization (mean exposure) and the standard deviation of the market capitalizations (standard deviation of exposures). Third, we would standardize each asset's exposure by its group (i.e., industry) mean and group standard deviation.

Chan, Karecski, and Lakonishok (1998) suggest an alternative approach for standardization. Their methodology consists of three steps.

Step 1 Define the universe of assets over which a particular group of exposures is to be standardized.

Step 2 Rank exposures.

Step 3 Rescale the ranked exposures so that their values lie between 0 and 1.

$$\text{Standardized exposure} = \frac{\text{Rank of raw exposure} - 1}{\text{Maximum (Rank of raw exposure} - 1)}$$

How Asset Exposures Are Used in a Linear Factor Model In the case of the linear factor model, asset exposures measure the sensitivity between returns on factors (e.g., momentum) and the asset's return. To show this, let's consider a three-asset, two-factor example: One of the factors is market size, while the other is an industry—computer hardware. Moreover, assume that we use the first method when it comes to standardizing exposures. We assume that asset 1 has an exposure of 1.0 standard deviation to market size and is in the computer hardware industry. Assets 2 and 3 have exposures of –1.0 and 0.5 standard deviations to market size and both are not in the computer hardware (HW) industry. The linear factor model posits the following relationship:

$$\begin{aligned}
\text{Asset 1's total return} &= 1.0 \times \text{Return to market size} \\
&\quad + 1 \times \text{Return to computer HW} \\
&\quad + \text{Asset 1's specific return} \qquad (20.28) \\
\text{Asset 2's total return} &= -1.0 \times \text{Return to market size} \\
&\quad + \text{Asset 2's specific return} \\
\text{Asset 3's total return} &= 0.5 \times \text{Return to market size} \\
&\quad + \text{Asset 3's specific return}
\end{aligned}$$

Equation (20.28) shows that asset 1's total return is positively related to the return on the market size factor. This means that, holding all other things constant, an increase in the return to market size will lead to an increase in asset 1's return. Similarly, the same increase will lead to a decrease in asset 2's return, again, holding all things equal. The exposures govern the sensitivity between the returns on the factors and the returns on the assets. Figure 20.3 shows the relationship between the time exposures and total returns computed.

Note that in the linear factor risk model, we try to explain the cross section of asset returns at a point in time (time t) in terms of exposures as of the previous period.

SOME IMPORTANT PRACTICAL CONSIDERATIONS

Futures Some assets represent composites—that is, they consist of one or more assets. An example of this is a futures contract on a stock index (e.g., S&P 500 futures). In this case, the overall risk (and return) provided by the futures contract depends on the value of the underlying index (e.g., S&P 500 index). We recommend that practitioners compute the exposure of this contract to factors as follows:

Step 1 Identify each asset contained in the underlying index.

Step 2 Compute the factor exposures of each asset using the methodology described earlier.

Step 3 Multiply the weight of each asset in the index by the asset exposure.

Step 4 The futures contract's exposure to a particular factor is given by the sum of the values computed in step 3 for that factor.

ADRs and GDRs American depositary receipts (ADRs) are securities traded in the United States and issued by U.S. depository institutions that represent equity shares of foreign-based companies. For U.S. investors, ADRs provide an alternative to investing in overseas equities directly without the inconveniences such as currency conversion and foreign settlement procedures. For non-U.S. investors, ADRs provide an alternative way to own shares of a company without holding its stock locally. Holders of ADRs, will not have exposure to the same level of currency risk as those who hold the underlying stock in its original country of domicile.

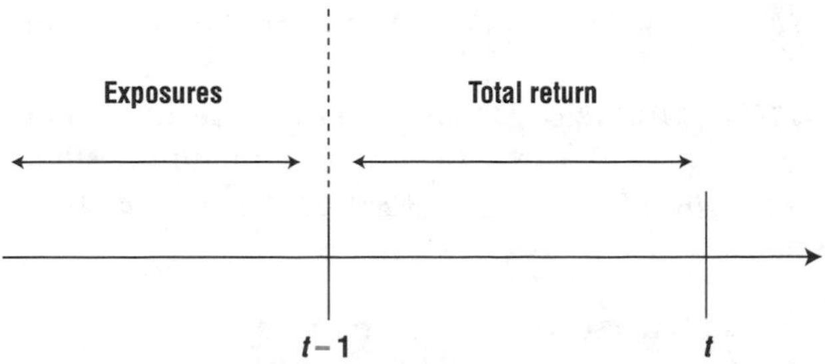

FIGURE 20.3 Time Line of Exposures

ADRs are treated in the same manner as U.S. securities for all legal and administrative purposes. The main advantages of ADRs are (1) there is no currency conversion in trading and receiving dividends, (2) they help in minimizing higher overseas transaction costs and custodial fees, and (3) there is uniformity in information available due to mandatory disclosures.

Histories In order to generate a time series of returns to factors, histories of exposures are required. Often, it may be difficult to obtain/procure comprehensive historical exposures. In addition, the definition of exposures can change over time, making it necessary to link old and new classifications. For example, the Internet became a new industry classification according to some schemes in 1999. In order to estimate the risk associated with investing in Internet stocks, the volatility of the returns to the Internet industry is required. This volatility estimate requires a time series of returns to the Internet industry, which, in turn, requires a time series of Internet exposures. If we need three years of history to estimate Internet volatility, one question would be, what was the return to the Internet industry in 1996?

In order to answer this question, we could find proxy industries that have similar price behavior to the Internet industry at a time when we have no exposures to the Internet. One example of such a proxy would be the commercial services industry. In this case, we would use the returns to this industry as a substitute for the unknown returns to the Internet industry.

Estimating Factor Returns

Equation (20.27) provides us with a mathematical description of a linear factor model. In this section we explain how we estimate the factor returns, $F^{\ell}(t)$, which are required to estimate risk. Briefly, a time series of factor and specific returns are generated as follows:

Step 1 Define a set of exposures to factors for each asset in the estimation universe.

Step 2 At each point in time (e.g., each day) run a cross-sectional regression of asset returns $[R^{\ell}(t)]$ on a set of exposures $[B^{\ell}(t-1)]$. This requires asset returns from period $t-1$ to t (where t denotes one day) and exposures as of period $t-1$. In some cases, however, exposures and asset returns are updated at different frequencies.

Step 3 A time series of factor returns, $F^{\ell}(t)$, and specific returns, $u^{\ell}(t)$, is generated by repeating these regressions over successive periods.

Define Assets Used in Estimating Factor Returns The estimation universe mentioned earlier is a group of security returns that are used to estimate the factor returns. It comprises one of four universes that we define in the factor return estimation process.

1. The *asset universe* is the set of all assets tracked.
2. The *estimation universe* represents the set of all assets used to estimate factor returns. Estimation universes can be defined in a variety of ways. For example,

in the United States we may define an estimation universe in terms of U.S. benchmark portfolios (e.g., Frank Russell 3000).

3. The *nonestimation universe* represents all the assets that have exposure and return information but do not qualify for the estimation universe. These assets may be excluded on the basis that they have extreme returns.
4. The *proxy universe* represents all assets that do not have exposure information or lack other data that are required to estimate factor returns. IPOs are examples of assets that fall in the proxy universe.

This information forms the basis for factor return estimation. Note that factor return estimation does not require *any* portfolio-level information.

Cross-Sectional Regressions Our main objective is to use a set of asset exposures to explain the cross-sectional dispersion of asset returns. At a point in time (e.g., a day), factor returns are estimated from the cross-sectional regression model in equation (20.23). Under standard assumptions, $u^{\ell}(t)$ is an N-vector of mean-zero specific returns with covariance matrix $\sigma^2(t)I$ where I is an $N \times N$ identity matrix. Note that we are assuming that the specific returns are homoscedastic—the variances are constant across security returns.

The ordinary least squares (OLS) estimate of $F^{\ell}(t)$ is given by

$$F^{\ell}(t) = \left[B^{\ell}(t-1)^T B^{\ell}(t-1)\right]^{-1} B^{\ell}(t-1)^T R^{\ell}(t) \tag{20.29}$$

Ordinary least squares estimation assumes that the covariance matrix of specific returns is $\sigma^2(t)I$, and that the variances of specific returns are constant across assets (i.e., returns are homoscedastic). In practice, this assumption is likely to be violated, which would lead to inefficient estimates as described by the OLS estimator. Alternatively expressed, a more reasonable description of the covariance matrix of specific returns, $u^{\ell}(t)$, is given by

$$\Sigma(t) = \begin{bmatrix} \sigma_1^2(t) & 0 & 0 & 0 \\ 0 & \sigma_2^2(t) & 0 & 0 \\ 0 & 0 & \ddots & 0 \\ 0 & 0 & 0 & \sigma_N^2(t) \end{bmatrix} \qquad \sigma_i^2(t) \neq \sigma_j^2(t) \qquad \text{for } i \neq j \tag{20.30}$$

We can transform $\Sigma(t)$ into a homoscedastic covariance matrix, $\sigma^2(t)I$, by making some assumption about the relationship between each asset's specific variance, $\sigma_n^2(t)$, and a "common variance," $\sigma^2(t)$. One specification is

$$\sigma_n^2(t) = v_n(t)\sigma^2(t) \tag{20.31}$$

where $v_n(t)$ is a scalar that captures differences in volatilities across assets. In this case,

$$\Sigma(t) = \sigma^2(t)\begin{bmatrix} v_1(t) & 0 & 0 & 0 \\ 0 & v_2(t) & 0 & 0 \\ 0 & 0 & \ddots & 0 \\ 0 & 0 & 0 & v_N(t) \end{bmatrix} = \sigma^2(t)P \tag{20.32}$$

Given the covariance matrix described in equation (20.32), we need to transform (20.30) to the model where the covariance matrix of $u^\ell(t)$ is $\sigma^2(t)I$. This transformation from a heteroscedastic to a homoscedastic model is done as follows.

From (20.32) it follows that $P^{-1/2}\Sigma(t)P^{-1/2} = \sigma^2(t)I$ or $\Sigma(t) = \sigma^2(t)P$. We transform the original heteroscedastic model into a homoscedastic model

$$R^*(t) = B^*(t-1)F^\ell(t) + u^*(t) \tag{20.33}$$

where
$$R^*(t) = P^{-1/2}R^\ell(t)$$
$$B^*(t-1) = P^{-1/2}B^\ell(t-1)$$
$$u^*(t) = P^{-1/2}u^\ell(t)$$

The specific returns in equation (20.33) are homoscedastic and the least squares estimate of $F^\ell(t)$, based on equation (20.33), is

$$\hat{F}^\ell(t) = \left[B^\ell(t-1)^T\Sigma(t)^{-1}B^\ell(t-1)\right]^{-1}B^\ell(t-1)^T\Sigma(t)^{-1}R^\ell(t) \tag{20.34}$$

$\hat{F}^\ell(t)$ is the weighted least squares (WLS) estimate of $F^\ell(t)$. Given $\hat{F}^\ell(t)$, estimates of specific returns are $u^\ell(t) = R^\ell(t) - B^\ell(t-1)\hat{F}^\ell(t)$. Taking a closer look at (20.33), note that for the nth asset, the transformed regression model is

$$\frac{R_n^\ell(t)}{\sqrt{v_n(t)}} = \frac{B_n^\ell(t)}{\sqrt{v_n(t)}}F^\ell(t) + \frac{u_n^\ell(t)}{\sqrt{v_n(t)}} \tag{20.35}$$

where $B_n^\ell(t)$ is a $1 \times K$ vector of exposures for the nth asset. Equation (20.35) shows that the larger (smaller) the scale factors $v_n(t)$, the less (more) weight is given to the asset returns. So, for example, if we set $v_n(t)$ equal to one over the log of market capitalization, then we would be weighting large-cap stocks more than small-cap stocks.

How do you choose $v_n(t)$ in practice? A common specification is to let $v_n(t)$ be a function of one of the regressors. For example, some empirical research has shown that large-cap stocks have smaller residual volatilities $[\sigma_n^2(t)]$ than small-cap stocks. To reflect this phenomenon—that is, to give more weight to large-cap stocks and less weight to small-cap stocks—we would set $v_n(t)$ equal the inverse of market capitalization of the nth stock[13]; refer back to (20.32). Table 20.4 provides a list of potential candidates for the weights.

---

[13]Alternatively, we could use 1 divided by the square root of market capitalization as the weight. Whether to use market capitalization or its square root is an empirical issue.

TABLE 20.4 Candidates for Weights in Weighted Least Squares Regression

Weight $[v_n(t)]$	Explanation
Inverse of market capitalization	Weigh large-cap stocks more. Empirical research has shown that large-cap stocks have lower specific risk than small-cap stocks.
Square root of inverse of market capitalization	Same as above.
Inverse of the volatility of residual return from market regression	Gives more weight to stocks that are better explained by the Capital Asset Pricing Model (CAPM). Residual is based on regression from historical time period.

By repeating the cross-sectional estimation each day over a period of time, say two years, we generate a time series of factor and specific returns. For example, suppose we run the cross-sectional regressions for T days ($t = 1, \ldots, T$). Then we would have the $T \times K$ factor return matrix $F^{\ell}(T)$ where the tth row is a row vector of K elements representing the K factor returns at time t. In addition we would have a $T \times N$ specific return matrix, $U^{\ell}(T)$, where the tth row is a vector of N-specific returns at time t.

All risk calculations are based on covariance matrices of factor and specific returns. We obtain estimates of these covariance matrices using the data in $F^{\ell}(T)$ and $U^{\ell}(T)$, respectively. We describe the methods used to generate the covariance matrix estimates later in the chapter in the section on predicted factor and specific return covariance matrices.

Factor-Mimicking Portfolios

In this section we explain an interesting relationship between the regressions described earlier, and a particular trading strategy. Understanding this relationship facilitates the interpretation of factor returns.

Factor returns generated from the cross-sectional regressions presented above are often described as returns to factor-mimicking portfolios. The term *factor-mimicking portfolio* comes from the idea that a portfolio of assets can be constructed in such a way that its behavior emulates the behavior of some factor. This portfolio is known as a long-short portfolio. A long-short portfolio consists of nearly equal amounts of long and short positions. Together, these positions have the ability to mimic particular factors. For example, a portfolio that consists of long positions in large-cap stocks and short positions in small-cap stocks is said to mimic the size factor. Large positive returns on such a portfolio show that large-cap stocks outperform small-cap stocks.

Similarly, we can emulate the behavior of, say, the value factor by constructing a portfolio that is long assets with very high earnings-to-price (E/P) ratios (high value) and short assets with low E/P values (low value). High positive returns on such portfolios demonstrate that high-value stocks outperform low-value stocks.

The reader may wonder how one can equate the return estimated from the cross-sectional regression specified by equation (20.34) and the return on a long-short portfolio. After all, they are both factor returns. Next, we show why the factor returns estimated from cross-sectional regression are returns on long-short portfolios or factor-mimicking portfolios. To keep things simple and to facilitate our example, we assume that there is only one factor that can explain returns, and that factor is market capitalization.

The cross-sectional return model, when there is only one factor, is given by

$$R^{\ell}(t) = b_n^{\ell}(t-1)F^{\ell}(t) + u^{\ell}(t) \tag{20.36}$$

where $b_n^{\ell}(t-1)$ is an $N \times 1$ vector of exposures and $R^{\ell}(t)$ is an N-vector of a cross section of asset returns. The weighted least squares estimator of $F^{\ell}(t)$—where the weights are market capitalizations—can be written as

$$F^{\ell}(t) = \frac{\text{covariance}\left[b_n^{\ell}(t-1),\ R^{\ell}(t)\right]}{\text{variance}\left[b_n^{\ell}(t-1)\right]} = \frac{\sum_{n=1}^{N} c_n(t-1)b_n^{\ell}(t-1)R^{\ell}(t)}{\sum_{n=1}^{N} c_n(t-1)b_n^{\ell}(t-1)^2} \tag{20.37}$$

where $c_n(\mathrm{t}-1)$ represents the market weight on the nth asset and we have imposed the assumptions that the exposures are standardized to have a cap-weighted mean of zero.[14] Now we can write the estimate of the factor returns as the weighted average of the original N asset returns.

$$\hat{F}^{\ell}(t) = \sum_{n=1}^{N} w_n(t-1)R^{\ell}(t) \tag{20.38}$$

where $w_n(t-1) = \dfrac{c_n(t-1)b_n^{\ell}(t-1)}{\sum_{n=1}^{N} c_n(t-1)b_n^{\ell}(t-1)^2}$

Equation (20.38) shows that the return to the market capitalization factor is essentially the return on a portfolio consisting of the N assets used in the cross-sectional regression. This portfolio has interesting properties that we now summarize.

- The return, $\hat{F}^{\ell}(t)$, represents the return on a portfolio that follows a zero net-investment strategy. This follows from the fact that the portfolio weights sum to zero, that is,

  $$\sum_{n=1}^{N} w_n(t-1) = 0$$

  In practice, such a strategy can be approximated by constructing a long-short portfolio.

[14]Note that both the mean and standard deviation are computed on a cross-sectional basis.

- The long positions—where $w_n(t-1) > 0$—correspond to positions in assets that have exposures (to market cap) above the average. That is, these positions are in large-cap assets.
- The short positions—where $w_n(t-1) < 0$—correspond to positions in assets that have exposures (to market cap) below the average. That is, these positions are in short small-cap assets.

Extending our analysis to the multivariate framework, the least squares estimate of factor returns is

$$F^{\ell}(t) = \left[B^{\ell}(t-1)^T B(t-1)\right]^{-1} B^{\ell}(t-1)^T R^{\ell}(t) = W_F R^{\ell}(t) \tag{20.39}$$

$W_F = (B^{\ell T}B)^{-1}B^{\ell T}$ is a $K \times N$ matrix of portfolio weights where each row represents a set of portfolio weights corresponding to a particular factor-mimicking portfolio. For example, the first row of W_F may correspond to portfolio weights that comprise the mimicking portfolio for the *market size* factor. The second row may contain the weights of the portfolio that mimics the *value* factor, and so on.

Note that $W_F B^{\ell}(t-1) = I$ (where I is the identity matrix). This means that each factor portfolio—that is, each row of W_F—has a unit exposure to its factor (the weighted average of exposures is equal to one) and zero exposure to all other factors.

In summary, we have shown that the least squares estimator of a cross-sectional regression of asset returns on size exposures is the return on a portfolio that is long large-cap assets and short small-cap assets. Therefore, factor returns represent returns on factor-mimicking portfolios.

Predicted Factor and Specific Return Covariance Matrices

Each cross-sectional regression generates one set of factor returns at a particular point in time. Repeating the cross-sectional estimation each day over a period of time, say two years, we generate a time series of factor and specific returns. Then we would have the $T \times K$ factor return matrix $F^{\ell}(T)$ where the tth row is a row vector of K elements representing the K factor returns at time t. In addition we would have a $T \times K$ specific return matrix, $U^{\ell}(T)$, where the tth row is a vector of K specific returns at time t. We begin (again) with the linear factor model for asset returns as shown in equation (20.23).

In order to compute predicted tracking error, we need a forecast of the covariance matrix of asset returns, $R^{\ell}(t)$, which we denote by $V^{\ell}(t)$. Taking the variance of $R^{\ell}(t)$, as specified in (20.23), yields

$$V^{\ell}(t) = B^{\ell}(t-1)\Sigma^{\ell}(t)B^{\ell}(t-1)^T + \Delta^{\ell}(t) \tag{20.40}$$

where $\Sigma^{\ell}(t)$ = $K \times K$ forecast factor return covariance matrix, which we estimate from the $T \times K$ matrix of factor returns $F^{\ell}(T)$

$\Delta^{\ell}(t)$ = $N \times N$ diagonal matrix with specific return variances along the diagonal that are estimated from the data in $U^{\ell}(T)$

This structure assumes that:

- Specific returns are uncorrelated variables.
- The correlation among assets is captured exclusively by the correlation among factors and the asset exposures.

In *ex ante* risk analysis we are interested in forecasts of covariance matrices of factor returns and specific returns. Let $\Sigma^{\ell}(t \mid t-1)$ and $\Delta^{\ell}(t \mid t-1)$ denote conditional estimates (forecast) of covariance matrices of factor and specific returns, respectively. Forecasts of $\Sigma^{\ell}(t \mid t-1)$ and $\Delta^{\ell}(t \mid t-1)$ may be obtained by ***different methods*—an important point to remember.** Therefore, the forecast of the asset return covariance matrix, which is used to estimate total risk and tracking error, may be actually a combination of two different forecast covariance matrices. Next, we explain how forecasts of the factor return covariance matrices are generated.

Factor Return Covariance Matrix Forecasts There are a variety of different methodologies that can be employed to estimate factor return covariance matrices. In this section, we explain one particular methodology that has gained widespread use. When forecasting covariances among factor returns we place relatively more weight on recent returns by weighting the data exponentially. This methodology is consistent with the empirical research that shows that the volatilities of financial returns tend to cluster over time.

Exponentially weighted covariance matrices are constructed as follows:

Step 1 Start with time series of daily returns on, say, 10 factors over the prior two years (504 days). Let $F^{\ell}(504)$ with element $f_k^{\ell}(t)$ (tth row, kth column of), denote a 504×10 matrix of factor returns (each row represents one day of factor returns and each column represents a time series of a different factor return). Moreover, the first row of $F^{\ell}(504)$ denotes the most recent day's factor returns whereas the last row represents the factor returns occurring 504 days ago. Each column of $F^{\ell}(504)$ is mean-centered (it has subtracted from it the equally weighted sample mean [taken over time]).

Step 2 Weight the factor returns in $F^{\ell}(504)$ so that the weight applied to returns at some past date is half the value it is currently. For example, suppose we set the half-life—the time it takes the weight to reach one-half its current value—to 25 days. In this case, we would apply the weight $\lambda^0 = 1$ to the most recent day's factor returns in row 1 of $F^{\ell}(504)$, λ^1 to the previous day's return, λ^2 to returns from two days ago, and so on, until 25 days prior, $\lambda^{25} = 0.50$. Solving for the weight λ, we get $\lambda = 0.50^{1/25} = 0.97$.

Now, when we form the covariance matrix estimate, we normalize the weights so that they sum to one. We construct new weights such that at ℓ days ago their value, ω_{ℓ}, is given by

$$\omega_{\ell} = \frac{\lambda^{\ell}}{\sum_{j=0}^{T-1} \lambda^j}$$

where $T = 504$

Using these weights we form the exponentially weighted factor return matrix $\tilde{F}$:

$$\tilde{F} = \begin{bmatrix} \sqrt{w_0}f_1(0) & \sqrt{w_0}f_2(0) & \cdots & \sqrt{w_0}f_K(0) \\ \sqrt{w_1}f_1(1) & \sqrt{w_1}f_2(1) & \cdots & \sqrt{w_1}f_K(1) \\ \vdots & \vdots & \cdots & \vdots \\ \sqrt{w_{504}}f_1(504) & \sqrt{w_{504}}f_2(504) & \cdots & \sqrt{w_{504}}f_K(504) \end{bmatrix}$$

Step 3 An exponentially weighted covariance matrix forecast is given by

$$\hat{\Sigma}(t \mid t-1) = \tilde{F}(t)^T \tilde{F}(t)$$

The principal advantage of using exponentially weighted forecasts is that they allow the covariance matrix to react quickly to recent market movements. However, some portfolio managers may find that the exponentially weighted covariance matrix forecasts are unreasonably volatile. In this case, we can decrease the decay rate so as to more evenly distribute the weight across historical observations.

As discussed at the beginning of this section, within the context of a linear factor model, the estimation of the total return covariance matrix requires that we estimate (1) the covariance matrix of factor returns and (2) the covariance matrix of specific returns. Next, we discuss the estimation of the covariance matrix of specific returns.

Specific Return Covariance Matrix Forecasts Specific risk estimates are a function of the estimate of the specific return covariance matrix. The specific return covariance matrix is simply a matrix of zeros with specific return variances along the diagonal. That is, in the calculation of specific risk, it is assumed that specific returns are uncorrelated with each other.

We write the forecast for the specific return covariance matrix of N assets at time t as

$$\Delta(t \mid t-1) = \begin{bmatrix} \delta_1^2(t \mid t-1) & 0 & 0 & 0 \\ 0 & \delta_2^2(t \mid t-1) & 0 & 0 \\ \vdots & 0 & \ddots & \vdots \\ 0 & 0 & \cdots & \delta_N^2(t \mid t-1) \end{bmatrix} \tag{20.41}$$

where the variance of the nth specific return at time t is given by $\delta_n^2(t \mid t-1)$. Note that, unlike the factor return covariance matrix,[15] the specific return covariance matrix has the same dimension as the number of assets (returns). Practitioners apply

[15]Recall that the dimension of the factor return covariance matrix is based on the number of factors.

different types of methodologies to forecast specific risk. One approach consists of three steps:

Step 1 Generate an estimate of each specific return variance using the exponential model described above. This results in N variance estimates where $s_n^2(t \mid t - 1)$ represents the nth estimate.

Step 2 Compute the average specific return variance estimate (taken over all N assets). Denote this value by $\bar{s}_n^2(t)$.

Step 3 The estimate of specific risk is given by a weighted combination of $s_n^2(t \mid t - 1)$ and $\bar{s}_n^2(t)$. In other words, we shrink each specific return variance computed in the first step to the average specific return.

$$\delta_n^2(t \mid t-1) = (1-\gamma)s_n^2(t \mid t-1) + \gamma\bar{s}_n^2(t)0 < \gamma < 1 \tag{20.42}$$

where γ is the shrinkage parameter.

On average, large-cap stocks tend to have smaller specific volatilities than smaller-cap stocks. Consequently, we observe the specific volatilities of large-cap stocks falling below the sample average—that includes both large and smaller-cap stocks—and the specific volatility estimator presented in (20.42) would tend to increase the specific volatilities of large-cap stocks and reduce the specific volatilites of smaller-cap stocks.

In order to minimize the effect that (20.42) has on the specific volatility of large-cap stocks, we can modify it so that it applies only to assets whose specific volatilities are greater than the average, $\bar{s}_n^2(t)$. In this case, (20.42) becomes

$$\delta_n^2(t \mid t-1) = \begin{cases} (1-\gamma)s_n^2(t \mid t-1) + \gamma\bar{s}_n^2(t) & \text{if } s_n^2(t \mid t-1) > \bar{s}_n^2(t) \\ s_n^2(t \mid t-1) & \text{if } s_n^2(t \mid t-1) \le \bar{s}_n^2(t) \end{cases}$$
$$\text{and } 0 < \gamma < 1$$

When estimating a specific returns covariance matrix, there are numerous practical issues that arise. Among them are:

- New assets may not have enough historical return data to estimate specific returns. Reasons for this may include initial public offerings (IPOs) and mergers/spin-offs. In this case, using some average of specific variances as a proxy may be reasonable.
- Specific variances may exhibit extreme outliers, to the extent that they dominate risk analysis. In this case, a large value of the shrinkage parameter may be required to mitigate the effect of such outliers on the resulting risk estimates.
- Specific return variances may be excessively volatile over time.

This concludes our discussion on estimating the covariance matrices of returns based on factor models. Next, we turn our attention to global equity factor models.

Global Equity Factor Risk Models

Thus far the information presented on equity factor risk models has covered both the local and global frameworks. We now turn our attention to global equity factor risk models. In this discussion, "global equity" refers to equities traded in markets covering North America, South America, Continental Europe, the United Kingdom, Japan, and the Pacific Rim. A global equity portfolio consists of equities that are traded in two or more of these regions. In principle, global equity can include any equity market. A global equity risk factor model involves a set of factors that can explain the risk in a portfolio that contains global equities.

Global equity factor models pose an important problem for portfolio managers because it is relatively difficult to define a set of factors that can describe the variation in a portfolio that consists of global equities. This is particularly the case when the global equity portfolio has pockets of concentrations. For example, a portfolio that consists of concentrations in exposures to Japanese and U.S. stocks requires a large amount of factors to properly describe its risk. One set of factors is needed to describe Japanese stocks, while another set of factors is needed to describe the U.S. stocks. Furthermore, we may consider a third set of factors to cover the covariation among the Japanese and U.S. stocks. Ideally, we would seek a smaller number of global factors to describe the risk; however, this set may be difficult to identify in practice.

Before we turn our attention to modeling global equity, we provide an overview of some research that has recently taken place on international equity models. This research has implications for building global equity factor models.

Country and Industry Effects Understanding the relative importance of country and industry effects has been an area of great interest among global equity portfolio managers. Historically, global equity management has been structured around country allocation. A two-step procedure is typically employed, with the first step being country allocation and the second the selection of industries and stocks within these countries.

The reason for the emphasis on country allocation stems from the belief that it is better to diversify among countries. From a statistical perspective, this belief is based on the empirical finding of low correlations among countries.[16] Researchers and practitioners offer three explanations as to why correlation among country returns is relatively low compared to correlation among industry returns.

1. ***Home bias or investor myopia.*** Instead of diversifying across all markets and holding a portfolio that mirrors the world portfolio, investors have historically strongly overweighted domestic securities in their portfolios. Country portfolios may in part reflect different sentiment among local residents, and investor sentiment varies from country to country. Home bias is often reinforced by regulatory constraints that require certain types of investors to hold their assets primarily, or even exclusively, in their home markets. This is true, for example,

[16]Holding all other things equal, the lower the correlation among assets, the greater the diversification benefit.

of Latin American pension funds and of insurance companies in a number of countries.

2. ***Industrial diversification.*** When using country indexes to determine the relative importance of country effects, it is important to note that country indexes differ in terms of sector composition. For example, relative to Switzerland, the Swedish index contains more firms in basic industries while Switzerland has more banks. So, each country really is a sector and correlations between sectors are low.
3. ***Country-specific economic shocks.*** Important economic shocks that affect firms differ across countries. This may be because the shocks are regional in nature, such as a change in fiscal or monetary policy that is specific to a country. Alternatively, it may be because national markets behave differently from global shocks. Either way, economic shocks can cause variation in stock returns that is country specific. In sum, the occurrence of shocks that affect banks in Switzerland differently from banks in Sweden is more important for explaining the low correlation between their country returns than the fact that Sweden has fewer banks.

More recent research has emphasized the increasing importance of industry factors for explaining risk relative to country factors. Most notable among this research have been publications by Aked, Brightman, and Cavaglia (2000); Munro and Jelicic (2000); and Rouwenhorst (1998a). The general conclusion from this research is that diversification across industries now provides greater risk reduction benefits than diversification across countries. Intuitively, arguments supporting an increasing role for industry factors in explaining risk fall along two lines:

1. Decline in trade barriers—for example, the General Agreement on Tariffs and Trade (GATT) and the North America Free Trade Agreement (NAFTA)—and economic policy coordination—for example, the Economic and Monetary Union (EMU).
2. Increasing globalization of firms' revenues and operations and the increasing proportion of intra-industry mergers and acquisitions.

When it comes to quantifying the relative importance of industry and country effects in explaining the variation of security returns, published research has been less than conclusive. We identify four reasons for this inconclusiveness:

1. Geographical scope of study (Europe vs. global; developed vs. undeveloped). Results vary with the choice of countries analyzed.
2. Industry classification (broad sectors vs. finer industries). Results can vary with the type of industry classifications scheme (e.g., Dow Jones STOXX vs. MSCI).
3. Historical period analyzed.
4. Definition of security exposure to a country. For example, some researchers define a security's exposure to a particular country in terms of a 0/1 indicator variable. Others assume that the security's beta is its country exposure. Results can clearly depend on the choice of exposure, and both definitions have their advantages and disadvantages.

Academics and industry professionals have conducted a wide array of research into measuring and identifying so-called global factor returns. The broad thrust of this research has focused on understanding better the relative importance of industry, country, and global factors. We summarize this literature in terms of five key points:

1. Holding all other things equal, the standard deviation of factor returns is a measure of the relative importance of a factor in explaining risk. The rationale is that if a factor is going to explain variability in returns it has to have some variability itself.
2. Improving industry classifications from "broad" to "narrow" appears to increase the relative importance of industries.
3. Over the past two years, industries appear to play a more significant role within Europe than they do worldwide.
4. Within Europe, the relative importance of industries has been increasing over time.
5. It is misleading to analyze the correlations of country and industry indexes over time because they do not provide hard evidence about the relative importance of industry and common factors. In short, it is difficult to disentangle industry and country effects from the returns on observed indexes. A factor model, which we explain later, allows one to separate country from industry effects.

Ultimately, the scope for active strategies along the industry dimension will be determined by the relative importance of industry factors in explaining security returns, by managers' ability to predict the future evolution of these factors, and by the degree of liquidity in industry indexes.

Country and Currency Effects Country and currency exposures depend on the geographical distribution of a firm's activities. For example, a company with a headquarters in the United States but with most of its costs and sales in Germany and Japan would have country exposures to Germany and Japan, and currency exposures to the euro and yen (vs. the U.S. dollar). In order to properly account for these exposures, a global equity factor model needs to incorporate both country and currency factors. Typically, and as shown below, country factors explain the cross-sectional variation in local returns. Currency factors, on the other hand, explain the total (currency plus local) returns.

Modeling Global Equities In a global equity model, risk is derived from estimating the covariance matrix of total returns, $R(t)$. This involves volatilities and correlations among a variety of factor returns, including industries, investment styles, countries, and currencies. In practice, there is a trade-off between the number of factors that need to be estimated in a properly specified global equity model and the number of historical data points (returns) required to estimate a covariance matrix.

We present four different methods of modeling global equities, which are variations of the linear cross-sectional factor model discussed earlier. These models are: (1) global equity (cross-sectional) factor model, (2) combined single region model (SRM), (3) block diagonal model, and (4) an enhanced block diagonal model.

1. ***Global equity (linear cross-sectional) factor model.*** In this model, there is one estimation universe, and one (complete) set of global factors is used to explain the cross-sectional variation in local stock returns. The term "global" is derived from the fact that returns to stocks issued in more than two countries around the globe are used in the cross-sectional regression to estimate factor returns. A primary advantage of this model is that it may not require a large number of factors. That is, the number of global factors is typically less than combining the factors from various single regions (such as the United States, Europe, and Japan). A potential drawback of this approach is the loss of power to explain the cross section of stock returns.
2. ***Combined SRM global model (full-information methodology).*** This model starts out with factor returns from each of the SRMs. For example, we may have a total of four SRMs, one each for the United States, (Western) Europe, Japan, and Asia except Japan. We estimate the factor return covariance matrix by combining factor returns across all SRMs. This covariance matrix is then combined with the specific variances from the SRMs to form the total covariance matrix.
3. ***Block diagonal model.*** Unlike the combined SRM model, we assume that the factor returns among different SRMs are uncorrelated and we estimate the factor return covariance matrix for each SRM separately. In fact, this is not a model of returns. Instead, it is a compilation of the various single region (local) covariance matrices. According to this approach, we start with the single region covariance matrices estimated using the techniques described earlier in the chapter. For example, we may estimate factor covariance matrices for the single regions: United States, Canada, continental Europe, United Kingdom, Japan, and Asia except Japan. Each region's factor covariance matrix represents a block. We then assume zero correlation among the blocks. So, for example, we assume that the U.S. equity market factors (and specific returns) are uncorrelated with the factors that explain the Canadian equity market. Specific risk is treated in an analogous manner to factor risk.

   A primary practical advantage of the block diagonal approach is that it provides managers with the same risk estimates as the single region models. So, for example, a U.S. equity portfolio's risk that is generated from a U.S. single region model is the same as that from the block diagonal model. An important disadvantage of the block diagonal approach is that it assumes zero correlation between major equity markets (such as the U.S. and Canadian markets).
4. ***Enhanced block diagonal model.*** According to this methodology, SRMs are used to estimate factor return risk similar to the way they were applied in the block diagonal model. However, it is no longer assumed that the factor returns across SRMs are uncorrelated. Rather, we estimate the correlations among factor returns of different SRMs and incorporate them into the block diagonal model. An algorithm has been developed and applied to ensure that the resulting factor return covariance matrix is fully consistent. A primary advantage of this approach is that it takes into account potentially important correlations among SRM factor returns. However, unlike the other methods discussed, this approach can be more computationally intensive.

Table 20.5 provides a brief comparison of these four methodologies.

TABLE 20.5 A Comparison of Methods

Methodology	Pros	Cons
Global equity risk model	Accounts for correlation (among factor returns) when estimating factor returns	Problems with portfolios that have highly concentrated exposures
Combined SRM	• Directly incorporates factor returns from SRMs • Handles portfolios with high concentrations	Large number of factors
Block diagonal model	• Risk estimates consistent with SRMs • Handles portfolios with high concentrations	Assumes zero correlation among SRM factor returns
Enhanced block diagonal model	• Addresses con in the block diagonal approach • Handles portfolios with high concentrations	Computationally intensive

Global Equity Factor Model In this approach, we define a set of global factors—which may simply be the entire set of single country factors—and estimate the covariance matrix of these factors and the respective specific volatilities. One specification of a global equity factor model can be written as

$$R(t) = R^{\ell}(t) + E_{ij}(t) + xc(t)$$
$$R^{\ell}(t) = G(t) + S(t-1)F_S(t) + I(t-1)F_I(t) + C(t-1)F_C(t) + u(t) \quad (20.43)$$

where $R^{\ell}(t)$ = $N \times 1$ vector of local excess returns from time $t-1$ to t. That is, the return expressed in local terms over the local risk-free rate. $R_n^{\ell}(t)$ is the return on the nth asset.

$G(t)$ = Constant term (across all assets) at time t. In certain situations—see Heston and Rouwenhorst (1994)—$G(t)$ represents a "global factor return"—that is, a return on a globally diversified portfolio of returns contained in $R^{\ell}(t)$.

$S(t-1)$ = $N \times M$ matrix of investment style exposures at time $t-1$. $S_n(t-1)$ is a vector of M investment styles for the nth asset.

$I(t-1)$ = $N \times J$ matrix of industry exposures at time $t-1$. $I_n(t-1)$ is a vector of J industry exposures for the nth asset.

$C(t-1)$ = $N \times K$ matrix of country exposures at time $t-1$. $C_n(t-1)$ is a vector of K country exposures for the nth asset.

$F_s(t)$ = $M \times 1$ vector of returns on investment styles (factor returns) from time $t-1$ to t. $F_{S,m}(t)$ is the return on the mth investment style.

$F_I(t)$ = $J \times 1$ vector of industry returns (factor returns) from time $t-1$ to t. $F_{I,j}(t)$ is the return on the jth industry.

$F_C(t)$ = $K \times 1$ vector of country returns (factor returns) from $t-1$ to t. $F_{C,k}(t)$ is the return on the kth country.

$u(t)$ = $N \times 1$ vector of specific returns (on local equity) from time $t-1$ to t.

For the nth asset, we have

$$R_n^{\ell}(t) = G(t) + S_n(t-1)F_S(t) + I_n(t-1)F_I(t) + C_n(t-1)F_C(t) + u_n(t) \quad (20.44)$$

where the subscript n refers to the nth asset and there are K ($k = 1, \ldots, K$) countries, J ($j = 1, \ldots, J$) industries, and M ($m = 1, \ldots, M$) investment styles. The model represented in equation (20.44) states that the local return on the nth asset is the sum of:

Global factor return, $G(t)$
Contribution from investment styles, $S_n(t-1)F_S(t)$
Contribution from industries, $I_n(t-1)F_I(t)$
Contribution from countries, $C_n(t-1)F_C(t)$

According to this specification we can write the return on the nth stock that belongs to the jth industry and kth country as

$$R_n^{\ell}(t) = G(t) + S_n(t-1)F_S(t) + F_{I,j}(t) + F_{C,k}(t) + u_n(t) \quad (20.45)$$

Equation (20.45) provides a rather restricted representation of reality even when viewed against the backdrop that models are supposed to simplify reality so that we can better understand and interpret complex phenomena. There are two major assumptions supporting (20.45):

1. ***Industry effects are global.*** Alternatively expressed, each stock is allocated to one industry that represents a global industry (e.g., global automotive). This assumption ignores potentially strong regional effects that could result from differences in capital-labor ratios across countries.
2. ***Securities in the same country have similar exposures to domestic* and *global factors.*** For example, Citigroup and JDS Uniphase are affected by the U.S. factor and the global factor in the same fashion. This is clearly unrealistic given the different exposure of each company to non-U.S. factors as reflected, for instance, in each company's proportion of foreign sales to total sales.

Equation (20.44) may be estimated using least squares regression. While it is beyond the scope of this chapter to explain the estimation process in detail, we review some important issues related to estimating (20.44).

- Since industry and country exposures sum to one across all stocks, we have two sources of perfect collinearity (including the constant vector). Therefore, we need to drop one industry and one country when estimating factor returns. In practice, one can get quite different estimates of factor returns depending on which variables are dropped from the regression.
- Rather than arbitrarily choosing an industry (country) to interpret the industry (country) factor returns, we may measure the industry (country) factor returns relative to a value-weighted portfolio. In practice, this means that to estimate equation (20.44) using weighted least squares, where the weights are the market

capitalization values, we need to impose two restrictions: (1) the sum of the market capitalization weighted industry factor returns is equal to zero, and (2) the sum of market capitalization weighted country factor returns is equal to zero.

- The constant in this regression is equal to the value-weighted return on the portfolio of all stocks in the cross-sectional regression. One interpretation is that the constant is the "global" factor return. In the case of a local model, note that if we add a constant term to the regression model, this would be equivalent to assigning a beta of one to each asset. In this case, the return on the local market is the estimate of the coefficient on the constant.

Combined SRM In the combined model, factor returns are first estimated for each single region model using the techniques outlined earlier in the chapter. The exact definition of the single region model, and in particular what geographical area it covers, is up to the developer. For developed markets, single region models are typically defined for Canada, United States, western continental Europe, United Kingdom, Japan, and Pacific Rim. The factor return covariance matrix used to estimate risk is generated from taking the union of all SRM factor returns. This approach directly accounts for correlation between all factors.

Block Diagonal Model In the block diagonal approach, there is no formal model of asset returns as in (20.44). Instead, this approach works as follows: Assume there are M ($m = 1, \ldots, M$) single region models (i.e., factor and specific return covariance matrices). For each single region model, the security return covariance matrix is expressed by

$$V^m(t) = B^m \Omega^m(t) B^{mT} + \Delta^m(t) \qquad \text{for } m = 1, \ldots, M \qquad (20.46)$$

where $V^m(t) = N_m \times N_m$ covariance matrix of security returns at time t for mth model.
$B^m = N_m \times K_m$ matrix of exposures to investment style, industry and local market for mth model.
$\Omega^m(t) = K_m \times K_m$ covariance matrix of factor returns at time t for mth model.
$\Delta^m(t) = N_m \times N_m$ diagonal matrix of variances of specific returns at time t for mth model.

In order to compute the risk of global equity portfolios, we generate an $N \times N$ matrix of security returns as follows:

First, construct the global covariance matrix contribution to the total covariance matrix. This term is given by

$$\Omega^{BD}(t) = \begin{bmatrix} B^1\Omega^1(t)B^{1^T} & 0 & 0 & 0 & 0 \\ 0 & B^2\Omega^2(t)B^{2^T} & 0 & 0 & 0 \\ 0 & 0 & \ddots & 0 & 0 \\ 0 & 0 & 0 & \ddots & 0 \\ 0 & 0 & 0 & 0 & B^M\Omega^M(t)B^{M^T} \end{bmatrix} \qquad (20.47)$$

Note that $\Omega^{BD}(t)$ incorporates the factor exposures from the SRMs.

Next construct the global matrix of specific variances. This term is given by

$$\Delta^{BD}(t) = \begin{bmatrix} \Delta^1(t) & 0 & 0 & 0 & 0 \\ 0 & \Delta^2(t) & 0 & 0 & 0 \\ 0 & 0 & \ddots & 0 & 0 \\ 0 & 0 & 0 & \ddots & 0 \\ 0 & 0 & 0 & 0 & \Delta^M(t) \end{bmatrix} \tag{20.48}$$

Finally, the global covariance matrix of security returns, based on the block diagonal factor return covariance matrix, is

$$V^G(t) = \Omega^{BD}(t) + \Delta^{BD}(t) \tag{20.49}$$

Currencies (and risk associated with currency exposures) can enter the block diagonal covariance matrix as a separate block. That is, it is assumed that currencies are uncorrelated with noncurrency factor returns so that the covariance matrix of asset returns can now be written as

$$V^{BD}(t) = \begin{bmatrix} V_1^{BD}(t) & 0 & 0 & 0 & 0 \\ 0 & V_2^{BD}(t) & 0 & 0 & 0 \\ 0 & 0 & \ddots & 0 & 0 \\ 0 & 0 & 0 & V_M^{BD}(t) & 0 \\ 0 & 0 & 0 & 0 & V_{ccy}^{BD}(t) \end{bmatrix} \tag{20.50}$$

where $V_{ccy}^{BD}(t)$ is a $C \times C$ covariance matrix of currency returns.

The main problem with the block diagonal covariance matrix is that it ignores potentially important correlations. For example, if one block represents the United States and another Canada, it clearly would not seem credible to assume zero correlation among these equity markets. A natural next step would be to improve upon the block diagonal approach so that we are completely consistent with the single region models while, at the same time, estimating important correlations among factor returns. This leads to the enhanced block diagonal methodology, which is discussed next.

Enhanced Block Diagonal Model In the enhanced block diagonal model, we attempt to provide the consistency that the SRMs offer while, at the same time, enabling us to estimate correlations between the SRM factor returns. In addition, we seek a methodology that is flexible enough to allow for situations where the blocks of the covariance matrix are estimated differently than the off-block elements. There are three situations where we may be required to use different estimation techniques for the block and off-block elements of the factor return covariance matrices. First, there may be too many factors when we consider the union of all SRM factor returns. This can lead to problems when estimating the combined SRM. Second, there may be situations where the SRM covariance matrices are available but not their underlying factor returns. In this case, we may need to use proxy factor returns to estimate cross-SRM correlations. Third, we may decide to use start dates or histories for the SRM factor return correlations that are different from the histories used to estimate the off-block correlations.

The steps required to produce the asset return covariance matrix based on the enhanced block diagonal methodology are:

Step 1 Estimate the block diagonal covariance matrix of factor and specific returns.

Step 2 Estimate the complete, full-information factor return covariance matrix using the combined SRM methodology. We generate this by first defining the union of all factor returns—across all SRMs—and then estimating the correlation among these factor returns.

Step 3 Complete the block diagonal factor return covariance matrix by filling in the off-diagonal blocks (i.e., the zeros) with the correlation estimates from the combined SRM matrix. An algorithm has been developed that performs this operation and that satisfies the following properties:

- The blocks of the original block diagonal matrix remain unchanged. This ensures that the individual SRMs are fully consistent with the enhanced block diagonal covariance matrix.
- The condition number of the completed block diagonal covariance matrix—the enhanced factor return matrix—is bounded to be less than or equal to some predefined value.[17] This ensures that the final covariance matrix has the proper statistical properties and that the resulting covariance matrix is fully consistent (i.e., pairwise correlations make sense) and positive definite.
- The completed covariance matrix converges to a positive definite matrix.

Step 4 Create the covariance matrix of asset returns by combining the enhanced factor return covariance matrix with the specific return covariance matrix.

MEASURING AND IDENTIFYING SOURCES OF RISK

In this section, we present various measures of predicted risk as defined in the linear factor model. These measures range from tracking error and portfolio volatility estimates to contributions to risk by asset. A portfolio's sources of risk are determined by:

- Each asset's exposure to some factor, regardless of whether that factor be the asset itself, some fundamental factor, or something else.
- The distribution of the returns on assets.
- The weight of each asset in the portfolio benchmark (if applicable).

[17]Stated another way, the smallest eigenvalue of the enhanced correlation matrix is set arbitrarily close to the smallest eigenvalue of the block diagonal matrix.

Portfolio Definitions

Thus far, the discussion in this chapter has been at a relatively abstract level. In this section, our focus shifts to portfolios and portfolio analytics. These analytics include the definition of portfolio returns and various portfolio measures of exposure.

There are four types of portfolios that we are concerned with—the managed portfolio, the benchmark portfolio, the active portfolio, and the market portfolio.

1. The managed portfolio is directed by the portfolio manager.
2. The benchmark portfolio is what the portfolio manager manages against. Examples of benchmark portfolios include the S&P 500 and the MSCI World.
3. The active portfolio is the difference between the managed and benchmark portfolios.
4. The market portfolio is supposed to be representative of the relevant market. Often, the benchmark and market portfolios are the same. In situations where they are different, risk and return may be calculated relative to the benchmark and market portfolios.

At each point in time we have the following quantities:

$P_n(t)$ Closing price of the nth asset as reflected in the base currency.

$q_n^p(t)$ Quantity—the number of shares held of the nth asset in the managed portfolio; this value can be positive, negative, or zero.

$\text{pos}_n^p(t)$ nth asset's position defined as price times quantity of shares held, that is, $P_n(t) \times q_n^p(t)$.

$\text{pos}^P(t)$ Total market value of the managed portfolio. By definition,

$$\text{pos}^P(t) = \sum_{n=1}^{N_p} \text{pos}_n^p(t)$$

where there are N_p assets in the managed portfolio; $\text{pos}^P(t)$ can be positive, negative, or zero.

$w_n^P(t)$ nth asset's weight in the managed portfolio. It's defined as

$$w_n^p(t) = \frac{\text{pos}_n^p(t)}{\text{pos}^p(t)}$$

We define similar quantities for the benchmark, the active, and the market portfolios where we use a superscript "b," "a," and "m" to denote benchmark, active, and market, respectively. That is,

$q_n^b(t)$ Quantity—the number of shares held of the nth asset in the benchmark portfolio.

$q_n^m(t)$ Number of shares outstanding of common stock, or the number of shares held of the nth asset in the market portfolio.

$w_n^b(t)$ nth asset's weight in the benchmark portfolio. Note that this weight is not necessarily a market cap weight.

$w_n^a(t)$ nth asset's weight in the active portfolio. Also known as the active weight, it is defined as the difference between the managed weight and the benchmark weight. That is, $w_n^a(t) = w_n^p(t) - w_n^b(t)$.

$w_n^m(t)$ nth asset's weight in the market portfolio, defined as

$$w_n^m(t) = \frac{\text{pos}_n^m(t)}{\text{pos}^m(t)}$$

Next, we define estimates of a portfolio's return. These estimates assume that there are no intraperiod cash flows or intraperiod trading. For example, if we are to compute a portfolio's one-day return, then we would assume that the two assumptions hold intraday. Using these definitions we define the portfolio return on a managed, benchmark, and market portfolio as follows.

For the managed portfolio, its one-period return from $t - 1$ to t is:

$$r_p(t) = \sum_{n=1}^{N_p} w_n^p(t-1)R_n(t) \tag{20.51}$$

For the benchmark portfolio, its one-period return from $t - 1$ to t is:

$$r_b(t) = \sum_{n=1}^{N_b} w_n^b(t-1)R_n(t) \tag{20.52}$$

For the active portfolio, its one-period return from $t - 1$ to t is:

$$r_a(t) = \sum_{n=1}^{N_a} w_n^a(t-1)R_n(t) \tag{20.53}$$

For the market portfolio, its one-period return from $t - 1$ to t is:

$$r_m(t) = \sum_{n=1}^{N_m} w_n^m(t-1)R_n(t) \tag{20.54}$$

Cash The term "cash" broadly applies to any amount that invests in some risk-free (or very low risk) account. In an equity portfolio, cash usually is defined as the sum of:

- The margin value of futures contracts. Portfolio managers equitize cash by buying futures contracts.
- Trade date cash. This represents the cash available to buy and sell securities on any particular day.
- The dollar (or equivalent) amount of repurchase agreements. Portfolio managers may lend funds short-term and earn interest (i.e., they enter reverse repurchase agreements). Reverses (lending) enter as positive cash whereas repurchase agreements are negative cash (borrowing).
- The dollar (or equivalent) amount of any other short-term instruments held. In the United States, for example, this includes the dollar value of holding Treasury bills.

In practice, cash enters the portfolio return calculation by simply changing the base (denominator) of the portfolio weight calculation. For example, consider a portfolio that has two assets with equity positions \$10 and \$2. Its portfolio weights are $^5/_6$ and $^1/_6$, respectively. Now, suppose we add $3 cash to the portfolio. In this case, the total portfolio value is $15, which results in portfolio weights of $^{10}/_{15}$ (equity position 1), $^2/_{15}$ (equity position 2) and $^3/_{15}$ (cash).

Cash is taken as riskless, so adding cash to a portfolio lowers its absolute risk (volatility) since it reduces the amount (weight) of the risky positions. In the previous example, the weights in the two equity positions decreased by $^3/_{16}$ and $^1/_{30}$. Note that although cash is a risk-less asset, it can increase risk when a portfolio's performance is measured against a benchmark and the benchmark portfolio holds risky assets. The impact of cash on a portfolio's tracking error is explored on page 390.

Futures When measuring risk, futures should be treated as distinct assets. In this section, our focus is on equity index futures. As explained earlier, futures are composite assets as their value is derived from an underlying asset(s). Take the example of a futures contract on the S&P 500. The return on this contract is a function of the return on the S&P 500 index that in turn is a function of returns on the assets which comprise the S&P 500.

An equity index futures exposure is its contract value. Its contract value is defined as the contract size times the index value. For example, the contract size of a June 2002 S&P 500 futures contract on March 21, 2002, was approximately $286,950. This is equal to the value of 1 point ($250) times the index's market value on that date (1,147.80). The exposure of holding 10 futures contracts would be $2,869,500.

The weight of the equity index future is given by ratio of its total exposure (e.g., $2,869,500) divided by the total market value of the portfolio. Note that the exposure is not the same as the futures market value. The futures total exposure is never incorporated in the computation of the portfolio's total market value.

ADRs and GDRs When evaluating the risk of American and global depositary receipts, some portfolio managers prefer to map these securities to their underlying parent companies. In other words, the exposures of the ADR or GDR are replaced by the exposures of the parent company. For example, suppose a portfolio held the BP Amoco ADR but not its parent (i.e., BP Amoco shares traded in the United Kingdom). In this situation, the ADR's exposures will be replaced by the parent company's exposures. The mechanics of mapping an ADR or GDR to its parent can be described in three steps. First, compute the portfolio weights of the ADR. Second, if the portfolio has positions in both the ADR and the parent company, compute the portfolio weights of both and combine them to get an aggregate weight. Third, use the parent company's exposures to represent the exposure of the aggregate position (i.e., the position that contains both the ADR and the parent).

One potentially important drawback to mapping an ADR to its parent involves currency risk. Suppose a portfolio with a base currency in British pounds holds shares in a stock that is traded locally in Russia. In addition, this portfolio manager holds the ADR of this company. Without combining positions, this portfolio would have two types of exchange rate risk—to the Russian ruble and to the U.S. dollar. By mapping the ADR to the parent company, the portfolio reduces its dollar exposure and increases its currency risk to the Russian ruble.

Currencies A portfolio's currency positions are derived from the quantity of shares of a particular asset that is held as well as any direct currency exposure. For example, a portfolio that has a reporting currency of Japanese yen may hold both U.S. cash as well as U.S. stocks. Positions in both contribute to the portfolio's overall position in USD.

Realized and Predicted Risk Calculations In the linear factor model framework, a portfolio risk statistic is a function of a forecast covariance matrix that, itself, is a function of asset exposures and factor and specific return covariance matrices. This model allows us to decompose risk into factor and specific components. Before we discuss portfolio risk calculations based on the linear factor model, it is important to note the differences between realized (*ex post*) and predicted (*ex ante*) risk calculations.

The calculation of a portfolio's realized risk (or tracking error) consists of two steps.

Step 1 A time series of the portfolio's actual (realized) returns is obtained. Typically, there are two sources of these actual returns.

1. Officially reported returns as maintained by a firm's accounting systems or as computed by a custodian. These returns are usually what appear in monthly statements that report the portfolio's performance.
2. Estimates of the officially reported returns.[18] These returns are mostly used in cases where daily performance reporting is required and no official returns are available. In this case, a portfolio's return is approximated by using returns as of time t and weights as of time $t - 1$.

For example, an estimate of a portfolio's active returns over a 20-day period are expressed as

$$r_a(t) = w^a(t-1)^T R(t) \qquad \text{for } t = 1, \ldots, 20 \qquad (20.55)$$

where $r_a(t)$ and $w^a(t-1)$ represent the active portfolio return and weights, respectively.

Step 2 Compute the standard deviation, or some other risk statistic, of the time series of actual returns. For example, realized tracking error is defined as the standard deviation of actual active returns.

Unlike realized risk calculations, predicted risk calculations rely only on the most recent set of portfolio holdings. For example, a predicted tracking error calculation at time $t-1$ for some future period would use portfolio weights as of time $t-1$. This is an important difference since by using only the most recent holdings we are allowed to carry out risk decompositions (explained later).

Next, we discuss predictive risk calculations in the context of the linear factor model.

Factor Model Framework

We work with the global linear factor model presented earlier in the chapter in the section on global framework. There, the cross section of returns, expressed in some base currency, is modeled according to:

[18] See the section on cash for more information on portfolio returns.

$$R(t) = B^{\ell}(t-1)F^{\ell}(t) + u^{\ell}(t) + E_{ij}(t) + xc(t) \tag{20.56}$$

where, in the discussion below, we assume that asset returns have exposures to the following classes of factors: investment styles, industries, countries, and currencies. Let's rewrite (20.56) so that the exchange rate returns appear as factors. To do so we add columns of ones and zeros to the exposures matrix $B^{\ell}(t-1)$ and rows (of returns) to the vector $F^{\ell}(t)$.

$$R(t) = B(t-1)F(t) + u^{\ell}(t) \tag{20.57}$$

where $F(t) = [F^{\ell}(t)|E_{ij}(t) + xc(t)]$ and $B(t-1)$ incorporates the exposures to currency factors. In practice, we may choose to ignore the cross term $xc(t)$.

The forecast covariance matrix of asset returns, as of time $t-1$, is based on forecasting the variance of the N-vector $R(t-1)$ as specified by equation (20.57). The forecast covariance matrix of $R(t-1)$ is

$$V(t \mid t-1) = B(t-h)\Sigma(t \mid t-1)B(t-h)^T + \Delta(t \mid t-1) \tag{20.58}$$

where $h > 1$ and $\Sigma(t \mid t-1)$ is the covariance matrix of factor returns which include investment styles, industries, countries, and currencies. The notation "$t \mid t-1$" reads as "the time t forecast given information up to and including time $t-1$." $\Delta(t|t-1)$ is the specific return variance matrix. We can think of the factor return covariance matrix as a four-by-four block expressed thus:

$$\Sigma(t \mid t-1) = \begin{bmatrix} \text{Investment styles (IS)} & \text{Ind \& IS} & \text{Cty \& IS} & \text{Ccy \& IS} \\ \text{IS \& Ind} & \text{Industry (Ind)} & \text{Cty \& Ind} & \text{Ccy \& Ind} \\ \text{IS \& Cty} & \text{Ind \& Cty} & \text{Countries (Cty)} & \text{Ccy \& Cty} \\ \text{IS \& Ccy} & \text{Ind \& Ccy} & \text{Cty \& Ccy} & \text{Currencies (Ccy)} \end{bmatrix} \tag{20.59}$$

Equation (20.59) shows that each class of factors represents a block along the diagonal of $\Sigma(t \mid t-1)$. The off-diagonal elements involve the interaction among the factor returns. When we measure the risk of a portfolio, the part coming from factors is, in effect, a sum of components of the matrix in (20.59) that are weighted by the factor exposures, that is, $B(t-h)$.

Equipped with expressions for the covariance matrix of stock returns, we can formulate the expression for the variance of the managed and active portfolios.

Portfolio Risk Measures The variance of the managed portfolio return is given by the expression

$$\begin{aligned} \sigma_p^2(t) &= w^p(t)^T V(t \mid t-1) w^p(t) \\ &= b^p(t-1)\Sigma(t \mid t-1)b^p(t-1)^T + w^p(t-1)^T\Delta(t \mid t-1)w^p(t-1) \end{aligned} \tag{20.60}$$

where $b^p(t-1) = w^p(t-1)^T B(t-h)$. Equation (20.60) provides a measure of a managed portfolio's total risk (squared). In practice, this number is usually reported in standard deviation terms, that is, $\sigma_p(t)$. The portfolio's factor and specific risk components are given by

$$\sigma^2_{\text{factor},p}(t) = b^p(t-1)\Sigma(t \mid t-1)b^p(t-1)^T \tag{20.61}$$

$$\sigma^2_{\text{spec},p}(t) = w^p(t-1)^T\Delta(t \mid t-1)w^p(t-1) \tag{20.62}$$

Note that risks, as defined in terms of standard deviations, are not additive. That is, the factor risk and specific risk do not sum to the managed total risk. Were we to measure risk using variances—see equation (20.60)—in place of standard deviations, then the risks would be additive. In practice, the standard deviation is used as a measure of risk since its units are in returns and not returns squared.

Similarly, the forecast variance of the return on the active portfolio is

$$\sigma^2_a(t) = b^a(t-1)\Sigma(t \mid t-1)b^a(t-1)^T + w^a(t-1)^T\Delta(t \mid t-1)w^a(t-1) \tag{20.63}$$

Equation (20.63) provides a measure of an active portfolio's total risk (squared). In practice, this number is usually reported in standard deviation terms, that is, $\sigma_a(t)$, and is known as tracking error. The active portfolio's factor and specific risk components are given by

$$\sigma^2_{\text{factor},a}(t) = b^a(t-1)^T\Sigma(t \mid t-1)b^a(t-1) \tag{20.64}$$

$$\sigma^2_{\text{spec},a}(t) = w^a(t-1)^T\Delta(t \mid t-1)w^a(t-1) \tag{20.65}$$

A Risk Budget and Hot Spots One way to evaluate a portfolio's positions is in terms of their contributions to risk. In order to understand the meaning of these contributions, it is useful to think of a portfolio's risk defined in terms of a risk budget. Simply put, a risk budget is the amount of risk that a portfolio manager can allocate to different factors or securities.

A portfolio manager managing her portfolio against a benchmark would consider the portfolio's tracking error as representing 100 percent of its overall risk. With a risk budget, we decide how much risk should come from different factors and/or assets. The sum of the contributions to risk from each of the factors and assets is equal to 100 percent.

It is important to note that a portfolio's risk budget is separate from the absolute level of risk that the portfolio incurs. For example, a portfolio might have a target tracking error of 5 percent, but currently its realized (and predicted) tracking error is running about 4 percent. In this example, the portfolio has 100 basis points of unused risk that it could employ in order to improve its chances of increasing returns.

Contributions to risk are defined by assets (stocks), investment style factors, industry factors, countries, and currencies. (In fact, any factor falls into the framework we discuss in this section.) Contributions to a portfolio's risk (e.g., tracking error) measure a position's marginal impact on that portfolio's risk. They answer questions such as, if we change a position's size by 2 percent, how much does the portfolio's tracking error change? What proportion of my portfolio's overall risk budget comes from a bet geared to the U.S. momentum factor? And how is the risk in my portfolio allocated across different securities and sectors?

As contributions to risk measure the marginal effect on risk, they are typically defined in terms of (mathematical) derivatives. This is not to say, however, that there are not alternative ways of computing contributions to risk. We may compute contributions to risk using numerical simulation rather than derivatives. Both approaches have their advantages and disadvantages. The primary advantage of the mathematical approach is that the calculations are extremely fast because you have closed-form results for the contributions to risk.

The mathematical derivatives that we employ measure the percentage change in risk for a given percentage change in position value. These derivatives are based on the factor model expression for tracking error (squared).

$$\sigma_a^2(t) = b^a(t-1)\Sigma(t \mid t-1)b^a(t-1)^T + w^a(t-1)^T\Delta(t \mid t-1)w^a(t-1) \quad (20.66)$$

Using this expression, we can answer the following three questions:

Question 1: How much does tracking error change when there is a change in the number of shares held in the nth stock position? A related question is, how much does the nth position contribute to the overall tracking error?

Question 2: How much does tracking error change when there is a change in the exposure to the kth factor? How much does the kth factor contribute to the total tracking error?

Question 3: What is the breakdown of total tracking error to factor and specific risk?

We address each question separately.

Contributions to Risk by Asset To answer the first question we need to find an expression for the change in tracking error, $\sigma^a(t)$, for a given change in the nth element (asset) of $w^a(t-1)$, which we represent by $w_n^a(t-1)$. The N_a-vector of *absolute* marginal contributions to tracking error (ACTE) is given by the derivative of the portfolio's tracking error with respect to the position vector $w^a(t-1)$,

$$\text{ACTE}(t) = \frac{\partial\sigma^a(t)}{\partial w^a(t-1)} = \frac{V(t \mid t-1)w^a(t-1)}{\sigma^a(t)} \quad (20.67)$$

where the nth element of ACTE(t), denoted $\text{ACTE}_n(t)$, is the nth asset's absolute marginal contribution to tracking error. Since $\sigma^a(t)^2 = w^a(t-1)^T V(t \mid t-1)w^a(t-1)$, if we premultiply (20.67) by $w^a(t-1)^T$, we get

$$w^a(t-1)^T\,\text{ACTE}(t) = \frac{w^a(t-1)^T V(t \mid t-1)w^a(t-1)}{\sigma^a(t)} = \sigma^a(t) \quad (20.68)$$

Or we can write equation (20.68) as

$$\sum_{n=1}^{N_a} w_n^a(t-1)\text{ACTE}_n(t) = \sigma^a(t)$$

That is, the tracking error is equal to the weighted average of the absolute marginal contributions to tracking error, where the weights are defined as the active portfolio weights. Dividing both sides of (20.68) by tracking error yields

$$\sum_{n=1}^{N_a} \frac{w_n^a(t-1)\text{ACTE}_n(t)}{\sigma^a(t)} = 1 \tag{20.69}$$

or

$$\sum_{n=1}^{N_a} \text{RCTE}_n(t) = 1 \tag{20.70}$$

where

$$\text{RCTE}_n(t) = \frac{w_n^a(t-1)\text{ACTE}_n(t)}{\sigma^a(t)}$$

represents the *relative* marginal contribution to tracking error (RCTE). RCTE measures the relative change in tracking error given the relative change in active weights. Mathematically, RCTE is defined

$$\begin{aligned}\text{RCTE} &= \frac{\partial\sigma^a(t)/\sigma^a(t)}{\partial w^a(t-1)/w^a(t-1)} = \left[\frac{w_n^a(t-1)}{\sigma^a(t)}\right]\frac{\partial\sigma^a(t)}{\partial w^a(t-1)} \\ &= \frac{w_n^a(t-1)}{\sigma^a(t)} \times \text{ACTE}(t)\end{aligned} \tag{20.71}$$

As (20.71) shows, RCTE measures the relative change in tracking error given a relative change in weight. Hot spot reports (Litterman 1996) are based off of the RCTE calculation.

Let's consider a numerical example. Suppose that an asset's active weight in a portfolio is 50 basis points and that the current predicted tracking error (annualized) is 3.5 percent. Assuming an absolute marginal contribution to tracking error of 8 percent would imply that the relative contribution to tracking error for this asset is 1.1428 percent.

$$\text{RCTE}_n(t) = \frac{0.0050}{0.035} \times 0.08 = 0.011428 \tag{20.72}$$

The RCTE for the nth asset, interpreted as 1.143 percent of the portfolio's risk budget, is consumed by this asset. Alternatively, if we focus on the ACTE, we find that if we increase our position in this asset by 200 bps (i.e., from 0.50 percent to 2.50 percent), then the tracking error increases by 16 bps. A similar decrease in the position would lead to a decrease in tracking error.

A key distinction between ACTE and RCTE lies in the way a change in position is defined. Suppose the current active weight in a position is –0.5 percent (an underweight). An increase in this weight, from a RCTE perspective, would mean making this weight more negative (e.g., going from –0.5 percent to –1.0 percent). In

ACTE, an increase in this weight would mean making it less negative (e.g., going from –0.5 percent to 0).

Since RCTE measures the relative change in risk, given a relative change in weight, a *positive RCTE* means that if the current active weight is:

- Positive, an increase in this weight (making it more positive) would lead to an increase in tracking error.
- Negative, a decrease in this weight (making it less negative) would lead to a decrease in tracking error.

Similarly, a *negative RCTE* means that if the current active weight is:

- Positive, an increase in this weight (making it more positive) would lead to a decrease in tracking error.
- Negative, a decrease in this weight (making it less negative) would lead to an increase in tracking error.

Table 20.6 summarizes the relationship between RCTE and ACTE.

In addition to computing an asset's change on the total tracking error, we can, in the context of a linear factor model, measure an asset's change on the factor and specific components of total tracking error. From the decomposition of tracking error into factor and specific components, we have

$$\begin{aligned} \text{ACTE}(t) &= \frac{V(t \mid t-1) w^a(t-1)}{\sigma^a(t)} \\ &= \underbrace{\frac{B^\ell(t-h)\Sigma(t \mid t-1)B^\ell(t-h)^T w^a(t-1)}{\sigma^a(t)}}_{\text{Factor component}} + \underbrace{\frac{\Delta(t \mid t-1) w^a(t-1)}{\sigma^a(t)}}_{\text{Specific}} \end{aligned} \tag{20.73}$$

Equation (20.73) has the benefit of having the factor and specific contributions add up to the total contribution to tracking error. A disadvantage with using

TABLE 20.6 Comparison of RCTE and ACTE

Current Value	Change in Active Weight	Change in Tracking Error
RCTE		
Positive	Negative weight becomes more negative	Increase
	Positive weight becomes more positive	Increase
Negative	Negative weight becomes more negative	Decrease
	Positive weight becomes more positive	Decrease
ACTE		
Positive	Negative weight becomes less negative	Increase
	Positive weight becomes more positive	Increase
Negative	Negative weight becomes less negative	Decrease
	Positive weight becomes more positive	Decrease

(20.73) as a risk decomposition, however, is that it is not easy to interpret the factor and specific components because they are not defined in the same way as ACTE (that is, not defined by a derivative).

An alternative way to find the factor and specific component of an asset's change on total tracking error is to first define the total factor and specific component of tracking error and then take derivatives of each with respect to the asset positions. The factor component of tracking error (squared) is given by

$$\varphi^a(t)^2 = w^a(t-1)^T B^\ell(t-h)\Sigma(t \mid t-1)B^\ell(t-h)^T w^a(t-1) \tag{20.74}$$

The nth asset's contribution to the factor component of tracking error is represented by the nth element of

$$\text{ACTE}_{\text{factor}}(t) = \frac{\left[B^\ell(t-h)\Sigma(t \mid t-1)B^\ell(t-h)^T\right]w^a(t-1)}{\varphi^a(t)} \tag{20.75}$$

and

$$\sum_{n=1}^{N_a} w_n^a(t-1) \times \text{ACTE}_{\text{factor},n}(t) = \varphi^a(t) \tag{20.76}$$

The specific component of tracking error is

$$\delta^a(t)^2 = w^a(t-1)^T \Delta(t \mid t-1) w^a(t-1) \tag{20.77}$$

It follows from equation (20.77) that the nth asset's contribution to the specific component of tracking error is represented by the nth element of

$$\text{ACTE}_{\text{specific}}(t) = \frac{\Delta(t \mid t-1)w^a(t-1)}{\delta^a(t)} \tag{20.78}$$

and

$$\sum_{n=1}^{N_a} w_n^a(t-1) \times \text{ACTE}_{\text{specific},n}(t) = \delta^a(t) \tag{20.79}$$

Note that $\sigma^a(t) \neq \varphi^a(t) + \delta^a(t)$ but rather $\sigma^a(t)^2 = \varphi^a(t)^2 + \delta^a(t)^2$.

As done previously, we can define relative contributions to tracking error.

$$\text{RCTE}_{\text{factor}}(t) = \frac{w^a(t-1)}{\varphi^a(t)}\text{ACTE}_{\text{factor}}(t) \quad \text{and} \quad \sum_{n=1}^{N_a} \text{RCTE}_{\text{factor},n}(t) = 1 \tag{20.80}$$

$$\text{RCTE}_{\text{specific}}(t) = \frac{w^a(t-1)}{\delta^a(t)}\text{ACTE}_{\text{specific}}(t) \quad \text{and} \quad \sum_{n=1}^{N_a} \text{RCTE}_{\text{specific},n}(t) = 1 \tag{20.81}$$

Contributions to Risk by Industry, Investment Style, or Other Factor In the previous section we computed the absolute and relative marginal contribution to the factor component of tracking error for a given change in the underlying asset position. Next, we compute the impact on tracking error from changing a portfolio's exposure to a factor. We begin by defining a $1 \times K$ vector of active factor exposures $b^a(t-1)$.

$$b^a(t-1) = w^a(t-1)^T B(t-h)$$
$$= \begin{bmatrix} \underbrace{\sum_{n=1}^{N_a} w_n^a(t-1)B_{n,1}(t-h)}_{\text{factor \#1}} \sum_{n=1}^{N_a} w_n^a(t-1)B_{n,2}(t-h)\cdots \\ \sum_{n=1}^{N_a} w_n^a(t-1)B_{n,k}(t-h)\cdots \sum_{n=1}^{N_a} w_n^a(t-1)B_{n,K}(t-h) \end{bmatrix} \tag{20.82}$$

Absolute marginal factor contributions to tracking error (AFCTE) are computed with respect to each of the K elements in $b^a(t-1)$. Specifically, the contribution to total tracking error from each of the K factors is given by the $K \times 1$ vector.

$$\text{AFCTE} = \frac{\partial \sigma^a(t)}{\partial b^a(t-1)} = \frac{\Sigma(t \mid t-1) b^a(t-1)^T}{\sigma^a(t)} \tag{20.83}$$

There are two things to note about the absolute marginal contributions to tracking error by factor:

1. AFCTE is a $K \times 1$ vector whose kth element is the marginal contribution to tracking error from the kth factor.

$$\text{AFCTE}_k = \frac{\partial \sigma^a(t)}{\partial b_k^a(t-1)} = \frac{\Sigma(t \mid t-1) b_k^a(t-1)^T}{\sigma^a(t)} \tag{20.84}$$

2. AFCTE does not contain any specific risk terms because specific risk does not contain any factor exposures.

AFCTE can also be written in relative terms, that is, as an RFCTE. The kth term of the relative marginal factor contribution to tracking error (RFCTE_k) is

$$\text{RFCTE}_k = \frac{\partial \sigma^a(t) / \sigma^a(t)}{\partial b_k^a(t-1) / b_k^a(t-1)} = \frac{b_k^a(t-1)^T}{\sigma^a(t)} \times \text{AFCTE}_k \tag{20.85}$$

Note that the sum of the RFCTE_k's is equal to the proportion of factor risk in tracking error. That is,

$$\sum_{k=1}^{K} \text{RFCTE}_k = \sum_{k=1}^{K} \frac{b_k^a(t-1)^T}{\sigma^a(t)} \times \text{AFCTE}_k = \frac{\varphi^a(t)^2}{\sigma^a(t)^2} \tag{20.86}$$

Note that the term $b_k^a(t-1)$ is a weighted average of exposures (for a particular factor) of all assets in the active portfolio. So, when we refer to taking a derivative with respect to the kth exposure we are not specifying whether that derivative is with respect to the active portfolio weights or the asset exposures. Similarly, we can compute the relative specific contribution to tracking error—(RSCTE(t)). That is, for the nth asset, its relative specific contribution to tracking error is

$$\text{RSCTE}_n(t) = \frac{w_n^a(t-1)\Delta(t \mid t-1)w^a(t-1)}{\sigma^a(t)^2} \tag{20.87}$$

Note that the sum over all assets of the $\text{RSCTE}_n(t)$'s is equal to the proportion of specific risk in tracking error. That is,

$$\sum_{n=1}^{N_a} \text{RSCTE}_n(t) = \frac{\delta^a(t)^2}{\sigma^a(t)^2} \tag{20.88}$$

Therefore, the sum of RSCTE's over all assets plus the sum of RFCTE's over all factors is equal to one (or 100 percent).

When determining a portfolio's sources of risk, it is important that we can drill down to the most detailed level. Sometimes its not enough to know how much a factor (e.g., price momentum) contributes to a portfolio's tracking error. Instead, we may need to know what assets are most responsible for a particular factor's risk contribution. Alternatively stated, suppose our goal is to lower our portfolio's risk that is coming from the price momentum factor. In order to do so we would need to reduce exposure to assets that contribute highly to price momentum's contribution to tracking error.[19] This is not the same as simply reducing the weights in assets that have high exposure to price momentum. Rather, we need to reduce the weight in the risky assets that contribute to the price momentum factor's contribution to risk.

In order to determine which assets contribute to a particular factor's risk, we need to measure the nth asset's relative contribution to the kth factor. This measure is given by

$$\text{RFCTE}_{n,k} = \frac{w_n^a(t-1) \times B_{n,k}(t-h)^T}{\sigma^a(t)} \times \text{AFCTE}_k \tag{20.89}$$

This expression tells us how much risk the nth asset contributes to the kth factor. Note that when we sum $\text{RFCTE}_{n,k}$ over all stocks, the result is the factor's contribution to tracking error.

$$\sum_{n=1}^{N_a} \text{RFCTE}_{n,k} = \text{RFCTE}_k \tag{20.90}$$

[19]Here, we assume that overweight positions have high price momentum exposure.

Having the ability to work with (20.88) is very important for hot spot reporting because it allows portfolio managers to view their portfolios' risk in a variety of ways.

Important Note: Contribution to Risk by Sector Sectors contain one or more industries. In practice, it is common to report exposures by sector as well as contribution to tracking error by sector. For a particular sector, its exposure is simply the sum of all industry exposures that belong to that sector. Similarly, for a particular sector, the sum of its respective industry contributions to risk is equal to that sector's contribution to risk.

For example, suppose that a sector consists of two industries—industry A and industry B—and a portfolio has an active exposure of 25 percent to industry A and –25 percent (underweight) to industry B. Since these industries are (the only industries) in the same sector, the portfolio's sector exposure is zero. Moreover, suppose that both industries have a contribution to risk of 30 percent. (Note that the total contributions to risk over both industries is not 100 percent because we are assuming that the portfolio has exposure to other industries.) When we add the two industry contributions to risk, we find that the contribution to risk from the sector is 60 percent. Mathematically, we have established the following result. Let there be S_i ($s = 1, \ldots, S_i$) industries in the ith sector. In this example, the sum of the industry exposures for a particular sector is zero: that is,

$$\sum_{s=1}^{S_i} b_s^a(t-1) = 0 \tag{20.91}$$

Now, the contribution to tracking error from a sector computed as the sum of contributions to tracking error by the individual industries is given by

$$\sum_{s=1}^{S_i} \frac{b_s^a(t-1)}{\sigma^a(t)} \times \text{AFCTE}_s \tag{20.92}$$

In our example, (20.92) is equal to 0.60.

Predicted Beta

A portfolio manager seeking a forward-looking view of how the managed portfolio varies with a market or benchmark portfolio can look at the portfolio's predicted beta. In order to derive a portfolio's predicted beta, we refer back to the market model introduced in the section on macroeconomic factors. The market model for the nth asset return is

$$R_n(t) = \alpha_n(t) + \beta_n(t) r_m(t) + e_n(t) \tag{20.93}$$

where $R_n(t)$ = Excess return on the nth asset over the risk-free rate at time t.
$r_m(t)$ = Return on a market portfolio over the risk-free rate.

$\beta_n(t)$ = Beta—a measure of the covariation between asset return and return on market portfolio.
$e_n(t)$ = Mean-zero, random component known as residual return. This return is uncorrelated with the market return.
$\alpha_n(t)$ = Alpha—captures difference between market component and asset return.

Using the definition, $r_m(t) = w^m(t-1)^T R(t)$, we can derive an expression for predicted beta. For the nth asset, its predicted beta is:

$$\beta_n(t \mid t-1) = \frac{v(t \mid t-1)^T w^m(t-1)}{\sigma^m(t)^2} \tag{20.94}$$

where $v(t \mid t-1)$ is an $N \times 1$ vector of covariances, representing the nth row of the covariance matrix $V(t \mid t-1)$. To better understand the definition of predicted beta, consider the case where the market portfolio consists of two assets and we are interested in finding the predicted beta for these two assets. In this case, $r_m(t) = w_1^m(t-1)R_1(t) + w_2^m(t-1)R_2(t)$ and

$$\begin{aligned}
\beta_1(t \mid t-1) &= \frac{\sigma_1^2(t \mid t-1)w_1^m(t-1) + \sigma_{12}^m(t \mid t-1)w_2(t-1)}{\sigma^m(t)^2} \\
\beta_2(t \mid t-1) &= \frac{\sigma_{21}^2(t \mid t-1)w_1^m(t-1) + \sigma_2^2(t \mid t-1)w_2(t-1)}{\sigma^m(t)^2}
\end{aligned} \tag{20.95}$$

In terms of a linear factor model, the expression for predicted beta is given by

$$\begin{aligned}
\beta(t \mid t-1) &= \frac{V(t \mid t-1)w^m(t-1)}{\sigma^m(t)^2} \\
&= \frac{\left[B(t-1)^T \Sigma(t \mid t-1)B(t-1)^T\right]w^m(t-1)}{\sigma^m(t)^2} + \frac{\Delta(t \mid t-1)w^m(t-1)}{\sigma^m(t)^2}
\end{aligned} \tag{20.96}$$

Here, $\beta(t \mid t-1)$ is an $N \times 1$ vector of predicted betas. A portfolio's beta is defined as the weighted average of individual betas $\beta_p(t) = w^p(t-1)^T\beta(t \mid t-1)$. Similar results hold for the benchmark and active portfolios.

Note from (20.96) that predicted beta consists of two components—factor and specific. This is a useful result because we can determine the source of a portfolio's beta. If a large amount of a portfolio's beta is due to factor exposure, then we can reduce its overall exposure to the market by reducing its factor exposure. On the other hand, if the specific risk component dominates a portfolio beta, then a manager should not focus on factors to reduce market exposure.

Predicted beta is also known as *fundamental beta* since its value depends on asset exposures to fundamental factors through the term $B(t-h)$. Another measure that relates a portfolio's return to a benchmark return is known as the predicted R-squared.

Measuring the Risk of Futures Exchange and Traded Funds Positions

Some equity portfolio managers use futures as a key component of their portfolio construction process. When cash comes into an account, some portfolio managers may choose to "equitize" this cash. That means they purchase futures in an amount that gives them the same exposure as the cash value. So, for example, if a portfolio received a \$50 million cash inflow, a portfolio manager may go long S&P 500 futures to the amount of a \$50 million exposure.

Since futures can play such an important role in portfolio construction, it's critical to understand how to measure the risk of futures positions within the context of an equity factor model. Before understanding the way that futures positions affect portfolio risk, we first need to analyze how a futures position impacts a portfolio's value.

The market value of a futures contract is its initial margin plus any variation margin. Variation margin results from the mark-to-market (MTM) feature of futures contracts. For example, variation margin increases as the futures contract moves out-of-the-money. We consider an example using a futures contract on the S&P 500 index.

Currently, each S&P 500 futures contract is worth 250 times the current market value of the spot S&P 500 index. So, if the value for the index is \$1,500, then the market exposure of the S&P 500 futures contract is \$375,000. Assuming a margin requirement of 5 percent, a portfolio manager would have to put down about \$18,750. Naturally, if a portfolio manager purchases *N* futures contracts, then the market value would be *N* times \$375,000 and the initial margin would be *N* times \$18,750.

At the end of each trading day, the mark-to-market of the futures contract is based on the formula MTM = 250 × (Close-of-business price of futures contract – Beginning-of-day price of futures contract).

So, if the futures price at the beginning of the day is \$1,500 and it closes at \$1,450, then the MTM would be a loss of \$12,500.

$$\text{MTM} = 250 \times (\$1{,}450 - \$1{,}500) = -\$12{,}500$$

As futures are settled each day, the variation margin in this case is \$12,500 and this amount would be added to the initial margin amount.

A future's position weight in a portfolio is defined as its total market exposure (\$375,000) divided by the portfolio's total invested capital. For example, suppose that a portfolio consists of two stock positions and one futures position. The futures position has a total market exposure of \$375,000 and the stock positions are currently valued at \$100,000 and \$200,000. In this case, the total capital invested is \$318,750 and the portfolio weights are: 31.4 percent (\$100,000/\$318,750), 62.7 percent (\$200,000/\$318,750), 117.6 percent (\$375,000/\$318,750), and 5.9 percent ($18,750/$318,750). Note that the sum of the portfolio weights does not equal 100 percent.

A popular methodology, and one used in some commercially available risk systems, measures the risk of futures by assuming a no-arbitrage condition. According to this approach, entering into a futures contract involves converting the futures position into a long spot position on the underlying asset (e.g., S&P 500) and an equivalent short cash position. This methodology assumes that holding a short-dated futures contract is equivalent (in both risk and return terms) to borrowing cash at the spot price and buying the underlying asset.

For example, an S&P 500 futures position with a total market value of $500,000 would enter a portfolio as a short $500,000 cash position and a long $500,000 position in the underlying S&P 500 spot composite. By treating futures in this way, we note that:

- The portfolio's market value remains unchanged.
- The total market value of equity positions increases by the amount of the futures position.
- Adding a futures position is indistinguishable from adding a set of the underlying assets.

An alternative methodology for measuring the risk of futures positions would treat these positions as separate and distinct whose risk and return are driven by an underlying composite. Futures positions would be mapped to the underlying equity exposures, returns, and prices. Since entering into a futures contract is costless, the futures position does not affect the cash in the portfolio, except for the margin that is allocated to enter into the futures contract.

To understand this approach to modeling futures, refer to the previous example of an S&P 500 futures position with a total exposure of $500,000. In this case, we would increase the portfolio's cash position by the initial margin and compute the weight on the futures contract as $500,000 divided by the portfolio's total invested capital.

Exchange-traded funds (ETFs) are securities that represent underlying composite portfolios but are traded on exchanges like stocks. Two examples of ETFs are Russell iShares and Standard & Poor's Depositary Receipts, or "spiders" (SPDRs).

SPDRs are exchange-traded securities, or units (like a mutual fund), that represents ownership in the SPDR unit investment trust. The SPDR trust was established to accumulate and hold a portfolio of common stocks that is intended to track the price performance and dividend yield of the S&P 500 composite index. Hence, it is reasonable to expect the market value of a SPDR to move closely with the S&P 500. SPDRs are engineered to provide a security whose market value approximates one-tenth of the value of the underlying S&P 500 index. SPDRs are created and redeemed with an actual portfolio of securities and in quantities of 50,000 SPDR creation units.

SPDRs or any other ETFs should be modeled the same way as common stock. That is, an ETF takes in positions, prices, and returns, and computes weights and related risk and return statistics.

When computing risk, ETFs and futures on composite assets require a specific type of handling. Specifically, an adjustment needs to be made so as to not overestimate the contribution of risk from a composite asset. This adjustment is required because a portfolio may hold an asset (e.g., IBM) and then hold a futures contract on a composite portfolio that contains that asset (e.g., S&P 500). Without such an adjustment, we are not guaranteed zero specific risk in the presence of a perfect hedge.

In order to correctly measure specific risk when dealing with futures and ETFs, we need to create a new set of managed weights. These new weights—represented as an *N*-vector—are computed as follows:

$$w^p_{\text{mod}}(t-1) = w^p_{\text{ex future}}(t-1) + w^p_{\text{future}}(t-1) \times w^p_u(t-1) \tag{20.97}$$

where $w^p_{\text{ex future}}(t-1)$ = Original managed weights, excluding the futures position
$w^p_u(t-1)$ = Managed weights on the underlying assets in the futures or ETFs
$w^p_{\text{future}}(t-1)$ = Weight of the futures contract in the managed portfolio; defined as the futures market exposure divided by the portfolio's net worth

To understand how (20.97) works, suppose that a portfolio held a common stock outright and its weight in the portfolio is 3 percent (excluding the futures). In addition, the portfolio holds futures contracts on a composite portfolio. The weight of the futures contract in the portfolio is 5 percent and the weight of the asset in the composite portfolio is 4 percent. In this case, we have $w^p_u(t-1) = 4\%$; $w^p_{\text{future}}(t-1) = 5\%$; and $w^p_{\text{ex future}}(t-1) = 3\%$.

Note that when a futures position is not held with respect to a particular asset, then $w^p_{\text{future}}(t-1) = 0$ and $w^p_{\text{mod}}(t-1) = w^p_{\text{ex future}}(t-1)$, and the modified weights are the same as the original portfolio weights without the futures.

How Does Cash Affect Tracking Error?

At some point, an equity portfolio will hold some amount of cash. In this section we study the role that cash plays in the tracking error of an equity portfolio. First, we need to be clear on the definition of cash. By cash, we mean the local risk-free investments. Investments in foreign risk-free assets (i.e., foreign cash) have currency risk associated with them and, therefore, do not fall under our definition of cash. Second, we need to be clear on the definition of risk. While it is straightforward to understand the impact of changes in cash to a portfolio's volatility, it is not so simple when it comes to understanding the role of cash in affecting tracking error.

As explained in the section on cash, an increase (a decrease) in the amount of cash in a portfolio decreases (increases) the weights of the equity positions. Hence, since cash is assumed to be a riskless asset (it has zero volatility and zero correlation), increases in cash tend to reduce a portfolio's volatility. This effect comes basically from reducing the weights in the risk positions and increasing the weight in the riskless position. This is an intuitive result.

Now, when measuring tracking error, we need to understand how changes in cash affect a portfolio's active weights. Recall that active weights are defined as the difference between managed and benchmark portfolio weights. And we know that the larger (smaller) the active weights are in absolute value, the larger (smaller) a portfolio's tracking error is. Since—holding all other things equal—an increase in cash reduces a portfolio's managed weights in equities, the impact on tracking error depends on the original values of the active weights and whether the corresponding stocks are positive or negative contributors to tracking error. Take a particular stock, for example, whose active weight, prior to any change in cash, is close to zero and is a positive contributor to tracking error. Holding all other things equal, if we were to add enough cash to the portfolio, then that stock's active weight would become negative, and thus add to tracking error. If, on the other hand, the stock starts off with a small overweight, then it would be possible to add enough cash to the portfolio to make this stock's active weight zero. In this case (holding all things equal) the stock's contribution to the portfolio's tracking error would decrease.

In summary, the impact that changes in cash have on a portfolio's tracking error depends on the original (i.e., prior to adding cash) values of the active weights and the stocks' contributions to tracking error. Broadly, if most of a portfolio's tracking error is coming from overweights, then an increase in cash will decrease (increase) the portfolio's tracking error. Similarly, if most of a portfolio's tracking error is due to underweights, then an increase (a decrease) in cash will reduce the managed portfolio weights and increase the absolute value of the active weights even more, thereby leading to higher tracking error.

An Example

We conclude the section with an example of a risk decomposition as provided by Goldman Sachs' PACE system. Figure 20.4 shows the first page of a PACE Risk Monitor Summary report for a hypothetical portfolio as of December 31, 2001.

The report shows that the portfolio's value on this day is $488,481,650. Its benchmark portfolio (i.e., the portfolio that is used in calculating tracking error) is the S&P 500. This portfolio currently contains 106 assets and 2.63 percent of its total value is in cash. Looking at the left-hand side of the top box in this report, we see that its annualized predicted tracking error (US Predicted TE) is 4.81 percent. The target TE for this portfolio is 4.50 percent, so this portfolio is running slightly above target. For comparison, this report shows a predicted tracking error from an alternative model (US RMG Daily TE). According to this model, the predicted tracking error is 4.84 percent. Reading down, we come to a box called "Risk Decomposition." This information shows that about 49.94 percent of the risk is specific and the remaining (50.06 percent) is coming from factors. In particular, 23.04 percent and 27.02 percent of the total tracking error is attributed to industries and investment styles, respectively.

Continuing down the page, we come to a table that shows contribution to risk by asset (stock). These contributions are based on the RCTE calculations. For example, Intel is the highest contributing stock to tracking error. It consumes 7.14 percent of the overall risk budget and has an underweight (versus the benchmark) of 114 basis points. Similarly, Oracle is also an underweight (its ac-

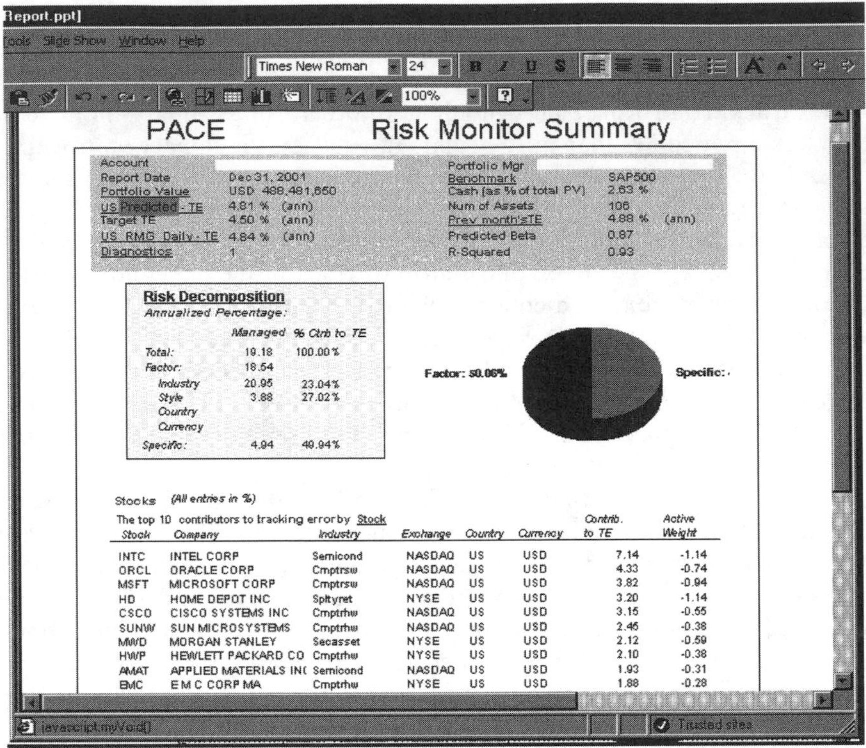

PACE Risk Monitor Summary

Account		Portfolio Mgr	
Report Date	Dec 31, 2001	Benchmark	SAP500
Portfolio Value	USD 488,481,650	Cash (as % of total PV)	2.63 %
US Predicted - TE	4.81 % (ann)	Num of Assets	106
Target TE	4.50 % (ann)	Prev month'sTE	4.88 % (ann)
US RMG Daily - TE	4.84 % (ann)	Predicted Beta	0.87
Diagnostics	1	R-Squared	0.93

Risk Decomposition

Annualized Percentage:

	Managed	% Ctrb to TE
Total:	19.18	100.00 %
Factor:	18.54	
Industry	20.95	23.04 %
Style	3.88	27.02 %
Country		
Currency		
Specific:	4.94	49.94 %

Stocks (All entries in %)

The top 10 contributors to tracking error by Stock

Stock	Company	Industry	Exchange	Country	Currency	Contrib. to TE	Active Weight
INTC	INTEL CORP	Semicond	NASDAQ	US	USD	7.14	-1.14
ORCL	ORACLE CORP	Cmptrsw	NASDAQ	US	USD	4.33	-0.74
MSFT	MICROSOFT CORP	Cmptrsw	NASDAQ	US	USD	3.82	-0.94
HD	HOME DEPOT INC	Spltyret	NYSE	US	USD	3.20	-1.14
CSCO	CISCO SYSTEMS INC	Cmptrhw	NASDAQ	US	USD	3.15	-0.55
SUNW	SUN MICROSYSTEMS	Cmptrhw	NASDAQ	US	USD	2.46	-0.38
MWD	MORGAN STANLEY	Secasset	NYSE	US	USD	2.12	-0.59
HWP	HEWLETT PACKARD CO	Cmptrhw	NYSE	US	USD	2.10	-0.38
AMAT	APPLIED MATERIALS INC	Semicond	NASDAQ	US	USD	1.93	-0.31
EMC	E M C CORP MA	Cmptrhw	NYSE	US	USD	1.88	-0.28

FIGURE 20.4 Risk Decomposition Example

tive weight is negative 74 basis points), and it consumes 4.33 percent of the overall risk budget.

THE RISK ESTIMATION PROCESS

Measuring risk requires that we quantify the future distribution of portfolio[20] and constituent returns. In this section we present an eight-step process for the practical implementation of an equity factor risk model. We continue to assume that a portfolio's return can be decomposed into common factor and specific components, and that the distribution of portfolio returns depends on only its mean and variance (i.e., first two moments). In addition, we assume that the factor model is applicable to the U.S. equity market. Hence, the information required to compute risk includes covariance matrices, factor exposures, and portfolio holdings (i.e., portfolio weights).

The standard deviation of the portfolio return yields the total portfolio risk estimate. Since a portfolio's return is modeled in terms of factor and specific components, we decompose total risk into factor and specific risks. We can further decompose factor risk into investment styles, industries, sectors, and so on.

[20]In this context, a portfolio return is simply a weighted average of all stock returns in that portfolio. Each stock's weight represents its contribution, in value, to the portfolio.

As discussed previously, a portfolio manager may manage a portfolio relative to some benchmark portfolio. The risk of a managed portfolio relative to its benchmark is calculated by computing the standard deviation of the difference between the managed portfolio and benchmark returns. This yields the relative risk measure that is commonly referred to as tracking error.

Suppose that a manager currently uses the market model to measure risk and attribute return. The manager's stock selection ability can be measured by the residual return—the difference between the managed portfolio return and the market's systematic component (market beta times market return). The standard deviation of the systematic component is a measure of systematic risk. The standard deviation of the residual return measures residual risk. Residual risk can be further decomposed into residual factor (i.e., the factors that can explain the residual returns) and residual specific risk.

Figure 20.5 presents a flowchart of the risk estimation process supporting a U.S. equity factor model. This process, which is presented in eight parts, extends to other markets as well as across markets.

We explain each of the eight steps in the risk estimation process:

Step 1 Source and collect exposure and market data. Exposure data may include industry classifications, fundamental data (e.g., book values), earnings estimates, and macroeconomic variables. Market data refers to daily asset prices and total returns as well as trading volume.

Step 2 Transform the raw exposure information and market data into asset exposures that will be used to estimate the parameters of the factor model. In the U.S. market, there are three basic types of exposures: (1) industry, (2) investment style, and (3) market.

Step 3 Construct an exposure matrix[21] (for each factor we have one exposure per asset) that consists of industry exposures, style exposures, and a possible new set of exposures that are generated from running time-series regressions of stock returns on market returns. This regression generates a market beta that we can use to measure a stock's exposure to the local market.

Step 4 Determine which assets qualify for our estimation universe. The estimation universe represents a set of assets that will be used to determine the parameters of the factor model (i.e., the factor returns). The estimation universe may change quite a bit over time. One reason why an asset would not qualify for a particular estimation universe is that there is not enough historical information on its stock returns and/or company information.

Step 5 Estimate factor returns by running a cross-sectional regression of asset returns—as defined by the estimation universe—on their factor exposures. The coefficients in this regression are estimates of factor returns.

Step 6 Run cross-sectional regressions each day over some sample period. Repeating these regressions over successive periods of time generates a time series of factor and specific returns. We use these time series of returns to estimate

[21]If we had N stocks and K factors then our exposure matrix would be an $N \times K$ matrix of exposures.

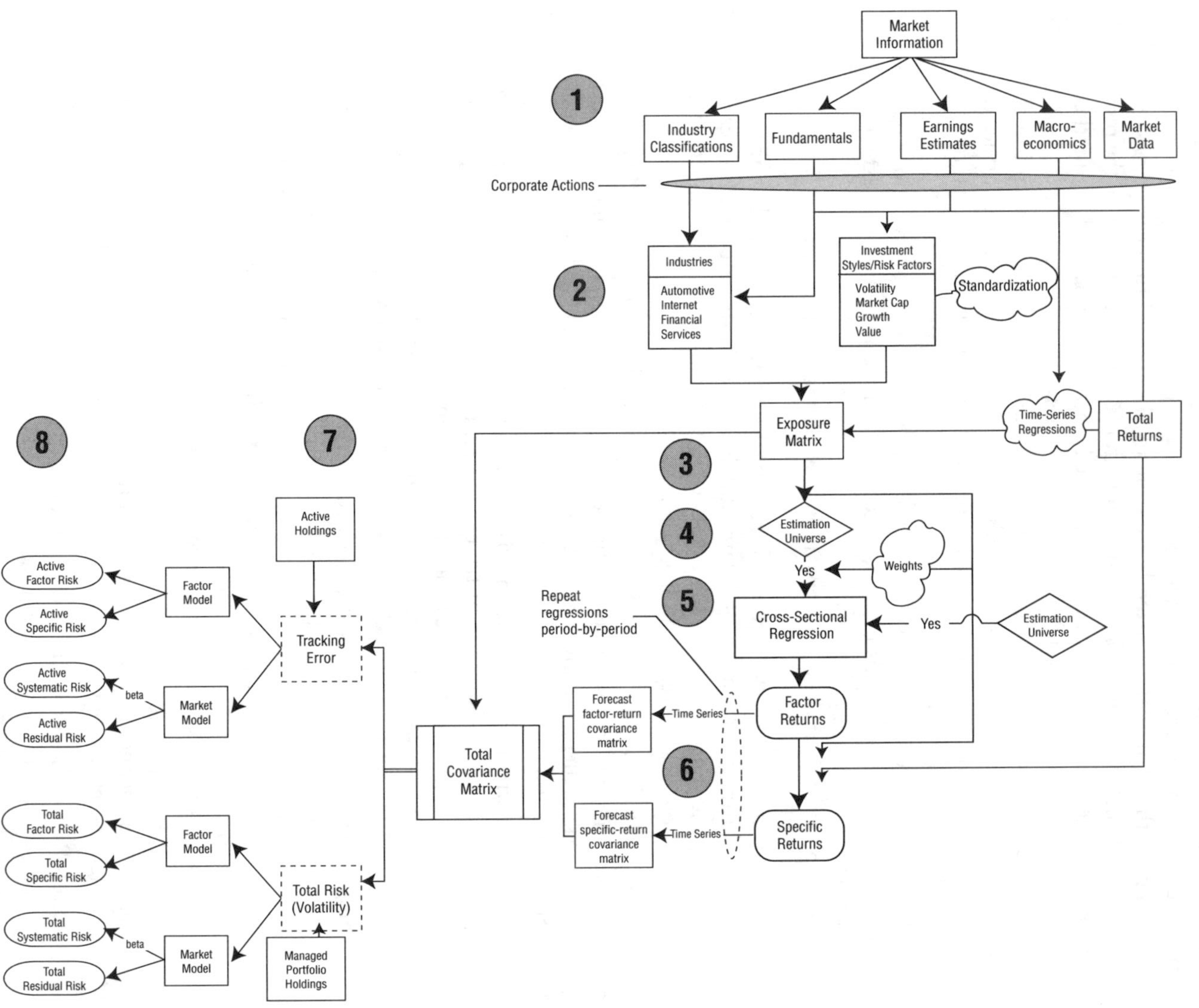

FIGURE 20.5 Example of the Risk Computational Process Based on a U.S. Equity Model

factor and specific return covariance matrices (separately). These covariance matrices are predictions of future movements and comovements of returns.

Step 7 At this point we begin to construct our risk estimates that are a function of holdings, exposures, and variance and covariance statistics. Thus far we have loaded all the information we need except for holdings. In order to compute portfolio weights:

- We take the number of shares held for that asset on a particular date (e.g., 100 shares held on November 15, 1999) and multiply this amount by the close-of-business price for the 15th (e.g., $10).
- We compute the total market value of the portfolio by taking the sum of all individual assets' market values (computed in the previous step).
- Each asset's portfolio weight is given by the ratio of its market value to the market value of the entire portfolio.

On each day we need to load portfolio files for all the accounts as well as benchmark portfolios.

For each asset, we compute its managed weight (its weight in the managed portfolio), its benchmark weight (its weight in the benchmark portfolio), and its active weight (defined as the difference between the managed and benchmark weights). Note that in the case where an asset is not held in the benchmark, its benchmark weight is zero and the active weight is equal to the portfolio weight. Conversely, for assets that are in the benchmark but not in the portfolio, their active weight is equal to the negative of the benchmark weight.

Given the portfolio weights, active weights, exposures, and covariance matrices, we compute forecasts of portfolio risk and tracking error.

Step 8 In this example, the final step in the risk estimation process involves finding the sources of risk. For example, we can decompose tracking error and portfolio volatility into various sources including the local market, industries, and investment styles.

SUMMARY

This chapter presented an overview as well as a detailed look into the linear factor model. The overview was presented in the form of a taxonomy of equity factor models. We classified factor models into those with observed and unobserved factor returns.

Next, we took an in-depth view of the linear cross-sectional factor model. We presented both local and global specifications. As part of this discussion we defined the various types of asset exposures used in linear factor equity models.

The linear cross-sectional factor model forms the basis of risk calculations. We presented these risk calculations, introduced both relative and absolute contributions to risk, and showed how risk can be attributed to factors and assets.

Finally, we summarized the practical implementation of the linear cross-sectional model. The eight-step process includes the data collection and the computations.

PART Four

Traditional Investments

CHAPTER 21

An Asset-Management Approach to Manager Selection

David Ben-Ur and Chris Vella

INTRODUCTION: THE IMPORTANCE OF INVESTMENT PHILOSOPHY

The starting point for any successful investment process is a sound, coherent, tested investment philosophy that is held as an article of faith by the team of professionals implementing it. Similarly, manager selection requires a set of "first principles" in seeking to research and identify such managers who can be expected to outperform their peers and the benchmark, thus creating alpha for clients in the future.

The manager-selection endeavor—its goals, structures, tools, and processes—is analogous to the security selection and portfolio construction process pursued by analysts and portfolio managers at active equity and fixed income investment organizations. In this framework, managers are viewed as businesses and multi-manager structures as portfolios of highly liquid assets. The insights gained from this philosophy form a strong cultural and intellectual basis for approaching the manager-selection problem, and, in our view, will yield a high-quality process with demonstrable investment results over time.

In seeking to apply a buy-side research approach to manager selection, any manager-selection team has at its disposal a powerful source of best practices: the asset managers with whom the team interacts each day.

How does an asset-management philosophy apply to a manager-selection team? Consider the following generic asset-selection process. The process can be broken into several distinct subcomponents:

1. Universe determination:
   - Determine the investable universe for the discipline.
2. Idea generation:
   - Quantitative screens.
   - Industry sources (conferences, trade publications, referrals).
3. Analysis of securities:
   - Quantitative modeling (historical and pro forma).
   - Fundamental analysis (management discussions, industry and business analysis).
   - "Triangulation" (via competitors, suppliers, customers, and other sources).

4. Security ranking and selection:
   - Team-based debate of each security's merits; assignment of "buy/hold/sell" rating.
   - Decision-making process for inclusion/exclusion.
5. Portfolio construction:
   - Sizing of positions.
   - Matching security weights to overall portfolio risk and return targets.
   - Application of sophisticated risk management techniques.
6. Monitoring:
   - Updates with management.
   - Continued industry and company triangulation.
   - Monitoring of risk positioning and portfolio structure.

When infused with the best practices of elite money-management organizations and applied to a manager-selection business, this generic process takes on a shape that is distinct from traditional manager due diligence. For a manager-selection group, the asset-management approach to manager selection strongly impacts group structure, culture, work flow, investment tools, and even recruiting—in short, this philosophy remakes the manager-selection team in the image of an asset-management group.

The current chapter deals with the first four steps of this generic process; Chapter 22 focuses on the portfolio construction process. At each step, we describe how insights gleaned from elite asset-management organizations can inform and sharpen the investment process, with the ultimate goal of generating superior investment results for institutional and individual clients.

MANAGER SELECTION USING AN ASSET-MANAGEMENT APPROACH

The opportunity set of managers and products is nearly as vast as the opportunity set of securities in the equity market. As of March 31, 2002, there were over 7,000 mutual funds registered for investment in the United States, and there were more than 10,000 offshore funds registered outside the United States. This does not include locally registered mutual funds, separate accounts, and private partnerships. The task of identifying the best money manager in a particular arena can be quite daunting at first glance and is similar to a portfolio manager's task in finding the most promising company for a portfolio out of thousands of potential choices. In both cases, a systematic approach to a massive database of information is utilized to reduce the amount of time and effort expended on ultimately unattractive options.

The first step in paring the universe of managers is to identify and screen for a specific type or style of manager. This step is analogous to quantitative screens employed by most asset managers to identify a universe of securities appropriate to the manager's style. For example, just as a U.S. large-cap value manager must sift through roughly 1,000 large-cap securities to determine which ones exhibit value characteristics, the manager-selection team must sift through thousands of U.S. equity managers to identify the roughly 300 that invest specifically in large-cap value securities. Like many asset-management organizations, the manager-selection group seeks to isolate the right style of investment using both measurable metrics and intangible considerations. Measurable metrics include the manager's official database classification and quantitative screening; the main qualitative consideration is a subjective overlay by the investor based on industry knowledge and subjective interpretation of the quantitative data.

The manager's self-classification should be used, but not to the exclusion of other metrics. A manager might believe that its investment style is, for example, truly large-cap value, but that manager's definition of value may differ dramatically from other value managers or, in certain cases, from the basic characteristics of traditional value benchmarks. The quantitative screening typically eliminates this type of manager from the analysis. At this stage quantitative screens embrace a number of factors, including style consistency, risk-adjusted performance over rolling periods of time, performance consistency, downside risk (or drawdown) analysis, and substyle analysis (to differentiate, for example, a deep value manager from a relative value manager). These screens are analogous to an asset manager's search of databases for companies meeting specific return on equity, net income, and valuation criteria. There are two key factors that the manager-selection team looks for in identifying successful managers from a quantitative perspective: superior risk-adjusted performance in various market environments and over a full market cycle and consistent results relative to an appropriate benchmark.

Any quantitative screen, no matter how powerful and robust, should serve only as a starting point; for both asset managers and manager-selection groups, quantitative pitfalls abound. For manager pickers, survivorship bias (the tendency of database providers to expunge the entire track record of products that shut down) represents a significant drawback of manager databases. Furthermore, pure quantitative screens fail to provide fundamental information about the investment manager, the experience of the team, the team's length of time at the firm, the depth of firm resources, the ownership structure of the firm, and so forth. A returns-based screen will also exclude information on how the track record was built—for example, the assets under management.

These pitfalls speak to the need for a qualitative overlay to the screening process. Often asset-management teams will qualitatively add and delete companies from their screens based on their history with the management team, prior experience investing in the security, or industry knowledge. Similarly, the manager-selection process should allow for making subjective additions to the list and deletions from the screened list of managers. Such qualitative overrides could derive from any number of sources: There may be a new team from a different organization taking over a bad track record that should be added to the list of managers. There may be a manager with an outstanding track record that screened very well but lost several key investment professionals and should therefore be eliminated from the list. A great team with a solid track record might be housed within a parent company that the manager-selection team knows to be ineffective at retaining talent; such a manager might be eliminated from the process. In summary, a good manager-selection screening process, like a good asset-management investment process, should take into account both observable, objective performance and risk criteria and less formal but equally important qualitative considerations. Managers that meet these joint criteria receive a request for proposal (RFP) and become eligible to proceed to the next phase of the investment process.

FUNDAMENTAL ANALYSIS

The heart of many traditional asset-management processes is fundamental analysis. This stage becomes even more important when assessing asset managers, whose strategic assets are the individuals managing the money and the processes they put into place. The primary forum for fundamental analysis is the on-site meeting with the manager.

The purpose of the on-site meeting is manifold. The selection team seeks to observe and absorb an organization's physical setting, corporate culture, quality of personnel, and, importantly, the quality of interpersonal relations and communications.

A competent manager-selection team uses several techniques to arrive at a deep understanding of these factors. First, all meetings should take place without the presence of sales or marketing personnel. These individuals—particularly the highly skilled ones—tend to redirect the conversation to highlight the manager's strengths or to "spin" or explain away its weaknesses. Speaking with individuals one-on-one allows for a more candid, less directed discussion. Additional insight comes from asking the same sets of questions to different individuals. Solid, healthy organizations tend to generate very similar answers from different individuals, whereas contrasting answers or angles often signify poor communications or political undertones.

The roster of meetings is also important. Just as savvy asset-management analysts will meet with many individuals in a company (CEO, CFO, line managers, etc.), the selection team should seek to meet not only the portfolio managers and analysts, but, where applicable, the CEO, chief investment officer, director of research, operations and technology personnel, and traders. In addition, young recruits to the firm—often individuals straight out of college—tend to represent a strong leading indicator of corporate health. In a strong firm, these individuals are accomplished and motivated, and have a clear sense of their role and trajectory within the organization. At less attractive firms, new hires tend to be less qualified, shorter-term in their horizon, and less focused on broad firm-level issues. Meeting with such people—from all parts of the organization—is an important piece in the on-site mosaic.

The selection team should employ several other techniques during the on-site visit. A view of the physical layout allows for inferences about communication, hierarchy, and group culture. Similar inferences can be drawn by end-of-day sessions with the entire investment team (as opposed to individuals) and by scheduling meetings that run late in the day; leaving a firm at seven o'clock in the evening affords an invaluable perspective on the work ethic of the firm. By asking the same series of questions to portfolio managers and research analysts, the selection team can assess the degree that similar investment philosophy and process has permated the entire organization. Often identification of these small nuances can be attained through an on-site visit to the organization.

The goal of the on-site visit is to ensure familiarity with both the overtones and the undertones of the corporate culture, structures, and processes. At the same time, most managers will appreciate the care, effort, and time taken by a team that mounts a significant effort; by day's end, strong professional and network relationships have been formed.

TRIANGULATION

The next step in manager evaluation is gathering information on the manager from numerous external sources in order to compare and contrast stories from different sources. Similar to the way a portfolio manager would conduct background checks on a company through questioning customers, suppliers, and the competition, we would also interview the competition (other portfolio managers with a similar investment style), customers (clients of the portfolio manager), and suppliers (sell-side research analysts and corporate management). The objective is to gather facts from various sources in order to confirm or refute a consistent positive pattern the team has developed on a particular manager.

Competitors, while clearly biased in their viewpoints, often reveal pertinent information about their peers. This information must be used carefully due to the biases involved; however, at times this information can lead to meaningful insights. For example, competitors will often have insight into whom they are seeing frequently in finals and who is winning business. Competitors often know which firms are losing talent and which firms are gaining it; they can also provide information on which organizations are great breeding grounds for solid analysts.

Information from customers can take several forms. Savvy manager-selection teams typically insist on reference checks from not only existing clients, but also new clients and terminated clients. The type of reference check typically speaks volumes about the manager under review. Managers who offer as references personal friends in the business or individuals or entities that do not have a solid understanding of the manager typically do so for lack of better references. Higher-quality reference checks would involve a seasoned professional with unique insights into the manager under review. New clients have often recently completed the same type of search currently being undertaken by the manager-selection team; as such, these conversations tend to be very useful in understanding how the new client became comfortable with the manager issues. Finally, terminated clients can at times be difficult to reach or may not be willing to offer much information, but every once in a while there is very useful information embedded in the conversation. Consistency in the information gathered is a key to identifying managers worth pursuing further, and inconsistent information at this stage will help identify managers with significant issues.

A third source of external "triangulation" information is the supplier community. When evaluating money managers, suppliers of information to portfolio managers tend to consist of sell-side analysts and corporate management. Each manager uses the sell side and corporate management to different degrees. No two managers are the same in this regard, so one must be very careful to assign the appropriate weight to these conversations. For example, a manager that uses the sell side extensively and talks to brokers on a daily basis should be well regarded by the Street and should have excellent sell-side reference checks; lack of such references could signal a problem. If a portfolio manager rarely uses sell-side research, such as a quantitative manager that relies on purely objective data or a bottom-up manager that relies solely on its own research, he or she should be able to provide excellent corporate management references. As always, one must be cognizant of the biases imbedded in these views. Sell-side analysts may want to direct new business to their largest client, and corporate management may have similar interests in mind; for example, they may be quite favorable if a manager own a large stake in their business.

QUANTITATIVE ANALYSIS

Most asset managers include quantitative modeling in their research—whether as the backbone of the process (as for quantitative strategies) or as a crucial decision-making input (as in traditional fundamental approaches). In either case, the quantitative analysis provides a systematic framework for evaluating investment opportunities on both a stand-alone and a comparative basis. A best-practices approach to manager selection involves the development of a comprehensive quantitative package that is produced for each manager involved in the investment process. Such a package provides an in-depth view of the manager from two key perspectives: a point-in-time (current) snapshot and, crucially, a historical overview.

When a manager is selected to participate in a search, the RFP package should include a request for monthly returns since inception and, importantly, full monthly holdings since inception. This information is thoroughly analyzed through multiple risk and style analysis systems. A thorough quantitative package is four-dimensional in nature: It looks at managers on both a stand-alone and a comparative basis, and it looks at managers during the current snapshot and over the longer course of history. Along these dimensions, the following characteristics should be examined:

- Returns-based attribution, not only by sector, but also by style, such as, in the case of equities, market cap, price-earnings (P/E) ratio, dividend yield, price-book (P/B) ratio, and earnings growth category.
- Factor attribution of *returns*, including security selection, factor exposures, beta exposures, and sector exposures.
- Factor attribution of *risk*, including security selection, factor exposures, beta exposures, and sector exposures.
- Returns-based analysis, including correlation studies, style exposures, drawdown analysis, and upside/downside capture.

The manager-selection team is looking to identify consistency in the sources of alpha generated by the manager under analysis. The quantitative package is developed in order to help pinpoint areas of weakness and strength in the process that have filtered through to the portfolio's results—for example, a manager whose five-year track record is in the top quartile relative to peers, though 95 percent of the alpha generated came from one sector where the relevant research analyst has recently left for a hedge fund. This example is clearly an exaggeration; however, the quantitative package provides the manager-selection team with the data to dig very deep into historical drivers of performance, and allows the team to ask portfolio managers specific questions to better understand the degree to which the manager understands these drivers and the risks taken within the portfolio to achieve success or failure over a specific time period. The package ultimately serves as both a decisionmaking tool and a historical benchmark for future manager performance and positioning.

INVESTMENT DECISION MAKING

The amount of information gathered throughout this process is massive, and one can easily become lost in the minutiae of each manager evaluated. All managers have positives and negatives associated with some part of the analysis; the goal is to identify all issues, compare managers to an appropriate peer group, determine the future risks, and evaluate whether those risks are worth the investment with the manager. The ultimate goal is to identify managers that will provide clients with alpha over the next several years. There are a few important factors that deserve focus throughout the final decision-making process: the application of a quantitative rating to all aspects of a firm, the involvement of several investment professionals in the investment process and final decision making, and the encouragement of debate among investment professionals on the merits and issues of each manager.

The rating of external managers should be standardized across each asset class and subclass. By standardizing the key factors, the manager-selection team is able to cross-fertilize ideas across teams (such as U.S. equities and international equities) and undertake healthy cross-team debates on multi-asset-class organizations. Each category should be assigned a rating—say, of 1 to 4. This scale would help to avoid defaulting to an average rating and force investment professionals to rate managers above or below the average for each category. Possible categories for rating include organization, investment philosophy, investment process, portfolio manager, research capabilities, risk management, robustness of product, user-friendliness, and overall rating.

The categories suggested are all-encompassing in order to give a full picture of an organization and pinpoint the areas of strength and areas of weakness or concern. Each category should be fully defined in order to standardize the research product for all managers. The investment process category, for example, could entail some or all of the following subcategories:

- Sensible investment process:
  - Vis-à-vis investment philosophy.
  - Vis-à-vis makeup of team, organization.
- Idea generation:
  - Screens.
  - Access to Street research.
  - Network—corporate management.
- Quality of research:
  - Models.
  - Company evaluation criteria.
  - Access to management.
  - Access to and utilization of tools.

- Effective communication between various parties:
  Are the best ideas getting into the portfolio?
  Is the process working effectively and efficiently?
- Consistency in approach.
- Sell discipline.

These subcategories need not be individually rated but rather help the team keep the appropriate framework in mind as a rating is assigned.

Each investment professional involved in a particular manager review or search should determine his or her ratings independently. A larger investment meeting should be held to debate the final rating of each category for each manager involved in the search process. A typical investment meeting should be intense, investment-oriented, and open to vigorous debate. Such meetings could take as long as one full day and are rarely shorter than four hours.

CONCLUSIONS

The asset management approach to manager selection imparts many benefits, both tangible and intangible, to the manager-selection team. First and foremost, it provides a systematic, results-driven framework in which to pursue strong investment results for clients. In addition, this approach provides ancillary and mutually reinforcing benefits, including:

- Strong relationships and open access to money managers who are appreciative of and familiar with the investment approach.
- Enhanced information networks via multiple "touch-point" contacts in each organization.
- Promotion of a dynamic investment-management culture within the manager-selection team; this culture in turn helps to attract and retain outstanding investment professionals within the manager selection group.
- A philosophy that lends itself to an asset-management business structure, in which payment is based on assets and performance rather than a consulting-style retainer fee. This structure, in turn, aligns the interests of the manager-selection group and the client.
- A daily, asset-management-like perspective on manager monitoring, which in turn drives greater manager knowledge and, ultimately, improved investment results.

For any asset-management business—including one in which the assets being managed are investment portfolios—this last benefit is perhaps the most important from a commercial and client-satisfaction standpoint.

CHAPTER 22

Investment Program Implementation: Realities and Best Practices

J. Douglas Kramer

The structuring of a thoughtful investment program is a time-consuming and complex task that requires not only the adherence to sound theoretical investment philosophy described throughout this book but also the navigation of practical realities during implementation. This chapter will address the interrelationship among the following practical issues: How does the size of an investment program impact the ability to implement investment policy? How should investors think about fees? What are the most cost-efficient methods to rebalance or transition managers? What are the real risks of asset allocation drift? In the context of those risks, how often should investors rebalance their asset allocation and manager lineup?

The size of an investment program is the single largest determinant of how an investment program can be implemented. Most significantly, the size of the plan can have a material impact on the distribution of risk in an investment program. Furthermore, plan size has a significant role in determining not only manager selection but also how funds will be invested with the managers: direct separate accounts or commingled vehicles (e.g., mutual funds, partnerships, etc.). Lastly, plan size determines the economies of scale and hence investors must adjust their implementation choices according to plan size in order to maximize after-fee total rate of return.

Classifying investment plans into four sizes facilitates the discussion of the impact of plan size on implementation.[1]

1. Superlarge programs: >$10 billion.
2. Large programs: $1 billion to $10 billion.
3. Medium-size programs: $100 million to $1 billion.
4. Small programs: <$100 million.

[1]Please note that the following discussion applies generally to institutional portfolios. Individual investors should consider the concepts discussed throughout this chapter taking into consideration the issues of taxes, financial planning, and trust and estate work, as well as other idiosyncratic needs.

PLAN SIZE: IMPLEMENTATION IMPACT ON RISK

The size of an investment plan can have a significant impact on the distribution of risk within the overall portfolio. The two main classes of investment risk we will address in this context are market risk (i.e., benchmark risk) and active management risk (see Chapter 13).

In the context of market risk, the size of a plan has historically had a material impact on which asset classes have been available for investment. Typically, smaller plans have had less diversification at the asset class level, limiting their investments to traditional domestic equity and bonds. In the context of Chapters 25 to 28, we recommend that smaller plans diversify into new and alternative asset classes to improve risk-adjusted returns. Additionally, the proliferation of commingled vehicles has provided smaller-program investors with access to asset classes that previously have not been available. Asset classes that are typically overlooked by the smaller plans include: real estate, high-yield bonds, international equities, emerging market equities and fixed income, hedge funds, and private equity. Many investors and investment committees at the smaller end of the size spectrum feel obligated to use separate accounts to prove their active customized fiduciary oversight role. The problem with this practice is that separate account fees on small accounts are typically quite expensive, which leads investment committees to overallocate capital to individual managers in order to hit fee break points and account minimums at the expense of good diversified investment policy. The risk associated with this practice at the smaller end of the size spectrum is the resulting concentration of active manager risk.

Concentrated active management risk can result from too few active managers, in many cases one per asset class. The subsequent lack of diversification of active manager risk at the total portfolio level can reduce the expected total return by limiting the plan's comfort with concentrated, potentially high-return managers. While there is nothing inherently wrong with significant active management risk, investors and investment committees recognize that unlike market risk, active risk creates a divergence of their performance from that of their peers. This peer risk generally leads plans to feel comfortable with between 100 and 300 basis points of active risk, an amount that does not significantly increase the volatility of total plan returns.

In the context of Chapters 13 and 14, we discussed the importance of creating an overall risk budget with the key objective of diversifying active management risk. Given the relatively small appetite for active risk of most plans, it is important to try to create as much return as possible per unit of active risk. It is especially important at the smaller end of the program size spectrum to make sure active management risks are desired, understood, monitored, and adequately diversified during implementation.

On the other end of the size spectrum, large and superlarge plans typically have sophisticated internal and external investment resources to create complex diversified portfolio structures. Larger plans may appear properly diversified across asset classes on paper but have significant implementation challenges. One of the biggest challenges to larger plans is finding enough complementary high-quality managers to implement policy in smaller-capitalization and high-transaction-cost asset classes.

As the investment program's asset allocation and risk budget are developed, it is commonplace to see the largest plans investing as much as 5 percent to high-yield bonds, 5 percent to publicly traded real estate, 5 to 10 percent to small-capitalization stocks, and 5 percent to emerging-market equities—all classic lower-capitalization, lower-capacity, and high-transaction-cost asset classes. In Chapter 21, we discussed the importance of investment managers capping product capacity in these asset classes in order to maintain product quality. Because of the low capacity of high-quality products, a $10 billion plan could need two or three high-yield managers, two or three real estate investment trust (REIT) managers, five to seven small-capitalization managers, and two or three emerging-market equity managers in order to be fully invested in the asset class.

The tension between the need to implement an asset allocation and the lack of high-quality supply to implement the asset allocation creates significant manager selection work. Many times, this supply/demand imbalance causes the number of managers in the largest plans to be significant. As the number of managers in the plan increases, so does the diversification of active management risk. While on the surface this sounds attractive, in the largest plans with significant numbers of active managers across asset classes the benefit of diversification must be balanced against the risk of hiring lower-quality managers as well as the increased costs associated with higher numbers of active managers.

As discussed in Chapters 12 and 13, investors should construct portfolios so that the correlation of excess returns among managers works to reduce active risk to acceptable levels. However, in the largest plans where the number of managers is highest due to the aforementioned reasons, the marginal opportunities to reduce risk are dampened by the sheer number of managers and the ensuing diversification. Outlined in Figure 22.1 is an example of how large plans get marginally less diversification benefit (i.e., lower tracking error) from adding new managers to the plan.

As discussed in Chapter 13, investors overseeing the largest plans must be vigilant in their demand for and monitoring of risk-budgeted tracking error. Active

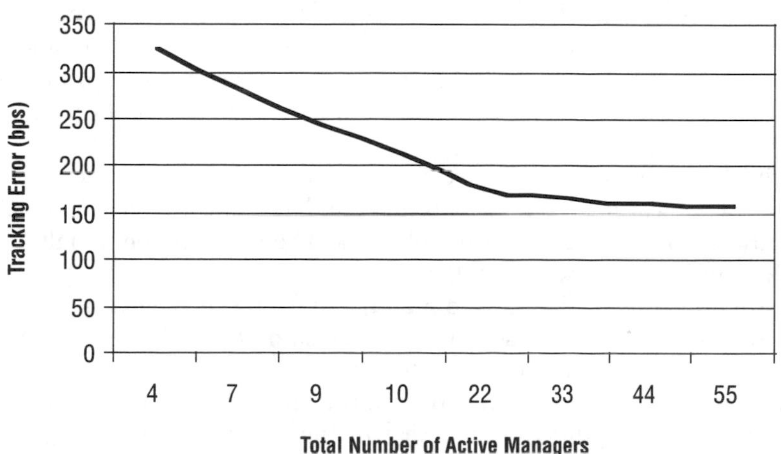

FIGURE 22.1 Total Fund Tracking Error

managers earn fees for the excess return that they are expected to create, and generation of excess return requires risk taking. In the context of an overall portfolio, each manager must generate enough tracking error to create excess return, but not so much that it leads to a concentration of risk that reduces the plan's ability to add other sources of excess return or degradation of their information ratios.

PLAN SIZE: IMPLEMENTING SEPARATE ACCOUNTS VERSUS COMMINGLED VEHICLES

Plan size has a significant impact on what type of investment vehicle should be considered for an investment program. Logically, the largest, most sophisticated programs typically use separate accounts to implement investment policy, as their large asset size gives them access and fee scale to the most sophisticated investment managers.

Furthermore, separate accounts facilitate customization, allowing investors to specify custom guidelines. Many investors think about guideline customization in the context of sector exposures (e.g., exposure to Japan must be ±10 percent around benchmark) or social restrictions (e.g., no sin stocks). However, there are other important examples of customization. For example, in certain contexts one of the key benefits of a separate account is that investors can specify customized tracking error targets in the investment guidelines. While most managers have a standard process that leads to a given tracking error and we are not advocating changing a manager's inherent investment philosophy, we are highlighting how separate accounts allow for hands-on specification of risk parameters that in some cases will allow a manager to dial up or down risk. Such adjustments are not available to investors who participate in commingled vehicles. Consistent with the need to create a thoughtful overall risk budget, separate accounts can allow for adjusting manager risk so that the total mix optimizes return in the context of the overall balanced risk budget.

Customization has its implementation drawbacks, however. Specifically, large numbers of separate accounts require significant oversight, as each manager must be monitored on a stand-alone basis and in the context of the overall plan. This oversight, described in detail in Chapter 15, requires significant human and technological resources. Moreover, asking a manager to create a customized product that is not a standard part of his or her process can create implementation risks on the part of the manager.

For those plans that do not have the resources to select and monitor a large number of investment managers there is an abundance of commingled vehicles that provide different kinds of investment solutions. The simplest commingled vehicles are single-manager mutual funds that provide investors, especially small and medium-size programs, with access to high-quality active management. It is important for investors in these mutual funds to understand the fund's objectives, guidelines, and benchmark. Similar to separate accounts, mutual fund performance can be measured in the context of excess return, tracking error, and information ratio. These statistics can, in turn, be included in the program's risk budget. Single-manager mutual funds are not just for smaller plans; many medium and large plans use mutual funds to cost-effectively satisfy allocation to smaller asset classes. One drawback, however, of the mutual fund approach is that, as previously mentioned, smaller programs that invest in one single-manager mutual fund per asset class tend to have a higher concentration of active management risk in the overall plan. Another drawback is the requirement to monitor the manager's performance, style consistency, risk, and so forth.

In response to these issues that exist in single-manager mutual funds, there now exist a number of commingled vehicles in the marketplace that combine managers together to diversify active management. These commingled vehicles, known as multimanager portfolios, combine managers usually in the same asset class and/or style (e.g., large-cap value, high-yield fixed income) and are actively managed by a sponsor. The sponsor assumes fiduciary oversight of the portfolio and can actively fire and hire managers within the vehicle. Multimanager portfolios provide investors with access to a more diversified set of managers all within the same vehicle.

Best practice in multimanager portfolio construction attempts to maximize the expected return per unit of risk of the portfolio, which requires not only understanding manager style, but also risk budgeting and the quantitative monitoring of return volatilities and correlations across managers. Many multimanager portfolios in the marketplace are not created with this precision or risk monitoring, but rather they are created by marketing organizations that market access to a combination of well-known investment management brands. While multimanager portfolios can provide access to good managers, the improper combination of managers can result in a concentrated risk profile that detracts from expected excess returns. Importantly, multimanager portfolios are not just for smaller and medium-plans. Larger plans can use multimanager portfolios in certain asset classes to streamline their investment process by outsourcing manager selection and portfolio construction within the multimanager portfolio, thus allowing the investment team to focus on areas where they have relevant expertise or interest. Additionally, many investment teams use multimanager portfolio where the investment process is more complex or less well known and where the asset class is complex, volatile, or less mature than other asset classes. As with single-manager mutual funds, investors can use the portfolio level excess return, tracking error, and information ratio targets as inputs into the overall risk budget.

PLAN SIZE: COSTS

While the level of costs associated with running an investment program can vary dramatically based on the size of the program, the categories of cost are predominately the same. Investment programs create costs from:

- *Investment management*—the costs paid directly to those managing the portfolio.
- *Custody*—the costs paid to the custodian bank for holding the assets.
- *Transaction costs*—the costs paid to brokers and intermediaries for providing liquidity.
- *Administration*—the costs paid to the CFO, pension fund oversight department, consultants, lawyers, accountants, transfer agents, payment agents, technology, and so on.

Smaller programs typically do not have the economies of scale to efficiently address each category of cost and hence need to pool assets with other plans through the use of commingled vehicles in order to prevent costs from significantly detracting from performance. While most of this expense control for smaller plans is intuitive, one underestimated benefit from the use of commingled vehicles is reduced transaction costs for larger plans. Some asset classes are very illiquid and hence have very high transaction costs. If there are significant cash flows in the investment program, a single manager with concentrated positions can incur very significant transaction costs from market impact. In this context commingled vehicles spread the capital more widely and can reduce the market impact on individual securities.

In addition to the use of commingled vehicles to reduce costs, large programs have other tools at their disposal. In the course of an investment program there will always be manager transitions due to asset allocation changes as well as the hiring and firing of investment managers. The movement of dollars among asset classes or managers creates significant transaction costs that can and should be managed. For example, terminating Large Cap Value Manager A in favor of Large Cap Value Manager B creates significant portfolio transactions during the transition. While there is most likely holdings overlap and those securities can be transferred in-kind, there will be a significant portion of the portfolio that needs to be sold and new securities to be purchased. If the new manager simply sold unwanted securities on the open market, the portfolio would be subject to commissions and, depending on the liquidity in the market, significant price impact (i.e., selling/buying in a lower-liquidity stock, causing poor price execution). Medium to superlarge plans have service providers available that can help reduce these costs. Specifically, programs can employ transition management firms to help them reduce costs during portfolio changes.

Transition managers provide access to centralized pools of cheap liquidity where buyers and sellers come together to communally reduce transaction costs. Transition managers reduce costs by crossing assets among contributors, thus not exposing transactions to the open market. Not all assets in a portfolio can be crossed within the transition pool, and hence some open-market transactions are required. However, in aggregate, utilizing a transition manager's crossing network can significantly reduce transition costs.

ASSET ALLOCATION DRIFT AND COMPLETION MANAGEMENT[2]

In a large plan with many specialized managers, unintentional asset allocation risk is often quite large. While there are many activities that create unintentional asset allocation risk, the first and most important is drift. Drift occurs when the value of underlying portfolio holdings moves away from the strategic benchmark due to differences in asset class returns and the fact that fixed benchmark weights reset at the end of every month.[3] For example, imagine a 60 percent stock/40 percent bond

[2]Special thanks to Mark Carhart for this section.

[3]If left unspecified, multi-asset-class benchmarks reset to their fixed proportions at the same frequency as performance is reported, typically monthly. Increasingly, clients are specifying that benchmark weights drift with asset valuations over longer horizons, permitting benchmark reset frequencies such as quarterly, semiannually or annually.

TABLE 22.1 Average Unintentional Drift Risk

Rebalance Frequency	Annualized Drift Risk
Quarterly	0.22%
Semiannually	0.27
Annually	0.40
Biannually	0.70

portfolio of index funds that is exactly at benchmark at the end of one month. If stocks outperform bonds by 4 percent over the next month—approximately a one standard deviation event—at the end of the month its new allocation will be 60.9 percent/39.1 percent.[4] This 0.9 percent mismatch equals about 0.19 percent of unintentional tracking error to the strategic benchmark.

Naturally, the risk in drift increases in the time between rebalances. Table 22.1 shows the average unintentional drift risk from different rebalance frequencies based on historical simulations. On average, plans that rebalance once a quarter experience 0.22% drift risk, while those rebalancing only once a year incur 0.40% in unintentional risk. This assumes that the underlying asset returns are the same as the benchmark. Actively managed underlying assets will cause even larger deviations and drift risk.

Even worse, the drift risk is the worst kind of risk because it is highly correlated with the strategic benchmark. In the previous example, that 0.19 percent of tracking error translates into a 0.17 percent increase in total portfolio volatility. Such an increase in volatility is equivalent to a 200 basis point increase in uncorrelated active risk on the total portfolio. In other words, the drift from a rather typical one-month return on stocks and bonds has the same impact on total risk of the plan as the entire active risk budget for an average plan!

Table 22.2 demonstrates the significance of the correlation between drift and benchmark risk. We simulated returns for an aggressive U.S. plan with a large pool of active managers and fixed benchmark weights for U.S. large-cap, mid-cap, and small-cap stocks, international stocks, U.S. bonds, and international bonds.[5] We found that rebalancing only once per quarter meant that 14 percent of the time the absolute return from unintentional drift exceeded the absolute return from intentional active risk. Rebalancing only once per year increased the frequency to an astounding 39 percent of the time.

When hearing this, our clients sometimes ask whether there is any additional return to intentionally following a drift strategy, in spite of the clear increase in risk. Although not rebalancing might be thought of as an asset class momentum

[4]For this example, we assume annual stock and bond volatilities are 20 percent and 5 percent, and that stock–bond correlation is 0.1.

[5]Example was based on an existing client. Their benchmark is 32 percent U.S. large-cap, 12 percent U.S. mid-cap, 14 percent U.S. small-cap, 17 percent international equity, 15 percent U.S. bonds, and 10 percent international bonds. The example assumes 26 individual managers across these six asset classes with active risk averaging approximately 9 percent for each equity manager and 2.5 percent for each bond manager.

TABLE 22.2 Simulated Returns for Aggressive U.S. Plan

Rebalance Frequency	Frequency That Absolute Return from Drift Exceeds Absolute Active Return
Quarterly	14%
Semiannually	24
Annually	39
Biannually	50

strategy, the returns to the strategy appear to be zero or slightly negative. Across hundreds of simulations for a variety of benchmarks and rebalance frequencies, we find the average return is about –5 basis points per year.

But these averages mask the highly visible and important periods where asset allocation drift is much worse. Consider a 60/40 plan with no asset allocation drift at the beginning of 1987. This plan would have entered October 1987 with a 7 percent stock overweight, resulting in an additional 1.4 percent loss in October 1987. The Long Term Capital Management (LTCM) blowup of 1998 and September 11, 2001, events created similar impacts on portfolio performance from not rebalancing.

Of course, drift risk isn't the only cause of asset allocation risk. Cash sitting in managers' accounts, currency deviations driven by stock selection activities, and manager or benchmark transitions also create unintentional risk that is frequently left unmanaged.

The solution to controlling these risks for larger plans is a completion manager. A completion manager coordinates the portfolio's overall asset allocation and is charged with explicitly minimizing unintentional asset allocation risk. Complex schemes with frequent cash flows may use their custodian as a specialized completion manager given their proximity to the information flows in the portfolio.

The ideal method for implementing a completion strategy is through liquid equity index futures, bond index futures, and currency forwards. This approach is optimal due to the ease of trading and low transaction costs. Currently, there are approximately 40 global index securities that are liquid enough for completion strategies. To indicate the magnitude of cost savings, for a normal trade size of $5 million, the cost of trading equity index futures is approximately 90 percent less than an equivalent trade in physicals. These derivatives also make it possible to manage the completion portfolio with limited capital due to the minimal margin and collateral requirements. (See Chapter 25 for further discussion on futures implementation issues.)

These arguments strongly favor the use of liquid derivatives to implement a completion strategy, but a rebalance strategy may also be implemented using cash instruments, with a natural reduction in efficiency. For example, some institutions use so-called "swing" portfolios.[6] A swing portfolio generally requires a substantial carve-out, often 10 to 20 percent of the overall portfolio. This capital is typically invested in index funds to bring the overall portfolio back toward its strategic

[6]The swing portfolio approach is much more common in Japan than in the United States.

benchmark, reallocating as needed. The availability of index funds, the cost of trading the funds, as well as the size of the swing portfolio all determine the efficacy of a cash-implemented swing portfolio.

Implementing a sound investment plan requires adherence to a well-designed investment policy. Well-designed investment policies require not only a good academic framework but also navigating the practical realities described in this chapter during implementation.

CHAPTER 23

Equity Portfolio Management

Andrew Alford, Robert Jones, and Terence Lim

OVERVIEW

Equity portfolio management (EPM) has evolved considerably since Benjamin Graham and David Dodd published their classic text on security analysis in 1934. For one, the types of stocks available for investment have shifted dramatically, from companies with mostly physical assets (such as railroads and utilities) to companies with mostly intangible assets (such as technology stocks and pharmaceuticals). Moreover, Modern Portfolio Theory and the Capital Asset Pricing Model, in conjunction with new data sources and powerful computers, have revolutionized the way investors select stocks and create portfolios. Consequently, what was once mostly an art is increasingly becoming a science: Loose rules of thumb are being replaced by rigorous research and complex implementation.

Of course, these new advances, while greatly expanding the frontiers of finance, have not necessarily made it any easier for portfolio managers to beat the market. In fact, the increasing sophistication of the average investor has probably made it more difficult to find—and exploit—pricing errors.[1] There are no sure bets, and mispricings, when they occur, are rarely both large and long lasting. Successful managers must therefore constantly work to improve their existing strategies and to develop new ones. Understanding fully the equity management process is essential to accomplishing this challenging task.

These new advances, unfortunately, have also allowed some market participants to stray from a sound investment approach. It is now easier than ever for portfolio managers to use biased, unfamiliar, or incorrect data in a flawed strategy, one developed from untested conjecture or haphazard trial and error. Investors, too, must be careful not to let the abundance of data and high-tech techniques distract them when allocating assets and selecting managers. In particular, investors should not allow popular but narrow rankings of short-term performance to obscure important differences in portfolio managers' style exposures or investment processes. To avoid these pitfalls, it helps to have a solid grasp of the constantly advancing science of equity investing.

[1]Studies show that the majority of professional money managers have been unable to beat the market. For example, see Malkiel (1995).

This chapter provides an overview of EPM aimed at current and potential investors, analysts, investment consultants, and portfolio managers. We begin with a discussion of the two major approaches to EPM: the traditional approach and the quantitative approach. The remaining sections of the chapter are organized around four major steps in the investment process: (1) forecasting the unknown quantities needed to manage equity portfolios—returns, risks, and transaction costs; (2) constructing portfolios that maximize expected risk-adjusted return net of transaction costs; (3) trading stocks efficiently; and (4) evaluating results and updating the process.

These four steps should be closely integrated: The return, risk, and transaction cost forecasts, the approach used to construct portfolios, the way stocks are traded, and performance evaluation should all be consistent with one another. A process that produces highly variable, fast-moving return forecasts, for example, should be matched with short-term risk forecasts, relatively high transaction costs, frequent rebalancing, aggressive trading, and short-horizon performance evaluation. In contrast, stable, slower-moving return forecasts can be combined with longer-term risk forecasts, lower expected transaction costs, less frequent rebalancing, more patient trading, and longer-term evaluation. Mixing and matching incompatible approaches to each part of the investment process can greatly reduce a manager's ability to reap the full rewards of an investment strategy.

A well-structured investment process should also be supported by sound economic logic, diverse information sources, and careful empirical analysis that together produce reliable forecasts and effective implementation. And, of course, a successful investment process should be easy to explain; marketing professionals, consultants, and investors all need to understand a manager's process before they will invest in it.

TRADITIONAL AND QUANTITATIVE APPROACHES TO EPM

At one level, there are as many ways to manage portfolios as there are portfolio managers. After all, developing a unique and innovative investment process is one of the ways managers distinguish themselves from their peers. Nonetheless, at a more general level, there are two basic approaches used by most managers: the traditional approach and the quantitative approach. Although these two approaches are often sharply contrasted by their proponents, they actually share many traits. Both apply economic reasoning to identify a small set of key drivers of equity values; both use observable data to help measure these key drivers; both use expert judgment to develop ways to map these key drivers into the final stock-selection decision; and both evaluate their performance over time. What differs most between traditional and quantitative managers is how they perform these steps.

Traditional managers conduct stock-specific analysis to develop a subjective assessment of each stock's unique attractiveness. Traditional managers talk with senior management; closely study financial statements and other corporate disclosures; conduct detailed, stock-specific competitive analysis; and usually build spreadsheet models of a company's financial statements that provide an explicit link between various forecasts of financial metrics and stock prices. The traditional approach involves detailed analysis of a company and is often well equipped to cope with data errors or structural changes at a company (e.g., restructurings or acquisitions). However, because the traditional approach relies heavily on the judgment of analysts, it is subject to potentially severe subjective biases such as selective perception, hindsight bias, stereotyping, and overconfidence that can reduce forecast quality.[2] Moreover, the traditional approach is costly to apply, which makes it impracticable for a large investment universe comprising many small stocks. The high cost and subjective nature also make it difficult to evaluate, because it is hard to create the history necessary for testing. Testing an investment process is important because it helps to distinguish factors that are reflected in stock prices from those that are not. Only factors that are not yet impounded in stock prices can be used to identify profitable trading opportunities. Failure to distinguish between these two types of factors can lead to the familiar "good company, bad stock" problem in which even a great company can be a bad investment if the price paid for the stock is too high.[3]

Quantitative managers use statistical models to map a parsimonious set of measurable factors into objective forecasts of each stock's return, risk, and cost of trading. The quantitative approach formalizes the relation between the key factors and forecasts, which makes the approach transparent and largely free of subjective biases. Quantitative analysis can also be highly cost-effective. Although the fixed costs of building a robust quantitative model are high, the marginal costs of applying the model, or extending it to a broader investment universe, are low. Consequently, quantitative portfolio managers can choose from a large universe of stocks, including many small and otherwise neglected stocks that have attractive fundamentals. Finally, because the quantitative approach is model-based, it can be tested historically on a wide cross section of stocks over diverse economic environments. While quantitative analysis can suffer from specification errors and overfitting, analysts can mitigate these errors by following a well-structured and disciplined research process.

On the negative side, quantitative models can be misleading when there are bad data or significant structural changes at a company (i.e., "garbage in, garbage out"). For this reason, most quantitative managers like to spread their bets across many names so that the success of any one position will not make or break the strategy. Traditional managers, conversely, prefer to take fewer, larger bets given their detailed hands-on knowledge of the companies and the high cost of analysis. A summary of the major advantages of each approach to equity portfolio management is presented in Table 23.1.[4] Given that our expertise is quantitative equity

[2]For a discussion of the systematic errors in judgment and probability assessment that people frequently make, please see Kahneman, Slovic, and Tversky (1982).

[3]For a good discussion of the traditional approach, please see White, Sondhi, and Fried (1998).

[4]For an excellent comparison of clinical (traditional) and actuarial (quantitative) decision analysis, please see Dawes, Faust, and Meehl (1989). They find clinical analysts do a good job identifying a set of relevant factors, but actuarial analysts do a better job assigning weights to each of several factors. For a comparison of traditional and quantitative portfolio managers, please see Jones (1998).

TABLE 23.1 Major Advantages of the Traditional and Quantitative Approaches to Equity Portfolio Management

Traditional Approach	
Depth	Although they have views on fewer companies, traditional managers tend to have more in-depth knowledge of the companies they cover. Unlike a computerized model, they should know when data are misleading or unrepresentative.
Regime shifts	Traditional managers *may* be better equipped to handle regime shifts and recognize situations where past relationships might not be expected to continue (e.g., where back tests may be unreliable).
Signal identification	Based on their greater in-depth knowledge, traditional managers can better understand the unique data sources and factors that are important for stocks in different countries or industries.
Qualitative factors	Many important factors that may affect an investment decision are not available in any database and are hard to evaluate quantitatively. Examples might include: management and their vision for the company; the value of patents, brands, and other intangible assets; product quality; or the impact of new technology.
Quantitative Approach	
Breadth	Because a computerized model can quickly evaluate thousands of securities and can update those evaluations daily, it can uncover more opportunities. Further, by spreading their risk across many small bets, quantitative managers can add value with only slightly favorable odds.
Discipline	While individuals often base decisions on only the most salient or distinctive factors, a computerized model will simultaneously evaluate all specified factors before reaching a conclusion.
Verification	Before using any signal to evaluate stocks, quantitative managers will normally back test its historical efficacy and robustness. This provides a framework for weighting the various signals.
Risk management	By its nature, the quantitative approach builds in the notion of statistical risk and can do a better job of controlling unintended risks in the portfolio.
Lower fees	The economies of scale inherent in a quantitative process usually allow quantitative managers to charge lower fees.

management, we will primarily apply a quantitative framework for describing the EPM process in the rest of this chapter.

FORECASTING STOCK RETURNS, RISKS, AND TRANSACTION COSTS

Developing good forecasts is the first and perhaps most critical step in the investment process. Without good forecasts, the difficult task of forming superior portfolios becomes nearly impossible. In this section we discuss how to use a quantitative approach to generate forecasts of stock returns, risks, and transaction costs. These forecasts are then used in the portfolio construction step described in the next main section.[5]

Forecasting Returns

The process of building a quantitative return-forecasting model can be divided into four closely linked steps: (1) identifying a set of potential return forecasting variables, or signals; (2) testing the effectiveness of each signal, by itself and together with other signals; (3) determining the appropriate weight for each signal in the model; and (4) blending the model's views with market equilibrium to arrive at reasonable forecasts for expected returns.

Identifying a list of potential signals might seem like an overwhelming task; the candidate pool can seem almost endless. To narrow the list, it is important to start with fundamental relationships and sound economics. Reports published by Wall Street analysts and books about financial statement analysis are both good sources for ideas. Another valuable resource is academic research in finance and accounting. Academics have the incentive and expertise to identify and carefully analyze new and innovative information sources. Academics have studied a large number of stock price anomalies, and Table 23.2 lists several that have been adopted by investment managers.

For portfolio managers intent on building a successful investment strategy, it is not enough to simply take the best ideas identified by others and add them to the return-forecasting model. Instead, each potential signal must be thoroughly tested to ensure it works in the context of the manager's strategy across many stocks and during a variety of economic environments. The real challenge is winnowing the list of potential signals to a parsimonious set of reliable forecasting variables. When selecting a set of signals, it is a good idea to include a variety of variables to capture distinct investment themes, including valuation, momentum, and earnings quality. By diversifying over information sources and variables, the portfolio manager has a good chance that if one signal fails to add value another will be there to carry the load.

When evaluating a signal, it is important to make sure the underlying data used to compute the signal are available and largely error free. Checking selected observations by hand and screening for outliers or other influential observations is a useful way to identify data problems. It is also sometimes necessary to transform a signal—for instance, by subtracting the industry mean or taking the natural loga-

[5]Some portfolio managers do not develop explicit forecasts of returns, risks, and transaction costs. Instead, they map a variety of individual stock characteristics directly into portfolio holdings. However, there are limitations with this abbreviated approach. Because the returns and risks corresponding to the various characteristics are not clearly identified, it is difficult to ensure the weights placed on the characteristics are appropriate. Further, measuring risk at the portfolio level is awkward without reliable estimates of the risks of each stock, especially the correlations between stocks. Similarly, controlling turnover is hard when returns and transaction costs are not expressed in consistent units. And, of course, it is difficult to explain a process that occurs in one magical step.

TABLE 23.2 Selected Stock Price Anomalies Used in Quantitative Models

Growth/value: Value stocks (high book/price, earnings/price, cash flow/price) outperform growth stocks (low B/P, E/P, CF/P).

Fama and French (1992)
Lakonishok, Shleifer, and Vishny (1994)
Dechow and Sloan (1997)
LaPorta, Lakonishok, Shleifer, and Vishny (1997)
Daniel and Titman (1997)
Fama and French (1998)

Post-earnings-announcement drift: Stocks that announce earnings that beat expectations outperform stocks that miss expectations.

Foster, Olsen, and Shevlin (1984)
Rendleman, Jones, and Lutane (1982)
Bernard and Thomas (1989)
Bernard and Thomas (1990)
Collins and Hribar (2000)

Short-term price reversal: One-month losers outperform one-month winners.

Jegadeesh (1990)
Lo and MacKinlay (1990)

Intermediate-term price momentum: Six-month to one-year winners outperform losers.

Jegadeesh and Titman (1993)
Chan, Jegadeesh, and Lakonishok (1996)
Rouwenhorst (1998b)
Hong, Lim, and Stein (2000)
Grundy and Martin (2001)
Jegadeesh and Titman (2001)

Earnings quality: Stocks with cash earnings outperform stocks with noncash earnings.

Sloan (1996)
Collins and Hribar (2000)

Analyst earnings estimates and stock recommendations: Changes in analyst stock recommendations and earnings estimates predict subsequent stock returns.

Stickel (1991)
Bercel (1994)
Womack (1996)
Francis and Soffer (1997)
Barber, Lehavy, McNichols, and Trueman (2001)

rithm—to improve the "shape" (i.e., symmetry) of the distribution. To evaluate a signal properly, both univariate and multivariate analysis is important. Univariate analysis provides evidence on the signal's predictive ability when the signal is used alone, whereas multivariate analysis provides evidence on the signal's incremental predictive ability above and beyond other variables considered. For both univariate and multivariate analysis, it is wise to examine the returns to a variety of portfolios formed on the basis of the signal. Sorting stocks into quintiles or deciles is popular, as is regression analysis, where the coefficients represent the return to a portfolio with unit exposure to the signal. These portfolios can be equal-weighted, cap-weighted, or even risk-weighted depending on the model's ultimate purpose. Finally, the return forecasting model should be tested using a realistic simulation that controls the target level of risk, takes account of transaction costs, and imposes appropriate constraints (e.g., the non-negativity constraint for long-only portfolios). In our experience, many promising return-forecasting signals fail to add value in realistic back tests—either because they involve excessive trading; work only for small, illiquid stocks; or contain information that is already captured by other components of the model.

The third step in building a return-forecasting model is determining each signal's weight. When computing expected returns, more weight should be put on signals that, over time, have been more stable, generated higher and more consistent returns, and provided superior diversification benefits. Maintaining exposures to signals that change slowly requires less trading, and hence lower costs, than is the case for signals that change rapidly. Other things being equal, a stable signal (such as the ratio of book-to-market equity) should get more weight than a less stable signal (such as one-month price reversal). High, consistent returns are essential to a profitable, low-risk investment strategy; hence, signals that generate high returns with little risk should get more weight than signals that produce lower returns with higher risk. Finally, signals with more diversified payoffs should get more weight because they can hedge overall performance when other signals in the model perform poorly.

The last step in forecasting returns is to make sure the forecasts are reasonable and internally consistent by comparing them with equilibrium views. Return forecasts that ignore equilibrium expectations can create problems in the portfolio construction step. Seemingly reasonable return forecasts can cause an optimizer to maximize errors rather than expected returns, producing extreme, unbalanced portfolios. The problem is caused by return forecasts that are inconsistent with the assumed correlations across stocks. If two stocks (or subportfolios) are highly correlated, then the equilibrium expectation is that their returns should be similar; otherwise, the optimizer will treat the pair of stocks as a (near) arbitrage opportunity by going extremely long the high-return stock and extremely short the low-return stock. However, with hundreds of stocks, it is not always obvious whether certain stocks, or combinations of stocks, are highly correlated and therefore ought to have similar return forecasts. The Black-Litterman model was specifically designed to alleviate this problem. It blends a model's raw return forecasts with *equilibrium expected returns*—which are the returns that would make the benchmark optimal for a given risk model—to produce internally consistent return forecasts that reflect the manager's (or model's) views yet are consistent with the risk model. (For a discussion of how to use the Black-Litterman model to incorporate equilibrium views into a return-forecasting model, please see Chapter 7.)

Forecasting Risks

In a portfolio context, the risk of a single stock is a function of the variance of its returns, as well as the covariances between its returns and the returns of other stocks in the portfolio. The variance-covariance matrix of stock returns, or risk model, is used to measure the risk of a portfolio. For EPM, investors rarely estimate the full variance-covariance matrix directly because the number of individual elements is too large, and for a well-behaved (i.e., nonsingular) matrix, the number of observations used to estimate the matrix must significantly exceed the number of stocks in the matrix.[6] Instead, most equity portfolio managers use a factor risk model in which individual variances and covariances are expressed as a function of a small set of stock characteristics—such as industry membership, size, and leverage. This greatly reduces the number of unknown risk parameters that the manager needs to estimate.

When developing an equity factor risk model, it is important to include all of the variables used to forecast returns among the (potentially larger) set of variables used to forecast risks. This way, the risk model "sees" all of the potential risks in an investment strategy, both those managers are willing to accept and those they would like to avoid. Further, a mismatch between the variables in the return and risk models can produce less efficient portfolios in the optimizer. For instance, suppose a return model comprises two factors, each with 50 percent weight: the book-to-price (B/P) ratio and return on equity (ROE). Suppose the risk model, on the other hand, has only one factor: B/P. When forming a portfolio, the optimizer will manage risk only for the factors in the risk model—B/P but not ROE. This inconsistency between the return and risk models can lead to portfolios with extreme positions and higher-than-expected risk. The portfolio will not reflect the original 50–50 weights on the two return factors because the optimizer will dampen the exposure to B/P, but not to ROE. In addition, the risk model's estimate of tracking error will be too low because it will not capture any risk from the portfolio's exposure to ROE. The most direct way to avoid these two problems is to make sure all of the factors in the return model are also included in the risk model (although the converse does not need to be true—there can be risk factors without expected returns).

A final issue to consider when developing or selecting a risk model is the frequency of data used in the estimation process. Many popular risk models use monthly returns, whereas some portfolio managers (including us) have developed proprietary risk models that use daily returns. Clearly, when estimating variances and covariances, the more observations, the better. High-frequency data produce more observations and hence more precise and reliable estimates. Further, by giving more weight to recent observations, estimates can be more responsive to changing economic conditions. As a result, risk models that use high-frequency returns should provide more accurate risk estimates. (For a detailed discussion of factor risk models, please see Chapter 20.)

Forecasting Transaction Costs

Although often overlooked, accurate trade-cost estimates are critical to the EPM process. After all, what really matters is not the gross return a portfolio *might*

[6]With N stocks, the variance-covariance matrix has $N(N + 1)/2$ elements, consisting of N variances and $N(N - 1)/2$ covariances. For an S&P 500 portfolio, for instance, there are $500 \times (500 + 1)/2 = 125{,}250$ unknown parameters to estimate—500 variances and 124,750 covariances.

receive, but rather the actual return a portfolio *does* receive after deducting all relevant costs, including transaction costs. Ignoring transaction costs when forming portfolios can lead to poor performance because implementation costs can reduce, or even eliminate, the advantages achieved through superior stock selection. Conversely, taking account of transaction costs can help produce portfolios with gross returns that exceed the costs of trading.

Accurate trading-cost forecasts are also important after portfolio formation, when monitoring the realized costs of trading. A good transaction-cost model can provide a benchmark for what realized costs should be, and hence whether actual execution costs are reasonable. Detailed trade-cost monitoring can help traders and brokers achieve best execution by driving improvements in trading methods—such as more patient trading or the selective use of alternative trading mechanisms.

Transaction costs have two components: (1) explicit costs, such as commissions and ticket charges; and (2) implicit costs, or market impact. Commissions and ticket charges tend to be relatively small, and the cost per share does not depend on the number of shares traded. In contrast, market impact costs can be substantial. They reflect the costs of consuming liquidity from the market, costs that increase on a per-share basis with the total number of shares traded.[7] Forecasting price impact is difficult. Because researchers observe prices only for completed trades, they cannot determine what a stock's price would have been without these trades. It is therefore impossible to know for sure how much prices moved as a result of the trades. Price impact costs, then, are statistical estimates that are more accurate for larger data samples.

One approach to estimating trade costs is to directly examine the complete record of market prices, tick by tick.[8] These data are noisy due to discrete prices, nonsynchronous reporting of trades and quotes, and input errors. Also, the record does not show orders placed, just those that eventually got executed (which may have been split up from the original, larger order). Lee and Radhakrishna (2000) suggest empirical analysis should be done using aggregated samples of trades rather than individual trades at the tick-by-tick level.

Another approach is for portfolio managers to estimate a proprietary transaction cost model using their own trades and, if available, those of comparable managers. If a sufficient sample is available, this approach is ideal because the resulting

---

[7]Market impact costs arise because suppliers of liquidity incur risk. One component of these costs is inventory risk. The liquidity supplier has a risk/return trade-off, and will demand a price concession to compensate for this inventory risk. The larger the trade size and the more illiquid or volatile the stock, the larger are inventory risk and market impact costs. Another consideration is adverse selection risk. Liquidity suppliers are willing to provide a better price to uninformed than informed traders, but since there is no reliable way to distinguish between these two types of traders, the market maker sets an average price, with expected gains from trading with uninformed traders compensating for losses incurred from trading with informed traders. Market impact costs tend to be higher for low-price and small-cap stocks for which greater adverse selection risk and informational asymmetry tend to be more severe.

[8]For example, see Breen, Hodrick, and Korajczyk (2000).

model matches the stock characteristics, investment philosophy, and trading strategy of the individual portfolio manager.[9]

To demonstrate how transaction costs can vary across trade characteristics, we estimated a nonlinear regression model on a large sample of our own trades. The sample represented over 60,000 trades over the nine months from October 2001 to June 2002. We measured costs using *implementation shortfall.* For purchases, implementation shortfall is equal to the decision price (or the price at the time we decided to trade) minus the average execution price (including commissions), all expressed as a proportion of the decision price. For sales, the terms in the numerator are reversed: Implementation shortfall is the execution price minus the decision price, divided by the decision price. Thus, with slippage (i.e., positive transaction costs), implementation shortfall is negative for both buys and sells. For example, if the decision price is $10 and a purchase is executed at $10.15, then the implementation shortfall is –0.015, for a cost of 1.5 percent.

To predict trade costs, our model uses five proxies for trading liquidity: order size, average trading volume, market capitalization, stock price volatility, and stock price level. We also control for contemporaneous sector returns, since marketwide price movements usually account for much of the difference between the decision price and the execution price, although ex ante these movements are generally unpredictable. Figure 23.1 presents the model's cost estimates, expressed as a proportion of trade value, for trading two baskets of stocks: (1) a large-cap basket comprising the stocks in the S&P 500 and (2) a small-cap basket comprising the stocks in the FR 2000 index. Figure 23.1 also shows the liquidity characteristics of an average large- and small-cap stock as of June 2002.

Not surprisingly, the cost of trading a basket of large-cap stocks is lower than the cost of trading a basket of small-cap stocks with similar liquidity. For example, a $500-million basket of S&P 500 stocks is expected to incur transaction costs of about 18 basis points. A trade this size represents about 1.3 percent of the average daily volume of the underlying stocks. In contrast, the average cost of trading a $25 million basket of Russell 2000 stocks, which represents 1.1 percent of average daily volume, is 25 basis points. Liquidity is more costly for small-cap stocks because their prices are more volatile, their prices are lower, and their average daily trading volume is smaller. Moreover, as the concave curves in Figure 23.1 show, trading costs increase with order size, but at a decreasing rate.

---

[9]There is a large academic literature on measuring transaction costs. One paper that is especially relevant to portfolio managers interested in developing a model based on their own trades is Keim and Madhavan (1997), who investigate the impact of investment style on total transaction costs for a sample of 21 institutions over the period January 1991 to March 1993. They study transaction costs by trade direction (i.e., buyer- vs. seller-initiated trades) and investment style: value-fundamental, technical-momentum, and index. The study concludes that total transaction costs are increasing in order size, and decreasing in firm size and the magnitude of the stock price. Further, costs differ by investment style. Technical and index investors, who demand immediacy, incur higher costs than the more patient value investors.

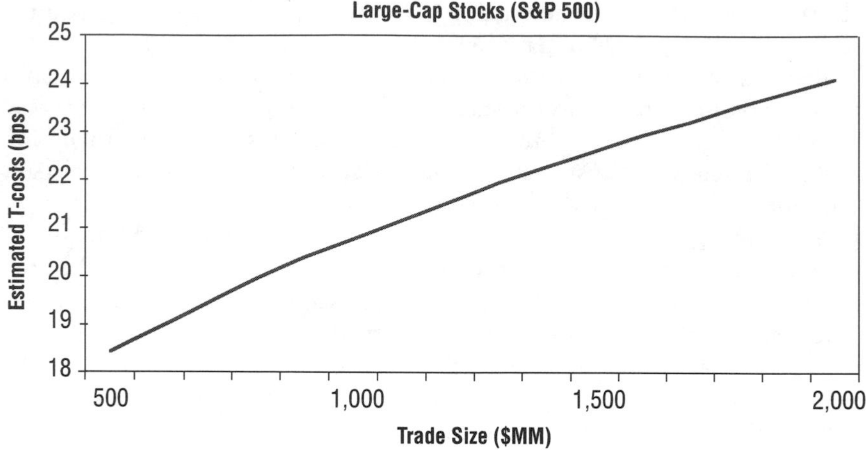

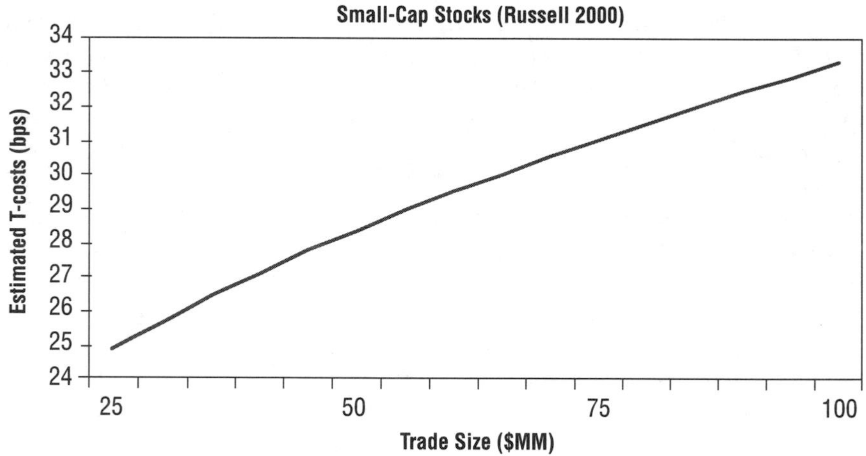

Average Characteristic (Weighted by Benchmark Weight)	Large-Cap (S&P 500)	Small-Cap (Rusell 2000)
20-day volatility (annualized)	56.4%	63.1%
Average daily volume traded	$363 million	$4 million
Average price	$37.67	$19.93
Proportional quoted half-spread	7 basis points	29 basis points

FIGURE 23.1 Transaction Costs for Large-Cap versus Small-Cap Stocks

CONSTRUCTING PORTFOLIOS

In this section we discuss how to construct portfolios based on the forecasts described in the preceding section. In particular, we compare ad hoc, rule-based approaches to more formal portfolio optimization. The first step in portfolio construction, however, is to specify the investment goals. While having good forecasts (as described in the previous section) is obviously important, the investor's goals define the portfolio management problem. These goals are usually specified by three major parameters: the benchmark, the risk/return target, and specific restrictions such as the maximum holdings in any single name, industry, or sector.

The benchmark represents the starting point for any active portfolio; it is the client's neutral position—a low-cost alternative to active management in that asset class. For example, investors interested in holding large-cap U.S. stocks might select the S&P 500 or Russell 1000 as their benchmark, while investors interested in holding small-cap stocks might choose the Russell 2000 or the S&P 600. Investors interested in a portfolio of non-U.S. stocks could pick the FTSE 350 (U.K.), TOPIX (Japan), or MSCI EAFE (world minus North America) indexes. There are a large number of published benchmarks available, or an investor might develop a customized benchmark to represent the neutral position. In all cases, however, the benchmark should be a reasonably low-cost, investable alternative to active management.

Although some investors are content to merely match the returns on their benchmarks, most investors allocate at least some of their assets to active managers (see Chapter 14 on how to allocate the active risk budget among active and passive strategies). In EPM, active management means overweighting attractive stocks and underweighting unattractive stocks relative to their weights in the benchmark.[10] Of course, there is always a chance that these active weighting decisions will cause the portfolio to *underperform* the benchmark, but one of the basic dictums of modern finance is that to earn higher returns, investors must accept higher risk—which is true of active returns as well as total returns.

A portfolio's *tracking error* measures its risk relative to a benchmark. Tracking error equals the time-series standard deviation of a portfolio's *active return*—which is the difference between the portfolio's return and that of the benchmark. A portfolio's *information ratio* equals its average active return divided by its tracking error. As a measure of return per unit of risk, the information ratio provides a convenient way to compare strategies with different active risk levels.

An *efficient portfolio* is one with the highest expected return for a target level of risk—that is, it has the highest information ratio possible given the risk budget. In the absence of constraints, an efficient portfolio is one in which each stock's

[10]The difference between a stock's weight in the portfolio and its weight in the benchmark is called its "active weight," where a positive active weight corresponds to an overweight position and a negative active weight corresponds to an underweight position. For instance, if the weight of a stock is 3 percent in the portfolio but only 2 percent in the benchmark, then the active weight is 1 percent, an overweight. On the other hand, if the portfolio weight is zero (i.e., the stock is not held) and the benchmark weight is 1 percent, then the active weight is –1 percent, an underweight.

marginal contribution to expected return is proportional to its marginal contribution to risk. That is, there are no unintended risks, and all risks are compensated with additional expected returns. How can a portfolio manager construct such an efficient portfolio? We compare two approaches: (1) a rule-based system and (2) portfolio optimization.

Building an efficient portfolio is a complex problem. To help simplify this complicated task, many portfolio managers use ad hoc, rule-based methods that partially control exposures to a small number of risk factors. For example, one common approach—called *stratified sampling*—ranks stocks within buckets formed on the basis of a few key risk factors, such as sector and size. The manager then invests more heavily in the highest-ranked stocks within each bucket, while keeping the portfolio's total weight in each bucket close to that of the benchmark. The resulting portfolio is close to neutral with respect to the identified risk factors (i.e., sector and size) while overweighting attractive stocks and underweighting unattractive stocks.

Although stratified sampling may seem sensible, it is not very efficient. Numerous unintended risks can creep into the portfolio, such as an overweight in high-beta stocks, growth stocks, or stocks in certain subsectors. Nor does it allow the manager to explicitly consider trading costs or investment objectives in the portfolio construction problem. Portfolio optimization provides a much better method for balancing expected returns against different sources of risk, trade costs, and investor constraints. An optimizer uses computer algorithms to find the set of weights (or holdings) that maximize the portfolio's expected return (net of trade costs) for a given level of risk. It minimizes uncompensated sources of risk, including sector and style biases. Fortunately, despite the complex math, optimizers require only the various forecasts we've already described and developed in the prior section.[11]

To demonstrate the benefits of optimization, we compare two portfolios: one constructed using stratified sampling and the other constructed using an optimizer. The return and risk forecasts are from our CORE U.S. models.[12] The benchmark and investment universe for both portfolios is the S&P 500 index. The stratified sampling (or rule-based) method divides stocks into eight buckets, two market-capitalization segments within each of four macro sectors. Within each bucket, stocks were ranked by expected return: Stocks in the bottom third were given a weight of

[11]Mathematically, an optimizer solves a formula such as the following (where b denotes stock weights in the benchmark; w denotes the optimal stock weights in the final portfolio; a denotes the return forecasts; S denotes the covariance risk matrix; and F denotes the stocks' characteristics):

Max $w'\ a$, subject to

$(w - b)'\ S\ (w - b) <$ (Target tracking error)^2

$| F'\ w - F'\ b | <=$ bounds on sector positions and other stock characteristics

$w_i > 0$ (no short positions)

$\Sigma_i\ w_i = 1$ (budget constraint that stock weights must sum to one)

[12]The CORE U.S. return model comprises six investment themes: profitability, valuation, earnings quality, momentum, management impact, and fundamental research. The CORE U.S. risk model is based on a factor structure that includes all of these investment themes, as well as other factors without expected returns (size, beta, etc.).

zero; stocks in the middle third were given a neutral weight equal to their weight in the S&P 500 benchmark; and stocks in the top third were given the remaining weight in proportion to their original benchmark weight.

Table 23.3 presents some summary characteristics for the two portfolios. The optimized portfolio was designed to have the same predicted tracking error as the rule-based portfolio—namely, 2.8 percent. This immediately highlights one advantage of optimization: It can easily target a specific level of tracking error, while managers who use stratified sampling would need to design a completely different set of rules to hit a different tracking error objective. The optimized portfolio is also more efficient: It has a much higher expected alpha (3.4 percent versus 2.1 percent) and information ratio (1.22 versus 0.73) for the same level of risk. Further, risk is spread more broadly: The 10 riskiest positions in the rule-based portfolio consume 60 percent of the total risk budget, versus just 37.5 percent for the optimized portfolio. Also, more of the risk budget in the optimized portfolio is due to the factors that are expected to generate positive excess returns: 45.4 percent versus 23.2 percent. Finally, the forecast beta for the optimized portfolio is closer to 1.00, as unintended sources of risk (such as the market timing) are minimized.

We can also show the benefits of portfolio optimization graphically. As stated previously, in an efficient portfolio without constraints, each stock's marginal contribution to risk should be proportional to its expected return. This means a plot of each stock's relative contribution to risk against its contribution to portfolio alpha should lie on a straight line. In practice, the plot is not a perfectly straight line, even for an optimized portfolio, because of portfolio constraints (e.g., no net short positions). As shown in Figure 23.2, the plot for the optimized portfolio falls much closer to the 45-degree line than the plot for the rule-based portfolio—making it significantly more efficient.

Another benefit of optimizers is that they can efficiently account for transaction costs, constraints, selected restrictions, and other account guidelines, making it much easier to create customized client portfolios. Of course, when using an optimizer to construct efficient portfolios, reliable inputs are essential. Data errors that add noise to the return, risk, and transaction cost forecasts can lead to portfolios in which these forecast errors are maximized. Instead of picking stocks with the highest *actual* expected returns, or the lowest *actual* risks or transaction costs, the optimizer takes the biggest positions in the stocks with the largest errors, namely the stocks with the greatest overestimates of expected returns or the greatest underestimates of risks or transaction costs. A robust investment process will screen major data sources for outliers that can severely corrupt one's forecasts. Further, as described in

TABLE 23.3 Summary Portfolio Characteristics

	Stratified Sampling	Optimized Portfolio
Tracking error	2.8%	2.8%
Expected excess return	2.1%	3.4%
Expected information ratio	0.73	1.22
Risk budget used by top 10 stocks	60.0%	37.5%
Percent of risk from return factors	23.2%	45.4%
Portfolio beta	1.03	1.01

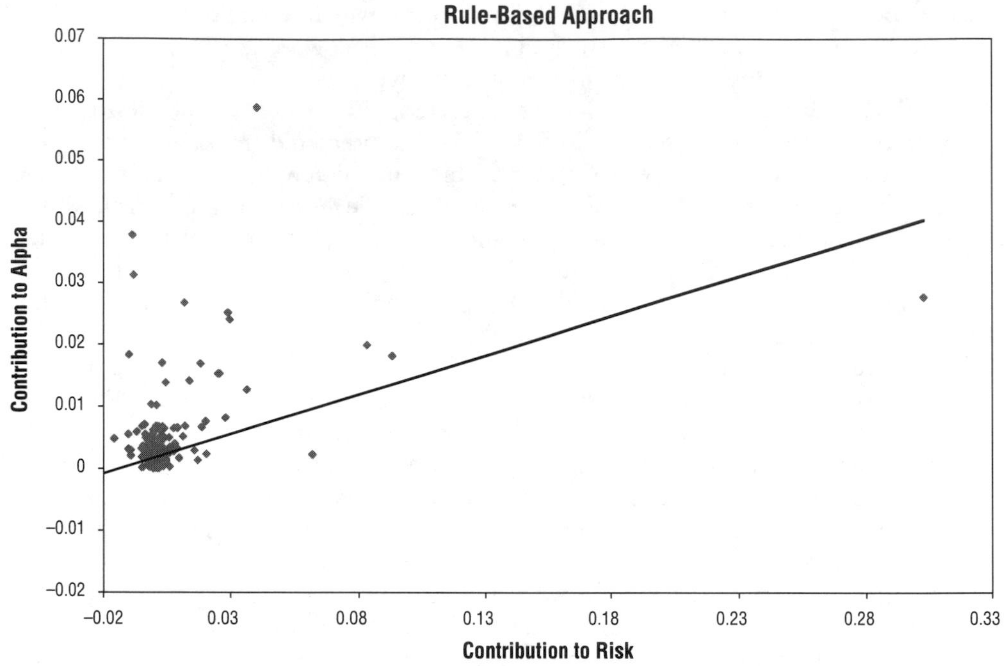

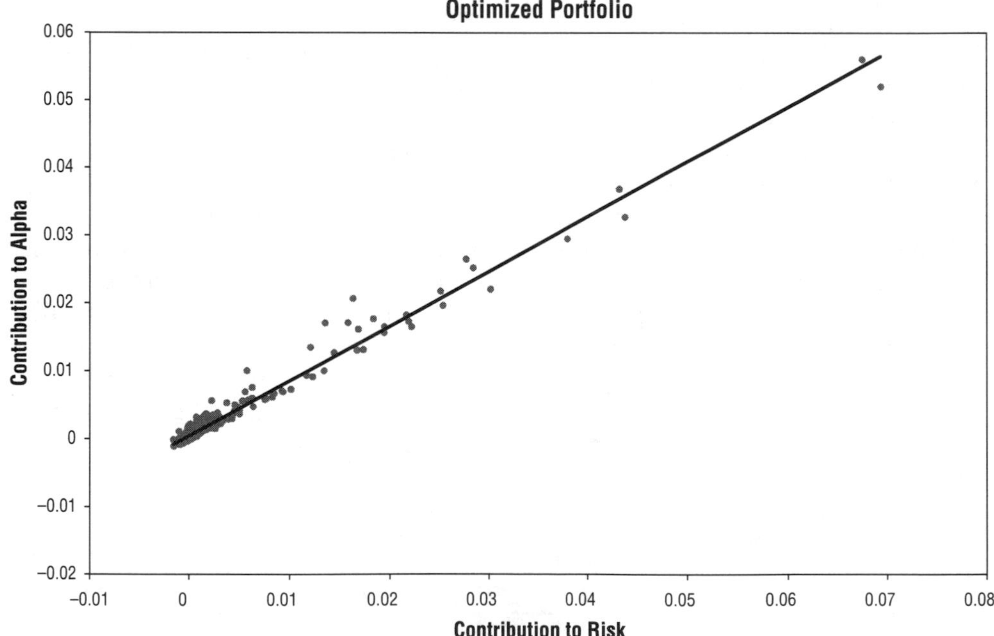

FIGURE 23.2 Rule-Based Approach versus Optimized Portfolio

the previous section, return forecasts should be adjusted for equilibrium views using the Black-Litterman model to produce final return forecasts that are more consistent with risk estimates, and with each other. Finally, portfolio managers should impose sensible, but simple constraints on the optimizer to help guard against the effects of noisy inputs. These constraints could include maximum active weights on individual stocks, industries, or sectors, as well as limitations on the portfolio's active exposure to factors such as size or market beta.

TRADING

Trading is the process of executing the orders derived in the portfolio construction step. To trade a list of stocks efficiently, investors must balance opportunity costs and execution price risk against market impact costs. Trading each stock quickly minimizes lost alpha and price uncertainty due to delay, but impatient trading incurs maximum market impact. In contrast, trading more patiently over a longer period reduces market impact but incurs larger opportunity costs and short-term execution price risk. Striking the right balance is one of the keys to successful trade execution.

The concept of striking a balance suggests optimization. Investors can use a trade optimizer to balance the gains from patient trading (e.g., lower market-impact cost) against the risks (e.g., greater deviation between the execution price and the decision price; potentially higher short-term tracking error). Such an optimizer will tend to suggest aggressive trading for names that are liquid and/or have a large effect on portfolio risk, while suggesting patient trading for illiquid names that have less impact on risk. A trade optimizer can also easily handle most real-world trading constraints, such as the need to balance cash in each of many accounts across the trading period (which may last several days).

A trade optimizer can also easily accommodate the time horizon of a manager's views. That is, if a manager is buying a stock primarily for long-term valuation reasons, and the excess return is expected to accrue gradually over time, then the optimizer will likely suggest a patient trading strategy (all else being equal). Conversely, if the manager is buying a stock in expectation of a positive earnings surprise tomorrow, the optimizer is likely to suggest an aggressive trading strategy (again, all else being equal). The trade optimizer can also be programmed to consider short-term return regularities, such as the tendency of stocks with dramatic price moves on one day to continue those moves on the next day before reversing the following day. For example, if a manager wants to buy a stock that was up significantly yesterday, it may pay to wait until tomorrow to execute the trade given the likelihood it will decline tomorrow relative to today's price.

To induce traders to follow the desired strategy (i.e., that suggested by the trade optimizer), the portfolio manager needs to give the trader an appropriate benchmark, which provides guidance about how aggressively or patiently to trade. Two widely used benchmarks for aggressive trades are the closing price on the previous day and the opening price on the trade date. Because the values of these two benchmarks are measured prior to any trading, a patient strategy that delays trading heightens execution price risk by increasing the possibility of deviating significantly from the benchmark. Another popular execution benchmark is the volume-weighted average price (VWAP) for the stock over the desired trading period, which could be a few minutes or hours for an aggressive trade, or one or more days for a patient trade. However, the VWAP benchmark should only be used for trades that are not too large relative to total volume over the period; otherwise, the trader may be able to influence the benchmark against which he or she is evaluated.

Buy-side traders can increasingly make use of alternative trading venues such as electronic communication networks (ECNs), which take advantage of available liquidity to match buyers and sellers directly. Further, ECNs provide buy-side traders more anonymity and greater control over their order flows. ECNs tend to be better for patient trades, however, since a trade might not get executed in an aggressive time frame given the small odds of finding a cross for certain trades. Principal package trading is another way to lower transaction costs relative to traditional agency methods.[13] Principal trades may be crossed with the principal's existing inventory positions, or allow the portfolio manager to benefit from the longer trading horizon and superior trading ability of certain intermediaries.

EVALUATING RESULTS AND UPDATING THE PROCESS

Once an investment process is up and running, it needs to be constantly reassessed and, if necessary, refined. The first step is to compare actual results to expectations; if realizations differ enough from expectations, process refinements may be necessary. Thus, managers need systems to monitor realized performance, risk, and trading costs and compare them to prior expectations.

A good performance monitoring system should be able to determine not only the degree of over- or underperformance, but also the sources of these excess returns. For example, a good performance attribution system might break excess returns down into those due to market timing (having a different beta than the benchmark), industry tilts, style differences, and stock selection. Such systems are available from a variety of third-party vendors. An even better system would allow the manager to further disaggregate returns to see the effects of each of the proprietary signals used to forecast returns, as well as the effects of constraints and other portfolio requirements. And, of course, any system will be more accurate if it can account for daily trading and changes in portfolio exposures. Currently, such systems are not available from outside vendors and need to be developed in-house.

Investors should also compare realized risks to expectations. At Goldman Sachs, we have developed the concept of the green, yellow, and red zones to compare realized and targeted levels of risk; see Litterman, Longerstaey, Rosengarten, and Winkelmann (2000). Essentially, if realized risk is within a reasonable band

[13]Please see Kavajecz and Keim (2002).

around the target (i.e., the green zone), then we can assume our risk management techniques are working as intended and no action is required. If realized risk is further from target (the yellow zone), the situation may require closer examination, and if realized risk is far from target (the red zone), some action is usually called for. Of course, we also use in-house systems to monitor *sources* of risk (as we do sources of return) to make sure we are not getting excessive risk from unintended sources, and that we are getting enough risk from our intended sources.

Finally, it is important to monitor trading costs. Are they above or below the costs assumed when making trading decisions? Are they above or below competitors' costs? Are they too high in an absolute sense? If so, managers may need to improve their trade cost estimates, trading process, or both. There are many services that can report realized trade costs, but most are available with a significant lag, and are inflexible with respect to how they measure and report these costs. With in-house systems, however, managers can compare a variety of trade cost estimation techniques and get the feedback in a timely enough fashion to act on the results.

The critical question, of course, is what to do with the results of these monitoring systems: When do variations from expectations warrant refinements to the process? This will depend on the size of the variations and their persistence. For example, a manager probably would not throw out a stock-selection signal after one bad month—no matter how bad—but might want to reconsider after many years of poor performance, taking into consideration the economic environment and any external factors that might explain the results. It is also important to compare the underperformance to historical simulations. Have similar periods occurred in the past, and if so, were they followed by improvements? In this case, the underperformance is part of the normal risk in that signal and no changes may be called for. If not, there may have been a structural change that might invalidate the signal going forward—for example, if the signal has become overly popular, it may no longer be a source of mispricing.

Similarly, the portfolio manager needs to consider the source of any differences between expectations and realizations. For example, was underperformance due to faulty signals, portfolio constraints, unintended risk, or random noise? The answer will determine the proper response. If constraints are to blame, they may be lifted—but only if doing so would not violate any investment guidelines or incur excessive risk. Alternatively, if the signals are to blame, the manager must decide whether the deviations from expectations are temporary or more enduring. Finally, if it is just random noise, no action is necessary. Similarly, any differences between realized and expected risk could be due to poor risk estimates or poor portfolio construction, with the answer determining the response. Finally, excessive trading costs (versus expectations) could reflect poor trading or poor trade cost estimates, again with different implications for action.

In summary, ongoing performance, risk, and trade cost monitoring is an integral part of the EPM process and should get equal billing with forecasting, portfolio construction, and trading. Monitoring serves as both quality control and a source of new ideas and process improvements. The more sophisticated the monitoring systems, the more useful they are to the process. And although the implications of monitoring involve subtle judgments and careful analysis, better data can lead to better solutions.

SUMMARY

The EPM process, which may once have been an art, is now increasingly a science. Each step in the process—forecasting, portfolio construction, trading, and monitoring—has grown increasingly complex and competitive with the advent of better tools and data, more sophisticated investors, and ever-greater resources devoted to the problem. Going forward, we expect traditional and quantitative investing to converge; successful investors will make full use of the best available tools. In fact, most traditional managers already use some quantitative screens and portfolio risk estimates. Best practices will increasingly include methods currently used primarily by quantitative managers—such as optimization, back testing, and statistical modeling—as well as methods that are now the primary domain of traditional managers—such as the in-depth analysis of qualitative investment criteria. In fact, Benjamin Graham, the "father of modern security analysis," had long seen the benefits in both approaches:

> *The first, or predictive, approach could also be called the qualitative approach, since it emphasizes prospects, management, and other nonmeasurable, albeit highly important, factors that go under the heading of quality. The second, or protective, approach may be called the quantitative of statistical approach, since it emphasizes the measurable relationships between selling price and earnings, assets, dividends, and so forth. . . . In our own attitude and professional work we were always committed to the quantitative approach.* (The Intelligent Investor, 1973, page 199)

To succeed in EPM in the future, then, investors need strong technical skills, a thorough understanding of investment theory, a widening base of knowledge, discipline, humility, and plain old common sense. They also need to devote considerable resources to each step in the process, and to sweat the details. As any student of the game knows, blocking and tackling wins ball games. For most casual investors, we suggest hiring skilled professionals or investing passively. For those who want to stay in the game, however, it is time to embrace the science of investing.

CHAPTER 24

Fixed Income Risk and Return

Jonathan Beinner

INTRODUCTION

In this chapter, we will examine the sources of risk and return in the fixed income markets. In many ways, the fixed income markets are more complex than the equity markets as there are many dimensions to consider when constructing a fixed income portfolio. There are so many questions to ask yourself, whether you are investing in a fixed income portfolio or you are an active fixed income portfolio manager. Should I own short maturities or long maturities? Should I own government bonds or corporate bonds or some combination? If I invest in mortgage-backed securities (MBSs), am I taking on some unintended risk? Should I invest internationally? If so, should I hedge the currency exposure? These questions and more will *not* be answered for you in this chapter. What we will try to do is to give the reader a sense of what questions should be asked when thinking about the fixed income component of an overall portfolio.

First, we will discuss the various risks that bond portfolios may be exposed to in order to understand what drives fixed income returns and volatility. Next, we will examine the fixed income benchmarks that are used by many market participants to define the desired neutral exposures to each of the major fixed income risks. Then we will identify the main strategies that active fixed income managers use to achieve higher returns than a passive indexed portfolio. And last, we will describe and then demonstrate the process that we in Goldman Sachs Asset Management (GSAM) use to determine an optimal allocation of these active strategies to maximize the information ratio, given a client's investment objectives and constraints.

SOURCES OF FIXED INCOME RISK

Before we begin the discussion of the various risks taken in fixed income portfolios it is necessary to understand what risk means in a fixed income context. After all, fixed income instruments have fixed cash flows and therefore no risk. Right? Also, many have said that it doesn't matter if the price of a bond goes down because you can always just hold it to maturity and therefore the price volatility of a bond is not important. While it is true that due to the nature of fixed income securities they are generally less volatile than equity securities, understanding what drives fixed income prices and returns is critical to building efficient bond portfolios. In fact, even the highest credit quality held-to-maturity portfolios bear risk, and one portfolio can achieve very different long-term returns than another due to different exposures to risk.

As with most financial assets, fixed income returns have two components: income and capital appreciation/depreciation. What distinguishes fixed income returns from the other asset classes is that most of the total return comes from the income component rather than the price component. That being said, the price component of the return can distinguish good portfolio performance from bad portfolio performance. Also, an investor can easily increase the income component of the portfolio, but generally it will come at the expense of higher volatility of the price component.

So, what drives this price component? First of all, remember that the price change of a bond can be approximated by the formula:

$$\text{Change in price} = (\text{Change in yield}) \times (\text{Duration}) \times (-1)$$

where the duration of a bond is effectively a weighted average of the time until each cash flow payment where the weights are equal to the present value of each cash flow. So in order to determine what drives the risk and return of the price component of fixed income returns, we must examine the risk exposures that drive changes in fixed income yields.

We will now examine the major sources of risk in most fixed income portfolios.

Interest Rate Risk

Interest rate risk is probably the most widely known and widely discussed risk in the fixed income world. It is the risk that the yield of a bond will change due to changes in the otherwise risk-free bond with the same cash flows. Usually the risk-free yield curve is determined by the yield of credit-risk-free government bonds. However, some market participants (GSAM included) have switched to using the swap yield curve instead of the government yield curve due to significant technical factors that have driven government yields out of line with other high credit quality fixed income instruments. Regardless, the concept of interest rate risk is the same, which is that there is a baseline interest rate for a cash flow at each maturity and if this rate changes in the market, the price of the bond will change with it.

There are a number of reasons that credit-risk-free interest rates change, but most changes are due to macroeconomic factors such as current and expected future monetary and fiscal policy, economic growth, level of inflation, and so on.

Note also that investors buying fixed income securities in different countries bear different interest rate risks because of the differences in the yield curves and in the macroeconomic and inflationary environments.

The measurement that is usually used to quantify a portfolio's exposure to interest rate risk is duration. Duration is effectively the amount in percent that a bond is expected to rise/fall due to a 1 percent decrease/increase in interest rates.

Yield Curve Risk

Yield curve risk is sometimes also known as term structure risk. This is the risk that a portfolio's value will change due to a change in the shape rather than the level of the yield curve. Multiple portfolios can be constructed to have the same duration but with very different exposures to yield curve risk. The most widely known portfolio structures are bulleted (with most of the cash flows paid at one point in the future), barbelled (with a cluster of securities with long maturities offset with short maturities), and laddered (with maturities spread out across the maturity spectrum).

As with interest rate risk, the key drivers of yield curve risk are macroeconomic factors. If the central bank is easing monetary policy and/or markets are concerned about future inflation, generally the yield curve will steepen. Also, technical factors can play a large role in yield curve risk. For example, in the early part of 2000, the long end of the U.S. yield curve inverted due to the lack of supply of long bonds and the fact that the U.S. Treasury was buying back long Treasuries in the secondary market.

The measure that is often used in quantifying yield curve risk is partial duration or key-rate duration. This measure indicates how much of a portfolio's total duration comes from cash flows in each part of the yield curve. At GSAM, we break out each portfolio's duration into partial durations at 10 different yield curve nodes: 3-month, 6-month, 1-year, 2-year, 3-year, 5-year, 7-year, 10-year, 20-year, and 30-year.

Sector Risk

Sector risk is the volatility of returns due to yield changes derived from changes in spread between the sector in question and the baseline yield curve (either the government or swap curve).

A multitude of factors drive spreads of the various fixed income sectors to tighten and widen, but generally the spread changes are due to significant changes in issuance of the sector or an increase or decrease in other risks that are prevalent in that sector such as credit risk for corporate bonds or volatility and prepayment risk for mortgage-backed securities.

The measure that is most often used to describe a portfolio's exposure to spread risk of a particular sector is contribution to duration (CTD). CTD is the market value weighted average duration of a portfolio's holdings of the sector multiplied by the market value weight of the portfolio held in that sector. For example, if a portfolio holds a 20 percent position in corporate bonds and the average duration of the corporates held is four years, then the CTD of corporates in the portfolio is 0.8 years (20% × 4). The reason this methodology results in a more effective measure than using just the market weight of the portfolio is because one can determine the impact on return by simply multiplying the CTD by the change in the market spread for the sector. For sectors that exhibit substantial probabilities of default, though, market weight may be a better measure of sector risk because the prices of these securities are more dependent on the probability of default than on the level of interest rates.

Table 24.1 lists the major sectors found in most fixed income portfolios and the historical volatility of their spreads.

Credit Risk

Credit risk is the risk borne by the fixed income investor that the cash flows that the issuer has contracted to pay will not be paid due to the inability or unwillingness of the issuer to do so. Market prices and yields change due to the market's assessment of the probability that the issuer will default on its obligations. If the market believes that the likelihood that an issuer will default has increased, the yield of the bond will go up to compensate for this higher level of risk. Credit risk is usually defined using credit ratings from a nationally recognized statistical rating organization (NRSRO) such as Moody's and Standard & Poor's as shown in Table 24.2.

As you can see, historically speculative-grade credits (rated below BBB/Baa) and also known as high-yield or junk bonds) have experienced significantly higher levels of default than investment-grade debt.

Volatility Risk

Many fixed income portfolios have exposure to volatility risk either explicitly or implicitly. To be exposed to volatility risk is to have the portfolio's value impacted

TABLE 24.1 Major Sectors and Historical Volatility of Their Spreads

Sector	Main Risks of Sector	Historical Annualized Spread Volatility (1 Std. Dev.)
Domestic sovereign (i.e., U.S. Treasury)	Interest rate	N/A
Agency/supranational/ quasi-government	Interest rate, spread	17 bps
Mortgage-backed securities (MBS)	Interest rate, spread, volatility, prepayment	36 bps
Asset-backed securities (ABS)	Interest rate, spread	24 bps
Investment grade corporates	Interest rate, spread, credit	38 bps
High-yield corporates	Interest rate, spread, credit	173 bps
Emerging market debt	Interest rate, spread, credit	409 bps

TABLE 24.2 Credit Ratings and Credit Risk

Moody's Rating	Standard & Poor's Rating	Historical Default Rate
Aaa	AAA	0.04%
Aa	AA	0.10
A	A	0.17
Baa	BBB	0.39
Ba	BB	1.58
B	B	4.35
<B	<B	8.54

not by the change in the level of interest rates but rather by how much interest rates move or are expected to move in either direction. In other words, a portfolio that is positively exposed to volatility benefits by large swings in interest rates and a portfolio that is negatively exposed (i.e., short volatility) benefits when interest rates are more stable than expected.

Volatility exposure arises when the portfolio has instruments with asymmetric payoffs: An interest rate movement in one direction generates a larger gain than the loss associated with the equal but opposite interest rate move. Volatility exposure is typically achieved either by using instruments that have explicit exposure to volatility such as options on fixed income securities or by using securities that exhibit sensitivity to volatility due to imbedded options such as callable and putable bonds. A good example of a sector that creates volatility exposure is the MBS market. Because the home mortgage borrowers backing a standard residential mortgage-backed security can refinance their mortgages if mortgage rates decline, the holder of the MBS is effectively short a call option. Therefore, holders of most MBSs have a short exposure to volatility.

There are two different risk exposures that generally arise when investing in options or securities with embedded options: gamma and vega (the names come from the Black-Scholes option pricing model). Gamma exposure is the market value impact from experiencing a change in interest rates. If you are long volatility, you experience a gain when the market moves, because in an interest rate rally the instrument will increase more than is suggested by its duration, and in a sell-off the instrument will decline less than is suggested by its duration. The measure that is often used to quantify gamma exposure in a fixed income portfolio is convexity. The units of the convexity measure for bonds are actually years^2 because it is effectively the second derivative of the bond's price with respect to a change in interest rates. However, convexity is typically thought of as a percentage measure where the approximate price return impact due to convexity exposure given a change in interest rates is determined by the formula:

$$\text{Price gain from convexity} = \tfrac{1}{2} \times \text{Convexity} \times \text{Change in interest rates}^2$$

The other exposure that is created by investing in fixed income instruments that exhibit volatility risk is vega risk. The price change in an instrument that results from vega exposure is due to a change in the market expectation of future volatility of interest rates. The market price of a fixed income option will increase if the market expects interest rates to be more volatile over the remaining life of the option. In the fixed income world, the measure frequently used to quantify vega risk is volatility duration, which is defined to be the percentage change in the price of the instrument due to a 1 percent change in expected future (or implied) volatility.

Prepayment Risk

Prepayment risk is a risk that is somewhat unique to the residential MBS market. As described in the preceding section, the borrowers underlying a mortgage-backed security can prepay their mortgages at face value and replace them with other mortgages at a lower rate. Therefore, an investor in an MBS security is short the option that the borrowers are long. The interesting thing about the prepayment option is that it is not efficiently exercised. Because mortgage-backed securities are backed by hundreds or thousands of individual borrowers, these securities are not "called" in the same way that a callable corporate or agency debt security is called. The MBS holder receives the prepayment of principal on only the percentage of underlying loans that are actually prepaid by the underlying borrowers. In times of falling interest rates, prepayment rates generally increase but there is usually some significant percentage of borrowers who do not take advantage of the opportunity to refinance into a lower mortgage rate. There are several reasons why someone would not refinance despite the economic incentive to do so, including credit impairment, refinancing costs, tax implications, or a lack of knowledge regarding the refinancing opportunity.

Due to the complexity of the prepayment option embedded in mortgage-backed securities, market participants have developed sophisticated models that attempt to predict the percentage of a mortgage pool that will pay off given a series of market variables, security characteristics, and prepayment history. Despite the best intentions of many well-respected statisticians, there is not a perfect prepayment model. This is because the coefficients of the variables that determine prepayment behavior and even the variables themselves change over time. Also, even if the model does a good job of predicting the average prepayment rate for a subset of the mortgage universe, individual pools of mortgages will have realized prepayment rates that could deviate substantially from the average just due to the random sampling of loans out of a larger distribution.

The imperfect nature of prepayment models gives way to the existence of prepayment risk. Prepayment risk is not the risk that prepayment rates increase if interest rates fall and some portion of the security's principal is paid off in a lower-rate environment. This phenomenon is captured by the volatility risk of the security in the same way that a standard callable bond pays earlier if interest rates fall. In other words, if the prepayment option were exercised efficiently and we could perfectly predict the level of prepayments given a set of variables, then there would be no prepayment risk. There would be only volatility risk. We define prepayment risk as the return volatility arising from the over- or underestimation of actual prepayment rates.

There are a number of measures that can be used to quantify prepayment risk. One measure is *prepayment duration*, which is defined as the percentage change in price due to a 10 percent increase in projected prepayment rates. Different MBS securities can have very different levels of prepayment duration, including both positive and negative exposures. Typical mortgage-backed pass-throughs have prepayment durations that range between –0.1 and –0.6. Structured securities that have a more leveraged exposure to prepayment risk can have much larger levels such as interest-only strips with prepayment durations ranging between –6.5 and –9.0, and principal-only strips exhibiting prepayment durations of 2.0 to 2.5.

Currency Risk

Currency risk is the exposure that an investor bears when investing in financial instruments denominated in a currency that is not the investor's base currency. Although not specific to the fixed income asset class, currency risk is prevalent in bond portfolios that have holdings across multiple markets and is becoming more common in single country portfolios as well. Even if the price of a fixed income security is unchanged over the investment period, the investor can achieve much higher or lower returns if the currency that the security was denominated in appreciates or depreciates relative to the base currency. Due to the volatile nature of exchange rates relative to most other fixed income risks, if an investment is exposed to currency risk, the return will be impacted more by the change in the exchange rate than by any other factor.

Currency risk can be mitigated or effectively eliminated using currency hedging techniques. The most widely used technique is to hedge using currency forward contracts where the investor will sell the currency of the nonbase-currency investment forward and simultaneously purchase the investor's base currency. This will offset any loss if the currency invested in depreciates relative to the base currency, since the investor has already effectively exchanged the currency at the exchange rate at the time of purchase of the security.

The measure that is most appropriate to quantify currency risk is simply the percent of the portfolio's market value (net of any currency hedges) that is exposed to each currency.

Security-Specific Risk

While the list of fixed income risks described so far is not exhaustive, these risks explain much of the volatility of returns of most fixed income securities. Security-specific risk can be thought of as the volatility of a bond's return that cannot be explained by the other fixed income risk factors.

Security-specific risk generally arises due to changes in the supply and demand balance of that security or due to changes in the market's perception of the credit quality of the issuer of the security. Several recent examples of market prices changing due to security-specific issuers are:

- Enron and WorldCom bond prices dropped dramatically more than prices of bonds with comparable credit ratings, as the market believed that there was a high probability of a debt default from the issuers.
- The price of Brazilian external sovereign debt declined significantly, as the market was concerned about the outcome of an upcoming presidential election and the fiscal policies of the victor.
- Collateralized mortgage obligations (CMOs) are structured mortgage-backed securities. The price of floating rate CMOs backed by Ginnie Mae (GNMA) mortgage pools increased because there was a large demand for this particular structure by European financial institutions.
- A number of securities have significantly outperformed the rest of the market because of short squeezes. Short sellers must borrow securities from long holders of the bonds. If there is too much demand to borrow an issue, the short sellers must bid up the price in order to avoid failing on the transaction.

It is important to note that unlike in the equity market, security-specific risk in the fixed income market is negatively skewed. In other words, the downside risk in bonds is generally much greater than the upside potential. With the exception of distressed debt investing, the buyer of a fixed income security expects to receive the promised coupon payments and eventually par value at maturity. A bond that is believed to have a high probability of maturing at par can trade at a premium to par value, but it is very rare that a bond will trade well above, say, 120 percent; and even if it does it is likely due to duration risk (i.e., a long-duration bond rallies a lot after interest rates fall significantly), not security-specific risk. Conversely, if a bond defaults or the market assigns a high probability to default, the market price can go below 50 percent of par value. Due to this asymmetric payoff of fixed income securities, it is very important to maintain proper diversification in bond portfolios that are exposed to any meaningful amount of credit risk.

The measure typically used for security-specific risk is either contribution to duration (CTD) for securities in low-risk sectors like governments and MBSs or market value percentage for riskier securities such as corporate bonds and emerging-market debt (EMD).

As you can see, the types of risks that a fixed income portfolio manager needs to be aware of are many and quite varied. Understanding what risks are in a bond portfolio and what the potential impacts of these exposures are is critical to being able to build portfolios that are consistent with the investor's risk and return objectives.

FIXED INCOME BENCHMARKS

Generally speaking, the choice of benchmark is the most important factor in determining the risk profile and the ultimate returns of a fixed income portfolio. Since, as we will discuss later, it is somewhat difficult to achieve very high levels of tracking error relative to a fixed income benchmark, the risk of even an actively managed portfolio will be mostly determined by the risk of the benchmark.

Of the risks that were described in the previous section, the four risk exposures that define most fixed income benchmarks are duration, sector, credit, and currency risks. The remaining risks mentioned (yield curve, volatility, prepayment, and security-specific) are generally a result of the decision on the first four since most fixed income benchmarks are constructed using market capitalization weights of the securities in the sectors and maturity ranges that have been chosen to achieve the desired duration, credit quality, and sector allocation. Table 24.3 shows a list of some of the more widely used benchmarks in the fixed income world. As you can see, the types of fixed income benchmarks are wide-ranging and span the entire spectrum of fixed income risks that we have described. Another important item to note is that with the exception of benchmarks with mostly below-investment-grade credit quality, the main determinant of fixed income volatility is interest rate risk. Also, diversifying interest rate risk globally reduces volatility, while adding currency risk (i.e., using an unhedged currency benchmark) increases volatility.

Of course, many investors construct their own customized benchmark indexes by combining all or portions of some of the more widely used benchmarks. This allows them to tailor their benchmarks (and the portfolios that are managed to those benchmarks) to have the desired types and amounts of risk. For example, an investor who wanted a Treasury benchmark but wanted a duration of one year could create a customized benchmark that was equal to 50 percent of the Merrill Lynch

TABLE 24.3 Widely Used Benchmarks

Benchmark	Duration Years	Sector Contribution to Duration (years) Govt.	Corp.	MBS	High-Yield	EMD	Credit Average Rating	Volatility Convexity	Historical 10-Year Returns (Ending 6/02) %	Historical Volatility % Std. Dev.
JPMorgan 3-Month US$ Cash Index	0.1		0.1				AAA	0.00	5.24	0.42
Merrill Lynch 6-Month U.S. T-Bill Index	0.4	0.4					AAA	0.34	4.97	0.44
Merrill Lynch 1–3-Year U.S. Treasury Index	1.6	1.6					AAA	0.04	6.02	1.66
Salomon Brothers Mortgage Index	3.1			3.1			AAA	–2.27	7.27	2.94
Lehman Brothers Intermediate Treasury Index	3.2	3.2					AAA	0.16	6.66	2.97
Lehman Brothers Intermediate Aggregate Index	3.2	0.9	1.0	1.3		0.1	AA+	–0.71	7.02	2.99
Lehman Brothers Aggregate Index	4.3	1.7	1.4	1.1		0.1	AA+	–0.36	7.35	3.73
Lehman Brothers Intermediate Corporate Index	4.4		4.4				A	0.27	7.26	3.77
Lehman Brothers High Yield Index	4.7				4.7		B+	0.23	5.99	6.57
Lehman Brothers Global Aggregate Index (hedged to US$)	4.8	3.0	1.1	0.7			AAA–	0.09	7.70	3.12
Lehman Brothers Global Aggregate Index (unhedged in US$)	4.8	3.0	1.1	0.7			AAA–	0.09	6.13	4.76
Lehman Brothers Government/Credit Index	5.3	2.9	2.4				AA	0.56	7.35	4.21
JPMorgan Emerging Market Bond Index—Plus*	5.8					5.8	BB	0.30	8.62	18.15
JPMorgan Global Government Index	5.8	5.8					AAA	0.38	7.47	3.17
Salomon Brothers Long Treasury Index	10.8	10.8					AAA	1.75	8.93	7.93

*Return is since the inception of the index in December 1993.

1–3-Year U.S. Treasury Index and 50 percent of the Merrill Lynch 6-Month U.S. T-Bill Index. Or an investor who liked the risk profile and diversification of the Lehman Aggregate but did not want to invest in securities rated below A could use a customized benchmark that would be the Lehman Aggregate excluding BBB-rated securities.

ACTIVE MANAGEMENT STRATEGIES

Once an investor decides on the appropriate benchmark, the next decision is whether to have the portfolio passively managed to try to match the returns of the benchmark or to have the portfolio manager actively manage the portfolio using various strategies with the objective of achieving a higher return than that of the benchmark.

As with any asset class, active management of a portfolio is simply tactically changing the risk exposures of the portfolio in order to either achieve the highest level of return given a targeted level of risk or achieve a targeted level of return while taking the least amount of risk. When describing risk and return, we generally define these terms as relative to the defined benchmark rather than as an absolute level. However, if one is managing an "absolute return" strategy such as a hedge fund, the concepts still work. In these cases, whether it is stated explicitly or not, the risk exposures of the portfolio are effectively being compared to a cash benchmark that has no risk, such as a T-bill- or a London Interbank Offered Rate (LIBOR)-based benchmark. Because of this focus on relative positioning versus a benchmark, we would use the terms "long" and "short" to be equivalent to overweight or underweight positions relative to the benchmark.

The next section examines the most widely utilized active management strategies for fixed income portfolios. You should note that each of the strategies matches up to one or more of the fixed income risk exposures described earlier.

Duration Timing Strategy

This strategy is effectively a market timing strategy where the portfolio manager positions the portfolio to have a longer or shorter average duration than the benchmark. A manager would choose to expose the portfolio to more interest rate risk (i.e., be longer) than the benchmark if he or she had a view that the bond market will outperform cash. When evaluating this type of trade, it is always important to determine what the market is "pricing in" in terms of implied forward interest rates. In a typical upward sloping yield curve, forward interest rates are generally higher than current interest rates. It is this implied forward rate that the manager is betting against when instituting a duration exposure.

Yield Curve Positioning Strategy

We would define a yield curve positioning strategy as one where the manager overweights the contribution to duration (CTD) of one or multiple parts of the yield curve and offsets these long positions with underweights of other parts of the yield curve. We would generally expect this strategy to be run market neutral (i.e., net duration of zero), since any residual market exposure would be considered part of the duration timing strategy. One example of a yield curve positioning trade would be to be long 0.5 years in the 2-year part of the curve and short 0.5 years in the 10-year part of the curve. This would be the type of trade that a manager would put on if he or she expected the yield curve to steepen. Another example of a yield curve trade would be to be long 1.0 year in the 5-year part of the curve and 0.5 year short in both the 2-year and the 10-year. This type of trade might be established if the manager thought that the 5-year was priced cheaply given the slope of 2's to 10's.

Sector Allocation Strategy

This strategy is defined as the manager taking overweight and underweight positions in the various fixed income sectors relative to the chosen benchmark. A manager would choose to be overweight a sector based on the relative spread advantage to other sectors and/or an expectation of future spread tightening. A sector may experience spread tightening due to either technical factors such as reduction in supply or an anticipated flow of funds into the sector, or fundamental factors such as an improvement in corporate earnings (for corporate bonds) or a reduction in convexity risk (for MBSs). One example of a sector allocation trade is an underweight of 0.5 years in the MBS sector in the case where the manager anticipates spread widening in mortgages. Another example would be an overweight of 5 percent in high-yield corporate bonds executed when the manager believes that the incremental yield offered by the high-yield sector more than compensates for the additional credit risk. Remember that for targeting risk positions in the high-quality sectors such as governments and mortgages, we use CTD, and for sectors with high credit risk we use market value percent because we believe that risk in the high-credit-quality sectors is roughly linear with duration while duration in the low-credit-quality sectors is not necessarily the best measure of future volatility.

Security Selection Strategies

Security selection strategies are a series of strategies in which the manager is selecting individual securities within each of the sectors in which the portfolio is invested. Security selection strategies are generally believed to generate the best risk-adjusted returns because the manager can diversify across many different active decisions rather than just a small number of bets. There are many different reasons that a manager will expect one security to outperform another, such as fundamental credit quality views, new issue premiums, mispriced mortgage cash flows, and attractive dealer bids or offerings.

Country Allocation Strategy

Many fixed income portfolios can invest in markets around the globe. The country allocation strategy is one where the manager takes active long and short positions in bonds priced off of the yield curve of one country versus bonds priced off of the yield curve of another country. As with the yield curve strategy, we would generally run this strategy to be market neutral with respect to global interest rates. In other words, the net of the long and short positions in various countries would not be expected to perform better or worse in rallying markets versus declining markets. Also, any currency exposure generated by the country allocation trades would be hedged using currency forwards in order to distinguish the bet on relative interest rates from a bet on exchange rates. Examples of country allocation trades are selling Japanese bonds to buy German bonds or selling U.S. bonds to buy Canadian bonds.

Currency Allocation Strategy

In addition to the flexibility to invest in bonds markets around the world, many investors allow active fixed income managers to implement views on exchange rates between one currency and another. This strategy is usually implemented by using currency forward contracts that explicitly expose the portfolio to one currency versus another or by leaving securities denominated in currencies that are expected to appreciate unhedged or only partially hedged.

Although the above list of active fixed income strategies is not fully comprehensive, these strategies most likely comprise the vast majority of risks that active bond managers trade in the portfolios that they manage. Managers will utilize different strategies and will allocate different levels of risk to those strategies based on the resources that they have and the confidence that they have in each strategy. Also, within each strategy, managers will use very different inputs to make active investment decisions. The next section will show how we combine the active strategies in such a way as to achieve the most optimal investment results.

COMBINING ACTIVE STRATEGIES USING RISK BUDGETING

The ability to determine trade ideas that on average add value is most certainly critical to being able to outperform a passive benchmark. However, determining how to size an exposure can be almost as important. Unfortunately, every trade idea will not always work out positively even if based on high-quality research and a disciplined decision-making process. Given this fact, allocating risk efficiently across investment ideas and investment strategies can result in the highest quality returns. In this section, we will show the process that we go through to decide the allocation of risk across the various active strategies.

This process of risk budgeting has seven steps:

Step 1 ***Determine the benchmark.*** The benchmark determines the neutral point for each of the risks in the portfolio. Active views will be taken relative to the benchmark, so it is important to know what the allocation of risk is in the benchmark at all times.

Step 2 ***Determine the investment constraints.*** Most investors will put explicit limits on what type of exposures they will allow in the portfolio. Sometimes these are absolute limits such as "maximum 30 percent in corporate bonds," and other times they are relative to the benchmark such as "the duration of the portfolio must be within one year of the benchmark duration." Many investors will put some type of limit on duration, credit quality, sector allocations, issuer allocations, and currency exposure. Recently, some investors have given more flexibility to their managers on individual types of risks and have instead provided the manager a constraint on total volatility relative to the benchmark in the form of a tracking error target.

Step 3 ***Determine the permissible active investment strategies.*** Once the constraints are known, the manager can determine what investment strategies can be utilized for the portfolio. For example, if the client does not allow any currency exposure, then obviously the currency strategy would not be implemented for that portfolio. Similarly, if a mandate does not allow for securities rated below investment grade, then the high-yield sector would not be part of the sector allocation strategy and of course there would be no security selection strategy within the high-yield sector.

Step 4 ***Determine an appropriate maximum amount of tracking error for each available strategy.*** The combination of the benchmark and the constraints will determine how much the risk exposure of the portfolio could deviate from the benchmark. Also, the manager may impose his or her own constraint on risk to a strategy based on capacity issues and prudence. The maximum tracking error is determined by multiplying the average deviation of the particular risk times the estimated volatility of that risk. For example, let's say that a particular U.S. fixed income mandate has a one-year limit on the duration deviation from the benchmark. The volatility of U.S. interest rates is about 1 percent per year. If the manager always had the maximum bet (i.e., either long one year or short one year) at all times, then the average tracking error would be about 100 basis points (1 year times 1 percent). However, for most strategies, the information ratios of the strategies will be higher if the managers take large positions when they have the most conviction and smaller positions when they have a view but with less conviction. Therefore, in this case, we would assign a constraint on the duration strategy of about 70 bps, which would correspond to an average 0.7 year exposure and would allow for the maximum one-year bet at times of maximum conviction. We go through a similar exercise for each investment strategy, examining what size of active positioning (on average) can be achieved and then estimating how much tracking error would result from that average position.

Step 5 ***Estimate the excess return per unit of risk for each strategy as well as the correlation of excess returns between strategies.*** The estimation of the amount of added return for each basis point of tracking error, or information ratio, is basically a measure of how good the manager believes the strategy will be going forward. Every strategy should have a positive information ratio, or else it would not make sense to include it in an active investment process. Determining the information ratio of a strategy is not an easy task and will always have some uncertainty around it. However, a manager can make an educated estimate by combining past results of actual or back-tested performance of the strategy with a forward-looking view that incorporates the manager's assessment of the current opportunities in the market.

Generally, our view is that security selection strategies can achieve the highest information ratios, followed by sector strategies and then followed by market timing strategies. Estimating correlations between the returns of the various strategies is also very important in determining the appropriate mix of strategies at the portfolio level. Again, a mix of historical results and intuition about the future can help determine these correlation estimates. For example, it makes sense that security selection strategies should not exhibit much correlation at all with other strategies because the manager's top-down view does not necessarily factor into individual security opinions. On the other hand, it might be expected that the duration strategy would have some positive correlation with the sector allocation strategy because the manager's macroeconomic opinion will be an input into both decisions.

Step 6 ***Determine the target excess return or the target tracking error.*** This is a necessary input, as the allocation of risk will seek either to maximize the excess return given a target level of risk or to minimize the tracking error needed to achieve a target level of excess return. Some clients give one target or the other, some give both, and some give neither. In the first two cases, the manager must make sure that the targets are achievable given the constraints. In cases where clients give no explicit risk or return targets, managers must use their judgment given their understanding of the clients' objectives.

Step 7 ***Determine the optimal amount of risk to each strategy.*** Finally, once you determine what strategies can be used, how much could be allocated to each strategy, how good you are at generating returns in each strategy, how you expect them to move together, and how much risk or return you are looking to achieve, you are ready to determine the appropriate allocation. We use a mean-variance optimization technique that utilizes all of the above inputs and results in an allocation of tracking error to each strategy that will maximize the information ratio.

In order to demonstrate this process, we will perform a few examples of this optimization technique. For purposes of this illustration, we will use several inputs:

1. The portfolios are managed to the Lehman Brothers U.S. Aggregate Index.
2. The portfolios are long only and do not allow explicit leverage.
3. The estimated information ratios for the active strategies are:

Duration	0.2
Yield curve	0.3
Sector allocation	0.4
Security selection for government/MBS/ABS/agency	0.7
Security selection for corporate/high-yield/EMD	0.5
Country allocation	0.4
Currency	0.4

4. The correlations of the strategies range from 0.0 to 0.3.

We have run the optimization for two different sets of constraints (see Table 24.4).

Table 24.5 shows the output from the optimization for Portfolio 1 where risk was allocated across the allowable strategies with three different targets for tracking error of 50, 75, and 100 basis points.

TABLE 24.4 Two Sets of Constraints

	Portfolio 1—Core High-Quality	Portfolio 2—Core Plus
Duration	Index +/– 0.5 years	Index +/– 2.0 years
Minimum credit quality	BBB–/Baa3	No minimum
High-yield maximum	Not allowed	10%
Emerging market debt maximum	Not allowed	10%
Other sectors	Benchmark +/– 20%	No constraint
Non-$ bonds	Not allowed	Maximum 20%, maximum 10% unhedged

There are a number of items to note in the table. You can see that for each strategy, the level of excess return from that strategy is equal to the allocated tracking error multiplied by the information ratio detailed earlier. For example, in the 75 bps tracking error case, the optimization has suggested an allocation of 48.2 bps to the sector allocation strategy, which contributes 19.3 bps of expected excess return (48.2 times the assumed information ratio of 0.4). Also note that while the total portfolio excess return is equal to the sum of the excess returns from each strategy, the total tracking error is much less than the sum of the tracking errors from each strategy. This is because of the benefit of diversifying risk across a number of strategies that are not highly correlated. Another item of note is that the total portfolio information ratio declines as risk increases. This is generally the case for any portfolio optimization given a set of constraints.

Lastly, note that while 100 bps was targeted for the optimization in the rightmost column, the total tracking error is only 87.3 bps. This is because the

TABLE 24.5 Portfolio 1 Optimization Results

		Target Tracking Error					
		50		75		100	
	Maximum Tracking Error	Excess Return	Tracking Error	Excess Return	Tracking Error	Excess Return	Tracking Error
Duration	35	1.1	5.3	2.3	11.3	7.0	35.0
Yield curve	25	5.5	18.2	7.5	25.0	7.5	25.0
Sector	50	9.1	22.7	19.3	48.2	20.0	50.0
Security—government/MBS/ABS/agency	25	17.5	25.0	17.5	25.0	17.5	25.0
Security—corporate/high-yield/EMD	40	15.2	30.4	20.0	40.0	20.0	40.0
Country	0	0.0	0.0	0.0	0.0	0.0	0.0
Currency	0	0.0	0.0	0.0	0.0	0.0	0.0
Total portfolio		48.3	50.0	66.5	75.0	72.0	87.3
Information ratio		1.0		0.9		0.8	

maximum level of tracking error was reached for every strategy and this resulted in only 87.3 bps of tracking error. There is simply no additional risk to take given the portfolio constraints. This is often the case for portfolios that do not allow investments below investment-grade because most high-credit-quality fixed income securities are highly correlated and it is hard for the returns of a diversified portfolio to deviate substantially from the benchmark, with the exception of returns resulting from duration risk. In this example, we limited the duration band to 0.5 years. The tracking error could be raised if that constraint was lifted, but the information ratio would deteriorate meaningfully.

Table 24.6 shows the output from the optimization for Portfolio 2. Because of the more flexible investment constraints, the optimization was run at target tracking errors of 50, 100, and 200 basis points.

In this case, the maximum tracking error for most of the strategies was higher than for Portfolio 1 because the investment constraints allowed for both larger size and broader types of risk. Notice that at the same level of tracking error, the information ratio is higher for Portfolio 2 than for Portfolio 1. This is because Portfolio 2 allows for more diversified sources of risk. Also, because Portfolio 2 is allowed to trade in more volatile markets such as high-yield, emerging-market debt, and currency, it is able to achieve much higher levels of tracking error if that is what the investor desires.

This analysis is just a sample of how this process works. It is portable to any benchmark with any set of constraints. This risk budgeting strategy could also be used to run hedge fund portfolios that exhibit tracking error of 1,000 basis points or more. To be able to achieve such high levels of risk, the manager must be investing exclusively in high-risk markets and/or utilizing leverage to be able to increase the amount of risk taken in the active strategies that are being used.

Keep in mind that this is not the end of the investment process. It is merely the beginning. To achieve the return objectives that result from these risk allocations,

TABLE 24.6 Portfolio 2 Optimization Results

		Target Tracking Error					
		50		100		200	
	Maximum Tracking Error	Excess Return	Tracking Error	Excess Return	Tracking Error	Excess Return	Tracking Error
Duration	140	0.8	4.2	2.1	10.4	7.4	37.0
Yield curve	25	4.3	14.3	7.5	25.0	7.5	25.0
Sector	160	7.1	17.8	17.7	44.3	62.9	157.3
Security—Government/ MBS/ABS/agency	25	17.5	25.0	17.5	25.0	17.5	25.0
Security—corporate/ high-yield/EMD	60	11.9	23.8	29.7	59.3	30.0	60.0
Country	25	7.6	19.0	10.0	25.0	10.0	25.0
Currency	70	7.6	19.0	19.0	47.5	28.0	70.0
Total portfolio		56.9	50.0	103.5	100.0	163.3	200.0
Information ratio		1.1		1.0		0.8	

the manager must now effectively run each of the strategies to achieve the estimated added value. Another important factor is that you will note that these risk allocations are done at the strategy level, not the actual risk exposure level. The risk allocations and correlations are averages rather than spot estimates. Therefore, it is important to understand the expected risk at each point in time based on the actual exposures that are in the portfolio. It may be the case that although you have estimated that two strategies are uncorrelated on average, the specific trades that have resulted from the strategies at a given point in time are expected to be highly correlated. In this instance, the manager should be aware of the potential increase in tracking error and actively decide whether it is appropriate to exhibit more than average risk at that time or to dial back one or both of the exposures. Also, as time goes by, the manager may change his or her estimates on the information ratio of the strategies, the correlations between the strategies, or the maximum amount of risk that can be taken based on new performance information, increases or decreases in resources dedicated to each strategy, a change in market volatility, or a belief that the future opportunities to add value in a particular strategy have gone either up or down relative to prior expectations.

Hopefully, we have given the reader a sense of the issues to consider when investing in the rather complex fixed income markets.

PART Five

Alternative Asset Classes

CHAPTER 25

Global Tactical Asset Allocation

Mark M. Carhart

INTRODUCTION

The goal of a global tactical asset allocation (GTAA) strategy is to improve the overall return per unit of risk in a client's portfolio through active management of asset allocation deviations. A GTAA strategy alters the asset allocation in the portfolio both to reduce a portfolio's unintentional asset allocation risk and to add excess return through intentional asset allocation deviations. Because the strategy's goal is twofold, it is often constructed as two separable pieces: (1) a rebalancing or *completion* portfolio, of which the sole objective is to reduce asset allocation risk in the portfolio, and (2) a *pure overlay* portfolio that is designed to capture excess return through global tactical asset allocation deviations.

Both the completion and pure overlay elements of a GTAA program can be customized to the specific needs of every portfolio. These include the portfolio's strategic asset allocation, its existing active and passive investment portfolios, and also client-specific objectives and investment constraints such as targeted active risk and constraints on leverage or position sizes. The degree of customization in GTAA often makes the strategy difficult to classify into a particular asset class, as the uses of it differ so widely across investors' portfolios.

The purpose of this chapter is to set forth the key elements of GTAA, while at the same time explaining the nuances of GTAA that make the strategy so appealing to various clients. In the following pages, we walk through the modern GTAA strategy in detail, explain and show through examples how clients and investment managers should best implement GTAA, and demonstrate how powerfully a GTAA program improves a portfolio's risk/reward profile.

After a brief history of GTAA, the chapter continues in four primary sections: the structure of a GTAA program, the empirical evidence supporting GTAA, practical implementation issues that face clients and managers, and finally, expectations for a GTAA program.

HISTORY OF GTAA

As long as investors have been buying and selling securities, they have also been timing the market. One of the early and great market timers was Charles Henry

Dow, the founder of the *Wall Street Journal*. Toward the end of the nineteenth century, Dow wrote down his views on stock market predictability in editorials, which eventually became a set of rules coined the "Dow Theory."[1]

However, as there have been advocates of market timing, there have also been skeptics. Benjamin Graham writes that an investor that "places his emphasis on *timing*, in the sense of forecasting, . . . will end up as a speculator and with a speculator's financial results"[2] (italics in original). I think we know what he meant by that.

Strong academic interest in broad stock market predictability would not occur until the 1970s, when sufficient data and analytical tools existed to reliably test for predictability in stock returns. Early papers (e.g., Fama's 1970 classic work laying out the Efficient Markets Hypothesis[3]) found limited evidence of profitable trading strategies in U.S. stocks. By the late 1970s, however, inconsistencies in the Efficient Markets Hypothesis began to appear, as academics quantified the strong negative relation between future stock prices and short-term interest rates.[4]

Institutional interest in an exclusive market timing strategy began in the mid-1970s in response to the 1973–1974 bear market and in large part driven by academic research.[5] William Fouse, who was then at Wells Fargo, marketed this strategy as Tactical Asset Allocation (TAA). The bear market alone did not create an environment for TAA. An additional key ingredient was the advent of the stock index and bond futures markets in the United States, markets that offered a low-cost and efficient method for implementing stock and bond tactical reallocations. Interest in TAA further blossomed after the 1987 crash as most TAA managers were positioned for a market correction.

Global TAA strategies appeared in the late 1980s and early 1990s, as additional evidence on global asset predictability accumulated, and the number and liquidity of foreign futures markets increased dramatically.[6] Global strategies added additional sources of value. Not only could they offer global market timing, but they also provided opportunities from country-level selection decisions in equities, bonds, and currencies. Unfortunately, by the late 1990s, the poor performance of many global asset allocators caused the industry to struggle. In particular, managers with a focus on valuation models and market timing underperformed—they underweighted equities in a period of strong equity performance—casting a negative light

---

[1]www.e-analytics.com/cd.htm, a web site maintained by Charles Kaplan of Equity Analytics, Ltd.

[2]Graham, Benjamin, 1959, *The Intelligent Investor* (2nd revised edition), Harper & Brothers, 25.

[3]Fama, Eugene F., 1970, "Efficient Capital Markets: A Review of Theory and Empirical Work," *Journal of Finance* 25, 383–417.

[4]A good example of these papers is Fama, Eugene F., and G. W. Schwert, 1977, "Asset Returns and Inflation," *Journal of Financial Economics* 5, 115–146.

[5]For a more complete discussion of Wells Fargo and the development of TAA, see Siegel, Laurence B., Kenneth F. Kroner, and Scott W. Clifford, 2001, "The Greatest Return Stories Ever Told," *Journal of Investing* 10, 91–102.

[6]In an extensive literature search, we found that the first use of the term GTAA to describe this strategy occurred in 1988: Givant, Marlene, 1988, "Taking a World View: $100 Million Fund Starts Global Allocation Strategy," *Pensions and Investment Age*, June 13, 2.

on the industry as a whole. Weak market returns since 2000 have increased the popularity of GTAA, and it is steadily becoming a mainstream product for the largest, most sophisticated institutional investors.

STRUCTURE OF A GTAA PROGRAM

Part 1: Completion

As a result of increased specialization of active managers and the breadth of product offerings, the number of investment managers in institutional portfolios has increased dramatically. For example, where balanced managers dominated the marketplace 20 years ago, we now routinely observe managers that might only focus on small-capitalization value stocks in the United States. One institutional client for which we manage assets divides its strategic benchmark into 14 different pieces, with multiple managers within each of these. In this specialized-manager structure, who manages the portfolio's overall asset allocation? Often this is neglected, but this need not be the case as the completion element of GTAA can provide the glue for a diversified multimanager investment portfolio.

A completion portfolio is designed to explicitly remove unintentional asset allocation risk. Described in Chapter 22 in more detail, multiple activities can create unintentional asset allocation risks. The first and probably most important is drift relative to benchmark in the underlying portfolio allocations caused by fluctuations in asset valuations.[7] Depending on how frequently clients "true up" their portfolios, drift risk can contribute upwards of 50 percent of total active risk, effectively swamping the intentional active risk from traditional security selection activities. Of course, returning the portfolio to its strategic benchmark is not free, as transaction costs eat up some of the benefits of rebalancing. Cash sitting in managers' accounts, currency deviations driven by stock selection activities, and manager or benchmark transitions also create unintentional risk that is frequently left unmanaged.

While institutions sometimes hire firms to handle subsets of these activities, the most natural and generally least costly approach is to place these responsibilities with a GTAA manager. The GTAA manager can monitor and remove unintentional benchmark deviations due to drift, cash holdings, transitions, and even contributions to and redemptions from the portfolio. More elaborate possibilities include implementing an overall currency hedge, moving alpha ("porting" it) from one asset class to another, and managing intermediate-term changes in strategic exposure driven by trustee boards or investment committees. In very complex portfolios, or portfolios with frequent cash flows, institutions might consider using their custodian as a specialized completion manager separate from a GTAA program. In these cases, the potential additional transaction costs from the completion and GTAA

[7]If left unspecified, multi-asset-class benchmarks reset to their fixed proportions at the same frequency as performance is reported, typically monthly. Increasingly, clients are specifying that benchmark weights drift with asset valuations over longer horizons, permitting benchmark reset frequencies such as quarterly, semiannually, or annually.

managers holding offsetting positions is balanced by the quality of completion offered by proximity to the information flows in the portfolio. Regardless of who manages the completion program, liquid futures and forwards are critical in reducing the transaction costs of rebalancing.

Part 2: Pure Overlay

As described in the introduction to the chapter, the pure overlay element of a GTAA program is designed to generate excess returns through intentional active deviations in sectors, countries, or asset classes. Generally, a GTAA strategy can be viewed as making two major types of decisions:

1. Asset class timing (includes stocks versus bonds versus cash, small-cap versus large-cap stocks, value versus growth stocks, emerging versus developed stocks and bonds, credit timing, etc.). Often, this type of decision is referred to as TAA.
2. Country or sector decisions within asset classes (includes country selection in developed and emerging equity, fixed income and currency markets, as well as the potential for sectors within equity markets, and maturity within fixed income markets). These are the global relative-value decisions that give meaning to the "G" in GTAA.

The relative importance of these two types of decisions is a critical feature of a well-managed GTAA program. Whereas the traditional TAA programs focused exclusively on the first type of decision, GTAA's ability to add value derives primarily from the second type of decision. The most successful, modern GTAA strategies predominate their risk in the latter, primarily country-selection decisions.

Because country-selection strategies potentially trade in many more securities than asset class timing alone, we expect a higher risk-adjusted return from them. In the nomenclature of Grinold's (1989) "Fundamental Law of Active Management," there is greater *breadth* in the country-selection strategy.[8] Breadth is the number of independent assets in the investment opportunity set. Of course, a strong *information coefficient*—the predictability of the assets in the strategy—can offset a loss of breadth. As we demonstrate later, the empirical evidence actually finds a lower forecasting ability in the time series of asset class returns as compared to the relative value of country returns, further raising the importance of the country-selection decision in GTAA.

The most common implementation of GTAA today uses all the liquid equity index futures, bond futures, and currency forwards in developed markets globally deployed in four different strategies: (1) TAA among global stocks, bonds, and cash; (2) country selection within global stock markets; (3) country selection within global bond markets; and (4) currency selection within global currency markets.

[8]Grinold, Richard C., 1989, "The Fundamental Law of Active Management," *Journal of Portfolio Management* 15, 30–37.

Currently, the liquid futures and forward instruments in the developed countries comprise approximately 35 securities.[9]

Theoretical Explanations for Asset Class and Country Predictability

One question one might ask is whether we should expect to be able to forecast the returns on countries and asset classes. At one level we could simply draw the analogy to active management within asset classes and ask why if active management can add value *within* asset classes should it not be able to add value *across* countries or asset classes? However, we can be more constructive than this. We believe that the tradable assets within GTAA should be forecastable on a theoretical basis both because of market equilibrium and because of market inefficiency.

An equilibrium model informs us about the relationship between risk and expected return. Individual investors within the aggregate market have different perceptions of risk that lead to risk-sharing equilibriums in which some investors buy risks that others sell. For example, a bank's short-term liabilities make it risky to hold long-term bonds, whereas a pension plan generally has longer-term liabilities that cause it to prefer longer-maturity bonds. The relative supply of these types of investors (among other influences, naturally) creates the slope of the yield curve.

Imagine now a mean-variance investor with a portfolio whose overall volatility is increased the same amount whether additional investments are made in short- or long-term bonds. This investor would prefer the highest-yielding bonds, regardless of maturity. A GTAA strategy managed for this investor, then, could add value by simply overweighting markets where the return to risk is high, and underweighting those where the return is low. This "risk" story is often given for observed return premiums such as value stocks and high-yield bonds.

In addition, the risk premiums vary through time and across countries due to changing aggregate supply and demand, as well as the absence of perfectly linked country business cycles. These phenomena create further opportunities to predict returns and do not depend on market inefficiency.

We also believe that forecastability derives from market inefficiency, by which we mean that markets deviate from their equilibrium levels. In spite of the elegance of the Efficient Markets Hypothesis, we believe there are strong reasons to expect market inefficiency, especially across global capital markets where there is relatively less capital chasing after market inefficiencies than within a given country's markets. In particular, we believe inefficiencies occur due to long-term overreaction and short-term underreaction to information, market segregation, tax effects, and

[9]Liquid stock index futures markets currently exist in Australia, Belgium, Brazil, Canada, Europe, France, Germany, Hong Kong, Italy, Japan, Korea, Malaysia, the Netherlands, Singapore, South Africa, Spain, Sweden, Switzerland, Taiwan, the United States, and the United Kingdom. Bond futures are liquid in Australia, Canada, Europe, Japan, Switzerland, the United States, and the United Kingdom. The liquid currency markets among developed countries are the Australian dollar, Canadian dollar, European Union euro, Hong Kong dollar, Japanese yen, New Zealand dollar, Norwegian krone, Singapore dollar, Swedish krona, Swiss franc, U.S. dollar, and U.K. pound sterling.

non–economically motivated players in capital markets. In any case, to characterize markets as efficient or inefficient is perhaps too sharp a distinction. A more realistic version of market efficiency would admit that investment activities such as GTAA are required to push markets toward equilibrium valuations and that efficient markets still allow for some degree of profitable activities designed to take advantage of what are traditionally considered market inefficiencies.

Investor behavior drives long-term overreaction and short-term underreaction to information. Who wants to own—much less acknowledge that they own—a stock that dropped significantly in price? Often these are companies with poor operating results where news stories convey only pessimism about the companies' future prospects. The same often holds for asset classes and countries. Japan, for example, which has endured a decade of economic decline in the 1990s and the beginning of the twenty-first century, shows only sluggish growth. As it happens, we believe investors have overreacted to the Japanese story, and believe Japanese equity prices will rise relative to the rest of the world.

The underreaction effect is based on a well-documented finding that investors underreact to new information in the short term. The primary result supporting this conclusion is the so-called "post-earnings-announcement drift."[10] In the nine-month period following an earnings surprise—whether positive or negative—the firm's stock price drifts relative to the aggregate market in the same direction as the earnings surprise. Post-earnings-announcement drift also holds in country equity markets, with negative earnings-surprise countries drifting downward relative to the world, and positive surprise countries drifting upward.

Market segregation means that there are constraints on the free flow of capital across countries or markets. For example, in Korea 20 years ago, due to regulatory restrictions it was difficult for Koreans to hold foreign securities and for foreigners to hold Korean securities. This caused a disequilibrium in global capital markets, as Koreans could not diversify their portfolios and therefore demanded a higher return for Korean equity risk. The diligent foreign investors who determined ways around these restrictions benefited in two ways. First, they earned higher returns than the rest of the world due to the higher price of equity risk, and second, they earned even higher returns as the market desegregated and the price of equity risk declined, further pushing upward Korean stock prices. Market segregation still exists in some developed markets today. Canada, for example, continues to limit the amount of foreign property that Canadian investors may own.

Finally, there are governments and central banks that are non–economically motivated participants in global capital markets. Central banks routinely use currency trades and monetary policy to influence exchange rates. However, free-floating exchange rates guarantee that the aggregate market participants will ultimately determine the equilibrium exchange rates. In that sense, central bank activity in currency markets is at best a short-term policy of "leaning against the wind" that capital markets eventually correct. Governments also periodically in-

[10]See Foster, Georg, Chris Olsen, and Terry Shevlin, 1984, "Earnings Releases, Anomalies and the Behavior of Security Returns," *Accounting Review*, October, 574–603, and Bernard, Victor, and Jacob Thomas, 1989, "Post-Earnings Drift: Delayed Price Response or Risk Premium?" *Journal of Accounting Research* 27, 1–36.

tervene in equity and bond markets. During the LTCM crisis of 1998, the Hong Kong Monetary Authority (HKMA) bought approximately 5 percent of the outstanding equity in Hong Kong stocks over a two-week period in an attempt to stabilize equity prices.[11]

THE EMPIRICAL EVIDENCE

The theoretical justifications are nice, but one might ask, is there empirical support for these effects in country and asset class returns? The answer is yes, and the evidence is very strong.

Let's focus on two specific sources of predictability: value and momentum. By value, we mean buying cheap assets and shorting expensive assets. If the previous section is correct, a value strategy should work for several reasons. For example, a simple valuation model should discern differing equity risk premiums across countries and would overweight higher-risk-premium countries where valuations are relatively lower. Alternatively, investor overreaction to negative information may temporarily depress a specific country's equity market. Still another possibility is market segmentation, which results in relatively more attractive valuations in the segregated equity markets.

Predictability across Global Equity Markets Using Valuation Measures

Using only countries in developed global equity markets, imagine that we measure value using a very simple value metric: the book-to-price (B/P) ratio. We form a long/short portfolio of country equity indexes using the reported value of this measure, without any adjustments for accounting, discount rate, or tax effects across countries. At the beginning of each month, our long/short portfolio consists of equal-weight long positions in the one-third of countries with the highest B/P and equal-weight short positions in the third with the lowest B/P. Let us rebalance this portfolio monthly. Table 25.1 presents summary statistics on the portfolio's performance over the 22-year period from the beginning of 1980 to the end of 2001.

The average annual excess return on this equity country selection portfolio is 4.9 percent, which means that on average, the cheapest third of equity countries outperforms the most expensive third of equity countries by 4.9 percent per year. In addition, volatility of 11.9 percent implies that the annual excess return on this portfolio exceeds zero in about 66 percent of years. The ratio of annual return to risk on the long-short portfolio represents the information ratio (IR) on this simple strategy without transaction costs. (We address transaction costs later.) As it turns out, this simple strategy earns an IR of 0.41, which is significantly positive from a statistical viewpoint. The probability that this IR would have been achieved by

[11]The HKMA purchases amounted to $9 billion compared to Hong Kong's total equity market capitalization of around $200 billion at the end of 1998. *Source:* HKMA Annual Report 1998.

TABLE 25.1 GTAA Long/Short Portfolio Summary Statistics

	Equity Country Selection Long/Short Portfolios		Stock Selection Long/Short Portfolios		Bond Country Selection Long/Short Portfolios		Currency Selection Long/Short Portfolios	
Statistic	Book/Price	1-Year Momentum	Book/Price	1-Year Momentum	Yield Curve Slope	1-Year Momentum	5-Year Reversal	1-Year Momentum
Mean annual return	4.9%	13.2%	15.8%	9.7%	1.0%	0.4%	3.9%	3.5%
Annualized volatility	11.9%	13.1%	10.4%	18.3%	4.8%	3.9%	7.9%	9.1%
Information ratio	0.41	1.01	1.52	0.53	0.21	0.12	0.50	0.38
T-statistic	1.94	4.74	6.28	2.19	0.92	0.51	2.33	1.78
Probability value for mean > 0	2.68%	0.00%	0.00%	1.47%	17.87%	30.36%	1.02%	3.78%

chance if B/P was a meaningless forecast variable is only 2.68 percent.[12] Had we made adjustments for country-specific tax, accounting, and regulatory differences, the performance of this strategy might be improved significantly.

Predictability within Global Equity Markets Using Valuation Measures

It is interesting to compare the predictability across country stock markets to the predictability in stocks within countries using the same exact measure. For every developed stock market, we create a within-country long/short portfolio using B/P for individual stocks, capitalization-weighted long positions in the highest third of companies, and capitalization-weighted short positions in the lowest third.[13] This results in 23 within-country equity long/short portfolios. We then equal weight these country long-short portfolios to derive a global stock-selection value effect.

Not surprisingly, the stock-selection effect also works within countries, with a much larger statistical significance than the country-selection effect. Table 25.1 reports these results. The average spread in return on stocks within countries is 15.8 percent, and the volatility of the global stock-selection portfolio is 10.4 percent, resulting in an IR of 1.52 and a probability value on the stock-selection effect of 0.00 percent.

While the value effect within equity markets is large, it is not as large as we might expect given the higher number of assets used in the stock-selection strategy. In the country-selection long/short portfolios, our average opportunity set was 18 countries, whereas the breadth of opportunities is 8,352 in the stock-selection portfolios. The breadth in the stock-selection portfolios is 464 times larger! According to Grinold's Law, all else being equal, the IR on the stock-selection strategy should be larger by a factor of 22, which is the square root of the ratio of breadths in the two strategies. In fact, the ratio is only three. This means that what the country-selection strategy loses in breadth, it mostly makes up for in forecasting accuracy. Recently, Peter Hopkins and Hayes Miller substantiated this finding when reviewing the performance attribution on global equity managers: The managers in their data set experienced far more success in forecasting countries than in forecasting stocks.[14]

The diversification in country indexes probably drives the significantly higher forecast accuracy in country selection relative to stock selection. Whereas a forecasting model in an individual stock will be notoriously uncertain, the residual risks from individual stock models wash out in a broad portfolio, resulting in more precise forecasts. In addition, Grinold's (1989) breadth is technically the number of *independent*

[12]The information ratio multiplied by the square root of the number of years in the sample (n) is distributed student-t with n degrees of freedom. We show p-values from a one-tailed test for the hypothesis that the mean return to the strategy is positive.

[13]Whereas an equal-weight portfolio of countries is quite feasible, and equal-weight portfolio of 7,500 global stocks is not. We use capitalization-weighted portfolios here to be more representative of the opportunity set.

[14]Hopkins, Peter J. B., and C. Hayes Miller, 2001, "Country, Sector, and Company Factors in Global Equity Portfolios," AIMR Research Foundation Monograph.

investment decisions, and it is obvious that individual stock returns are not completely independent. Another possible explanation is that the dearth of large global players reallocating capital across countries means that country-selection opportunities are larger. The data support all of these explanations.

Predictability across Global Bond and Currency Markets Using Valuation Measures

Now let us turn to the evidence in global bond and currency markets, where valuation effects also exist. We repeat the long/short portfolio construction methodology using the bond and currency markets in the developed world, once again buying the cheapest third and shorting the most expensive third. We measure value in bonds by the slope of the yield curve, and in currencies by trailing five-year excess returns, which is a simple purchasing power parity measure. Our tests include all the independent bond and currency markets in the developed world, and, except for Germany prior to the creation of the euro, exclude the sovereign country bonds and currencies that eventually adopted the common European currency. These amount to nine country markets and 11 currencies. Table 25.1 also reports these results.

Consistent with global equity markets, there is a valuation effect in both global bond and currency markets. The information ratio is 0.21 in bonds and 0.50 in currencies, with probability values of 17.9 percent and 1.0 percent, respectively. The fewer number of independent assets within these asset classes probably reduces their information ratios relative to equity markets, consistent with Grinold's Law. Clearly, taken together, the evidence in global asset returns strongly supports predictability from valuation models.

Interestingly, in spite of the fact that value measures work across all three primary asset categories as well as within equity markets, the performance on each of these value portfolios constructed from different assets is not highly correlated. In fact, the average correlation is –0.04.

We used very simple measures of valuation to demonstrate that significant predictability in country returns exists. When actually implemented, these strategies can be further improved through elementary country-specific adjustments. Clearly addressing differences in taxes, regulation, and economic environment only strengthens the empirical evidence for predictability.

Predictability in Stock versus Bond Returns Using Valuation Measures

What about timing the market? As it turns out, valuation is also a key driver of expected future total returns on stocks relative to bonds. Taking U.S. data starting in 1926, we simulate a well-known and simple valuation model for timing stocks relative to bonds. We use the "Fed model," which compares the earnings yields on stocks to the interest yield on bonds. In particular, we create an earnings yield gap measure by subtracting yields to maturity on intermediate-term bonds from trailing earnings-price ratios on the S&P 500. In each month, we take a position in stocks equal to five times the earnings yield gap and an offsetting position in intermediate-term bonds. For example, the earnings yield at the end of December 1999 was 3.29

percent while intermediate-term interest rates were 6.45 percent, giving an earnings yield gap of –3.16 percent. Therefore, the strategy would have resulted in a 15.8 percent short stock position and 15.8 percent long bond position at the beginning of January 2000.

As shown in Figure 25.1, the success of this simple strategy is striking. The information ratio on the earnings-yield-gap timing model is 0.43, which yields a highly significant probability value of 0.01 percent due to its extremely long history. In addition, the strategy is correctly positioned coming out of the bear market of 1973–1974, and is substantially underweight during the crash of 1987. The earnings yield gap is negative, though, for the four-year period starting at the beginning of 1996, thus missing out on one of the greatest continuous market appreciations on record. We believe this is one reason why many TAA managers struggled in the late 1990s.

One important facet of any forecasting model is robustness. By robust, we mean that the same factor or investment theme forecasts asset returns both across and within countries, across various asset classes, and across different time periods. Robust forecasting variables are less subject to data-mining biases and therefore are more likely to perform well out of sample. The more intuitive and consistent the factor, the more likely future performance will be strong. As shown earlier, the valuation investment theme is a very robust strategy.

Predictability Using Momentum Measures

To further support the case of predictability, let us turn to the evidence on predictability using momentum. Momentum means using measures of short-term performance to predict future performance. Recent past returns should forecast

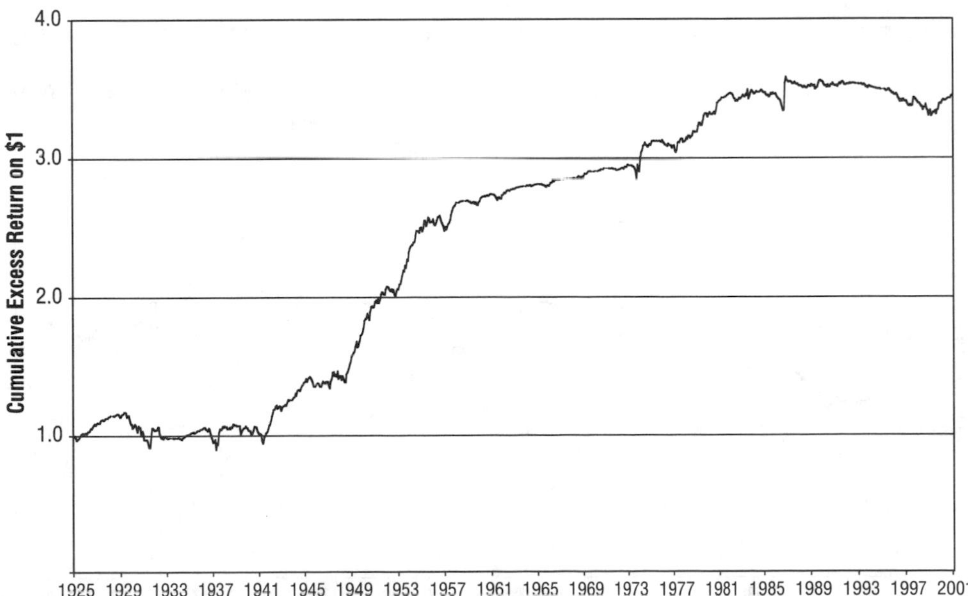

FIGURE 25.1 Cumulative Excess Return on a U.S. Stock/Bond Timing Strategy

future returns if investors underreact to short-term information, or if some non–economically motivated market participants are "leaning against the wind."

For simplicity, we define momentum as the prior year's total return. Once again, we form long/short portfolios in global equity, bond, and currency markets, long the highest third based on prior year return, and short the lowest third based on the same measure.

We show these results in Table 25.1. As before, the momentum effect is robust across countries in all three asset classes, as well as within countries' stock markets. The statistical significance of the momentum factors is even stronger than the valuation factors. In addition, the momentum effect across country equity markets is almost twice that within country equity markets, as measured by their relative information ratios. In this case, the information coefficient for momentum in country selection is more than 40 times greater than in stock selection!

Here, let us interject the importance of diversification. Both valuation and momentum measures predict future asset returns, and neither is a complete story by itself. It stands to reason that an even better approach would use both of these variables. In fact, diversification across investment themes is exceedingly powerful in GTAA. To take just one example, consider a global equity country-selection strategy that equally weights the B/P and one-year return strategies. As shown in Figure 25.2, the combined strategy exhibits similar volatility to the single-measure strategies, yet it generates cumulative excess returns over our 22-year period that are three times higher than the momentum portfolio alone.

While we reviewed two simple forecasting measures, there exist a number of additional intuitive investment themes that forecast asset class and country returns, and an exceptionally large universe of specific forecasting measures within each of

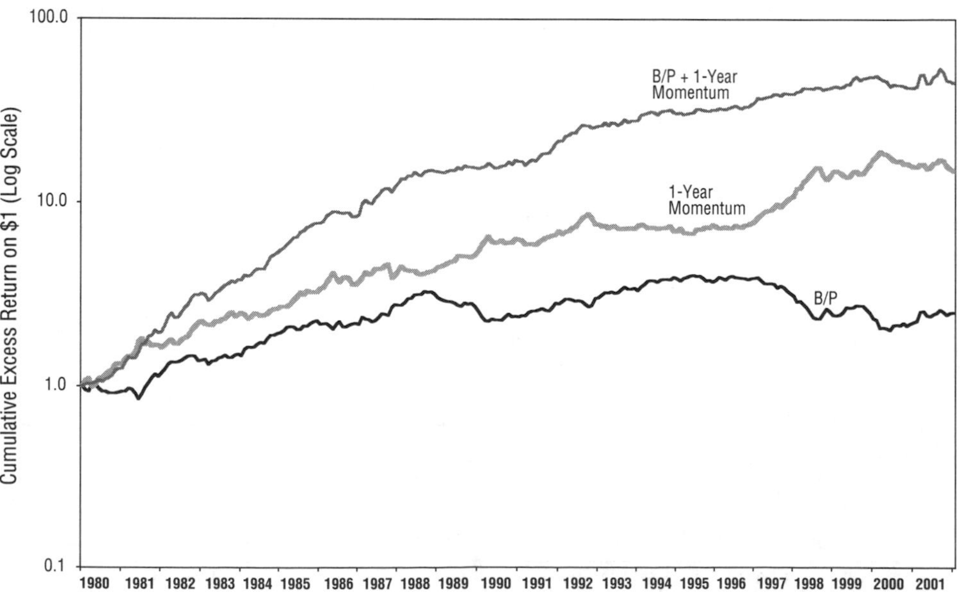

FIGURE 25.2 Cumulative Excess Return on Global Equity Country Long/Short Portfolios

these. Other investment themes that we believe drive future investment performance are macroeconomic growth, fund flows, and proxies for risk premiums.

IMPLEMENTATION ISSUES

Portfolio Construction

The forecast models of country and asset-class returns drive the desire to create deviations from the strategic asset allocation in a GTAA portfolio. However, knowing that cheap countries outperform expensive ones on average is not enough. We must also use a method of portfolio construction that translates our forecasts into meaningful estimates of expected return. We desire portfolios that balance risk and return, but traditional mean-variance optimizers struggle to construct reasonable portfolios due to the inconsistency between estimates of expected return and risk. To avoid these undesirable results, users of optimizers often impose constraints, which unfortunately also hinder the optimizer's ability to find the best portfolio.

As described more fully in Chapter 7, the Black-Litterman asset allocation model provides the natural solution to this problem by estimating expected returns more consistent with risk assumptions. It achieves this by blending views from forecasting models with the market's implicit equilibrium views to create a new set of expected returns. In principle, the model works by "shrinking" the weights on extreme views toward equilibrium, and the weights on correlated views toward each other. The degree of shrinkage depends on how much confidence we place in our forecasting model views relative to the market's implicit views. The resulting expected returns more consistently reflect estimated volatilities and correlations. In this way, the Black-Litterman approach produces better-specified expected returns and results in better-balanced portfolios than traditional methods, while requiring fewer artificial constraints.

Conceptually, a GTAA portfolio is constructed in two steps. First, the completion portfolio is built to minimize tracking error to the benchmark, and second, the pure overlay portfolio is created to maximize expected return per unit of intentional active risk. In practice, we solve for these two portfolios jointly along with transaction costs projections in order to create an aggregate GTAA overlay portfolio that maximizes expected return per unit of risk net of transaction costs. Determining the completion and pure overlay positions at the same time minimizes overall transaction costs.

After using Black-Litterman to estimate expected returns, the actual joint completion and pure overlay portfolio optimization is straightforward:

$$\underset{\{w\}}{\mathrm{Max}}\{\mathrm{E}[R]'(w-b) - \lambda\,(w-b)'\Sigma(w-b) - \phi\, t(w-w_0)\}$$

where E[R] represents the vector of Black-Litterman expected returns, w represents the vector of asset weights, b represents the vector of benchmark weights, Σ represents the covariance matrix of asset returns, $t(\ )$ represents the transaction cost function that depends on the size of trades, w_0 represents the vector of current weights, and λ and ϕ represent the risk aversion and transaction cost aversion parameters calibrated for the desired risk and GTAA-process-specific transaction costs.

Intuitively, $E[R]'(w - b)$ is the expected excess return over the benchmark, $(w - b)'\Sigma(w - b)$ is the tracking error relative to benchmark of the combined completion and overlay portfolio, and $t(w - w_0)$ is the estimated total transaction costs implied by a given optimal portfolio. Then, for attribution purposes, the completion portfolio is defined as

$$\underset{\{w_c\}}{\text{Min}}\{(w_c - b)'\Sigma(w_c - b)\}$$

where w_c represents the vector of weights in the completion portfolio. This optimization also yields the pure overlay weights, which are defined as $w - w_c$. Note that while every asset in the benchmark is represented in w and w_c, only the subset of assets with liquid futures and forwards are traded, so the tracking error of the completion portfolio is not zero. Also, this is a purely hypothetical completion portfolio that ignores transaction costs, since transaction costs are already considered in the total GTAA optimization. If the completion and pure overlay portfolios are managed separately, transaction costs must be considered in each of them independently.

Given the reduced transaction costs, does it always make sense to combine the completion and pure overlay portfolios? Although generally managing these two portfolios together is easier and less costly, this is not always the case. The exceptions are typically very large and complex portfolios, or portfolios with significant contributions and redemptions. In these cases, the custodian or a specialized completion manager is often closer to the information flow and can more quickly and more accurately remove unintentional asset allocation risk, and the gains from reducing transaction costs from netting are typically small since the pure overlay portfolio is usually not rebalanced every time there is a new cash inflow or outflow.[15]

Where Does GTAA Fit Into a Portfolio?

GTAA is generally implemented in a small overlay account using liquid derivative instruments such as futures and forwards, although the strategy can also use swaps or cash instruments such as country index funds to increase the opportunity set.

Why? The small account size required is a tremendous advantage from a risk budgeting viewpoint. This is because in practice the dollars allocated and limited tracking error of traditional managers severely limit the achievable active risk in a portfolio. It is exactly this problem that drives investors to seek absolute return strategies. Another practical motivation for limiting the size of the GTAA overlay

---

[15]In practice, one could rebalance both completion and overlay every time anything changed in the underlying holdings of the portfolio. Because there is noise in any model's expected return estimates, trading too frequently results in trading on noise, and therefore only reduces performance. Based on our experiences with our forecasting models, we believe the optimal rebalance frequency for a pure overlay account is somewhere between three and seven weeks.

portfolio is to minimize the disruption to underlying portfolio managers, since a GTAA account can often be carved out of existing cash assets in a portfolio.

The actual size requirements vary depending on the degree of completion required, the amount of active risk desired, and the sensitivity of the client to making periodic contributions to the strategy. As a general rule of thumb, a pure overlay portfolio requires a minimum of 3 percent capital for every 1 percent active risk, and the completion portfolio requires about 1 percent. In a GTAA overlay portfolio, the capital is used as initial margin and as a cushion for investment performance.

The GTAA active risk budget also varies across client portfolios. Since GTAA is uncorrelated with other active risks,[16] a risk budgeting exercise will generally place significant risk capital in the strategy. Of course, the assumed information ratio on the strategy also critically determines its size; it is common to set this equal to the average IR on other active management activities. In our experience, clients typically choose GTAA active risk on their overall portfolios between 0.25 percent (contributing about 2 percent of the total active risk) to 2.0 percent (contributing more than half of the total active risk), although the potential for GTAA active risk is virtually unlimited.[17] The most common target is 1.0 percent on the overall portfolio, in which case GTAA consumes about one-quarter of the active risk budget and requires about 5 percent of the portfolio's assets. To clarify, this risk target represents volatility on the client's overall portfolio, not volatility relative to the value of the overlay account. Relative to the overlay account alone, the volatility in this example would amount to 20 percent per year. As this example demonstrates, GTAA is almost always the most efficient source of active risk in a portfolio.

Should Global Currency Management Be Included in GTAA?

Historically, many institutions have created separate currency and GTAA overlay portfolios. This separation is unnatural, since currency allocation is an integral element of GTAA. We also believe separating currencies from GTAA is suboptimal. First, the best currency managers are also often the best GTAA managers since the best quantitative approaches apply equally well to currencies. Second, separating the two mandates increases the size of the assets that must be devoted to the program since both the currency and GTAA overlay portfolios need a buffer for profits and losses, and the diversification benefit from combining the two overlay accounts results in a smaller total profit/loss buffer. Third, the total management fees will generally be lower in a GTAA mandate that includes currency management than in two separate mandates, one for currencies and one for GTAA without currencies. This is especially true if the two overlay accounts each earn performance fees, since the client may end up paying performance fees in years that the total excess returns are negative. Finally, there are potential efficiency gains from managing GTAA and currencies jointly, since a fully specified GTAA program can exploit correlations between currencies and hedged equity and fixed income markets. (See Jorion 1994, 2002.)

---

[16]We measure this in a later section of this chapter.

[17]The practical limit occurs when the clients place 100 percent of their assets in GTAA and the strategy is run at its maximum tracking error of approximately 40 percent.

The Advantages of Implementing Using Futures and Forwards

The minimal margin requirements for futures and forward contracts makes the overlay implementation of GTAA possible. The initial margin on futures is generally 2 to 10 percent, and the initial collateral on forward and swap contracts is equally small. But use of these derivative instruments offers another advantage: high liquidity and low transaction costs.

The liquidity in futures markets today is immense. Liquid futures exist in all of the major global markets and asset classes, and are commensurate in size with trading in underlying cash instruments. Table 25.2 reports average trading volumes in futures and cash markets around the world today. Liquidity in global currency forward markets is similar in magnitude, making it possible to trade significant positions quickly with minimal market impact.

On average across all major global equity markets, traded futures market volume is 83 percent that of cash market volume, amounting to approximately $90 billion a day. Average daily global bond futures market volume amounts to over twice this. While market volumes in bond cash markets are tougher to measure, in the U.S. 10-year and 30-year markets, futures market volume is about 50 percent higher than cash markets.

While the overall trading volume in futures is similar to that in cash instruments, futures transaction costs are considerably lower. The one-way transaction cost is the sum of commissions and fees, one-half of the bid/ask spread, and the anticipated market impact from trading a given size order. Figure 25.3 depicts the relative round-trip transaction costs for a $5 million trade in stock index futures versus underlying stocks, on average across 15 developed equity futures markets.

The results are striking. Because the average futures contract size is more than 1,000 times the price of the average stock, the commission rates for futures are approximately 90 percent less than for stocks. The bid/ask spread and market impact are also much smaller in futures, about one-fifth the level in stocks. Two elements drive the spread and market impact costs: liquidity and the potential for traders to hold private information that is not reflected in prices. The liquidity impact simply means that to trade in larger sizes over short horizons, prices must move adversely to entice additional liquidity on the other side. The larger the trading volume in a given market, the smaller will be the liquidity impact. This suggests the liquidity impact of futures is similar to, if not a bit smaller than, stocks.

The private information problem, on the other hand, is much more pronounced in individual stocks. This is because private information is firm specific by its very nature, and the value of that information is many times greater when trading the specific firm's stock than when trading a stock index in which the stock represents only a small fraction. This causes the bid/ask spread and market impact cost for underlying stocks to greatly exceed that for stock index futures. And while we've shown the difference between market impact in stocks and futures for a moderately sized order, trades in larger sizes further increase the cost of trading stocks relative to stock index futures.

The most obvious disadvantage of using futures to implement GTAA is that the completion portfolio cannot track the benchmark as well as the underlying cash

TABLE 25.2 Average Daily Trading Volume ($mm) in Global Cash and Futures Markets

		Equities[a]			Bonds			
Country	Index	Futures Market Volume	Cash Market Volume	Ratio of Futures/Cash Volume	Bond	Futures Market Volume[b]	Cash Market Volume[c]	Ratio of Futures/Cash Volume
Australia	SPI 200	559	1,168	48%	10-year government bond	1,089		
Canada	S&P/TSE 60	132	4,538	3	10-year government bond	456		
Europe	DJ Euro STOXX 50	6,907						
France	CAC 40	3,405	3,260	104	10-year euro notional bond	8,515		
Germany	DAX	7,127	2,930	243	Euro-Bund	75,841		
Hong Kong	Hang Seng	1,233	878	140				
Italy	MIB 30	2,538	1,621	157				
Japan	Nikkei 225/TOPIX	5,195	5,623	92	10-year government bond	31,441		
Korea	KOSPI 200	5,294	3,050	174				
Netherlands	AEX	1,169	2,272	51				
Spain	IBEX 35	1,071	1,467	73	10-year government bond	129		
Sweden	OMX	318	1,556	20				
Switzerland	SMI	802	1,478	54	10-year government bond	97		
Taiwan	MSCI Taiwan	492	3,811	13				
United Kingdom	FTSE 100	3,751	5,313	71	10-year government bond	5,323		
United States	S&P 500	39,408	67,567	72	10-year government bond	33,345	31,141	107%
	Russell 2000/Nasdaq 100	8,992			30-year government bond	23,432	7,246	323
Totals		88,393	106,532	83%		179,667		148%

[a]Goldman Sachs & Co., Index and Derivatives Perspective, April 2002. Data represent daily averages for Q1 2002.
[b]Carr Futures. Data represent daily averages for Q1 and Q2 2002.
[c]U.S. Federal Reserve Board. Data represent daily averages for U.S. government coupon bonds for Q2 2002.

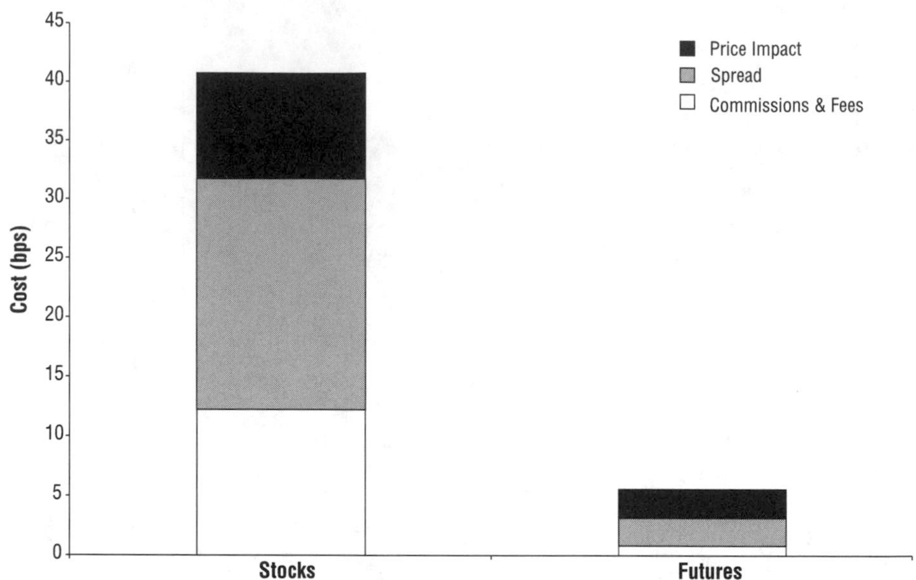

FIGURE 25.3 The Round-Trip Cost of Trading $5 Million in Physical Stocks versus Stock Index Futures

instruments used to calculate the benchmark. The additional tracking error derives from three sources. First, futures do not exist in all countries and asset classes. Second, existing futures have been created for the most popular local indexes of large stocks, but these indexes often do not coincide with the indexes used by institutions in their global portfolios. Third, even if a futures contract exists on the very index used in the benchmark, the futures contract does not track the underlying index perfectly due to short-term mispricing between the two as well as differences in tax treatment that can be significant in some countries. This tracking error is termed basis risk.

In spite of these issues, a completion portfolio of futures and forwards generally tracks a global multi-asset-class benchmark quite well. In Table 25.3, we show a recent snapshot of the completion portfolio for one of our existing clients. After incorporating all three sources of completion error described earlier, the projected tracking error on the completion portfolio is only 0.45 percent, which compares favorably to the tracking error of 2.18 percent before completion.

These arguments strongly favor the use of liquid derivatives to implement GTAA, but the strategy may also be implemented using cash instruments, with a natural reduction in efficacy. For example, it is common in some countries for institutions to use so-called "swing" portfolios. A swing portfolio generally requires 10 percent or more of the institution's overall portfolio and is invested entirely in passive underlying funds. The manager of the swing portfolio then reallocates capital among these funds to effect an overall asset allocation. The availability of index funds, the cost of trading them, and the size of the swing portfolio all determine the degree to which the GTAA process would be constrained and the performance would be reduced.

TABLE 25.3 Representative Completion Portfolio

Country	Benchmark Weight	Aggregate Underlying Managers' Weight	Unintentional Asset Allocation Deviations	Completion Portfolio Weight	Resulting Completion Deviations
Equities					
Australia	0.55%	0.06%	–0.49%	0.04%	–0.45%
Austria	0.31	0.00	–0.31	0.25	–0.07
Belgium	0.33	0.00	–0.33	0.03	–0.30
Canada	0.00	0.08	0.08	0.03	0.12
Denmark	0.25	0.04	–0.20	0.00	–0.20
DJ Euro STOXX 50	0.00	0.51	0.51	–1.93	–1.42
Finland	0.18	0.27	0.09	0.06	0.14
France	1.81	1.17	–0.64	0.92	0.28
Germany	2.52	0.48	–2.04	2.05	0.01
Greece	0.18	0.00	–0.18	0.08	–0.10
Hong Kong	0.23	0.08	–0.16	–0.22	–0.38
Ireland	0.15	0.59	0.44	0.00	0.44
Italy	1.69	1.07	–0.61	0.49	–0.12
Japan	6.10	5.15	–0.94	0.74	–0.20
Netherlands	0.52	1.53	1.01	0.00	1.01
New Zealand	0.08	0.00	–0.08	0.09	0.01
Norway	0.24	0.00	–0.24	0.00	–0.24
Portugal	0.16	0.00	–0.16	0.05	–0.11
Spain	0.82	0.54	–0.28	0.20	–0.08
Singapore	0.13	0.39	0.26	0.00	0.26
Sweden	0.30	0.36	0.06	–0.12	–0.06
Switzerland	0.35	1.57	1.22	0.00	1.22
Emerging markets	3.00	4.05	1.05	0.00	1.05
United Kingdom	2.09	3.23	1.14	–1.66	–0.52
U.S. Small Capitalization	3.01	5.40	2.39	–2.31	0.08
U.S. Large Capitalization	42.99	33.51	–9.48	9.11	–0.36
	68.00%	60.09%	–7.91%	7.91%	0.00%
Bonds					
Australia	0.03%	0.00%	–0.03%	0.03%	0.00%
Belgium	0.25	0.00	–0.25	0.00	–0.25
Canada	0.20	0.40	0.20	–0.15	0.05
Denmark	0.10	0.33	0.23	0.00	0.23
France	0.70	2.22	1.52	0.00	1.52
Germany	0.73	1.34	0.61	–1.95	–1.34
Italy	0.73	0.83	0.10	0.00	0.10
Japan	2.29	2.17	–0.12	0.12	0.00
Netherlands	0.19	0.23	0.04	0.00	0.04
Spain	0.28	0.00	–0.28	0.00	–0.28
Sweden	0.07	0.15	0.08	0.00	0.08
United Kingdom	0.43	0.43	0.00	0.00	0.00
United States	23.00	23.07	0.07	–0.22	–0.15
	29.00%	31.17%	2.17%	–2.17%	0.00%

(Continued)

TABLE 25.3 (*Continued*)

Country	Benchmark Weight	Aggregate Underlying Managers' Weight	Unintentional Asset Allocation Deviations	Completion Portfolio Weight	Resulting Completion Deviations
Currencies					
Australian dollar	0.58%	0.06%	–0.52%	0.52%	0.00%
Canadian dollar	0.16	0.48	0.32	–0.32	0.00
Danish krone	0.33	0.37	0.05	0.00	0.05
Euro	11.07	10.27	–0.80	0.76	–0.05
Hong Kong dollar	0.23	0.08	–0.16	0.00	–0.16
Japanese yen	8.01	7.32	–0.68	0.68	0.00
New Zealand dollar	0.24	0.00	–0.24	0.24	0.00
Norwegian krone	0.08	0.00	–0.08	0.08	0.00
Singapore dollar	0.13	0.39	0.26	–0.26	0.00
Swedish krona	0.36	0.51	0.16	–0.16	0.00
Swiss franc	0.35	1.57	1.22	–1.22	0.00
British pound	2.45	4.20	1.74	–1.74	0.00
U.S. dollar (cash)	3.00	8.74	5.74	–5.59	0.16
	27.00%	34.00%	7.00%	–7.00%	0.00%
Total	100.00%	100.00%	0.00%	0.00%	0.00%
Tracking error			2.18%		0.45%

An Example Table 25.4 shows a recent GTAA overlay portfolio for one of our clients. In this portfolio, the client permits trading in all Commodity Futures Trading Commission (CFTC)-approved equity index and bond futures,[18] developed market currency forwards, and country equity index funds. The client requires that holdings consist only of assets in the benchmark, and permits a limited degree of beta extension in both stocks and bonds through TAA. The active risk target is 2.5 percent.

The positions in this portfolio represent active country and asset class deviations derived from four independent GTAA strategies: (1) asset class timing, (2) country selection within global equities (hedged), (3) country selection within global bonds (hedged), and (4) currency selection. Based on our experience with each of these strategies as well as our expectations from Grinold's Law, we allocate risk across the four strategies, which results in the most risk from currencies, the second most from global equity markets, the third most from global bond markets, and the least from asset class timing.

[18]The U.S. Commodity Futures Trading Commission (CFTC)—in a futile and ridiculous attempt, in our view, to protect investors from themselves—does not permit U.S. investors to trade futures in undiversified indexes or on exchanges it deems unsafe to the investor. The Netherlands' AEX and Switzerland's SMI indexes are the most prominent global futures not approved by the CFTC.

TABLE 25.4 Representative GTAA Overlay Portfolio

Country	Contract	Overlay Weights	Risk Decomposition
Equities			
Australia	SPI 200 Futures	–3.16%	–5.09%
Belgium	Belgium MSCI Index fund	0.42	0.87
Canada	S&P/TSE 60 futures	–0.85	–2.32
Finland	Finland MSCI Index fund and DJ Euro STOXX 50 futures	–0.14	–0.28
France	CAC 40 futures and DJ Euro STOXX 50 futures	–0.91	–2.70
Germany	DAX futures and DJ Euro STOXX 50 futures	1.09	3.65
Hong Kong	Hang Seng futures	3.73	20.59
Italy	MIB 30 futures and DJ Euro STOXX 50 futures	–0.76	–2.24
Japan	TOPIX futures	2.62	11.21
Netherlands	Netherlands MSCI Index fund and DJ Euro STOXX 50 futures	0.21	0.59
New Zealand	New Zealand MSCI Index fund	–0.19	–0.27
Portugal	Portugal MSCI Index fund	–0.29	–0.41
Spain	IBEX 35 futures and DJ Euro STOXX 50 futures	0.46	1.46
Singapore	Singapore MSCI Index fund and Singapore MSCI futures	–1.57	–5.69
Sweden	OMX futures	–0.93	–2.14
Switzerland	Switzerland MSCI Index fund	–0.52	–1.26
United Kingdom	FTSE 100 futures	–1.89	–3.85
United States	S&P 500 futures	3.92	15.05
		1.26%	27.19%
Bonds			
Australia	Australia 10-year futures	0.38%	–0.02%
Canada	Canada 10-year futures	4.45	2.26
EMU countries	Germany 10-year Euro-Bund futures	–10.06	0.18
Japan	JGB 10-year futures	–19.20	5.56
Switzerland	Switzerland 10-year futures	–1.83	0.18
United Kingdom	Long Gilt futures	–7.39	1.41
United States	U.S. 10-year futures	21.78	15.77
		–11.87%	25.35%
Currencies			
Australian dollar	A$/US$ currency forward	3.30%	8.45%
Canadian dollar	C$/US$ currency forward	–1.81	–0.88
Euro	Euro/US$ currency forward	–0.35	0.02
Japanese yen	Yen/US$ currency forward	–1.55	0.10
New Zealand dollar	NZ$/US$ currency forward	3.21	8.28
Norwegian krone	Norwegian krone/US$ currency forward	5.14	3.06

(Continued)

TABLE 25.4 *(Continued)*

Country	Contract	Overlay Weights	Risk Decomposition
Singapore dollar	S$/US$ currency forward	3.35	1.38
Swedish krona	Swedish krona/US$ currency forward	10.46	15.72
Swiss franc	Swiss franc/US$ currency forward	−15.15	11.44
British pound	Pound/US$ currency forward	−2.64	−0.09
		3.96%	47.48%
Total			100.00%
Total active risk		2.48%	
Equity beta extension		0.02	
Bond beta extension		0.18	

At the time of this portfolio snapshot, we held active positions in 35 different securities in the overlay portfolio with a predicted tracking error of 2.48 percent. We held large equity overweights in the United States, Hong Kong, and Japan partially offset by large underweights in Australia, the United Kingdom, and Singapore. In bonds, overweights in the United States and Canada were offset by underweights in Japan, Euroland, and the United Kingdom. Our major currency positions were long the Swedish krona and Norwegian krone, and short the Swiss franc and U.K. pound sterling, with a net underweight in the U.S. dollar overall.

The position sizes were determined using the optimization problem described earlier, where returns are maximized subject to a total tracking error constraint as well as constraints on the tracking errors within each of the four GTAA strategies. Despite the very simple optimization problem, the portfolio's risk budget is fairly well balanced, as seen in the tracking error decomposition in the rightmost column. At the individual security level, there are 11 positions contributing more than 5 percent of risk in absolute terms. That this well-balanced portfolio can result from a simple optimization problem is a testament to the Black-Litterman asset allocation model, which was developed primarily to address the problem of unbalanced portfolio optimizations.

Leverage

Finally, note that in asset class timing, we held a beta extension of 0.02 in equities and 0.18 in bonds. By an equity beta extension of 0.02, we mean that the beta of our global equity portfolio with respect to the equity benchmark was 1.02. This implies that for every 10 percent increase in the MSCI World Index, our global equity portfolio should outperform by 0.20 percent. Beta extension better represents the market timing position in equities than the sum of weights because the weights themselves may indicate a misleading position. For example, a 2× overweight in a country with half the beta of second country where a 1× underweight is held actually represents a beta-neutral position, and therefore would not be expected to outperform when the global equity market increases or decreases.

Beta extension in bonds works analogously, and is equivalent to the concept of duration extension applied to a global portfolio.[19] Our bond beta extension of 0.18 means that for every 10 percent increase in the J.P. Morgan Global Government Bond Index, our global bond portfolio is expected to outperform by 1.80 percent.

One might ask whether holding a beta extension in both stocks and bonds represents leverage. The answer depends on which definition of leverage is used, and unfortunately, there are several. To appreciate this difficulty, consider a recent report from the Leverage & Derivatives Subcommittee of the Association for Investment Management and Research (AIMR) Investment Performance Council:

> *The discussion of [leverage] has been rather involved due to the fact that the use of leverage can be viewed from many different angles (e.g., trading portfolios, money manager, etc.). As a consequence, the Subcommittee has abandoned former approaches to give a rather specific definition of the term "Leverage." Instead, it will propose a rather general definition of the term. . . .*[20]

The committee recently arrived at a much oversimplified notion of leverage that any portfolio employing securities or strategies that *might* cause leverage must be leveraged:

> *In general, a portfolio is considered to be leveraged if certain instruments or strategies such as financing assets through liabilities (e.g., margin) or the use of futures, options, or other derivative instruments are employed. These strategies are implemented in order to alter the return impact ("exposure") that a unit move in certain underlying securities markets will have on the portfolio to an extent otherwise unachievable without the use of those instruments or strategies. Rather than being occasionally used (e.g., for insuring the value of the portfolio in case of a market crash), the potential use of these strategies is assumed to be an integral part of the investment strategy.*[21]

By this new AIMR definition, accounts using futures to reduce the beta of an investment account to bring it closer to the benchmark would be leveraged. In fact, by the AIMR definition, traditional bond managers cannot use derivatives of any kind to manage the duration of their portfolios without falling under the definition of leverage.

---

[19]Duration measures the price impact in a bond for a given interest rate change. In a bond index, duration is calculated assuming a parallel shift across all maturities in the index. Conceptually, one could define a global duration that would similarly assume a parallel shift that is equal across all maturities and all countries. However, such a concept would not accurately reflect the impact of shifts in global interest rates, as correlations across countries are substantially less than one, and interest rate volatilities can be quite different around the world.

[20]Update Report of the Leverage & Derivatives Subcommittee of the Investment Performance Council, March 1, 2002, AIMR.

[21]Update Report of the Leverage & Derivatives Subcommittee of the Investment Performance Council, June 1, 2002, AIMR.

Another common definition is that of *notional* leverage. Notional leverage is usually calculated by summing the market value of all physical noncash securities in the portfolio with the notional exposure of futures and forwards. If this notional value is greater than the market value of the total portfolio, the portfolio is notionally levered. For example, a portfolio with $99 million in physical holdings, $1 million in cash, $5 million in a long S&P 500 futures position, and $3 million in a short U.S. 10-year bond futures is notionally leveraged as its notional exposure of $101 million is larger than its total value of $100 million.[22]

We prefer a measure of leverage that addresses whether the characteristics of the portfolio could have been obtained holding entirely physical securities. Under this definition, using derivatives to alter portfolio characteristics will not be flagged as leverage unless derivatives are used to create portfolio characteristics that would not be possible without the use of derivatives. For example, beta extension is easily obtained by holding stocks with betas higher than the benchmark, and duration extension is created by holding bonds with maturities longer than the benchmark, so strategies using futures to create a certain degree of these exposures would not be termed leveraged. In fact, such strategies are already employed by many traditional managers in their portfolios without being interpreted as leverage.

THE EXPECTATIONS OF A GTAA PROGRAM

Performance

As noted at the beginning of this chapter, TAA and GTAA have experienced both strong and difficult performance periods over their histories. What should a client expect? The expectation for excess return is a function of the amount of active risk in GTAA as well as the manager's information ratio and investment style.

Long-term information ratios on the best GTAA managers are generally between 0.5 and 1.0, and in some cases even exceed 1.0. While this may seem excessively high, consider that (1) transaction costs are 90 percent lower than for traditional products, and (2) unlike the tremendous number of players and amount of capital chasing after securities within a country, the number and capital of global asset allocators is relatively small. This implies that market disequilibriums are likely to be larger, and perhaps to exist for longer periods. This also suggests that GTAA managers may have longer periods of underperformance, although a well-diversified strategy should experience shorter episodes of underperformance.

Performance comparisons across GTAA managers can be difficult due to the extremely customized nature of the strategy. However, for every GTAA account there exists a benchmark, so excess performance can be readily measured. We believe the information ratio on an AIMR-compliant asset-weighted GTAA composite is the best single performance measure, and this is readily compared across managers. We show the performance of our AIMR-compliant GTAA composite in Figure 25.4. The realized information ratio on this performance history is 1.14.

---

[22]The market value of futures contracts is zero because they are marked to market every day and the profit/loss is added to/taken from the cash in the account.

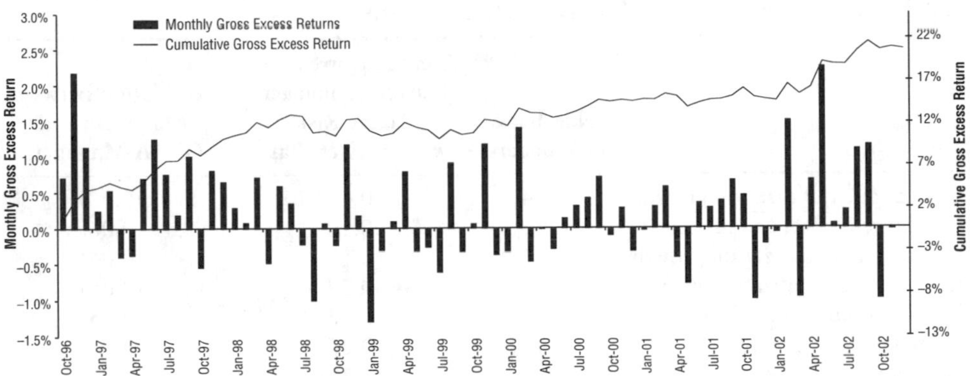

FIGURE 25.4 GSAM AIMR-Compliant GTAA Composite, October 1996 to October 2002

Some argue that IR is not the best metric to compare managers, especially traditional managers, because as they take more risk, their information ratio declines. However, the use of derivatives in GTAA means that there are few natural boundaries on position sizes or directions, unlike traditional security selection strategies where net shorts or extremely large positions are both more costly and less readily employed. Therefore, the IR on a GTAA portfolio should be relatively unaffected by targeted active risk.[23]

Fortunately for clients, GTAA active risk is not highly correlated with other sources of active risk. Table 25.5 demonstrates the low correlation of four GTAA managers with other traditional asset class managers.[24] Over the six-year period from 1996 to 2001, the correlation of these GTAA managers' active risk with the active risks of traditional managers was quite low, averaging only 0.01 across the major asset classes. This correlation is particularly low in light of the average correlation between manager active risks within asset classes of 0.20. Only domestic and international fixed income show average active risk correlations above 0.10, from which we infer that GTAA managers were taking duration bets similar to fixed income managers over this period. Correlations across GTAA managers appear to be low also. The correlation of GSAM's GTAA performance history is only 0.03 with the other GTAA managers.

Is GTAA Suitable for All Investors?

We believe GTAA is suitable for almost any institutional portfolio. However, clients that understand the importance of removing unintended risks, the use of derivatives, risk budgeting, and risk management most appreciate GTAA's benefits. The

[23]Notwithstanding any client-imposed constraints like range constraints or no net shorts.

[24]The traditional manager data are from Nelson's institutional manager database. We thank Dmitri Smolyanski at General Motors Investment Management Company for the database of GTAA managers.

TABLE 25.5 Correlation of Manager Active Returns

Asset Class	Number of Managers	Average Correlation between Manager Active Risk within Asset Class	Average Correlation between Managers and GTAA Managers
U.S. large-capitalization growth	224	0.17	(0.03)
U.S. large-capitalization value	206	0.16	0.06
U.S. small-capitalization growth	131	0.17	(0.04)
U.S. small-capitalization value	137	0.28	(0.08)
International equity	94	0.24	0.05
Domestic fixed income	48	0.27	0.16
High-yield	63	0.22	0.02
International fixed income	46	0.26	0.17
Total/Average	949	0.20	0.01

Sources: Nelson's; General Motors Investment Management Company.

minimum size of the portfolio is generally not a binding constraint, although in some markets the futures contracts have large denominations.[25] If the GTAA program on a small portfolio is implemented using two separable portfolios (completion and pure overlay), the efficacy of the customized completion portfolio depends on the size of the holes in the portfolio, but the overlay portfolio may be implemented through a commingled vehicle, obviating any concern about minimum portfolio size.

In general, GTAA can fit anywhere in a client's portfolio. Some clients carve out an entire slice of their strategic benchmark, while others prefer to carve the overlay out of an area of their portfolio that is passively managed or generates low active risk. While the GTAA manager will generally not have a preference, clients might prefer funding the overlay program from an area of their portfolio with low expected active return, such as U.S. large-capitalization equities or U.S. core fixed income. This result is often a natural outcome of the risk budgeting analysis.

GTAA as a Portable Alpha Strategy

GTAA can also be implemented as a portable alpha strategy on a specific piece of a client's portfolio, for example, as a portable alpha strategy over the global equity portfolio, or even over a U.S. enhanced index portfolio. Used in this fashion,

[25]The largest contracts are the 10-year Japanese government bond futures at $860,000 per contract, the S&P 500 futures at $200,000 per contract, and the Russell 2000 futures at $190,000 per contract. In some markets, miniature contract sizes have gained popularity, for example, in the S&P 500 where the S&P 500 EMini Index Futures trades at $40,000 per contract.

GTAA is just another source of active risk, but a special source in that so little capital is required. This makes it easy to combine with other sources of active risk within the same portfolio. This is in contrast to a common portable alpha strategy that transports alpha from a fixed income strategy onto an equity benchmark, because substantial capital is needed for the fixed income strategy in order to generate the excess return.

The completion portfolio in a GTAA program can also make portable alpha strategies possible. For example, a portfolio that desires more active risk from its equity managers but doesn't want to increase its strategic equity weighting can transfer capital from its fixed income managers to its equity managers, then undo this implicit stock/bond bet by selling equity index futures and buying bond futures in equivalent proportions. Essentially, the completion portfolio frees the linkage between a portfolio's strategic asset allocation and the asset classes where active risk is derived, obtaining a more optimal allocation of active risk.

Choosing a GTAA Manager

There exist approximately 25 investment firms globally that credibly offer TAA/GTAA services. Some of these have not committed the resources to offer a truly global product and therefore offer only domestic TAA, and some firms have not developed a global derivatives trading capability. However, about 10 major global players exist in the modern GTAA industry, with more than 80 percent of market share concentrated in the top four players.[26]

We believe a strong GTAA manager possesses the following key traits:

- A sound investment philosophy based on strong theoretical and proven empirical evidence.
- A quantitative approach that can be intuitively explained.
- A program that offers diversification in active risk across strategies, across investment themes, and across securities held in the portfolio.
- An appropriate risk budget that does not rely too heavily on market timing.
- An independent risk management group ensuring that investment philosophy and client guidelines are followed.
- A strong commitment to continued research as models and markets evolve.

SUMMARY

The modern global tactical asset allocation program really comprises two separate strategies, completion and pure overlay. The completion element of GTAA flexibly and cost-effectively manages unintended asset allocation risk with limited capital and minimal disruption to underlying investment managers. The pure overlay of GTAA adds value from opportunistic long and short positions in asset classes and countries.

[26]Based on our estimates from publicly available data.

GTAA is well motivated from both theoretical and empirical standpoints, and should be an important element of most institutions' investment programs. In spite of periodic poor performance in mostly value-oriented TAA managers, the largest and most successful GTAA managers have generated long-term information ratios above 0.5, which compares favorably with active management in other, more traditional asset classes.

Finally, the actual implementation of a GTAA program is straightforward and is readily customized to client-specific benchmarks, constraints, and objectives. Managed appropriately, GTAA helps to diversify total active risk and can significantly improve a portfolio's overall information ratio due to GTAA's high expected information ratio and low correlation with benchmarks and other active risks.

CHAPTER 26

Strategic Asset Allocation and Hedge Funds

Kurt Winkelmann, Kent A. Clark, Jacob Rosengarten, and Tarun Tyagi

INTRODUCTION

Many institutional investors are considering strategic allocations to hedge funds. Investors are interested in hedge funds for two reasons. First, they believe that hedge funds offer the opportunity to increase expected portfolio returns. Second, investors believe that hedge funds diversify total portfolio risk. In short, hedge funds are attractive to investors because they believe that hedge funds offer the potential to increase expected portfolio return at the expense of little or no change in expected portfolio risk.

While most investors would agree that hedge funds are attractive because of their potential to enhance risk-adjusted performance, they would also agree that allocations to hedge funds are difficult to analyze, largely because of the general lack of consistent data. Consequently, investors are faced with a dilemma: Because they believe that hedge fund managers can produce excess returns by exploiting informational inefficiencies, they believe that their portfolios should have hedge fund allocations. However, hedge fund allocations are difficult to analyze, in part because the same informational inefficiencies translate into inconsistent time series data.

This chapter expands on our equilibrium approach to strategic asset allocation and gives investors an intuitive framework that they can use to evaluate the role of hedge funds. As we've discussed in Chapter 9, standard portfolio advice is usually based on mean-variance analysis. Typically, an analyst uses historical time series data to estimate the expected return, volatility, and correlation of returns for various asset classes. Portfolio weights are then found by using these parameters in an optimizer.

However, practitioners have had reservations about fully embracing this approach. As shown in Chapter 9, optimal portfolio weights are incredibly sensitive to small changes in expected return assumptions. Chapter 9 shows further that historical average returns provide poor predictors of expected future performance. The strength of these reservations is intensified for hedge funds, due in part to the generally poor relative quality of hedge fund data.

Our approach to the role of hedge funds in some senses inverts the problem. Instead of asking what the portfolio weights should be on the basis of specific expected return assumptions, we instead ask what return can justify a specific allocation. The benefit of this approach to investors is that we rely on our ability to estimate volatility and correlation from time series data rather than attempting to estimate expected returns. As discussed in Chapters 9 and 16, volatility and correlation are more easily estimated from historical data than expected returns.

We call the returns required to justify a specific hedge fund allocation the implied "hurdle rates." We find the hurdle rates by making specific reference to the other holdings in an investor's portfolio. Hurdle rates can be viewed as setting the minimum expected return that an investor should require for a particular hedge fund allocation. They are useful because they can give investors a yardstick by which a specific hedge fund portfolio should be judged.

Our principal finding is that the implied hurdle rates for hedge fund portfolios can be quite low, especially for modest allocations. Moreover, our historical analysis suggests that some hedge fund portfolios have been able to achieve these hurdle rates. As a result, *our principal recommendation is that investors should include hedge funds as part of their strategic asset allocations.*

The remainder of this chapter is organized as follows. The next section discusses why we believe hedge funds can add value. We then address the issue of available hedge fund data. In the next two sections, we show how our equilibrium framework can be used to analyze hedge fund allocations. Implementation of the hedge fund program is covered in the subsequent sections, followed by concluding comments.

POTENTIAL ADVANTAGES OF HEDGE FUNDS TO INVESTORS

Why are hedge funds attractive to investors? At one level, this is an easy question to answer: A suitably constructed portfolio of hedge funds can be attractive because it has the potential to generate positive returns for the overall portfolio. However, in judging hedge fund performance we must ask the question "Attractive relative to what?" Posing the question in this way forces us to explicitly consider the underlying economics of hedge funds relative to other investment choices.

Since views on equity and fixed income markets are ultimately expressed through long and short positions in public securities markets, one natural comparison for hedge fund portfolios is the active risk taken by traditional active managers. We can reframe the question to ask what *structural* factors give hedge fund managers the capability to generate value relative to traditional active managers. In particular, we want to compare the risk and performance characteristics of hedge fund managers relative to cash with the risk and performance characteristics of traditional active managers relative to an index of publicly traded securities.

Why does it make sense to compare a hedge fund manager to a traditional active manager? After all, traditional active managers usually hold long positions in the securities in their portfolios and are measured versus an index, while hedge fund managers usually take long and short positions and are measured relative to cash. How can the two be compared?

Let's look at the return of the traditional active manager a little more closely, and in particular relative to cash. By adding and subtracting the manager's index, the active manager's return is reconstituted as a long position in the index, a long position in a long/short portfolio, and a short position in cash. The long/short portfolio is simply the difference between the security weights in the actual portfolio and the benchmark. The difference between the long/short portfolio and cash can now be compared to the excess return on hedge funds (i.e., the hedge fund return relative to cash rates).

There are three fundamental characteristics of hedge fund managers that give them the potential to add value relative to their traditional active management counterparts. First, hedge fund managers do not face the same constraint on short positions that traditional active managers face. For example, suppose that a hedge fund manager and a traditional active manager have the same views on two securities such that one stock appears as a long position (or overweight relative to the benchmark) and the other appears as a short position (or underweight relative to the benchmark). If the active manager has a net short constraint, then the potential to generate higher excess returns can be reduced. Table 26.1 illustrates this point with a simple hypothetical example.

The figures in Table 26.1 show the expected return for two optimized portfolios, based on the same assumptions regarding the returns to individual securities. Risk, as measured by the volatility of portfolio return, is the same for both portfolios. The first portfolio, labeled Unconstrained Optimal Portfolio, assumes that the managers can take long and short positions irrespective of size. The second portfolio, Constrained Optimal Portfolio, imposes a constraint on the size of the short positions. As Table 26.1 illustrates, the impact of the short constraint is to reduce the potential to add value: The expected return on the unconstrained portfolio is higher than that of the constrained portfolio for the same level of portfolio volatility.

TABLE 26.1 Impact of Short Constraints—A Hypothetical Example

	Correlation				
	Asset 1	Asset 2	Asset 3	Volatility	Expected Return
Asset 1	1.0	0.2	0.3	13.0%	10.0%
Asset 2	0.2	1.0	0.1	3.0	5.0
Asset 3	0.3	0.1	1.0	16.0	–5.0

	Unconstrained Optimal Portfolio	Constrained Optimal Portfolio
Asset 1	21%	29%
Asset 2	99	71
Asset 3	–20	0
	100%	100%
Expected return	8.0%	6.5%
Volatility	4.7	4.7

The second fundamental characteristic of hedge funds that can influence their ability to add value is the composition of the investment universe. Many traditional active managers are allowed to purchase only those securities that are part of their performance benchmarks. Since hedge fund managers do not have performance benchmarks, they are not limited in the same way. For example, a hedge fund manager and a traditional active manager may each have strong positive views on a particular security. Unless that security is part of the traditional active manager's investment universe, he or she may not be able to hold the stock in the portfolio.

Finally, although most hedge fund managers stick to one investment style, they are not necessarily restricted from making changes. Traditional active managers, by contrast, are usually restricted to the investment style for which they were selected. Consequently, a hedge fund manager has the ability to more quickly change portfolio characteristics to reflect changes in market conditions. For example, a hedge fund manager would potentially have the ability to switch from growth to value stocks, depending on the market cycle, in a way that a traditional active manager who is categorized by style cannot. Similarly, hedge fund managers may be able to dynamically adjust the level of market exposure in a way that a traditional active manager may not. (See Litterman and Winkelmann, 1996.) Thus, hedge fund managers could have the potential to generate outperformance through market timing that traditional active managers may not.

HEDGE FUND DATA

Determining the appropriate benchmark for a hedge fund has been a topic of some debate. Because hedge fund returns are driven more by human skill than by long-only indexes, each hedge fund's returns are as unique as the individuals who generate them. Despite this challenge, however, it is important to know how a manager's performance ranks against that of other managers who invest using similar methodologies and assets to express their views. For this reason, there has been a growing demand for hedge fund indexes and subindexes that can be used to gauge a manager's relative performance. Importantly, these indexes do not typically pass the tests that would be required for them to be considered to be benchmarks—for many, either constituents or constituent weights are not known in advance, and some contain funds in which investors cannot place capital.

There are several major hedge fund index providers that provide index and subindex performance information. Among these are Hedge Fund Research (HFR), Credit Suisse First Boston/Tremont, Altvest, Mar-Hedge, Van Hedge, Hennessee, and FRM/MSCI. In our judgment, there is no one "best" index that addresses all concerns. Prior to using any particular index, we recommend that great care be taken to understand the index's strengths and weaknesses, as well as the construction methodology.

Self-Reporting Biases

Hedge fund managers are not allowed to solicit business, so presence on a hedge fund database, and in an index, represents an opportunity to raise a fund's profile among potential investors. Consequently, in most hedge fund indexes the managers choose to report, which can introduce a number of potential biases. For example, a manager may stop reporting either because of very poor performance or because the manager has had strong performance and is no longer raising assets.

Some of the more significant concerns that should be understood include:

- ***Survivorship bias.*** Hedge fund managers are dropped from an index if they stop reporting to the index provider. It is clear that periods of nonreporting can coincide with periods of significant loss. Since this lost information is not included in the index's construction, index performance is biased upwards and downside volatility is possibly understated.
- ***Backfill bias.*** Hedge funds are added after they have a few successful years managing money, at which point their entire return history is put on the database. This biases the data toward firms that managed to survive the first few, difficult years.
- ***Investibility.*** Indexes potentially include funds that are no longer accepting new assets. The index is therefore not investible, so it is not a true benchmark.
- ***Transparency.*** Some index providers reveal the number of managers in each category but not the actual names of the managers. These indexes are therefore not known in advance, and so are not useful for true benchmarking. This feature makes comparing any one fund to the index less effective.
- ***Incorrect fund categorization.*** Funds can identify their own categories, and some funds report themselves in categories in which they do not manage capital.
- ***Frequency of reporting.*** For many traditional investment products, index performance can be calculated on a daily basis. Hedge fund indexes, by contrast, are typically reported only monthly. This occurs because many hedge fund managers report results only on a monthly basis. Monthly data tends to understate a fund's true peak-to-trough losses. It is not unusual to encounter short-term periods of significant loss that would be revealed if daily data, as opposed to monthly data, were available.
- ***Leverage measurement.*** With conventional indexes (e.g., the S&P), there is no ambiguity about what it means to be fully invested versus the index. The same degree of certainty does not exist with respect to hedge fund indexes. Differences in returns among managers are caused, to some degree, by different levels of leverage inherent in each manager's strategy. Of course, statistical methods can be used to infer the effective leverage of a manager relative to an index. For example, one can calculate the beta of any manager's returns to the index. However, there will likely be a wide confidence interval around any statistical estimate since the hedge fund index providers have only monthly data.
- ***Constituent weightings.*** Some indexes equal-weight the funds in their indexes, while others use weights based on assets under management. An equally weighted index is particularly suspect because this construction process gives equal weight to returns from both small and large funds. In fact, large funds and small funds, even if they operate in the same investment space, are often not comparable. To the extent that large returns may be easier to achieve on smaller rather than larger amounts of capital under management, this approach overstates the performance of the investment sector the index purports to measure.

- *Completeness.* Many of the most successful hedge managers choose to not report to index providers. Accordingly, the index may not be representative of what the universe of managers is actually achieving.

FRAMEWORK FOR EVALUATING HEDGE FUND ALLOCATIONS

How should investors think about hedge fund allocations? The very features that make hedge funds attractive (ability to transact in a large number of markets, ability to consider a wide variety of active strategies) also complicate the evaluation of a hedge fund program. In our view, since most investors already have a portfolio of assets, the most effective way to evaluate a hedge fund program is relative to those assets already held. That is, for a given portfolio of assets investors should assess the impact of a hedge fund allocation on the level and distribution of portfolio risk, then calculate the implied hurdle rate relative to cash of alternative hedge fund allocations, and finally determine whether a specific hedge fund program can achieve those hurdle rates.

Why do we choose to use portfolio risk characteristics as the basis for our analysis? The reason for this relates to how much information we feel that we can reliably extract from historical time series. While estimation of expected returns, volatility, and correlation are all complicated exercises, we believe that historical time series are better suited to the estimation of volatility and correlation than expected returns. This issue becomes even more important when we consider asset classes such as hedge funds, where data availability is even more limited.

To illustrate our approach, let's work through a simple example. Suppose that our current asset allocation is as shown in Figure 26.1. In many respects, this portfolio represents a stylized asset allocation of a hypothetical U.S. defined benefit program, albeit with a larger allocation to international equity than is typically seen in such plans. The asset allocation in Figure 26.1 has around 43 percent allocated to U.S. equity, which we will assume is held in a broad index such as the Russell 3000. Non-U.S. equity constitutes about 22 percent of the portfolio in Figure 26.1, which

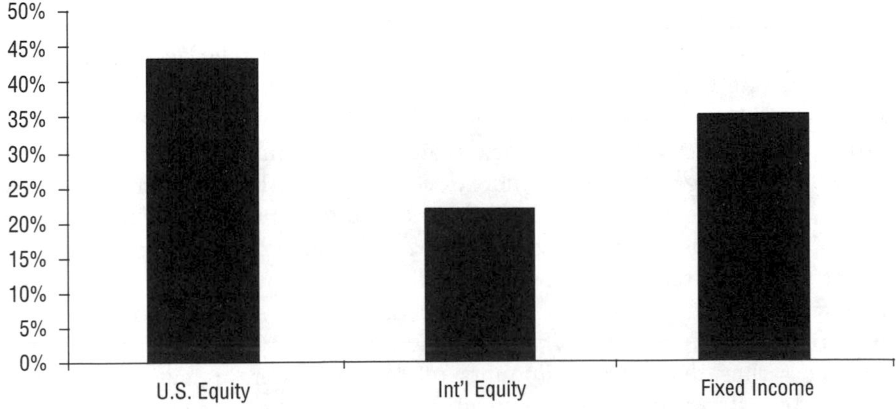

FIGURE 26.1 Hypothetical Asset Allocation

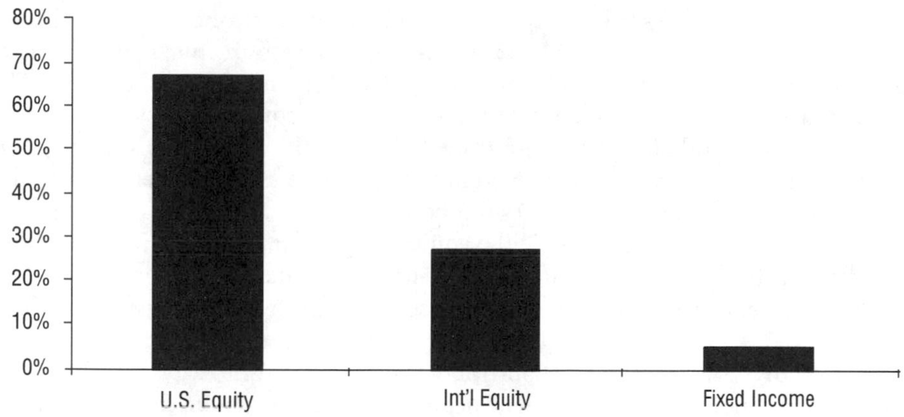

FIGURE 26.2 Portfolio Risk Decomposition

we will represent as exposure to MSCI non-U.S. Developed Equity. Finally, the fixed income allocation is about 35 percent, which we will assume is held in U.S. investment-grade bonds. Note that even though the example is from a U.S. investor's perspective, the approach generalizes to other currency perspectives. By combining the portfolio weights of Figure 26.1 with a covariance matrix of asset returns, we can calculate the overall portfolio volatility as 9.6 percent.

There are two natural questions we would like to answer about the portfolio allocations in Figure 26.1. First, we would like to know how the overall volatility of 9.6 percent is distributed across the various asset classes. Second, we would like to understand the impact on portfolio risk and return of allocating a portion of the portfolio away from each of the asset classes and into hedge funds.

Figure 26.2 shows the risk decomposition corresponding to the allocations of Figure 26.1. These figures show us how much of the portfolio's volatility, at the margin, can be attributed to each of the asset classes. Effectively, they show us how we are "spending" or "budgeting" our overall portfolio volatility of 9.6 percent. It is not too surprising that at the margin, almost 67 percent of the volatility is attributable to U.S. equity, given the portfolio's high equity allocation. The risk decomposition in Figure 26.2 is important, as it serves as a reference point for any portfolio reallocations: We want to know how the distribution of risk changes as we allocate portions of the portfolio to hedge funds.

DEVELOPING A HEDGE FUND ALLOCATION

Although some investors will make allocations to specific hedge funds, many more will instead make broad allocations to the asset class. Since the term "hedge funds" covers many alternative strategies, it is reasonable to first identify a potential hedge fund portfolio structure and then assess the volatility of this structure and its correlation with other asset classes. Ideally, the hedge fund portfolio would be structured so that the allocation of risk across hedge fund strategies would be consistent with an investor's views about expected returns.

Table 26.2 illustrates this point with two potential portfolios. The first portfolio, labeled Portfolio A, has equal weight assigned to each of four hedge fund sectors: relative value, event driven, equity long/short, and tactical trading. (The relative value sector is itself a blend of three strategies: equity market neutral, fixed income arbitrage, and convertible arbitrage.) The overall volatility of this portfolio is 6.1 percent. However, although equal investments are made in each sector, Table 26.2 also shows that each sector does not contribute equally to hedge fund portfolio volatility. In fact, in this example the equity long/short sector at the margin contributes about half of the risk in the hedge fund portfolio.

Although some investors would be comfortable with a disproportionate amount of risk allocated to just one strategy, many would not. In fact, analysis of the level of diversification in the portfolio provides a useful way to think about structuring the portfolio. Rather than beginning with portfolio weights and then calculating the risk decomposition, let's instead begin with a target of equal risk contributions and work backwards to find the corresponding portfolio weights.

The results of this exercise are shown in Portfolio B. We see that the portfolio weights can change significantly when we make diversification across strategies our goal. For example, the equally weighted portfolio has 25 percent of the portfolio value and 47 percent of the portfolio risk at the margin in equity long/short, while the equal risk weight portfolio has 25 percent of the portfolio volatility (at the margin) in equity long/short and only 14 percent of the portfolio value.

The portfolios in Table 26.2 are clearly two among many, and are meant to illustrate the following point: Investors should be careful to allocate risk to those hedge fund strategies that they think will offer the best opportunities to enhance risk-adjusted performance. For example, an investor with no specific information about the relative merits of one hedge fund sector versus another might be inclined to pick portfolio weights so that each hedge fund sector had an equal contribution to risk (e.g., Portfolio B). However, if an investor believed that one particular sector was likely to do better than another, then risk in the hedge fund portfolio should be shifted into the sector with the higher return expectations.

IMPLEMENTING THE HEDGE FUND ALLOCATIONS

There are two ways (at least!) that investors can implement their hedge fund allocations. The first is to make an outright allocation to hedge funds in the same way

TABLE 26.2 Equal Value Weight and Equal Risk Weight Portfolios

	Portfolio A		Portfolio B	
	Allocation	Contribution to Risk	Allocation	Contribution to Risk
Relative value	25%	12%	39%	25%
Event driven	25	24	22	25
Equity long/short	25	47	14	25
Tactical trading	25	17	26	25
Portfolio volatility	6.1%		5.2%	

that allocations are made to other asset classes (e.g., U.S. equity). Effectively, hedge funds are substituted for exposure to other asset classes.

Alternatively, investors can treat the hedge fund portfolio as a substitute for other active strategies (e.g. active U.S. large-cap equity or active U.S. fixed income). Suppose an investor wanted to substitute a hedge fund portfolio for a traditional active manager, say an active U.S. large-cap equity manager. If the hedge fund manager equitizes a portion of the cash (e.g., by purchasing futures contracts), and invests the rest in the specific hedge fund portfolio, the investor now has a portfolio that can be compared with a traditional active manager. This strategy is called a "portable alpha" strategy.

For our purposes, we'll assume that investors are substituting away from equity and fixed income and into hedge funds. The basic principles that are described in this case can be easily applied to analyze portable alpha strategies.

Let's look at the case where an investor decides to make outright allocations to hedge funds. In this case, the investor must consider the volatility of a hedge fund portfolio and its correlation with other asset classes. For discussion purposes, we'll assume that the hedge fund portfolio is the equal risk portfolio discussed earlier (i.e., Portfolio B). This portfolio has a volatility of 5.2 percent and a correlation with U.S. equity of 0.51.

An investor who chooses to make an outright allocation to hedge funds must also choose how to fund the allocation. That is, the investor must choose which asset class (or combination of asset classes) the hedge fund program substitutes for in the overall portfolio. In our simple example, there are three natural alternatives: (1) the investor can scale all other assets down proportionately; (2) the investor can substitute away from equity holdings and into the hedge fund portfolio; (3) the investor can substitute away from bonds and into hedge funds.

The impact on total portfolio volatility of each funding alternative is summarized in Figure 26.3. The chart plots alternative allocations to hedge funds and the resulting portfolio volatility for each of the three funding methods.

What happens when we substitute out of equity and into hedge funds? In our

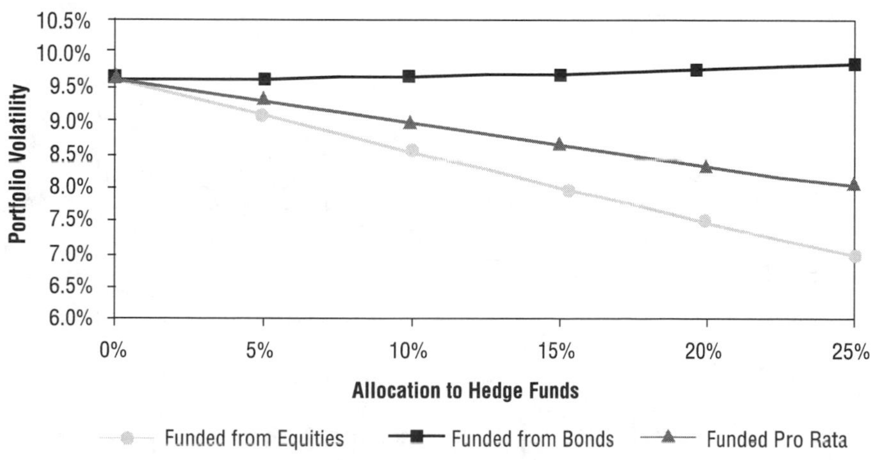

FIGURE 26.3 Portfolio Volatility and Hedge Fund Allocations

example, hedge fund volatility declines almost linearly. The principal reason for this is that we are effectively substituting an asset with low volatility (the hedge fund portfolio) for one with higher volatility (the equity portfolio or the total portfolio). In addition, the hedge fund portfolio is not perfectly correlated with the equity portfolio. Both of these effects mean that substituting into the hedge fund portfolio reduces total portfolio volatility. Clearly, if the hedge fund portfolio is riskier or more highly correlated with equity market returns, then total portfolio volatility will not be reduced by as much, or even at all, when we substitute into hedge funds.

Suppose, though, that an investor wanted to add hedge funds to the portfolio, but didn't want a change in total portfolio risk. Since the hedge fund portfolio (Portfolio B) in our hypothetical example has a bondlike volatility, the investor might substitute hedge funds for fixed income. For example, in Figure 26.3 allocations to hedge funds funded through reductions in fixed income leave the total portfolio volatility more or less unchanged. Again, this result depends on the structure of the hedge fund portfolio and our assumptions on hedge funds volatility and correlation. If the hedge fund portfolio is skewed toward higher-volatility strategies or strategies that are more highly correlated with equity markets (e.g., equity long/short), then total portfolio volatility will increase if the hedge fund allocation is funded out of fixed income.

The analysis of the impact on total portfolio volatility is important to investors for two reasons. First, it reinforces the point that investors should analyze the characteristics of their hedge fund portfolios prior to investing. The second reason Figure 26.3 is important is because it provides investors with an easy decision rule: How they fund the hedge fund allocation depends in part on how much risk they would like to take in the overall portfolio.

In addition to analyzing the impact on total portfolio volatility, investors should consider the impact of each funding alternative on the marginal contribution to total portfolio risk. Figure 26.4 illustrates this point by showing the mar-

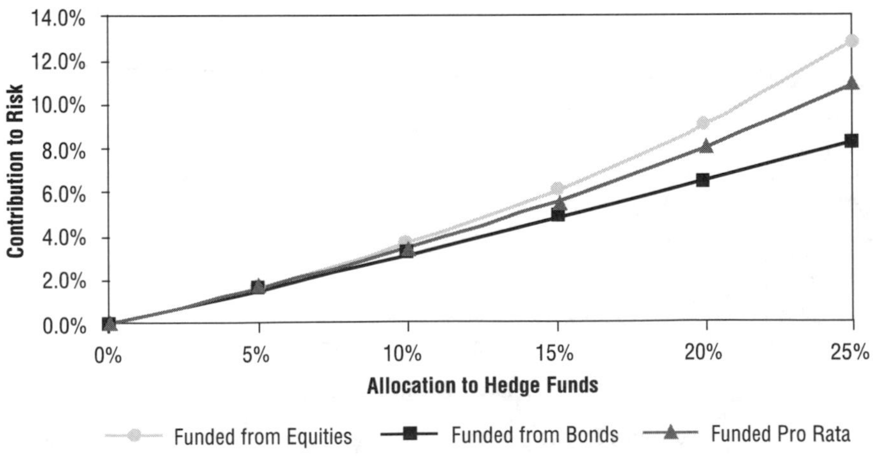

FIGURE 26.4 Hedge Fund Contribution to Risk

ginal contribution to risk (expressed in percentage terms) for each hedge fund allocation and under each scenario.

The important feature of Figure 26.4 is the illustration that the marginal impact on portfolio risk from hedge fund allocations can be quite small.[1] In this example, even a 20 percent allocation to hedge funds contributes less than 10 percent of the total portfolio risk at the margin, irrespective of which funding choice is made. Of course, this conclusion depends on the actual structure of the hedge fund portfolio. If the hedge fund portfolio were concentrated in a highly volatile sector (e.g., equity long/short), then we would anticipate a more significant marginal contribution to total portfolio risk at each hedge fund allocation.

Figures 26.3 and 26.4 suggest that *a hedge fund program can be designed to have a modest impact on total portfolio volatility and the distribution of portfolio risk*. What about the returns associated with hedge fund allocations?

Rather than focus on projecting future returns to hedge funds on the basis of historical averages, our preferred approach is to find the implied excess returns (i.e., returns over cash rates) associated with alternative allocations.[2] Implied returns are the returns that are implied by the optimality of the portfolio structure under the assumed correlation and volatility structure of all the asset classes in the portfolio. The results are shown in Figure 26.5, again using the same equal risk weight hedge fund portfolio. In keeping with the analysis of Figures 26.3 and 26.4, we also show the impact of alternative funding scenarios.

What is striking about the numbers in Figure 26.5 is how low the implied premiums actually are. For instance, the implied return for a 10 percent allocation to hedge funds is around 107 basis points, irrespective of which funding choice is used. In fact, the choice of how the hedge fund allocation is funded really begins to matter only at more significant hedge fund allocations.

For example, suppose that an investor allocated 25 percent to hedge funds. If the hedge fund allocation is made out of equities, then the implied hedge fund return is around 127 basis points. On the other hand, if the hedge fund portfolio is made out of bonds, then the implied return is 14 basis points lower. Similar to Figures 26.3 and 26.4, the relationship between the implied returns and the hedge fund allocation will depend on the actual structure of the hedge fund portfolio: A more volatile hedge fund portfolio (e.g., one that is concentrated in equity long/short managers) will have a higher implied return. Alternatively, a hedge fund portfolio that is not especially highly correlated with the other assets (e.g., concentrated in commodities futures trading) will have a lower implied return at every allocation.

The implied returns shown in Figure 26.5 are best interpreted as hurdle rates. In other words, they are the minimum returns required by the investor to hold the hedge fund allocation and all other asset classes in the indicated proportions. Of course, higher returns on hedge funds would be preferred (and perhaps even expected). In

---

[1]The marginal contribution to risk from a hedge fund depends on its weighting in the portfolio, its level of volatility, and its correlations with the other assets in the portfolio.

[2]Implied returns can be found for any set of portfolio weights as $R = \lambda\Omega X$. In this equation, R is a vector of asset returns, Ω a covariance matrix of asset returns, X a vector of portfolio weights, and λ a risk aversion parameter.

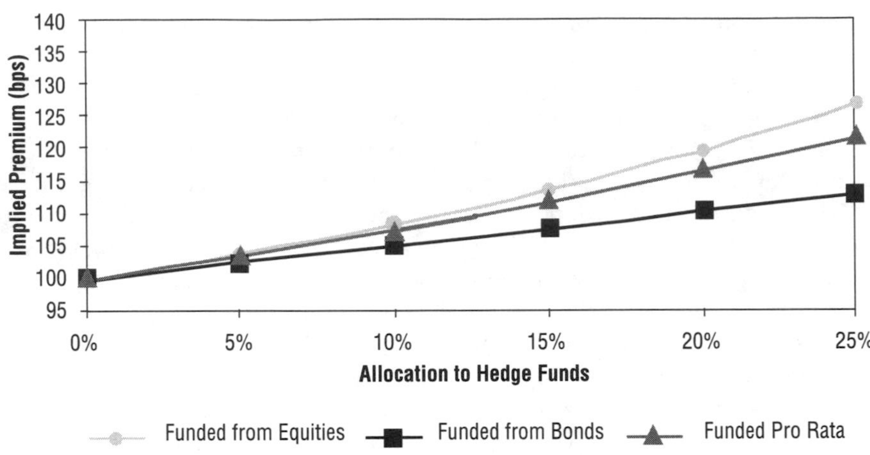

FIGURE 26.5 Implied Hedge Fund Hurdle Rates

some senses, then, it is reasonable for an investor to ask whether a particular implementation of a hedge fund program can achieve these hurdle rates.

EVALUATING IMPLIED HURDLE RATES

How can we use the implied hurdle rates? Our implied hurdle rates correspond to the minimum return required to invest at a particular level in a hedge fund portfolio with specific risk characteristics. In our example, the risk characteristics are those of the portfolio with an equal contribution to risk from each hedge fund strategy. The risk characteristics of the hedge fund strategies, in turn, were developed from time series of hedge fund indexes. At one level, we might think about making passive investments to each of the hedge fund strategies by investing in the indexes.

However, this choice is not available to us—we cannot implement a hedge fund allocation by passively investing in a hedge fund index. Thus, an investor can reasonably ask whether a portfolio of particular hedge funds can be constructed whose historical volatility and correlation resemble the characteristics of the indexes, and whose historical performance at least matches the implied hurdle rates.

A simple way to approach these issues is to begin with an evaluation of the risk characteristics and then analyze the historical performance. Our purpose in evaluating historical volatility is to determine whether it is feasible to construct a portfolio of hedge funds for each strategy whose volatility matches that of the hedge index for that strategy.

Our analysis of historical volatility focused on manager-specific returns in the following hedge fund strategies—event driven, equity long/short, convertible arbitrage, equity market neutral, fixed income arbitrage, and tactical trading (convertible arbitrage, equity market neutral, and fixed income arbitrage are the subsectors of the relative value sector). Table 26.3 shows the number of managers in each hedge fund sector and the data source. Although our database covered manager returns from January 1994 through May 2001, we chose to reduce the number of

TABLE 26.3 Hedge Fund Managers (1/94–5/01)

Strategy	Source	Number of Managers
Event driven	TASS	179
Equity long/short	TASS	622
Convertible arbitrage	TASS	71
Equity market neutral	TASS	177
Fixed income arbitrage	TASS	89
Tactical trading	Barclays	1,355

Sources: TASS Research; Barclays CTA index.

managers used in the study to a more relevant subset. In particular, we selected only those managers that had reported at least nine consecutive months of performance, and excluded managers for which we had missing monthly performance data points. (It is important to keep in mind that managers reported returns over differing time periods and that most managers did not report returns over the entire period indicated in Table 26.3).

For each strategy, we then developed samples of equally weighted portfolios. Our objective was to determine how many managers were necessary within each strategy to match the volatility of the strategy index. For the purposes of this analysis, we decided to consider the individual components of the relative value sector. That is, rather than focus on relative value, we looked at convertible arbitrage, fixed income arbitrage, and equity market neutral.

For event driven, equity long/short, convertible arbitrage, equity market neutral, and fixed income arbitrage, the CSFB/Tremont index was used, while the Barclays CTA index was used for tactical trading. (The CSFB/Tremont indexes use only a subset of the managers in the TASS Research database.) We further restricted the sample to use only those managers who had a complete history of data for the three-year period from June 1998 through May 2001. On the basis of these data, we formed 1,000 samples of 5, 10, and 20 managers for each strategy, and calculated portfolio risk characteristics.

Table 26.4 summarizes our analysis. For each hedge fund strategy and each portfolio size (measured by number of managers), we show the median and the mean portfolio volatility, as well as the median and mean manager volatility. The table also shows the average correlation of excess returns between the managers for each hedge fund strategy. For comparison purposes, we also show the corresponding index volatility, calculated over the same time period. (The volatility differences between the indexes and the portfolios can be explained, in part, by the weighting schemes—the indexes are approximately capitalization weighted while the portfolios are equally weighted.)

As Table 26.4 clearly illustrates, an investor does not need to hold all of the managers in each hedge fund sector to approximate index-level volatility. Part of the explanation for this lies in the low levels of manager-specific correlation for some of the sectors. For example, the average correlation between manager returns in the fixed income arbitrage sector is around 0.19. Clearly, a low level of correlation across managers can help to reduce the volatility in a hedge fund portfolio.

While this result is good news for investors, it is also cautionary. Our results

TABLE 26.4 Hedge Fund Portfolio Volatility (6/98–5/01)

	# of Managers	Index Volatility	Median Volatility Portfolio Size			Mean Volatility Portfolio Size			Median Manager Volatility	Mean Manager Volatility	Mean Manager Correlation
			5	10	20	5	10	20			
Event driven	106	9.0%	6.8%	6.8%	6.8%	7.9%	7.3%	7.0%	6.4%	10.6%	0.40
Equity long/short	292	16.5	16.4	14.9	13.9	16.9	15.2	14.0	22.5	25.7	0.24
Convertible artbitrage	50	6.5	5.9	5.8	5.5	6.8	5.9	5.5	7.2	9.7	0.28
Equity market neutral	47	2.5	5.6	4.2	3.3	5.7	4.3	3.3	10.5	10.8	0.03
Fixed income arbitrage	18	5.7	5.9	5.2	4.8	6.0	5.3	4.8	6.7	9.6	0.19
Tactical trading	298	7.6	12.0	10.5	9.7	12.4	10.7	9.8	17.0	19.4	0.16

TABLE 26.5 Adjusted Historical Hedge Fund Performance (1/94–5/01)

Strategy	Index Level Alpha	T-Statistic (Alpha)	Index Level Beta	T-Statistic (Beta)	Residual Volatility	Total Volatility
Event driven	3.6%	1.77	0.25	6.55	5.4%	6.6%
Equity long/short	3.1	0.86	0.52	7.65	9.5	12.3
Convertible arbitrage	4.8	2.60	0.04	1.17	4.9	5.0
Equity market neutral	5.0	4.59	0.10	4.83	2.9	3.3
Fixed income arbitrage	1.0	0.62	0.03	0.87	4.3	4.3
Tactical trading	1.1	0.36	–0.03	–0.47	8.2	8.2

Source: CSFB/Tremont.

suggest that investors can achieve indexlike volatility without holding an exceptionally large number of hedge fund managers within each sector. However, to achieve these volatility levels, investors must also ensure that the correlation of returns across managers within each sector is relatively low. Consequently, our results also suggest that investors will need to rely on thoughtful portfolio construction tools to develop an initial hedge fund portfolio, and robust risk management systems to ensure that the hedge fund portfolio remains within its prescribed risk tolerances.

What about historical performance? The objective of our analysis in this case is to verify whether a portfolio of hedge fund managers can achieve the implied hurdle rates shown in Figure 26.5. Those hurdle rates range between 100 and 125 basis points over cash rates, for allocations between 5 and 25 percent.

One easy step we can take is to assess the historical performance for each hedge fund strategies index. For example, we can regress the historical performance (measured as excess return over cash) of each hedge fund on historical U.S. equity performance (also excess return over cash) and evaluate whether each hedge fund strategy added value after adjusting for the performance of the overall equity market. We'll call the performance after all the adjustments the strategy's "alpha."

The results of this analysis, summarized in Table 26.5, are comforting. Over the period January 1994 through May 2001, the historical performance for each hedge fund strategy is positive, after adjusting for cash rates and market returns. (All return numbers are annualized.) In some sectors, the value added historically is quite high. For example, the alpha (or adjusted performance) for equity long/short is 310 basis points.

Although each strategy's alpha is positive (and in some cases high), we can still ask whether it was generated by chance. To answer this question, we'll calculate the t-statistic for each adjusted performance. For a simple rule of thumb, we'll regard an alpha as statistically different from zero if the t-statistic is greater than two in absolute value.[3] That is, when the alpha is positive and the t-statistic is greater than two, then we are more inclined to regard the historical performance as representing

[3]We are measuring statistical significance with a 95 percent confidence interval.

something other than chance. In contrast, a positive alpha that is not statistically significant could be merely happy coincidence rather than manager skill.

In our case, two of the six strategies (convertible arbitrage and equity market neutral) have statistically significant historical alphas. For example, the equity market neutral alpha is 500 basis points and the t-statistic is 4.59. By contrast, the equity long/short alpha is 310 basis points, but the t-statistic is 0.86. On the basis of these figures, we are more inclined to regard the equity market neutral composite performance as representing something other than chance.

Index performance statistics are composites of many individual managers. The figures summarized in Table 26.5 suggest some historical variation across hedge fund strategies in producing alpha. However, even though the composite performance in a particular strategy does not have a statistically significant alpha, there may be managers in that strategy who have been able to generate significant outperformance.

A simple way to approach this issue is to do the same type of analysis that was done on each hedge fund index, except at the manager level. In other words, we can find the alpha for each manager in each strategy and determine whether the manager's alpha is positive and statistically different from zero. Just as with the analysis at the index level, we'll find the alpha for each manager by regressing the manager's historical performance on the performance of the U.S. equity market, after adjusting both for the level of cash returns. As before, when the alpha is positive and the t-statistic is greater than two, we are inclined to regard the historical performance as representing something other than chance.

In Table 26.6 we show the distribution of t-statistics for the alphas for the managers in each hedge fund strategy. We have focused on the t-statistics for only those managers who had positive alphas, since we want to know whether there are some managers who historically were able to add value through skill rather than chance. These alphas were estimated from the larger manager universe, and covered a longer time period. (Many managers reported returns over differing time periods, and most managers did not report returns over the entire time period indicated in Table 26.6.)

It is quite clear from Table 26.6 that some managers had statistically significant alphas. For example, in equity long/short 71 percent of the managers had positive

TABLE 26.6 Historical Manager-Specific Alpha (1/94–5/01)

Strategy	Number of Managers	% Managers with Positive Alpha	% Managers Statistically Significant out of Those with Positive Alpha
Event driven	179	82%	59%
Equity long/short	622	71	33
Convertible arbitrage	71	80	77
Equity market neutral	177	62	49
Fixed income arbitrage	89	66	42
Tactical trading	1,355	57	12

Source: TASS Research.

alphas of which around 33 percent had t-statistics greater than two. However, it is important to remember that a positive and significant historical performance does not constitute a prediction that those same managers will be able to add value in the future.[4]

How does our analysis help us evaluate the implied hurdle rates? In our opinion, investors can draw three principal inferences.

First, the fact that the historical adjusted performance for each hedge fund sector substantially exceeds the implied hurdle rates suggests that the hurdle rates have been achievable, particularly for modest allocations.

Second, the fact that there is some variation across strategies in the significance of the historical adjusted performance suggests to us that investors are advised to carefully consider how to develop, monitor, and maintain their hedge fund portfolios.

Finally, the variation in significance in historical performance across managers within each hedge fund sector seems to us to imply that investors will need to be quite careful in how they select specific hedge fund managers.

CONCLUSION

Many institutional investors are perplexed by the challenges associated with investing in hedge funds. Paradoxically, the characteristics of the asset class that make it an attractive investment also confound careful analysis. In this chapter, we have shown that our equilibrium framework can be extended in a way that gives investors the ability to make reasoned allocations to hedge funds.

In common with the overall theme of this book, our framework relies on the principles of applied portfolio theory. Since hedge fund returns are more difficult to estimate than hedge fund volatility and correlation, our portfolio advice relies instead on hedge fund risk characteristics. In addition, our portfolio advice relies on an investor's existing portfolio as a neutral reference point. Thus, our approach gives investors a framework for deciding how much incremental return they must receive on hedge funds relative to the other assets in the portfolio to justify a particular allocation. We view these returns as implied hurdle rates for hedge fund allocations.

Applying our framework to a stylized version of a typical U.S. institutional investor's portfolio, we conclude that *the implied hurdle rates for hedge fund allocations are quite small.* Indeed, the implied hurdle rates for modest allocations to hedge fund portfolios diversified across strategies are in the range of 100 to 125 basis points over cash. Our analysis of specific hedge fund managers is indicative that at least historically, investors could have constructed portfolios to achieve or even

[4]In the presence of sufficient data, it is often useful to stratify the data into favorable and unfavorable equity market periods and separately calculate the beta in each of these scenarios. If a hedge fund portfolio becomes more (positively) correlated with equity markets in difficult environments, the implied equilibrium hurdle rate of return for that manager should increase as well.

exceed these hurdle rates. However, our analysis also shows how important manager selection is to achieving these hurdle returns.

Investors have a number of available investment alternatives for which data are not readily available. Hedge funds are just one example of these alternatives. However, our analysis should be reassuring, as it demonstrates that investors can still find reasonable portfolios without abandoning basic portfolio principles. These basic principles can also be used to analyze other alternative asset classes.

CHAPTER 27

Managing a Portfolio of Hedge Funds

Kent A. Clark

Chapter 26, "Strategic Asset Allocation and Hedge Funds," suggests a framework for evaluating an allocation to hedge funds within a broader investment portfolio. This chapter explores the management of a portfolio of hedge funds, first defining hedge funds, and then offering a framework for evaluating hedge funds and addressing portfolio construction issues.

Managing a portfolio of hedge funds is similar to managing any portfolio, and involves all of the same steps. The clear difference is that the assets traded are interests in hedge funds rather than individual securities.

First, the universe of investable assets needs to be defined and, if possible, classified into groups of similar assets to facilitate analysis. Second, the portfolio manager must develop views on the investment characteristics of each asset. Third, a risk budget is set and the assets are assembled into a portfolio. Finally, the assets and the portfolio are monitored on an ongoing basis to ensure that the investment characteristics continue to be consistent with the investor's goals. If we were to substitute "hedge fund" for "asset" in this brief outline, we would have summarized the process of managing a portfolio of hedge funds.

As discussed in previous chapters, investment returns derive either from benchmark exposure or from alpha. In equilibrium, risks uncorrelated with the market return do not earn a risk premium, so alpha cannot be earned consistently. For the most part, however, investors appear to reject this idea. Although indexing, which creates pure benchmark exposure, is increasingly popular, it is still the case that a significant proportion of investment assets are held in actively managed investments, in which the investment manager attempts to add returns in excess of benchmark returns. A lively academic debate considers whether excess returns can be consistently earned, and if so, whether they derive from anomalies, frictions, or exposures to previously unidentified risk factors. This debate is beyond the scope of the discussion here.

An investment in any asset class can run along a continuum that ranges from pure indexing to pure active management. In pure indexing, the investor attempts to recreate the returns of a benchmark index either by exactly replicating index holdings or by creating a basket of securities that very closely track the benchmark index's returns. Active managers attempt to add alpha, loosely defined as returns in excess of benchmark returns, by deviating from benchmark holdings, either by reweighting benchmark securities or by holding securities not represented in the benchmark. Active management itself ranges from enhanced indexing to pure active management. With enhanced indexing, the investment manager aims to closely replicate index returns, volatility, and correlation characteristics while adding a small amount of alpha. In contrast, in pure active management, the investor pays no attention to any benchmark and simply attempts to generate returns by the implementation of his or her views. Hedge funds are designed to represent this purest form of active management.

WHAT IS A HEDGE FUND?

A hedge fund is an unconstrained, loosely regulated investment vehicle for which a portion of manager compensation is a performance fee. Hedge funds are intended to be unadulterated exposure to active management, reflecting only the managers' views on future asset returns, and not reflecting any concept of benchmark index.

- *Constraints.* Hedge funds are vehicles that allow investment managers to engage in pure active management, with no consideration of a benchmark, and unconstrained with respect to the use of short selling (see Figure 27.1), leverage, instruments, and strategies. Consequently, hedge funds are sometimes referred to as belonging to "skill classes" rather than asset classes. The attraction of hedge funds is that they offer investors an opportunity to both enhance expected returns as well as reduce risk.
- *Regulation.* In the United States, the Securities and Exchange Commission does not regulate hedge funds. As a result, hedge fund investing is restricted to qualified investors who can meet certain net worth and income standards. These requirements are intended to distinguish sophisticated investors who are able to effectively evaluate the risks of unregulated vehicles. Due to this freedom from regulatory oversight, however, hedge fund managers are not allowed to solicit clients.

Hedge funds exploit an investment technique known as short selling, or selling an asset that the investor does not own with the intention of repurchasing it later. The investor may expect that the asset's price will drop, resulting in an outright profit, essentially reversing the timing of the old piece of stock market advice from "buy low and sell high" to "sell high and buy low." Alternately, the investor may sell an asset short as a hedge against another asset, or in order to exploit the relative price movements between two assets.

As an example, the mechanics of short-selling stock in the United States are straightforward, but important to understand. Short sellers employ a "prime broker" who locates the borrowable stock and acts as custodian of the stock. The investor identifies the asset to sell short and notifies their prime broker of the intent. The broker then locates a "shortable" security, one that the owner has already agreed may be borrowed and sold short. The prime broker borrows the asset and sells it, using the proceeds as collateral for the shorted security. In addition, in the United States, the short seller must post margin, or further security for the short-sold asset, in accordance with Regulation T. The short seller must pay a borrowing fee, plus any income paid on the asset, to the owner who loaned the security.

FIGURE 27.1 The Mechanics of Short Selling
Source: Tremont Advisers, Inc.

- ***Fee structure.*** Hedge fund fees include a fixed management fee, a proportional participation performance fee, and a high-water mark. The fixed management fee typically ranges from 0 to 2 percent of assets annually. The performance fee is expressed as a percentage of the fund's returns, allowing the hedge fund manager to participate in the fund's returns. Performance fees range from 20 percent to 50 percent of fund returns and are subject to a high-water mark. That is, if the fund's net asset value (NAV) is below the level at which a performance fee was last paid (referred to as the high-water mark), the manager does not receive any performance fee until the fund's NAV once again rises above the high-water mark.

  The performance fee structure is equivalent to the hedge fund manager owning a proportion of the fund and a put option, where the ownership share is equal to the participation rate of the performance fee. Suppose the performance fee allows the manager to receive 20 percent of the hedge fund's returns. This is analogous to the manager owning 20 percent of the fund. In addition, however, the manager holds a put option on the fund, with a strike price equal to the high-water mark, since the manager does not participate in any losses in the fund.

These three characteristics—the lack of constraints, the lack of regulation, and the performance fee—are the common defining features of hedge funds. There are a number of other characteristics that many hedge funds share that affect investors.

- ***Lack of transparency.*** Hedge funds have a reputation for being very secretive, opaque investments. Most will not reveal the assets held, with particular care taken to protect information about short positions. Often, investors will receive periodic letters reviewing performance and exposures, but frequently even leverage is not included in the correspondence. Some of the most guarded funds will not even reveal the types of strategies being managed, let alone the models or trading strategies employed. The secrecy of hedge funds reflects a trade-off between two competing objectives. Investors prefer a high level of transparency so that they can better understand the investment process and the manager's philosophy, and have confidence in the ability of a manager to earn superior returns. Hedge fund managers, though, typically invest in strategies that have limited capacity and are concerned that transparency will lead to increased flow of capital into these strategies, reducing the opportunity to add value.
- ***Short lives.*** The half-life of hedge funds is about two and a half years (Brown, Goetzmann, and Park 1999). A few funds have failed with large losses and eye-grabbing headlines. More often, the outcome is less dramatic, driven by the fact that most of the potential economics for a hedge fund manager are in the incentive fee. A fund with poor performance, even if modestly positive, may not be viable. When the fund is below its high-water mark, the situation is exacerbated, since the fund has to earn returns—without incentive compensation—simply to get back to even.
- ***Illiquidity.*** Hedge fund investments are usually illiquid, with redemption windows at least as infrequent as monthly. In addition, redeeming investors must notify the hedge fund manager well in advance of the redemption date, further

decreasing liquidity. Consequently, a long-term view will need to be taken in evaluating, and investing in, hedge funds.

- ***Capacity constraints.*** Hedge funds with excellent performance and robust investment processes may find the demand by investors to be greater than the estimated capacity of the strategy. Since most of the revenue for a successful hedge fund comes from performance fees rather than the fixed management fee, many managers reach the point where it is in their best interest to turn away new investment. In fact, extremely successful hedge funds may even return capital to investors, preferring to maintain the ability to generate excellent returns on a smaller capital base to having more assets under management. The fact that some managers close their funds means that the investable universe of hedge funds is a subset of the whole. The resulting inability to invest in many hedge funds implies that the returns of indexes attempting to measure the performance of the hedge fund universe may not be attainable, even for large institutional investors.

Notably, none of these characteristics mentioned addresses the issue of what investment strategies are associated with hedge funds. Figure 27.2 briefly summarizes some broad hedge fund strategies, stratified along four sectors. This is not an exhaustive list of hedge fund strategies, nor is it a definitive classification system. It does, however, provide a structure within which to analyze hedge funds.

DEFINING THE INVESTMENT UNIVERSE

Investors contemplating an allocation to hedge funds are first faced with the fact that there is no single, exhaustive listing of hedge funds, and that the universe is large and continually changing as hedge funds go in and out of business. TASS Research speculates that a conservative estimate of assets under management in hedge funds is between $500 million and $600 million, and an often-quoted statistic suggests there are over 6,000 hedge funds in existence. Probably there are about half this number of strategies, with multiple share classes.

Since no single listing of managers exists, the investor must create the investment universe using a combination of commercially available databases and ad hoc information gathering. Commercial providers of hedge fund data rely on managers to report their data and styles, resulting in a number of biases to the databases (see Chapter 26 for further discussion). As well, most managers who are closed to new investment do not report their returns to the databases.

To better understand the magnitude of this problem, consider two commercially available databases—Hedgefund.net and TASS. Each has an equity long/short category. Hedge funds in this category invest long and short in equities, with the goal of delivering excellent risk-adjusted returns. After adjusting for multiple share classes and misclassified managers, there are 684 funds in Hedgefund.net's long/short equity category and 677 funds in the TASS long/short equity category. Overlap between the two databases is 249 funds, so clearly neither database is comprehensive.

A further complication of defining the investment universe is determining exactly what falls within the category of "hedge fund." Notably, the definition of

Hedge funds can be classified into a number of different sectors and strategies. Goldman Sachs categorizes hedged funds into four sectors, each of which include a number of strategies. The four sectors are: relative value, event driven, equity long/short, and tactical trading.

Relative Value	Event Driven	Equity Long/Short	Tactical Trading
Convertible Arbitrage	Merger Arbitrage	Geography (United States, Japan, Europe)	Managed Futures
Equity Arbitrage	Special Situations	Industry (Technology, Energy)	Global Macro
Fixed Income Arbitrage	High-Yield/ Distressed Debt	Style (Value, Growth, Small)	

Relative Value: Managers generally identify relationships between securities. When the current pricing relationship deviates from the manager's expectations, trades are structured that will profit when prices revert to their normal relationships. Strategies include convertible bond arbitrage, equity arbitrage, and fixed income arbitrage. Equity arbitrage includes statistical arbitrage and equity market neutral strategies.

Event Driven: Managers identify corporate events they expect to affect valuations, and construct trades to extract value when the event occurs. The predominant strategy in this area is merger arbitrage, in which the manager typically buys shares in the target company and sells short shares in the acquiring company, with the expectation that any spread between valuations will disappear upon completion of the merger. Other strategies include special situations, high-yield, and distressed debt.

Equity Long/Short: Managers develop views on stocks and express those views by going either long or short in amounts that reflect the manager's conviction about the view. Managers can further express conviction about the views by varying the amount of capital invested, and are able to express directional views by adjusting the net long or short exposure of the portfolio. Most managers tend to have a long bias, but short-biased managers do exist. Specializations within the equity long/short sector are typically along geographic or industry lines.

Tactical Trading: Includes both macro managers and managed futures. Macro managers typically develop views on broad economic themes and then implement those views with a variety of instruments. Using either systematic or discretionary approaches, managed futures traders develop views on a variety of markets and typically implement those views through futures contracts and interbank currency forwards.

FIGURE 27.2 Hedge Fund Classifications
Source: Tremont Advisers, Inc.

hedge funds provided earlier was silent on the issue of what strategies qualify as hedge fund strategies, with the only common characteristics seeming to be loose regulation, lack of constraints, and performance fees. Investors may want to further qualify funds they consider for the hedge fund allocations of their portfolios, possibly eliminating managers who are long-only, or who invest in certain securities or regions. Other limitations with respect to style, strategy, and leverage may also help limit the universe to a manageable number of funds.

DEVELOPING VIEWS ON HEDGE FUNDS

The heterogeneity of hedge fund strategies, or at least of strategy implementation, represents both an opportunity and a challenge. The opportunity arises from finding hedge fund managers who are able to exploit unique informational or analytical advantages. The challenge is making choices among very diverse approaches.

Evaluation of a hedge fund manager requires consideration of both compensated and uncompensated risks. Compensated risks are the investment risks a manager takes in order to generate returns to the fund. Key drivers of the manager's ability to deliver return for the investment risk are the investment strategy and the people executing the investment strategy. Uncompensated risks are created by the hedge fund organization and business. While these risks cannot increase returns, they can certainly lead to manager distraction or fund failure.

The goal of manager evaluation is to assess whether a given hedge fund has an investment "edge." The manager's edge is the group of characteristics that will help deliver attractive risk-adjusted returns over time.

Investment Strategy

Investment strategy is the central focus of hedge fund evaluation. A thorough understanding of the hedge fund manager's strategy, style, and approach is essential prior to investing. The process begins with an evaluation of the general investment proposition's potential to generate returns. For example, suppose the hedge fund's returns depend on being able to predict the growth of an economic variable, and a careful evaluation of the strategy suggests that the economic variable in question is not predictable. In this case, the hedge fund would be discarded simply because the venture seems unlikely to generate returns, regardless of the relative qualities of the manager and organization.

After determining that a fund is operating in a field in which it should be possible to generate returns, attention turns to evaluating the fund's strategy and its approach to implementing the strategy. A variety of factors will be considered in this evaluation.

Consideration is given to how the manager develops investment views, including information sources and analytical tools used. Does the hedge fund have informational, analytical, or size advantages, and are these advantages sustainable? Implementation of the views, including trade structuring and execution, portfolio construction, rebalancing, risk monitoring, and use of leverage are all important. The decision-making process is important, particularly if there is a portfolio management team with more than a single key person.

All managers have a style identified with their strategy. Understanding each manager's investment style will help in combining managers to create a portfolio that is not overly exposed to any single return-driving factor. Also, understanding investment style helps frame return expectations, particularly when the style is out of favor. Style analysis is both an analytical and a quantitative undertaking—analytical because manager style may change over time and because the history of returns may be too short to evaluate the style quantitatively. Furthermore, the investor is usually unable to observe the hedge fund's positions, so must infer the style from interviews or return histories.

People

Hedge fund investments are typically partnerships, and choosing partners in any business venture is an important task. Investments in hedge funds ultimately hinge on the people involved in managing the investments and business.

The experience, education, and track record of the people involved in the hedge fund are important characteristics to be evaluated. Hedge fund managers are an eclectic group of people, with varied educational and trading backgrounds. Many successful managers have previously worked on the proprietary trading desks of investment banks, while others have been Wall Street research analysts or traditional portfolio managers, or have had careers in other industries altogether. There is no single route to success, but relevant experience is preferred.

More than just investing expertise is required. Ability to manage a company is key, whether the main investor is running the business or a specialist is hired to do so. In cases where there is more than one person involved, the question arises of how well they will get along and how differences will be resolved.

Organization

A hedge fund's organizational structure and business plan can affect investment returns, and must be carefully analyzed prior to committing capital to the manager. Organizational distractions can disrupt the investment decision makers' ability to focus on managing the portfolio. Conversely, effective internal controls can provide important safeguards against fraudulent practices in the fund.

Hedge fund management companies range in size and scope, from start-up sole proprietorships to large financial institutions that offer hedge funds as part of broad product lines. Successful managers of all organizational sizes exist, but the organization must be consistent with the needs and aspirations of the hedge fund itself. Appropriate trading infrastructure has to be in place. The manager needs to have legal counsel, and appropriate compliance structures are necessary.

A typical scenario for new hedge funds is a successful portfolio manager leaving a large organization to start up his or her own fund. This may raise concerns because the manager is leaving the support and infrastructure of the larger organization. Whether the manager will be able to overcome these challenges is clearly germane to the hedge fund's success.

The manager's plan for growth is an important consideration, especially in light of the long investment horizon required of many hedge funds. Does the manager have in place hiring plans consistent with asset growth? The manager's forecast of capacity and his or her plans to monitor capacity constraints at appropriate intervals can affect when the hedge fund closes. Fund size has to be evaluated in the context of the strategy, since the nature of assets and trading style will dictate the appropriate fund size. A manager trading a low-turnover strategy in large-capitalization U.S. stocks should have much larger potential capacity than one who trades emerging-market stocks with high turnover.

A key consideration in hedge fund investing is the alignment of interests between the hedge fund's employees and investors. The extent to which employees are themselves investors in the fund is an important variable in the decision to invest with a hedge fund. Investors want not only key principals to be investors, but also research analysts and others involved in the investment process and business management.

Distribution of ownership among employees is another issue, since more distributed ownership helps retain key people, improving organizational stability and continuity.

Track Record

In addition to the analytical assessment of the investment strategy, there are a number of quantitative aspects of the fund's returns and portfolio. These include volatility, style characteristics, downside risk, and worst-case loss. Particularly interesting is whether returns and style are consistent with the strategy articulated by the hedge fund manager.

If sufficient data are available, an evaluation of the return/risk trade-off offered by the hedge fund is usually performed. Expected absolute performance is important, and must be adequate to ensure the investors achieve their goals. However, looking only at absolute performance ignores the role of risk taking by the hedge fund. The prospective hedge fund investor will appraise whether the amount of return per unit of risk offered by the fund is consistent with the investment strategy and degree of leverage in the fund.

The analysis of past returns raises the issue of performance persistence for hedge funds. Although a careful analysis of past returns is an important input to the decision-making process, chasing past performance has a number of pitfalls.

Reviewing the year-over-year migration of hedge fund managers from one performance quartile to another helps to understand the hazard of placing too much weight on past performance. For example, there were 313 equity long/short managers with a full year of returns data in the TASS database for 1999 and 2000. Of the 78 managers in the top quartile of returns in 1999, only 14 (18 percent) were in the top-performing quartile for 2000. In fact, 35 (45 percent) of 1999's top-quartile managers ended 2000 in the bottom-performing quartile of managers in 2000, and the absolute best-performing fund in 1999 was the absolute worst-performing fund in 2000. This fund returned 334 percent in 1999 and –69 percent in 2000, for a net return over the two years of 3.5 percent. Unfortunately, an investment made at the beginning of 2000 based solely on 1999 returns would have ended badly.

Hedge funds have tremendous scope to change their investment approaches. Many hedge funds have very flexible operating guidelines, allowing managers to change important characteristics of the investment strategy, including instruments traded and leverage. As well, investment strategies themselves change, as innovative new financial products make it possible to mitigate some risks while focusing more closely on others. Looking only at past performance does not incorporate these changes.

Finally, as previously mentioned, hedge funds with the best track records tend to be closed to new investment. Chasing past performance may lead to frustration over lack of access to the funds with the best return histories.

Figure 27.3 summarizes some of the information examined in evaluating a hedge fund's track record. This event-driven fund is compared to the S&P 500, a traditional equity market index, as well as the Tremont Event Driven peer index.

	Jan	Feb	Mar	Apr	May	Jun	Jul	Aug	Sept	Oct	Nov	Dec	Annual
2000									0.70%	−2.45%	4.44%	0.24%	2.84%
2001	0.48%	2.34%	4.44%	−1.78%	0.95%	2.76%	−1.98%	1.35%	−1.00	0.63	−0.22	0.29	8.37
2002	0.83	0.29	0.93	−0.14	−0.97	2.39	−2.82						0.43

	Manager	CSFB/ Tremont Event Driven	S&P 500
Annualized Return	6.06%	0.74%	−22.33%
Standard Deviation	6.58	4.60	17.20
Drawdown	−2.82	−6.63	−38.39
Sharpe Ratio	0.33	−0.67	−1.60
Return-to-Drawdown	2.15	0.11	−0.58
Beta to S&P 500	−0.20	0.14	
Annualized Alpha	−2.94	0.63	

	2000	2001	2002	Annualized Return
Manager	2.84%	8.37%	0.43%	6.06%
CSFB/Tremont Event Driven	−0.91	7.84	−5.09	0.74
S&P 500	−12.68	−11.88	−19.92	−22.33

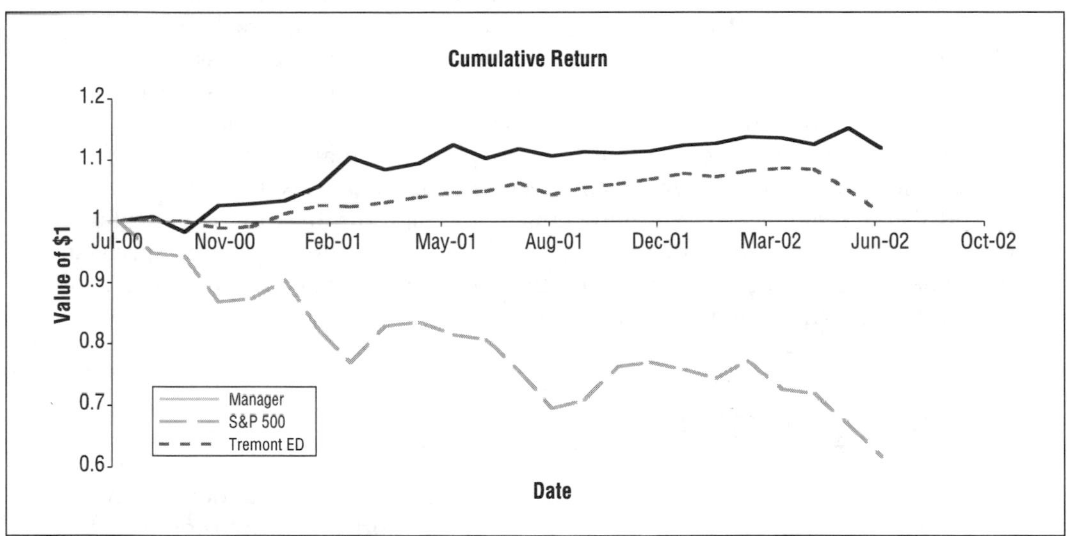

FIGURE 27.3 Sample Analysis of Track Record
Source: Tremont Advisers, Inc.

The goal is to evaluate the nature of returns, risks taken, and to what extent returns are repeatable. Various measures of risk and return to unit of risk are evaluated.

Figure 27.3 includes monthly returns, helpful in assessing consistency of returns, and in evaluating performance in months when exogenous events or market displacements may have occurred. In addition, two measures of risk appear, standard deviation and largest drawdown. Largest drawdown measures the largest percentage loss the manager experienced, regardless of time. In this example, the fund lost 2.82 percent in a single month. However, the drawdown could have occurred over any number of months. The units of return received per unit of risk are summarized by Sharpe ratio and return-to-drawdown ratio. Both are helpful in gauging whether the risk taken was adequately compensated, and are particularly useful when comparing funds.

Beta to the S&P 500 and alpha are included to help evaluate whether the hedge fund added value beyond a passive investment in the equity market. In the case of this fund, the beta is negative, but so is the alpha. Since the S&P 500 has had negative returns over the period of measurement, the investor may decide that, despite the negative alpha, value was added by having a negative beta and positive returns. This highlights the fact that these quantitative measures need to be considered in the context of fund strategy and the market environment. A graph of cumulative returns is included to help visualize performance.

More information and analysis may be collected to help assess the relative merits of the hedge fund's track record, including comparisons to other managers with similar strategies.

Final Evaluation

The final view on the hedge fund will combine inputs and insights gathered while researching the investment strategy, people, organization, and track record. The view should include an assessment of the fund's strengths and weaknesses as well as expectations for return. Importantly, expectations for worst-case loss need to be laid out prior to investing to help frame future monitoring of the manager. Anticipating a worst-case loss of 5 percent from a hedge fund that is expected to deliver 20 percent net returns per year does not seem reasonable, for example. Such expectations will ultimately lead to disappointment and high turnover in the portfolio of hedge funds. Expectations for potential positive returns should also be specified, since unexpectedly large positive or negative returns may be an indication the manager is taking unanticipated risks.

PORTFOLIO CONSTRUCTION

Creating a portfolio of hedge funds needs to begin with a clear understanding of the investor's objectives and the fit of the hedge fund portfolio into his or her overall portfolio. The goal is to set a risk budget consistent with these objectives, and then allocate the budget to a portfolio of managers that are most likely to deliver returns that fulfill the objectives. In addition to expectations for return and volatility, investors should understand how large a loss they are comfortable sustaining in their hedge fund portfolio, as well as their liquidity requirements.

These goals will help derive a strategic allocation to the various hedge fund sectors. Diversification at the sector level is an important source of risk reduction, so all four sectors should at least be considered in portfolio allocations. Table 27.1 shows correlation, risk, and return of the four hedge fund sectors defined previously, as well as for the equal-risk allocation discussed in Chapter 26. Correlations and beta to the S&P 500 are also presented. Correlations range from as low as 0.08

TABLE 27.1 Correlations between Hedge Fund Sectors, January 1994 to July 2002

	Relative Value	Event Driven	Long/ Short	Tactical Trading	Equal Risk	S&P 500
Relative Value	1.00					
Event Driven	0.64	1.00				
Long/Short	0.36	0.66	1.00			
Tactical Trading	0.16	0.08	0.23	1.00		
Equal Risk	0.66	0.73	0.75	0.67	1.00	
S&P 500	0.29	0.58	0.61	0.04	0.48	1.00
Beta	0.06	0.24	0.46	0.03	0.15	1.00
Mean	6.2%	6.9%	8.7%	7.0%	7.0%	7.5%
Standard deviation	3.2%	6.4%	11.8%	9.9%	4.8%	15.6%
Sharpe ratio	1.97	1.09	0.73	0.71	1.46	0.48

Data sources: Data are CSFB/Tremont indexes. The Relative Value index combines the CSFB/Tremont Convertible Arbitrage, Equity Market Neutral, and Fixed Income Arbitrage indexes in a 40%, 40%, and 20% weighting, respectively.

between the event-driven and tactical trading strategies to a high of 0.66 between the equity long/short and event-driven sectors.

Further, correlations between strategies, as presented in Table 27.2, are also potentially modest. Using three strategies within the relative value sector, correlations range from 0.07 to 0.58.

The indexes on which these returns are based have very short histories compared to comparable indexes for equity and fixed income investments. Decisions will likely need to be based on a combination of historical data and judgment to arrive at allocations to the various hedge fund sectors.

Tactical overweights and underweights to strategies and sectors are also possible, and are a potential source of value added. Views on strategies and sectors can be derived from bottom-up analysis, studying the return potential of individual managers, or from a top-down perspective, by understanding the effects on expected returns of macroeconomic, financial, and supply and demand conditions. The ability to add value from tactical allocations is impeded by fund illiquidity, which imposes potentially long horizons on any positions taken. If the view is indeed expected to play out over a long period, or if the investor can plan to have

TABLE 27.2 Correlations between Relative Value Strategies, January 1994 to July 2002

	Convertible Arbitrage	Equity Market Neutral	Fixed Income Arbitrage
Convertible Arbitrage	1.00		
Equity Market Neutral	0.34	1.00	
Fixed Income Arbitrage	0.58	0.07	1.00

Source: Tremont Advisers, Inc.

capital inflows over the short term, allowing tactical positions to be unwound, then it may be possible to capitalize on these views.

When sector and strategy allocations have been decided, the investor determines allocations to individual funds. Again, the risk budget is spent on hedge funds in accordance with the views previously developed. Hedge funds for which higher returns are expected, or for which there is more conviction about a given level of return, should receive a greater share of the portfolio's risk budget.

Hedge funds should have exposure only to a manager's views with little permanent exposure to any asset class. Consequently, over a long enough time, correlations across funds are expected to be low, and the benefits of diversification are expected to be large. This is in contrast to combinations of long-only managers, for which benchmark volatility dominates total portfolio volatility and drives correlations.

For example, consider a typical actively managed, long-only, large-cap U.S. equity portfolio benchmarked to the S&P 500 index, with a volatility of about 17 percent. If the managed portfolio has a beta of one and a tracking error of 5 percent, then the index accounts for 92 percent of portfolio volatility. This suggests that the preponderance of risk in a traditional portfolio is attributed to the choice of benchmark index, not to investment manager impact. In addition, if we consider two portfolios managed in this way, with betas of one to the benchmark and with uncorrelated idiosyncratic risks, the correlation between the two managers is also 0.92, so the benefits of diversification are low. In contrast, arguably, 100 percent of a hedge fund portfolio's risk is due to the manager's views and effect on the portfolio, and correlations are expected to be commensurately low between hedge fund managers. It is important to note that this is characteristic of active risk and return, so the same low correlation argument holds for the active portion of long-only manager returns.

Table 27.3 shows the mean correlation across hedge fund managers for a number of strategies. Within-strategy manager correlation ranges from a low of 0.03 to a high of 0.40. To put this into perspective, the median correlation of stocks in the S&P 500 over a recent five-year period was approximately 0.19. Using the S&P 500 as the universe, the median correlation of stocks in the same sector was 0.35, and within the same industry was 0.42. Hedge fund correlations are analogous to the correlations of

TABLE 27.3 Manager Correlations within Strategies, June 1998 to May 2001

Strategy	Number of Managers	Mean Manager Correlation
Event driven	106	0.40
Equity long/short	292	0.24
Convertible arbitrage	50	0.28
Equity market neutral	47	0.03
Fixed income arbitrage	18	0.19
Tactical trading	298	0.16

Data sources: Data for all but tactical trading are drawn from the TASS database. Tactical trading data are from the Barclay CTA database.

individual securities, and the benefits of diversification within a hedge fund portfolio are expected to be similar to the benefits of diversification within a stock portfolio.

The tremendous challenge in portfolio construction again arises from short return histories commonly found for hedge funds. Hedge funds with attractive long-run return histories are often closed to new money, so hedge fund investors may find themselves putting together portfolios of managers with short return histories of varying lengths. In addition, strategies change as managers respond to market conditions, incubate new strategies, and modify their investment approaches. Once again, using judgment as well as quantitative methods is extremely important. In some cases, the greatest use of quantitative tools is as a means of checking return and risk assumptions for reasonableness.

Few hedge funds are managed to a consistent level of volatility or beta. Typically, only funds based on quantitative processes target beta and standard deviation of returns, while most other managers use heuristic approaches to portfolio construction. In addition, many hedge fund managers vary portfolio risk characteristics as a part of their investment process, based on their views. Most vary total exposures, and many vary market exposure. Consequently, long-term volatility and correlation assumptions for portfolio construction purposes may be difficult to assess, and decisions based on short-term risk characteristics present the hazard of quick changes in portfolio risk.

Further complicating matters is the fact that measuring risk is not straightforward for some hedge fund strategies. An example is merger arbitrage. A typical merger arbitrage trade involves purchasing shares in the target of an announced acquisition and selling short shares of the acquiring firm, in proportions consistent with the terms of the bid. For example, if the acquirer offers two shares for each share of the target, then the merger arbitrageur would purchase one share of the target and sell short two shares of the acquirer to be neutral. The spread in value between the long and short positions of this trade represents the market's assessment of the likelihood that the deal will break. The wider the spread, the more probability the market assigns to a failed bid. In fact, the major risk of a merger is that the deal breaks, and the spread on the neutral position above widens. This risk is not captured in typical equity risk models, and is not necessarily symmetrically distributed. Suppose that the spread is 6 percent, and the spread may widen to 20 percent if the deal breaks. The arbitrageur can earn the 6 percent spread or can see the spread widen to 20 percent and lose 14 percent.

In light of these data shortcomings, building a portfolio of hedge funds is not simply a quantitative optimization problem. Nevertheless, expected returns and risks need to be balanced in arriving at the final portfolio. Using the views developed for each manager, the hedge fund investor must weigh expected returns against expected contribution to portfolio risk. Keeping in mind the caveats previously addressed, quantitative measures of risk will probably be considered. In addition, careful analysis of the expected payoffs to each hedge fund's strategy will be incorporated into the final decision.

Potential constraints that will be forced on the portfolio arise from closed managers and fund illiquidity. The fact that some of the investors' favorite hedge funds may be closed clearly reduces expected returns. Illiquidity can also remove a fund from consideration, or can cause the investor to require higher expected returns to justify investing in the hedge fund.

MONITORING

Hedge fund investing requires a commitment to monitoring hedge funds and the portfolio of hedge funds. Monitoring involves both a quantitative and a qualitative approach. Returns data and other available data may be used to evaluate each hedge fund's return profile for consistency with the stated investment strategy. In addition, regular contact with the manager will foster dialogue and understanding of the manager's approach and adherence to that approach.

Much of hedge fund monitoring is intended to detect style drift. Style drift occurs when the hedge fund's investments are inconsistent with its articulated strategy. This drift could take any one of a number of forms, including changes in the types of assets in the manager's universe or changes in the manager's portfolio construction rules or risk process. Although some changes may be welcomed, investors should be aware of shifts so that expectations and portfolio allocations can be adjusted accordingly. In some cases, style drift may justify termination of the manager.

For investors who receive only fund net asset values, style drift may be detected by observing returns and noticing outsized positive or negative returns, or that the strategy does not exhibit expected correlations. If a greater degree of portfolio transparency is available, and if sufficient infrastructure and analytical tools are in place, analysis of portfolio positions is an excellent means of evaluating the hedge fund's adherence to the stated style.

Organizational changes may adversely affect returns. Material changes in personnel, assets under management, or service providers are examples of organizational changes of which an investor will want to be aware.

In addition to monitoring individual hedge funds, the portfolio of funds must be reviewed to assess whether it continues to meet its objectives, and to ensure that allocations to funds continue to appropriately balance expected return and contribution to risk. Changes in fund strategies or markets may alter correlations between funds as well as their expected returns and risk, changing the portfolio's risk/return profile. Consequently, monitoring will attempt to flag changes in expected return and risk for the portfolio of hedge funds.

ONGOING PORTFOLIO MANAGEMENT

After initiation, investors reevaluate their portfolios and may choose to reallocate capital. For the most part, this is simply a matter of continually running through the process of manager evaluation and portfolio construction. Regular decisions are made about increasing and decreasing allocations to managers and strategies, with the extremes being addition of new hedge funds or termination of existing managers. Reasons for terminating a manager include poor returns, organizational turmoil, and style drift. There is an important and unique consideration related to the performance fee and high-water mark, however, that arises in deciding to adjust hedge fund allocations.

Suppose a \$1 million investment has been made in Hedge Fund A, but that this manager has lost 20 percent of the fund's assets since the investment was made. NAV is now \$800,000. The hedge fund investor wants to replace Hedge Fund A with Hedge Fund B, which executes roughly the same strategy, but has performed better over the same period. If A's and B's strategies are going to be highly correlated in the future, then the investor needs to consider the "free ride" that will be enjoyed in not having to pay the performance fee to Hedge Fund A. The free ride occurs because the investor does not have to pay performance fees until Hedge Fund A's NAV returns to the high-water mark. Consequently, from the $800,000 NAV, the investor can receive a return of 25 percent without paying fees. In contrast, suppose the investor terminates Hedge Fund A and invests in Hedge Fund B, and that Hedge Fund B returns 25 percent gross. Assuming a performance fee of 20 percent, the investor receives only 20 percent net returns. Clearly, if Hedge Fund A and Hedge Fund B have identical gross returns over the next year, the net returns to Hedge Fund A will be higher than those to Hedge Fund B since no performance fee will be paid to Hedge Fund A. The implication of this is that there may be an incentive at the margin to not actively trade hedge funds.

FUNDS OF HEDGE FUNDS

For investors who do not have the resources or expertise to invest in a portfolio of hedge funds, there are funds of hedge funds. These investment firms may operate in one or all of the four hedge fund sectors outlined in Figure 27.2.

A fund of funds may be able to obtain better access to information and to managers than may individuals investing on their own behalf. Funds of funds also offer the opportunity to invest in a diversified portfolio with a low minimum amount. Most hedge funds require a minimum investment of $1 million. A fund of funds makes it possible for investors to have well-diversified hedge fund portfolios for lower investment amounts than would otherwise be the case. Finally, the fund of funds offers access to professional investment management, including manager evaluation, portfolio construction, and monitoring.

CHAPTER 28

Investing in Private Equity

Barry Griffiths

What is private equity, and why should investors consider it as part of an overall portfolio? In this chapter, we will consider private equity to be any ownership interest not publicly traded, anywhere in the world, except for real estate. Under this definition, private equity is an enormous asset class, including everything from local dry-cleaning shops to very large industrial enterprises, and from new start-ups with one or two employees and no revenues to firms of long standing with thousands of employees and stable revenue streams.

Compared with public equity, private equity has some advantages as an investment. Fundamentally, the fact that these companies are private means that information about them may not always flow efficiently. This creates an opportunity for managers with superior skill or information to generate unusually large returns. On the other hand, this very lack of widely available information makes it more difficult to apply the equilibrium approach developed in this book.

In this chapter we will discuss the basic rationale for private equity investments, the mechanics of investing in private equity, and limitations on information about valuation and returns. Finally we shall examine an approach to including private equity in a global asset allocation strategy.

WHY PRIVATE EQUITY?

Private equity sometimes has the reputation of being an alternative asset class, with the suggestion that it is somehow new or strange. A moment's reflection will show that this is not the case. Markets for publicly traded assets are relatively new, with histories of up to a few centuries and substantial size starting only in the nineteenth century. Most prior economic ownership, therefore, must have been private. And indeed, private equity today is in many ways an old-fashioned asset class.

The basic assumptions underlying modern finance usually start with the following ideas:

- Information about economic opportunities spreads quickly to all market participants.
- Markets are highly liquid.

- Transaction costs are low.
- As a result, arbitrage opportunities are severely limited and transient.

In private equity, none of these basic assumptions are true. Although this fact can be a handicap to analysis, it can also be the source of excess returns to investors who understand the private equity market.

Private equity managers can have an informational advantage in assessing transactions and making investment decisions. In public markets, information is thoroughly regulated and available to many potential investors. In private markets, information is less readily available and much less transparent. The sales of most private companies, for example, are not widely advertised—private equity investors with a large network of contacts and deal sources hear about more deals and have the ability to access those deals. In addition, few private companies issue annual reports or discuss their performance or financial condition. This lack of information means that those investors who engage in thorough and skilled due diligence can make better decisions than other buyers. They can spot hidden value or uncover problems that will influence their views of companies and valuations.

Private equity investors also have a chance to add value and make a difference to both start-up companies and larger businesses in need of restructuring or repositioning. Unlike public market investors, who are generally passive owners of small interests in companies, the best private equity investors often control companies and boards of directors, choose management, drive strategy, and affect operational and financial decisions. They also generally can decide how and when to exit an investment, an important advantage that can have a significant effect on investment returns. In addition, while the lack of liquidity in private markets carries risks, private equity investors are often compensated for this risk by often being able to acquire companies at prices lower than comparable, publicly traded companies. The lower prices sometimes come from a less efficient sales process—private equity investors may buy companies outside of auctions where there is less competition and much less information on market prices.

Finally, unlike their public counterparts, private companies do not live under the scrutiny of thousands of investors who are highly focused on quarterly results. Private equity investors have a fairly long-term view of investments (typically five years or more), and are willing to accept short-term losses and significant capital investment projects that they believe will create value when they choose to exit the investment.

TYPES OF PRIVATE EQUITY INVESTMENT

It is often thought that private equity investments are either new-company startups or possibly transactions in which existing public companies are taken private. In fact, there are a large number of strategies in private equity investing, as depicted in Figure 28.1. These span the entire life of an enterprise, from a seed-stage startup, through development and expansion, to possible turnaround and distressed investments.

It is not surprising that these various private equity strategies have different economic sources of risk and return. For example, companies that involve innovations in technology or business models might be expected to have returns that are

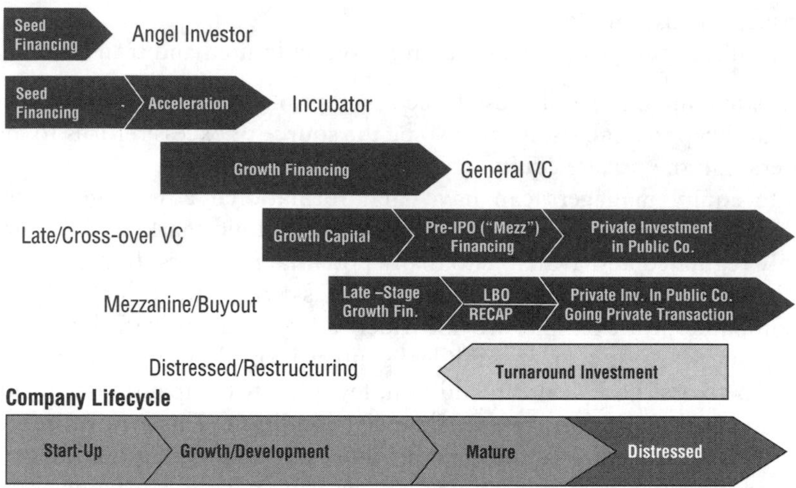

FIGURE 28.1 What Is Private Equity?

based substantially on the effectiveness of the innovation, and would have relatively little to do with trends in the public equity market. Businesses of this kind could be classic start-up or venture investments, but could just as easily be growth or turnaround deals.

Other kinds of private investments might have returns that are substantially based on the public equity market. In one obvious case, some buyout investments involve nothing more than applying a higher degree of financial leverage than similar public companies. In such a case, it is clear that the returns will be highly correlated with the public market. Less obviously, some start-up or venture investments are really just copies of other recent successful start-ups. To the extent that such an investment has little that is really new in its sources of risk and return, it might be expected to be reasonably highly correlated with some portion of the public equity market. This was seen clearly in the Internet and telecom bubbles of 1998–2000, when many copycat start-ups were found to have returns strongly correlated with returns in the public market.

We can see that different portfolios of private equity may have very different risk characteristics. Risk in private equity is thought to be related to several factors, including:

- Strategy (as described earlier)
- Industry or sector
- Company size
- Geography

Thus, a portfolio of private equity investments consisting of nothing but California-based, early-stage technology start-ups with enterprise value under $10 million might be expected to have very different risk characteristics from a portfolio of buyouts of European industrial companies in turnaround situations. Either portfolio might be expected to differ markedly from a mixed portfolio that incorporates a blend of sectors, industries, company sizes, and locations. And none of these would be expected to closely resemble a portfolio of whatever commitments the world's private equity investors made in a given year.

MECHANICS OF PRIVATE EQUITY INVESTMENT

Private equity investments are not readily accessible to investors in the same way that publicly traded equity investments are. Where publicly traded securities can be bought and sold at any time, without necessarily changing control of the firm, private companies have no such open market. Most private equity transactions are between individuals or firms, and typically involve a change of control—that is, the new investors generally buy the company from the previous owners.

However, some portion of private equity investments are accessible to financial investors. The most common way this is done is through partnership interests. A partnership will be formed with a general partner, who usually has some form of experience and expertise in a particular kind of private equity investment. The financial investors are limited partners, who don't usually provide cash when the partnership is formed but instead make commitments to provide cash when called upon. These commitments are for a limited size and for a limited period of time (typically five years).

When the general partner finds an attractive investment, he or she will make a capital call on the commitments of the limited partners in order to finance the purchase. The general partner then manages the investment for some period of time, which may involve working with corporate management of the investment, installing new management, helping with operational matters, or adding value in other ways. Finally the investment is liquidated, often by an initial public offering (IPO) or sale to another buyer, and the proceeds are distributed to the partners. This cycle often takes five years or more for each such investment, although shorter investments are also possible.

The limited partners typically pay fees to the general partner for managing the investments. In addition, the general partner usually receives a fraction of the profits, if any, on each investment (commonly in the vicinity of 20 percent). This fraction of profits is often called a *carried interest.*

Once a commitment to a private equity partnership is made, it is not readily exited. General partners will not usually release limited partners from commitments, as this would compromise their ability to make investments on behalf of the partnership. Although there are some secondary buyers for limited partnership interests, these transactions are often time-consuming and usually require the consent of the general partner for the transfer.

VALUATION AND RETURN STATISTICS IN PRIVATE EQUITY

Since private equity investments do not trade regularly, there are difficulties in establishing valuations for them, and consequent difficulties in estimating return statistics for private equity as a class. Most private equity partnerships follow simple rules when reporting investment values between transactions. Typically, an investment will be held at cost, or at the value of the most recent significant transaction by an outside investor. When an investment goes public, is sold, or goes out of business, the obvious valuations can be applied. In addition, general partners often have wide discretion in applying modified valuations when circumstances appear to warrant doing so.

Thus, if there are no transactions in a private business for some period of time, the valuations reported to investors can be seriously out-of-date. For example, consider the case of a business that is able to finance expansion out of its own cash flow. Additional rounds of investment may not be required for some years, so that the reported valuation may not change at all while the true economic value of the business increases markedly. By contrast, a failing business may not be able to raise additional capital, and so its valuation might be held at cost until it ceases operations.

In an entire partnership, it is unusual for all of the investments to have transactions at any one time, so the valuation of the partnership as a whole is almost always out-of-date to some extent. The only times at which the valuations of a partnership can be wholly relied on are at inception (when no investments have yet been made) and at termination (when all investments have been liquidated and the proceeds distributed). Since private equity valuations are always out-of-date, periodic return series for single investments or partnerships are highly unreliable. And, since periodic return series are highly unreliable, so too are estimates of mean return, volatility, or covariance with any other asset.

As a result, the most commonly quoted measure of performance in private equity is internal rate of return (IRR), which is computed from cash flows (whenever they occur) and the residual value of the investments on the date of calculation. By the time an investment or partnership is fully liquidated, the IRR will be reliable, since it uses only fully observable values (cash flows and dates). However, it is of limited utility compared with periodic returns, since it cannot be inferred when or how the gains were actually made.

Because IRR can be reliably measured over the life of a partnership, but periodic returns and risk statistics generally cannot, it can be difficult for private equity investors to fully understand the risk/return trade-offs being made by fund managers. Sometimes, investors may be led to concentrate only on IRR, without asking what the economic sources of risk and return in a partnership might be. Because good statistics are hard to come by, successful private equity investing requires close attention to the economic fundamentals of the underlying investments.

Since private equity is exactly that—private—there is no central reporting organization for valuation or returns. Indeed, private equity partnerships often view their valuation and return statistics as proprietary information, and may have prohibitions against sharing data. There are a few organizations that try to compile data about IRR across the private equity industry, but only a fraction of partnerships share data in this way.[1] Thus, estimates of risk and return in private equity as a class are quite unreliable compared with their counterparts in public markets.

[1]Typically these organizations report statistics of IRR—mean, median, standard deviation, and quartiles are common. It should be noted that standard deviation of IRR is not an estimate of volatility, as it measures dispersion of return among partnerships rather than through time.

HISTORICAL RETURNS IN PRIVATE EQUITY

In Table 28.1 and Figure 28.2, we show historical returns to private equity as reported in the Venture Economics database. As noted earlier, this information has serious limitations, but it is among the best available. We show the internal rate of return that was reported by partnership investment vehicles. In order to deal with the problem of lagged valuations, we break out liquidated partnerships separately from unliquidated partnerships. Liquidated partnerships have exited all of their investments and distributed the proceeds to the investors; these funds were formed mostly between 1980 and 1994. Unliquidated partnerships still have some amount of investments contained in the partnership vehicle, and so the reported IRR depends in part on the valuation determined by the general partners. These funds were formed mostly in the 1990s.

It is clear that these partnerships, whether liquidated or unliquidated, have a strong central tendency, with a median value near 10 percent (after fund fees and carried interest have been accounted for). This is very close to the long-term return of the S&P 500, and suggests that private equity as a class probably does not have significant long-term, aggregate returns in excess of public equity—although, as noted earlier, individual private equity managers may have such returns.

It is also clear that there is a high degree of dispersion among private equity funds in terms of their reported IRRs. The top quartile of private equity funds is located near 20 percent; the bottom quartile is near 0 percent. This dispersion is quite large compared to results for public asset classes.

It is often suggested that the two major kinds of private equity funds—venture and buyout, broadly construed—may have different returns. In any given year this is almost certainly true, but in the aggregate, over time, this appears not to be the case. If we look at the data for liquidated funds from the Venture Economics database, we can see that in the aggregate the distribution of reported returns is roughly similar (see Table 28.2), given the high degree of dispersion and the limited amount of data. In each case, the median return is near 10 percent, but the range between upper-quartile and bottom-quartile funds is near 15 percent.

All of the liquidated funds analyzed here were formed before the stock price bubble of 1998–2000. As more funds are liquidated we may find that the history of

TABLE 28.1 Historical Returns to Private Equity

	U.S. Liquidated	U.S. Unliquidated	Europe Liquidated	Europe Unliquidated
Sample size	345	1,178	84	580
Maximum	243.9%	726.2%	107.9%	265.5%
Upper decile	26.5%	45.6%	21.7%	30.7%
Upper quartile	17.7%	19.8%	13.4%	16.0%
Median	10.1%	5.8%	5.6%	4.9%
Lower quartile	2.6%	–5.2%	–1.1%	0.0%
Minimum	–72.6%	–100.0%	–43.5%	–100.0%
Standard error	1.2	1.4	2.1	1.3

Data source: Thomson Venture Economics.

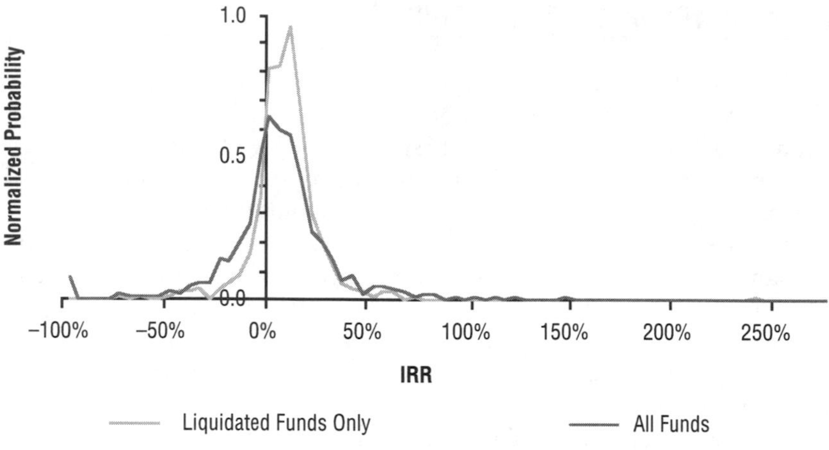

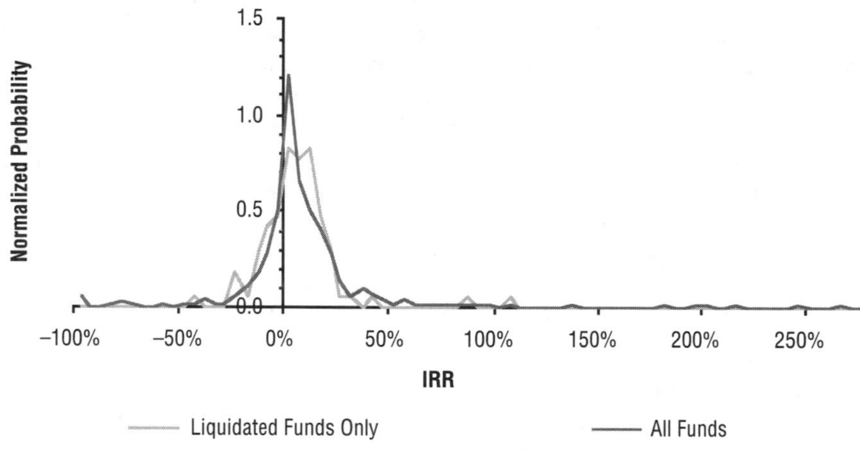

FIGURE 28.2 Distribution of Returns to Private Equity
Data source: Thomson Venture Economics.

TABLE 28.2 Distribution of Reported Returns

	Buyout Liquidated	Venture Liquidated	Buyout Unliquidated	Venture Unliquidated
Sample size	102	327	410	1133
Maximum	243.9%	107.9%	137.8%	726.2%
Upper quartile	22.4%	14.6%	16.2%	19.8%
Median	12.8%	7.9%	5.6%	5.2%
Lower quartile	5.5%	1.3%	–4.1%	–2.6%
Minimum	–42.2%	–72.6%	–100.0%	–100.0%
Standard error	3.4	0.9	1.2	1.5

Data source: Thomson Venture Economics.

relative returns changes somewhat, although it is difficult to predict exactly how. However, it does not appear that an investor should count on systematically different returns from buyout and venture funds.

SOURCES OF RETURN IN PRIVATE EQUITY

Based on the preceding discussion, we can draw several conclusions about building a model of private equity for purposes of asset allocation.

- Standard risk and return statistics for private equity cannot be measured with any degree of reliability.
- Because of the stale valuations, illiquidity, and long commitment periods of the asset class, market weights cannot be used to infer equilibrium expectations.
- Because of the different kinds of private equity strategies, any two portfolios may have different risk and return profiles.
- Risks in private equity are partly, but not solely, related to risk in the public equity markets.
- Returns in private equity are partly related to returns in the public markets, but are partly the result of excess information or skill on the part of the private equity manager.

These conclusions suggest that it would be a mistake to look for a single right answer in making private equity allocations. Instead, it might be better to look for a set of "good enough" answers that depend on the characteristics of the portfolio of private equity that a given investor can create.

Let us provisionally adopt a simple model for returns in a private equity portfolio, decomposing private equity returns into equilibrium and nonequilibrium sources. Suppose that the investor has a portfolio of public equity. The excess returns, r_e, for this portfolio have some equilibrium excess return μ_e and volatility σ_e, as discussed in earlier chapters. The investor wishes to substitute some fraction w of private equity. We will assume that the returns in this particular private equity portfolio have components due to the equilibrium expected return, and due to additional nonequilibrium sources.

$$r_p = \beta r_e + \alpha + \varepsilon \tag{28.1}$$

where β = Market multiplier that accounts for the component of equilibrium return from this public equity portfolio to this private equity portfolio

α = Nonequilibrium component of expected return, due to the investor's superior skill or information operating in the private market

ε = Component of risk in this private equity portfolio that is independent of the public market, with volatility σ_n

It can be seen that the total expected excess return for the private equity portfolio is

$$\mu_p = \beta\mu_e + \alpha \tag{28.2}$$

and the total volatility is

$$\sigma_p^2 = \beta^2\sigma_e^2 + \sigma_n^2 \tag{28.3}$$

As a result, the cross-correlation coefficient ρ between these public equity and private equity portfolios is given by

$$\rho = \frac{\beta\sigma_e}{\sigma_p} \tag{28.4}$$

In both equation (28.2) and equation (28.3) we can see that the expected excess return and the volatility of the private equity portfolio are partly related to the public market, and partly due to investor skill or information (on the one hand) and risks unrelated to the public market (on the other).

What values should be assumed for the parameters α, β, and σ_n? Once again, this will depend on the skill of the investor and the approach taken to diversification, but some observations seem possible.

First, let us consider β. Since private equity is, after all, some kind of equity, a value near 1 seems *a priori* reasonable. For companies that have a strongly innovative component to their business models, a lower value might be expected. For companies that just use a higher degree of financial leverage with no real sources of innovation, or companies that are just copies of recent, successful companies, a value of β closer to 2 might be expected. In addition, the carried interest paid on investments in partnerships can reduce the effective β by about 20 percent. We have performed some simulations that suggest that a value consistent with the Venture Economics database would be near 0.7, but this is subject to all of the qualifications cited earlier regarding the limitations of publicly available data in private equity. Thus, much as in the public equity market, private equity investors can produce portfolios of high or low β, depending on their choices in constructing their portfolios.

Next, let us consider σ_n. Clearly a very small or poorly diversified portfolio of private equity could have a very large value of σ_n, perhaps in the vicinity of 100 percent, which would be consistent with single stocks of companies that have recently gone public. A larger, more diversified portfolio of private equity might have a significantly smaller value. At the lower extreme, a portfolio of 20 partnerships, each with 20 investments, could have

$$\sigma_n = \frac{100\%}{\sqrt{20 \text{ partnerships} \cdot 20 \text{ companies}}} = 5\% \tag{28.5}$$

We have performed some simulations that suggest that a value for a large, well-diversified private equity portfolio, consistent with the Venture Economics database, might be near 15 percent, but once again this is subject to all of the qualifications cited earlier regarding the limitations of the publicly available data. Certainly values of up to 25 percent would not be unreasonable for some private equity portfolios.

Finally, let us consider α. Although the market inefficiencies described earlier make positive values of α possible, this is by no means guaranteed. In addition, investors in private equity partnerships must pay fees, typically reducing expected return by 2 to 3 percent. We have performed some simulations that suggest that a value of α very near zero would be consistent with the data in the Venture Economics database, once again noting the limitations of the data. Here again, different private equity investors can produce portfolios with very different values of α, depending on their choices in manager selection and portfolio construction.

What of manager skill? Examination of the historical data suggests that particular managers with excess skill or information may be able to deliver α of up to 10 percent or even higher (while others, as noted, may have negative α). To the extent that these managers with unusual skill are doing unusual deals, this may also have the effect of lowering β, although in this case the non-public-market risk term σ_n may increase. As has been observed in previous chapters, this can be a good trade—σ_n represents relatively cheap risk, while the public-market component controlled by β is the relatively expensive part.

OPTIMAL ALLOCATION EXAMPLES

In the general, multi-asset case, the model described earlier can be used to augment the global covariance matrix and calculate optimal weights for private equity. However, some additional insight can be gained by considering a simple two-asset situation, where the investor simply wishes to substitute private equity for some fraction w of an existing public-equity portfolio.

Using the results of Chapter 4 and the model defined earlier, we see that the optimal weight for private equity (as a fraction of the total equity portfolio) is given by

$$w_o = \frac{\alpha + \left(\lambda\sigma_e^2 - \mu_e\right)(1-\beta)}{\lambda\left[\sigma_n^2 + (1-\beta)^2\sigma_e^2\right]} \tag{28.6}$$

Here λ is the risk-aversion parameter described earlier in the book.

This is an interesting result for several reasons. First, from the numerator it can be seen that there are essentially two reasons to allocate to private equity. The first is if the private equity portfolio has some positive source of return, α, unrelated to returns in the public market. The second is that if the private equity portfolio has β less than 1, there is also a diversification rationale for an allocation to private equity.

Second, it is interesting to examine the behavior of this allocation for its dependence on the market β. The most important point is that since the multiplier $\lambda\sigma_e^2 - \mu_e$ must be positive, then w_o must decrease as β increases. Thus we see that the rationale for an allocation to private equity must rely in large part on its nonequilibrium innovative components, such as new or innovative businesses.

Third, look at the simplifications that arise if $\beta = 1$. In this case, it can be seen that

$$w_o|_{\beta=1} = \frac{\alpha}{\lambda\sigma_n^2} \tag{28.7}$$

Here we see that if the private equity portfolio has unit dependence on the public equity market, then the allocation to private equity depends only on the specific return and specific volatility of the private equity portfolio, and not on total return or total volatility.

Fourth, consider the special case when the expected excess return for the private equity portfolio is exactly equal to the expected excess return for the public equity portfolio—that is, when

$$\alpha = (1 - \beta)\mu_e \tag{28.8}$$

It is clear that this case is equivalent to selecting a private equity allocation to minimize total volatility in the combined (private plus public) equity portfolio. In this situation, the optimizing allocation to private equity is

$$w_{\min\,vol} = \frac{1-\beta}{\left(\frac{\sigma_n}{\sigma_e}\right)^2 + (1-\beta)^2} \tag{28.9}$$

for any λ. This reinforces our observation that an allocation due solely to diversification effects is only observed for private equity portfolios with β less than 1 with respect to the public equity market.

The graphs in Figure 28.3 illustrate the fraction of the total equity portfolio that might be allocated to private equity, depending on the statistics that are assumed to be achieved for the particular private equity portfolio under consideration. As earlier in the book, in these examples we assume a risk aversion parameter of 2.857, expected excess returns to public equity of 4.1 percent, and public equity volatility of 15.9 percent.

It can be seen that for β less than 1, the allocations to private equity are essentially straight lines, depending principally on the ratio between specific return and specific volatility, as discussed earlier. For β of 1.5, however, the penalty for high dependence on equilibrium public returns is clearly visible.

Some of these allocations may be surprisingly large compared with recommendations seen elsewhere. However, it is clear from this analysis that the optimal allocation to private equity depends on the particular characteristics of the private equity portfolio under consideration, rather than just on the label attached to it. For those investors who can realistically expect to achieve an α of 3.0 percent or more (modest with respect to the dispersion of returns among private equity funds), with β no higher than 1.5, then an allocation to private equity of at least 10 percent of the total equity portfolio is readily justified.

It should be emphasized that these results are for the two-asset case only, and without considering liquidity constraints. Somewhat different results will obtain for the multi-asset case, but the basic analysis is the same and uses the same machinery developed earlier in the book. Since private equity is highly illiquid, investors making allocations to private equity need to carefully consider their needs

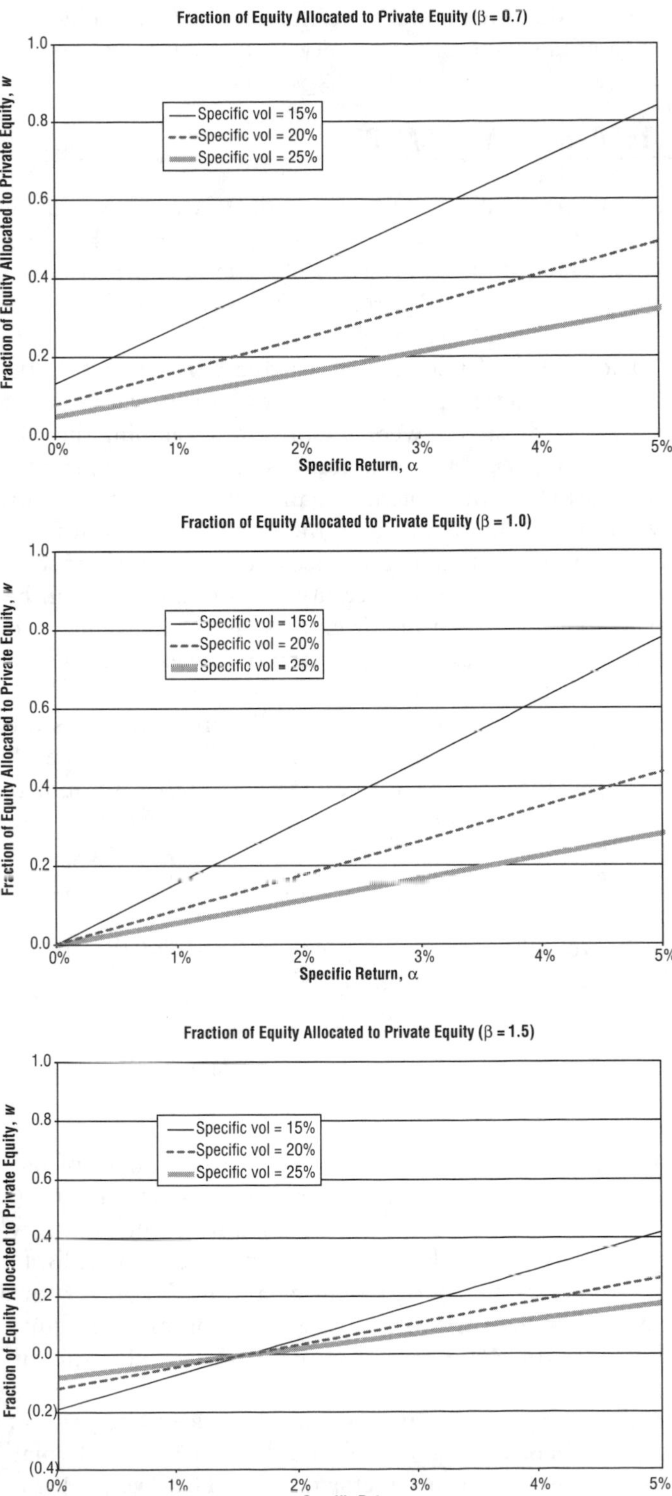

FIGURE 28.3 Fraction of Equity Allocated to Private Equity

for liquidity and the additional liquidity constraints introduced by the need to meet any unfunded commitments to private equity partnerships.

EFFECT OF SUBOPTIMAL ALLOCATION

At this point a fundamental difficulty is observed. We can derive the optimal allocation to private equity as a consequence of estimated statistics, but we have also observed that the estimated statistics are not very reliable. Furthermore, the range of illustrated results (allocation of 10 percent to 50 percent of the equity portfolio to private equity) is rather broad to be useful.

One way to address this difficulty is to calculate the impact on the statistics of the overall equity portfolio if it should turn out that the private equity portfolio has different statistics from those that were assumed in developing the allocation. If reality differs from assumptions, the situation is said to be *suboptimal*. Then the investor can decide whether the potential gains (if the estimates turn out to be accurate) are worth the additional risks (if the estimates turn out to be inaccurate).

For example, suppose that an investor decides, on the basis of some set of parameters, to select a weight w to private equity. (Note that there will be a variety of sets of parameters that may result in any given weight.) As we have shown, this allocation will generally be based (at least in part) on the expectation that the specific return α to the private equity portfolio will be positive.

However, suppose that the α that is actually obtained turns out to be zero. Then the optimal thing to have done (had the true value of α been known at the time of allocation) would have been to allocate a smaller amount to private equity, and possibly none. In this case the investor will have paid a price in terms of increased total equity volatility, without receiving the expected benefit in terms of increased return. What is the impact on total equity volatility of some positive weight w?

The combined volatility for the total equity portfolio that results from a selected weight w, here called σ_T, is given by

$$\left(\frac{\sigma_T}{\sigma_e}\right)^2 = (1-w)^2 + 2\beta w(w-1) + w^2\left[\beta^2 + \left(\frac{\sigma_n}{\sigma_e}\right)^2\right] \tag{28.10}$$

This function is given in Figure 28.4 for the same ranges of parameters discussed earlier. It can be seen that for low weights on private equity (for example, $w = 10\%$), over the range of parameters discussed here, the volatility of the combined equity portfolio increases by no more than a factor of 1.06. (For example, if σ_e were about 16 percent, then σ_T would be about 17 percent for any beta betweeen 1.0 and 1.5.) Many investors have weights on private equity that are up to 10 percent of their total equity portfolios, or even higher, possibly reflecting this observation.

For intermediate weights on private equity the price to be paid, in terms of increased volatility, is steeper. For $w = 25\%$ and β up to 1.0, total volatility is in the same range—an increase of up to a factor of 1.07. However, if β turns out to be 1.5, the increase in total volatility is a factor of 1.19. Thus, it probably makes sense to have a weight on private equity as high as 25 percent only if the investor

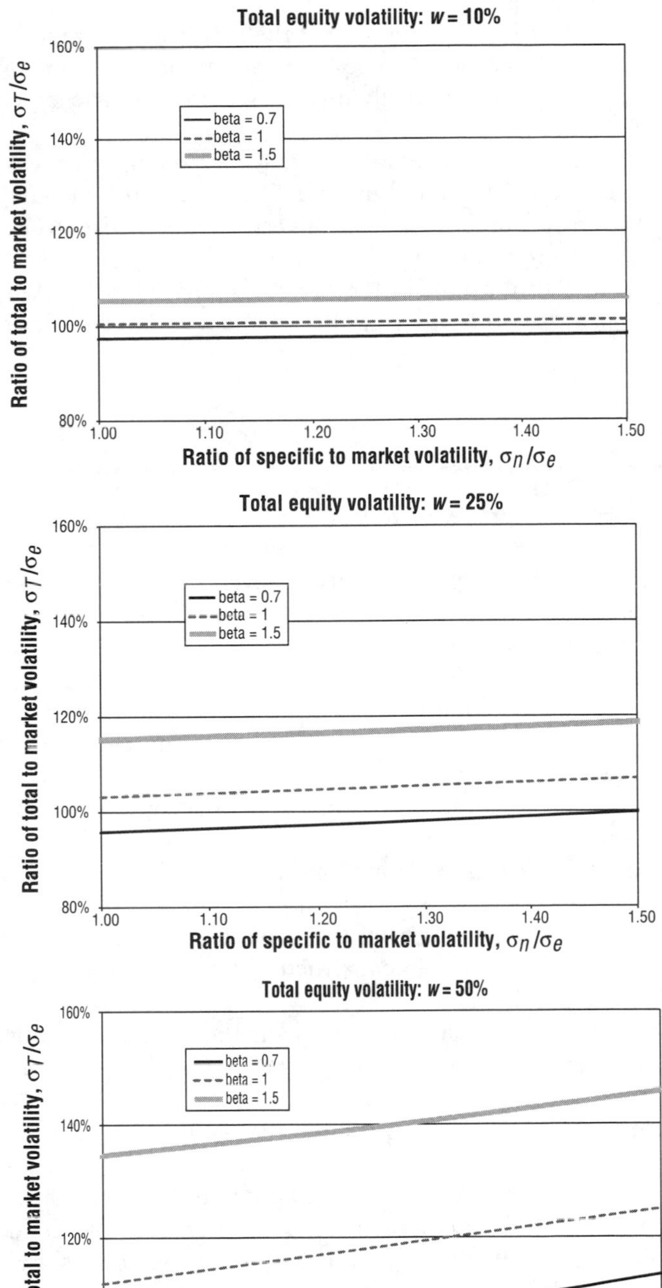

FIGURE 28.4 Total Equity Volatility

is confident of the α that he can obtain, or if the investor is confident that β is not much higher than 1.0. Once again, some investors do have weights on private equity as high as this, but they are usually investors with extensive experience in private equity.

For higher weights on private equity, there is a high degree of sensitivity to the true parameters. For $w = 50\%$ and β up to 1.5, total volatility of the equity portfolio increases by a factor of up to 1.5. An investor who chooses to put 50 percent of her total equity portfolio in private equity must be very confident that she can control the risk and return profile of the private equity portfolio. Otherwise, it is very possible to incur a significant volatility penalty without a corresponding increase in return.

KEY IDEAS

The key ideas in this chapter are the following:

- Private equity differs from public equity in several ways:
  1. In private equity, information does not flow freely.
  2. Private equity is highly illiquid.
  3. Transaction costs are high.
- These factors create the opportunity (but not a guarantee) for higher returns.
- The same factors cause private equity valuations, and resulting returns statistics, to be unreliable.
- Available data on internal rate of return generated by private equity partnerships suggest that median rates of return are roughly comparable to the public equity market, but dispersion among fund managers is much higher than in the public market.
- As a result, the risk and return in any private equity portfolio depend very strongly on how that portfolio is constructed—estimates for private equity as a class are of limited utility.
- We suggest that private equity can be modeled as having a mixture of characteristics that depend on equilibrium returns in the public equity market, and on nonequilibrium non-public-market factors.
- Using a simple two-asset model, we show that simple diversification is usually an inadequate rationale for investing in private equity—these investments only make sense when there is a reasonable likelihood of additional return due to superior information or skill on the part of the private equity manager.
- In order to invest successfully in private equity, great care must be taken to understand the underlying sources of risk and return in the selected private equity investment.
- For specific returns (alpha) of at least 3 percent, and beta no greater than 1.5, it may be optimal to allocate at least 10 percent of the total equity portfolio to private equity, and possibly as much as 50 percent of the total equity portfolio.
- Allocations toward the lower end of this range have only modest penalties for suboptimal allocations, in the event that the parameter estimates that are used turn out to be incorrect. However, the penalties increase markedly toward the high end of the range.

PART Six

Private Wealth

CHAPTER 29

Investing for Real After-Tax Results

Don Mulvihill

Chapters 29 through 32 focus on investment management for individual or family investors. Tax considerations, spending requirements, and estate planning issues greatly complicate the development and implementation of investment strategies. Our goals will be (1) to show that the principles developed in the preceding chapters are relevant to individual investors and (2) to demonstrate ways to accommodate these complicating factors in our formulation of investment analysis.

Individual investors generally seek to preserve and grow the real, after-tax value of their estates. We will focus on investment strategies for wealthy individuals. Such individuals will generally not consume all of their wealth and thus will leave an estate. Integrating estate-planning issues with investment strategies will be a recurring theme in our discussion. Tax rates are always changing and vary from one state to the next. For simplicity, we will assume marginal tax rates of 40 percent on ordinary income and short-term gains and 20 percent on long-term capital gains.[1] We will use these rates in all examples in the following chapters, unless otherwise noted. We will assume a 50 percent estate tax rate.

The efficient frontier is a good visual aid for understanding portfolio management issues. The activities of investment managers and financial advisors generally fall into one of two categories: (1) develop more efficient portfolios by improving the expected return per unit of risk (i.e., shift the efficient frontier upward) or (2) help investors identify and reach the point on the efficient frontier that is appropriate to their circumstances. Many investors and their advisors find it difficult to integrate taxation, estate planning, spending, and inflation issues into their investment analysis. Consequently, they follow a strategy of first seeking to maximize risk-adjusted nominal pretax returns and then dealing with tax, estate, and spending issues. Given the enormous impact of income and estate taxes, this approach is almost certain to lead to inefficient asset allocation and portfolio strategies.

Bob Litterman made the following points concerning risk in Chapter 2:

[1]At the time we wrote this, President Bush has just announced a proposal to eliminate tax on dividends. The calculations made throughout this book assume that dividends are taxable.

- Risk is the energy that in the long run drives investment returns.
- Individuals have limited tolerance for risk. This is related to their capacity to endure both short-term and long-term fluctuations in wealth.
- Risk is therefore a scarce resource that should be budgeted and apportioned in order to get the most expected return for a given level of risk.

Investment management involves first identifying the desired level of risk and then building investment portfolios that maximize the expected return for that level of risk. Taxable investors will easily understand that taxes reduce expected investment *returns*. If you earn a return, the government will take some of it from you. What may be less obvious is that taxes also affect and generally reduce *risk*. Consider the impact of capital gains taxes on equity returns. When stock market returns are high, investors often have a lot of realized capital gains and thus pay a lot of taxes. When market returns are flat there are few realized gains and tax liability is small. When market returns are negative investors often have net realized losses that generate valuable credits in the form of tax loss carryforwards. After-tax returns are generally less volatile and thus less risky than pretax returns.

Taxable investors face income, capital gains, and, in most cases, transfer taxes. Each individual or family is unique. Each has plans for the disposal of one's wealth and an estate structure designed to facilitate those plans. Investors begin from different points. Many investors accumulated their wealth in the form of concentrated low-basis stock holdings and must deal with transition issues. These types of considerations will affect the conversion of expected pretax to expected after-tax risk and return. In order to develop a strategy that maximizes expected after-tax return for a give level of risk, it is necessary to integrate these investor-specific considerations into calculations of after-tax risk and return. As a result, each investor has a unique efficient frontier. Each of the next three chapters will be devoted to gradually integrating various complicating factors into the formulation of an investor-specific efficient frontier. This framework provides three benefits.

1. It provides investors with a practical and customized tool for identifying a target level of risk. This comes from describing risk in terms of the dispersion of future after-tax wealth forecasts.
2. It allows taxable investors to integrate income, capital gains, and transfer taxes into investment decisions in order to optimally allocate the budgeted level of risk.
3. It suggests ways that investors can enhance expected after-tax return for a given level of risk by better understanding the interplay among estate planning, income tax planning, asset allocation, and portfolio management.

The axes of a conventional efficient frontier chart are expected return and risk. In order to integrate income and transfer tax considerations, we are going to develop an efficient frontier chart that plots expected future after-tax wealth against risk. There are many options embedded in the 40,000 pages of the U.S. tax code. The efficient frontier chart that we will develop will plot the trade-off between expected future after-tax wealth and risk assuming the investor has made optimal use of some of these options as they apply to that investor's situation. In the course of developing this chart, we will demonstrate that taking advantage of the flexibility in the tax code will allow for meaningful improvement in real after-tax wealth accumulation.

Chapter 30 reviews the historic returns of U.S. stocks, bonds, and bills over the past 76 years and adjusts these returns for the impact of income taxes and inflation. These adjusted returns are used to create an efficient frontier that plots expected future real after-tax wealth against volatility in the distribution of expected future wealth. This will be based on just these three asset classes. Our analysis will demonstrate that the conversion from nominal pretax returns to real after-tax returns reduces the perceived riskiness of stocks and increases the perceived riskiness of bills. The reader should get a sense of how difficult it can be to grow wealth net of the impact of taxes and inflation.

Chapter 31 integrates estate-planning issues into risk and return calculations. Entities such as retirement accounts, charitable trusts, grantor trusts, and foundations have unique income and estate tax characteristics. *Asset location* refers to the positioning of the various components of an asset allocation plan among the various entities that make up an investor's estate. Careful asset location can enhance the transfer of wealth to heirs and/or charities by taking advantage of the income and estate tax characteristics of these entities. The traditional efficient frontier assumes optimal allocation of assets. Chapter 31 develops an efficient frontier that also assumes the optimal location of assets. This efficient frontier will reflect the combinations of asset *allocation* and asset *location* that give the highest expected result per unit of risk. The construction of the efficient frontier will reflect the investor's plans for long-term wealth transfer. The chart will plot the expected real net transfer of wealth to designated heirs and/or charities against the volatility of the expected real net transfer.

Chapter 32 analyzes the impact of taxes on equity portfolio management. Capital gains taxes are due only when a security is sold. The investor generally controls the decision to sell and therefore can defer taxes. Linking the deferral of taxes to plans for the ultimate disposal of the assets can enable an investor to avoid taxation on unrealized gains. This creates a tension between the desire to enhance pretax returns through active portfolio management and the desire to enhance after-tax returns through tax deferral. Chapter 32 explores ways to deal with this conflict and also reviews tax loss harvesting as a mechanism for enhancing after-tax returns from equities.

The remainder of this chapter develops a planning framework that reflects the objectives of wealthy investors and allows for the integration of the factors that complicate investment planning for taxable investors. Inflation and spending requirements are considered within that framework. There is a general review of how taxes are assessed and ways investors can reduce tax liabilities. The chapter concludes with an analysis of how to calculate after-tax returns in a manner that reflects the investor's specific planning framework.

PLANNING FRAMEWORK

At its most basic level, investment management for tax-exempt investors is a two-dimensional problem. The dimensions are risk and return. Investment management, at its core, involves adjusting the expected risk/return trade-off in an attempt to get to a desirable point on the efficient frontier. Individual investors face a multidimensional problem. Taxes, estate planning, and nonfinancial considerations related to estate planning make an already complex problem much more complex.

Wealthy individuals will generally not consume all of their wealth. Consumption patterns vary a great deal from one investor to the next, but as a general statement it is true that the wealthier the individual, the greater the proportion of the estate that will go to heirs or charity. A wealthy individual can be thought of as a steward of wealth. Their wealth exceeds their consumption needs, so they are managing their estates on behalf of future beneficiaries. These could be any combination of charities, immediate heirs, and future generations.

The first step in investment management for individuals is to formulate the problem in a way that accommodates these complicating factors and maintains a focus on the key variables of risk and return. Most wealthy investors can formulate their problem as:

> *Subject to funding my consumption needs, maximize the risk-adjusted real value of wealth that will be received, net of income and transfer taxes, by my intended heirs and charitable beneficiaries.*

This formulation is useful because it allows investors to evaluate estate planning, asset allocation, and portfolio management strategies in a consistent manner. Any potential decision can be analyzed in terms of its impact on the expected after-tax real proceeds received by heirs and charities. The expectation of after-tax proceeds can be viewed as a distribution. It has a mean, a median, and a standard deviation. This formulation brings us back to our familiar trade-off between return and risk. It enables us to apply the tools of modern portfolio management to the issues facing individual investors. For example, if an investor is considering a change in asset allocation policy, the proposal can be evaluated in terms of its impact on the distribution of expected future net proceeds. Does the proposed change in asset allocation policy increase or decrease the expected mean? Does it widen or narrow the distribution of expected outcomes? Taxation, estate plans, and spending requirements complicate the calculation of expected after-tax return and expected after-tax risk. One of the key differences between managing the assets of taxable and tax-exempt investors is that these calculations are investor-specific for taxable investors. While these calculations may be complex, they are required in order to properly apply modern portfolio theory to the issues of a taxable investor.

TAXATION

There are four key forms of taxation to be considered (as of December 2002):

1. ***Income tax*** is applied to taxable interest and dividends using the ordinary tax rate.
2. ***Capital gains tax*** is applied to realized gains and losses. Positions held one year or less are taxed as short-term using the ordinary tax rate. Positions held more than one year are taxed as long-term using the long-term tax rate. Capital gains taxes can be avoided through charitable giving or death. If appreciated assets are given to charity, there is no capital gains tax due on the appreciation. If appreciated assets are held until death, the cost basis is "stepped up" to the current market value, eliminating the potential tax liability. These elements of

the tax code are important to wealthy investors who will not consume much of their wealth.

3. ***Gift tax*** is applied to gifts made to heirs and other noncharitable beneficiaries by a living donor. The tax rate is graduated but quickly reaches 55 percent. There is a lifetime exemption that is currently $1,000,000 per donor. This is scheduled to rise to $3,500,000 by 2009. A husband and wife can be considered separate donors, thus doubling the amount of wealth that could be passed to children free of transfer tax. In addition to this lifetime exemption, individuals may give up to $11,000 per year to an unlimited number of recipients. This will not count against their lifetime exemptions. Thus, a husband and wife could each give up to $11,000 per year to each child and grandchild. The annual allowance plus the lifetime exemption are sufficient to allow most Americans to avoid paying pay gift or estate taxes.
4. ***Estate tax*** is similar to and intertwined with the gift tax. Gift and estate taxes are sometimes referred to as transfer taxes. Estate taxes are applied to bequests to noncharitable recipients from the estate of a deceased person. There is a lifetime exemption, which is the same exemption applied to the gift tax. Any usage of this exemption to avoid tax on gifts reduces the exemption left to apply to the estate tax. There are two important distinctions between the gift and estate taxes.

    (1) Appreciated assets given by a living donor will retain their cost basis. Thus, the recipient will have a contingent tax liability on such assets and will be liable for capital gains taxes if the assets are sold at a price greater than the original cost basis. Conversely, appreciated assets in the estate of a deceased person receive a step-up in basis. The cost basis of the assets is increased to the market value at the time of the donor's death. This wipes out capital gains tax liability on appreciated assets.

    (2) Estate tax is calculated on a tax-inclusive basis (i.e., the tax is applied to the entire amount of the estate including the portion that will be used to pay the tax). Table 29.1 illustrates this point. There is a clear tax advantage to giving wealth to children sooner, by gift, rather than later by bequest. This can create tensions within a family, sometimes with cruel consequences.

This is a very brief summary of the key elements of the tax code affecting investors as of August 2002. The federal tax code is extremely complex with over 40,000 pages. It is safe to say that 250 million Americans are subject to a tax code than no human being can fully understand! The tax code is constantly being revised. The complexity is a function of the various objectives pursued by the legislators who write the tax code. These include raising revenue, encouraging and discouraging certain activities and targeting redistribution of wealth. The complexity of the tax code seems to accumulate much like barnacles on a ship. It appears the legislators care little about the administrative burden that their unnecessarily complex tax code imposes upon individuals and businesses. This is unfortunate because the enormous aggregate cost of compliance is a squandering of society's resources on an unproductive activity.

Transfer taxes are in an unusual state of flux. They are currently scheduled to gradually decline for nine more years, then go to zero for one year, then revert back

TABLE 29.1 Comparison of Gift and Estate Tax

Assume that all lifetime exemptions have already been used and use a 50% rate.

Gift Tax		Estate Tax	
Parent gives child $1,000,000	$1,000,000	Parent dies and leaves $1,500,000 to child	$1,500,000
Parent owes 50% gift tax	$500,000	Estate owes 50% estate tax	$750,000
Net to child	$1,000,000	Net to child	$750,000
Total cost to parent	$1,500,000	Total cost to parent's estate	$1,500,000
Child's net/total cost	66%	Child's net/total cost	50%
Effective tax rate	33%	Effective tax rate	50%

to the full 55 percent rate in the following year. This level of uncertainty plays havoc with estate planning.

Tax considerations impact analysis in several ways.

1. Not all returns are equal. Municipal bond interest is generally free of federal tax. Income and dividends are taxed immediately at ordinary tax rates while appreciation is taxed if and when realized at either short- or long-term tax rates.
2. Disposal plans affect taxation. Capital gains taxes on unrealized gains can be avoided if appreciated assets are given to charity or held until death.[2]
3. Reallocation is costly. Equities tend to appreciate, so the reallocation of an individual's assets may require the payment of capital gains taxes. This is one of the most significant differences relative to investment planning for tax-exempt investors. This issue is particularly relevant for individuals who create their wealth through the ownership of a business. A public offering or stock swap can create the situation where much of the individual's wealth is in a single low-cost-basis stock. Sale of the position to diversify and reduce risk will require a large capital gains tax payment. There are estate planning and hedging strategies that can reduce the tax burden required to diversify from a concentrated and appreciated position.
4. Estate planning structures complicate the calculation of expected after-tax return. Individuals often have various entities within which they can hold assets. Examples include grantor trusts, charitable trusts, family limited partnerships, retirement accounts, and foundations. Each has its own income, gift, and estate tax characteristics. For example, an IRA defers taxation on all returns, converts all returns to ordinary income, and is not eligible for the step-up basis at death. Thus, the expected *after-tax* return of an asset, factoring in both income and transfer taxes, can vary greatly depending on the type of entity in which it is held.

[2]The tax-free step-up in basis eliminates tax liability on unrealized gains at death. This feature of the tax code is related to the estate tax and might be eliminated if the estate tax is eliminated.

Taxes represent a formidable challenge to an investor seeking to preserve and grow the value of an estate on behalf of his or her heirs. Roughly speaking, the government wants about one-third of what you earn and half of what you have when you die. Individuals often view the IRS as an enemy who relentlessly confiscates a significant portion of their income. This is a reasonable assessment for ordinary income items such as salary and interest. However, investors interested in capital appreciation have a more complex relationship with the IRS. In this situation the IRS can be viewed as a partner whose influence can be at times costly and at other times beneficial. We have no choice but to live with this partner, so it is important to understand how the IRS operates. In a world without taxes, an investor who owns an asset sees a direct relationship between the future price of the asset and his gain or loss (e.g., the investor's return is 10 percent if the asset appreciates by 10 percent). The situation changes when the IRS becomes our partner. With the introduction of long-term capital gains taxes, the tax man says: "If you earn a positive return, give me 20 percent of it; if you earn a negative return, I will refund 20 percent of the loss."

This is the essence of our relationship with the IRS with respect to appreciation. However, our uninvited partner adds four important caveats—and three of these actually favor the taxpayer:

- *The timing option.* Capital gains taxes are due only when an investment is sold. You decide when to cash in your chips and settle up with the IRS.
- *The short-term option.* The IRS will bear 40 percent of the loss if you earn a negative return during the first year. If you earn a positive return, you can let the gain ride, holding the position for at least one year. When you eventually sell, the IRS takes only 20 percent of the gain.
- *The disposal option.* The IRS waives its claim to capital gains tax on your appreciation on assets you give to charity or hold until death (the step-up in basis).

The fourth caveat limits the tax man's generosity:

- *No absolute subsidy.* The IRS will not subsidize overall net losses. Realized losses can only be netted against gains or carried forward to offset future gains.[3] The IRS will bear part of a realized loss only if the investor has other realized gains against which to net the loss.

Taxes lower the expected return on investments. Capital gains taxes make the government a de facto partner in all investment activities. The terms of this partnership are complicated, and a number of its terms can be worked to the investor's benefit. The option of a tax-free step-up in basis, the ability to defer recognition of gains and accelerate recognition of losses, asset allocation and asset location

[3]Taxpayers are allowed to deduct up to $3,000 in realized losses from ordinary income. Excess losses can be carried forward.

choices, the use of leverage, the opportunity to use tax-deferring entities and other tax-related choices all provide opportunities to reduce the impact of taxes on wealth accumulation.

An important aspect of managing wealth for individuals is to make optimal use of these options. These options are very different from traded options in that they are not priced. They are free. The government put the options into the tax code. Making good use of them can risklessly enhance the after-tax accumulation of wealth.

INFLATION

Inflation is an important consideration. Money is given to future beneficiaries for a reason. The hope is that a bequest will help heirs to buy a home, pay for grandchildren's education, purchase cars, and so on. Likewise, the hope is that charitable beneficiaries can use the gift to purchase goods and services in pursuit of their objectives. Inflation relentlessly reduces the amount of homes, education, and other goods and services that an estate can provide. Further, spending requirements are likely to rise over time with inflation and will thus claim an increasing proportion of an estate that fails to grow at the rate of inflation.

Inflation is a silent destroyer of wealth. Its impact is never listed on brokerage statements, investment reports, or tax returns. Nevertheless, it has reduced the value of estates by an average of 3.0 percent per year since 1925. There have been periods when inflation has been much higher. Inflation averaged 7.3 percent per year during the 1970s. More recently, inflation averaged 2.9 percent during the 1990s. This is considered to be benign, yet, even at these levels, the purchasing power of a dollar is reduced by almost 40 percent over 20 years' time. Today's 3.0 percent expected inflation exceeds the after-tax return currently offered by many bonds and money market securities. A negative real return does not serve the goal of preserving and growing the real value of an estate. In the next chapter we will see how "safe" investments such as Treasury bills have rarely provided a positive real after-tax return.

Inflation affects investment planning in two ways. The first is obvious. Inflation reduces the real value of future dollars. The second is that inflation affects future spending requirements. An investor who currently withdraws a fixed amount from his portfolio to meet his annual spending needs should expect that this amount will grow with the rate of inflation, all other things being equal. This introduces a new risk. Unexpected inflation tends to reduce the market value of financial instruments while at the same time increasing spending requirements. This combination can increase spending as a percentage of the portfolio's value. A spending policy that had seemed reasonable could become unsustainable.

SPENDING

Some investors use their financial assets to fund their living expenses, while others can use ongoing employment income. Spending requirements have an impact similar to inflation and taxation in that they detract from the preservation and growth of an estate. Spending tends to be inflexible. Declining markets will reduce the value of an estate, and therefore if spending remains unchanged it will consume a larger percentage of the individual's assets. Spending requirements will tend to rise with inflation. This can intensify the adverse impact of inflation. Markets often react badly to a surge in the rate of inflation. Declining nominal market returns, declining real asset values, and increased spending requirements would obviously be a difficult combination, possibly leading to accelerating sales of assets at depressed prices.

The feasibility of a spending policy must be considered in combination with the impact of taxation and inflation. Preservation of an estate's real value requires that investment returns are at least equal to the sum of taxation, inflation, and spending. If we assume that income and capital gains taxes will take about 30 percent of investment returns, then spending should not exceed (70% × Pretax investment return) – Inflation. If we plug in some numbers that seem reasonable based on historic averages, an 8.0 percent pretax investment return and 3.0 percent inflation would allow for spending 2.6 percent of a portfolio's value. This calculation does not allow for spending increases linked to inflation. Based on horizon and expected inflation, the sustainable spending rate is something less than 2.6 percent.

When considering sustainable spending policies, investors should consider the range of possible outcomes rather than simply the mean expected return. In an environment of low or negative portfolio returns, fixed real spending requirements will consume an increasing portion of the portfolio's value. This can lead to an accelerating downward spiral. At the end of Chapter 30 we will show that even modest spending requirements can cause significant deterioration in worst-case forecasts.

CALCULATING AFTER-TAX RETURNS

Investment decisions should be based on expected after-tax returns. Investment horizon, the method by which an asset is disposed of, and the tax characteristics of the entity that holds an asset all affect the calculation of expected after-tax return. Let us use an equity index fund to illustrate. We will expect a 2 percent dividend yield and 8 percent annual appreciation. Dividends will be paid at the end of the year, they will be subject to income tax, and the net dividend will be reinvested. All appreciation will be unrealized until the fund is sold.

Horizon

The investor expects to sell after one year. Taxes will be 40% × 2% + 20% × 8% = 2.4%.

The expected after-tax return is 7.6%.

We define the effective tax rate as 1 – (After-tax return/Pretax return).

In this case, the effective tax rate is 24%.

Let us now change the assumption to a five-year holding period. This will allow appreciation to compound on a pretax basis. Table 29.2 shows the expected growth in value and cost basis.

The sale will produce gross proceeds of $155.28 and will require a capital gains tax of 20 percent of the surplus over the cost basis. This yields net proceeds of $145.67. This is an annualized after-tax return of 7.81 percent. Deferring the payment of capital gains taxes increased the expected after-tax return from 7.60 percent to 7.81 percent. This reduced the effective tax rate to 21.9 percent. Extending the example to 10 years produces an expected after-tax return of 8.03 percent, an effective tax rate of 19.7 percent. A 25-year holding period produces an 8.47 percent expected after-tax return, an effective tax rate of 15.3 percent. Deferral reduces the impact of capital gains taxes.

Disposal

The previous example assumed that the investor would sell at the end of the horizon. What if the investor did not sell? There are only four ways an investor can dispose of a security: Sell it, give it to an heir while the donor is alive, give it to an heir upon the donor's death, or give it to a charity. Only selling requires immediate payment of capital gains tax. If the asset is transferred to an heir while the donor is alive, the heir assumes the existing cost basis of the asset. If the asset is given to charity or held until death, capital gains taxes are avoided. Many wealthy investors will not consume much of their wealth, and therefore many of their assets may be disposed of by death or charitable giving. We will use the term *bequest mode* to describe the situation in which an investor expects to eventually dispose of an asset in a way that does not require the payment of capital gains taxes. This is the alternative to *liquidation mode* in which an investor is managing an asset with the expectation that it will eventually be sold. In this case, capital gains taxes can be deferred but ultimately must be paid. Referring to the tax options described earlier, an investor in liquidation mode may employ the timing option to defer capital gains tax and thus achieve a greater after-tax return. An investor in bequest mode can derive more benefit from the timing option by combining it with the disposal option. A buy-and-hold strategy can be particularly powerful when an investor is operating in the bequest mode. The after-tax expected return of the index fund is 9.2 percent in the bequest mode regardless of holding period. There is ongoing taxation of dividends while appreciation is not taxed. The effective tax rate is only 8 percent. This assumes that all appreciation

TABLE 29.2 Expected Growth in Market Value and Cost Basis

Year	Dividend	Income Tax	Cost Basis	Market Value
0			100.00	100.00
1	2.00	0.80	101.20	109.20
2	2.18	0.87	102.51	119.25
3	2.38	0.95	103.94	130.22
4	2.60	1.04	105.50	142.20
5	2.84	1.14	107.21	155.28

can be compounded without any realization. In fact, most index funds make small periodic distributions of realized gains.

Entity

Let us now assume that the index fund is held within a 401(k) or similar tax-advantaged entity. In this case, all forms of return including income, realized gains, and unrealized gains are allowed to compound on a tax-deferred basis. Eventually the investor will begin to withdraw from the account and the withdrawals will be subject to ordinary income tax. This is true regardless of the nature of the returns within the account. Generally funds will be withdrawn gradually over a period of many years. To simplify the calculation and allow a comparison to the preceding examples, we will assume a lump-sum withdrawal at the end of the holding period. We will also net out the tax benefit derived from making a pretax salary contribution to the retirement account. We are interested only in the impact of deferral on investment returns after the money is deposited into the account.

$$\text{Expected after-tax return} = \{[(1 + R)^Y \cdot (1 - T) + T]^{(1/Y)}\} - 1$$

where R = Expected total return
Y = Holding period in years
T = Tax rate

The longer the holding period, the greater the value derived from pretax compounding.

5 years	$\{[(1 + 10\%)^5 \cdot (1 - 40\%) + 40\%]^{(1/5)}\} - 1 = 6.44\%$
10 years	$\{[(1 + 10\%)^{10} \cdot (1 - 40\%) + 40\%]^{(1/10)}\} - 1 = 6.94\%$
25 years	$\{[(1 + 10\%)^{25} \cdot (1 - 40\%) + 40\%]^{(1/25)}\} - 1 = 8.03\%$

The after-tax expected return is very low for short holding periods because the conversion of appreciation to ordinary income drives the tax rate toward 40 percent

Table 29.3 shows the expected after-tax returns for various asset classes in differing situations based on assumptions regarding expected returns and the composition of the returns. The expected after-tax returns are a function of the pretax returns and composition of returns as described at the top of the table. The results will change as these assumptions change. What will not change is that the conversion of an expected pretax return to an expected after-tax return will vary greatly based on horizon, disposal plans, and entity. Asset allocation plans should be based on these specific after-tax returns rather than a generic after-tax return based on full and immediate taxability. Asset allocation analysis should be integrated with asset location analysis. Many wealthy individuals have complex estate structures that may include entities such as charitable remainder trusts, grantor trusts, foundations, insurance policies, and so on. Each of these entities will have unique income, transfer, and estate tax characteristics. Optimally locating the components of an asset allocation plan among these entities can significantly increase the after-tax wealth received by future heirs and charities. Asset location is another of the free

TABLE 29.3 Expected After-Tax Returns in Various Situations

Asset	Expected Pretax Return and Composition	
Money market fund	3%	3% taxable income
Tax-exempt bond	4	4% tax-exempt income
Treasury bond	6	6% taxable income
High-yield bond fund	9	7% taxable income, 2% annual appreciation, 50% annual turnover
Passive equity	10	2% dividend yield, 8% annual appreciation, 5% annual turnover
Active equity	11	2% dividend yield, 9% annual appreciation, 30% annual turnover

5% turnover on passive equity is consistent with historic change in the composition of the S&P 500.

	Expected After-Tax Return, Five-Year Holding Period		
	Liquidation Mode	Bequest Mode	Tax-Deferred Mode
Money market fund	1.80%	1.80%	1.84%
Tax-exempt bond	4.00	4.00	2.47
Treasury bond	3.60	3.60	3.76
High-yield bond fund	5.81	5.89	5.76
Passive equity	7.79	9.00	6.44
Active equity	8.54	9.17	7.13

	Expected After-Tax Return, 25-Year Holding Period		
	Liquidation Mode	Bequest Mode	Tax-Deferred Mode
Money market fund	1.80%	1.80%	2.04%
Tax-exempt bond	4.00	4.00	2.81
Treasury bond	3.60	3.60	4.46
High-yield bond fund	5.82	5.83	7.11
Passive equity	8.24	8.74	8.03
Active equity	8.65	8.79	8.96

options embedded in the tax code. We will discuss how this can be used with powerful results in the next chapter.

CONCLUSIONS

1. Wealthy investors generally have more than enough wealth to meet their spending needs. Thus, the financial goal is to maximize what can be transferred to heirs and/or charities net of income, transfer, and estate taxes. Estate and transfer taxes have such great impact that an investment planning framework must take them into account.

2. The tax code is complex but contains a great deal of flexibility. Investors can take advantage of various options in the tax code to meaningfully reduce the impact of taxes.

3. Inflation and spending join taxation as barriers to the growth of real wealth. The impact of each should be included in a planning framework.

4. Investors should base decisions on risk-adjusted expected after-tax returns. The conversion of expected pretax risk and return to after-tax risk and return depends on a number of investor-specific considerations. Two different investors might have very different expected after-tax results from the same investment.

CHAPTER 30

Real, After-Tax Returns of U.S. Stocks, Bonds, and Bills, 1926 through 2001

Don Mulvihill

Our expectations for future returns from stock and bond markets are highly influenced by their historic returns. Most investors are familiar with the average nominal past results but less familiar with the more relevant information: past real, after-tax results. Individuals generally quote nominal rates when discussing market returns and bond yields. Newspaper and television reporters use nominal rates to describe stock market results. Investment advisors and brokers use nominal returns in performance reports and advertisements. It seems that the entire financial services industry is focused on nominal numbers. A reader is unlikely to find a single quotation of real, after-tax results anywhere in the *Wall Street Journal*. However, real after-tax results are more relevant to taxpaying investors. An interesting exercise is to adjust historic market returns to reflect the impact of inflation and taxes. The adjusted results demonstrate how difficult it is to grow wealth net of the combined impact of taxes and inflation. It is even more difficult when spending requirements are included.

HISTORIC RETURNS ADJUSTED FOR INFLATION AND TAXES

We examined data on monthly U.S. stock and bond market returns since 1926 (Ibbotson Associates, 2003). The United States has had many bullish and bearish markets over the past 76 years. Overall, it has been a rewarding experience for investors as the stock market has multiplied wealth. This period contained many different market scenarios, thus making analysis more valuable. However, one should keep in mind that this was a period of extraordinary growth of the economic and political power of the United States. Future returns may not be as robust. The last two decades of the century were particularly robust. Surging corporate earnings and rising price-to-earnings multiples have produced market returns greater than 20 percent in 11 of the 20 years. In addition to creating wealth, this boom gave many investors inflated expectations of future investment returns.

We will look at three asset classes: stocks, bonds, and cash. These will be represented by the past performance of large-cap domestic stocks, intermediate-term government bonds, and Treasury bills as reported by Ibbotson Associates. Our analysis of what past investors would have earned assumes that investors owned broadly diversified portfolios whose returns were equal to the reported market returns.

An important statistical caveat is in order. We will use this data to analyze holding periods of as long as 25 years. Using monthly starting points, we have over 600 different 25-year holding periods in our 76 years of data. However, they overlap. There are only three independent 25-year holding periods.

Past results are not necessarily indicative of future results although they can serve as a useful reality check against either extreme optimism or pessimism. The purpose of our analysis of historical data is not to forecast either future absolute returns or relative returns among asset classes. It is to demonstrate (1) the enormous differences between nominal and real, after-tax return, (2) the uneven impact of taxes on different asset classes, (3) the impact of time on the perception of risk, and (4) the impact of fixed real spending requirements.

The average annual returns since 1926 (calculated as geometric means) are shown in Table 30.1. An investor trying to decide on the allocation between stocks and bonds might conclude that the long-term expected return of stocks is about double that of bonds. This fact would then be weighed against the greater volatility of stocks in determining the trade-off that best suited the investor's objectives. However, during this period, inflation averaged 3.06 percent per year. An adjustment for inflation produces the results shown in Table 30.2.

Inflation changes the situation a great deal. Real returns are much lower. The historic real return of stocks is nearly four times that of bonds. The adjustment for inflation might provide greater motivation for ownership of stocks versus bonds.

The next step is to adjust returns for the impact of taxes. This is a subjective process. Tax rates have varied a great deal over the past 76 years. At times they have been higher than current rates, but at other times they have been lower.

TABLE 30.1 Average Nominal Returns 1926 through 2001

	Nominal
Stocks	10.68%
Bonds	5.33
Cash	3.81

Source: Ibbotson Associates.

TABLE 30.2 Impact of Inflation

	Nominal	Real
Stocks	10.68%	7.41%
Bonds	5.33	2.21
Cash	3.81	0.73

Source: Ibbotson Associates.

Calculating results using the various tax rates in effect at different points in time would produce results that may not be relevant to an investor who today faces a 38.6 percent federal tax rate. However, calculating historic after-tax returns using today's tax rates ignores the interplay between tax rates and the relative demand for stocks and bonds. Past returns would likely have been different if today's tax rates were in place. Another complicating variable is the long-term trend toward lower dividend yields. Dividends are currently taxed as ordinary income, while appreciation is taxed at the lower capital gains rate. Thus, a greater portion of past stock returns were subject to ordinary taxation than is likely to be the case going forward. This requires some sort of simple, subjective compromise.

- Government bond and Treasury bill returns will be subject to a 30 percent tax rate. This is reasonable because municipal bonds often trade at yields about 70 percent of comparable maturity government bonds. A high-bracket taxable investor is likely to buy a municipal bond rather than a government bond subject to about 40 percent tax.
- Stock returns consist of dividends and appreciation. Dividends are currently taxed as ordinary income, while appreciation is usually taxed at long-term rates when the security is sold. In the previous chapter we demonstrated that deferral of capital gains taxes over long periods can meaningfully reduce the effective tax rate. Ordinary tax rates have fluctuated a great deal over the past 76 years, and so has the portion of stock returns from dividends. Our assumption is that investors hold broadly diversified stock portfolios that have returns in line with the overall market. We will further assume that these investors are sensitive to taxes and thus favor long holding periods. We will subject stock returns to 20 percent tax in our analysis.

Any attempt to convert historic returns to an after-tax basis requires some arbitrary assumptions. This approach seems reasonable. There is no point in being overly precise because, as demonstrated in the preceding chapter, the actual taxation of an asset depends on the factors of timing, disposal, and entity. This exercise is intended only to give us a rough idea of how taxes may alter expected returns and change relative risk/return ratios of different asset classes.

Taxes are applied to nominal returns, not real returns. If a bond yields 6 percent, the investor owes tax on the 6 percent yield even if inflation is consuming one-half or more of the nominal return. The combined impact can be seen in the adjusted data shown in Table 30.3.

TABLE 30.3 Combined Impact

	Nominal	Real	Real After-Tax
Stocks	10.68%	7.41%	5.57%
Bonds	5.33	2.21	0.66
Cash	3.81	0.73	–0.39

Source: Ibbotson Associates.

TABLE 30.4 Combined Impact of Inflation and Taxes

	Low Inflation	Higher Inflation
Nominal T-bill yield	3.00%	6.00%
Expected inflation	2.00	5.00
Real return	1.00	1.00
Taxes at 40%	1.20	2.40
After-tax nominal	1.80	3.60
After-tax real	–0.20	–1.40

Real after-tax returns will tend to decline in inflationary periods because taxes are levied on nominal returns. Short-term interest rates often move with the expected rate of inflation. Assume Treasury bill rates are 1 percent above the expected rate of inflation and thus provide a 1 percent real pretax return. Table 30.4 shows that an increase in the expected rate of inflation will lead to a decline in real after-tax returns even if real pretax returns are unchanged.

On an after-tax basis neither cash nor bonds have done much to help an investor grow the purchasing power of his or her estate. Stocks, however, have provided growth in real value. Figure 30.1 visually demonstrates the significant differences between nominal, real, and real after-tax returns. Notice how the relationship between

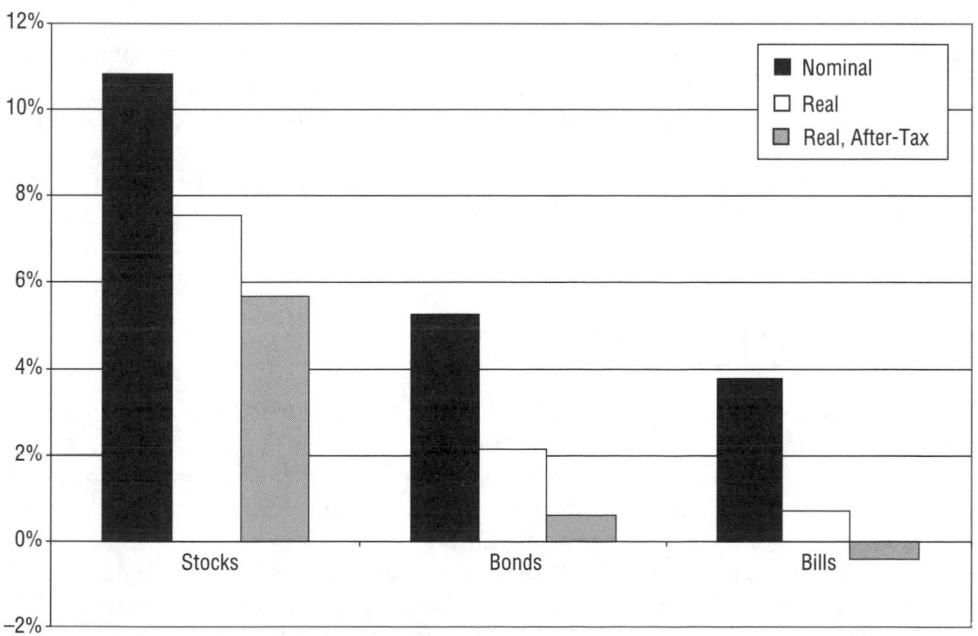

FIGURE 30.1 Returns 1926 through 2001
Source: Nominal and inflation data from Ibbotson Associates; tax adjustments by Goldman Sachs.

stock and bond returns changes. Based on nominal pretax returns, investors might feel they are looking at a menu of investments, each with a unique level of risk. Do you want the petite filet, the regular size, or the carnivore special? They all sound good. The choice depends on your appetite for risk. However, looked at on a real after-tax basis, only one choice is likely to be very satisfying. The menu has changed a great deal. Do you want to maintain some cash balances? That will cost you. Do you want some insurance to lock in your level of wealth without too much risk? Bonds may be the answer. But if you want meaningful growth, better consider stocks or other higher-return assets.

There are various participants in global bond and money markets. Pension funds and central banks are tax-exempt. Banks and insurance companies are subject to regulatory constraints that limit their participation in equity markets, driving them toward bonds and money markets. It may be the case that these participants establish market-clearing yield levels that make little sense to taxable clients.

These data suggest that the equity risk premium has averaged about 7 percent on a pretax basis and 5 percent on a real after-tax basis. A number of observers believe that the premium has declined in recent years. Broader ownership of equities and more efficient capital markets may have contributed to this decline. Another distinction between past results and the current situation is that dividend yields have declined a great deal. In earlier times, investment analysts used dividend discount models to estimate the value of companies. Today, the P/E ratio is a more common measure of valuation. This decline is partly the result of the tax code. The effective tax rate on equities declines as dividends make up a smaller portion of total return. This means that the effective tax rate on equities has declined relative to taxable bonds and money market securities. Consequently, the after-tax equity risk premium is increasing relative to the pretax risk premium. This is an interesting phenomenon for the immediate purpose of our analysis. It is more troubling on a broader level. A tax code that encourages companies to retain earnings rather than distribute them to shareholders is likely to lead to a less efficient allocation of society's capital resources and thus to a lower growth rate. As we write this, President George W. Bush has proposed eliminating tax on dividends. This change would obviously alter the calculation of expected after-tax return and would likely lead to an increase in dividend yields.

INFLATION AND "SAFE" ASSETS

Inflation reduces the purchasing power of an estate. Figure 30.2 shows the annual rate of U.S. inflation during the past 76 years.

There have been two serious inflationary episodes. The first was associated with shortages during and after World War II. The second covered almost all of the 1970s and was caused, in part, by rising oil prices and rapid growth of the money supply. During each of these periods, inflation significantly reduced the real value of estates. During the 10 years ending December 1979, the purchasing power of $1 was cut in half. In recent years inflation has been averaging about 3 percent. This destroys most or all of the after-tax return currently offered by many bonds and money market securities.

Figure 30.3 shows that bonds had two periods of exceptionally good returns.

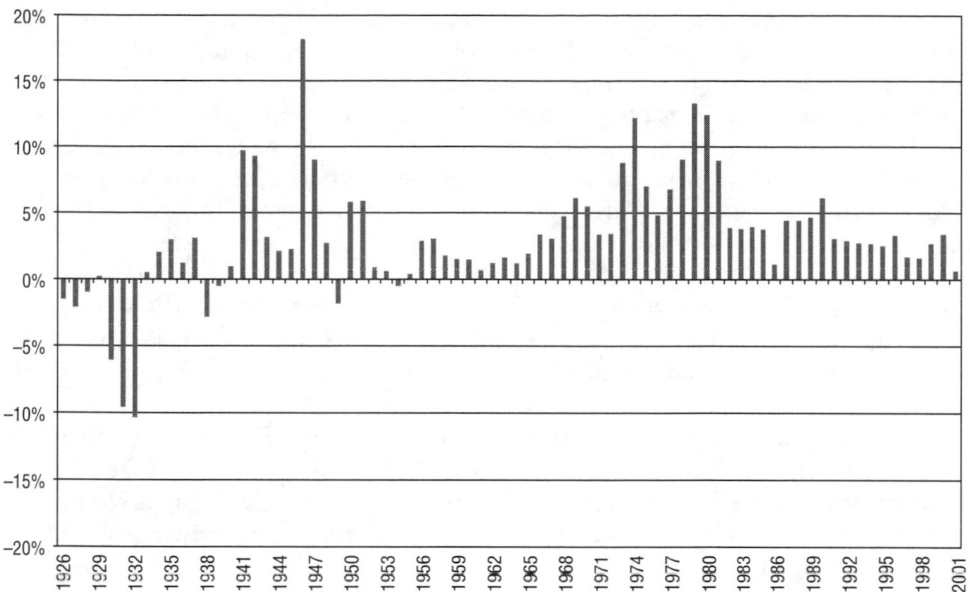

FIGURE 30.2 Annual U.S. Inflation, 1926 through 2001
Source: Ibbotson Associates.

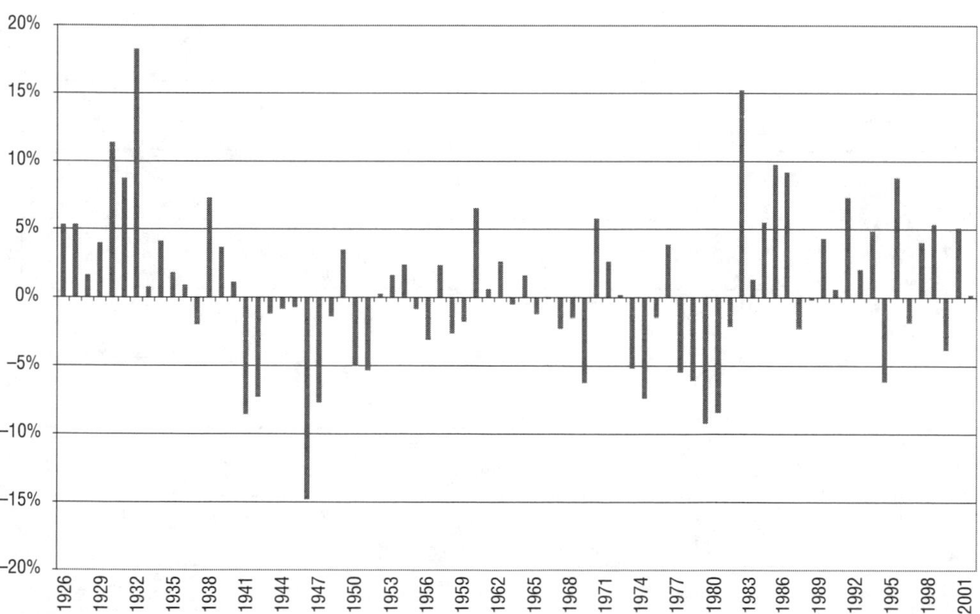

FIGURE 30.3 Annual Real, After-Tax Bond Returns, 1926 through 2001
Source: Nominal and inflation data from Ibbotson Associates; tax adjustments by Goldman Sachs.

The first was in the years following the 1929 stock market crash. Prices rose as bond yields declined to almost zero in response to a sharp decline in industrial activity and credit demand. The second period commenced in 1982 and followed the decision of the Federal Reserve, chaired by Paul Volker, to slow and control money supply growth. In between, there was a 41-year period in which bonds generally produced negative real, after-tax returns. Forty-one years is a long time! This was a dismal period for bond investors. Market yields trended higher and culminated in the inflationary period of the 1970s.

Many investors consider Treasury bills to be the safest of all investments. However, when adjusted for taxes and inflation, it is clear that Treasury bills can produce significant negative returns. Figure 30.4 shows the adjusted returns of Treasury bills over the same period of time. These returns were even worse than those of bonds.

Treasury bills have no credit risk and little interest rate risk. However, they offer no hedge against unexpected inflation. During most of the past 76 years, a taxable investor holding Treasury bills would have suffered a decline in real wealth. In 1946, a Treasury bill investor would have lost 15 percent of his or her real wealth in just one year due to the postwar inflation. Over the 10 years ending at year-end 1982, a Treasury bill investor would have lost almost one-quarter of the real value of his or her principal. Because of the ever-present risk of inflation, investors should not consider Treasury bills or any other investment to be riskless.

The U.S. Treasury introduced Treasury Inflation-Protected Securities (TIPS) in 1997. These are designed to provide a hedge against inflation. Like other Treasury

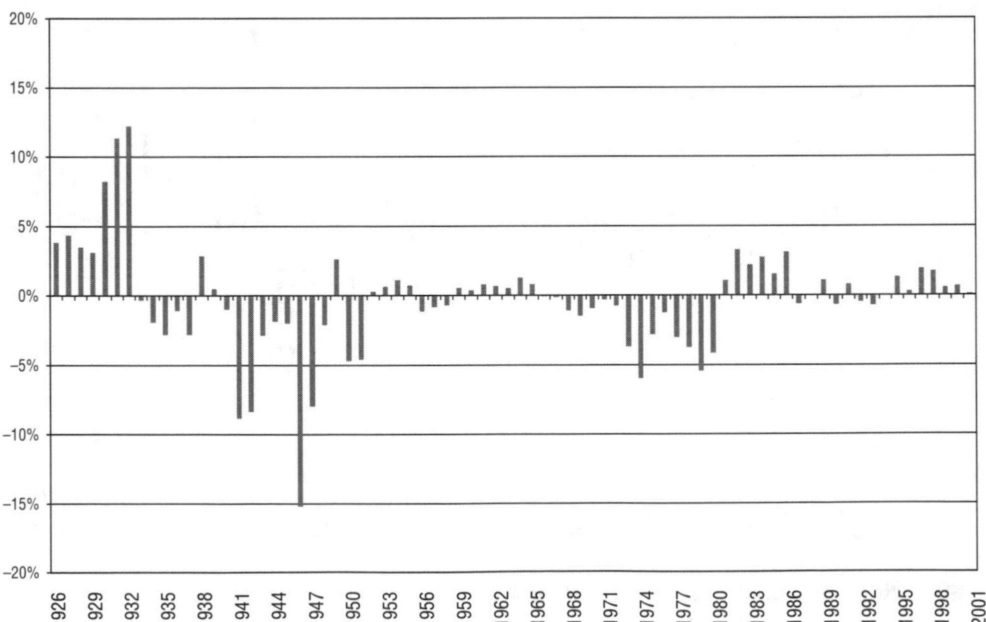

FIGURE 30.4 Annual Real, After-Tax Treasury Bill Returns, 1926 through 2001
Source: Nominal and inflation data from Ibbotson Associates; tax adjustments by Goldman Sachs.

bonds, they have a fixed coupon rate, pay interest on a semiannual basis, and repay principal at maturity. What is unique is that the principal amount is regularly adjusted to reflect monthly changes in the consumer price index (CPI). If you assume that prices tend to rise, then the principal amount of the bond will rise as the principal is adjusted up. At maturity, the investor will receive the inflation-adjusted amount of principal. TIPS offer an attractive inflation hedge to tax-exempt investors. As of August 2002, the coupon rate is about 3 percent. A return of 3 percent over the rate of inflation may be very attractive to investors such as pension funds that have liabilities influenced by the rate of inflation.

Taxes reduce the effectiveness of TIPS as an inflation hedge. Investors are taxed on their interest payments when received, plus are assessed tax on any upward adjustment in the principal amount. The tax on adjustments to the principal amount is levied at the time of the adjustment, even though the investor will not receive the principal until maturity. The adjustments are taxed as ordinary income. Assume prices rise, with the CPI rising 10 percent in a single year. An investor who had purchased a TIPS with a 3 percent coupon rate at par at the beginning of the year would see the notional principal amount of the security adjusted from 100 to 110. The investor would receive about \$3.30 in interest. This plus the \$10 adjustment in the principal value would create \$13.30 in taxable income. At 40 percent tax, the liability is \$5.32. The investor has a bond with par value of \$110, \$3.30 in interest, and \$5.32 in tax liability for a net of \$107.98. This is an after-tax return of about 7.98 percent versus inflation of 10 percent. TIPS are not a good inflation hedge when the portfolio is directly subject to taxation at high rates. TIPS may be an effective hedge if held within a tax-exempt entity such as a foundation. When held within tax-deferred retirement accounts, the effectiveness is greater than in a taxable account but less than in a tax-exempt account.

RISK ADJUSTED FOR TAXES AND INFLATION

The two previous sections demonstrated that over the past 76 years (1) real after-tax returns were significantly less than nominal returns and (2) cash and bond investments have provided minimal growth in real after-tax wealth. Now, let us turn our attention to risk and see how adjusting for taxes and inflation affect risk calculations.

Figure 30.5 shows the risk and return trade-offs of bills, bonds, and stocks based on both nominal and adjusted historic returns. Note that the riskiness of stocks declines when returns are adjusted for taxes. This is because the absolute amount of taxes is high during periods of strong market returns and low or negative during weak markets.

The nominal return of Treasury bills is essentially riskless over one-year holding periods. An investor who buys a Treasury bill and holds it until maturity will earn exactly what was expected. However, the real, after-tax return of Treasury bills is not riskless because of the impact of inflation.

Readers should not focus too closely on the absolute values plotted in Figure 30.5. They are the result of our arbitrary assumptions regarding tax rates. What is significant is the direction in which the data points shift as we move from nominal results to real, after-tax results.

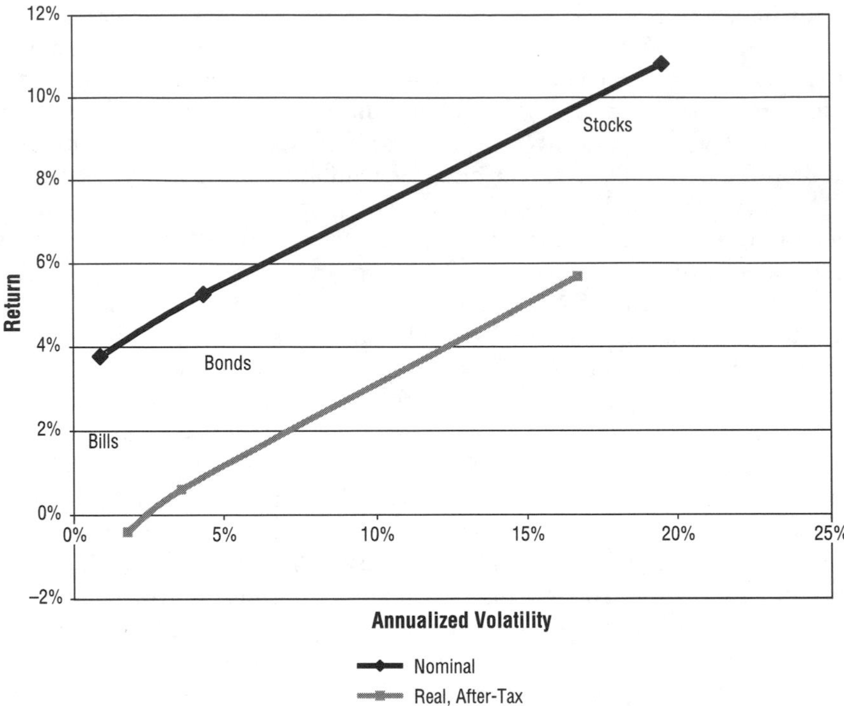

FIGURE 30.5 Impact of Taxes and Inflation on Risk and Return
Source: Nominal and inflation data from Ibbotson Associates; tax adjustments by Goldman Sachs.

- The riskiness of stocks declines because the absolute amount of tax varies with market returns. Taxes are high in strong markets and low or effectively negative in weak markets. This reduces the volatility in after-tax results.
- The riskiness of "safe" investments increases because the impact of inflation introduces uncertainty into the future real value of money market and fixed income investments.

RISK AND TIME

Figure 30.5 shows risk as measured by the volatility of *annual* returns. The choice of time horizon significantly affects the risk calculation. Longer-term returns are more predictable than annual returns. Random volatility tends to cancel out over time, converging on the expected average return. Furthermore, market returns from one year to the next may not be completely independent events. Market returns have tended to be "mean reverting" during the period we have studied. There is some controversy on this point. However, data from the past 76 years support the mean-reversion concept. In particular, long-term cumulative returns have not been as volatile as the annual volatilities would suggest. A total of 76 years of data yields only three independent 25-year periods, and so the statistical support for mean reversion is weak. However, the concept is intuitively appealing.

We can imagine what factors would contribute to mean reversion of returns. Stock market returns are influenced by growth in corporate earnings and changes in average P/E ratios. Each has tended to fluctuate around long-term averages. For example, periods of investor exuberance produce higher than normal P/E ratios, while periods of investor pessimism can produce lower than normal P/E ratios. Stock market returns can fluctuate significantly from one year to the next as economic growth and P/E ratios oscillate around their long-term averages. Such oscillations would contribute to mean reversion in market returns. Figure 30.6 shows how longer horizons narrow the range of annualized returns. Annual stock returns have varied widely, ranging from a negative 54 percent during the 12 months ended 6/30/32 to a maximum of positive 140 percent, which occurred in the subsequent 12-month period, ending 6/30/33. That's volatility! That is also an extreme example of mean reversion. Over longer periods of time, cumulative returns have converged toward their long-term average. During this time period, which included the Great Depression, there was never a 25-year period in which the diversified stock market failed to increase real after-tax wealth.

There is a similar argument for mean reversion of bond market returns. Over the past 76 years, bond yields have generally been in a range of about 5 percent to 7 percent. A period of rising market yields will produce negative bond returns. However, if market yields subsequently decline to their normal range, there will be a period of unusually high bond returns.

The distribution of bond and bill returns exhibits a similar pattern, although the one-year returns are far less volatile that those of stocks. However, a long-term investor should recognize that the real, after-tax returns of bonds and bills have converged toward low or negative averages. Figure 30.7 shows the distribution of 25-year returns for all three asset classes. Stocks consistently provided growth in real, after-tax wealth; bonds rarely provided any growth in real, after-tax wealth; and Treasury bills have never provided an increase in real, after-tax wealth. This leads to the trade-off between safety and effectiveness. In nominal terms, all asset classes have positive expected returns and thus would appear to contribute to the goal of wealth accumulation. But, when we shift to wealth stewardship focused on real, after-tax results, we find that money market and fixed income securities may be ineffective and possibly counterproductive. This is an important consideration for the investor who is interested in long-term results.

Investors who base investment decisions on nominal, annual return and risk data are likely to conclude that T-bills are riskless, bonds have modest risk, and stocks are very risky. And it is absolutely true that during short investment horizons, stock and bond returns can vary, with stocks being particularly volatile. However, an investor who is focused on the long-term preservation and growth of the real value of an estate may come to a very different conclusion. Since 1926, there has never been a 25-year period in which stocks failed to increase real wealth, there have been few periods in which bonds increased real wealth, and "safe" Treasury bills almost always reduced real wealth. To be more precise, it was the issuer of the Treasury bills, the government, that destroyed the wealth through taxation and monetary policy.

Individual investors often use risk analysis to get an idea of potential worst-case scenarios. An understanding of the relationship between time and risk is very important in this regard. Riskier asset classes have higher expected returns but

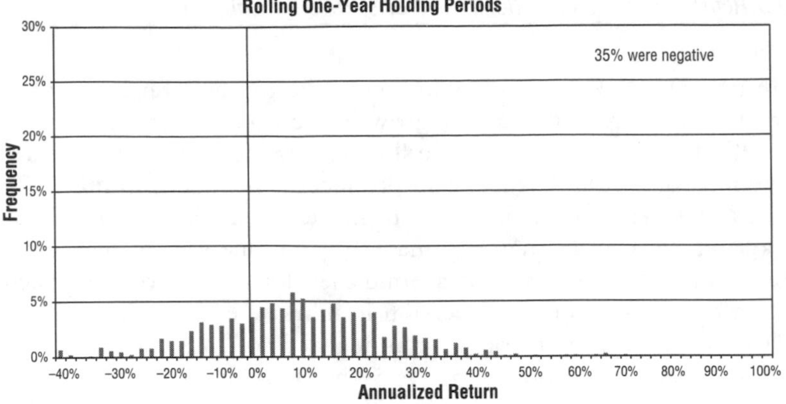

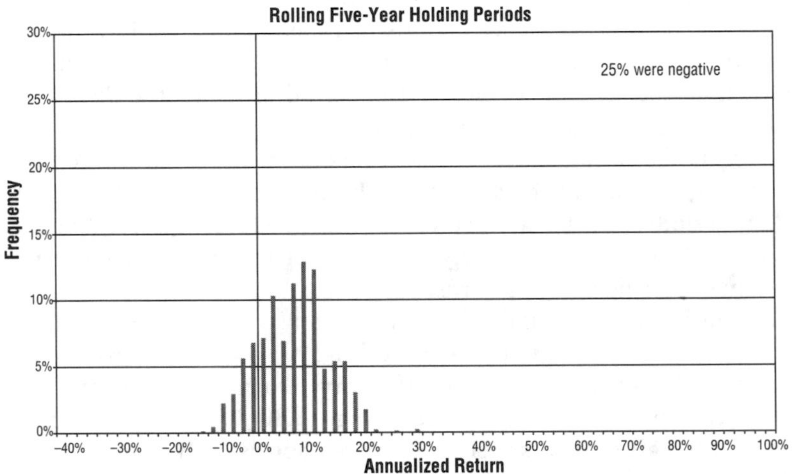

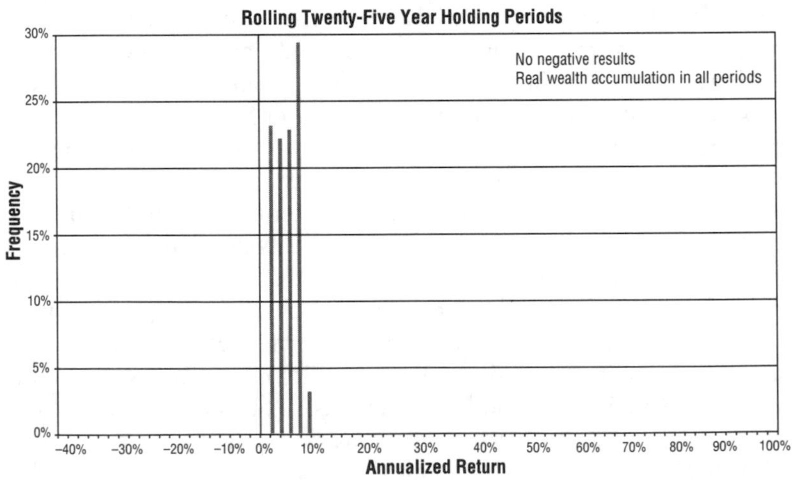

FIGURE 30.6 Longer Horizons Narrow the Range of Annualized Returns: Distribution of Real, After-Tax Returns on U.S. Stocks, 1926 through 2001

Source: Nominal and inflation data from Ibbotson Associates; tax adjustments by Goldman Sachs.

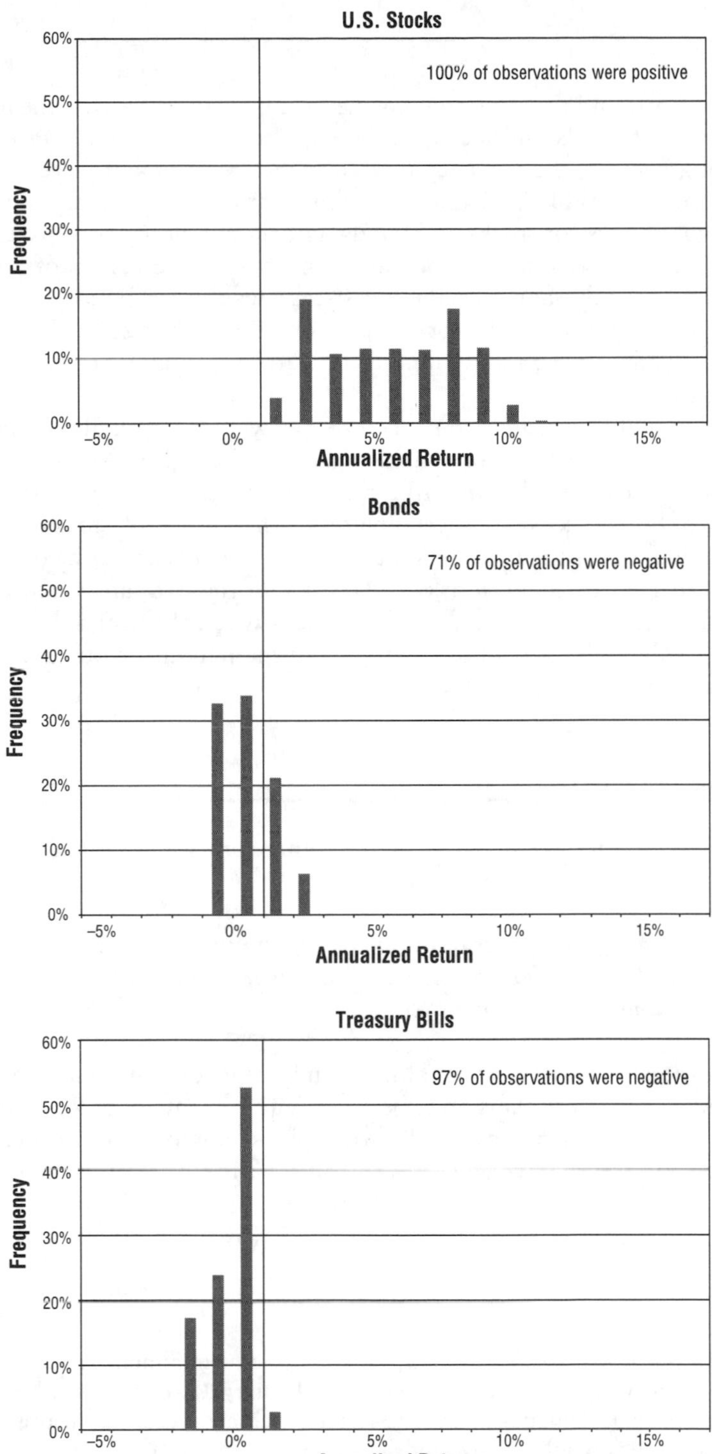

FIGURE 30.7 Distribution of 25-Year Returns for All Three Asset Classes: Real, After-Tax Returns; Rolling 25-Year Holding Periods; 1926 through 2001

Source: Nominal and inflation data from Ibbotson Associates; tax adjustments by Goldman Sachs.

greater volatility around those returns. As the time horizon increases, the higher expected return compounds and increases the expected future value. Once the time horizon is long enough, the tendency toward higher returns will increase even the worst-case scenarios. Table 30.5 illustrates this relationship by comparing historical real after-tax results for stocks and bonds. For short holding periods, the worst-case results of stocks were much worse than the worst-case results of bonds. For 10-year holding periods, however, the worst-case results for bonds were actually lower than the worst-case results for stocks. For 25-year horizons, the worst-case results for stocks had twice the wealth accumulation of bonds despite the greater volatility of stock returns.[1]

Investors should be sensitive to interim risk as well as terminal risk. For example, an investor with a 25-year horizon might look at the rightmost column in Table 30.5 and observe that there has never been a 25-year period in which stocks failed to produce real, after-tax wealth accumulation. The choice of stocks over bonds might seem obvious. But the investor should also consider whether he or she would have the tolerance for the interim risk. The results for the two- and three-year holding periods demonstrate that there were instances when the real value of a stock portfolio fell to about 40 percent of the original principal during one of the 25-year holding periods.

APPLICATION

Let us complete this analysis by applying the framework we described in the previous chapter. A wealthy investor's goal is:

> *Subject to funding my consumption needs, maximize the risk-adjusted real value of wealth that will be received, net of income and estate taxes, by my intended heirs and charitable beneficiaries.*

We will estimate the after-tax wealth that might have been accumulated under a range of asset allocation plans and spending requirements over 20-year holding periods. We will consider five asset allocation plans ranging from conservative to aggressive (see Table 30.6). We will define a conservative investor as having 40 percent in stock, 40 percent in bonds, and 20 percent in cash. We will define an aggressive investor as having 80 percent in stock, 15 percent in bonds, and 5 percent

[1]Tables 30.5 through 30.11 show average, maximum, and minimum results for various rolling holding periods. The first such period begins January 1926. The next begins February 1926 and so forth. Calculating an average result by merely averaging the results of these various holding periods would overweight the data in the middle of the data set. The first month and last month of the data set will each be used in just one holding period. The second and next to last months would each be used in two holding periods. Months in the middle of the data set would be used in many different holding periods. In order to avoid any distortion, we calculated the average results by compounding the average returns in the underlying data set. The maximum and minimum results are based on the results of the rolling holding periods.

TABLE 30.5 Real, After-Tax Expected and Observed Growth of $1 Million

Holding Period (Years)	1	2	3	4	5	10	25
Stocks							
Expected	1,060,600	1,124,872	1,193,040	1,265,338	1,342,017	1,801,010	4,353,019
Observed maximum	2,400,045	2,186,773	2,297,655	3,188,544	3,440,334	3,935,114	10,816,923
Observed minimum	462,453	364,485	349,213	469,250	613,319	632,078	1,233,192
Bonds							
Average	1,005,600	1,011,231	1,016,894	1,022,589	1,028,315	1,057,432	1,149,825
Observed maximum	1,182,842	1,292,251	1,483,053	1,577,964	1,600,319	1,797,595	1,398,647
Observed minimum	838,657	776,638	746,191	704,298	693,334	607,862	635,643

Source: Nominal and inflation data from Ibbotson Associates; tax adjustments by Goldman Sachs.

TABLE 30.6 Five Asset Allocation Plans

	Stocks	Bonds	Bills
Conservative	40.00%	40.00%	20.00%
Semiconservative	50.00	33.75	16.25
Moderate	60.00	27.50	12.50
Semiaggressive	70.00	21.25	8.75
Aggressive	80.00	15.00	5.00

in cash. We will also identify three points on the continuum between conservative and aggressive.

We will use a 20-year holding period and consider the results that would have been achieved in each of the 673 20-year holding periods based on monthly data from 1926 to 2001. We will assume monthly rebalancing so that the target asset class weights are maintained. In practice, this might be difficult to achieve without adverse tax consequences, but we will nevertheless maintain our assumed tax rates of 30 percent on bonds and bills and 20 percent on stocks.

We will begin with the assumption of no spending draining wealth from the portfolio. We will assume a $1,000,000 initial value. Table 30.7 shows the distribution of nominal pretax wealth accumulated in these 20-year periods. Table 30.8 shows the distribution of real, after-tax wealth accumulation. The "terminal minimum" is the lowest ending value that was observed in any 20-year period. The "interim minimum" is the lowest point to which principal sank at any point within any of the 20-year periods. A conservative investor never saw nominal principal sink below 84 percent of the original amount. The aggressive investor had situations in which the nominal principal value had fallen to about 65 percent of the original amount.

This chapter is being written in late 2002 when stock prices are in the third year of a bear market. A number of investors who had identified themselves as aggressive and liked stocks because of their long-term expected excess returns are suddenly becoming less aggressive. One risk of adopting an aggressive posture is that you do not have the tolerance for interim volatility, and you will switch to a

TABLE 30.7 Nominal Pretax Ending Wealth

$1 million starting value; 20-year holding periods; no spending from portfolio

	Expected		Observed		
	Amount	Annualized	Terminal Maximum	Terminal Minimum	Interim Minimum
Conservative	4,006,457	7.19%	11,292,739	1,894,950	842,612
Semiconservative	4,489,137	7.80	13,359,046	1,895,414	792,248
Moderate	5,026,733	8.41	15,736,158	1,864,478	743,423
Semiaggressive	5,625,130	9.02	18,456,735	1,803,537	697,157
Aggressive	6,290,803	9.63	21,553,998	1,715,355	653,340

Source: Nominal and inflation data from Ibbotson Associates.

TABLE 30.8 Real After-Tax Ending Wealth

$1 million starting value; 20-year holding periods; no spending from portfolio

	Expected		Observed		
	Amount	Annualized	Terminal Maximum	Terminal Minimum	Interim Minimum
Conservative	1,703,177	2.70%	2,962,304	783,104	654,136
Semiconservative	1,897,423	3.25	3,457,124	809,596	652,272
Moderate	2,103,882	3.79	4,023,525	830,364	583,951
Semiaggressive	2,321,830	4.30	4,669,807	849,446	502,581
Aggressive	2,550,273	4.79	5,404,874	866,702	431,080

Source: Nominal and inflation data from Ibbotson Associates; tax adjustments by Goldman Sachs.

more conservative posture following a decline in market prices. This locks in the loss and creates the possibility of lower terminal results than might have been possible if a more conservative posture had been adopted from the beginning.

One of our goals in these chapters on taxable client portfolio management is to show how the principles of modern portfolio management can be applied while accommodating the impact of taxation. Figure 30.8 plots the expected values from Table 30.8 against the standard deviations of the results observed for the many 20-year holding periods that we studied. This is a first step in developing an efficient

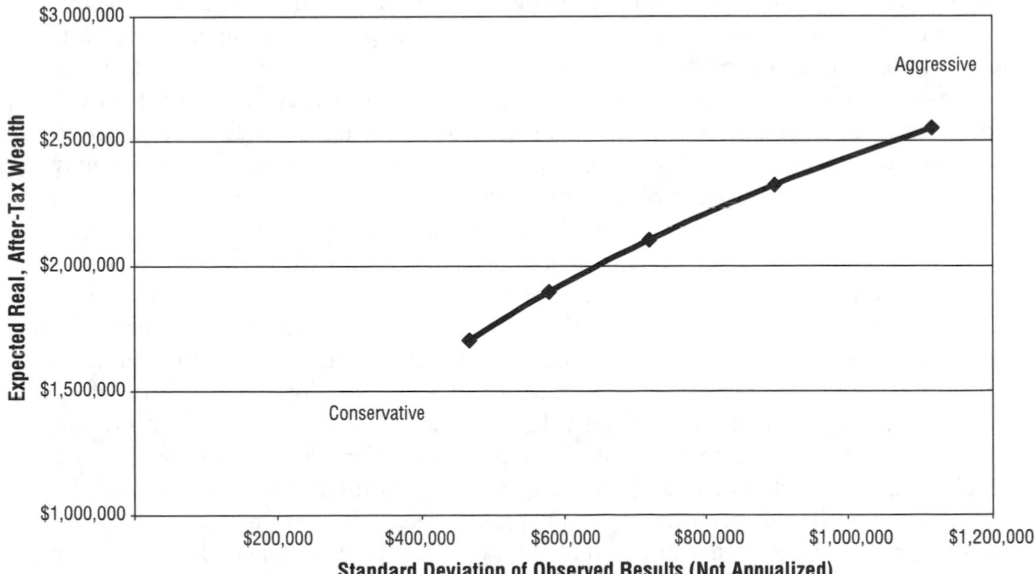

FIGURE 30.8 Real, After-Tax Wealth and Volatility over 20 Years ($1 Million Initial Value)
Source: Nominal and inflation data from Ibbotson Associates; tax adjustments by Goldman Sachs.

frontier for taxable investors. We have incorporated a holding period, thus capturing some of the benefits of mean reversion. We have projected wealth adjusted for taxes and inflation. We have expressed risk in terms of the volatility of ending results.

There is a great deal of useful and perhaps surprising information in this chart.

- It demonstrates that it is difficult to grow wealth net of taxes and inflation. Twenty years is a long time by most individuals' standards. This data covered some very robust markets, but two of the combinations, on average, were unable to achieve even a doubling of real wealth. This was based on the assumption that *none* of the portfolio was used to meet spending requirements. As described later, even modest spending requirements will have a big impact on wealth accumulation.
- The minimum results were almost identical for each combination, and the riskier combinations actually had higher terminal minimum results. When looking at asset allocation issues, many individuals attempt to identify their ideal risk levels based on estimates of worst-case outcomes. The assumption is that the riskier strategies have inferior worst-case outcomes. That is true only for short holding periods. The interim low points for the riskier strategies are likely to be meaningfully lower than their worst-case terminal result. When we extend the holding period to 20 years, results tend to converge toward long-term averages. The higher expected return of riskier strategies compounds and raises even the worst-case outcomes.

Many individuals use their investment portfolios to fund their ongoing expenditures. We next want to see how a spending requirement will alter these results. We will model the impact of spending based on the following assumption. We will continue to use 20-year holding periods. We will set spending as a percentage of the portfolio's initial value. Thereafter, spending will rise with the rate of inflation and will not respond to changing portfolio values. Spending will increase with inflation but not increase in response to very good markets nor will it be cut back in response to poor markets. This is probably a good approximation of investors' desires but may not be a good approximation of investors' actual behavior. Tables 30.9, 30.10, and 30.11 demonstrate the impact of spending. A comparison to Table 30.8 shows that even modest spending requirements would have had meaningful impact. Conservative strategies could not, on average, have supported more than a 2 percent initial spending requirement without the expectation of a decline in real wealth. One of the key differences among Tables 30.8 through 30.11 is the deterioration of minimum results. Our model assumed that spending would continue to grow with the rate of inflation regardless of market conditions. In other words, the investor would not cut back on spending if investment results were poor. Under this assumption, worst-case results become much worse. Even modest spending requirements can meaningfully increase the decline of principal value in weak markets. If assets are sold off at depressed prices, those assets cannot contribute to a recovery in principal value in any subsequent market rebound. This point is best illustrated in Table 30.11, where the interim worst-case results were about the same as the terminal worst-case results. In these simulations, the worst cases were the result of market conditions reducing the

TABLE 30.9 Real, After-Tax Ending Wealth

$1 million starting value; 20-year holding periods; 1% initial spending

	Expected		Observed		
	Amount	Annualized	Terminal Maximum	Terminal Minimum	Interim Minimum
Conservative	1,360,825	1.55%	2,595,485	630,265	549,532
Semiconservative	1,537,089	2.17	3,049,142	651,402	544,236
Moderate	1,725,126	2.76	3,569,878	671,181	532,819
Semiaggressive	1,924,286	3.33	4,165,583	689,457	484,499
Aggressive	2,133,665	3.86	4,844,725	706,095	414,492

Source: Nominal and inflation data from Ibbotson Associates; tax adjustments by Goldman Sachs.

TABLE 30.10 Real, After-Tax Ending Wealth

$1 million starting value; 20-year holding periods; 2% initial spending

	Expected		Observed		
	Amount	Annualized	Terminal Maximum	Terminal Minimum	Interim Minimum
Conservative	1,018,473	0.09%	2,228,667	473,239	418,692
Semiconservative	1,176,755	0.82	2,641,160	491,755	417,454
Moderate	1,346,369	1.50	3,116,231	506,462	414,944
Semiaggressive	1,526,741	2.14	3,661,359	519,696	411,184
Aggressive	1,717,057	2.74	4,284,576	531,345	397,904

Source: Nominal and inflation data from Ibbotson Associates; tax adjustments by Goldman Sachs.

TABLE 30.11 Real, After-Tax Ending Wealth

$1 million starting value; 20-year holding periods; 3% initial spending

	Expected		Observed		
	Amount	Annualized	Terminal Maximum	Terminal Minimum	Interim Minimum
Conservative	676,121	−1.94%	1,869,352	282,497	279,907
Semiconservative	816,421	−1.01	2,233,178	292,534	285,854
Moderate	967,612	−0.16	2,662,585	301,085	283,944
Semiaggressive	1,129,197	0.61	3,157,135	308,035	280,914
Aggressive	1,300,449	1.32	3,724,427	313,276	276,792

Source: Nominal and inflation data from Ibbotson Associates; tax adjustments by Goldman Sachs.

value of the portfolio to the point that subsequent periods of good returns could not overcome the impact of spending. The value of the portfolio continued to decline until the end of the holding period as spending consumed principal.

CONCLUSIONS

Real, after-tax returns are relevant to a taxable investor who seeks to preserve and grow the real value of an estate. Because the differences between nominal and real after-tax returns have been so great, investors should not make investment decisions based on expected nominal results.

Over the past 76 years, government bonds and Treasury bills have more or less preserved real wealth but have provided no real growth.

Inflation adds an element of uncertainty to all returns. The real return of even Treasury bills is uncertain and has been quite volatile during periods of surging inflation. There is no riskless security. The real, after-tax return of stocks is less volatile that the nominal return because the absolute amount of tax varies with market returns, thus narrowing the distribution of outcomes.

Long-term returns of stocks, bonds, and Treasury bills have been more stable than one would expect from compounding observed annual volatility. This suggests there has been a mean-reversion tendency. Most investors use risk parameters to estimate the potential for bad results. Mean reversion plus the higher average return for equities leads to the observation that for sufficiently long holding periods, perhaps 10 years, the observed worst real, after-tax results of equities have been better than those of bonds or bills. Based on the historic returns, if a portfolio is required to support ongoing spending requirements, it is the "safer" asset allocation strategies that have been more likely to produce destruction of the estate's value. However, the interim volatility of riskier strategies will be greater. Investors should consider the expected interim volatility in the value of a portfolio as well as the expected volatility of terminal results.

We demonstrated that an investor can derive an efficient frontier chart that contains adjustments for income taxes and inflation. We plotted the expected future real after-tax value of a portfolio against the volatility of the estimates based on historic market returns. In this chapter we did not consider estate or transfer taxes, nor did we consider tax-advantaged entities. In the next chapter we will seek to derive a similar efficient frontier chart that also takes into account estate and entity issues.

CHAPTER 31

Asset Allocation and Location

Don Mulvihill

The tax code allows for various entities related to retirement savings, estate planning, and philanthropy. Examples include 401(k) plans, grantor trusts, charitable remainder trusts (CRTs), and charitable foundations. These are only a few of the many entities available. We will not attempt to provide even a basic overview of estate planning in this book. It is too complex a subject. We will use these four entities to demonstrate the value of asset location strategies. This concept was briefly discussed in Chapter 29. Asset location refers to the positioning of the various components of an asset allocation plan among the various entities that make up an investor's estate. We have defined the goal of investing as:

> *Subject to funding my consumption needs, maximize the risk-adjusted real value of wealth that will be received, net of income and estate taxes, by my intended heirs and charitable beneficiaries.*

The growth of wealth and its transfer to heirs or charities is affected by ongoing income and capital gains tax as well as any transfer taxes. The entities described above have various tax characteristics. Their usefulness varies by asset class. Financial assets can be broadly grouped into four categories by the nature of their return.

Return	*Asset Class/Strategy*
1. Tax-exempt income	Municipal bonds, tax-exempt money market securities.
2. Taxable income, dividends and short-term gains	Government and corporate bonds, taxable money market securities, bank accounts, real estate investment trusts (REITs), hedge funds, preferred stock.
3. Realized long-term gains	Actively managed public equities, private equity funds.
4. Unrealized appreciation	Equity index funds, tax-efficient equity strategies.

This is a simplification because many assets produce both income and gains, but the categorization is helpful in understanding asset location. The key is to match the tax characteristics of the entity to the return characteristics of the asset class or strategy. This should be done with reference to the investor's long-term disposal plans and related transfer tax considerations. Let us consider two situations to illustrate this point.

SITUATION 1: GOAL IS MAXIMIZING CHILDREN'S WEALTH

Mr. and Mrs. Jones have $25 million in financial assets. They are in their mid-60s. For planning purposes, they are using a 20-year combined life expectancy. Their goal is to maximize what can be passed to their four children. Their expenses include $250,000 annual living expenses that should grow with inflation and $80,000 per year based on Mr. and Mrs. Jones each giving $10,000 per year to each child. Mr. and Mrs. Jones have:

- Direct ownership of $15 million in cash and securities.
- A 401(k) plan with $2 million from which they will withdraw $100,000 per year.
- A grantor trust, now owned equally by the four children, with $8 million.

SITUATION 2: GOAL IS MAXIMIZING LONG-TERM GIFTS TO CHARITY

Mr. Smith has $100 million in financial assets plus another $55 million of charitable assets under his control. He is 70 years old and single. For planning purposes he is using a 15-year life expectancy. He has started a personal foundation and also created a charitable remainder trust. He has $2 million in annual living expenses that are expected to grow with inflation. He has:

- Direct ownership of $75 million in cash and securities.
- A 401(k) plan with $5 million from which he will withdraw $500,000 per year.
- A charitable remainder trust with assets of $50 million. The trust will pay Mr. Smith $2.8 million per year for 10 years. The present value of this annuity is $20 million. Thus, we consider $20 million of the $50 million to be part of Mr. Smith's personal wealth and the remaining $30 million to be part of the charitable assets under his control.
- The Smith foundation has $25 million in assets.

The residual of the CRT will go to Mr. Smith's foundation in 10 years. At his death, all his personal assets will go to the foundation.

The remainder of this chapter is devoted to exploring how each can benefit from asset location strategies. We will demonstrate this by developing an efficient frontier chart that assumes optimal asset allocation and location. We will begin with a brief review of the tax characteristics of the four entities in our examples.

401(K) PLAN

A 401(k) plan is a common retirement savings vehicle. This vehicle allows investors to defer tax on salary income contributed to the plan and allows for tax deferral on all income and gains earned within the plan until they are withdrawn. When money is withdrawn it will be subject to ordinary income tax regardless of the nature of returns within the plan. Investors generally must begin to withdraw assets when they reach age 70. The advantage of a 401(k) is tax deferral and the pretax compounding that it allows. Assuming an 8 percent return, 25 years of deferral reduces the effective tax rate from 39.1 percent to 21.8 percent.[1] The disadvantages of a 401(k) are (1) it converts long-term gains into ordinary income, and (2) the investor does not get the step-up in basis in which the government waives capital gains tax on unrealized appreciation in the estate of a deceased person. Income producing investments such as bonds and REITs benefit from the deferral offered by a 401(k) plan and suffer little from the disadvantages since they produce little appreciation. An equity index fund, on the other hand, produces a lot of unrealized capital appreciation plus some ongoing dividend income. The deferral of tax on dividends is helpful, but turning long-term gains into ordinary income and giving up the possible benefits of the step-up in basis can actually reduce the investor's expected after-tax return. As a general rule, investments that generate a lot of ongoing ordinary income derive more benefit from 401(k)s and similar entities.

In our examples we will assume that each investor will annually withdraw a fixed amount equal to 10 percent of the current balance. Mr. and Mrs. Jones, together, will withdraw $100,000 at the end of each year.[2] Mr. Smith will withdraw $500,000 at the end of each year. We will deduct 40 percent for income taxes and credit the balance toward their annual spending requirements.

GRANTOR TRUST

A grantor trust is an entity that allows one person to transfer a gift to another while still retaining some control of the trust. The Joneses gave assets to their children through a grantor trust. The terms of the trust allow the parents some control over the timing of the children's access to the trust assets. The creation of the trust was a gift to the children that would likely have required the payment of $4 million in transfer tax if we assume a 50 percent gift and estate tax rate. However, now that the trust is established, the assets are out of the parents' estate and will not be subject to estate tax at their deaths. Further, and this is the point relevant to our analysis, the parents may continue to pay the trust's income and capital gains tax without that payment being construed as a gift subject to transfer tax. This

[1]The effective tax rate is 1 – (After-tax return/Pretax return). In this example, the after-tax return is $\{[(1.08^{25})(1 - .391)] + 1\}^{1/25} - 1$. The +1 element is added to distinguish deferral of tax on investment return from deferral of tax on salary income contributed to the plan.

[2]Mr. and Mrs. Jones would be better off not withdrawing anything from the retirement account until forced to at age 70.5. To simplify our calculations, we will assume they begin withdrawing now.

arrangement reduces future estate tax liability in two ways. First, because the assets are now out of the parents' estate, any subsequent appreciation will not be subject to estate tax at their deaths. Second, because the parents can pay the trust's taxes, future estate tax liability is reduced. If the parents pay $1 in income tax, the estate tax liability is reduced by $0.50. The grantor trust's principal balance will grow at the pretax rate rather than the after-tax rate. We will soon demonstrate that, under current tax laws, a grantor trust can greatly enhance the transfer of wealth to the next generation.

CHARITABLE REMAINDER TRUST (CRT)

A CRT is a vehicle commonly used to diversify a low-cost-basis stock holding while making a partial gift to charity. Mr. Smith has just contributed $50 million worth of Smith Industries stock to a CRT he created. This stock had a cost basis of about zero, so we will treat it as zero in our analysis. If Mr. Smith had sold it he would have had to make an immediate capital gains tax payment of 20 percent of $30 million. Instead, Mr. Smith created the CRT, contributed the stock, and arranged for the CRT to pay him 10 annual payments of $2,800,000. At the end of the 10 years the balance of the CRT will go to a charity that Mr. Smith has designated. Mr. Smith has designated his foundation as the future recipient. The IRS requires that Mr. Smith determine the present value of this annuity and deduct it from $50 million in order to determine the amount of charitable donation Mr. Smith has made. The IRS identifies the appropriate discount rate based on the Treasury yield curve. We will assume a 6.64 percent rate. This gives the annuity a present value of $20 million. Thus, Mr. Smith can claim a charitable deduction of $30 million today even though the charity will not get any money for 10 years and the actual amount that the charity will receive is not determined.

Mr. Smith will control the management of the CRT. The manager will immediately sell the Smith Industries stock and use the proceeds to build a diversified portfolio. This sale creates no direct tax liability for Mr. Smith. At the end of each of the next 10 years, Mr. Smith will receive $2,800,000. The tax characterization of this payment will be based on the "tiering of income" rules. The IRS will look at the nature of income within the CRT and attribute the most highly taxed sources, in sequence, to Mr. Smith. For example, if this year the CRT had

$1,000,000	of interest income and dividends
$600,000	of short-term gains
$49,000,000	of long-term gains

then Mr. Smith will have

$1,000,000	of ordinary income and dividends
$600,000	of short-term gains
$1,200,000	of long-term gains
$2,800,000	

The tiering of income rules create a perverse form of leveraging. If Mr. Smith's annuity payment is equal to 5.6 percent of the CRT's total value, then a 1 percent income and dividend yield would cause 1%/5.6% = 18% of Mr. Smith's annuity payment to be subject to ordinary income tax. This is an important consideration. In many cases, investors use CRTs to obtain immediate diversification while deferring the payment of long-term capital gains tax on an appreciated single-stock position. However, the investor may not ultimately benefit if the process of deferral causes a significant portion of the gain to be effectively recharacterized as ordinary income. CRTs should be managed to minimize taxable income and short-term gains.

FOUNDATION

A foundation is an entity created to pursue philanthropic activities. A single donor funds a private foundation. That donor has the ability to influence how the portfolio is managed and to what charitable activities distributions are made. Portfolio management policies must be focused on the benefit of the charity and must meet "reasonable person" standards. A foundation is not part of an individual's estate. Assets contributed to the foundation are generally treated as charitable donations, subject to certain limitations. In general, an individual may claim a charitable deduction for gifts up to 30 percent of their income, if the gift is to a public charity, and up to 20 percent if the gift is to a private foundation.

Appreciated assets given to a foundation will not be subject to capital gains tax. The foundation generally must distribute at least 5 percent of its assets to charitable activities each year although we will ignore that in our calculations. The foundation is free of tax except for certain modest excise taxes that we will also ignore in our analysis. Mr. Smith contributed some low-cost-basis shares of Smith Industries to fund this foundation. He was able to claim the market value of the shares as a deduction against income tax. He owed no capital gains tax. The foundation was then able to immediately sell the shares and reinvest into a more diversified portfolio without incurring any tax.

We now want to analyze asset allocation and asset location strategies for the Jones family and for Mr. Smith. We will begin with the Joneses. We will target the expected future wealth of their children in 20 years' time, assuming that at that point both Mr. and Mrs. Jones have died and left their remaining assets to their children. We will assume a 50 percent estate tax although we note that the estate tax is currently under review by Congress. We will allocate among six assets with certain assumptions regarding expected return and volatility (Table 31.1) and correlations (Table 31.2). We will assume a 3 percent inflation rate.

In order to demonstrate the value of estate planning and then the value of asset location strategies, we will examine the Jones family's situation in three scenarios. We will begin by assuming no estate planning or retirement entities. All $25 million will be held in the parents' name and will be subject to ongoing income tax. The ending balance in 20 years will be subject to 50 percent estate tax. Annual spending will start at $250,000 and will grow at 3 percent per year, reflecting our assumption for inflation. In addition, there will be $80,000 of annual gifts. We will assign

TABLE 31.1 Expected Returns and Volatility

	Nominal Pretax Return	Real, After-Tax Return	Pretax Volatility
Diversified public equity	9.75%	4.68%	17.24%
Private equity fund	12.62	6.89	34.72
Taxable 10-year AA bond	5.13	0.07	4.74
Tax-exempt 5-year bond	3.52	0.51	5.67
Taxable money market fund	4.75	−0.15	0.45
Hedge fund	8.53	2.47	8.75

TABLE 31.2 Expected Correlations

	Diversified Public Equity	Private Equity Fund	Taxable 10-Year AA Bond	Tax-Exempt 5-Year Bond	Taxable Money Market Fund	Hedge Fund
Diversified public equity	1.00					
Private equity fund	0.47	1.00				
Taxable 10-year AA bond	0.14	0.04	1.00			
Tax-exempt 5-year bond	0.17	0.08	0.78	1.00		
Taxable money market fund	−0.01	−0.02	0.17	0.16	1.00	
Hedge fund	0.39	0.22	0.23	0.28	0.29	1.00

no future value to these gifts. Finally, to allow for a fair comparison, we will gross up the parents' wealth by $4 million to $29 million to reflect the transfer tax they would pay in order to move $8 million into the grantor trust. We are ignoring lifetime gift allowances and some of the more creative methods for transferring wealth in order to keep this example simple. The reader might think we have already failed in that quest, but this is a very simplified example compared to what a practitioner would typically deal with. These assumptions yield the efficient frontier shown in Figure 31.1.

Based on the 8 percent volatility solution, the nominal weighted portfolio pretax return is 7.36 percent. However, the impact of estate taxes, income taxes, inflation, and spending combine to produce an expected decline in real wealth from $29 million to just $20.6 million. In our example, the expected nominal wealth, net of estate taxes, was $37.3 million. Discounting for 3 percent annual inflation yields the forecast $20.6 million. The estate tax was very onerous. In this example, the entire estate was subject to estate tax and the amount due was $37.3 million.

The next step is to introduce the Joneses' estate plan. As described previously, they have $15 million in direct accounts, $2 million in the retirement account, and $8 million in a grantor trust owned by the children. The parents' spending will begin at $250,000 per year and will be partially met by $100,000 annual withdrawals from the retirement account. These withdrawals will be subject to 40 percent income tax. The parents will make $80,000 in annual gifts and will pay the taxes of the grantor trust. There will be uniform asset location in this example. The asset al-

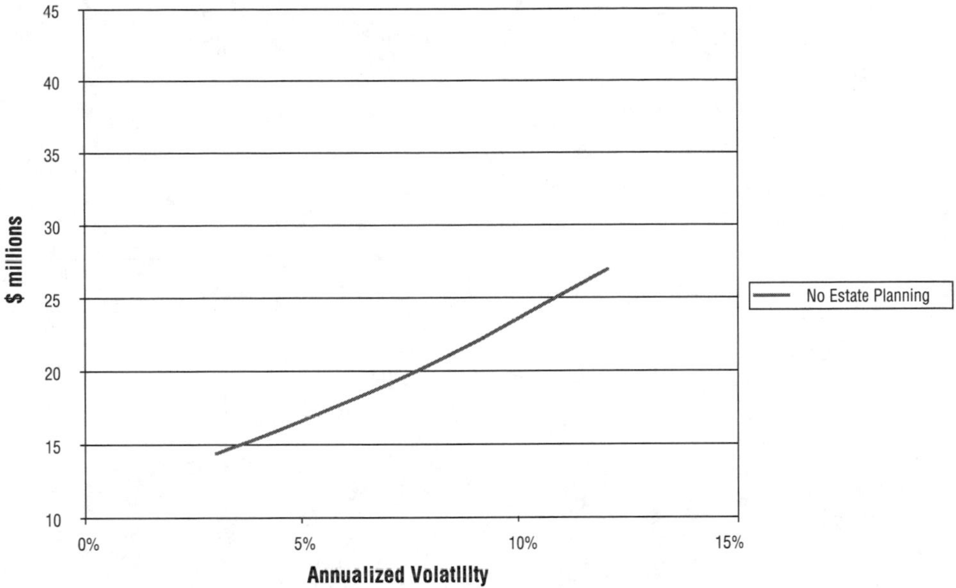

FIGURE 31.1 The Jones Family's Efficient Frontier: Expected Real Wealth of Children in 20 Years Net of Income and Transfer Taxes

location mix will be identical within each of the three entities. If there is a 10 percent allocation to public equity, 10 percent of each entity will be allocated to public equity. We will, however, allow each entity to choose between taxable and municipal bonds as appropriate.

Figure 31.2 shows the improvement in the efficient frontier derived from the estate plan. Based on the 8 percent volatility solution, the expected future real wealth increased by 28 percent, from \$20.6 million to \$26.3 million. Most of the increase came in a meaningful reduction of estate taxes from \$37.3 million to just \$12.1 million (in nominal dollars).

Now we will introduce asset location. We will use optimization techniques to find the ideal mix of assets and location for varying levels of risk. The optimizer will be allowed to manipulate the allocation to asset class and location according to the following instructions:

Maximize: Expected future value net of income and transfer taxes

Subject To:

Initial grantor trust assets = \$8 million

Initial direct assets = \$15 million

Initial retirement assets = \$2 million

Cash in direct assets ≧ 4% of direct assets

Total hedge fund ≦ 10% of total assets

Total private equity ≦ 15% of total assets

Total initial risk ≦ X

Total final risk ≦ 1.1 * X

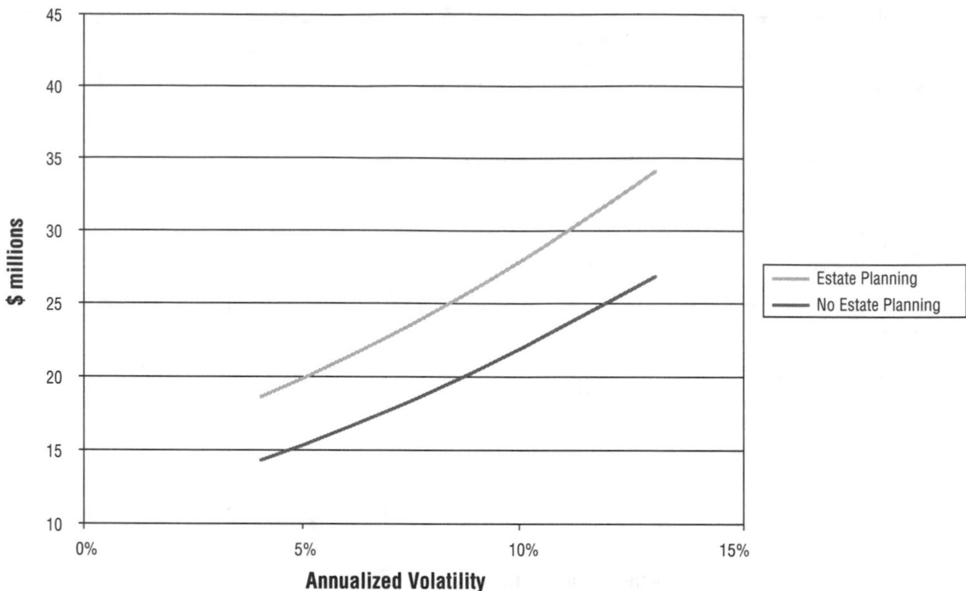

FIGURE 31.2 Impact of Estate Planning: Expected Real Wealth of Children in 20 Years Net of Income and Transfer Taxes

The optimizer uses standard programming techniques to find the best solution to the stated problem. The best solution is the mix of asset allocation and location that gives the most expected future value of net income and estate taxes while abiding by the constraints specified earlier. We imposed limits on the allocation to illiquid assets and required that there be some cash in Mr. and Mrs. Jones' personal account. These are typical requirements. From a practical point of view, investors do want to limit their allocation to illiquid investments.

We mapped the efficient frontier by optimizing at different levels of total risk.[3]

[3]The optimization process treats each entity as a separate pool of assets. Within each pool we assume there is continuous rebalancing to maintain the target asset allocation *of that entity*. In the case where there are no entities, and also in the case where each entity has the same asset allocation, portfolio risk should remain constant over time. However, in the case of optimized asset location, each entity will have a different asset allocation mix. Over time, the relative sizes of the entities will change and therefore the overall asset allocation and risk level will change. The optimization process tends to place the riskier, more appreciating assets into the tax-advantaged entities. Over time, these entities are expected to grow faster and therefore there is a tendency for the overall risk level to increase. The degree to which overall portfolio risk increases is related to the excess performance of risky assets over less risky assets. In practice, this comes down to the performance of equities. When equities do well, the risk level will tend to increase and vice versa.

Continuous rebalancing to retain the target level of risk is one option available to an investor. However, that would require a complex multiperiod optimization process. For the sake of simplicity, we decided to impose a constraint that the expected risk level could not drift up by more than 10 percent; that is, if the target initial risk level is 8 percent, the ending risk level should not exceed 8.8 percent.

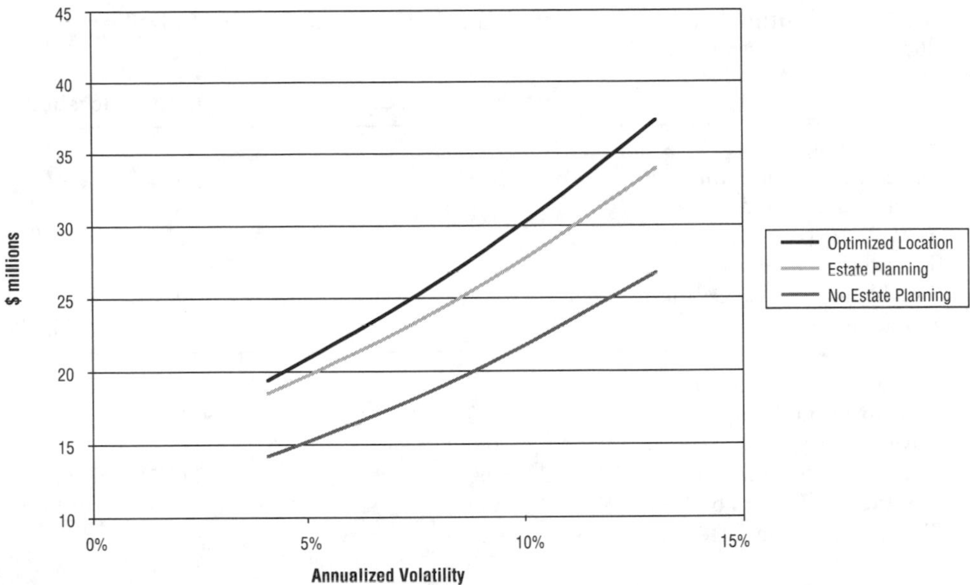

FIGURE 31.3 Benefits of Optimized Location: Expected Real Wealth of Children in 20 Years Net of Income and Transfer Taxes

Figure 31.3 demonstrates the results. The introduction of asset location allows for further improvement in the efficient frontier. Using the 8 percent volatility solution as a point of comparison, the expected future wealth rose an additional 9 percent to $28.6 million. This is the equivalent of adding 0.43 percent to the annualized after-tax nominal return on all assets. Table 31.3 highlights the changes in future wealth and asset allocation.

Table 31.4 shows the optimal asset allocation and location for the 8 percent

TABLE 31.3 Jones Family: Improvements in Expected Future Wealth

All results in $ millions and are based on 8% annual volatility solution.

	No Estate Plan	Estate Plan	Optimized Location
Expected nominal estate tax liability	–$37.3	–$12.1	–$10.6
Expected nominal ending wealth	$37.3	$47.7	$51.6
Expected real ending wealth	$20.6	$26.3	$28.6
Asset Allocation			
Diversified public equity	31.0%	31.9%	27.5%
Private equity fund	12.7	11.8	13.5
Taxable 10-year AA bond	0.0	7.0	1.1
Tax-exempt 5-year bond	26.0	10.5	31.3
Taxable money market fund	20.3	28.7	16.6
Hedge fund	10.0	10.0	10.0
	100.0%	100.0%	100.0%

TABLE 31.4 Optimal Asset Allocation and Location for 8 Percent Volatility Solution—Jones Family

	Entity Allocation		Overall Allocation	
Direct Holdings				
Diversified public equity	26.1%		15.7%	
Private equity fund	17.6		10.6	
Taxable 10-year AA bond	0.0		0.0	
Tax-exempt 5-year bond	52.2		31.3	
Taxable money market fund	4.0		2.4	
Hedge fund	0.0%	100.0%	0.0%	60.0%
401(k) Retirement Account				
Diversified public equity	0.0%		0.0%	
Private equity fund	0.0		0.0	
Taxable 10-year AA bond	0.0		0.0	
Tax-exempt 5-year bond	0.0		0.0	
Taxable money market fund	100.0		8.0	
Hedge fund	0.0%	100.0%	0.0%	8.0%
Grantor Trust				
Diversified public equity	37.0%		11.9%	
Private equity fund	9.1		2.9	
Taxable 10-year AA bond	3.4		1.1	
Tax-exempt 5-year bond	0.0		0.0	
Taxable money market fund	19.2		6.1	
Hedge fund	31.3%	100.0%	10.0%	32.0%
				100.0%

volatility solution. The ideal solution includes (1) shifting the higher-return assets into the grantor trust in order to avoid estate taxes on the appreciation they generate, and (2) shifting the more tax inefficient investments into the retirement account or grantor trust where they enjoy tax deferral or tax subsidization via estate tax savings.

The optimal solution has two tendencies. First, it shifts more of the expected return into the grantor trust. This reduces future estate tax liability by having more of the family's appreciation outside of the parents' estate. Second, it shifts more tax liability into the grantor trust. This is helpful because income and capital gains tax payments are partially subsidized by future estate tax savings. The family is going to own instruments that generate tax liability. It is better to position them in the grantor trust so that the parents can pay the income tax while allowing the children's assets to grow and compound at pretax rates. In the case where we imposed uniform asset allocation on each entity, the pretax return of the parents' directly held assets was 7.44 percent while the grantor trust was 7.72 percent. The small difference was due to the parents' greater use of municipal bonds. In the optimized solution, the pretax return of the parents' holdings declined to 6.80 percent while the grantor trust rose to 8.51 percent. A grantor trust is a powerful estate-planning vehicle, and it is far more powerful when used in an optimal manner.

It is interesting to note how the retirement account was used. The chief tax benefit of retirement accounts is the ability to defer income tax on salary for many years. However, the tax benefits on investments held within the retirement account are mixed and decline as the owner gets older. All return earned or accrued within the retirement account will be subject to ordinary income tax when it is withdrawn. Any balance left over when both parents have died will be subject to ordinary income tax. The remaining balance will then be subject to estate tax and will not have the benefit of the step-up in basis. Given that Mr. and Mrs. Jones have begun to withdraw from the account and have only a 20-year life expectancy, the power of deferral is diminishing. Given this situation, it makes little sense to shift highly appreciating assets that generate long-term capital gains rather than ordinary income into the retirement account. The return will be taxed as ordinary income and the appreciation will be subject to estate tax. Consequently, the optimal solution derived the most benefit from the tax characteristics of the retirement account by shifting the money market allocation into the retirement account. This asset class is subject to ordinary income tax and so will benefit from the deferral that the retirement account can provide.

We will now perform the same analysis for Mr. Smith. His objective is to maximize the future value of the foundation. Mr. Smith recognizes that all of his assets will eventually go to the foundation. Thus, his personal assets and the foundation's assets should be run in a coordinated fashion. Figure 31.4 shows the same three efficient frontiers for Mr. Smith. Note that estate planning does not provide as large an increase as was the case with the Jones family. That is because Mr. Smith expects to give all his assets to his foundation and therefore there will be no estate taxes due. Mr. Smith benefits from estate planning because a part of

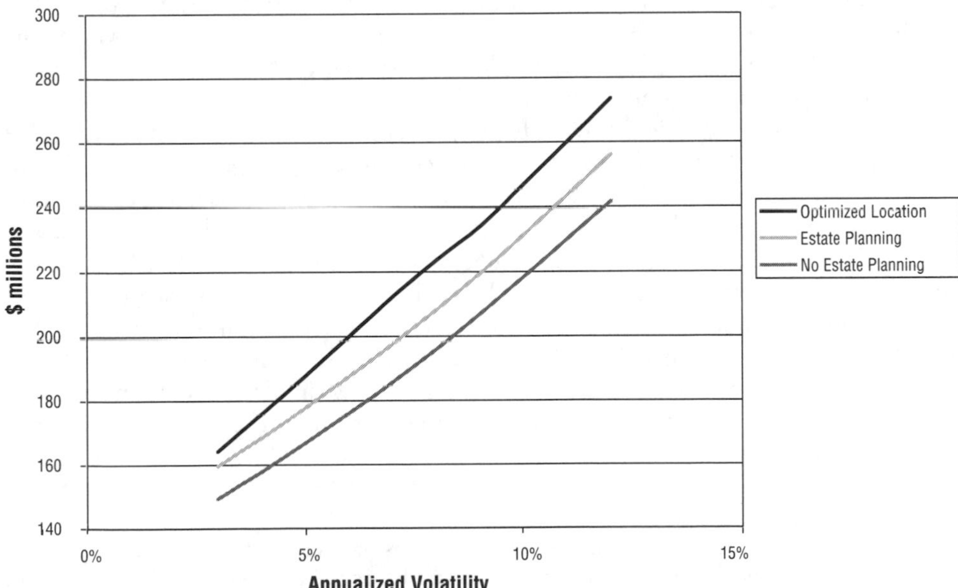

FIGURE 31.4 Mr. Smith's Efficient Frontier: Expected Real Value of the Foundation in 15 Years Net of Income and Transfer Taxes

TABLE 31.5 Smith Foundation: Ending Wealth and Asset Allocation

All results in $ millions and are based on 8% annual volatility solution.

	No Estate Plan	Estate Plan	Optimized Location
Expected nominal estate tax liability	$0.0	$0.0	$0.0
Expected nominal ending wealth	$305.9	$324.9	$348.8
Expected real ending wealth	$196.4	$208.6	$223.9
Asset Allocation			
Diversified public equity	31.8%	32.1%	28.2%
Private equity fund	12.1	10.1	10.5
Taxable 10-year AA bond	0.0	12.3	0.0
Tax-exempt 5-year bond	24.8	11.5	22.4
Taxable money market fund	21.3	24.0	28.9
Hedge fund	10.0	10.0	10.0
	100.0%	100.0%	100.0%

the assets under his control can be managed free of income and capital gains tax. Asset location shifts more of the more tax inefficient assets into the foundation. Table 31.5 provides ending wealth and asset allocation under the three scenarios. Table 31.6 shows asset allocation and asset location in the optimized location scenario at 8 percent volatility.

Mr. Smith is in a very different position from the Jones family because estate taxes do not affect his plans. Consequently, the percentage increases in future wealth derived from the introduction of an estate plan are not nearly as great. Estate planning merely shifts a portion of his wealth from taxable to tax-exempt status. In general, the faster he gives his wealth to the charity, the greater will be the future value of the charity. In our example, we assumed that there would be no further donations until Mr. Smith's death.

Asset location strategies allowed for improvement in the expected future value of the foundation. Optimized location produced an expected real future value of $223.9 million, which was 7 percent greater than the uniform asset allocation solution. This was achieved by shifting the tax inefficient hedge fund into the foundation.[4] Minimizing the ordinary income generated in the CRT maximized the benefit derived from the CRT. Remember that the tiering of income rules mean that ordinary income or short-term gains in the CRT cause significant increases in Mr. Smith's tax liability on distributions he receives from the CRT. Consequently the CRT is invested in public equity, which has only a low dividend yield, and municipal bonds. As was the case with the Joneses, the best use of the retirement account

[4]In practice, Mr. Smith's foundation might be viewed as having too aggressive an asset allocation mix. Even though Mr. Smith intends to donate his remaining assets to the foundation, the foundation must be run according to prudent-person rules. In a real situation, it might be necessary to impose some additional constraints that produce a more balanced asset allocation strategy for the foundation.

TABLE 31.6 Optimal Asset Allocation and Location for 8 Percent Volatility Solution—Mr. Smith

	Entity Allocation		Overall Allocation	
Direct Holdings				
Diversified public equity	0.0%		0.0%	
Private equity fund	0.0		0.0	
Taxable 10-year AA bond	0.1		0.0	
Tax-exempt 5-year bond	46.3		22.4	
Taxable money market fund	53.0		25.6	
Hedge fund	0.6%	100.0%	0.3%	48.4%
401(k) Retirement Account				
Diversified public equity	0.0%		0.0%	
Private equity fund	0.0		0.0	
Taxable 10-year AA bond	0.0		0.0	
Tax-exempt 5-year bond	0.0		0.0	
Taxable money market fund	100.0		3.2	
Hedge fund	0.0%	100.0%	0.0%	3.2%
Charitable Remainder Trust				
Diversified public equity	79.3%		25.6%	
Private equity fund	0.0		0.0	
Taxable 10-year AA bond	0.0		0.0	
Tax-exempt 5-year bond	20.7		6.7	
Taxable money market fund	0.0		0.0	
Hedge fund	0.0%	100.0%	0.0%	32.3%
Foundation				
Diversified public equity	16.3%		2.6%	
Private equity fund	23.6		3.8	
Taxable 10-year AA bond	0.0		0.0	
Tax-exempt 5-year bond	0.0		0.0	
Taxable money market fund	0.0		0.0	
Hedge fund	60.1%	100.0%	9.7%	16.1%
				100.0%

was to hold a lower-yielding asset that generates ordinary income. The optimal location strategy increases the expected future value of the foundation by reducing Mr. Smith's ongoing income tax liability. In the case of uniform asset allocation in each entity, Mr. Smith was projected to pay \$38.5 million in income and capital gains taxes over the 15-year period. In the optimized solution, this declined to \$23.9 million.

Table 31.7 compares the optimal 8 percent volatility results for the two investors. The calculation of annualized return is net of both income and estate taxes. Mr. Smith's annualized return is much greater because he will not pay estate taxes. The asset allocation solutions are not that different but the asset location solutions were very different, reflecting differences in the goals and objectives. Minimizing estate tax

TABLE 31.7 Optimal 8 Percent Volatility Solutions

	Jones	Smith
Annualized nominal return	3.69%	5.56%
Annualized real return	0.67	2.48
Asset Allocation		
Diversified public equity	27.5	28.2
Private equity fund	13.5	10.5
Taxable 10-year AA bond	1.1	0.0
Tax-exempt 5-year bond	31.3	22.4
Taxable money market fund	16.6	28.9
Hedge fund	10.0	10.0
	100.0%	100.0%

liability was the key strategy for the Joneses while minimizing income and capital gains tax liability was important to Mr. Smith.

CONCLUSIONS

Integration of tax considerations into investment decisions is critical to achieving optimal results. The two subjects are so intertwined that they cannot be dealt with separately.

The estate tax can be the biggest barrier to the transfer of wealth to heirs. There are various estate planning entities that can reduce estate tax liability. Asset location strategies can derive far more utility from these estate planning entities. Shifting appreciation from parents' accounts to children's accounts can be accomplished by having the children hold more of the family's public and private equity. Entities that allow the parents to pay the taxes due on the children's investments can enhance results by allowing the children's assets to grow at the pretax rate. This slows the growth of the parents' assets but, in combination, it reduces estate tax liability by having more of the overall after-tax appreciation occur outside of the parents' estate.

Investors who have more philanthropic intentions are less concerned with estate tax issues and more concerned with minimizing income tax. The less tax they pay, the more that can go to charity. A strategy of shifting more highly taxed investments into tax-advantaged entities such as foundations or CRTs will accomplish this.

Asset location strategies can meaningfully enhance results without necessarily taking on any more risk. Each investor is unique and requires customized analysis and planning.

CHAPTER 32

Equity Portfolio Structure

Don Mulvihill

Equities make up the largest part of many investors' portfolios and an even larger part of their expected total return. In the previous chapters we have observed:

- Equities generally provide long-term growth in real wealth. Their expected real, after-tax return is much greater than that of bonds or money market instruments.
- Taxes are a major impediment to growing wealth. After-tax returns compound at a much slower rate. For example, over 25 years, 10 percent per year turns $1 into $10.8, while 8 percent per year produces only $6.8.
- Asset location strategies can reduce the impact of taxation. Matching the return characteristics of an investment to the tax characteristics of an estate planning or retirement entity can enhance after-tax returns and the transfer of wealth to heirs or charities.

These factors support the view that minimizing the tax on equity returns should be an important consideration in investment strategies for taxable investors. Equities are interesting because, unlike bonds or bills, the investor can generally control when taxes are due. Appreciation is the main component of equity returns. Capital gains taxes on appreciation are due only when a stock is sold. Since the investor generally controls the decision to sell, investors can defer tax liabilities for many years. Tax deferral is powerful because it allows wealth to compound on a pretax basis. Tax deferral can be even more powerful when it can lead to tax avoidance. The step-up in basis eliminates capital gains tax liability on appreciated assets held by an individual who has died. The government waives capital gains taxes on appreciated assets given to charity. Many wealthy investors (1) will always have an allocation to equities and (2) will dispose of a significant portion of their wealth through death and/or charitable giving. Put these two factors together and you have a strong case for buy-and-hold equity strategies that allow market returns to compound with minimal capital gains taxes.

There is an obvious tension between the desire to minimize taxes and the desire to enhance returns through active management. Active management implies turnover and the realization of taxable gains that could have been deferred through a buy-and-hold strategy. In this chapter we will analyze that tension and look at ways to organize equity investing in order to enhance the portion of active management returns that accrue to the investor rather than the IRS.

Mr. Street is a successful equity portfolio manager. Over the past 15 years his portfolios have returned 12 percent per year while the market has returned only 10 percent. Mr. Street claims to be tax efficient because his annual turnover is only 30 percent. Would a taxable investor have benefited from Mr. Street's services or would the investor have been better off in an index fund? To answer that we must ascertain (1) whether the investor would have held the stock in a taxable or tax-advantaged account and (2) whether the investor expected to eventually sell the portfolio and pay capital gains tax or dispose of the assets through death or charitable giving, thus avoiding capital gains tax.

All or most of the additional return created by Mr. Street's portfolio management skill would have accrued to the investor if the assets were held in a tax-free entity such as a foundation or a tax-deferred retirement account. Turnover and realization of gains has no tax impact in these entities. The outcome would be different if the portfolio was subject to direct taxation. Ten percent out of the 12 percent annual return came just from being in the market. Mr. Street deserves credit only for the extra 2 percent return. In order to earn that additional return, Mr. Street periodically turned over the portfolio, subjecting all the appreciation to capital gains tax. Thirty percent annual turnover implies about a three-year average holding period. Three years is not very long, so a taxable investor who hires Mr. Street should accept the fact that, over time, substantially all appreciation will be subject to capital gains tax. This is very different from a buy-and-hold index strategy that would have allowed the 10 percent return to compound on a pretax basis. The index fund would have returned more on an after-tax basis. We present three tables that compare the growth of a portfolio assuming 9 percent annual appreciation and a 1 percent dividend yield. Table 32.1 reflects a passive strategy. We assigned a 5 percent annual turnover to reflect unavoidable turnover due to mergers, acquisitions, and benchmark changes. Table 32.2 reflects active management with 30 percent

TABLE 32.1 Portfolio Growth and Return for Buy-and-Hold

9% annual appreciation; 1% dividend yield; 5% turnover

						Annualized After-Tax Return	
Year	Dividend	Realized Gain	Tax	Market Value	Cost Basis	Bequest	Liquidation
				$1,000,000	$1,000,000		
1	$10,000	$ 4,500	$ 4,900	1,095,100	1,009,600	9.51%	7.80%
2	10,951	9,203	6,221	1,198,389	1,023,533	9.47	7.86
3	11,984	14,136	7,621	1,310,607	1,042,032	9.44	7.92
4	13,106	19,327	9,108	1,432,560	1,065,357	9.40	7.97
5	14,326	24,807	10,692	1,565,125	1,093,797	9.37	8.02
10	22,219	57,809	20,449	2,423,633	1,325,265	9.26	8.22
15	34,248	104,360	34,571	3,732,739	1,749,893	9.18	8.36
20	52,622	172,458	55,541	5,732,896	2,456,188	9.12	8.46
25	80,720	274,187	87,125	8,792,064	3,582,505	9.08	8.54

TABLE 32.2 Portfolio Growth and Return for Active Management with No Excess Return

9% annual appreciation; 1% dividend yield; 30% turnover

						Annualized After-Tax Return	
Year	Dividend	Realized Gain	Tax	Market Value	Cost Basis	Bequest	Liquidation
				$1,000,000	$1,000,000		
1	$10,000	$ 27,000	$ 9,400	1,090,600	1,027,600	9.06%	7.80%
2	10,906	48,346	14,032	1,185,628	1,072,821	8.89	7.85
3	11,856	65,854	17,913	1,286,278	1,132,618	8.75	7.88
4	12,863	80,828	21,311	1,393,595	1,204,997	8.65	7.91
5	13,936	94,206	24,416	1,508,539	1,288,724	8.57	7.93
10	20,628	155,839	39,419	2,229,672	1,866,048	8.35	7.99
15	30,419	232,753	58,718	3,287,423	2,744,333	8.26	8.02
20	44,838	343,605	86,656	4,845,511	4,043,765	8.21	8.03
25	66,087	506,537	127,742	7,141,798	5,959,879	8.18	8.04

turnover. In this table we did not account for fees and we assumed the active manager's return was identical to the market return. In Table 32.3 reflects active management with net excess return of 2 percent per year. In each case we applied the turnover to the average level of appreciation in the portfolio. We also assumed that all realized gains were long-term.

The passive portfolio grew to $8.8 million while the active portfolio grew to only $7.1 million. If the investor was operating in bequest mode (i.e., disposed of the assets through charitable giving or death), the passive portfolio's annualized return was 9.08 percent versus 8.18 percent for the active portfolio. Tax deferral added 0.90 percent to the after-tax return. If the investor was operating in liquidation

TABLE 32.3 Portfolio Growth and Return for Active Management with 2% Excess Return

11% annual appreciation; 1% dividend yield; 30% turnover

						Annualized After-Tax Return	
Year	Dividend	Realized Gain	Tax	Market Value	Cost Basis	Bequest	Liquidation
				$ 1,000,000	$1,000,000		
1	$10,000	$ 33,000	$ 10,600	1,109,400	1,032,400	10.94%	9.40%
2	11,094	59,710	16,380	1,226,148	1,086,825	10.73	9.47
3	12,261	82,260	21,357	1,351,930	1,159,989	10.57	9.52
4	13,519	102,196	25,847	1,488,314	1,249,858	10.45	9.56
5	14,883	120,651	30,084	1,636,828	1,355,309	10.36	9.59
10	23,838	214,379	52,411	2,617,451	2,117,233	10.10	9.67
15	38,026	345,817	84,374	4,174,588	3,367,683	10.00	9.71
20	60,632	552,091	134,671	6,656,077	5,367,864	9.94	9.72
25	96,670	880,369	214,742	10,612,265	8,558,072	9.91	9.74

mode, then there would be a final tax liability equal to the 20 percent capital gains tax rate applied to the difference between the ending market value and ending cost basis. This would narrow the gap but the passive portfolio would still be ahead by 8.54 percent versus 8.04 percent. When we allow for 2 percent excess return, the active manager does return more than the passive strategy. In the case of bequest mode, it is 9.91 percent versus 9.08 percent. In the case of liquidation mode, the successful active manager produced 9.74 percent versus 8.54 percent. Table 32.4 demonstrates how the tax code punishes active management of equities. It is more difficult to add value on an after-tax basis than a pretax basis. In this example, about one-half of Mr. Street's excess return was lost because Mr. Street's portfolio turnover accelerated the payment of taxes.

If an active manager can achieve additional appreciation through skillful portfolio management, the additional appreciation will generate additional taxes. We can calculate how much additional appreciation an active manager must generate in order to simply match the after-tax return of a passive strategy. The results are shown in Figure 32.1. The shape of the chart shows that any turnover greater than about 15 percent leads to meaningful tax impact. Much of the tax damage is done in the first 20 percent of turnover. The reason is that the impact of pretax compounding is related to holding period, which is the inverse of turnover. Five percent turnover implies a 20-year holding period. Thus, there is little difference between 30 percent turnover, which some consider to be low, and 75 percent turnover. Neither allows for much pretax compounding. These calculations all assume that turnover is tax-indifferent. Turnover is applied to the average level of appreciation in the portfolio. If turnover is applied in a tax-conscious manner, these relationships will change. For example, a policy of aggressively harvesting unrealized losses might lead to very high turnover in a weak market but would actually enhance the after-tax return.

Adopting active strategies in a taxable portfolio is similar to paying a cover charge to enter a casino. The investor agrees to subject market returns to taxation in the hope that the active management will generate sufficient excess returns to cover the taxes. Even if the active strategies are successful, the benefit to the investor is only the net of the excess return and the taxes. A portfolio structure that shields much of the market's return from tax consequences of active management will allow the investor, rather than the IRS, to enjoy the benefit of any excess returns generated by active management.

A "core and satellite" portfolio structure is the combination of a large diversified portfolio managed with a tax-sensitive strategy plus one or more concentrated

TABLE 32.4 Annualized Pretax and After-Tax Returns, 25-Year Holding Periods

		After-Tax Return	
	Pretax	Bequest	Liquidation
Passive	10%	9.08%	8.54%
Active, no excess return	10	8.18	8.04
Active, 2% excess return	12	9.91	9.74

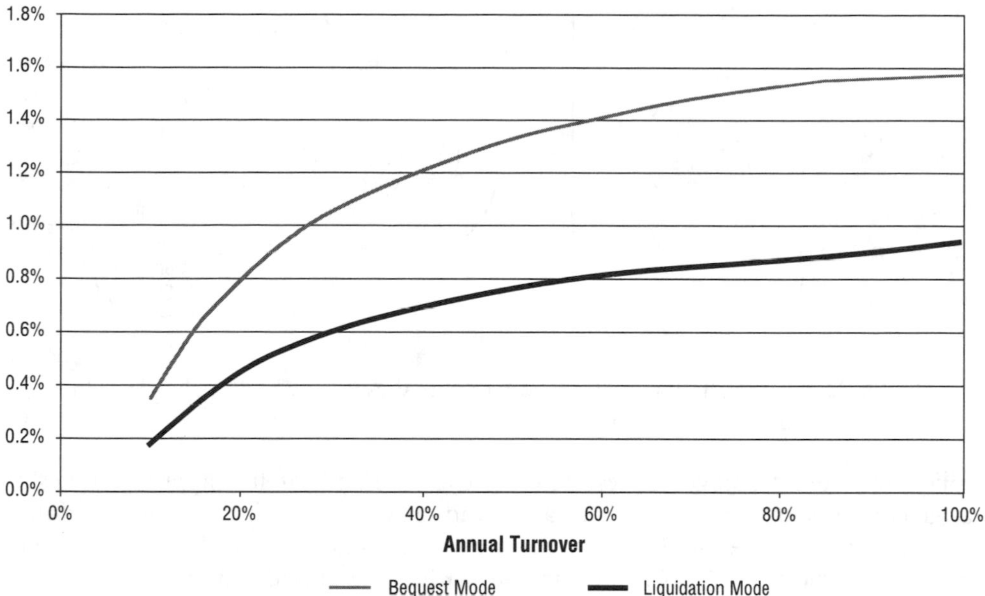

FIGURE 32.1 Tax Hurdle: Excess Pretax Return Required to Match the After-Tax Return of a Passive Strategy

and aggressive actively managed portfolios. The core portfolio allows the market's return to compound on a pretax basis. The after-tax return can be further enhanced through systematic tax loss selling. The satellite portfolios may allow for more extraordinary returns from active management but will likely generate a lot of realized gains. Two examples of satellite portfolios are:

1. A market-neutral hedge fund that is long some stocks and short others, and balanced to eliminate market exposure. The investor will owe tax on any returns that the hedge fund manager can generate, but that will not subject the returns of the core index fund to taxation. This arrangement separates active management from equity exposure.
2. A specialty fund such as active small cap. The portfolio manager can manage the portfolio aggressively because the core index fund has already created diversification. The strategy will generate realized gains but may also generate excess returns.

The core and satellite approach should allow much of the market's return to compound on a pretax basis in the core portfolio. In addition, it may allow for more effective asset location strategies. Breaking the equity holdings into a tax-efficient core and tax-inefficient satellites may allow for positioning the tax-inefficient satellites within tax-advantaged entities.

The last point is particularly important. In many cases there are legal or practical considerations that limit how much of an investor's wealth can reside inside of tax-advantaged entities. Thus, there is a limit to how much of the investment port-

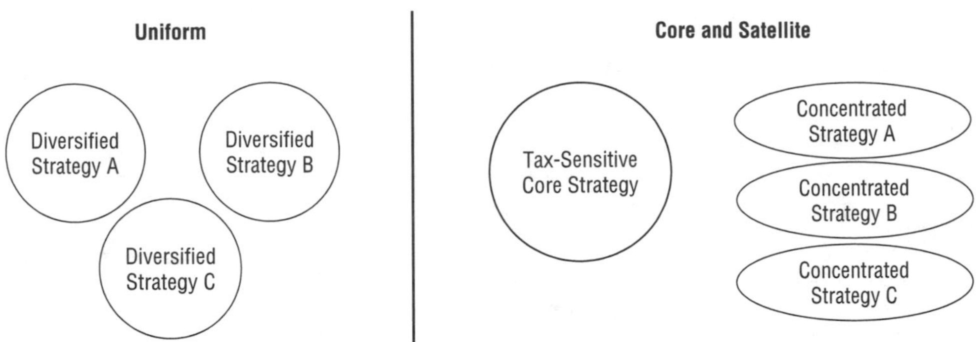

FIGURE 32.2 Uniform Equity Portfolio Structure versus Core and Satellite Structure

folio can take advantage of these entities. The core and satellite approach takes a large component of the equity allocation and creates a tax-efficient core portfolio that does not require the shield of a tax-advantaged entity. This allows more scope for placing the tax-inefficient investments within the tax-advantaged entities. We introduced Mr. Smith in the preceding chapter. He controls $155 million in assets. Of this, $80 million is in tax-advantaged entities. If he had a 60 percent allocation to equities, the total equity holdings would be $93 million. It will not all fit within the tax-advantaged entities. But, if he adopted a core and satellite structure with 50 percent of the equity holdings in the core, he could hold the core in his personal account. There would be $46.5 million in satellite portfolios. These could all fit within the tax-advantaged entities and still allow room for hedge funds or other tax-inefficient asset classes.

Let us compare after-tax wealth generation between the two structures shown in Figure 32.2. In the uniform structure there are three active strategies. Each runs a diversified portfolio with an expected tracking error of 5 percent. The three managers are given identical amounts and their strategies are uncorrelated. The tracking errors will tend to net and the overall tracking error to the benchmark is 2.89 percent. In the core and satellite structure, 50 percent of the equity allocation is put into an index strategy. The remainder is divided equally among the three managers. Each manager will have a 10 percent tracking error. The overall expected tracking error should also be 2.89 percent. We will analyze these two structures in the context of Mr. Smith's desire to maximize the future value of his foundation.

In the preceding chapter, Mr. Smith's menu of investment choices included public equity. We will assume that was in the uniform structure. We shall now add two additional choices, as described in Table 32.5.

TABLE 32.5 Three Equity Strategies

	Pretax Return	After-Tax Return	Pretax Volatility	After-Tax Volatility	Annual Turnover
Uniform	9.75%	8.00%	17.24%	16.40%	30%
Core index	9.00	8.16	17.00	16.06	5
Satellite aggressive	10.50	8.39	17.95	16.40	50

We plotted a new efficient frontier for Mr. Smith that reflects the benefits of the core and satellite approach. We required that equal amounts be invested in the core index and the aggressive satellites. Figure 32.3 shows the new efficient frontier.

Table 32.6 shows the asset allocation and location results for the 8 percent volatility solution, comparing the uniform equity struture to the core and satellite equity portfolio structure. The ideal mix includes using the tax-efficient core in Mr. Smith's personal account and the higher-yielding but tax-inefficient satellite strategies in the tax-advantaged entities. This arrangement allows Mr. Smith to retain, for his foundation, 100 percent of any excess return generated by active portfolio management. Switching to the core and satellite equity structure increased the expected real value of the foundation from $223.9 to $225.7 million without increasing expected risk.

We assumed that the core portfolio was a simple buy-and-hold index strategy. The after-tax return of the index strategy can be enhanced with a systematic tax loss harvesting strategy. Tax loss harvesting takes advantage of flexibility in the tax code. The investor decides whether and when to sell a stock. Thus, the investor can decide whether to realize a gain or a loss. Stocks tend to appreciate over time, so a buy-and-hold strategy is effective at deferring capital gains taxes on the appreciation. A more effective utilization of this flexibility is to realize losses and not realize gains. For example, Mr. Smith will implement his core portfolio strategy by purchasing a diversified portfolio of 250 stocks. Eleven months later he looks at the portfolio: 150 stocks have risen in value, 25 are about unchanged, and 75 have declined in value. The decliners are down by an average of 20 percent. The unrealized loss is equal to 6 percent of the total portfolio value. Mr. Smith also owns several hedge funds.

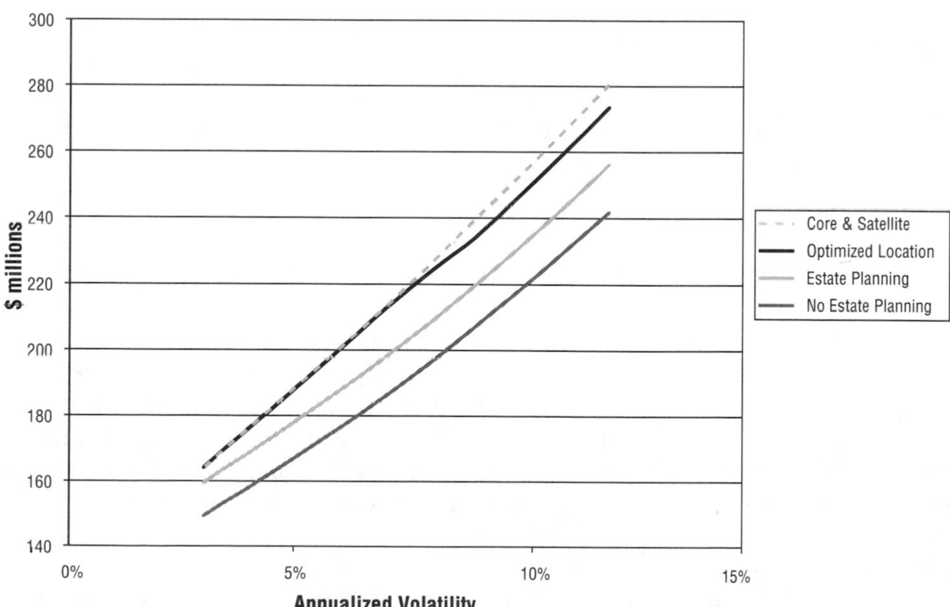

FIGURE 32.3 Mr. Smith's Efficient Frontier: Expected Real Value of the Foundation in 15 Years Net of Income and Transfer Taxes

TABLE 32.6 Comparison of Uniform Structure and Core and Satellite Structure

Asset Allocation		Asset Location			
		Direct	401(k)	CRT	Foundation
Uniform Equity Structure					
Public and Private Equity					
Uniform diversified public equity	28.2%	0.0%	0.0%	25.6%	2.6%
Core equity	—	—	—	—	—
Satellite equity	—	—	—	—	—
Private equity fund	10.5%	0.0%	0.0%	6.7%	3.8%
	38.7%				
Fixed Income and Money Market					
Taxable 10-year AA bond	0.0%	0.0%	0.0%	0.0%	0.0%
Tax-exempt 5-year bond	22.4%	22.4%	0.0%	0.0%	0.0%
Taxable money market fund	28.9%	25.6%	3.2%	0.0%	0.0%
	51.3%				
Alternative Investments					
Hedge funds	10.0%	0.3%	0.0%	0.0%	9.7%
Core and Satellite Equity Structure					
Public and Private Equity					
Uniform diversified public equity	0.0%	0.0%	0.0%	0.0%	0.0%
Core equity	16.5%	16.5%	0.0%	0.0%	0.0%
Satellite equity	16.5%	0.0%	0.0%	12.0%	4.5%
Private equity fund	10.1%	10.1%	0.0%	0.0%	0.0%
	43.1%				
Fixed Income and Money Market					
Taxable 10-year AA bond	0.1%	0.0%	0.1%	0.0%	0.1%
Tax-exempt 5-year bond	18.4%	18.4%	0.0%	0.0%	0.0%
Taxable money market fund	28.4%	3.4%	3.2%	20.3%	1.6%
	46.9%				
Alternative Investments					
Hedge Fund	10.0%	0.0%	0.0%	0.0%	10.0%

These are likely to generate realized short-term gains. If Mr. Smith were to sell the stocks that have declined in value within his core equity portfolio and reinvest into similar stocks, he would realize a short-term capital loss. If that loss could be netted against the realized gains distributed by the hedge funds, Mr. Smith will reduce his current year tax liability. That tax savings enhances his current and future wealth. The tax loss harvesting transaction will reduce the cost basis of his equity portfolio. However, because he intends to eventually give the equities to his foundation, he is not concerned with their cost basis. In this case, applying 40 percent ordinary tax rate to the realized short-term loss would provide Mr. Smith with the equivalent of an extra 2.4 percent after-tax return from his core equity portfolio. This extra return comes not from taking additional risk but rather by being more clever in utilizing the tax code's flexibility.

There are two general approaches to tax loss harvesting. The difference involves how to deal with the "wash sale" rule. If a taxable investor sells a security at a loss and purchases the same security within 31 days, the investor must net the sale price against the most recent purchase price rather than the original purchase price. In effect, the realized loss is disallowed and the unrealized loss is carried forward. One approach to dealing with the wash sale rule is to purchase similar but not substantially identical securities. For example, an investor who owns shares in Merck, a pharmaceutical company, might sell the shares of Merck at a loss and immediately reinvest in Pfizer, another pharmaceutical company. Switching from Merck to Pfizer will likely have little impact on the portfolio's risk profile. The other approach is to wait the 31 days. An investor could sell Merck, wait 31 days, and then repurchase Merck. This has the advantage of maintaining the portfolio's risk profile over time. However, for the 31-day interval a part of the portfolio is out of the market and underinvested in equities. Some investors will purchase equity index futures or exchange-traded funds as a way to maintain equity exposure. The drawback to this variation is that unwinding the hedge position may generate short-term gains if the market has risen during the 31-day period.

Tax loss harvesting has two benefits. First, it generates additional after-tax return. Second, it reduces the risk of the portfolio. Tax loss harvesting generates the most realized losses in declining markets and fewer realized losses in strong markets. The investor utilizes the tax code flexibility to allow the IRS to share in losses but not in gains! Equity markets tend to appreciate and thus the ability to harvest losses from a portfolio declines with time. In our experience, an investor might realize losses of 10 percent of a portfolio in the first year, 7 percent in the second year, 5 percent in the third year, and declining amounts thereafter. Actual results will vary with market conditions. Losses will be larger in weak markets and smaller in strong markets. Even in modestly good markets there are usually some stocks or sectors that are doing poorly and provide the opportunity for tax loss harvesting. We believe that systematic tax loss harvesting applied to a broadly diversified portfolio is expected to cumulatively generate realized losses equal to 30 percent of the portfolio's initial value. About two-thirds of these will be short-term in nature. Tax loss harvesting will generally yield few losses after about five years. Table 32.7 shows how tax loss harvesting can increase after-tax return. Compare this to Table 32.1 that showed the growth of a simple buy-and hold-strategy. Tax loss harvesting adds the most value when the investor is in bequest mode, thus able to eventually dispose of the assets in a manner that avoids capital gains tax liability. If the investor is operating in liquidation mode, then tax loss harvesting creates tax deferral but not tax avoidance. Losses generate tax savings but also reduce the portfolio's cost basis. Once the portfolio is finally liquidated, the reduced cost basis will generate a larger terminal tax liability.

A tax loss harvesting strategy will create meaningful benefits for Mr. Smith because it fits nicely with his plan to eventually give his assets to his foundation. On the other hand, the Jones family would derive less benefit because the children will hold most of the family's equities by the time Mr. and Mrs. Jones die. The step-up in basis does not apply to equities held by the children in the grantor trust. We assumed the Joneses had no philanthropic intentions.

We will add tax loss harvesting to the core equity portfolio. We can map out one last efficient frontier for Mr. Smith, shown in Figure 32.4. We applied the core and satellite portfolio structure and tax loss harvesting to the Jones family example as well and derived two new efficient frontiers, shown in Figure 32.5.

TABLE 32.7 Portfolio Growth and Return for Passive Management with Tax Loss Harvesting

9% annual appreciation; 1% dividend yield; 5% underlying turnover

			Harvested Losses					Annualized After-Tax Return	
Year	Dividend	Realized Gain	Short-Term	Long-Term	Tax	Market Value	Cost Basis	Bequest	Liquidation
						$1,000,000	$1,000,000		
1	$10,000	$ 4,500	–$100,000		–$35,100	1,135,100	1,049,600	13.51%	11.80%
2	11,351	9,383	–60,000	–40,000	–$25,583	1,274,193	1,095,917	12.88	11.29
3	12,742	14,648	–40,000	–30,000	–$13,974	1,415,586	1,137,280	12.28	10.79
4	14,156	20,285		–20,000	$5,719	1,551,425	1,166,002	11.60	10.19
5	15,514	26,253		–10,000	$9,456	1,697,111	1,198,313	11.16	9.82
10	24,098	62,189			$22,077	2,628,694	1,447,095	10.15	9.11
15	37,150	112,799			$37,420	4,049,097	1,905,908	9.77	8.96
20	57,085	186,764			$60,187	6,219,197	2,670,678	9.57	8.91
25	87,570	297,198			$94,468	9,538,203	3,891,434	9.44	8.89

Underlying turnover refers to mergers, acquisitions, and benchmark changes that cause turnover in otherwise passive portfolios. This does not include turnover due to tax loss harvesting.

This table assumes that taxes are paid from the account and the tax savings derived from tax loss harvesting are credited to the account.

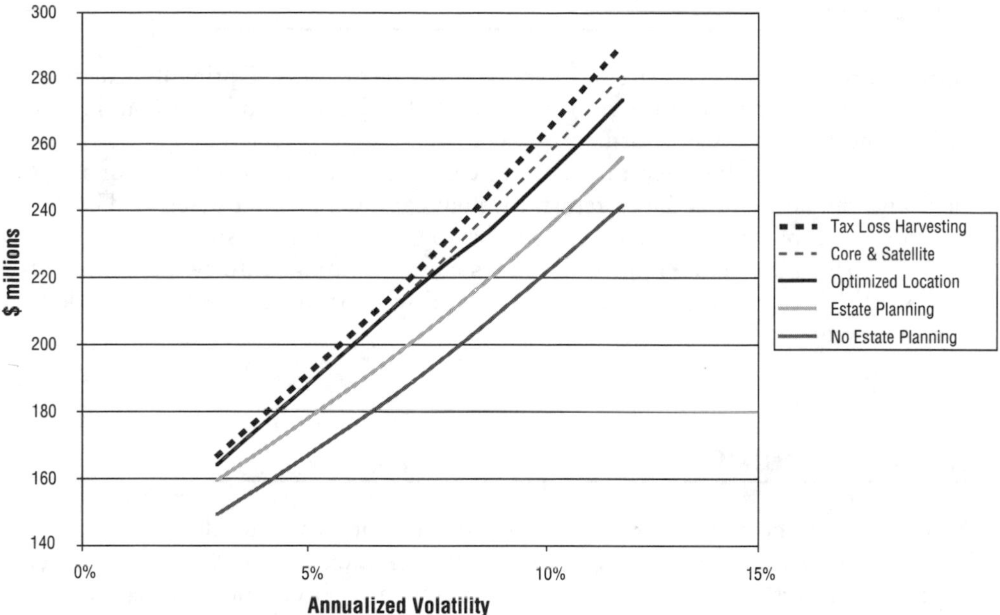

FIGURE 32.4 Mr. Smith's Efficient Frontier: Expected Real Value of the Foundation in 15 Years Net of Income and Transfer Taxes

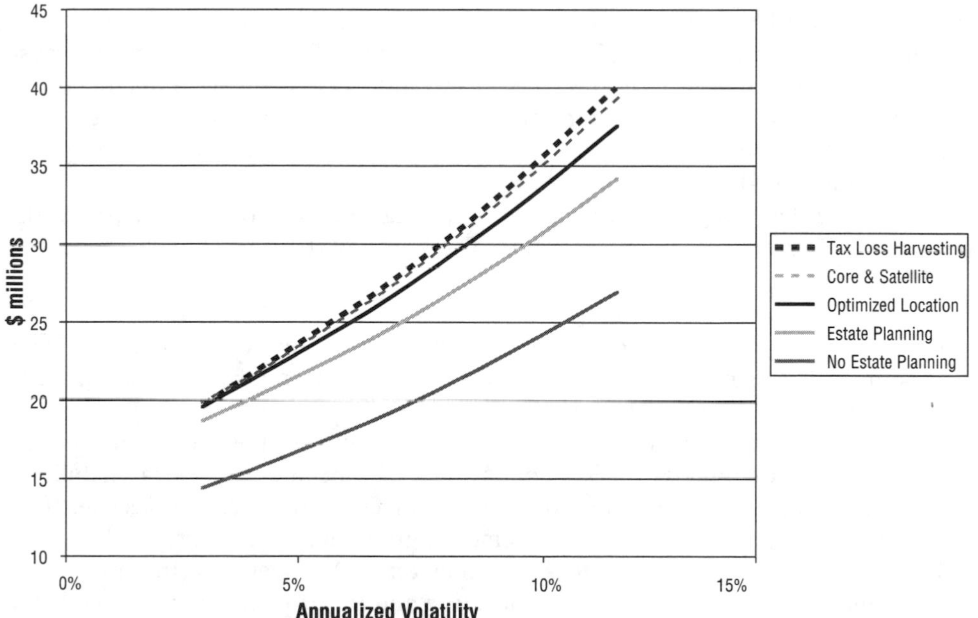

FIGURE 32.5 The Jones Family's Efficient Frontier: Expected Real Wealth of Children in 20 Years Net of Income and Transfer Taxes

CONCLUSIONS

Equities are an important part of most investors' portfolios. Optimally exercising the taxpayer's control over the recognition of realized gains and losses could meaningfully increase after-tax return.

There is tension between the desire to enhance return through active management and the desire to enhance return through capital gains tax deferral. The core and satellite approach allows investors to better manage this tension.

The core and satellite approach breaks equity holdings into two components with very different tax characteristics. This allows for more effective asset location strategies.

OVERALL CONCLUSIONS

We can review the progress we have made during the past four chapters by looking at the increase in expected wealth transfer for each family. We created an efficient frontier that integrates estate planning and investment decisions. We demonstrated that optimal integration can produce significant improvement in the efficient frontier. The investor can expect to transfer more wealth for a given level of risk, or could expect to transfer the same amount of wealth with less risk. Using the 8 percent volatility solution as a reference point, from no estate planning through to full use of asset location, equity portfolio structure and tax loss harvesting generated a 44 percent increase in the expected future real wealth of the Jones children. The same process increased the expected future real value of the Smith foundation by 17 percent. The Joneses derived a greater increase because they were faced with the 50 percent estate tax. Table 32.8 demonstrates this progress. What is important to keep in mind is that the progress was achieved without increasing risk. Integration of investment and tax planning created the additional return.

We have demonstrated a process for applying modern portfolio theory to the special requirements of taxable investors. The four key steps are:

1. Frame the problem according to the investor's long-term objectives. This sounds simple but is often overlooked. The proper framework can bring much clarity to investment planning.
2. Investors have choices regarding asset allocation, asset location, and equity management strategies. These choices affect income and transfer tax liabilities. Understand how these options relate to the investor's long-term objectives. Optimally exercising these options can meaningfully enhance results.
3. The efficient frontier will differ for each investor. An investor's efficient frontier should represent a series of asset allocation and location mixes that provide the highest possible expected after-tax result for a given level of risk. The efficient frontier is based upon optimal exercise of the various tax options. Build a mathematical model that relates expected return, risk, a correlation matrix,

TABLE 32.8 Enhanced Wealth Transfers Based on 8 Percent Volatility Solutions

	No Estate Plan	Estate Plan	Asset Location	Core and Satellite	Tax Loss Harvesting
The Jones Family					
Children's Expected Wealth in 20 Years					
Nominal ($ millions)	37.3	47.5	51.6	53.2	53.7
Real ($ millions)	20.6	26.3	28.6	29.5	29.8
Annualized Return Net of Income and Estate Taxes					
Nominal	1.26%	3.26%	3.69%	3.85%	3.90%
Real	–1.69%	0.25%	0.67%	0.82%	0.87%
Mr. Smith					
Foundation's Expected Value in 15 Years					
Nominal ($ millions)	305.9	324.9	348.8	351.6	359.1
Real ($ millions)	196.4	208.6	223.9	225.7	230.5
Annualized Return Net of Income and Estate Taxes					
Nominal	4.64%	5.06%	5.56%	5.61%	5.76%
Real	1.59%	2.00%	2.48%	2.54%	2.68%

and estate structure to the investor's long-term goals. Figure 32.6 demonstrates the optimal efficient frontier for each of the two investors we studied. The efficient frontiers are very different.

4. Implement portfolio strategies in a tax-efficient manner. This is particularly true of equities because investors can control the timing of capital gains tax liability. The tax code makes it difficult to add value from active management in directly taxed accounts. A broadly diversified core portfolio enhanced with tax loss harvesting is likely to provide the best results in the presence of taxes. Investors should seek ways to shift less tax-efficient strategies into entitites that reduce or eliminate taxation. The concept of a tax-efficient core portfolio residing in the investor's directly owned account complemented with aggressive satellites in the tax-advantaged entities is likely to derive the most benefit from the equity allocation.

This modeling process allows investors to analyze many issues on the basis of the impact on long-term results. Some examples of how this can be applied:

- ***Portfolio management.*** Managers generally seek to change the expected return, risk, or correlation matrix. They seek additional return per unit of risk, or they seek to reduce correlation to other asset classes. Expectations regarding portfolio management can be captured in terms of revisions to the expected return, risk, and correlation matrix. The model can then be used to identify how the

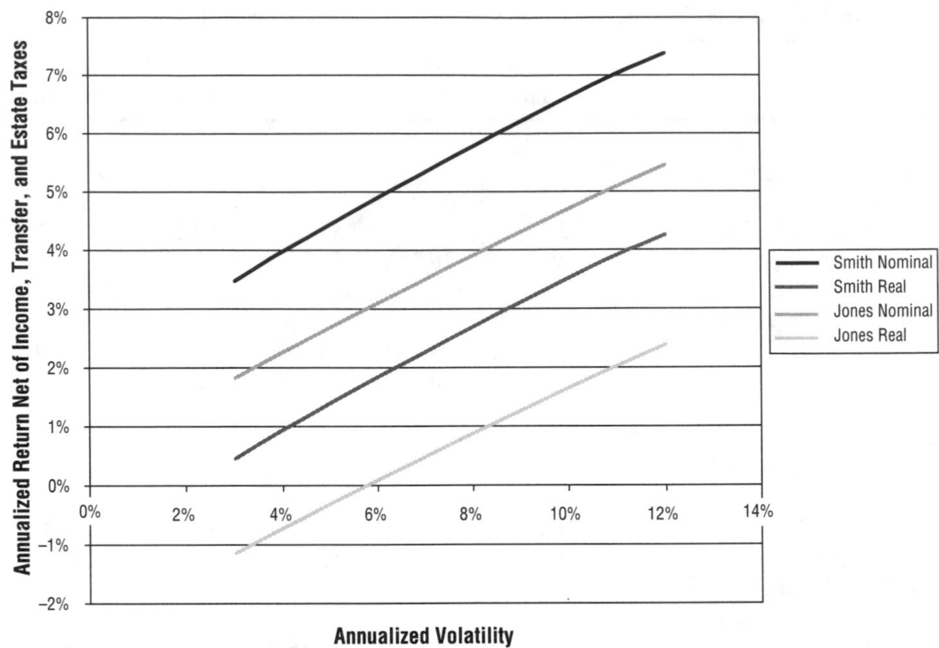

FIGURE 32.6 Optimal Efficient Frontiers

investor could alter asset allocation or location to obtain the most favorable impact on expected long-term results.

- *Asset allocation.* The model relates risk to expected real long-term after-tax results. This is done to capture the powerful impact of estate taxes. It has the added benefit of focusing on what is most relevant to the investor. The classic efficient frontier relates risk to return. Return, however, is an intermediary variable. The investor is interested in wealth and will likely make asset allocation decisions on the basis of the expected wealth and the volatility of the expected wealth.
- *Estate planning.* We took the existing estate plan as fixed in our two examples. However, this modeling process can be used to evaluate changes to estate plans as well. For example, if Mr. Jones was considering buying a life insurance policy as a mechanism for reducing estate taxes, he could first observe his efficient frontier based on the existing estate plan. Then he would alter the model to include the life insurance policy and calculate a new efficient frontier. This efficient frontier would reflect the optimal use of that policy within the context of his other estate entities. A comparison of the efficient frontiers would allow for evaluation of the likely benefit of the life insurance policy on his long-term wealth transfer to his beneficiaries.
- *Concentrated stock positions.* Some investors have a significant portion of their wealth in a single stock with very low cost basis. This is often the result of the sale of a business or stock-based compensation. These investors face the issue of achieving diversification and risk reduction for the least amount of tax. If Mr. Smith's personal assets included a large position in low-cost-basis shares

> of Smith Industries, he could use this process to determine his best choices. He would alter the model to reflect the additional asset class. He would assign it an expected return, a volatility, and correlation to other assets. He would change the model to reflect the fact that reducing the allocation to Smith Industries will require the immediate payment of capital gains taxes. He would then map out the efficient frontier that he faces given the embedded tax liability in his existing holdings. The curve would likely be steeper, reflecting the fact that he would have to pay capital gains taxes to achieve risk reduction.

Taxable investors seek to maximize risk-adjusted expected after-tax wealth. The goal is not to maximize pretax return, nor is it to minimize taxes. There is a tension between the desire to maximize pretax return and after-tax return. This tension can be frustrating to investors and advisors whose background is in the management of pension funds and other tax-exempt assets. Properly managing taxable investor assets requires a much greater level of customization and an understanding of income and estate tax issues. Each investor is unique. Not only do they each have unique goals and estate plans, but they also have unique holdings. Customization includes an attention to each client's cost basis and holding periods on existing assets. The process that we have developed allows investors to optimally navigate this tension by relating investment decisions to after-tax results. It allows modern portfolio theory to be properly applied to taxable investors.

NOTES

Readers should not focus on the actual allocation mixes that we identified as optimal in these examples. The output reflected our inputs regarding expected return, risk, and correlations. In particular, allocations among the highly correlated taxable bond, municipal bond, and money market classes could swing dramatically based on small changes to these parameters. Changes in asset allocation within this group would likely have minimal impact on long-term results. What the reader should observe is the general tendencies of the optimal solution, especially the placement of tax-inefficient entities within tax-advantaged entities.

Readers should recognize that modeling estate plans can be complex. Errors in the model can produce inaccurate results. At the same time, our experience in modeling has sometimes produced results that seemed odd but in fact were correct. The interplay between the tax characteristics of different entities is complex and the impact not always intuitive. The optimization process that we use includes year-by-year projections of each entity's balance and tax liability. Studying these projections often leads to insights into the unexpected interplay between the entities.

Bibliography

Adler, M., and B. Dumas. 1983. "International Portfolio Choice and Corporation Finance: A Synthesis." *Journal of Finance* 38:925–984.

AIMR. 2002 (March 1). "Update Report of the Leverage & Derivatives Subcommittee of the Investment Performance Council." Charlottesville, VA: Association for Investment Management and Research.

AIMR. 2002 (June 1). "Update Report of the Leverage & Derivatives Subcommittee of the Investment Performance Council." Charlottesville, VA: Association for Investment Management and Research.

Aiyagari, R., and M. Gertler. 1991. "Asset Returns with Transaction Costs and Uninsured Individual Risk: A Stage III Exercise." *Journal of Monetary Economics* 27:309–331.

Ankrim, E. M., and C. H. Hensel. 1994. "Multicurrency Performance Attribution." *Financial Analysts Journal* (March/April):29–35.

Antoniou, A., I. Garrett, and R. Priestley. 1998. "The Macroeconomic Variables as Common Pervasive Risk Factors and the Empirical Content of the Arbitrage Pricing Theory." *Journal of Empirical Finance* 5:221–240.

Arnott, R. D., and P. L. Bernstein. 2002. "What Risk Premium Is Normal?" *Financial Analysts Journal* 58 (March/April):64–83.

Barber, B., R. Lehavy, M. McNichols, and B. Trueman. 2001. "Can Investors Profit from the Prophets? Consensus Analyst Recommendations and Stock Returns." *Journal of Finance* 56(2):773–806.

Barra. 1998. "Single Country Equity." In *Risk Model Handbook*. Berkeley, CA: Barra.

Becker, G. 1997. "Why a Crash Wouldn't Cripple the Economy." *BusinessWeek* (April 14):26.

Bercel, A. 1994. "Consensus Expectations and International Equity Returns." *Financial Analysts Journal* 50(4):76–80.

Berkley, S., and N. Gendron. 2002. "A Guide to the Lehman Global Family of Fixed Income Indices." Lehman Brothers Fixed Income Research.

Bernard, V., and J. Thomas. 1989. "Post Earnings Announcement Drift: Delayed Price Response or Risk Premium?" *Journal of Accounting Research* 27(Suppl.): 1–36.

Bernard, V., and J. Thomas. 1990. "Evidence That Stock Prices Do Not Fully Reflect the Implications of Current Earnings for Future Earnings." *Journal of Accounting and Economics* 13:305–340.

Black, F. 1989. "Universal Hedging: Optimizing Currency Risk and Reward in International Equity Portfolios." *Financial Analysts Journal* 45 (July/August):16–22.

Black, F. 1990. "How I Discovered Universal Hedging." *Investing* 4 (Winter): 60–64.

Black, F. 1993. "Estimating Expected Returns." *Financial Analysts Journal* 49: 36–48.

Black, F., and R. Litterman. 1992. "Global Portfolio Optimization." *Financial Analysts Journal* 48 (September/October):28–43.

Bollerslev, T. 1986. "Generalized Autoregressive Conditional Heteroscedasticity." *Journal of Econometrics* 31:307–327.

Breen, W., L. S. Hodrick, and R. A. Korajczyk. 2000. "Predicting Equity Liquidity." Working Paper #205. Chicago: Northwestern University, Department of Finance.

Brinson, G. P., and N. Fachler. 1985. "Measuring Non-U.S. Equity Portfolio Performance." *Journal of Portfolio Management* (Spring):73–76.

Brown, K., and W. V. Harlow. 2002. "Staying the Course: The Impact of Investment Style Consistency on Mutual Fund Performance." Working paper available from the author at McCombs School of Business, University of Texas, Austin; see also www.bus.utexas.edu/~brownk/Research/styleconsistent-wp.pdf.

Brown, S. J. 1989. "The Number of Factors in Security Returns." *Journal of Finance* 5:1247–1262.

Brown, S. J., W. N. Goetzmann, and J. Park. 2001. "Careers and Survival: Competition and Risk in the Hedge Fund and CTA Industry." *Journal of Finance* 56 (October):1869–1886.

Campbell, J., and J. Cochrane. 1999. "By Force of Habit: A Consumption-Based Explanation of Aggregate Stock Market Behavior." *Journal of Political Economy* 107:205–251.

Carhart, M. 1997. "On Persistence in Mutual Fund Performance." *Journal of Finance* 52(1):57–82.

Carino, D. R. 1999. "Combining Attribution Effects over Time." *Journal of Performance Measurement* (Summer):5–14.

Cavaglia, S., C. Brightman, and M. Aked. 2000. "On the Increasing Importance of Industry Factors: Implications for Global Portfolio Management." *Financial Analysts Journal* (September/October):41–54.

Chamberlain, G., and M. Rothschild. 1983. "Arbitrage, Factor Structure, and Mean-Variance Analysis on Large Asset Markets." *Econometrica* 51: 1281–1304.

Chan, L. K. C., N. Jegadeesh, and J. Lakonishok. 1996. "Momentum Strategies." *Journal of Finance* 51(5):1681–1713.

Chan, L. K. C., J. Kareceski, and J. Lakonishok. 1998. "The Risk and Return from Factors." *Journal of Financial and Quantitative Analysis* 33:159–188.

Chen, N.-F., R. Roll, and S. A. Ross. 1986. "Economic Forces and the Stock Market." *Journal of Business* 59:383–403.

Christopherson, J. A., W. E. Ferson, and D. Glassman. 1998. "Conditioning Manager Alphas on Economic Information: Another Look at the Persistence of Performance." *Review of Financial Studies* 11(1):111–142.

Collins, D. W., and P. Hribar. 2000. "Earnings-Based and Accrual-Based Market Anomalies: One Effect or Two?" *Journal of Accounting and Economics* 29(1): 101–123.

Connor, G., and R. A. Korajczyk. 1986. "Performance Measurement with the Arbitrage Pricing Theory: A New Framework for Analysis." *Journal of Financial Economics* 15:373–394.

Connor, G., and R. A. Korajczyk. 1988. "Risk and Return in an Equilibrium APT: Application of a New Test Methodology." *Journal of Financial Economics* 21:255–290.

Connor, G., and R. A. Korajczyk. 1993. "A Test for the Number of Factors in an Approximate Factor Model." *Journal of Finance* 48:1263–1291.

Constantinides, G. M., and W. E. Ferson. 1991. "Habit Persistence and Durability in Aggregate Consumption: Empirical Tests." *Journal of Financial Economics* 29(2):199–240.

Daniel, K., and S. Titman. 1997. "Evidence on the Characteristics of Cross-Sectional Variation in Stock Returns." *Journal of Finance* 52(1):1–33.

Dawes, R. M., D. Faust, and P. E. Meehl. 1989. "Clinical versus Actuarial Judgement." *Science* 243 (March 31):1668–1674.

Dechow, P. M., and R. G. Sloan. 1997. "Returns to Contrarian Investment Strategies: Tests of Naive Expectations Hypotheses." *Journal of Financial Economics* 43(1):3–27.

De Santis, G., and B. Gerard. 1997. "International Asset Pricing and Portfolio Diversification with Time-Varying Risk." *Journal of Finance* 52(5):1881–1912.

De Santis, G., and E. Tavel. 1999. "Conditional Covariance Estimation in QS." Goldman Sachs Asset Management. Mimeographed.

Elton, E. J., M. J. Gruber, S. J. Brown, and W. N. Goetzmann. 2002. *Modern Portfolio: Theory & Investment Analysis*, Sixth Edition. New York: John Wiley & Sons.

Engle, R. F. 1982. "Autoregressive Conditional Heteroscedasticity with Estimates of the Variance of the United Kingdom Inflation." *Econometrica* 50:987–1007.

Engle, R. F. 2002. "Dynamic Conditional Correlation: A Simple Class of Multivariate GARCH Models." *Journal of Business and Economic Statistics* 20(3): 339–350.

Epstein, L. G., and S. E. Zin. 1991. "Substitution, Risk Aversion, and the Temporal Behavior of Consumption and Asset Returns: An Empirical Analysis." *Journal of Political Economy* 99(2):263–286.

Fama, E. F. 1970. "Efficient Capital Markets: A Review of Theory and Empirical Work." *Journal of Finance* 25:383–417.

Fama, E. F., and K. R. French. 1992. "The Cross-Section of Expected Stock Returns." *Journal of Finance* 47(2):427–465.

Fama, E. F., and K. R. French. 1993. "Common Risk Factors in the Returns of Stocks and Bonds." *Journal of Finance* 33:3–56.

Fama, E. F., and K. R. French. 1996. "Multifactor Explanations of Asset Pricing Anomalies." *Journal of Finance* 51:55–84.

Fama, E. F., and K. R. French. 1998. "Value versus Growth: The International Evidence." *Journal of Finance* 53(6):1975–1991.

Fama, E. F., and K. R. French. 2002. "The Equity Premium." *Journal of Finance* 57(2):637–659.

Fama, E. F., and J. Macbeth. 1973. "Risk, Return and Equilibrium: Empirical Tests." *Journal of Political Economy* 81:607–638.

Fama, E. F., and G. W. Schwert. 1977. "Asset Returns and Inflation." *Journal of Financial Economics* 5:115–146.

Ferson, W. E., and R. A. Korajczyk. 1995. "Do Arbitrage Pricing Models Explain the Predictability of Stock Returns?" *Journal of Business* 3:309–347.

Ferson, W. E., and R. W. Schadt. 1996. "Measuring Fund Strategy and Performance in Changing Economic Conditions." *Journal of Finance* 51:425–462.

Foster, G., C. Olsen, and T. Shevlin. 1984. "Earnings Releases, Anomalies and the Behavior of Security Returns." *Accounting Review* 59 (October):574–603.

Francis, J., and L. Soffer. 1997. "The Relative Informativeness of Analysts' Stock Recommendations and Earnings Forecast Revisions." *Journal of Accounting Research* 35(2):193–211.

Fung, W., and D. Hsieh. 1997. "Empirical Characteristics of Dynamic Trading Strategies: The Case of Hedge Funds." *Review of Financial Studies* 10(2): 275–372.

Givant, M. 1988. "Taking a World View: $100 Million Fund Starts Global Allocation Strategy." *Pensions and Investment Age* (June 13):2.

Graham, B. 1959. *The Intelligent Investor*, Second Revised Edition. New York: Harper & Brothers.

Graham, B. 1973. *The Intelligent Investor: A Book of Practical Counsel*, Fourth Revised Edition. New York: Harper & Row.

Graham, B., and D. Dodd. 1934. *Security Analysis*. New York: McGraw-Hill.

Grauer, F., R. Litzenberger, and R. Stehle. 1976. "Sharing Rules and Equilibrium in an International Capital Market under Uncertainty." *Journal of Financial Economics* 3:233–256.

Grinblatt, M., and S. Titman. 1989. "Portfolio Performance Evaluation: Old Issues and New Insights." *Review of Financial Studies* 2:393–421.

Grinblatt, M., and S. Titman. 1994. "A Study of Monthly Mutual Fund Returns and Performance Evaluation Techniques." *Journal of Financial and Quantitative Analysis* 29(3):419–444.

Grinold, R. C. 1989. "The Fundamental Law of Active Management." *Journal of Portfolio Management* 15:30–37.

Grinold, R. C., and R. N. Kahn. 1999. *Active Portfolio Management: A Quantitative Approach for Producing Superior Returns and Selecting Superior Returns and Controlling Risk*, Second Edition. New York: McGraw-Hill.

Grundy, B. D., and J. S. Martin. 2001. "Understanding the Nature of the Risks and the Source of the Rewards to Momentum Investing." *Review of Financial Studies* 14(1):29–78.

Hamilton, J. D. 1994. *Time Series Analysis*. Princeton, NJ: Princeton University Press.

Harvey, C. R. 1997. "WWWFinance: Quantitative Performance Evaluation." Available at www.duke.edu/~charvey/Classes/ba350_1997/perf/perf.htm.

Haugen, R. A., and L. B. Nardin. 1996. "Commonality in the Determinants of Expected Stock Returns." *Journal of Financial Economics* 41:401–436.

He, G., and R. Litterman. 1999. "The Intuition behind Black-Litterman Model Portfolios." Goldman Sachs Investment Management Series.

Heston, S. L., and K. G. Rouwenhorst. 1994. "Does Industrial Structure Explain the Benefits of Industrial Diversification?" *Journal of Financial Economics* 36:3–27.

Heston, S. L., and K. G. Rouwenhorst. 1995. "Industry and Country Effects in International Stock Returns." *Journal of Portfolio Management* 21 (Spring):53–58.

HKMA Annual Report 1998. Hong Kong Monetary Authority.

Hong, H., T. Lim, and J. C. Stein. 2000. "Bad News Travels Slowly: Size, Analyst Coverage, and the Profitability of Momentum Strategies." *Journal of Finance* 55(1):265–295.

Hopkins, P. J. B., and C. H. Miller. 2001. *Country, Sector, and Company Factors in Global Equity Portfolios*. AIMR Research Foundation Monograph. Charlottesville, VA: Association for Investment Management and Research.

Ibbotson Associates. 2003. *Stocks, Bonds, Bills and Inflation® 2003 Yearbook*. Chicago: Ibbotson Associates, Inc.

Ibbotson, R., and Peng Chen. 2002. "Stock Market Returns in the Long Run: Participating in the Real Economy." Yale ICF Working Paper 00-44. New Haven, CT: International Center for Finance at Yale School of Management.

Ibbotson, R., and R. Sinquefield. 1976. "Stocks, Bonds, Bills, and Inflation: Year-by-Year Historical Returns (1926–1974)." *Journal of Business* 49(1):11–47.

Index and Derivatives Perspective. 2002 (April). New York: Goldman Sachs & Co.

InterSec Research. 2001. "Investment Industry Research: The U.S. Tax-Exempt Cross-Border Marketplace." Stamford, CT.

Investment Company Institute. 1997. "Valuation and Liquidity Issues for Mutual Funds." Washington, DC: ICI.

Jagannathan, R., and R. A. Koraczyk. 1986. "Assessing the Market Performance of Managed Portfolios." *Journal of Business* 59(2):217–235.

Jagannathan, R., E. R. McGrattan, and A. Scherbina. 2000. "The Declining US Equity Premium." *Federal Reserve Bank of Minneapolis Quarterly Review* 24(4): 3–19.

Jegadeesh, N. 1990. "Evidence of Predictable Behavior of Security Returns." *Journal of Finance* 45(3):881–898.

Jegadeesh, N., and S. Titman. 1993. "Returns to Buying Winners and Selling Losers: Implications for Stock Market Efficiency." *Journal of Finance* 48(1): 65–91.

Jegadeesh, N., and S. Titman. 2001. "Profitability of Momentum Strategies: An Evaluation of Alternative Explanations." *Journal of Finance* 56(2):699–720.

Jensen, M. C. 1968. "The Performance of Mutual Funds in the Period 1945–1964." *Journal of Finance* 23(2):389–416.

Johnson, R. A., and D. W. Wichern. 1998. *Applied Multivariate Statistical Analysis*, Fourth Edition. Englewood Cliffs, NJ: Prentice Hall.

Jones, R. C. 1998. "Why Most Active Managers Underperform (and What You Can Do about It)." In *Investment Guides for Plan Sponsors: Enhanced Index Strategies for the Multi-Manager Portfolio*, edited by Brian Bruce. New York: Institutional Investor.

Jorgenson, D. W., and B. Fraumeni. 1989. "The Accumulation of Human and Non-Human Capital, 1948–84." In *The Measurement of Saving, Investment, and Wealth* (NBER Studies in Income and Wealth, vol. 52), edited by R. E. Lipsey and H. S. Tice, pp. 227–282. Chicago: University of Chicago Press.

Jorion, P. 1986. "Bayes-Stein Estimation for Portfolio Analysis." *Journal of Financial and Quantitative Analysis* (September):279–292.

Jorion, P. 1994. "Mean/Variance Analysis of Currency Overlays." *Financial Analysts Journal* 50(3):48–56.

Jorion, P. 2002. "Portfolio Optimization with Constraints on Tracking Error." *Financial Analysts Journal* (forthcoming).

Jorion, P., and W. N. Goetzmann. 1999. "Global Stock Markets in the Twentieth Century." *Journal of Finance* 54(3): 953–980.

Kahneman, D., P. Slovic, and A. Tversky. 1982. *Judgement under Uncertainty: Heuristics and Biases*. New York: Cambridge University Press.

Kavajecz, K. A., and D. B. Keim. 2002. "Packing Liquidity: Blind Auctions and Transaction Cost Efficiencies." Working paper available from the authors at The Wharton School, University of Pennsylvania, Philadelphia.

Keim, D. B., and A. Madhavan. 1997. "Transactions Costs and Investment Style: An Inter-Exchange Analysis of Institutional Equity Trades." *Journal of Financial Economics* 46(3):265–292.

King, M., E. Sentana, and S. Wadhwani. 1994. "Volatility and Links between National Stock Markets." *Econometrica* 62:901–933.

Knez, P. J., R. Litterman, and J. Scheinkman. 1994. "Explorations into Factors Explaining Money Market Returns." *Journal of Finance* 49(5):1861–1882.

Lakonishok, J., A. Shleifer, and R. W. Vishny. 1994. "Contrarian Investment, Extrapolation, and Risk." *Journal of Finance* 49(5):1541–1578.

LaPorta, R., J. Lakonishok, A. Shleifer, and R. Vishny. 1997. "Good News for Value Stocks: Further Evidence on Market Efficiency." *Journal of Finance* 52(2):859–874.

Lee, C., and B. Radhakrishna. 2000. "Inferring Investor Behavior: Evidence from TORQ Data." *Journal of Financial Markets* 3:83–111.

Litterman, R. B. 1996. "Hot Spots and Hedges." Goldman Sachs Risk Management Series. Published in *Journal of Portfolio Management* 22(5):52–75.

Litterman, R., and R. Gumerlock. 1998. *The Practice of Risk Management.* London: Euromoney Publications PLC.

Litterman, R., J. Longerstaey, J. Rosengarten, and K. Winkelmann. 2000. "The Green Zone . . . Assessing the Quality of Returns." *Journal of Performance Measurement* 5(3)29–50.

Litterman, R., and K. Winkelmann. 1996. "Managing Market Exposure." Goldman Sachs Risk Management Series.

Lo, A. W., and A. C. MacKinlay. 1990. "When Are Contrarian Profits Due to Stock Market Overreaction?" *Review of Financial Studies* 3:175–208.

Lucas, R. E., Jr. 1978. "Asset Prices in an Exchange Economy." *Econometrica* 46(6):1429–1445.

McGrattan, E. R., and E. C. Prescott. 2001. "Taxes, Regulation, and Asset Prices." Working Paper 610. Minneapolis: Federal Reserve Bank of Minneapolis.

Malkiel, B. G. 1995. "Returns from Investing in Equity Mutual Funds, 1971 to 1991." *Journal of Finance* 50:549–572.

Markowitz, H. 1952. "Portfolio Selection." *Journal of Finance* 7(1):77–91.

Markowitz, H. 1959. *Portfolio Selection: Efficient Diversification of Investments.* New York: John Wiley & Sons (also New Haven, CT: Yale University Press, 1970; Oxford: Basil Blackwell, 1991).

Markowitz, H. 1987. *Mean-Variance Analysis in Portfolio Choice and Capital Markets.* Oxford: Basil Blackwell.

Mehra, R., and E. C. Prescott. 1985. "The Equity Premium: A Puzzle." *Journal of Monetary Economics* 15:145–161.

Merton, R. C. 1980. "On Estimating the Expected Return on the Market." *Journal of Financial Economics* 8:323–361.

Merton, R. C. 1990. *Continuous-Time Finance.* Oxford: Basil Blackwell.

Mirabelli, A. 2000/2001. "The Structure and Visualization of Performance Attribution." *Journal of Performance Measurement* (Winter):55–80.

Modigliani, F., and L. Modigliani. 1997. "Risk-Adjusted Performance." *Journal of Portfolio Management* 23 (Winter):45–54.

Morgan Stanley Capital International. 2001. "MSCI Enhanced Methodology: Index Construction Objectives, Guiding Principles and Methodology for the MSCI Provisional Equity Index Series."

Moskowitz, T., and A. Vising-Jorgensen. 2002. "The Returns to Entrepreneurial Investment: The Private Equity Premium Puzzle." *American Economic Review* 92 (September).

Munro, J., and D. Jelicic. 2000. "The Relative Importance of Industry and Country Influences." Faculty and Institute of Actuaries Investment Conference paper, June. Available at www.actuaries.org.uk/files/pdf/library/proceedings/investment/2000conf/relimportpap.pdf.

Myners, P. 2001. "Institutional Investment in the United Kingdom—A Review." A report addressed to The Rt Honorable Gordon Brown, MP, Chancellor of the Exchequer, HM Treasury, London; available at www.hm-treasury.gov.uk/media//843F0/31.pdf.

Nadbielny, T. S., M. Sullivan, and M. De Luise. 1994. "Introducing the Salomon Brothers World Equity Index." Salomon Brothers.

Newey, W. K., and K. D. West. 1987. "A Simple Positive Semi-Definite, Heteroskedasticity and Autocorrelation Consistent Covariance Matrix." *Econometrica* 55:703–708.

"The *P&I* 1000: Our Annual Look at the Largest Pension Funds." 2002. *Pensions & Investments* (January 21).

Rendleman, R. C., C. P. Jones, and H. A. Lutane. 1982. "Empirical Anomalies Based on Unexpected Earnings and the Importance of Risk Adjustments." *Journal of Financial Economics* 10(3):269–287.

Roll, R. 1977. "A Critique of the Asset Pricing Theory's Tests; Part I: On Past and Potential Testability of the Theory." *Journal of Financial Economics* 4:129–176.

Roll, R., and B. Solnik. 1977. "A Pure Foreign Exchange Asset Pricing Model." *Journal of International Economics* 7:161–179.

Rosenberg, B., and W. McKibben. 1973. "The Prediction of Systematic and Specific Risk in Common Stocks." *Journal of Financial and Quantitative Analysis* 8(2)317–333.

Rouwenhorst, K. G. 1998a. "European Equity Markets and EMU: Are the Differences Between Countries Slowly Disappearing?" Yale ICF Working Paper. New Haven, CT: International Center for Finance at Yale School of Management.

Rouwenhorst, K. G. 1998b. "International Momentum Strategies." *Journal of Finance* 53(1):267–284.

Satchell, S., and A. Scowcroft. 2000. "A Demystification of the Black-Litterman Model: Managing Quantitative and Traditional Portfolio Construction." *Journal of Asset Management* 1(2):138–150.

Scheidt, D. 2001 (April 30). Letter to Craig S. Tyle (Division of Investment Management [SEC]: April 2001 Letter to the ICI Regarding Valuation Issues). Available at www.sec.gov/divisions/investment/guidance/tyle043001.htm.

Sharpe, W. 1991. "Capital Asset Prices with and without Negative Holdings." *Journal of Finance* (June):489–509.

Sharpe, W. 1992. "Capital Asset Prices with and without Negative Holdings." In *Nobel Lectures, Economic Sciences 1981–1990*, edited by K.-G. Mäler, pp. 312–332. World Scientific Publishing.

Siegel, J. J. 1972. "Risk, Interest Rates and the Foreign Exchange." *Quarterly Journal of Economics* 89:173–179.

Siegel, L. B., K. F. Kroner, and S. W. Clifford. 2001. "The Greatest Return Stories Ever Told." *Journal of Investing* 10:91–102.

Sloan, R. G. 1996. "Do Stock Prices Fully Reflect Information in Accruals and Cash Flows about Future Earnings?" *Accounting Review* 71(3):289–315.

Solnik, B. H. 1974. "An Equilibrium Model of the International Capital Market." *Journal of Economic Theory* 8:500–524.

Stambaugh, R. F. 1982. "On the Exclusion of Assets from Tests of the Two-Parameter Model: A Sensitivity Analysis." *Journal of Financial Economics* 10:237–268.

Stambaugh, R. F. 1997. "Analyzing Investments Whose Histories Differ in Length." *Journal of Financial Economics* 45:285–331.

Stein, C. 1955. "Inadmissability of the Usual Estimator of the Mean of a Multivariate Normal Distribution." In *Proceedings of the Third Berkeley Symposium on Probability and Statistics*, pp. 197–206. Berkeley, CA: University of California Press.

Stickel, S. E. 1991. "Common Stock Returns Surrounding Earnings Forecast Revisions: More Puzzling Evidence." *Accounting Review* 66(2):402–416.

Sullivan, M., M. De Luise, K. Sung, and P. A. Kerr. 2002. "Global Stock Market Review: May 2002." Salomon Smith Barney Equity Research: Global Equity Index (June 13).

U.S. Federal Reserve Board. 1947–2001. *Flow of Funds Accounts of the United States*. Washington, DC: Federal Reserve Board.

White, G. I., A. C. Sondhi, and D. Fried. 1998. *The Analysis and Use of Financial Statements*, Second Edition. New York: John Wiley & Sons.

Womack, K. 1996. "Do Brokerage Analysts' Recommendations Have Investment Value?" *Journal of Finance* 51(1):137–167.

Working Group. 1996. "Risk Standards for Institutional Investment Managers and Institutional Investors." Capital Risk Market Advisors; available at www.cmra.com/html/the_risk_standards.html.

Zitzewitz, E. 2002. "Who Cares about Shareholders? Arbitrage-Proofing Mutual Funds." Working paper available from the author at the Stanford Graduate School of Business, Stanford, CA.

Index

Absolute marginal contributions to tracking error (ACTE), 380–383
Absolute marginal factor contributions to tracking error (AFCTE), 384
Absolute return strategy, 444
Accounting agents, valuations, 289–290
Active management:
  characteristics of, generally, 22, 25–26, 105, 154, 181
  country allocation strategy, 445–446
  currency allocation strategy, 446
  duration timing strategy, 444
  goal of, 212
  risk budgeting and, 446–451
  sector allocation strategy, 445
  security selection strategies, 445
  yield curve positioning strategy, 444–445
Active portfolio, defined, 374–375
Active return, 174
Active risk:
  correlations of, 479–480
  implications of, 26, 153, 168
  investments, structured *vs.* traditional, 198–199
  management, structured *vs.* traditional, 193–197
  management selection, 199–209
  in risk budget, 171–185
Active trading, 125
Actuarial decision analysis, 418
Actuarial mortality tables, 111
Administration costs, 411
After-tax wealth:
  after-tax returns, calculation of, 541–544
  appreciation, 539
  capital gains, 536–539, 541–542
  components of, 534
  estate tax, 537–538, 544–545
  gift tax, 537–538
  income tax, 536
  inflation, 540–541, 545, 564
  planning framework, 535–536
  spending, 540–541, 545, 562
  subsidies, 539
  taxation considerations, 536–540, 544
  transfer tax, 537, 544–545
Agency bonds, 99
Aggressive investors/trades, 10, 431–432, 558, 560
Allocation, *see* Asset allocation
Alpha, 154, 159, 174–179, 181, 185, 188, 275–277, 343, 387, 457, 498, 501, 510, 524–525, 530
Alternative asset classes:
  characteristics of, 153
  global tactical asset allocation (GTAA), 455–482
  hedge funds, portfolio management, 501–515
  private equity investments, 516–530
  strategic asset allocation, hedge funds, 483–500
Altvest, 486
American depositary receipts (ADRs), 319, 376
Analyst earnings estimate anomaly, 421
Annual growth rate, 50
Annual returns, 547, 554–558
Annuities, 568
Appreciation, 539, 548, 565, 579, 582
Arbitrage, 490
Arbitrage trading, 295

Asset allocation:
  characteristics of, 14–15, 22
  drift, 412–414
  global tactical, 455–482
  paradigm, 106
  in risk management, 24–25
  strategic, *see* Strategic asset allocation
  wealth generation, 592
Asset classes:
  alternative, 105, 453–530
  Black-Litterman approach, 76–79
  currency hedging, impact of, 140–151
  implications of, 19, 21
  in market portfolio, 100–103
  risk characteristics, 108–109
  risk management, 25
  timing, 458, 474
Asset consumption, 49
Asset demands, 49
Asset exposures, equity risk factor models:
  country, 351–353
  currency, 353
  industry, 350–351
  investment style/risk, 351
  in linear factor model, 354–355
  local market, 351–353
  standardizing, 353–354
Asset grouping, return attribution:
  contributions to returns, 332–333
  international portfolio, 322–327
Asset-level contributions, return attribution, 320–322, 327–328
Asset location strategies, 571–579
Asset management:
  forecasting models, 76–78
  importance of, 28
Asset pricing, 48
Asset universe, 356
Association for Investment Management and Research (AIMR), 477
Asymptotic principal component (APC), 345, 347
Auditing tools, 293
Average returns, 107
Backfill bias, 487
Bank accounts, 565
Barbelled portfolios, 192, 437
Becker, Gary, 102
Benchmark(s):
  performance measurement, 278
  portfolio, defined, 374–375
  in portfolio construction, 427
  in risk budgeting, 446–447
  in risk management, 25–26, 28
Bequest mode, 542, 587
Bermuda, 352
Beta, 30, 42–43, 87–88, 101, 147, 149, 155, 174, 176, 200, 221–222, 276–277, 303, 343, 352–353, 386–388, 476
Beta-neutral, 476
Bid/ask spread, 289, 472
Black, Fischer, 56, 73, 76
Black-Litterman models:
  active risk, 184–185
  global asset allocation model, *see* Black-Litterman global asset allocation model
  global tactical asset allocation, 467
Black-Litterman global asset allocation model:
  active risk, 184–185, 191
  development of, 76–77
  expected returns, 77–84, 431
  German equity market, 79–80, 82–84
  global minimum-variance portfolio, 87–88
  Japanese equity market, 84
  optimal portfolio weights, 76, 78, 81, 86–87
  overview, 76–78
  parameter changes, impact of, 85–87
  risk constraints, 87–88
  unconstrained mean-variance optimization, 81
  unconstrained optimal portfolio, 77, 80–81, 83–85, 87
Black-Scholes option pricing model, 246, 439

Block diagonal global equity factor model, 367–369, 371–372
Bond/equity split, 104, 109–110, 124
Bond futures, 414, 470–471
Bond investments, *see* Bond portfolio
  Capital Asset Pricing Model (CAPM), 40
  portfolio risk, 36–38
Bond market:
  after-tax wealth applications, 558–564
  annual returns, 547, 554–558
  historic returns, 546–550
  inflation, impact on, 547, 549–553
  investment horizon, 558
  risk-adjusted returns, 553–554
Bond portfolio, generally:
  duration of, 110, 112, 123–125, 130, 436
  liabilities, 114
Book-to-market equity, 422
Book-to-price (B/P) ratio, 423, 461, 463
Bottom-up asset allocation, 26
Broker-dealers, 287–288
Broker quotes, 289–290, 292, 294
Budgeting, in risk management, 252
Bulleted portfolios, 437
Bush, President George W., 550
Business plan, 256
Buy-and-hold strategies, 196, 542, 579–580, 587
Buy-side traders, 432

Callable bonds, 440
Capital appreciation, 436, 567
Capital Asset Pricing Model (CAPM):
  components of, 36–37
  development of, 36
  expected returns, 40
  global equilibrium, 77
  implementation of, 103
  international, 56, 66
  market portfolio, 91, 100–101, 103
  optimal portfolio, 41–42
  risk aversion, 38–39
  risk premium, 42–43
  testing, 103
  time period, 37
  uncorrelated assets, 152, 155
Capital depreciation, 436
Capital gains/capital gains tax, 30, 47, 534, 536–539, 541–542, 565, 569, 579–580, 585
Capital markets, 460
Capital market theory, 179
Carried interest, 519
Carve-outs, 414
Cash, generally:
  Capital Asset Pricing Model (CAPM), 37, 40
  completion management, 414–415
  effects on tracking errors, 390–392
  equity risk factor models, 375–376
  global tactical asset allocation (GTAA), 470, 472
  international portfolios, 319
Cash flow, 27, 280, 435, 437
Cash flow projections, 112
Cautious investors, 10
Central banks, 460–461, 550
Charitable gifts, 566
Charitable remainder trust (CRT), 566, 568–569, 576, 578
Chen, Peng, 45, 47–48
Children, wealth creation strategies, 566, 570, 574
Clinical decision analysis, 418
Closing price, 295, 431
Collateral, 470
Collateralized mortgage obligations (CMOs), 441
Combined single region model (SRM), global equity factor model, 367–369, 371–373
Commercial real estate, 101–102
Commingled vehicles, 410–412
Commissions, 472
Commodities, 20–22, 25, 103, 153
Commodity Futures Trading Commission (CFTC), 474
Common stock, 99
Completion management, 414–415
Completion manager, 468
Completion portfolio, GTAA, 455, 457–458

Compounding, 564, 582
Compounding period, return attribution, 313
Computer software:
- portfolio optimization, 161, 297
- return attribution, 313

Concentrated active management, 26
Confidence levels, 185–190
Conservative investors, 561
Consumer price index (CPI), 553
Consumption habits, 52
Contingency planning, 254
Contribution to duration (CTD), 437, 442, 444
Controllers, functions of, 290
Convertible arbitrage, 490, 494–495, 498
Convexity, volatility risk, 439, 445
Core portfolio, 582–586
Corporate bonds, 53, 437, 445, 565
Corporate credit, 99
Correlated assets, 153
Correlation(s):
- covariance matrix estimation, 230–232
- in modern portfolio theory (MPT), 12–13, 20–22

Cost basis, 586
Country allocation strategy, 323–324, 445–446
Country asset exposures, 351–353
Country contributions, return attribution:
- international portfolios, 323–325
- single region, 306

Country currency weight, 323–324
Country effect:
- global equity risk factor models, 365–367
- global factor model, return attribution, 320–322

Country indexes, 92
Country of domicile, 351, 355
Country of issuance, 351–352
Country sector weight, 324–325
Country selection, global tactical asset allocation (GTAA), 458, 459, 474
Country stock selection, 324
Covariance, 12, 32, 37–38, 40–43, 58, 62–64, 70
Covariance matrices/matrix:
- characteristics of, generally, 78
- decomposition, 242–243, 246–247
- equity risk factor models, 337–338, 342, 357–358, 361–364, 387, 395
- estimation, *see* Covariance matrix estimation
- factor model framework, 378
- global equity factor model, 372

Covariance matrix estimation:
- alternative methods, 245–248
- applications, generally, 224–227, 237–239
- computations, 225
- correlations and, 241–243, 248
- decay rate, 236, 239–241, 243
- financial data, 227–231
- generalizations, 239–243
- histories of different length, 243–245
- normal distributions, 240–241
- risk model, 248
- using daily data, 232–235, 238, 248
- volatilities, 225, 232, 241–243, 248
- weighting observations, 235–237, 242–243

Credit ratings, 438, 441
Credit risk:
- implications of, 27, 251, 438, 445, 552
- monitoring, 267–268

Credit-risk-free interest rates, 436
Credit spread, 30
Credit Suisse First Boston (CSFB)/Tremont, 486, 495
Cross-portfolio pricing comparisons, 293
Cross product:
- defined, 60
- matrix, equity risk factor model, 347–348
- return attribution, 320–321

Cross-section modeling, equity risk factor models, 341, 345
Currencies, global equilibrium, 30, 56–75
Currency allocation strategy, 446

Currency asset exposures, 353
Currency contributions, return attribution:
  international portfolio, 320–322, 325
  single region, 306
Currency effect, global equity risk factor model, 367
Currency exposure, equity risk factor models, 376–377
Currency forwards, 414, 446
Currency hedging, 104–105, 140–149, 441, 457
Currency markets, forecasts across valuation measures, 464
Currency overlay, 469
Currency risk, 355, 440–441
Currency selection, global tactical asset allocation (GTAA), 474
Currency surprise, 320–322
Custodians, 411, 468
Custody, 411
Customized investment plans, 410
Customized portfolios, 429
Cyclical industries, 31

Daily data, risk monitoring program, 216
Data collection, in valuation, 288
DAX equity index, 301
Decay rate, covariance matrix, 236, 239–241, 243
Default, 31, 438
Default premium, 338–339, 344
Deferred taxes, 542–543, 567
Defined benefit plans, 102, 488–489
Degree of confidence, 85, 87, 172–173, 190
Dependencies, in risk plan, 254–255
Depreciation, global equilibrium, 60–61
Derivatives, 25, 28, 39, 224, 290, 468, 470–476
Developed markets, 93, 213, 371
Dilution effect, 296
Discount rates, 50
Disposal plans, 538, 542–543
Distressed debt investing, 442
Diversification:
  active risk management, 199
  levels, 104–105, 110
Dividend(s):
  implications of, 46, 52, 281, 548, 565
  payout ratios, 48
  reinvestment, 541
Dodd, David, 416
Dollar-weighted returns, 281
Domestic equities:
  active risk management, 202
  portfolio risk, 14–19
  strategic asset allocation, 122–123
Dow, Charles Henry, 455–456
Downside scenarios, risk budgets, 257
Dow Theory, 456
Duration timing strategy, 444
Dynamic asset allocation, 113, 121, 125–126

Earnings growth, 48
Earnings quality anomaly, 421
Earnings to share price (E/P), 339–341, 359
Earnings-yield-gap timing model, 465
Economic and Monetary Union (EMU), 366
Economic growth, 247
Economic shocks, 366
Efficient frontier, 533–354, 561–562, 564, 571–573, 585, 587–591
Efficient market, 33, 42, 101
Efficient Markets Hypothesis, 456, 459
Efficient portfolio, 427–429
Eigenvalues, 346
Electronic communications networks (ECNs), 432
Emerging markets, 46, 93, 160–162, 213
Emerging-market debt (EMD), 442, 450
Empirical analysis, 424
Employee demographics, implications of, 111
Energy prices, 30
Enhanced active management, 26

Enhanced block diagonal global equity factor model, 367–369, 372–373
Entity, after-tax returns, 543–544
Equilibrium approach, generally:
  benefits of, 3–6
  Capital Asset Pricing Model (CAPM), 36, 77
Equilibrium expected returns, forecasting, 422
Equity allocations:
  overfunded, 119, 120, 122, 125
  underfunded, 118–121, 130
Equity index funds, 565
Equity index futures, 414, 470–471
Equity investments:
  Capital Asset Pricing Model (CAPM), 40
  portfolio risk, 36–38
Equity long/short sector, hedge funds, 490, 494–495, 498
Equity market, 30
Equity market neutral, 490, 494–495, 498
Equity-only equilibrium, 79
Equity portfolio management (EPM):
  forecasts, 419–426
  overview, 416–417
  portfolio construction, 427–431
  quantitative approach to, 418–419
  results evaluations, 432–434
  returns, forecasting, 417, 420–422
  risk monitoring, 432–433
  risks, forecasting, 417, 422–423
  trading, 431–432
  traditional approach to, 417–419
  transaction costs, forecasting, 423–425
  updating investment process, 432–434
Equity portfolio structure, 579–590
Equity premium puzzle, 48, 51
Equity risk, 130
Equity risk factor models:
  American depositary receipts (ADRs), 355–356, 376
  background, 341–342
  covariance matrices, 361–364
  currencies, 376–377
  estimating factor returns, 356–359
  factor-mimicking portfolios, 340, 359–361
  factor returns and exposures, 338–340
  futures, 355, 376
  GDRs, 355–356, 376
  global, 365–373
  histories, 356
  linear cross-sectional factor model, 348–355
  observed factor returns, 342–344
  overview, 334–335
  portfolio definitions, 374–376
  portfolio risk statistics, 377
  risk estimation, 392–395
  risk measurement, 378–392
  risk sources, 373–378
  simple, example of, 335–337
  unobserved factor returns, 345–348
Equity risk premium (ERP):
  defined, 45
  equilibrium estimates of, 48–53
  frictions, 52
  habit persistence, 52
  historical perspective, 45–48
  implications of, 550
  investment policy and, 53–54
  strategic asset allocation, 109
  utility function, 50–52
Estate planning, 538–541, 544–545, 572–576, 590, 592
Estate tax(es), 537–538, 544–545, 568, 574–578
Estimation universe, 356–357, 393
Euro, 62, 142, 147, 151, 349
European Public Real Estate Association (EPRA), 101–102
Event driven sector, hedge funds, 490, 494–495
Ex ante/ex post equity returns, 52
Exceptional active return, 304, 306
Excess returns, *see* Expected returns
  covariance matrix estimation, 227
  implications of, 107
  private equity, 523
  risk budgeting, 447–448

Exchange rates, 57, 60–62, 284, 301, 349, 441
Exchange-traded funds (ETFs), 25, 389–390
Expected active return, 303
Expected returns:
  Black-Litterman global asset allocation model, 77–86
  Capital Asset Pricing Model (CAPM), 36
  covariance matrix estimation, 226
  credit risk and, 268
  global equilibrium, 56–75
  market portfolio construction, 100–101
  modern portfolio theory (MPT), 12–13, 16–20, 23
  risk budget, 255–256
  uncorrelated assets, 161–168
Exposure matrix, 346, 393

Factor loadings, 338–339
Factor-mimicking portfolios (FMPs), 340, 359–361
Factor model, return attribution:
  contributions to returns, 331
  global, 321–322
  implications of, 247
  linear, 303, 309, 311–319
Factor returns:
  contributions, 301, 304, 306
  covariance matrix forecasts, 362–363
  equity risk factor models, 338–341, 347
  estimating, 356–359
  global, 367
Fair value, 288–289, 294–296
Fama, Eugene, 45, 53, 344
Federal Reserve, 552
Fed model, 464
Feedback, indirect, 222–223
Fiduciaries, 408
Financial accounting controls, 252, 277
Financial budgets, 252, 257, 277
Financial institutions, risk management strategies, 28–29, 249
Financial planning, 277
Financial risk management, 28–29
Financial statements, 417
Financial theory, 4
Financial Times Stock Exchange (FTSE), All World indexes, 91–92
Fiscal policy, 436
Fixed income arbitrage, 490, 494–495
Fixed income market, 74, 78
Fixed income portfolios:
  active management strategies, 444–451
  benchmarks, 442–444
  risk budgeting, 446–451
  risk sources, 435–442
Fixed-income securities, 99, 104–105, 130, 145, 555
Forecasting:
  equity portfolio management (EPM), 417, 419–426
  factor model framework, 378
  global tactical asset allocation (GTAA), 461–467
  models, 76–78, 226–227, 262, 264–266, 273
  returns, 417, 420–422
  risks, 417, 422–423
  transaction costs, 423–425
Foreign bond portfolios, 140–142
Foreign exchange (FX), currency hedging, 145
Foreign exchange hedge, 60
Foreign exchange market, 349
Foreign exchange rates, 292. *See also* Exchange rates
Foreign market changes, 30
Forward contracts, 60, 319, 325, 468, 470, 472
Forward premium, 320, 322, 325
Foundation, 566, 569–570, 575–578, 590
401(k) plan, 543, 567, 575
Fouse, William, 456
Frank Russell Company, 313
Free float, 92, 94, 98
French, Kenneth, 45, 53, 344
Frictions, 52
FRM/MSCI, 487
FTSE 300, 92

FTSE 350, 427
Fundamental analysis, 402–403
Fundamental beta, 387–388. *See also* Beta
Fundamental factors, equity risk factor models, 338–339, 341, 345
Funding ratio, 128–130, 133–135
Futures accounts, 153
Futures contracts, 60, 376, 388, 459, 468, 470–472
Futures exchange and traded fund positions, measuring risk of, 388–390

Gamma exposure, 439
GDRs, 355, 376
General Agreement on Tariffs and Trade (GATT), 366
Generalized autoregressive conditionally heteroscedastic (GARCH) processes, 245–246
General partners, 519
Geometric returns, 319
Germany:
  equity market, 79–80, 82–84
  European Public Real Estate Association (EPRA), 102
  global equity risk factor model, 367
Gift tax, 537–538
Ginnie Mae (GNMA), 441
Global bond market, forecasting across using valuation measures, 464
Global bonds, Lehman Global Aggregate index, 98–100
Global capitalization weighted portfolio, 151
Global equilibrium expected returns:
  Capital Asset Pricing Model (CAPM), 55–56
  equilibrium condition, 70–75
  exchange rates and, 61–66
  general model, 57–61
  matrix algebra, 63–64, 67–70, 74
  optimal portfolio, 63–65
Global equities modeling:
  block diagonal factor model, 367–369, 371–372
  combined single region model (SRM), 367–369, 371–373
  comparison of, 369
  enhanced block diagonal, 367–369, 372–373
  global equity factor model, 367–371
Global equity, generally:
  diversification, 122–123, 130
  factor model, 367–371
  index, 20
Global equity markets:
  forecasting across using valuation measures, 461, 463
  forecasting within using valuation measures, 463
Global equity portfolio:
  characteristics of, generally, 92, 365
  local indexes, 95–98
  Morgan Stanley Capital International (MSCI) equity indexes, 93–97
  Salomon Smith Barney Global Equity Index (SSBGEI), 91–93
Global factor model, 321–322
Global Industry Classification Standard (GICS), 94, 350–351
Global interest rates, 445–446
Global markets, 14
Global minimum-variance portfolio, 87–88
Global multi-asset-class benchmark, 472
Global stock-selection portfolio, 463
Global tactical asset allocation (GTAA):
  asset class, 455, 459–461
  benchmarks, 480–482
  completion element, 455, 457–458
  completion portfolio, 473–474
  country predictability, 459–461
  customization, 455, 479–480
  empirical evidence for, 461–467
  expectations, 478–481
  global currency management, 469
  history of, 455–457
  implementation, 467–478
  leverage, 476–478
  manager selection, 481–482
  overlay portfolio, 474–476
  performance, 478–480
  portable alpha strategy, 480–481

portfolio construction, 467–468, 479–480
program structure, 457–461
pure overlay element, 455, 458–459, 467
purpose of, 455
size requirements, 468–469
theoretical explanations for, 459–461
using forwards, 470, 472
using futures, 470–472
Goal-setting, in risk plan, 253
Goetzmann, Will, 46
Goldman Sachs Asset Management (GSAM):
green zone, 270–272, 432
portfolio analysis and construction environment (PACE), 262, 264–267, 293, 298, 304–306, 310–311, 391–392
red zone, 432–433
yellow zone, 432–433
Goldman Sachs Commodities Index, 103
Gordon growth model, 45
Government bonds, 45, 73, 98–99, 344, 436, 546–548, 565
Graham, Benjamin, 416, 434, 456
Grantor trust, 566–568, 570, 574–575, 587
Great Depression, 555
Green Sheet, 217–222, 272
Green zone events, 214, 216, 222, 270–273, 432–433
Grinold's Law, 458, 463–464
Gross domestic product (GDP), 46, 48, 93
Group weight, 307, 326
Growth factors, 436
Growth managers, 197, 213
Growth rate, 344
G-7, currency hedging, 147

Habit persistence, 52
Half-life, 236, 241, 243, 503
Heartland:
High Yield Muni Bond, 292
Short Duration High Yield Mini, 292
Hedgefund.net, 504
Hedge Fund Research (HFR), 486
Hedge funds:
allocation development, 489–490
characteristics of, generally, 78, 103–105, 153, 286–287, 444, 502–504, 565
classifications, 505
evaluation framework, 488–489
fee structure, 503
funds of, 515
hurdle rate evaluation, 488, 494–500
implementing allocations, 490–494
information resources, 486–488, 504
investment strategy, 506
investment universe, 504–505
leverage, 487
management characteristics, 484–486
managerial style, 506
monitoring, 514
organizational structure, 507–508
overview, 501–502
people involved, 507
portfolio construction, 510–513
portfolio management, 501–515
potential advantages of, 483–486, 499
self-reporting biases, 486–488
track record, 508–510
Hedging, 28, 56, 73, 112, 474
Held-to-maturity portfolios, 436
Hennessee, 486
High-yield bond index, 338, 344
High-yield bonds, 438, 445
High-yield markets, 217
Hindsight bias, 418
Historical data:
active risk management, 193–195, 200, 208–210
covariance matrix estimation, 247
currency hedging, 147
optimal risk budget, 177–178, 181–183, 188
significance of, 30, 107, 109
Historical simulations, 265, 269, 413
Historical volatility, 31, 350, 438
Historic returns, 12, 546–550
Holding periods, 547–548, 558, 560, 582

Home bias, 145–146, 365–366
Hong Kong Monetary Authority (HKMA), 461
Hopkins, Peter, 463
Hot spots:
  equity risk factor models, 379–386
  in risk management, 34–35
Human capital, 102
Hurdle rates:
  defined, 181, 484
  hedge fund evaluations, 488, 494–500
  portfolio risk, 18–21, 23

Ibbotson, Roger, 45, 47–48
Ibbotson Associates, 547
Illiquidity, 267, 503–504, 513, 526
Implementation shortfall, 425
Implied forward interest rates, 444
Implied hurdle rates, hedge funds, 494–499
Implied returns:
  currency hedging, 147–149
  hedge funds, 493
  risk budget development, 179–184
  uncorrelated assets, 162–164
Implied views, in portfolio risk, 19, 22–23, 166
Implied volatilities, 246–247
Incentive fees, 289
Income, taxable, 565. *See also* Ordinary income
Income tax, 52, 534, 536, 543, 568
Independent valuation:
  accounting agents, 289–290
  importance of, 285–286
  oversight group, responsibilities of, 286, 291–293
  oversight philosophy, 285–291
  price verification, 290
  separate oversight, 290
Individual investors, active risk management, 196
Individual retirement accounts (IRAs), 52, 538
Industrial diversification, 366
Industry asset exposures, 350–351, 353–354
Industry classifications:
  asset exposures, 354, 356
  global equity risk factor models, 366
Industry contributions:
  equity risk factor models, 386
  return attribution, 320–322, 325–326, 328
Industry effect, global equity risk factor models, 365–367, 370
Industry factors, equity risk factor models, 345
Inflation, 11, 30, 45, 344, 436–437, 540–541, 545, 547, 549–553, 564
Inflation risk, 57
Information ratio:
  active risk management, 195, 199, 206–208
  global equity markets forecasts, 461
  global tactical asset allocation (GTAA) portfolio, 479
  performance measurement, 273, 275
  risk budget development, 181, 185, 187, 189
Initial public offering (IPO), 519, 540
Institutional funds:
  international diversification, currency hedging, 136–151
  market portfolio, 91–103
  strategic asset allocation, 104–135
  uncorrelated return sources, 152–168
Institutional investors, active risk management, 196, 198
Institutional portfolios, 25
Insurance companies, 550
Insurance coverage, 254
Interaction effect, return attribution, 307–308
Interest rate risk, 436, 442, 552
Interest rates, 30, 49–50, 292, 549
Intermediate-term price momentum anomaly, 421
Internal control, 260, 289
Internal rate of return (IRR), 520–521
Internal rate of return (IRRATE), 281–282

Internal Revenue Service (IRS), 539, 568, 582, 587
International CAPM, 56, 66
International diversification:
  home bias and, 137–140
  strategic asset allocation, 105
International equities, portfolio risk, 14–19
International portfolio, return attribution, 319–327
Intuition, 12, 22, 34, 36, 40, 62, 87, 119, 122
Investment Benchmark Reports (Venture Economics/Thomson Financial), 102
Investment Company Act of 1940, 287
Investment decision-making strategies, 10–11, 22–23, 29, 405–406
Investment horizon, 45, 470, 541–542, 555
Investment philosophy, 399–400
Investment plan:
  components of, 24, 254
  implementation of, 25–27
  monitoring, 27
  size of, *see* Investment plan size
Investment planning, 540
Investment plan size:
  costs, 408, 411–412
  implementation impact on risk, 408–410
  separate accounts *vs.* commingled vehicles, 410–411
Investment program implementation:
  asset allocation drift, 412–414
  completion management, 414–415
  overview, 407
  plan size, 408–412
Investment style contributions, return attribution:
  international portfolio, 320–322, 326–327
  single region, 307
Investment styles:
  asset exposure, 351–353
  hedge funds, 506
  types of, 320–322, 326–327, 432
Investor myopia, 365–366
Japan:
  covariance matrix estimation applications, 234
  equity market, 84, 107, 162, 165–166
  global equilibrium excess returns, 57–65
  global equity risk factor model, 367
  government bonds, 98
  optimal portfolio construction, 107
  strategic asset allocation, 160
  TOPIX, 101, 427
Jorion, Philippe, 46, 469
J.P. Morgan Global Government Bond Index, 477
Junk bonds, 438

Labor income, 102
Laddered portfolios, 437
Large-cap stocks, 198, 364, 425–426
Leaning against the wind, 466
Least squares regression, 370
Legal risk, 27, 251
Lehman:
  Global Aggregate index, 98–100
  Long Government and Credit Index, 115, 117, 124–125
  U.S. Aggregate Index, 125, 444, 448
Leptokurtic distribution, 228
Leverage/leveraging:
  constraint, 87
  global tactical asset allocation (GTAA), 476–478
  implications of, 276, 450, 569
  private equity investments, 518, 524
Liability analysis, in strategic asset allocation:
  dynamic, 125–126
  modeling, 111–112, 131–133
  static, 113–115
  uncertainty, 110–111
Life expectancy, 566
Likelihood functions, 241, 243
Limited partners, 519
Limited partnerships, 102

Linear cross-sectional factor model:
  asset exposures, 350–355
  global framework, 349–350
  local framework, 348–349
Linear factor model, return attribution:
  components of, 247, 303, 309
  multiperiod attribution, 311–319
Linearity, in portfolio, 31, 100–101
Lintner, John, 36
Liquidation, private equity, 519–520
Liquidation mode, 542, 581–582
Liquidity, generally:
  awareness, 269
  duration, 267
  implications of, 472
  risk, 27, 251
Local market asset exposure, 351–353
Log returns, 313–316
London InterBank Offer Rate (LIBOR), 74, 444
Long position, 21, 361, 484
Long Term Capital Management (LTCM), 414, 461
Long-short portfolio, 359–360
Long-term investors, 555
Lottery, 11

Macroeconomic factors:
  defined, 48
  equity risk factor models, 338–339, 341, 344
  interest rate risk and, 436
  yield curve risk, 437
Managed portfolio:
  defined, 374–375
  risk measures, 378
Management costs, 411
Management fees, 25–26, 28, 154, 289
Management philosophy, 270
Manager selection:
  asset-management approach, 400–402
  fundamental analysis, 402–403
  global tactical asset allocation, 481
  investment decision making, 405–406
  investment philosophy, 399–400
  investment style, 401
  qualitative analysis, 401
  quantitative analysis, 404–405
  self-classification, 401
  triangulation, 403–404
Manager-selection team, 402, 405
Managerial styles:
  active, 26
  structured *vs.* traditional, 193–197
Marginal contribution, portfolio risk, 19–21, 33, 38, 40, 161, 173, 200, 261, 263, 492–493
Mar-Hedge, 486
Market capitalization:
  asset exposure, 353–354
  Black-Litterman global equilibrium approach, 79–80, 83
  covariance matrix estimation, 225
  equity risk factor models, 358, 360
  free float, 92, 94, 98
  global equilibrium, 59, 66, 70, 72–73
  global equity factor model, 371
  global equity portfolios, 92
  Morgan Stanley Capital International (MSCI) global equity indexes, 93–94
  risk premium, uncorrelated assets, 160
  Salomon Smith Barney Global Equity Index (SSBGEI), 93
  significance of, 4, 6, 37, 40–41, 43
Market distress, 242
Market factors, equity risk factor models, 338, 341–344
Market inefficiency, 459
Market makers, 292
Market neutral, 444
Market-neutral hedge funds, 153, 583
Market portfolio:
  assets in, 101–103
  construction of, 100–103, 388
  defined, 374–375
  global bonds, 98–100
  global equity, 91–98
  strategic asset allocation, 108

Market risk, 43, 154, 190, 251
Market segregation, 459
Market shocks, 241
Market size, equity risk factor models, 361
Market spread, 437
Market timing, 300–301, 304, 432, 444, 448, 456, 464, 476
Market value, 582
Markowitz, Harry, 12, 40
Mark-to-market (MTM), 388
Matrix algebra, global equilibrium, 67–70, 74
Matrix pricing, 289, 294
Maturity premium, 344
Maximum likelihood estimates, 243
Mean reversion, 554, 562, 564
Mean-variance optimization, 81, 131, 256
Merger arbitrage, 513
Merrill Lynch:
- 1–3-Year U.S. Treasury Index, 444
- 6-Month U.S. T-Bill Index, 444

Miller, Hayes, 463
Mispricing, 286, 295–296
Model risk, 260
Modern portfolio theory (MPT):
- common applications, 10–13
- cost-benefit analysis, 9–10
- insights, generally, 32–33
- return on investment, 8, 11–12
- as risk management strategy, generally, 7–9, 12
- size of return, 13, 22

Modified Bank Administration Institute (modified BAI) method, 281
Modified Dietz method, 281, 283
Momentum, generally:
- factor, 355
- GTAA forecasts, 465–467

Monetary policy, 31, 436
Money market securities, 10, 550, 555, 565
Monte Carlo simulation, 128–130, 229–230, 265–266, 269
Monthly data, risk monitoring program, 214, 216
Moody's, 438
Morgan Grenfell Asset Management, 285
Morgan Stanley Capital International (MSCI):
- All Country World Index (ACWI), 91–93, 95, 98
- covariance matrix estimation, 228
- EAFE, 78, 177, 188, 427
- emerging markets index (EMF), 93
- Equity Index Series, 93–94
- Global Industry Classification Standard (GICS), 351
- Greece index, 93
- index construction, 94, 97
- Morocco, 93
- World index, 94–96, 98, 476

Mortality rates, 111
Mortgage-backed securities (MBS), 99, 435, 439–440, 442, 445
Mortgage pools, 440–441
Mossin, Jon, 36
Multimanager portfolios, 411
Multiperiod return attribution:
- linking returns, 311–313
- linking sources of returns, 313–319

Multiple-asset portfolios, 22
Multivariate analysis, 421
Multivariate normal distribution, 227–228, 239
Municipal bonds, 538, 565, 593
Mutual funds, 103, 286, 295–296, 400, 410–411

Nasdaq Composite Index, 282–283
Nationally recognized statistical rating organization (NRSRO), 438
Natural resources, 103, 105
Negative alpha, 510
Negative RCTE, 382
Nelsons Database, 177–178, 479–480
Net asset value (NAV), 285–286, 295–296, 514–515
New York Stock Exchange, 295
Nikkei 225, 92

Noise:
  covariance matrix estimation, 238
  volatility, 111–112, 114–115, 118, 120
Nominal returns, 549–550, 553
Nonestimation universe, 357
Nonlinear portfolio, 31
Normal distribution, 32, 227–228, 239–241, 243
Normalized returns, 271
North America Free Trade Agreement (NAFTA), 366
Notional leverage, 478
Null hypothesis, 53

Objectives, long-term, 590
Oil, 103
One-period returns, 313–315, 318–319
Opening price, 431
Operational risk, 27, 251
Optimal asset allocation, wealth creation, 571–578
Optimal portfolio:
  Capital Asset Pricing Model (CAPM), 40–43
  characteristics of, generally, 12, 16, 23, 33, 39–41
  construction, 297
  covariance matrix estimation, 226
  global equilibrium, 66, 70
  weights, in strategic asset allocation, 106
Option pricing, 246, 439
Ordinary income, 548, 577
Ordinary least squares (OLS) regression, 357–358
Organizational culture, 259
Oscillation, implications of, 228–229, 238, 555
Overconfidence, 418
Overlay, *see* Pure overlay
Overreaction, long-term, 459–460
Over-the-counter (OTC) securities, 289

Partnerships, private equity, 519–521
Passive index portfolios, 25, 435
Passive management, 26, 202–203, 206–210, 480, 588
Passive portfolios, 581–582
Peer group, in performance measurement, 276–278
Pension funds:
  asset distribution, 112–113
  funding probabilities, 128–130
  liabilities, 52, 111, 125–126
  overfunded, 127, 130
  payout structure, 125–127
  required returns, 126–128
  risk plan for, 255
  static analysis, 113–115
  tax-exempt, 550
  underfunded, 126, 128, 130
Percent returns, 313–315
Performance attribution, 260, 273, 299
Performance contribution, 299
Performance measurement, calculation of, 280–281. *See also* Performance measurement tools
Performance measurement tools:
  alpha, 275–277
  benchmarks, 275–276
  green zone, 270–273
  information ratio, 273, 275
  meaningfulness of, 269–270
  multiple, 268–269
  peer group, 276–277
  returns, attribution of, 273
  Sharpe ratio, 273, 275
Planning, in risk management, 252
Plan Sponsor Network (PSN), 193
Plan sponsors:
  active management, 213
  functions of, 211–212
  risk monitoring, 221
Portable alpha, 480–481, 491
Portfolio analysis:
  alternative assets, 153–154
  risk contributions, 156, 162
  risk premium, 154–155
Portfolio diversification, 9, 11, 13
Portfolio management:
  characteristics of, generally, 28
  wealth generation and, 590–592

Portfolio optimization:
  portfolio construction and, 417, 428–430, 467–468
  strategy overview, 19–20
Portfolio risk:
  currency hedging, 145
  decomposition of, 34–35
  implications of, 13–14, 17, 21
  measurement, 378–379
Portfolio valuations, periodic reviews of, 293
Positive RCTE, 382
Post-earnings-announcement drift,421, 460
Practice of Risk Management, The (Litterman/Gumerlock), 251, 259
Predicted beta, 387
Predicted R-squared, 388
Preferred stock, 565
Prepayment duration, 440
Prepayment risk, 439–440, 442
Price comparisons:
  against independent model prices, 292–293
  pricing sources, 291–292
Price/earnings (P/E) ratio:
  annual returns, 555
  estimated risk premium, 45
  expansion, 47, 52
  growth, 47
  historic returns, 546
Price reversals, 422
Price verification, 290
Pricing:
  methodologies, 289
  override/manual price procedures, 289
  valuation oversight philosophy, 286–288
Pricing in, defined, 444
Principal component analysis (PCA), 345–348
Principal package trading, 432
Private equity, *see* Private equity investments
  characteristics of, 25, 104–105
  defined, 102
  market portfolio and, 102–103
Private equity funds, 565
Private equity investments:
  characteristics of, generally, 516–517, 530
  historical returns, 521–523
  mechanics of, 519
  optimal allocation examples, 525–528
  purpose of, 516–517
  return sources, 523–525
  returns statistics, 519–520
  risk, 518
  suboptimal allocation, 528–530
  types of, 517–519
  valuation, 519–520
Private wealth:
  after-tax results, investing for, 533–545
  after-tax returns for U.S. stocks, bonds, and bills, 546–564
  asset allocation and location, 565–578
  equity portfolio structure, 579–593
Probabilities, in risk management, 31
Probability distributions, 32, 81, 83, 227–228, 239
Productivity growth, 50
Profitability, risk-adjusted, 256
Proxy universe, 357
Public equities, 565
Public equity market, 102, 518
Pure overlay, global tactical asset allocation (GTAA), 455, 458–459, 467

Quantitative analysis, management selection, 404–405
Quantitative management, equity portfolio management (EPM), 418–419
Quantitative modeling, 87

RACS, *see* Risk-adjusted change in surplus (RACS)
Raw exposure, 350
Real estate, generally:
  investments, 25, 78, 100–105
  publicly traded, 101–103

Real estate investment trusts (REITs), 409, 565, 567
Real interest rate, 344
Reallocation, 538
Rebalance strategy, 413–414, 417
Recession, impact of, 31
Recruitment, management selection process, 403–404
Red zone events, 214, 216, 432–433
Reference checks, management selection process, 403–404
Refinancing, 440
Regression analysis:
  characteristics of, 422
  covariance matrix estimation, 244–245
  cross-sectional, 309, 345, 357–360, 393
  equity risk factor models, 339, 346–347
  performance measurement, 275–276
Relative marginal contribution to tracking error (RCTE), 381–382
Relative marginal factor contribution to tracking error (RFCTE), 384–385
Relative specific contribution to tracking error (RSCTE), 385
Relative value sector, hedge funds, 490, 494
Remedial planning, 254
Reoptimization, 106
Repurchase agreements, 375
Residual return, 174, 327–329
Residual risk, 176, 393
Retirement planning, 575
Return attribution:
  algorithms, to align official and estimated returns, 328–329
  asset grouping, 298, 306–311, 332–333
  defined, 297, 299
  factor model, 298, 301–306, 309, 331
  international portfolios, 319–327
  in performance measurement, 273, 327–328
  purpose of, 298–300
  residuals, 327–329
  returns computation, 300–301, 331–333
  single region (local model), 301–319
Return-free strategy, 202
Return on equity (ROE), 47–48, 253–254, 256–258, 278, 423
Returns, *see specific types of returns*
  after-tax, 541–544
  computation of, 283–284
  dollar-weighted, 281
  normalized, 271
  risk capital, 277
  stocks *vs.* bonds, forecasts using valuation measures, 464–465
  time-weighted, 282–283
  uncorrelated assets, *see* Returns for uncorrelated assets
Returns for uncorrelated assets:
  optimal portfolio weights, 162–163, 165–166
  optimal risk allocations, 164–165
  portfolio analysis, 156–160
  risk decomposition, 161, 164, 166
  strategic asset allocation, 163–168
Returns on risk capital (RORC), 253–254, 256–258, 278
Risk, *see specific types of risk*
  allocation, 27, 172
  characteristics of, 534
  defined, 249, 277
  forecasting models, 262, 264–266
  sources of, generally, 33–34, 152–168, 251, 313–319, 373–378, 435–442, 523–525
  types of, 27, 251
Risk-adjusted change in surplus (RACS), strategic asset allocation, 114–115, 120–123, 130–131
Risk and return assumptions:
  active risk management, 201
  strategic asset allocation, 115–125
Risk aversion:
  Black-Litterman global equilibrium approach, 83
  global equilibrium and, 63, 72, 75

implications of, 33, 37–38, 40, 42, 49–51, 56, 109, 155, 179
private equity investments, 525
Risk budget/budgeting:
active management strategies, 446–451
active risk level, 171–185
active risk spectrum, 192–210
covariance matrix estimation, 248
data analysis, 176–179
development of, 24, 26–27, 171–173
equity risk factor models, 334–395
example of, 256–257
global tactical asset allocation (GTAA), 476
hedge funds and, 512
implied confidence levels, 185–190
implied returns, 179–184
independent valuation, 285–296
investment policy, 185–190
optimal active risk budget development, 171–191
optimal allocation, 14
optimality and, 173
and portfolio, 429
purpose of, 255–256, 277–278
return attribution, 297–333
risk management, total fund level, 211–223
risk monitoring, 221–222, 249–284
risk/return analysis, 13
security selection, 221
separate investment accounts, 410
uncorrelated assets, 166
views, 185–190
Risk capital, 253–254, 257, 262–264, 277
Risk contributions, 156, 162
Risk culture, 260–261
Risk decomposition, *see* Portfolio risk, decomposition of
analysis, 269
covariance matrix estimation, 226
equity risk factor models, 383, 391
GTAA portfolio, 475–476
implications of, 34–35, 147, 164, 166, 172, 199, 224, 254, 263–264, 391–392
return attribution and, 298–299
risk monitoring program, 221–222
uncorrelated assets, 161
Risk diversification standards, 277
Risk estimation, 392–395
Risk exposure, 351
Risk footprint, 215
Risk-free assets, 37, 49
Risk-free rate, 39, 48, 58, 114–115, 159, 175, 303
Risk-free strategy, 202
Risk-free yield curve, 436
Risk function, 15–16
Riskless asset, 45
Risk management:
benchmarks, 28
decomposition of risk, 34–35
dimensions of, 251, 277
program implementation, *see* Risk monitoring program
purpose of, 27–28, 35
risk budget, *see* Risk budget/budgeting
risk plan, 253–255
significance of, 29–30
strategic asset allocation, 108–109
strategies, generally, 7–9, 12
stress test, 30–32
three-legged stool, 253–258
utility function, 32–33
Value at Risk (VaR), 28–29, 35
volatility, 35
Risk management unit (RMU):
credit risk monitoring, 268
examples of, 261–266
formation of, 258–259
objectives of, 251, 260–261
performance attribution, 273
performance measurement, 271, 275
philosophies/processes, 270, 279–280
risk budget, 278
Risk measurement:
asset allocation, 24–25
benchmarks, 25
risk budget, 24–27
risk tolerance, 25
significance of, 14–15, 24–26
source of risk, 33–34

Risk minimization strategies, 21–23, 156–157
Risk monitoring program:
credit risk, 267–268
Green Sheet, 217–222
green zone, 214, 216, 222, 270–273, 432–433
implementation of, 212
performance measurement, 249–252
purpose of, 212, 251, 257–258
rationale, 258–259
red zone, 214, 216, 432–433
risk budget, 221–222
yellow zone, 214, 216, 271, 273, 432–433
Risk plan, 253–255
Risk premiums:
global equilibrium, 75
implications of, 42–43, 156
risk budget development, 183
uncorrelated assets, 154
Risk reduction strategies, 152, 534
Risk/return trade-offs, 115, 120, 154, 520, 553
Risk tolerance, 25, 42–43, 57
Roll, Richard, 100
Rolling window technique, 229–230
R-squared statistics, equity risk factor models, 343–344, 388
Rule-based portfolio, 429–430
Russell iShares, 389
Russell 1000, 427
Russell 2000, 188, 427
Russell 2000 Value Index (R2000V), 299
Russell 3000, 92, 212, 214, 248, 488

Safe asset allocation, 552, 554, 564
Salary growth, implications of, 111
Salomon Smith Barney (SSB)
Developed World index, 93
Emerging Composite index, 93
Global Equity Index (GEI), 91–93, 95–96, 98
S&P 500, 30, 97, 196–197, 306, 328, 355, 388–389, 428, 464, 508, 510, 512
S&P 600, 427
Satellite portfolio, 582–586
Secondary market, 437
Sector allocation strategy, 445
Sector contributions, return attribution, 320–322, 325–326, 328
Sector risk, 437–438
Securities and Exchange Commission (SEC), 285, 287–288, 290, 296, 502
Securities selection:
global equity indexes, 97
risk budgeting, 447–448
strategies, 445
Security-specific risk, 441–442
Selective perception, 418
Self-insurance, 254
Sell signals, modern portfolio theory (MPT), 17–20
Senior leadership, functions of, 255
Senior management, functions of:
risk management, 260
valuation policies, 289–290
Serial correlation, covariance matrix estimation, 233, 237–239, 244
Settlement risk, 251
Shadow price, 249, 255
Sharpe, William F., 33, 36
Sharpe ratio:
currency hedging, 151
expected returns, 164
global diversification, 122
implications of, generally, 33, 75, 105, 113–114
implied, 166
performance measurement, 273, 275
strategic asset allocation, 110, 112, 120
uncorrelated assets, 155, 158–159, 163–166, 168
Short positions, 22, 28, 361
Short sales, 441, 502
Short-term price reversal anomaly, 421
Shrinkage, portfolio construction, 467
Siegel's paradox, 61–63, 69

Single region return attribution:
  asset grouping methodology, 306–311
  factor model based approach, 301–306, 309
  multiperiod attribution, 311
Sinquefield, Rex, 45
60/40 plans, 414
Skill classes, 502
Slope coefficients, in performance measurement, 275–276
Small-cap stocks, 198, 364, 425–426
Sovereign bonds, 99, 464
Sovereign debt, 441
Specialty funds, 583
Spectrum strategy, defined, 192
Spending policy, 540–541, 545, 562
Spiders, 389–390
Spreadsheet applications, 74, 161
Stale pricing exception reports, 293
Standard & Poor's, 351, 438
Standard & Poor's Depositary Receipts (SPDRs), 389–390
Standard deviations, 107, 120, 228, 230, 273, 275, 353–354, 377, 379, 413
Start-up companies, 517–518
Static analysis, 113–115
Stationarity, covariance matrix estimation, 228
Statistical factors, 341
Step-up in basis, 538–539, 567, 579
Stereotyping, 418
Sterling, 142, 147, 151
Stewardship, 555
Stock positions, concentrated, 592–593
Stock recommendation anomaly, 421
Stock selection, *see* Securities selection
  country, 324
  international portfolios, 326
  return attribution, 300, 304, 307–308
  strategies, 221–222
Stock-specific returns, 338
Stock swap, 538
Strategic asset allocation:
  decision points, 104–105
  dynamic analysis, 125–126
  equilibrium approach benefits, 108–109
  funding probabilities, 128–130
  hedge funds, 483–500
  investment decisions, 112–113
  modeling liabilities, 111–112
  required returns, 126–128
  risk and return assumptions, 115–125
  standard framework applications, 105–107
  static analysis, 113–115
  uncertain liabilities, 110–111
  uncorrelated assets, 163–166, 168
Stratified sampling, 428
Strengths, weaknesses, opportunities, and threats (SWOT) analysis, 253
Stress test, 30–32
Structural inefficiency, 188
Structured active management, 26
Structured investments, 198–199
Structured management:
  selection factors, 202–203, 205–210
  traditional management compared with, 193–197
Style bias, 428
Style drift, 263, 514
Subsidies, 539
Supply and demand, 3, 44, 49, 65, 511
Surplus risk, 117–120, 133–134
Survivorship bias, 46, 181–182, 487
Swap contracts, 60, 293, 468
Swap yield curve, 436
Swing portfolio, 414–415, 472
Systematic risk, 393

Tactical asset allocation (TAA), 456, 458, 465, 474, 478, 482
Tactical trading, hedge funds, 490, 494
TASS Research, 495, 504, 508
Taxation, *see specific types of taxes*
  equilibrium approach, 6
  global tactical asset allocation, 459
  liabilities, 534
  tax rates, 52, 542, 547–548, 553, 586–587

Tax code, 545
Tax deferral, 540, 581. *See also* Deferred taxes
Tax-exempt entities, 550
Tax-exempt income market securities, 565
Tax loss harvesting, 587–590
Technical factors, equity risk factor models, 341, 345
Theory:
  Black-Litterman global asset allocation model, 76–88
  Capital Asset Pricing Model (CAPM), 36–43
  equilibrium approach, 3–6
  equity risk premium, 44–54
  global equilibrium expected returns, 55–75
  modern portfolio theory (MPT), 7–23
  risk measurement, 24–35
Three-factor model, return attribution, 328
Tiering income, 568–569
Time horizon, 9, 29, 149, 256–257. *See also* Investment horizon
Time-series modeling, equity risk factor models, 341, 356, 377
Time-weighted returns, 282–283
Top-down asset allocation, 26, 98, 448
TOPIX, 101, 427
Total risk, 26
Tracking errors:
  active management, 200, 202, 204–205, 207–209, 449
  cash effects, 390–392
  defined, 249–250
  equity risk factor models, 380–383
  expectations, 263
  forecasts, 262
  management, structured *vs.* traditional, 193
  performance measurement, 273, 275
  portfolio construction and, 427
  risk budgeting, 174, 177, 189–190, 447–451
  risk monitoring, 213–216, 222, 249
Trade-cost monitoring, 424
Trade optimizer, 431
Trade-offs:
  active risk budget, 199
  risk/return, 115, 120, 154, 520, 553
Traditional investments:
  characteristics of, 198–199
  equity portfolio management, 416–434
  fixed income risk and return, 435–451
  investment program implementation, 407–415
  management selection, asset-management approach, 399–406
Traditional management:
  cash, 485
  equity portfolio management (EPM), 417–419
  global tactical asset allocation (GTAA), 479
  hedge funds and, 484–486, 491
  selection factors, 202–203, 205–210
  structured management compared with, 193–197
Transaction costs:
  adverse selection risk, 424
  decision price, 425
  explicit costs, 424
  global tactical asset allocation (GTAA), 457, 467–468, 470
  implications of, 4, 77, 172, 212, 221, 411–412, 414, 417, 424
  implicit costs, 424
  inventory risk, 424
  market impact, 424
Transfer taxes, 534, 537, 544, 565, 567, 570–572
Transition managers, 412
Treasury bills (T-bills), 344, 375, 444, 547–549, 552–553, 555, 564
Treasury Inflation-Protected Securities (TIPS), 552–553
Tremont Event Driven peer index, 508
Trend analysis, 260
Treynor, Jack, 36
Triangulation, management selection, 403–404

Truncated-sample estimation, 244
T-statistic, 497, 499
Two-manager structured equity program, 203

Uncertainty, 30, 49, 53, 87, 111
Uncorrelated assets, 166
Uncorrelated risk, 154, 157
Underreaction, short-term, 459–460
Undervalued stocks, 222
Uniform equity portfolio structure, 584–586
U.S. dollar, currency hedging, 142–151
U.S. equities, global equilibrium, 60–65
U.S. stocks:
  after-tax wealth applications, 558–564
  annual returns, 547, 554–558
  historic returns, 546–550
  inflation, impact on, 547, 549–553, 564
  risk-adjusted returns, 553–554
U.S. Treasury, 53, 437, 552
Univariate analysis, 421
Universal hedging, 56–57, 63, 72–73, 76
USD/GBP, 283, 300–301, 349
Utility function:
  equity risk premium, 49–51
  risk management and, 32, 37–38

Valuation:
  authorization, 288–289
  committee, 286, 290–291, 294
  fair, 295–296
  independent, *see* Independent valuation
  management reporting, 290–291
  oversight philosophy, 285–291
  portfolio risk and, 17–18
  price comparisons, 291–292
  prices, transaction prices *vs.*, 291
  ratified procedures, 288–289
  risk measurement and, 32
  statutory, 286–288
  uncorrelated assets, 155–156
  verification tools, 291
Value at Risk (VaR), 28–29, 225–226, 249–250, 253–254, 256, 268, 277–278, 335
Value factor, equity risk factor models, 361
Value investors, 425
Value stocks, 155
Van Hedge, 486
Variance analysis, 309–310, 328
Variance-covariance matrix, 224, 423
Variance monitoring, 252, 257–258
Vega risk, 439
Venture Economics, 524
View portfolio, 77, 85–87
Volatility:
  annualized, 29
  asset allocation drift and, 413
  bond market, 118
  covariance matrices, 364
  covariance matrix estimation, 225, 227–230, 232, 241–243
  equity risk factor models, 341
  fixed income securities, 435–436
  foreign bond portfolios, 140–142
  global equilibrium and, 61, 75
  hedge funds, 140–145, 488–489, 491–493, 495–497, 513
  historical, 31
  implications of, 8, 13–17, 19
  noise, 111–112, 114–115, 118, 120
  price comparisons, 292
  private equity investments, 528–530
  risk budget development, 183
  risk monitoring, 218
  strategic asset allocation, 105–107
  transaction costs and, 425
  uncorrelated assets, 163
Volatility exposure, 353, 439
Volatility risk, 438–439, 442
Volker, Paul, 552
Volume-weighted average price (VWAP), 432

Wash sale rule, 587
Wealth creation, 11

Wealth maximization strategies:
- charitable gifts, 566
- charitable remainder trust (CRT), 566, 568–569, 576, 578
- children, 566, 574
- foundation, 566, 569–570, 575–578
- 401(k) plan, 567, 575
- grantor trust, 566–568, 570, 574–575
- transfer taxes, 570

Weighted least squares (WLS) regression, 358

Weighting, generally:
- Capital Asset Pricing Model (CAPM), 37
- covariance matrix estimation, 235–237
- global bonds, 99
- global equilibrium, 76, 78, 81, 86–87
- hedge funds, 487
- in portfolio risk, 21–23

Wilshire REIT index, 101

Withdrawals, 401(k) plan, 567

Yellow zone events, 214, 216, 271, 432–433

Yen, 60–66, 142, 147, 151, 376

Yield curve:
- positioning strategy, 444–445
- risk, 437, 442
- sloping, 444

Zero-mean distribution, 83